Jaffe's diversity-based approach to public speaking works in every classroom!

More successfully than any other public speaking text, *this* book gives students the guidance and tools they need to become effective speakers in today's society. Clella Jaffe's success stems from her ability to effectively integrate diversity topics **within the context** of public speaking skills development. Her superb framework of speech development concepts, skills, and applications is praised by instructors nationwide.

Jaffe *shows* students how diversity impacts communication, how culture provides expectations about speaking and listening, **and** how students can use this knowledge to become effective, culturally sensitive speakers.

Fifth Edition PREVIEW

PREMIUM ONLINE RESOURCES
To package with each student text, see facing page for details.

Book Companion Website
A premium website that includes a broad range of resources for each text chapter.

Speech Builder Express™
A powerful online tool that guides students through every step of the speechmaking process.

InfoTrac® College Edition with InfoMarks®
An easily searchable online library that helps students research their speeches.

vMentor™
Live, one-on-one tutoring from speech experts.

New to this edition:

▶ **A new "Case Study"** followed by discussion questions that opens each chapter.

▶ **New sample speeches and examples**

▶ **Increased coverage** of ethics, commemorative speaking, plagiarism, Internet research, persuasion, and other key topics.

▶ **Chapter-by-chapter resources on the premium Book Companion Website,** which includes tutorial quizzes, interactive vocabulary, and more

Turn the page to begin your tour!

A conversation with author Clella Jaffe

About the author

Dr. Clella Jaffe is chair of the communication department at George Fox University in Newberg, Oregon. She has taught communication courses at George Fox as well as at St. John's University (Queens) and Oregon State University. For many years, she taught oral interpretation of literature and coached and judged forensic competitions. Her widely selling public speaking text is critically acclaimed for its effective integration of diversity into all facets of the public speaking course.

Dr. Jaffe, what made you decide to write a public speaking textbook?

When given the task of selecting a text for the public speaking course at Oregon State University, I studied many, many textbooks to find one with all the elements I considered essential: an emphasis on ethics, inclusion of diversity issues, a chapter on narrative, and a grounding in the rhetorical tradition. I could not find a text that included all four. I wondered if other professors felt the same need and frustration. At a Western States Communication Association meeting I saw a professor walk through the textbook displays, picking up one public speaking text after another and looking through the index. I heard her mutter, "Nothing on diversity." I knew, then that I was not alone in my frustration with available public speaking texts.

How does *Public Speaking: Concepts and Skills for a Diverse Society* differ from other public speaking texts?

This text presents groundbreaking coverage of diversity, which is integrated with principles from classical rhetoric and up-to-date theories such as narrative theory, dialogical theory, and invitational rhetoric. I am a member of the Ethics Commission of the National Communication Association, and ethical considerations are woven throughout the text. I like to think it is well rounded and blends theory and practical advice in an understandable and practical way.

Now that the book is in its Fifth Edition, how do you keep the text current and engaging to students?

I keep current on national and world events and on popular culture. I also attend national conventions and read communication journals for updates to the theoretical material in the text.

You have inspired thousands of students in your 20 years of teaching public speaking. What keeps teaching public speaking fresh and interesting for you and your students?

I truly love to teach public speaking, and I hope that's contagious. I also incorporate a lot of current events in my classroom by taping excerpts from broadcast news shows or referring students to a newspaper article. I enjoy helping students see course principles unfold on the daily news—principles such as diversity of opinion, civility (or lack thereof), the importance of narrative, of critical and comprehensive listening, of persuasion, of making a case for or against change. I think the principles of rhetoric are indispensable.

What lessons do you hope your students leave your course remembering?

I want them to know how to participate in the important dialogues that go on in our culture. I hope they can listen well, understand and evaluate the information and arguments they hear, and present their own ideas clearly and cogently.

Clella Jaffe . . . always at the cutting edge of speech instruction

---

CASE STUDY: LORNA OWENS'S MISSION

Lorna Owens has used her public speaking and listening skills as a lawyer, small business owner, motivational speaker, and community activist.

The inspiring eulogy and the glowing tributes at her father's funeral led Lorna Owens to reassess her life priorities. As she heard friends and relatives narrate the wonderful things he'd done throughout his life, she realized that no one could speak as positively about her. Owens, a native of Jamaica, was at the top of her game as a high-powered Florida lawyer, but her reflections led her to resign her position and start her own company. Eventually, she became a motivational speaker and life coach. Owens sponsors an annual event, "And the Women Gather," which brings together women (mostly professionals) who have fun while listening to interesting, inspirational speakers. Proceeds from the event go to two organizations: (1) the Guild of Women Achievers, which provides health care and health education to women who work in sweatshops in India, and (2) Women Behind Bars, a nonprofit, 90-day empowerment program that Owens organized to help women transition from prison to the community. Her eventual vision includes a full-service salon and day spa that will employ former inmates.[2]

Questions for Discussion

▸ How has Lorna Owens used public speaking throughout her several careers?
▸ How do you think listening has been a factor? For instance, when was listening important in her career as a lawyer? As a life coach, how did she rely on her audiences' listening to help her accomplish her goals?
▸ What advice do you think she would give you as you begin your public speaking course?
▸ How are speaking and listening important in helping people make social changes such as prison reform?
▸ How will you use speaking in your career? Listening?

public speaking when a person delivers a presentation to a group that listens, generally without interrupting the speaker's flow of ideas

The Miami Herald (via Knight-Ridder/Tribune News Service), March 14, 2005, pNA. Speaker helps women find a balance. Full Text: COPYRIGHT 2005. The Miami Herald Byline: Ana Veciana-Suarez.

NEW *Case Studies*
Engaging, relevant stories of real speechmakers that draw students into each chapter's topics

Every chapter of the Fifth Edition begins with a new *Case Study* that effectively shows students the great, practical value of effective speaking and listening skills. Each *Case Study* serves to engage students in chapter topics, at the same time offering invaluable, often-life-changing lessons learned by the real people discussed in the *Case Studies* . . . for example, a lawyer who heard inspirational eulogies at her father's funeral which led her to a new life as a motivational speaker . . . and a fitness trainer who incorporates a variety of visual aids into his workshop and seminar presentations.

An applied focus with many NEW Sample Speeches, videos, and examples throughout

Praised from its first edition for the value of its sample speeches and examples, this edition again delivers! Jaffe has replaced many of the previous edition's speeches and examples with current, engaging material that effectively reinforces skills development.

For example, a new speech on the benefits of pet ownership shows how a student's academic major guided her topic choice (Chapter 6). A new speech on driving while drowsy showcases an effective introduction and conclusion (Chapter 10). A new tribute to Barbara Jordan (Appendix C) illustrates commemorative speaking. Many speeches carried over from previous editions are now available on videotape.

SPEECH VIDEO

Log onto the book's website to watch the informative speech *Pumpkins* by Anna Riedl, answer questions for analysis, and evaluate the speech. An outline of the speech appears below and is also available on the book's website.

Student Learning: Book Website
A video clip of this speech is available on the book website for viewing and evaluation or guided critical analysis. The clip is also available on the Multimedia Manager CD-ROM.

Student Outline with Visual Aids with Commentary

PUMPKINS
Anna Riedl

General Purpose:	To inform
Specific Purpose:	To inform the audience about characteristics and facts about pumpkins.
Thesis Statement:	Although the pumpkin is well known by name, there are facts that many people may not know about pumpkins.
Preview:	Many facts about pumpkins are not well known, including their anatomy, variety, health benefits, and other interesting trivia.

Introduction

I. Did you know that pumpkins are 90% water?
[Display title slide.]
II. Although I've seen pumpkins all my life, I've never really thought much about them, and I'm sure many of you have not as well.
III. After going through pages of information on the Internet about pumpkins, I discovered many things I did not know about this squash.
IV. Today, I will share what I now know about their anatomy, variety, nutrients, and other interesting facts, so that we can all go into the festive October and November months with a little more knowledge of pumpkins.

The Pumpkin!

In this speech, Anna uses PowerPoint-generated slides throughout. The LCD display is on standby before she begins. She reactivates it and brings up each slide and each build by clicking the mouse.

Slides act as a transition between points. Each slide has a point-by-point build programmed in.

New coverage empowers today's speech students

The Fifth Edition is completely updated featuring expanded coverage in these key areas:

- ▶ **Dialogical Theory**—comparing and contrasting conversation with public speaking.

- ▶ **Plagiarism**—identifying various types of plagiarism and how to avoid them.

- ▶ **Listening**—including the D-R-E (Describe, Respond, Evaluate) method of providing feedback.

- ▶ **Commemorative Purpose**—revising the general purposes to include commemorative speaking.

- ▶ **Internet and Online Research**—updating and revising the section on Internet research; differentiating subject directories, search engines, and specialized databases in the Invisible Web.

- ▶ **Persuasion**—adding the Theory of Reasoned Action.

New to this edition

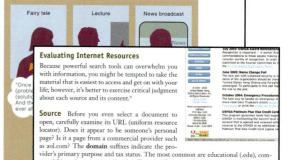

Strategies to Improve Listening

Being mindful of your thought patterns during the listening process can lead you to develop strategies for understanding and retaining material. Use a combination of resources from within your culture, along with nonverbal and note-taking skills.

Use Cultural Schemas

Listening schemas are sets of cultural expectations that can help you organize and understand messages (Figure 4.3). **Schemas** are mental plans, blueprints, or models you use to perceive information and then interpret, store, and recall it.[10] Think of how you listen to a story. You have a mental model of what a good story is like, and you use this

Fairy tale | Lecture | News broadcast

Evaluating Internet Resources

Because powerful search tools can overwhelm you with information, you might be tempted to take the material that is easiest to access and get on with your life; however, it's better to exercise critical judgment about each source and its content.[9]

Source Before you even select a document to open, carefully examine its URL (uniform resource locator). Does it appear to be someone's personal page? Is it a page from a commercial provider such as aol.com? The **domain** suffixes indicate the provider's primary purpose and tax status. The most common are educational (.edu), commercial (.com), government (.gov), military (.mil), nonprofit organization (.org), and foreign (.ca for Canada, .jp for Japan, and so on). Ask yourself which domain is most reliable for your particular topic. Ask who or what entity published the page. (For example, www.cdc.gov means the entity is a government website hosted by the CDC or Centers for Disease Control.) Decide if the entity supports your subject well, and choose links that seem the most appropriate, given your topic. Figures 7.1a and 7.1b show two Web pages about the same subject that differ by domain.

After you link onto the Web page, look for information about the author, institution, organization, or agency that accepts responsibility for the material on the site. If this is not immediately apparent, look for a home page or follow links such as "about us," "philosophy," or "background" that might provide information about the page's author. Take care to distinguish between primary or secondary, expert or peer sources.

BUILD YOUR SPEECH
YOUR FIRST SPEECH

I. Introduction
II. Body
III. Conclusion

I. INTRODUCE YOUR TOPIC

Your first speech may vary slightly from this pattern, but in general an introduction has these four major functions that date back to the first-century AD Roman educator Quintilian:[6]

- ▶ Draw audience attention to the topic.
- ▶ Relate the topic to their concerns.
- ▶ Link yourself to the subject.
- ▶ Preview the major points.

II. DEVELOP THE BODY OF YOUR SPEECH

Here, you present and develop your major ideas, using sufficient evidence for clarification and support. There are many ways to organize speeches, such as topical, problem-solution, cause-effect, and so on. These will be discussed in more detail in Chapter 9. Using these patterns results in a linear arrangement, as shown by this outline of a topical speech:

A. First main point
  1. Support
  2. Support

B. Second main point
  1. Support
  2. Support

Although linear patterns are common, your cultural background, your learning style, or your personality traits may lead you to visualize your speeches as moving in wavelike patterns or in spiraling forms. Chapters 9 and 17 illustrate both traditional and alternative organizational forms. You will also find narrative speech patterns in Chapter 15.

III. CONCLUDE MEMORABLY

To be most effective as a speaker, don't stop abruptly. Instead, provide a sense of closure that ties your ideas together and leaves your audience with something to take away with them. Conclusions often have these elements:

- ▶ A transition to the conclusion
- ▶ A reference to the introduction
- ▶ A summary of the major ideas
- ▶ A final memorable statement

And now, it's even easier for students to move from the book to its many online and media tools

Easy-to-spot prompts at the beginning of every *Build Your Speech* box guide students to **Speech Builder Express**™—our dynamic web-based speech outlining and organizing program. Online access to **Speech Builder Express,**™ **vMentor,**™ **InfoTrac**® **College Edition,** and the premium **Book Companion Website** are all available to each student with an access card that can be bundled with this book at the instructor's request (or purchased separately by students with used books). *See next page for details.*

Innovative and exclusive multimedia resources that enhance the student's learning experience

Help your students master their speech-building skills with **Speech Builder Express**™

This effective web-based program works in tandem with the book's ***Build Your Speech*** boxes, taking students through every step of the speech-building process.

- Nine simple steps provide a series of critical thinking questions that guide students to effective speech delivery.
- Links to video clips, InfoTrac® College Edition, and an online dictionary and thesaurus help students pull all aspects of their speeches together.
- Tutorial help is included for using visual aids and works cited.
- Any portion of the outline can be e-mailed to the instructor.

If you would like your students to have access to these Premium Online Resources at no additional charge, please use ISBN 0-495-16224-8 when placing your order. Access to the Premium Online Resources are not automatically packaged with this text.

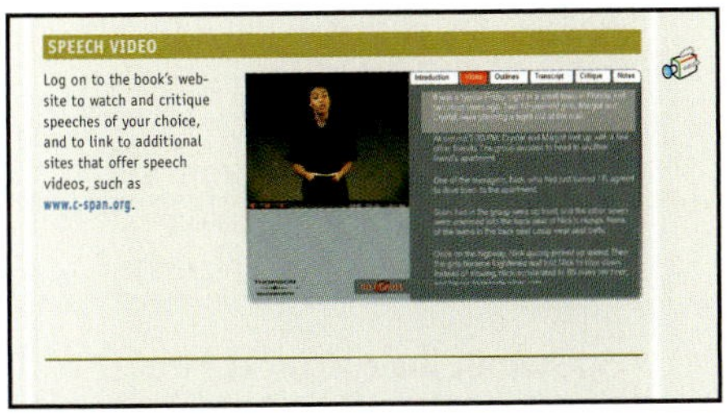

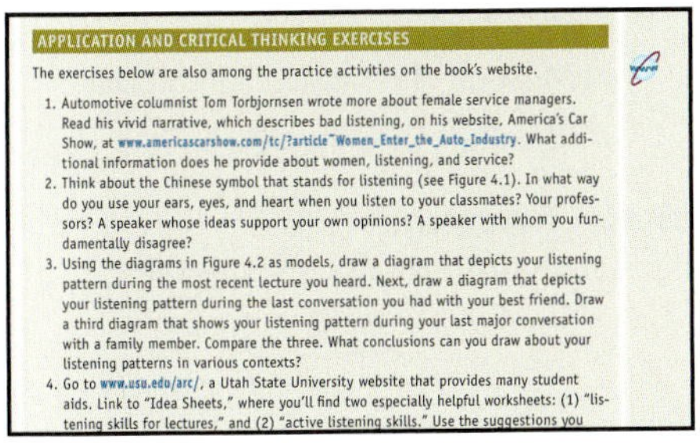

APPLICATION AND CRITICAL THINKING EXERCISES

The exercises below are also among the practice activities on the book's website.

1. Automotive columnist Tom Torbjornsen wrote more about female service managers. Read his vivid narrative, which describes bad listening, on his website, America's Car Show, at www.americascarshow.com/tc/?article~Women_Enter_the_Auto_Industry. What additional information does he provide about women, listening, and service?
2. Think about the Chinese symbol that stands for listening (see Figure 4.1). In what way do you use your ears, eyes, and heart when you listen to your classmates? Your professors? A speaker whose ideas support your own opinions? A speaker with whom you fundamentally disagree?
3. Using the diagrams in Figure 4.2 as models, draw a diagram that depicts your listening pattern during the most recent lecture you heard. Next, draw a diagram that depicts your listening pattern during the last conversation you had with your best friend. Draw a third diagram that shows your listening pattern during your last major conversation with a family member. Compare the three. What conclusions can you draw about your listening patterns in various contexts?
4. Go to www.usu.edu/arc/, a Utah State University website that provides many student aids. Link to "Idea Sheets," where you'll find two especially helpful worksheets: (1) "listening skills for lectures," and (2) "active listening skills." Use the suggestions you

Help your students see text concepts come to life through the **Book Companion Web Site**

http://communication.wadsworth.com/jaffe5

Premium online resources

This book's premium website includes a broad range of resources that help students to better understand chapter material, complete assignments, and succeed on tests. The site includes:

- Sample Student Speeches with critical viewing questions—all linked to the ***Study and Review*** section located near the end of each text chapter.
- Practice exercises—correlated to each chapter's ***Application and Critical Thinking Exercises.***
- Interactive flashcards and crossword puzzles correlated to the ***Key Terms*** section in the book—helping students reinforce their understanding of terms and concepts.

Give your students access to live one-on-one tutoring from a subject expert with **vMentor**™

vMentor enables students to interact with a tutor and other students using two-way audio, an interactive whiteboard when appropriate, and instant messaging.

Help your students choose and research their speech topics with **InfoTrac® College Edition with InfoMarks®**

Includes millions of current, full-text articles (not abstracts) from almost 5,000 diverse sources, such as top academic journals, newsletters, and up-to-the minute periodicals. The database also includes access to **InfoMarks**—stable URLs that can be linked to articles and searches.

More tools that help your students succeed!
Available for packaging with each text

Student Workbook
0-495-12747-7

by Clella Jaffe. Features extensive individual and group activities that support assignments suggested in the *Annotated Instructor's Edition* and the *Instructor's Resource Manual.*

Speech Builder Express™ Student Guide
0-495-00541-X

A user-friendly guidebook that helps students navigate the Speech Builder Express™ speech outlining and organizing software.

Election 2004: Speeches from the Campaign
0-495-00471-5

Features selected full speeches and excerpts from the 2004 Democratic and Republican conventions. A great way to help students understand the power and impact of effect speaking.

InfoTrac® College Edition Student Activities Workbook for Public Speaking
0-534-53045-1

Contains guidelines and an extensive selection of individual and group activities designed to help instructors and students get the most benefit from InfoTrac College Edition.

Premium Online Resources
To order packaged with each text:
0-495-18804-2

Give your students access to a wide array of interactive, multimedia learning resources with our exclusive Premium Online Resources. Integrated text icons prompt students to enhance their online learning via:

- **The Book Companion Website,** which includes a variety of sample speech videos, speech outlines, and a unique critique and evaluation feature.
- **InfoTrac® College Edition with InfoMarks,®** which helps students to choose and research their speech topics.
- **Speech Builder Express,™** which guides students through the outlining and organizing process.
- **vMentor™** for immediate tutorial help.

WebTUTOR Advantage Speech Tutor Express™ for WebTutor™ Advantage

Helps students master their public speaking skills. A web-based learning system that operates on both the WebCT and Blackboard platforms.

Opposing Viewpoints Resource Center

Available for a nominal fee when packaged with this book, the Opposing Viewpoints Resource Center exposes students to all sides of today's most compelling issues. For a demonstration, please visit http://www.gale.com/OpposingViewpoints.

A Guide to the Basic Course for ESL Students
0-534-56779-7

Assists the nonnative English speaker with FAQs, helpful URLs, and strategies for accent management and for overcoming speech apprehension.

The Art and Strategy of Service Learning Presentations
0-534-61754-9

Provides invaluable guidelines for connecting service-learning work with classroom concepts and offers advice for working effectively with agencies and organizations.

Engaging student resources

These resources can enhance your course and save you time!

Instructor's Resource Manual
0-495-12748-5
by Clella Jaffe. Includes suggested teaching tips, in-class activities, service learning opportunities, speaking assignments, performance evaluations, and a chapter-by-chapter *Test Bank*.

Annotated Instructor's Edition
0-495-12746-9
by Clella Jaffe. Features marginal annotations that integrate the extensive ancillary program. Includes discussion starters, service learning ideas, and online course suggestions for every chapter.

Instructor's Resource CD-ROM including Multimedia Manager and Computerized Test Bank
0-495-12749-3
An all-in-one Microsoft® PowerPoint® tool that contains ExamView® Computerized Testing Software, the *Instructor's Resource Manual*, and pre-designed PowerPoint® presentations. The PowerPoint files contain text, images, and cued videos of student speeches and can be customized to suit your course needs.

Turnitin®
This proven online plagiarism-prevention software promotes fairness in the classroom by helping students learn to correctly cite sources and allowing instructors to check for originality before reading and grading speeches. Turnitin quickly checks student speeches against billions of pages of Internet content, millions of public works, and millions of student papers and speeches—*and within seconds generates a comprehensive originality report!*

WebTutor™ ToolBox

WebTutor™ ToolBox for WebCT® and Blackboard®
Pairs all the content of the text's website and other multimedia tools with the sophisticated course management functionality of a WebCT or Blackboard product.

The Teaching Assistant's Guide to the Basic Course
0-534-56778-9
Addresses general teaching and course management topics, as well as specific strategies for communication instruction.

Student Speeches for Critique and Analysis on Video and DVD
Eight volumes that offer a variety of sample student speeches, including all speech types as well as non-native English speakers and the use of visual aids. Available on video and DVD. *Ask your Thomson Wadsworth representative for ordering information.*

Innovative instructor resources

Custom publishing made easy—
your course, your needs, your personalized solutions

As you consider the Fifth Edition of Jaffe's *Public Speaking,* keep in mind that **Thomson Custom Publishing** can help create personalized learning solutions for instructors like you—no matter what your course needs may be. There are times when your teaching needs are not fulfilled by a traditional text alone; and that is where custom publishing can help. With Thomson Custom Publishing, you can teach public speaking your way.

http://www.textchoice.com brings textbook customization to your desktop.

TextChoice, Thomson Custom Publishing's digital library, provides the fastest, easiest way for you to create your own learning materials. You may easily preview and select content from this as well as hundreds of other best-selling titles, choose material from one of our databases, and add your own material. Getting exactly what you want has never been so easy.

Your course, your way!

Experience the advantages

▶ An extensive database of content that includes materials suitable for every public speaking course.

▶ Chapters that can be mixed and matched from multiple titles.

▶ Automatic repagination and indexing.

▶ Instant, printable Table of Contents.

▶ Online viewing, page by page within minutes.

▶ Incorporation of your original material.

You can add your own material—course notes, supplements, lecture outlines, articles, study guides, problems, exercises, out-of-print books, and more—at the beginning or end of any chapter. **TextChoice** can insert blank pages wherever you wish to place your content, then your Thomson representative will collect the material from you. It's that easy.

To learn more, please contact your local Thomson Wadsworth representative.

www.wadsworth.com

www.wadsworth.com is the World Wide Web site for Thomson Wadsworth and is your direct source to dozens of online resources.

At www.*wadsworth*.com you can find out about supplements, demonstration software, and student resources. You can also send email to many of our authors and preview new publications and exciting new technologies.

www.wadsworth.com
Changing the way the world learns®

From the Wadsworth Series in Communication Studies

Public Speaking

FIFTH EDITION

Concepts and Skills for a Diverse Society

CLELLA JAFFE

GEORGE FOX UNIVERSITY

Australia • Brazil • Canada • Mexico • Singapore • Spain
United Kingdom • United States

THOMSON

WADSWORTH

THOMSON

WADSWORTH

Public Speaking: Concepts and Skills for a Diverse Society, FIFTH EDITION • Clella Jaffe

Publisher: Holly J. Allen
Acquisitions Editor: Jaime Perkins
Senior Development Editor: Renee Deljon
Assistant Editor: John Gahbauer
Editorial Assistant: Laura Localio
Senior Technology Project Manager: Jeanette Wiseman
Senior Marketing Manager: Kimberly Russell
Marketing Assistant: Alexandra Tran
Senior Marketing Communications Manager: Shemika Britt
Project Manager, Editorial Production: Catherine Morris
Creative Director: Rob Hugel
Executive Art Director: Maria Epes
Print Buyer: Rebecca Cross
Permissions Editor: Bob Kauser
Production Service: Gretchen Otto, G & S Book Services

Compositor: G & S Book Services
Photo Researcher: Terri Wright
Copy Editor: Janet Parkinson
Illustrator: John and Judy Waller, Carole Lawson, G & S Book Services
Text and Cover Designer: Norman Baugher
Cover Image: "Culture of the Crossroads" Mural © 1998 by Precita Eyes Muralists. Directed by Susan Kelk Cervantes (McDonald's Building, 24th Street at Mission, SF, CA). www.precitaeyes.org
Cover and Chapter-Opening Murals Photographer: Jonathan Fisher
Cover Printer: Phoenix Color Corp
Printer: R.R. Donnelley/ Willard

Library of Congress Control Number: 2005933208

ISBN 0-495-00656-4

Thomson Higher Education
10 Davis Drive
Belmont, CA 94002-3098
USA

For more information about our products, contact us at:
Thomson Learning Academic Resource Center
1-800-423-0563

For permission to use material from this text or product, submit a request online at **http://www.thomsonrights.com**.

Any additional questions about permissions can be submitted by e-mail to **thomsonrights@thomson.com**.

BRIEF CONTENTS

CONTENTS

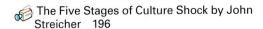
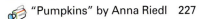

LIST OF SPEECHES

Please Note: *A transcript or outline of the following additional speeches does not appear in the book, but the text refers to most of these speeches, and a video of each is on the book's website along with transcripts, outlines, and note cards.*

George W. Bush, *Republican National Convention, 2004*

Hillary Carter-Liggett, *Shakespeare*

Jessica Howard, *Exemplum*

Shaura Neil, *Terrestrial Pulmonate Gastropods*

Barack Obama, *Democratic National Convention, 2004*

Paul Southwick, *Embryo Adoption*

Nathan Willingham, *John Goodman*

PREFACE

The civilization of the dialogue is the only civilization worth having and the only civilization in which the whole world can unite. It is, therefore, the only civilization we can hope for, because the world must unite or be blown to bits.

Robert Hutchins, 1967

A CULTURALLY informed book that never loses sight of its fundamental purpose, the fifth edition of *Public Speaking: Concepts and Skills for a Diverse Society*, like previous editions, trains students to be effective public speakers and listeners. The text's recognition of diversity deepens students' understanding of core concepts, theories, applications, and critical thinking proficiencies essential for listening and speaking in the twenty-first century. Understanding diversity is more important than ever because people from one cultural background increasingly find themselves in dialogue with people from other cultural backgrounds, and as media, communication, and transportation technologies become even more sophisticated, the pace of cross-cultural interaction increases.

I originally wrote this text to emphasize the intertwined relationship between public speaking and culture, because through public speaking we express, reinforce, transmit, influence, and blend different cultures. In fact, the very human characteristics speakers aim to influence—beliefs, values, attitudes, and actions—are precisely the basic elements of diversity. In the classroom, cultural backgrounds influence students' perceptions of the role of public speaking, their perceptions of themselves as speakers, their perceptions of their audiences, and their perceptions of other speakers. Culture also influences topic selection, research methods and resources, and reasoning styles. As a result, this text applies 2,500 principles of public speaking in a way that is sensitive to our ever-changing pluralistic society.

It's a privilege to write the fifth edition of this text. This edition reflects the many helpful suggestions of students and instructors who have used previous editions, and it provides a wide selection of new speeches, both student and professional. Events in the United States and around the world—the many natural and man-made disasters, the monumental policy shifts, and the rapidly evolving technological advances—continue to change social and political climates. These challenges and changes further warrant updates in the book and make us even more aware of the importance of effective public speaking and listening in a diverse society and world.

New to This Edition

I made a number of important changes in response to reviewers who provided feedback on this book's previous edition. I appreciate their suggestions greatly. Here are some highlights of what's new:

Case Studies. I've added a case study on a relevant aspect of public speaking near the beginning of each chapter to bring concepts to life and provide increased context for students. The case studies open with a narrative scenario and conclude with analytical questions that focus on everyday applications. Most of the case studies include a photograph of their subject. Throughout the chapters, I refer to the case studies to illustrate points of instruction.

New sample speeches. In the book and on the book's website, I have replaced or updated sample speeches for currency, variety, and even greater effectiveness. Nearly 40 percent of the sample speeches, by both student and professional speakers, are new, and more of the speeches or outlines are now available on video. For more information about the new speech videos on the book's website, see the Student Resources section later.

Thoroughly updated research coverage. Constant technological advances, combined with students' increasing technological sophistication, led to revision of Chapter 7, "Researching Your Speech in an Electronic Culture." The section on Internet research now precedes the one on library research to acknowledge that many students search online first; in addition, many materials previously accessible only in the library are now available online and in resources such as InfoTrac® College Edition. Coverage of Internet research tools further distinguishes between subject directories, search engines, and the Invisible Web, which includes billions of sites that search engines do not find.

Increased coverage of selected topics. I expanded coverage of important topics such as the dialogical theory, general purposes, thesis statements, previews, plagiarism, feedback, and reasoning to deepen students' understanding of each area. For example, I added a fourth general purpose: to commemorate. I identified several types of plagiarism that are especially common with Internet materials and added a section titled "Plagiarism and Culture." There's also new coverage of written feedback using the D-R-E (Describe, Respond, Evaluate) Method in the listening chapter, and you'll find coverage of document cameras in the visual aids chapter. The theory of reasoned action gives students another way to understand how people make decisions (Chapter 17).

New examples. To keep examples timely and interesting and to better support the concepts, I replaced examples for currency and greater effectiveness in each section.

New visuals. More than 30 percent of the text's photos are new, and figures have been added or modified where appropriate to better illustrate concepts. For example, Figure 6.3 has been modified in Chapter 6. A few visuals are also gone (the oral, literate, and electronic cultures in Chapter 1). Now, only one figure represents the spiral and the star organizational patterns.

Streamlined chapters. Finally, I've shortened and tightened the text's narrative explication, trimmed most of the Building Your Speech boxes to brief prompts that direct students to Speech Builder Express, and reduced and reformatted the chapter-ending material to improve its usability.

Proven Features of the Book

While presenting public speaking within the context of a pluralistic society and highlighting the ways that students are empowered through expressing their ideas in public settings, this book offers a range of distinctive features that have made it, I'm grateful to say, many instructors' preferred text and a favorite among students.

Rhetorical foundations. Chapter 2, "Giving Your First Speech: Developing Confidence," introduces students to the five canons of rhetoric, grounding their understanding of speechmaking in its classical Greek and Roman origins and highlighting that it needs to be approached as a process. The canons are mentioned throughout the text when appropriate. In addition, figures from classical rhetoric, such as St. Augustine, Aristotle, and Quintilian, take their place alongside Sonja

Foss and Cindy Griffin (invitational rhetoric), Walter Fisher (narrative theory), and Icek Ajzen and Martin Fishbein (theory of reasoned action).

Emphasis on diversity. This edition continues to emphasize diversity by describing public speaking and listening traditions from a range of perspectives. For example, my childhood experiences in New Mexico led me to include information about Navajo speaking traditions. And my adult years in an African American community and in New York City show up in examples, illustrations, and Diversity in Practice boxes.

Diverse sample speeches. To provide students with illustrative models of the speech concepts and techniques covered in this text, every chapter includes sample speech excerpts, transcripts, and outlines that represent the book's attention to diversity. Examples of topics include the African dun dun drum and the Vietnamese alphabet. This is the only textbook on the market to feature a student speech given through an interpreter (given in Spanish, interpreted into English.) Additionally, most chapters end with an annotated speech transcript or outline (by either a student or a professional speaker). Video of most sample speeches is available on the book's companion website, where students also have access to several interactive features (for more information, see the discussion of student resources below).

Civility and speechmaking. Chapter 3, Ethics and Diversity, emphasizes the importance of civility and speechmaking by addressing topics such as responses to diversity (condensed in this edition). The chapter builds on the discussion of dialogical theory in Chapter 1, and introduces concepts from Barnett and Kimberly Pearce and Amatai Etzioni in a section on dialogical theory. The chapter also includes a new professional speech on civil discourse.

Narrative traditions and strategies. Chapter 15, "Telling Narratives" is based in the narrative theory of communication that has been highly influential in communication studies during the last two decades. Students are introduced to the exemplum pattern, which has its roots in classical rhetoric.

Nontraditional speech organization patterns. Chapter 9, "Organizing Your Speech," includes distinctive coverage of nontraditional patterns, such as the star and the wave, to expand students' repertoire of organizational options.

Technology. Chapter 7, "Researching Your Speech in Electronic Culture," offers the most concentrated technology coverage, but because technology plays such a prominent role in today's students' lives, the book consistently presents topics, examples, and strategies that reflect our electronic, technologically advanced culture.

Quick-start guide for giving a first speech. A start-to-finish guide for students preparing for their first speeches appears in Chapter 2, "Giving Your First Speech: Developing Confidence." This highly praised chapter also includes guidelines and suggestions for overcoming public speaking anxiety.

Purposeful and Effective Pedagogy

In addition to chapter-opening lists of learning objectives, key term definitions in the margins of each chapter, and chapter-ending summaries, each chapter includes several acclaimed pedagogical features that improve student learning and performance:

▶ **Stop and Check boxes.** These critical thinking and application activities help students assess their progress throughout each chapter. Many of these activities include a suggested reading, available within the InfoTrac College Edition online database, to expand students' understanding of the topic and give them practice researching and locating quality support material. Others work in tandem with exercises available in the Student Workbook, and most are also available in electronic format on the book's companion website with additional interactive features.

▶ **Diversity in Practice boxes.** These boxes enhance the book's emphasis on diversity by presenting brief discussions of public speaking traditions from a range of perspectives on topics such as cultural listening styles (Chapter 4), prior credibility in other cultures (Chapter 5), Chicano murals as visual evidence (Chapter 8), African organizational patterns (Chapter 9), immigrants' accents (Chapter 14), and persuasion in other cultures (Chapter 17).

▶ **Build Your Speech boxes.** These skill-building activities help students apply text concepts to actual speechmaking, and can serve as starting points for completing actual speech assignments. Most of these activities prompt students to access Speech Builder Express, Thomson Wadsworth's award-winning online speech organization and outlining program.

▶ **Key Terms.** The perfect complement to the definitions provided in the margin of each chapter, the end-of-chapter list of key terms helps students check their acquisition of important vocabulary. Using the page number provided, students can easily reference the term with its definition in context. A complete glossary is provided on the book's companion website, where students can also study chapter concepts and terms online using interactive crossword puzzles and flashcards (the website is described more fully below).

▶ **Application and Critical Thinking Exercises.** Suitable for individual or group assignments, and for in-class discussion, these end-of-chapter questions help students better understand and critically evaluate the chapter content and further apply the skills they've learned.

Accompanying Resources: An Exclusive Teaching and Learning Package

Public Speaking: Concepts and Skills for a Diverse Society, Fifth Edition, offers a comprehensive array of supplements to assist in making the public speaking course as meaningful and enjoyable as possible for both students and instructors, and to help students succeed. Thomson Wadsworth has prepared the following descriptions of both the print and electronic resources available for your consideration.

Resources for Students

Strictly optional, these resources are bundled with student copies of the text only at your request, either free or at a small additional cost.

Guide to Online Resources for Public Speaking. Packaged with an access code for Thomson's 1pass portal, the *Guide to Online Resources for Public Speaking* provides a comprehensive overview of and introduction to the many valuable resources for students available online, including the book's premium companion website, InfoTrac College Edition, Speech Builder Express, and vMentor. This handy guide, which can be packaged with the text at no additional charge, offers helpful information about and strategies for using each of these valuable online resources. **Please note:** If you want your students to have access to these premium online resources, please order **ISBN: 0-495-16224-8.** Using this ISBN ensures that the guide and 1pass access code will be bundled with every new copy of the text at no additional charge to your students. Students with used books may purchase the guide and access code by visiting http://communication.wadsworth.com/jaffe5. Descriptions of each of the component online resources follow:

▶ **Public Speaking Premium Companion Website.** The premium companion website (accessed through Thomson's 1pass portal) features a wealth of interactive and multimedia learning resources, including video of over thirty complete student and professional speeches and several speech clips, all but a few included or referenced in the text. The videos help students prepare for their own speech performances and give effective feedback to their peers by providing practice in evaluating and critiquing introductory, informative, persuasive, and special-occasion speeches. After responding to the questions for analysis, students can email their responses to you and see how their answers compare to the author's evaluations.

The full-length speech videos are further enhanced with a scrolling outline feature that students can turn on to run next to the movie screen. When the scroll feature is on, synchronized highlighting tracks each speaker's progress through his or her speech outline. The videos also have a "Notes" feature that lets students record written comments while watching the video. At a student's command, the program pauses, enters a time-stamp that indicates where the video was paused, and offers the student prewritten notes to choose from or modify as well as the option of composing completely original notes. A transcript, full-sentence and key word outlines, and note cards are provided for the full-length student speech videos.

The Premium Website also includes numerous chapter-by-chapter interactive resources to help students understand and apply the text's instruction. These include live and updated Web links for every URL mentioned in the book, self- quizzes, key term crossword puzzles and flashcards, InfoTrac College Edition readings with critical questions, speech preparation and evaluation checklists, "Stop and Check" skill-building and critical thinking activities that are linked to the corresponding "Stop and Check" boxes in the book, and an online glossary. Finally, the premium website provides public speaking student resources, such as an interactive version of the *Personal Report of Communication Apprehension* (PRCA).

▶ **Speech Builder Express™ Speech Organization and Outlining Program.** This award-winning web-based tool coaches students through the speech organization and outlining process. By completing interactive sessions that help them write a thesis statement, develop main and subordinate points, integrate support material, craft transitions, plan visual aids, compose an introduction and conclusion, and prepare a bibliography, students can create full-sentence and keyword outlines, formatted according to the principles presented in the text. The program's prompts are customized depending on the type of speech a student is preparing and the many other variables of speech preparation, such as organizational pattern. Within the program, students also have access to embedded resources, such as text and video models, a timeline, a dictionary, and a thesaurus. **Speech Builder Express** works in tandem with the "Build Your Speech" activities in the text, giving students the step-by-step guidance that results in effective speech preparation and delivery. For more information about Speech Builder Express, visit http://sbe .wadsworth.com.

▶ **InfoTrac College Edition with InfoMarks™.** With their free four-month subscription to this online library's more than 18 million reliable, full-length articles, students can use keyword searches to retrieve almost instant results from over 5,000 academic and popular periodicals in the InfoTrac College Edition database. Students also have access to InfoMarks—stable URLs that can be linked to articles, journals, and searches to save valuable time when doing research—*and* to the InfoWrite online resource center, where they can access grammar help, critical thinking guidelines, guides to writing research papers, and much more. For more information about InfoTrac College Edition and the InfoMarks linking tool, visit http://www.infotrac college.com and click on "User Demo."

▶ vMentor gives your students access to virtual office hours—one-on-one, online tutoring help from a subject-area expert, at no additional cost with the text. In vMentor's virtual classroom, students interact with the tutor and other students using two-way audio, an interactive whiteboard for illustrating the problem, and instant messaging. To ask a question, students simply click to raise a "hand." **Again, please note:** For students to have access to these premium online resources at no additional charge, please be sure to order **ISBN: 0-495-16224-8.** Students who buy used books may visit http://communication.wadsworth.com/jaffe5 to purchase 1pass access separately. *Your local Thomson sales representative has more details.*

The following print and multimedia resources are also available for students and can be packaged with the text in a combination of your choice:

Speech Builder Express Student Guide. This user-friendly guidebook helps students use the Speech Builder Express speech outlining and organizing software. They receive help for every step—from choosing their speech topic, to selecting an appropriate organizational pattern, to incorporating visual aids, and beyond.

InfoTrac College Edition Student Activities Workbook for Public Speaking. The workbook features guidelines and an extensive selection of individual and group activities designed to help instructors and students get the most from InfoTrac College Edition. Referenced throughout the *Annotated Instructor's Edition.*

Election 2004: Speeches from the Campaign. Featuring selected full speeches and excerpts from the 2004 Democratic and Republican conventions, this dynamic CD-ROM is a great way to help students understand the power and the impact of public speaking—both when it's effective and when it fails. Students may view some of the conventions' more noted speeches, including those by Barack Obama, Arnold Schwarzenegger, Bill Clinton, and Laura Bush.

Student Workbook. Written by Clella Jaffe, this workbook complements and expands students' understanding of the main text's material. It features a welcome letter to the student and an introductory overview about the benefits of taking a public speaking course. It also features chapter-by-chapter activities, many of which expand on the text's Stop and Check and Build Your Speech activities and include scenario-based learning that facilitates both individual and group work. Chapter review self-tests with answer keys are also included. The workbook also contains speech assignment options, examples, and checklists. Speech preparation forms and checklists are formatted so they can be pulled out of the workbook and submitted.

A Guide to the Basic Course for ESL Students. This item can be bundled and is designed to assist the nonnative speaker. Featuring FAQs, helpful URLs, and strategies for accent management and speech apprehension, this resource is referenced throughout the *Annotated Instructor's Edition.*

The Art and Strategy of Service Learning Presentations, **Second Edition.** Written by Rick Isaacson and Jeff Saperstein of San Francisco State University, this brief book is an invaluable resource for students in basic courses that integrate a service-learning component. The handbook provides guidelines for connecting service-learning work with classroom concepts and advice for working effectively with agencies and organizations. It also provides model forms and reports and a directory of online resources.

Resources for Instructors

Public Speaking: Concepts and Skills for a Diverse Society, Fifth Edition, also features a full suite of resources for instructors. The following class preparation, classroom presentation, assessment, and course management resources are available:

Annotated Instructor's Edition (AIE). The *Public Speaking* AIE is a student text enhanced with marginal class-tested and reviewer-validated teaching tips and suggestions for integrating the extensive ancillary program. Fully cross-referenced with the *Instructor's Resource Manual*, the test bank, the ESL and Service Learning handbooks, the *Multimedia Manager/Instructor's Resource CD-ROM*, and the *Public Speaking* Premium Companion Website, this tool is a must-have for the first-time instructor or graduate teaching assistant and a great refresher for the veteran professor.

Instructor's Resource Manual. Cross-referenced with the *Annotated Instructor's Edition* and the student workbook, the *Instructor's Resource Manual* provides a comprehensive teaching guide. Written by Clella Jaffe, this manual features sample syllabi, as well suggested speaking assignments and criteria for evaluation. Each text chapter has the following resources: transition notes to the fifth edition, chapter goals, a chapter outline, suggestions correlating supplements and online resources, supplementary research notes, suggested discussion questions and specific suggestions for integrating student workbook activities and videos. The *Manual* also includes a printed test bank that features class-tested multiple-choice, true-false, short-answer, essay, and fill-in-the-blank test questions.

This manual is also available on the instructor website and the Multimedia Manager with Instructor Resources CD-ROM, which includes ExamView Computerized Testing. More information follows.

Instructor's Website. The password-protected instructor's website includes electronic access to the Instructor's Resource Manual, downloadable versions of the book's PowerPoint slides, and a link to the Opposing Viewpoints Resource Center. To gain access to the website, simply request a course key by opening the site's home page.

Multimedia Manager with Instructor Resources CD-ROM: A Microsoft® PowerPoint® Tool. This CD-ROM contains an electronic version of the Instructor's Resource Manual, the ExamView® Computerized Testing program, JoinIn on Turning Point question slides, and ready-to-use Microsoft® PowerPoint® presentations, prepared by Matthew Thompson of the University of Central Florida, based on material in the text. The PowerPoint slides contain text, images, and cued videos of speeches from the premium website and can be used as is or customized to suit your course needs. This all-in-one lecture tool makes it easy for you to assemble, edit, publish, and present custom lectures for your course. More information about ExamView and JoinIn follow:

▶ **Computerized Testing** enables you to create, deliver, and customize tests and study guides (both print and online) in minutes using the test bank questions from the Instructor's Resource Manual. ExamView offers both a *Quick Test Wizard* and an *Online Test Wizard* that guide you step-by-step through the process of creating tests, while its "what you see is what you get" interface allows you to see the test you are creating on-screen exactly as it will print or display online. You can build tests of up to 250 questions, using up to 12 question types. Using the complete word-processing capabilities of ExamView, you can even enter an unlimited number of new questions or edit existing ones.

▶ Thomson Wadsworth is now pleased to offer you JoinIn™ content for Response Systems tailored to *Public Speaking*, Fifth Edition, allowing you to transform your classroom and assess your students' progress with instant in-class quizzes and polls. Our exclusive agreement to offer JoinIn on Turning-Point® software lets you pose book-specific questions and display students' answers seamlessly within the Microsoft® PowerPoint® slides of your own lecture, in conjunction with the "clicker" hardware of your choice. Enhance how your students interact with you, your lecture, and each other.

Turnitin. This proven online plagiarism-prevention software promotes fairness in the classroom by helping students learn to correctly cite sources and allowing instructors to check for originality before reading and grading papers and speeches. Turnitin quickly checks student papers and speeches against billions of pages of Internet content, millions of published works, millions of student papers, and within seconds generates a comprehensive originality report.

WebTutor™ ToolBox for WebCT and Blackboard. Preloaded with content and available *free* via a PIN code when packaged with the text, WebTutor ToolBox pairs all the content of this text's rich premium book companion website with all the sophisticated course management functionality of a WebCT or Blackboard product.

Student Speeches for Critique and Analysis on Video and DVD. These volumes offer a variety of sample student speeches that your students can watch, critique, and analyze on their own or in class. All of the speech types are included, as well as speeches featuring nonnative English speakers and the use of visual aids.

The Teaching Assistant's Guide to the Basic Course. This guidebook is designed for today's communication teacher. Based on leading communication teacher training programs, the guide covers general teaching and course management topics, as well as specific strategies for communication instruction, such as providing effective feedback on performance, managing sensitive class discussions, and conducting mock interviews.

These resources are available to qualified adopters, and ordering options are flexible. Please consult your local Thomson sales representative for more information, to evaluate examination copies of any of these instructor or student resources, or to arrange product demonstrations. You may also contact the Wadsworth Academic Resource Center at 800-423-0563, or visit us at http://communication.wadsworth.com.

Acknowledgments

Every book is a co-created product in which an author relies on the encouragement of others. I owe a longstanding debt to former Oregon State University colleagues (Victoria O'Donnell, Sean Patrick O'Rourke, Anne Zach Ferguson, and dozens of graduate teaching instructors). My colleagues at George Fox University, Richard Engnell, Craig Johnson, and Ray Anderson, have consistently and patiently supported my writing, for which I am grateful. I also thank generations of students at Oregon State, St. John's (New York), and George Fox University who provided insights, examples, speeches, and support. Scott Johnson (Bethel College) and Mark Parravecchio deserve special recognition for their insights on the text. I extend special thanks too to Sandy Pensoneau of Wayne State University, as she created the web quizzes for students on the book's premium companion website.

Likewise, I want to thank the many people at or working with Thomson Wadsworth who helped bring this new edition and its many supplements to fruition: Holly Allen, Barbara Armentrout, Lucinda Bingham, Renee Deljon, Maria Epes, John Gahbauer, Stephanie Lee, Annie Mitchell, Jaime Perkins, Catherine Morris, Gretchen Otto, Kimberly Russell, Alexandra Tran, and Jeanette Wiseman.

I also would like to thank the reviewers who contributed valuable comments about this book's fourth edition and offered helpful suggestions for the fifth: Ferald J. Bryan, Northern Illinois University; Cynthia Brown-El, Macomb Community College; Amy R. Slagell, Iowa State University; Patricia O'Keefe, College of Marin; Kathryn Wylie-Marques, John Jay College, City University of New York; Franklin L. Gray, Ball State University; Tina Kistler, Santa Barbara City College; Michelle Burch, Clark State University; and Kathleen Farrell, Saint Louis University.

I would also like to thank the reviewers for previous editions of this book. Reviewers for the First Edition were Martha Ann Atkins, Iowa State University; Dennis Beaver, Bakersfield College; Carol Berteotti, University of Wisconsin–La Crosse; Carole Blair, University of California–Davis; Bruce G. Bryski, Buffalo State College; Jacquelyn Buckrop, Ball State University; Norma Flores, Golden West College; Charles Griffin, Kansas State University; Susan Hellweg, San Diego State University; Mark Hickson, University of Alabama–Birmingham; Janet Hoffman, Southern Illinois University at Carbondale; Susan Huxman, Wichita State University; Karla Jensen, Texas Tech University; Shelley D. Lane, Collin County Community College; Jo Ann Lawlor, West Valley College; Steven March, Pima County Community College; Victoria O'Donnell, Montana State University; Sean Patrick O'Rourke, Vanderbilt University; Patricia Palm McGillen, Mankato State University; Mark Morman, Johnson County Community College; Teresa Nance, Villanova University; Mary Pelias, Southern Illinois University; Mark Stoner, California State University–Sacramento; Patricia Sullivan, State University of New York at New Paltz; Marsha Vanderford, University of South Florida; Donald E. Williams, University of Florida; Lee Winet, State University of New York–Oswego; and Anne Zach Ferguson, University of California–Davis. Reviewers for the Second Edition were Thomas E. Diamond, Montana State University; Kevin E. McClearey, Southern Illinois University at Edwardsville; Susan Messman, Arizona State University; Karla D. Scott, Saint Louis University; Jessica Stowell, Tulsa Community College; and Lori Wisdom-Whitley, Western Washington University. Reviewers for the Third Edition were Clifton Adams, Central Missouri State University; Linda Anthon, Valencia Community College; Jay Baglia, University of South Florida; Carol Barnum, Southern Polytechnic State University; Lori Basden Arnold, Rowan University; Julie Benson-Rosston, University of Montana; John Bourhis, Missouri State University; Cheri Campbell, Keene State College; Faye Clark, Georgia Perimeter College; Risa Dickson, California State University at San Bernardino; Hal Fulmer, Georgia Southern University; Matthew Girton, Florida State University; Sherrie L. Guerrero, San Bernardino Valley College; Robert Gwynne, University of Tennessee–Knoxville; Fred Jandt, California State University at San Bernardino; Laura Nelson, University of Wisconsin–La Crosse; Jean E. Perry, Glendale Community College; Susie Richardson, Prince George's Community College; Paula Rodriguez, Hinds Community College; Scott Rodriguez, California State University at San Bernardino; Cathy Sargent Mester, Pennsylvania State University; Kristi A. Schaller, University of Hawaii; Ann M. Scroggie, Santa Fe Community College; Karni Spain Tiernan, Bradley University; David Walker, Middle Tennessee State University; June D. Wells, Indian River Community College; Nancy J. Wendt, Oregon State University; L. Keith Williamson, Wichita State University; and Marianne Worthington, Cumberland College. Reviewers for the Fourth Edition were James E. Bruce, University of Tennessee at Martin; Ferald J. Bryan, Northern Illinois University; Nanci Burk, Glendale Community College; Helen Chester, Milwaukee Area Technical College; Omar Guevara, California State University at Bakersfield; Janice D. Hamlet, Northern Illinois University; Jeff Przybylo, William Rainey Harper Community College; Diana D. Roberts, Community College of Southern Nevada; Lisa Waite, Kent State University; and Diane E. Waryas, Community College of Southern Nevada.

Writing takes a toll on an author's family. I am grateful for Jack, Sara, Josh, J. C., and all the little ones who make a difference in my life. Wadsworth has provided a series of editors who have guided this text throughout the five editions. Annie Mitchell and Renee Deljon were consistently patient and supportive. I was also blessed with Janet McCartney Parkinson as copy editor, Gretchen Otto as project manager for the book, and Terri Wright as photo researcher for this edition.

Clella Jaffe, Ph.D.

Public Speaking

Concepts and Skills for a Diverse Society

FIFTH EDITION

INTRODUCTION TO PUBLIC SPEAKING AND CULTURE

THIS CHAPTER WILL HELP YOU

▶ Explain three ways you can be empowered by studying public speaking

▶ Define culture in the context of public speaking

▶ Give reasons for studying public speaking from a cultural perspective

▶ Identify three ways culture affects public speaking

▶ Know how public speaking influences culture

▶ Understand aspects of the dialogical theory of communication

▶ Identify elements of the transactional model of communication

"Culture of the Crossroads" Mural © 1998 by Precita Eyes Muralists. Directed by Susan Kelk Cervantes. (McDonald's Building, 24th Street at Mission, SF, CA)

WHAT COMES TO MIND when you hear the words *public speaker?* Politicians? Clergy members? Stand-up comedians? Professors? True, these people all perform in public, but public speaking is not limited to formal settings. A coach's locker room speech, a firefighter's talk about home safety, and a camp counselor's campfire story are just a few less formal speechmaking situations. By definition, **public speaking** occurs when one person prepares and performs a speech for a group that listens, generally without interrupting the speaker's flow of ideas. Your public speaking course will help you think your way through the process of planning, presenting, and evaluating effective speeches. Throughout the term, you will assess your current skills, identify specific areas for improvement, and plan strategies to deal with the challenges of speaking and listening in a free society. As you create first one speech and then another, you will improve your skills by adding competencies and by refining those you already have.[1]

Although this text has *public speaking* in the title, speechmaking is only one element of the course you're taking. More often than not, you will be in the audience, listening to speeches in a world that is increasingly diverse. Improving your listening skills by learning to better understand and evaluate the messages you hear daily is another major course goal. The skills needed for these two roles—speaker and listener—are the focus of this text.

Chapter-at-a-Glance
This chapter begins by discussing how studying public speaking can empower students. The chapter proceeds to discuss why it is useful to study public speaking from a cultural perspective, how culture affects public speaking, and how public speaking influences culture. The chapter ends with the dialogical theory of communication and the transactional model.

CASE STUDY: LORNA OWENS'S MISSION

Lorna Owens has used her public speaking and listening skills as a lawyer, small business owner, motivational speaker, and community activist.

Courtesy Lorna Owens/Positive Vibe

The inspiring eulogy and the glowing tributes at her father's funeral led Lorna Owens to reassess her life priorities. As she heard friends and relatives narrate the wonderful things he'd done throughout his life, she realized that no one could speak as positively about her. Owens, a native of Jamaica, was at the top of her game as a high-powered Florida lawyer, but her reflections led her to resign her position and start her own company. Eventually, she became a motivational speaker and life coach. Owens sponsors an annual event, "And the Women Gather," which brings together women (mostly professionals) who have fun while listening to interesting, inspirational speakers. Proceeds from the event go to two organizations: (1) the Guild of Women Achievers, which provides health care and health education to women who work in sweatshops in India, and (2) Women Behind Bars, a nonprofit, 90-day empowerment program that Owens organized to help women transition from prison to the community. Her eventual vision includes a full-service salon and day spa that will employ former inmates.[2]

Questions for Discussion

▸ How has Lorna Owens used public speaking throughout her several careers?
▸ How do you think listening has been a factor? For instance, when was listening important in her career as a lawyer? As a life coach, how did she rely on her audiences' listening to help her accomplish her goals?
▸ What advice do you think she would give you as you begin your public speaking course?
▸ How are speaking and listening important in helping people make social changes such as prison reform?
▸ How will you use speaking in your career? Listening?

public speaking when a person delivers a presentation to a group that listens, generally without interrupting the speaker's flow of ideas

The Miami Herald (via Knight-Ridder/Tribune News Service), March 14, 2005, pNA. Speaker helps women find a balance. Full Text: COPYRIGHT 2005. The Miami Herald Byline: Ana Veciana-Suarez.

How Can This Course Help You?

Although you may not think of yourself as a "public speaker," chances are you have performed in public at least once—for example, a grade school "Show and Tell" talk, a club announcement, or a class report. You've undoubtedly listened to many speeches, and you have formed some ideas about what makes a presentation effective or ineffective. These experiences provide a foundation on which you can build additional competencies. Studying public speaking principles can empower you in a number of ways. Let's consider some of them.

Gain Confidence and Competence

If you are typical, the idea of giving a speech makes you at least somewhat anxious. For example, one student confessed:

> Nothing scares me worse than public speaking. I would rather shoot myself in the foot or go bungee jumping than speak in front of people. I spend days with my stomach in knots, and when I finally get up to speak, I feel like I can't breathe. My hands shake and my legs feel like jelly. ANNA

Apprehension is the dread or fear of having something bad happen. **Communication apprehension (CA)** is the fear of negative reactions you might experience because you speak out.[3] CA is linked to learning style preference[4] and to inborn temperament traits such as shyness.[5]

A specific type of CA is **public speaking anxiety (PSA),**[6] which has two dimensions: process anxiety and performance anxiety. **Process anxiety** is your insecurity about the how-to of speechmaking. For example, you may lack confidence when it comes to topic selection, research, or organizing your ideas. **Performance anxiety** is your concern about actually presenting your idea. For instance, you don't want to tremble or forget your speech entirely.

If you feel nervous about speechmaking, you're normal. A National Communication Association poll found that almost 40 percent of Americans confess to some PSA.[7] Because anxiety is so common, Chapter 2 presents information you can use to recognize and deal with it. Fortunately, you can be *competent* without feeling *confident*, because competence is the ability to succeed or to do something well. Three elements compose **communication competence:** motivation, knowledge, and skills[8] (see Figure 1.1). Motivation comes from within you, but studying this text, participating in classroom activities, fulfilling assignments, and actually giving speeches will help you develop the knowledge and skills you need to perform competently.

Many people, especially those with high levels of PSA, experience increased confidence after they complete the course,[9] as these testimonials suggest:

> Initially, I took the class to fulfill the requirement, but it was a valuable course! My confidence when speaking in front of people has increased significantly since the first day of class. MARY

> Getting up in front of the class . . . built up my confidence. MARTINA

STOP AND CHECK

ASSESS YOUR CURRENT COMPETENCE

On a sheet of paper, draw three overlapping circles. Label one *knowledge,* one *skills,* and one *motivation.* In each circle, write your current knowledge, skills, and motivations in the public speaking context. Then identify areas you want to improve within each category.

Instructor Resource: *TA's Guide*
For tips on reducing students' communication apprehension, see pp. 41–42 of the *Teaching Assistant's Guide to the Basic Course.*

Classroom Discussion/ Activity
Ask students to each think of three physiological reactions they experience while giving a speech. Compile a master list of reactions on the chalkboard or other display medium. Point out how many of the reactions they share with their classmates. This activity can serve as a springboard to a discussion or lecture on ways to manage common physiological reactions to speech anxiety. These include upset stomach, trembling in hands or legs, flushed face, sweating, narrowing of vision, loss of balance, rigid posture, dry mouth, and excessive salivation.

---

communication apprehension (CA) the fear or dread of negative responses you might experience because you speak out

public speaking anxiety (PSA) fear or dread specifically related to speaking in public

process anxiety fear due to lack of confidence in knowing how to prepare a speech

performance anxiety fear of forgetting or of presenting your speech poorly

communication competence the ability to communicate appropriately and successfully

Figure 1.1
Elements of Communication Competence
Communication competence combines three overlapping elements: motivation to communicate, knowledge about communication, and skills in speaking and listening.

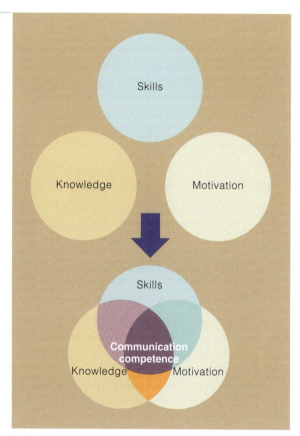

Develop Your Professional and Personal Skills

What do employers look for when they hire? Typically, they seek people who can listen effectively, present their ideas clearly, think critically, and exude enthusiasm. In one survey, 98 percent of personnel interviewers identified both verbal and nonverbal communication skills as important, and they overwhelmingly agreed that these skills are vital for higher-level positions.[10] You can use many of the skills you develop in this course in occupations as diverse as law, medicine,[11] management, teaching, and accounting.[12]

In addition to job success, the ability to present your thoughts clearly and persuasively enables you to voice your ideas about important social issues. You can probably identify many examples of individuals whose communication makes a difference. Students hold peace rallies and set up environmental workshops. People contribute to radio talk shows and send letters to newspaper editors.[13] On weblogs (**blogs**) and listservs, and in online chat rooms and other discussion forums, millions of people share ideas about everything from sport controversies to movies to the war on terrorism. Skillful communicators influence local, national, and international decisions.

Finally, public speaking skills are valuable in a variety of social situations. Narrating a "cousins' story" at a family reunion, telling a joke to a group of friends, and giving a wedding toast or a funeral eulogy are examples of situations where short, often impromptu speeches create and maintain strong, personal connections. For example, the opening case study showed how tributes given at her father's funeral caused Lorna Owens to reassess her life. As speaker after speaker described his many acts of compassion, she thought, "They're never going to say this about me."[14] She went home, reordered her priorities, reorganized her life, followed her visions, and became more involved with others.

blogs shortened form of weblogs

rhetoric the study of persuasion in its various forms, a term often used negatively

Increase Your Critical Thinking Skills

From ancient Greek and Roman academies to modern English and communication departments, the study of **rhetoric** has long played a central role. In fact, rhetoric is one of the original seven liberal arts. This may seem surprising, given the generally negative feeling people today have about the word. For instance, when asked to define *rhetoric*, Paula responded:

> Rhetoric is just talking. It's a negative word nowadays, but I don't think it always was. But presently it implies speaking just to fill up space, I think.
>
> PAULA

Phrases such as "empty rhetoric" or "Is this just rhetoric or will there be action?" probably influenced her definition. However, rhetoricians typically study persuasion in its many forms, including writing, advertising campaigns, rhetoric of film, and rhetoric of art. Because persuasive speaking has been important in every culture and every generation, this text covers both ancient and modern principles of rhetoric. (See the Diversity in Practice box on this page for more on the historical importance of public speaking.)

Studying rhetorical principles helps you develop critical thinking competencies. Ideally, by the time you graduate, you will be able to analyze information, sort through persuasive appeals, discriminate faulty arguments from valid reasoning, and follow ideas to logical conclusions. In the process you will learn to appreciate a diversity of opinions and presentation styles.[15] All these competencies open doors for you and your future.[16]

So what advantages does a course in public speaking offer? Your confidence increases as you face your fears and meet the challenge of preparing and giving speeches. You add to your communication abilities within a culture that values them. Finally, you develop critical thinking skills that enable you to sort through the ideas and persuasive appeals that surround you daily.

Classroom Discussion / Activity
Discuss the importance of critical thinking skills by analyzing a news reports or an ad. Begin by asking for first impressions—What does X say or suggest? Then ask students to identify the assumptions on which the story or ad relies. Ask for ways to question those assumptions. Finally, have students compare their first impressions with the results of their questioning and discuss the value of their critical analysis.

DIVERSITY IN PRACTICE
PUBLIC SPEAKING IN ANCIENT CULTURES

PUBLIC SPEAKING HAS ITS PLACE in every society. For example, fragments of the oldest book in existence, *The Precepts of Ke'gemni and Ptah-hotep* (ca. 2100 BC), provided young Egyptians with guidelines for both speaking and listening:[17]

- Speak with exactness, and recognize the value of silence.
- Listeners who have "good fellowship" can be influenced by the speeches of others.
- Do not be proud of your learning.
- Keep silent in the face of a better debater; refute the false arguments of an equal, but let a weaker speaker's arguments confound themselves.
- Do not pervert the truth.
- Avoid speech subjects about which you know nothing.
- Remember that a covetous person is not a persuasive speaker.

It was good advice then, and it's good advice now!

Why Take a Cultural Perspective?

Recent wars, national disasters, and terrorist incidents remind us that we live in a rapidly shrinking world where members of distinctly different cultures regularly come into contact. But not all diversity is global in scope; in national regions and local communities you encounter people with diverse ethnic backgrounds, faiths, political affiliations, economic circumstances, views about sexuality, and so on. Although your community or school may not seem especially diverse, you will better understand our nation and our world if you understand how diversity affects communication. That is why this text presents both the public speaking norms most common in the United States and the speaking traditions of other cultures in this country and abroad.

What exactly is a culture? **Cultures** are integrated systems of learned beliefs, values, attitudes, and behaviors that a group accepts and passes along from older to newer members. Don Smith,[18] founder of Daystar University in Kenya, compares a culture to an onion: It has visible outer layers (clothing, art, food, language, and so on) and embedded perceptual filters that influence how we view the world (ideologies, folk beliefs, attitudes, values, and so on).[19] Put another way, culture exists at a conscious as well as at an unconscious level; cultures include relatively stable elements, but they can and do change.

Although members of a society share many commonalities, each complex culture contains subgroups, or **co-cultures,** made up of people who diverge in some way from the mainstream. Think of all the co-cultural groups you can identify (for example, skinheads, Jehovah's Witnesses, bikers). Logging on to **www.yahoo.com**, going to its Web directory, and clicking on the Cultures and Groups link results in a listing of more than 1,100 cultures and 10,000 groups represented. Seeing the extensive list of links, and maybe even visiting some of the interesting sites they lead to, will help you better understand why this text integrates diverse perspectives throughout.

Taking a cultural approach increases your communication competence. Because you perform each speech within a specific situation to an audience that holds expectations regarding its length, appropriate delivery, and so on, you succeed best when you understand and adapt to cultural norms. This increases your **rhetorical sensitivity** and marks you as a person who "can adapt to diverse social situations and perform reasonably well in most of them."[20]

Culture Affects Public Speaking

Some cultural influences on public speaking are easily identifiable. But cultures also influence our speaking in less obvious ways by providing core resources, technological aids, and cultural norms (see Figure 1.2).

Cultures Provide Core Resources

According to communication professor W. Barnett Pearce,[21] each culture offers a pool of **core cultural resources,** or "logics of meaning and action," that define our obligations as well as our taboos. These systems of intertwined beliefs, attitudes, values, and behaviors underlie every area of life, including public speaking.

Beliefs are the ideas we mentally accept as true or reject as false. Values are our underlying evaluations of what is important, significant, moral, or right. Attitudes are our predispositions to evaluate, either negatively or positively, persons, objects, symbols, and the like. Finally, behaviors are the actions we consider appropriate or normal. Here are some foundational cultural resources for public speaking in the United States:

- A *belief* that we can change our society by speaking out and creating public policies instead of giving in to fate.
- A *value* that places individuality over conformity.
- Positive *attitudes* toward open forums and negative attitudes about suppressing dissent.
- Standards for predictable speaking and listening *behaviors* that vary according to context.

These core resources, and others like them, combine to create public speaking expectations. Because Americans typically value freedom and choice, we try to respect one an-

cultures integrated systems of learned beliefs, values, behaviors, and norms that include visible (clothing, food) and underlying (core beliefs, worldview) characteristics of a society

co-cultures subgroups of culture, characterized by mild or profound cultural differences, that coexist within the larger culture

rhetorical sensitivity the ability to adapt to a variety of audiences and settings and to perform appropriately in diverse social situations

core cultural resources beliefs, values, attitudes, and behaviors that provide a logical basis for a culture to define what is necessary, right, doubtful, or forbidden

Figure 1.2
Core Cultural Resources
Intertwined beliefs, values, attitudes, and actions comprise our core cultural resources.

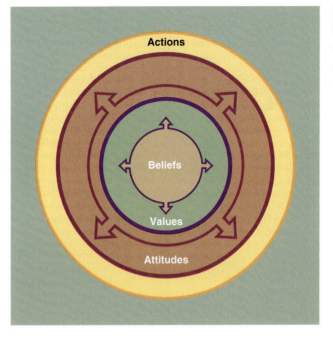

Instructor Resource: Power-Point
The *Multimedia Manager with Instructor Resources* CD-ROM includes a Power-Point slide of Figure 1.2.

other's ideas. Our beliefs that individuals are intelligent and reasonable lead us to influence others through persuasion rather than coercion. On the other hand, some cultural groups discourage their members from expressing their ideas freely, and many leaders choose force as a means of control.[22]

Cultures Provide Technological Aids

The technology available to a culture greatly affects how its members create and exchange messages. A strictly **oral culture** provides no technology for recording, storing, or transmitting ideas, so speakers and audiences must meet face to face. Members of oral cultures rely on poems and chants, proverbs and sayings, and stories and genealogies that help them learn and remember their values, beliefs, and traditions.[23]

In contrast, most cultural groups across the globe have at least some access to literacy and to electronic devices that allow them to record their ideas and convey them to audiences separated by both distance and time. You, fortunately, have libraries, electronically stored databases, the Internet, and other information sources you can use to gather speech materials. You can also write out your speaking notes, which frees you from the limitations of memory. In addition, electronic devices such as microphones, cameras, sophisticated recording machines, and more recent inventions like presentation software help you support your ideas in a variety of ways. Consequently, this text provides guidelines for using the many research, recording, and presentation technologies available in this culture.

Cultures Provide Expectations about Speaking and Listening

Cultures vary not only in the value they place on *expressiveness* and explicitness but also in their expectations regarding the *how, who,* and *what* of public speaking.

Cultures Vary in Expressiveness

Members of **nonexpressive cultures** value privacy and guard their emotions and ideas rather than express them indiscriminately. For example, people in Japan often associate silence with wisdom, and silence expresses power in various cultures throughout Asia.

Classroom Discussion/ Activity
Discuss how the abundance of technology in today's society has affected our oral communication and memory.

Classroom Discussion/ Activity
Ask students to describe the expressiveness of their own ethnic or home culture and to describe their experiences with cultures that have a different degree of expressiveness.

oral culture culture with no writing and no technology for recording messages apart from face-to-face interactions

nonexpressive cultures cultures that value privacy and encourage members to keep their emotions and ideas to themselves rather than to express them publicly

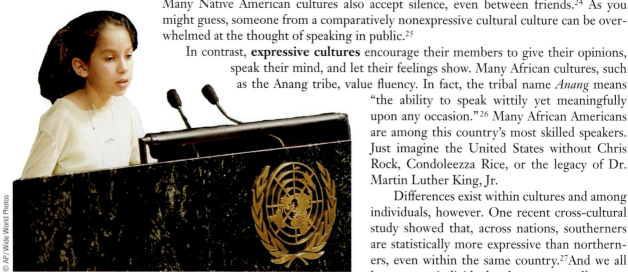

The voices of women, children, minorities, or the poor often are ignored or discounted. However, in May, 2002, Gabriela Azurduy Arrieta from Bolivia was one of two children who addressed the United Nations General Assembly at a special session devoted to children's issues. U.N. members, who hear mainly from adults, took their speeches seriously.

Many Native American cultures also accept silence, even between friends.[24] As you might guess, someone from a comparatively nonexpressive cultural culture can be overwhelmed at the thought of speaking in public.[25]

In contrast, **expressive cultures** encourage their members to give their opinions, speak their mind, and let their feelings show. Many African cultures, such as the Anang tribe, value fluency. In fact, the tribal name *Anang* means "the ability to speak wittily yet meaningfully upon any occasion."[26] Many African Americans are among this country's most skilled speakers. Just imagine the United States without Chris Rock, Condoleezza Rice, or the legacy of Dr. Martin Luther King, Jr.

Differences exist within cultures and among individuals, however. One recent cross-cultural study showed that, across nations, southerners are statistically more expressive than northerners, even within the same country.[27] And we all know some individuals who are naturally more reserved than others. In addition, rhetorically sensitive people commonly regulate their expressiveness to appear more or less outgoing, depending on the circumstances.[28] For example, the same man who normally creates a dramatic image by expressing his emotions and verbalizing his opinions sometimes withholds his expression to "be cool" and not let his thoughts or feelings show.[29]

Cultures Influence "Who" Speaks

In some cultures, only adult men, and sometimes just those men judged to be the oldest, wisest, or most knowledgeable, speak publicly.[30] This restriction virtually eliminates the voices of children, young people, non-experts, and women in public arenas. Cultures also may silence specific people or groups, such as the poor, ethnic minorities, or people with divergent political views, by ridiculing, misunderstanding, or punishing them for speaking out.[31] Fortunately, the Bill of Rights boldly proclaims the ideal of free speech; unfortunately, this ideal is not always realized in practice. However, you can cooperate with your classmates to make your public speaking classroom a safe place for everyone to speak and listen.

Classroom Discussion/ Activity
Ask students to discuss recent speaking experiences from a cultural perspective.

Cultures Guide the "How-To" of Speaking

A culture's core assumptions and norms work together to produce a preferred **communication style**.[32] The communication style common in the United States takes a *problem orientation*. It assumes that the world is rational and that we can find solutions to problems ranging from the global to the personal by acting on them. The style is also *direct*, featuring ideas that are logically organized in a way that gets to the point without "beating around the bush." A related characteristic is *explicitness*, or the use of clear, concise, and precise language instead of indirect or vague statements. The cultural values of equality and individuality result in *informality*, which is characterized by conversational delivery, and *personal involvement*, which leads speakers to identify with audiences by sharing personal experiences or finding other points of common ground. Your competency in many public speaking contexts will be judged against these norms.

expressive cultures cultures in which members are encouraged to give their opinions, speak their minds, and let their feelings show

communication style a culture's preferred ways of communicating, given its core assumptions and norms

Cultures Influence the "What" of Public Speaking

Some cultures discourage the expression of personal feelings and viewpoints; others find this desirable, even at the expense of "objectivity."[33] In the United States, we encourage people to debate one another on controversial topics. You probably can disagree with your friends and still remain friends. In contrast, traditional Chinese and Japanese speakers downplayed personal arguments, a behavior that may be traced to the Confucian idea of *hsin*, in which speakers and their words are inseparable. In these cultures, a public challenge could shame a person by casting doubt on his or her honesty.[34]

Cultural factors such as these can affect how comfortable you feel in a public speaking classroom that teaches Euro-American cultural norms. What is considered competent in a classroom or in a business setting may be quite different from your cultural traditions. If so, you may have to become **bicultural,** knowing the rules for competent speaking in the dominant culture while appreciating and participating in your own ethnic speech community. In the following example, a Nigerian woman living in the United States explains how she accomplishes this:

> At work, . . . I raise my voice as loud as necessary to be heard in meetings. At conferences where I present papers on "Women from the Third World," I make serious arguments about the need for international intervention in countries where women are deprived of all rights. . . . Yet as easily as I switch from speaking English to Ibo [her Nigerian language], . . . I never confuse my two selves.
>
> Hundreds of thousands of women from the third world and other traditional societies share my experience. We straddle two cultures, cultures that are often in opposition. Mainstream America, the culture we embrace in our professional lives, dictates that we be assertive and independent—like men. Our traditional culture, dictated by religion and years of socialization, demands that we be docile and content in our roles as mothers and wives—careers or not.[35]

As you can see, students from many traditions bring their contrasting expectations of "how to" speak into their college classrooms. Clearly, if they judge another tradition by their own culture's standards, misunderstandings and negative evaluations can result. This text presents standards commonly used to judge a speaker's competencies. But keep in mind that they are not the only ways of sharing ideas publicly.

Public Speaking Influences Culture

Cultures are not static. This means they can and do change, often through the efforts of skillful public speakers. Historically, people have spoken out against slavery and for women's suffrage; currently, public speakers debate educational questions, health care access, immigration laws, social security reform, and so on. As the case study at the beginning of the chapter pointed out, public speakers transmit, reinforce, repair, or transform their cultures.[36]

- Some *transmit* cultural resources to people who do not currently hold them. For example, volunteers prepare immigrants to become citizens by explaining the U.S. government, and pastors hold catechism classes to teach their church's beliefs.
- Other speakers *reinforce* or support existing cultural elements. They encourage listeners to "keep on keeping on" with their current behaviors or beliefs. Politicians who urge people to keep voting and inspirational speakers who urge donors to continue to support charities are in this category.
- When events threaten to tear apart communities, speakers attempt to *restore* matters to a healthy state by using words. For example, after a tragedy at a school, a principal

Instructor's Resource Manual For a list of videos that can be used to increase students' understanding of the relationship between culture and public speaking, see Chapter 1 in the *Instructor's Resource Manual* (available in print, online, and on the Multimedia Manager CD-ROM).

bicultural knowing and applying different rules for competent behaviors in two cultures

or other official usually hosts meetings that provide information essential for re-establishing the community's feelings of security.

▶ Speakers *transform* societies by bringing about social change. Prison reform, civil rights legislation, environmental protection—skilled speakers argued for all these changes. Even stable societies that are relatively functional can be improved, which leads people to speak out for better health care and social security reforms.

Whether the speaker's purpose is to transmit, reinforce, repair, or transform culture, we who live in dynamic and changing cultures depend on those who are willing to speak out and perpetuate positive cultural characteristics or, when necessary, to resist and change cultural elements that need improvement.

Public speaking competencies enable you to participate in transmitting, reinforcing, restoring, or transforming cultural resources. These people are trying to change existing educational policies.

STOP AND CHECK

RECOGNIZE YOUR CULTURAL SPEAKING TRADITIONS

What public speaking traditions does your cultural heritage provide? How expressive were you encouraged to be? Were you encouraged or discouraged from speaking because of your ethnicity, your age, your socioeconomic class, or your gender? If so, how? What topics are sensitive or taboo? How might your cultural traditions affect your participation and your comfort in this course?

To investigate this topic further, log on to InfoTrac College Edition to search for and read Celeste Roseberry-McKibben's article "'Mirror, Mirror on the Wall': Reflections of a 'Third Culture' American." Compare and contrast her list of "mainstream American" values with the information presented throughout this chapter.

A Theory and a Model of Communication

The word *communication* is so common that you may not think much about what actually happens when people communicate. However, scholars continue to probe the many interrelationships among speakers, messages, listeners, and situations. Many current theories and models emphasize both speakers and listeners who jointly and actively co-create meaning. We first look at the dialogical theory before turning to the transactional model of communication.

The Dialogical Theory of Communication

dialogical theory theory proposing that face-to-face conversation is the prototype that is foundational to all other communication

Theories are explanations by which scholars provide the general or abstract principles of a field of study. Think back to how you first learned to communicate. Chances are you spent a lot of time listening and then practicing words and phrases with parents and older relatives. According to the **dialogical theory** of communication, the give-and-take quality of these first conversations form the foundational pattern for all other communication activities, even public speaking.[37] In this theory, conversation and public speaking share many similarities and some differences:

▶ In both types of communication, nonverbal cues such as facial expressions, emphasis on specific words, gestures, and eye contact add meaning to the message.

▶ In both types, everyone involved must actively engage the ideas presented. Helmut Geissner coined the term *respons*-**ibility**[38] to explain the interactions and mutual responses that co-create meanings. In conversations, the partners work together to confirm that what is said is being understood. For example, you might hear something like this: "Let's stop at that store." "You mean Sears?" "Yeah, Sears." In contrast, audiences usually wait until the end of a public speech before they ask questions.[39]

▶ Conversations and public speeches each have predictable structures, functions, and lengths. The Russian scholar Mikhail Bahktin explained, "We 'pour' our speech into ready-made forms or **speech genres.** These forms are given to us in the same way in which our native language is given."[40] In other words, there are cultural ways to propose marriage or answer a phone (genres or forms of conversations), and there are cultural norms for giving an announcement or a eulogy (public speech genres).

▶ Meaning in both contexts depends on situational factors such as "[w]ho says what, where and when, why and for what, in what manner, with and for whom? . . . and who understands what, where and when, how, why, and for what, in what manner, with or from whom."[41] A conversation with your mother about a failed test differs from the conversation you have with your professor about that test. A resident assistant's report on student concerns given in a walnut-paneled boardroom to the university's board of trustees differs from a similar report by the same RA given in a sorority lounge where students munch donuts and drink coffee as they listen. Each situation affects the multiple meanings in the speech act.

▶ As a general rule, public speeches are more formal (although conversational delivery is desirable) and more carefully prepared than conversations.

Theories, in short, explain a phenomenon or process, and the dialogical theory helps explain the communication process. This theory builds on the prototype of dialogue as foundational to all other communication. However, because theories are generally abstract, many people prefer a diagram or model to help them better understand the concept.

The Transactional Model of Communication

The most common model is called the **transactional model of communication,**[42] because it depicts communication as a process in which the communicators create mutual meanings. This model, shown in Figure 1.3, is one way to think about what happens when you interact with others. It includes the following components, which I will define by showing what they look like when you give a speech:

▶ As a *sender-receiver* (or source), you originate or *encode* a message by selecting words (a verbal code) to represent your ideas. In your preparation, you consider your classmates (reflecting on what you know about them through previous interactions). For instance, you may know some of their majors, their years in school, and other pertinent information.

▶ Your *messages* are intentional. Sometimes you inform; sometimes you persuade. You intentionally choose language they understand, reasoning they accept, and illustrations that relate to their lives.

▶ In classroom speeches you use the *channel* of face-to-face, voice-to-ear interactions, and you use nonverbal channels such as gestures or tone of voice to enhance your message.

respons-**ibility** speakers' and listeners' mutual engagement with the ideas, which allows them to jointly forge meanings

speech genres cultural forms that we rely upon when we participate in a specific type of communication

transactional model of communication represents communication as a process in which speakers and listeners work together to create mutual meanings

▶ *Receivers-senders*, your classmates in this case, hear your words and *decode* or interpret them. Each brings a personal background and heritage, plus individual beliefs, values, worries, and judgments to class. Each filters your words through personal perceptions, thoughts, and feelings, and sometimes through the influence of other listeners.

▶ Your classmates send messages to you, called *feedback*. Some will ask questions; some may nod, frown, smile, or clap. You decode this feedback and adapt to it. For example, if you see confused faces, you might add details to clarify your point. If the audience seems bored, you might regain attention with an interesting example. In this transactional process of mutual sending-receiving-responding, you and your listeners cooperate in creating meaning.

▶ *Noise*, or static, can interfere with both the message and its reception. For instance, your words might be difficult to hear because you have a sore throat. Or a fire truck might go by the building (*external noise*) as you speak. *Internal noise*, such as listeners' worries over being overdrawn at the bank or their hunger pangs, can also disrupt the process.

▶ Your class takes place within a situational context that includes a classroom within a college or university. Room temperature, lighting, decorations, and seating arrangements are all factors that affect your presentation.

▶ Finally, as this chapter explained, your class takes place within a larger cultural framework, in which expectations about higher education and about public speaking influence what is considered appropriate and inappropriate in the context.

Although it is not perfect, the transactional model effectively shows communication as a complex, dynamic process. It depicts and clarifies some of the many variables that affect the way humans cooperate with one another to co-create meanings.

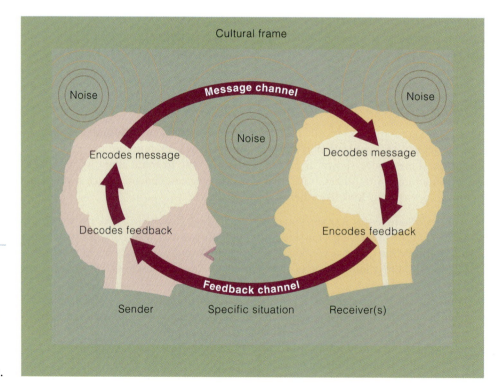

Figure 1.3
Transactional Model of Communication
The transactional model depicts communication as a dialogical process in which communicators co-create messages in culturally appropriate situations.

Summary

This chapter introduced the benefits you can gain by studying public speaking from a perspective of cultural diversity. This course will help you increase your competence and, perhaps, your self-confidence. It will also prepare you for participating actively in a culture that values skilled speakers and listeners. Finally, the study of rhetoric, a cornerstone of a liberal arts education, can equip you with critical thinking skills useful in everyday interactions.

By definition, culture includes both the visible and the underlying (embedded) aspects of a society, and culture influences public speaking in a number of ways. Your cultural and co-cultural traditions provide you with core resources that include beliefs, values, attitudes, and behaviors that influence how you create your own speeches and respond to others' messages. In addition, this technologically advanced society provides you with a variety of resources that you can use to research your topic and present your speech. Finally, your cultural heritage provides expectations regarding the *how*, the *who*, and the *what* of public speaking. Of course, within each culture, individual personalities and preferences also influence the ways we communicate.

Not only does culture affect public speaking, but public speaking also affects culture. We speak to transmit core cultural beliefs, values, and attitudes to newcomers who must learn appropriate behaviors in specific contexts. Some of us reinforce or support culture as it is; others repair or restore community when it is threatened. Others influence the removal or transformation of cultural elements that become outmoded or dysfunctional.

The chapter closed with dialogical theory and the transactional model of communication. Dialogical theory assumes that face-to-face conversations form the prototype for other types of speech, including public speaking. Although public speaking shares similarities with conversations, it also differs in significant ways. The communication model depicts in visual form the transactional nature of communication. It emphasizes that cooperation is required of both the originator of the message and the receiver if they are to *transact* or negotiate meaning. Public speakers originate the message but remain aware of the audience and adapt to feedback both as they prepare and as they speak. Listeners actively decode the information and encode feedback. All this communication, which can be negatively affected by both internal and external noise, takes place within a specific situation and cultural frame.

Student Learning: Speech Videos on the Website
Throughout the text, a video icon appears next to references to speech videos available on the book website for viewing and guided critical analysis. All speech video segments are also available on the Multimedia Manager with Instructor Resources CD-ROM.

STUDY AND REVIEW

The premium website for *Public Speaking* offers a broad range of resources that will help you better understand the material in this chapter, complete assignments, and succeed on tests. The website features

▶ Speech videos with critical viewing questions, speech outlines, and transcripts, and
▶ Interactive practice activities, self quizzes, and a sample final exam.

For more information about this text's electronic learning resources, consult your **Guide to Online Resources for Public Speaking** or visit http://communication.wadsworth.com/jaffe5.

Student Learning: Book Website
Under "Chapter Resources," students will find several tools for reviewing the information in this chapter, including a "Tutorial Quiz." You can have them email the results of this quiz to you as a participation or extra-credit activity.

KEY TERMS

The terms below are defined in the margins throughout this chapter. The book's website also provides interactive flashcards and crossword puzzles to help you learn these terms and the concepts they represent.

public speaking 2
communication apprehension
  (CA) 3
public speaking anxiety (PSA) 3
process anxiety 3
performance anxiety 3
communication competence 3
blogs 4
rhetoric 4
cultures 6
co-cultures 6

rhetorical sensitivity 6
core cultural resources 6
oral culture 7
nonexpressive cultures 7
expressive cultures 8
communication style 8
bicultural 9
dialogical theory 10
respons-ibility 11
speech genres 11
transactional model of communication 11

APPLICATION AND CRITICAL THINKING EXERCISES

The exercises below are among the practice activities on the book's website.

1. Sometimes people do not see themselves as public speakers because they define the word *public* too narrowly. They think of public speakers as politicians speaking at conventions but not as homemakers testifying before a local school board. Write your definition of "public." Then, make a list of specific publics you have already addressed and those you may address someday.

2. To gain experience in speaking publicly, prepare an announcement (using the guidelines in Appendix B) and deliver it to your classmates. You can find upcoming campus or community events in the newspaper, on posters, or on bulletin boards around campus.

3. Interview a person working in the field you hope to enter when you graduate. What opportunities exist for public speaking within that occupation? Ask if and how public speaking is related to the higher-paying, more prestigious jobs within the field.

4. What stereotypes do you hold about the word *rhetoric?* The Internet has many sources of information on this topic. Visit http://eserver.org/rhetoric/ and follow at least two links you find there. This will help you understand the value of rhetoric. Throughout the term, listen for the word *rhetoric* as it is used on radio or television. Watch for it as you read newspapers or magazines. Each time you encounter the word, decide whether it's being used negatively, positively, or neutrally. Note if any of the sources speak of rhetoric as essential in a free society.

5. Work with a group to evaluate the role of public speaking in creating and maintaining your college or university.

   ▸ What role did public speaking have as the founders launched your institution?
   ▸ How does your school currently use public speaking to recruit new students and donors?
   ▸ What role does ceremonial speaking, such as convocations or commencement addresses, have in maintaining the vision and the values of your institution?
   ▸ When issues threaten to divide your campus, how do groups and individuals use public speaking to negotiate differences?
   ▸ How does public speaking function to move your school from the present to the future?

6. In a small group, give examples to show how public speaking is similar to everyday conversation and how it differs. Use the dialogical theory and the communication model to guide your thinking.

7. I used your classroom speech to illustrate the transactional model of communication. Select a communication event from your own life and use that to identify and explain each element of the model.

SPEECH VIDEO

Log on to the book's web-site to watch and critique Alexandria Reed's delivery of the speech she gave at her twin brothers' graduation party. A transcript of the speech appears below and is also available on the book's website with the video.

Sample Speech

GRADUATION PARTY SPEECH
Alexandria Reed

Think about the last time someone gave you directions. They may have included the phrase "a fork in the road." Today, Jeffrey and Michael have come to that fork in the road. But first, let me share with you the journey that has brought them to this fork in the road.

Their journey began, not on different paths, but as one single cell: Jeffrey was born first, and Michael followed just 57 minutes later. They were close as babies. They even spoke their own "twin language" before they spoke English. The doctors almost had my parents separate them because they would only say the words they used to communicate with other; they didn't even say "Mommy" or Daddy." When they were toddlers they also liked to bite (particularly their older sister). Their word when they got mad must have been "nony" because they always yelled it before they bit someone. My mom learned to come running to my safety when she heard that from one of the twins.

They remained a "single unit." In fact, through elementary school, they were always in the same classroom. I have always referred to them as "the boys."

Their journey began to take them on different paths during middle school, and high school became a time for them to grow. Michael became involved with band and later with drama. He even became drum major his senior year. Jeffrey grew to love sports (especially basketball) and fell in love with cars. He is now restoring his own truck. "The boys" still hold a close bond and support each other's activities.

Now their journey brings them to a fork in the road. Next year Jeffrey will join me at Hope College, while Michael will attend the University of Michigan. Jeffrey will try out for the basketball team and Michael for the marching band. You can bet you will see Michael at some of Jeffrey's games and Jeffrey at the Michigan football games cheering on his brother.

Michael and Jeffrey, I am proud of each of our accomplishments. As you take this fork in the road, may the directions in your life always be clear. I look forward to seeing you succeed in all of your future endeavors.

CHAPTER 2

GIVING YOUR FIRST SPEECH: DEVELOPING CONFIDENCE

THIS CHAPTER WILL HELP YOU

▶ Develop skills to overcome process anxiety

▶ Explain the five canons of rhetoric: invention, disposition, style, memory, and delivery

▶ Develop strategies to deal with performance anxiety

▶ Develop strategies to deal with physiological anxiety

▶ Develop strategies to deal with psychological anxiety

▶ Learn skills for effective rehearsal

Detail from "Family Life and Spirit of Mankind" Mural © 1977 by Susan Kelk Cervantes and Judith Knepher Jamerson. (Leonard R. Flynn School, East Wall, Army Street at Harrison, SF, CA)

HEN ASKED, "What's the worst part about giving a speech?" students responded:

Standing in front of people, knowing that they are judging you.	CLAIRE
Babbling on and on when you don't know what to say.	MITRA
Knowing what to speak about.	JONATHAN
Being exposed.	HOLLY

Their answers reflect both process anxiety (not knowing how to create a speech) and performance anxiety (nervousness about actually giving the speech). The goal of this chapter is to help you decrease both types of anxiety by demystifying the speechmaking process and by giving you strategies for dealing with nervousness. Putting this information into practice will increase your overall speaking competence.[1]

CASE STUDY: REESE WILSON'S PUBLIC SPEAKING ANXIETY (PSA)

Chapter-at-a-Glance
This chapter begins with a description of the five classical canons of rhetoric: selecting appropriate content (invention), organizing material (disposition or arrangement), choosing effective language (style), gaining familiarity with the speech (memory), and presenting the material to an audience (delivery). The chapter concludes with a description of physiological responses to public speaking anxiety and specific strategies for managing it.

For a speech of self-introduction, each class member was assigned to tell a narrative that revealed something significant about him- or herself. (Chapter 15 describes narrative speeches in detail, and Chapter 16 gives instructions for a speech of definition that can feature a narrative.) Reese Wilson's speech of definition went like this:

When it comes to giving speeches, I may have been the most nervous person here, if it weren't for an event at high school graduation last year. According to Webster's Revised Unabridged Dictionary, *"overcome" is a verb meaning "to win a victory over." Roget's New Millennium Thesaurus adds, "to overcome" is "to gain the superiority." Some synonyms include "to conquer, crush, overpower, and defeat." Antonyms include "surrender and retreat." Overcome is often used in the context of facing a personal struggle.*

Because I had one of the top GPAs in my class, I was expected to give a speech at graduation. Ever since I was a sophomore in high school, I contemplated getting bad grades just to avoid this speech. On top of that, I was afraid because I had never used a microphone before. To give you an idea of how terrified I was, I was supposed to practice my speech at graduation rehearsal. When it was my turn, I got up to the podium and couldn't say a thing. Everyone told me it was easy, and encouraged me to just say "hi" or something, but I couldn't.

My dad and the high school counselor told me I didn't have to give a speech. (My dad later told me that he never thought I would do it in the first place.) They talked to me for a while, but it didn't help. Since I had been worrying about this speech for years, I had told a lot of people about it. Many said they would be praying for me, and I remembered that. Finally, I decided to pray that I would be able to overcome, a word which I didn't fully understand at the time. Eventually, I was able to say "hi" into the mike. That was enough for me; I gave up and went home to get some sleep.

The next day I graduated. When I heard my name called, I didn't know what happened, but the next thing I knew I was sitting down again. I didn't even remember the speech for a couple of hours because I was in shock. Apparently, I went up there, and spoke. I vaguely recall reading my speech, trying to keep my place with my finger, but I was shaking so badly I kept losing my place. Fortunately, things still went smoothly. It was meant to be a funny speech, and it felt good to make people laugh. Finally it was over.

If one of the quietest and most nervous people can overcome his fear and give a speech to a full gym at graduation, any of the shy people here can overcome and give a speech in a tiny classroom with only two video cameras. For me, it takes a little prayer, then just going and doing it.

After the course was over, Reese answered the following questions:

Did you feel more comfortable by the end of the semester? Why or why not?

I did feel more comfortable because I had gotten practice speaking in class, and the more I did it, the less anxiety I would feel.

What advice would you give someone else who has extreme anxiety about giving public speeches?

The relief of having done the speech and gotten it over with, along with the sense of accomplishment that comes with it, together outweigh any nervousness that may come before a speech.

Questions for Discussion

▶ What strategies did Reese employ to help him succeed, in spite of his terror about speaking?

▶ Throughout the semester, Reese consistently volunteered to speak first on his assigned day. How might this have helped his anxiety?

▶ Compare your level of anxiety with his and devise some strategies for managing your nerves on speech day.

Develop Skills to Overcome Process Anxiety

"Because the syllabus says your first speech is coming up next week, I'll describe the assignment today . . ." When you first hear these words, you may begin to experience tension.[2] Why? Perhaps it's fear of the unknown—you may feel like you're in unknown territory without a road map.[3] Fortunately, you can take some of the mystery out of the process by studying speech principles, observing others speak, and actually speaking yourself. As speechmaking becomes more familiar, you will probably experience less process anxiety and the panicky feelings that accompany it.

Think of it this way: When you learn any new skill, you follow the guidelines quite closely at first. Only after you have mastered the basics and feel more confident do you begin to take liberties. Remember when you first learned to write in cursive? You concentrated on every move, precisely forming each curve and loop. Eventually, you took more liberties and developed your own distinctive handwriting. Public speaking is similar. Early on, your instructor may teach you specific guidelines. However, after you gain some experience, you can be more creative in your preparation.

Rhetoric has a 2,500-year tradition in the West, rooted in classical Greek and Roman academies. As a result of closely studying the "how-to" of speechmaking, these early educators divided the process into five major stages, or categories: (1) creating the speech; (2) organizing speech materials; (3) choosing effective language; (4) learning the major

Instructor's Resource Manual
For research evidence on how best to handle public speaking anxiety, see Research Note 2.1 in this book's *Instructor's Resource Manual* (available in print, online, and on the Multimedia Manager CD-ROM).

Instructor's Resource Manual
See Teaching Idea 2.1, "The Canons of Rhetoric," in this book's *Instructor's Resource Manual* (available in print, online, and on the Multimedia Manager CD-ROM).

© Thomson Learning

Anxiety often results from not knowing how to create a speech. Learning and practicing the guidelines found in the five canons of rhetoric can reduce process anxiety.

ideas; and (5) delivering the speech. In each category they identified a **canon** (a set of principles, standards, norms, or guidelines) that students need to master to become effective orators. They called these five categories, and the principles within them, the five **canons of rhetoric.**[4]

Create Your Speech: The Canon of Invention

The **canon of invention** provides guidelines for creating the content of your speech. Just as an inventor designs a product that solves a particular problem, you will design a speech that meets a need for a specific audience in a specific situation. Principles in the canon of invention help you analyze your audience, select an appropriate topic and purpose, gather evidence, and develop reasonable and logical arguments and explanations. This text devotes nine chapters to this vital canon, but as a general introduction and to help you prepare your first speech, each principle is briefly discussed here.

Consider the Audience and the Setting

Your first task is to think about your classroom audience and the individuals within it. Look around and notice details that might influence your speaking choices. Of course, age and gender are fairly obvious, but look for additional features such as wedding rings, religious jewelry, or clothing that suggests specific interests or affiliations. Strike up conversations before or after class as a way to learn more about your classmates. It will help if you think of the whole group as a mini-culture that develops unique ways of interacting. (See the Diversity in Practice box for more on this point.) These strategies will help you think of your audience as individuals who make up a larger group.

Consider also the situation in which you will speak. Elements such as lighting, ventilation, acoustics, and room layout make a difference. Other factors, such as time of day, matter as well. Are your classmates typically hungry or sleepy during class? Being mindful of details such as these will help you move to the next task—choosing your subject and purpose.

DIVERSITY IN PRACTICE
YOUR CLASSROOM CULTURE

CULTURES ARE NOT ALWAYS NATIONAL or regional in scope. Groups— even those as small as your class— develop distinct ways of doing things, which means that each becomes a *mini-culture* with its own set of beliefs, values, and norms or rituals.[5] If this seems confusing, consider the differences between a speech class and a biology class. Or contrast two psychology classrooms. In one, the professor lectures every period; in the other, the professor uses discussions and small groups to present course concepts.

Similarly, one speech class may develop a warm, open, supportive climate in which class members believe that each student can succeed. They value one another's feelings, and they create rituals, such as learning one other's names and chatting as they gather. In contrast, another class might develop a closed, hostile, or competitive culture whose members ignore one another and sleep or study during other students' speeches.

Instructors usually identify their beliefs, values, and behavioral norms during the first class session. They typically state that public speaking is important, and they affirm openness, honesty, and diversity as fundamental values. They also provide expectations about respectful listening and speaking behaviors. Students contribute to the classroom culture by combining their beliefs about one another, their values, and how they act in the class.

canon a set of principles, standards, norms, or guidelines

canons of rhetoric principles, standards, norms, or guidelines for creating and delivering a speech

canon of invention principles for designing a speech that meets a need of a specific audience

Choose a Topic

"Oh, no! What will I talk about?" This may be one of your biggest questions, and later chapters will provide you with detailed guidelines covering topic choice. However, your first assignment probably will be either a self-introduction or the introduction of a classmate. Consequently, topic choice is partly done for you, but finding an interesting focus still will be a challenge. If you must introduce a classmate, set up an interview that will uncover one or more unusual facts about the person, and focus your speech around these details. A self-introduction may create more anxiety because *you* are in the spotlight. You must reveal something personal, and you must decide just what private details you are willing to share. With any speech assignment, consider these guidelines:

- Be sure you understand the expectations. You will be very embarrassed if you prepare a speech carefully only to discover on speech day that you've misunderstood the assignment. Pay special attention to the guidelines your instructor provides that explain the time limits and the general requirements for the speech. If you are confused, ask questions to clarify the expectations. Also, study the examples at the end of chapters throughout the text and in Appendix C, as well as those on the book's website, where you'll also find numerous videos of sample speeches for you to watch and critique. The examples will help you understand how other students successfully completed similar assignments.

- Reveal something unusual. Avoid boring your audience with something everyone has experienced; instead, search for a unique focus. Students have described unusual jobs (working as a pyrotechnician, setting off fireworks displays), vacations (a trip to New Zealand), and volunteerism (taking a therapy pet into nursing care facilities).

- Select a significant topic. Have you had life-changing experiences? Have you learned important lessons that others could also learn? Consider incorporating your personal adventures or insights into a speech. Find and watch Mona Bradsher's speech on the book's website. In it she describes her decision to return to school after a divorce. A transcript of the speech is also available at the end of the chapter and on the book's website.

- Consider a story format. Sharing a story is often a good way to connect with your audience. In fact, Chapter 15 describes narrative speaking in detail; there, you'll find a pattern that is especially effective for introductory speeches.

- Consider your listeners' sensibilities. Your purpose is not to shock your audience by revealing highly personal information or potentially embarrassing details. This is an opportunity to be culturally sensitive in your preparation; try to think from the diverse perspectives of audience members.

- Try out your ideas on people you trust. Discuss your audience and your assignment with close friends or associates. If you have two or three ideas, elicit opinions about each one.

If you have been thinking of your audience all along, you will have a good sense of what are and are not appropriate topics.

Identify Your Purpose

After you have selected your topic, identify your reason for speaking, given this particular audience. What response do you want from them? Your answer to this question determines your general purpose. Your early speeches will probably focus on one of the following four goals:

- Do you want your audience to learn something? If so, your general purpose is *to inform*.

- Do you want them to respond by believing or doing something? Are you trying to reinforce their beliefs or behaviors? Then your general purpose is *to persuade*.

▶ Do you want them simply to laugh and enjoy themselves? If so, your purpose is *to entertain*.

▶ Do you want to highlight and reinforce a particular cultural ideal? If so, your general purpose is *to commemorate*.

Of course, these purposes often overlap. In your introductory speech, your major goal will be to inform the class about either yourself or another classmate, but you should also be at least somewhat entertaining. And as Reese's self-introduction in the case study that opens Chapter 2 shows, it's often effective to highlight a cultural ideal such as perseverance.

Gather Speech Materials

Although you probably will be familiar with many of the topics you choose, you can fill the gaps in your knowledge by consulting outside resources. Go to the library or log onto its or another library's website to look for information in databases and on CD-ROMs, DVDs, VHS tapes, audiotapes, books, journals, newspapers, and magazines. Television and radio shows can also provide useful information. And of course, search the Internet. (A word of caution, however: The Internet is full of excellent as well as poor or even fraudulent data. Chapter 7 provides guidelines for thinking critically about the information you find online.) Finally, remember to take advantage of InfoTrac College Edition or similar periodical databases. InfoTrac College Edition, in particular, provides 24/7 access to over a million full-text articles (not just excerpts or abstracts) from thousands of journals, newspapers, and magazines.

An introduction generally relies less on outside research and more on personal experiences or on an interview with the subject. However, you may need to consult library resources to improve the speech. For example, Brigit knew about New Zealand from her visit to the country, but books and magazines provided her with additional information about its history and culture.

If you introduce a classmate, schedule an interview for an uninterrupted time in a quiet place—and then be on time. Bring a list of questions and tape-record your conversation (with permission only) or take notes as you talk. Be sure you understand what you are told by asking questions such as "Did I hear you correctly when you said you took your dog into convalescent homes?" or "Could you tell me how therapy pets are screened for safety?" To avoid any misunderstandings, summarize the major ideas as you conclude.

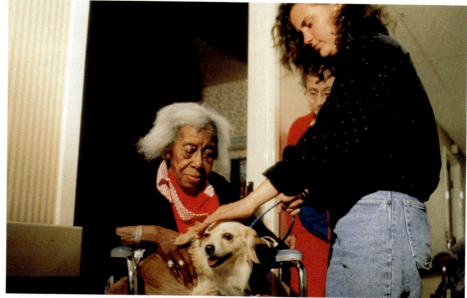

Interesting and unusual events or experiences such as volunteer work with a therapy pet make excellent speech topics. Gather information from interviews, library research, personal know-how, and electronic resources.

Organize Your Ideas: The Canon of Disposition or Arrangement

After you gather information, arrange your ideas so that they will make sense to your audience. The principles of speech organization make up the **canon of disposition** or **arrangement.** Of course, there are many ways to organize a speech, and cultures vary in their organizational patterns; this, in turn, influences cultural expectations.

Most speeches in the Western speaking tradition have three major parts: the introduction, the body, and the conclusion. An introduction orients your audience toward the subject. Next comes the body of the speech, the part that generally takes up most of your speaking time; here, you explain and develop your major ideas. Finally, a memorable conclusion rounds out the speech. Taken as a whole, the outline looks like this:

I. Introduction
II. Body
III. Conclusion

I. INTRODUCE YOUR TOPIC

Your first speech may vary slightly from this pattern, but in general an introduction has these four major functions that date back to the first-century AD Roman educator Quintilian:[6]

- Draw audience attention to the topic.
- Relate the topic to their concerns.
- Link yourself to the subject.
- Preview the major points.

II. DEVELOP THE BODY OF YOUR SPEECH

Here, you present and develop your major ideas, using sufficient evidence for clarification and support. There are many ways to organize speeches, such as topical, problem-solution, cause-effect, and so on. These will be discussed in more detail in Chapter 9. Using these patterns results in a linear arrangement, as shown by this outline of a topical speech:

A. First main point
  1. Support
  2. Support

B. Second main point
  1. Support
  2. Support

Although linear patterns are common, your cultural background, your learning style, or your personality traits may lead you to visualize your speeches as moving in wavelike patterns or in spiraling forms. Chapters 9 and 17 illustrate both traditional and alternative organizational forms. You will also find narrative speech patterns in Chapter 15.

III. CONCLUDE MEMORABLY

To be most effective as a speaker, don't stop abruptly. Instead, provide a sense of closure that ties your ideas together and leaves your audience with something to take away with them. Conclusions often have these elements:

- A transition to the conclusion
- A reference to the introduction
- A summary of the major ideas
- A final memorable statement

canon of disposition or **arrangement** guidelines for organizing a speech

Connect Your Ideas

Your major work is done, and it's time to weave your ideas together so that your speech flows smoothly from point to point. Words and phrases that link your ideas with one another are called **connectives.** Simple connectives include words such as *first, next,* and *finally.* More complex connectives, such as "After the initial shock of my accident, I began the painful rehabilitation process," summarize where your speech has been and where it is going. Connectives help your listeners keep their place in the speech by linking the various points to one another and to the speech as a whole.

Once you have gathered materials and selected an organizational pattern, you can then choose precise wording and learn your speech well enough to deliver it to an audience. The principles for these aspects of speechmaking are found in the final three canons of rhetoric: style, memory, and delivery.

Choose Suitable Language: The Canon of Style

When asked, "What do you think it means when someone says, 'I like your style?'" two students responded:

> You would most likely mean that you like the way I carry myself
> or the way I act.
> MATT

> It would probably mean that you like something about my personality
> or the way I handle things and people.
> JOSH

A dictionary would say they're right. Style can mean a person's individuality as expressed in his or her actions and tastes.[7] However, in rhetoric, **style** means language; the **canon of style** contains the principles for using language effectively in both speaking and writing. (That's why you consult style manuals in your writing classes.)

Put the finishing touches on your ideas by polishing the words you use, always with an ear tuned to your listeners. Here are a few general guidelines for effective use of language in public speaking:

- Choose vocabulary and grammar that fits both the occasion and the audience. This means adapting your vocabulary to audience characteristics such as occupation, age, or educational level.
- Omit offensive language such as swear words or language that demeans people.
- Choose understandable words. Either define technical jargon or replace it with more familiar terminology.
- Minimize slang expressions. Language used in public speeches is generally more formal than language used in everyday conversation.

More detailed information on the canon of style is provided in Chapter 13.

Learn and Present Your Speech: The Canons of Memory and Delivery

Because they lacked teleprompters and the like, Roman educators taught young orators elaborate techniques for learning their speeches by heart. However, the **canon of memory** is often called *the lost canon* because so few people in this culture rely on memory alone, and because **memorized delivery** is highly risky. Forgetting even a few simple words can lead to public embarrassment—something you definitely want to avoid! In general, stay away from **manuscript delivery,** in which you write out your entire speech and then read it to your audience. As you might imagine, reading your speech means you lose important eye contact with listeners. In the classroom, avoid spur-of-the-moment **impromptu delivery,** where you stand up and speak with little advanced preparation.

Classroom Discussion/ Activity
Use video clips to illustrate different speaking styles, such as a rap artist giving an award-acceptance speech; Martin Luther King Jr. or Jesse Jackson giving a civil rights speech; and a physician or scientist giving a jargon-filled speech at a medical convention.

---

connectives words and phrases that you use to tie your ideas together

style in rhetoric, style means language

canon of style principles for choosing effective language

canon of memory guidelines to help you remember your ideas

memorized delivery learning the speech by heart, then reciting it

manuscript delivery reading a speech

impromptu delivery speaking with little advanced preparation

Instead, use **extemporaneous delivery,** in which you carefully prepare an outline showing how you'll organize the major ideas of your speech. Before speaking, put key ideas, single words, phrases, and statistics on note cards. Use these cards to jog your memory as you give the talk, but choose the exact wording as you go. Chapter 14 elaborates on these four delivery methods, and Chapter 11 gives you additional information on content outlines and speaking outlines.

Rehearsal is a vital part of the preparation process. Find a quiet place where you can deliver your speech out loud, using your note cards. If possible, practice in the room where you'll actually speak. Recruit friends, family, roommates—anyone who can act as an audience, provide feedback, troubleshoot problems, and let you practice speaking in front of a group. Go through the speech several times, each time selecting slightly different words. Focus on looking away from your notes and communicating conversationally. Although practice may not make perfect, the more prepared you are, the better you will feel about your presentation.

Principles found in the **canon of delivery** provide guidelines on nonverbal behaviors, such as gestures and eye contact that strengthen your performance. (See Chapter 14.) In brief, you will be more skillful if you do the following during your speech:

▶ Make eye contact with your listeners.
▶ Have pleasant facial expressions.
▶ Avoid a monotone voice.
▶ Smile at appropriate times.
▶ Assume a posture of confidence.
▶ Incorporate appropriate gestures.
▶ Speak conversationally.
▶ Stay within the time limits.

Focus throughout not on giving something *to* your audience, but on creating something *with* them.

The guidelines found in the five canons of rhetoric build process competence. You learn to analyze your audience, select a topic and purpose, and gather materials (invention). Then you organize or arrange your ideas into meaningful patterns (disposition), choose appropriate language (style), and learn your major points (memory), so that you can present them effectively (delivery). Afterwards, you must deal with performance anxiety.

For additional information on the canons of rhetoric, follow links on the website The Forest of Rhetoric, at http://humanities.byu.edu/rhetoric/silva.htm.

Teaching Tip
Explain early on that the canon of memory does *not* mean memorizing the entire speech word-for-word.

Classroom Discussion/ Activity
Memoria is often considered the "lost" rhetorical canon because so little emphasis is placed upon memorization in our digital age. Engage students in a discussion of the topic of memory. Is there any value to learning how to memorize information?

Student Learning: Book Website
All URLs mentioned in the text are available as live, regularly maintained links on the book's website, located in the "Chapter Resources" list under "Web Links."

BUILD YOUR SPEECH
YOUR FIRST SPEECH

Using the five canons of rhetoric, prepare a self-introduction or the introduction of a classmate. Throughout your preparation, consider the following questions:

1. Do I understand the assignment?
2. Is my topic somewhat unusual? If not, do I have a unique or novel approach?
3. Is the topic significant enough to discuss?
4. How will I adapt this speech to this audience?
5. Which friends can I ask to listen to my ideas?

For additional help building your first and subsequent speeches log on to Speech Builder Express.

extemporaneous delivery preparing a speech carefully in advance but choosing the exact wording during the speech itself

canon of delivery rules or standards for presenting your speech

Develop Strategies to Overcome Performance Anxiety

Performance anxiety comes in two forms: physiological and psychological. **Physiological anxiety** is your bodily response to the feared event. **Psychological anxiety** manifests itself in worry, dread, and feelings of inadequacy about the performance itself. Eileen describes both types:

> I was anxious about my speech from the first moment I knew about it. I became most worried the night before and the day of the speech. I worry about how I present my speech, and I'm not very confident in my abilities. Once I stand in front of the class, I become rigid and my stomach is in knots. I generally turn red (shades) and talk differently (due to nerves).

This section discusses a number of specific skills you can use in combination to overcome both kinds of nervousness.[8]

Develop Strategies to Deal with Physiological Responses

You know from experience how your body responds to dangerous situations. A process called the **fight-or-flight mechanism** takes over, and adrenalin rushes in to help you fight the threat or run from the danger. Unfortunately, your body doesn't distinguish between physically threatening situations (where you actually need the extra physical energy to make your escape) and psychologically threatening experiences (where your increased heart rate, butterflies, and adrenaline rush only add to your stress). Ralph Behnke and Chris Sawyer[9] identify four milestones of anxiety-producing events: (1) *anticipation*, the pre-speaking period; (2) *confrontation*, beginning the speech; (3) *adaptation*, completing the speech; (4) *release*, after the speech. Anxiety peaks in the anticipation period and steadily decreases, disappearing in the release milestone, although some symptoms may linger.[10] (See Figure 2.1).

Here's how Emily described the process:

> As I sit in class, my anxiety level increases by the minute. Right before and as I walk to the front of the room, I use all my power to hide how nervous I am. I take a deep breath and start talking. During the beginning of my speech, anxiety is the worst. My nervous habits show through most in the beginning. As I continue my speech, it gets easier and I become more comfortable. By the conclusion, I'm usually cool, calm, and collected!

To counteract physical tension, engage in some form of physical exercise before class, such as lifting weights, brisk walking, or running. Listen to soothing music. Don't skip breakfast or lunch, and limit sugar and caffeine if these substances make you feel wired. When you get to the classroom, focus on relaxing your major muscle groups and breathe slowly and deeply just before you speak.

These additional tactics may ease your anxiety:

- Plan a compelling introduction to help carry you through the anxiety peak at the beginning of the speech. When you arrive in the classroom, silently repeat the goal of the speech, the main ideas, and your introduction so you will start well.
- Follow Reese's example in the opening case study and volunteer to go first; this decreases the length of the anticipation period.
- Use appropriate visual aids, especially at the start of your speech. They can ease your tension because they give the audience something to look at besides you.
- Deliver your introduction from notes, rather than reading it or reciting a memorized text. When you read, you risk disengaging your audience. A memorized introduction is hazardous because this is such a high-anxiety point in your speech.

physiological anxiety bodily responses to a perceived threat (increased heart rate, adrenaline rush)

psychological anxiety mental stress about a perceived threat

fight-or-flight mechanism physiological mechanism your body automatically activates when threatened to enable you to fight or to flee

Develop Strategies to Deal with Psychological Anxiety

Although you know better, you may listen to your internal voice that says, "I don't know what I'm doing. I'll forget halfway through. I probably won't get my ideas across. They'll see my knees shake." Self-talk is called **internal monologue (I-M).**[11] Although negative self-talk adds to your discomfort, it's not fatal. Researchers have identified two areas of vulnerability: your level of confidence (I've never done this before; I'm embarrassed about my looks; I'll flunk) and your expectations regarding the audience's reactions (they'll make fun of me; they don't want to hear what I have to say; they won't pay attention; they'd rather be somewhere else).[12]

Control Your Internal Monologue

You can learn to control I-M by a process called **cognitive modification,** in which you identify negative thoughts and replace them with positive ones.[13] Think positively in three areas: about the message, about the audience, and about yourself:

▶ To think positively about the message, select a topic that interests you and is beneficial to your audience. Give yourself enough time for research and organization. Be sure of your pronunciation; check the dictionary to make sure you know how to say unfamiliar words.

▶ To promote positive thoughts about the audience, remember that other students are probably just as nervous when they speak and that they are not experts in your subject. Assume that they want you to succeed, and focus on the purpose of your speech. (If your first language is not English, think of how your audience would feel if they had to give a speech in *your* native language.)

▶ Maintain a positive self-image by focusing on the things you do well. Remind yourself that your worth as a person is unrelated to your skill as a novice public speaker and that competence develops with experience.

Use Visualization

Another helpful strategy, one used by athletes and musicians, is called **visualization.** Visualization is a form of positive self-talk or mental strategizing in which you see yourself successfully performing a complex task. Professors Joel Ayres, Theodore Hopf, and their associates have taught thousands of students how to use visualization techniques to ease their PSA. They found that those who use these techniques during their preparation are less apprehensive and report fewer negative thoughts during their speeches.[14] The suggested process goes like this:

1. In a quiet place, picture all the details from the beginning to the end of your speech.
2. Mentally place yourself in the audience and pretend you are watching as you give your speech.
3. Imagine yourself as a competent, well-prepared performer who stands confidently, stresses important words, pauses effectively, and makes appropriate gestures.
4. Think about the audience responding positively with nods, smiles, and interest.

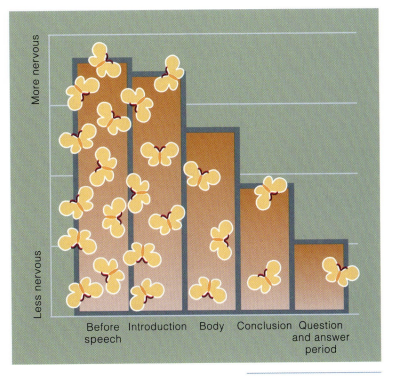

Figure 2.1

Performance Anxiety

Knowing that anxiety is greater at certain periods can help you control your nervousness by planning strategies that enable you to get through these periods.

Instructor Resource: Power-Point

The *Multimedia Manager with Instructor Resources* CD-ROM includes a Power-Point slide of Figure 2.1.

internal monologue (I-M) self-talk

cognitive modification identifying negative thoughts and replacing them with positive ones

visualization rehearsing by using your imagination to envision your speech from start to finish

5. Continue to visualize yourself finishing your speech, gathering your notes, making final eye contact with the audience, and leaving the podium or other speaking space.

6. Finally, imagine yourself back in the audience, delighted to be through!

Two key elements accompany successful visualization: You must create vivid images, and you must control the images you generate.[15]

Believe it or not, research shows that most highly anxious students finish a speech class feeling less anxious[16] because of the process of **habituation.** This means that anxiety lessens when an experience is repeated over time and the anticipated negative outcomes are not as bad as expected.[17] Jennifer's comments support this idea:

I think it was really good that we did so many speeches because when we did it so many times, I was less nervous each time.

habituation lessening of anxiety when an experience is successfully repeated over time

STOP AND CHECK

ASSESS YOUR PUBLIC SPEAKING ANXIETY

Take this test to self-assess your anxiety regarding public speaking. In the blank beside the statement, write the number of the response that best reflects your feelings.

0 = Strongly disagree
1 = Disagree
2 = Agree
3 = Strongly agree

_____ 1. I begin to get nervous the moment the speech is assigned.
_____ 2. I feel panicky because I don't know how to create a speech.
_____ 3. I usually feel nervous the day before I have to speak.
_____ 4. The night before the speech I can't sleep well.
_____ 5. I'm afraid people will think I'm dumb or boring or weird in some way.
_____ 6. On the morning of the speech, I am really tense.
_____ 7. I find it difficult to think positively about giving a speech.
_____ 8. I think my physical reactions are greater than those that other people experience.
_____ 9. During my speech I actually think I'll faint.
_____ 10. I continue to worry even after the speech is over.

Add Your Scores

_____ Total score

0–5   You are virtually fearless.
6–15   Your level of anxiety is quite normal.
16–25 Your level of anxiety may give you problems.
26–30 Consider making an appointment with your professor. Go back and look at the areas that bother you the most, and develop specific strategies from this chapter to help you with your unique stresses.

Classroom Discussion / Activity
Have a few students give brief impromptu speeches about their speaking anxieties. Ask the class suggest ways to handle these anxieties. This activity will help students realize that they are not alone in their fears or their physiological reactions to them.

Classroom Discussion / Activity
As a class, discuss ways the audience (class) can be supportive of speakers and not disruptive. Develop a "code of conduct" for speech days.

Student Learning: Book Website
This Stop and Check activity can also be found on the book's website, where it's located under "Chapter Resources."

Before your speech, find a quiet place to rehearse. Learn your main ideas, and practice giving the speech differently each time instead of trying to memorize it word for word.

© Mary Kate Denny/PhotoEdit

Summary

It is not enough simply to get up in front of an audience and talk; good speaking requires thought and preparation. The Greeks and Romans identified a set of principles or standards—a canon—for each of the five areas of speechmaking: invention, disposition, style, memory, and delivery. Use guidelines from the canon of invention to consider your audience's characteristics and interests, and take into account their responses to the time of day and temperature in your classroom. After that, select a unique, significant, and appropriate topic or focus. Decide whether your major purpose is to inform, persuade, or entertain; then gather information from oral, print, or electronic resources that will provide the materials you need to present your topic adequately.

Organize your ideas into a culturally meaningful pattern using norms from the canon of disposition to create an introduction, body, and conclusion. Choose appropriate wording (canon of style) and learn your major ideas (canon of memory) so that you can extemporaneously deliver your speech (canon of delivery).

Finally, plan strategies for dealing with your nerves. Know when to expect the highest levels of physical symptoms, and plan accordingly. Plan specific activities to counteract the physical tension brought on by the fight-or-flight mechanism. Then work on your psychological stress. Control your internal monologue by cognitive restructuring, substituting positive thoughts for negative ones. Visualize yourself performing your speech successfully from beginning to end. Use vivid images and control your imaginary scenario so that you succeed in giving your speech.

Doing these steps thoughtfully and thoroughly enables you to walk into your classroom with confidence on speech day, and they equip you with the necessary knowledge and skills to be a more competent public speaker.

STUDY AND REVIEW

The premium website for *Public Speaking* offers a broad range of resources that will help you better understand the material in this chapter, complete assignments, and succeed on tests. The website features

▶ Speech videos with critical viewing questions, speech outlines, and transcripts, and
▶ Interactive practice activities, self quizzes, and a sample final exam.

For more information about this text's electronic learning resources, consult your **Guide to Online Resources for Public Speaking** or visit http://communication.wadsworth.com/jaffe5.

KEY TERMS

The terms below are defined in the margins throughout this chapter. The book's website also provides interactive flashcards and crossword puzzles to help you learn these terms and the concepts they represent.

canon 20	impromptu delivery 24
canons of rhetoric 20	extemporaneous delivery 25
canon of invention 20	canon of delivery 25
canon of disposition or arrangement 23	physiological anxiety 26
connectives 24	psychological anxiety 26
style 24	fight-or-flight mechanism 26
canon of style 24	internal monologue (I-M) 27
canon of memory 24	cognitive modification 27
memorized delivery 24	visualization 27
manuscript delivery 24	habituation 28

APPLICATION AND CRITICAL THINKING EXERCISES

The exercises below are also among the practice activities on the book's website.

1. Consider the role of preparation and rehearsal in increasing your speaking competence. What effect does last-minute preparation have on competence? What effect does it have on anxiety? Knowing this, how do you plan to prepare for your next speech?

2. Rank from 1 to 5 (easiest to hardest), the five canons of rhetoric in order of difficulty for you personally.

   ____ Invention: audience analysis, topic selection, purpose, research
   ____ Disposition: organization or arrangement and connection of ideas
   ____ Style: choice of appropriate language
   ____ Memory: remembering what you want to say
   ____ Delivery: actually presenting your speech

   Which is easiest? Why? Which is hardest? Why? Identify specific strategies you can use to work on the areas that challenge you most.

3. Log on to **www.whitehouse.gov** and explore the site. How might links found on this site help you apply principles of invention such as topic selection and research?

4. At the top of a sheet of paper, write down an occupation that interests you. Then, along the left side of the page, list the five canons of rhetoric, leaving several spaces between each one. Beside each canon, identify ways that the skills developed within that canon will be useful in the job you named. For example, how will identifying a purpose or doing research help a nurse or an engineer? How will organizing ideas help a teacher or computer programmer?

5. Work with a group to analyze your classroom audience, using the suggestions on page 20. In light of material from Chapter 1 and from your own experiences, discuss some adaptations you might make to speak successfully to the class. For instance, how might the group influence your choice of topics? How might you adapt to diversity? How might the classroom itself, the time of day of the class, and other outside factors affect your speaking?

6. Classroom speakers generally use extemporaneous delivery; however, the other modes of delivery are sometimes more culturally appropriate. With a group, write down the four modes: memorized, manuscript, impromptu, and extemporaneous. Beside each, identify specific instances in which that mode would probably be the most effective. For instance: impromptu delivery goes with most wedding toasts; manuscript delivery work with graduation speeches. After you have identified several specific examples, discuss with your group some guidelines that you think speakers should follow for each type of delivery.

SPEECH VIDEO

Log on to the book's website to watch and critique Mona Bradsher delivering her Speech of Self-Introduction. A transcript of the speech appears below and is also available on the book's website.

Student Speech with Commentary

SELF-INTRODUCTION
Mona Bradsher

My name is Mona Bradsher. I'm a junior, although I'm older than most juniors at our school. In my speech, I want to introduce you to a very persuasive six-year-old. Through her, you'll learn why I have come back to finish my college degree after a ten-year break from school.

When I was eighteen, I started college like many of you. But, unlike most of you, I dropped out when I was twenty— in the middle of my sophomore year. I left school because I wanted to get married to a man named Jason. I'd met him the summer before, and we had fallen in love. Jason and I did get married and we had a daughter, Sasha.

In my case, the fairy tales were wrong: Jason and I didn't live happily ever after. We divorced just before our fifth wedding anniversary. So there I was— a twenty-five-year-old single mom with a child to raise. My income was pretty low, because I didn't have enough education to get a job that paid well. It was hard to get by on what I could make and the small amount of child support that Jason paid each month. We didn't go out for dinners or movies, but we did eat healthy meals at home. We didn't have money for a nice car, so we used the bus system. When Sasha was sick, I'd have to work extra hours to pay the doctor's bill and the cost of prescriptions. So it was tough, and I worried that as my daughter got older I wouldn't be able to support her on what I made. I felt really trapped.

Last year Sasha started school. One day she came home and told me her teacher had taught them about the importance of education. Sasha's teacher had put up a chart showing the difference between what high school graduates and college graduates make. Her teacher also talked about how education helps every person fulfill his or her individual potential and lead a fuller life. The teacher told all the children that education was the most important gift they could give themselves. So Sasha said to me, "Mommy, now that I'm going to school, why don't you go too?" At first I told Sasha that mommy had to work to pay for our apartment and food, but Sasha would have none of that. She insisted that I should go to school. I don't know how many of you have tried to argue with a very insistent six-year-old, but take my word for it: You can't win! Because my daughter was so persistent, I checked around and found out there is an educational loan program specifically for older students who want to return to school and complete their education. I qualified, and I'll keep getting the loan as long as I maintain a B average. So far, my average is above that because Sasha and I have a deal: We study together for three hours every night.

And that's why I'm here now. That's why I've come back to finish my degree after a ten-year break. I'm here because my daughter reminded me of the importance of education.

If I can learn an important lesson from a six-year-old, then I can learn other important lessons from the teachers at our university.

Mona's self-introduction, a personal experience narrative, explains why she is an "older than average" student in a class composed mainly of younger students.

She briefly summarizes her marriage and divorce, but she piles up details when she describes her life as a poor, single working mother. Notice how her vivid images get her listeners emotionally involved in her story.

Mona is tapping into strong cultural values— the value of education, of perseverance, and of hard work. She doesn't really tell students, "Don't get married too young; stay in school." But her narrative persuasively argues that the choice she made brought difficulties she could have avoided if she had stayed in school. (Chapter 15 provides more details on the functions of narratives.)

ETHICS AND DIVERSITY

Detail from "Family Life and Spirit of Mankind" Mural ©
1977 by Susan Kelk Cervantes and Judith Knepher Jamerson. (Leonard R. Flynn School, East Wall, Army Street at
Harrison, SF, CA)

THIS CHAPTER WILL HELP YOU

▶ Define ethical communication

▶ Describe three responses to diversity

▶ Identify characteristics of dialogical
  speaking and listening

▶ Explain three guidelines for speaking
  in a democracy

▶ Discuss ethical responsibilities of
  listeners

▶ Give examples of two kinds of unethical
  behavior

"*D*EMOCRACY IS *organized conflict.*" This startling definition by a former city councilor and mayor, Pam Plumb, further says that "disagreement and different points of view are actually the very foundation of democracy."[1] Put another way, the purpose of democracy is to bring together divergent points of view and allow participants to fashion solutions that bring about good results for the greatest number of people. Unfortunately, forging a civil society is often messy and unpleasant, and people of differing viewpoints frequently encounter ethical challenges in their often contentious deliberations.

In our diverse society, you regularly make ethical communication choices. When you defend your beliefs or remain silent, when you respectfully listen or refuse to hear someone with a different perspective, when you check facts or knowingly pass on faulty information, when you credit your sources or plagiarize speech materials, you are making ethical choices.

Professor Vernon Jensen describes **ethical communication** as the conscious decision to speak and listen in ways that you, in light of your cultural ideals, consider right, fair, honest, and helpful to others as well as yourself.[2] Because the U.S. Constitution guarantees freedom of speech, you are at liberty to express your ideas even if they disgust or offend others—but you must balance your rights with your responsibilities. You can't legally yell "FIRE!" in a crowded theater, for example, nor can you legally damage another person's reputation by spreading information you know to be false. Professor Jensen suggests that you focus on both rights and responsibilities, which he calls **rightsabilities.**[3]

Maintaining this dual focus is often difficult. Think of the many individuals and groups who believe and behave in ways that dramatically differ from your beliefs and actions. Some differences seem irreconcilable, which can lead to tension between you and those with whom you might otherwise have much in common.[4] This tension leads to a number of ethical questions. On what basis do we determine right and wrong in public discourse? Should you leave some things unsaid? When? Who decides? What responsibilities do you have as a listener or as a researcher? This chapter presents some principles that have emerged out of discussions about these ethically challenging questions. We will first examine common responses to diversity and then discuss guidelines for ethical speaking, listening, and researching in a complex culture.

Chapter-at-a-Glance
This chapter describes the ways that culture influences ethics. Ethical speaking involves a dialogical theory of communication in which diversity is respected. Listeners as well as speakers have ethical responsibilities in the communication process. The chapter ends with a discussion of plagiarism and fabrication.

ethical communication the conscious decision to speak and listen in ways that you, in light of your cultural ideals, consider right, fair, honest, and helpful to others as well as to yourself

"rightsabilities" phrase coined by Professor Vernon Jensen to highlight the tension that exists between our right to free speech and our responsibility for our speech

heckling taunting, insulting, ridiculing, or shouting down another person

CASE STUDY: HECKLING

Hecklers sometimes resort to extreme means such as a pie in the face to protest a view they disagree with.

© VISSER ROBERT/CORBIS SYGMA

University audiences are sometimes expressive and rowdy, and students on many campuses have loudly booed both "conservative" and "liberal" speakers. Not long ago, protestors threw pies at four different conservative speakers and threw salad dressing at another. Occasionally, intense **heckling** forces a speaker to stop mid-speech.

An event at a college in the Midwest illustrates this. Chris Hedges, a war correspondent and *New York Times* reporter, was the commencement speaker. He chose an antiwar topic, and he strongly criticized the U.S.

military ideals of heroism that military recruiters commonly use. When he referred to recruits as unemployed "boys" from places like Mississippi and Arkansas and sprinkled in words such as "betrayal" and "tyranny over the weak" to describe U.S. foreign policy in Iraq, the crowd grew restless. After a while, someone unplugged his microphone, but Hedges continued to speak and the microphone was turned on once more. Some graduates then turned their backs on him; others started shouting their disagreement; a few headed up the aisles toward the stage. One student burst into tears and left, and another tossed his cap and gown onto the stage and stormed out. Eventually, someone again unplugged the mike, and the college president asked Hedges to conclude.

Reactions fell into two main camps. Some listeners felt that failure to listen to ideas, even unpopular ones, would result in "the death of the university." They were horrified at audience behaviors that deprived them of hearing the speaker. Others felt that Hedges had violated unspoken rules regarding time and place. To them, a commencement speaker should celebrate the graduates' achievements. One said, "The day belongs to the students. It doesn't belong to a political view."[5] Overall, what should have been a joyful occasion turned into a debacle.

Questions for Discussion

▶ What do you think the listeners' motivations were for their behaviors?
▶ Do you think Hedges' topic was out of place? Why or why not?
▶ What ethical responsibilities do audience members have toward a speaker? Toward other listeners? Toward their own political opinions? Which should assume the most importance in this setting? Explain your choice.
▶ After a similar incident at a different university involving a conservative speaker, one letter to the editor argued that heckling or booing a liberal speaker draws more media response than when the speaker is conservative.[6] Do you agree? Why or why not?
▶ In what settings might Hedges' speech have been welcomed?
▶ Is there ever a place for heckling? If so, when or where might it be appropriate? If not, why not?

Responses to Diversity

To illustrate the range of differences between individuals and national groups, Porter and Samovar[7] created a minimum-maximum scale (see Figure 3.1). The "minimum" end of the scale shows comparatively small differences between co-cultural groups. At the "maximum" end are national groups differing in language, history, religious traditions, form of government, and core philosophy. Diversity, even at minimal levels, can divide people and result in hearings, open disputes, or marches; differences at the maximum end can lead to boycotts, sanctions, even wars. Resistance, assimilation, and accommodation are three common responses to diversity.

Resisting groups or individuals defend their own beliefs and traditions against change; in extreme cases, they attack their opponents.[8] The intensity of these attacks ranges from physical assaults, death threats, terrorism, or war to milder challenges that ignore, discount, or ridicule divergent ideas. In public arenas, we attack with words. Dispute and contention are so pervasive that Deborah Tannen terms U.S. culture an "argument culture."[9] As a linguist, Tannen is especially sensitive to the war metaphors that frame public discourse. For example, we engage in culture wars: wars of ideas, battles between the sexes, battles over Supreme Court nominees—hundreds of issues are framed in conflict terms. Resistance can be positive, however. In fact, resisting groups and individuals often confront social, environmental, and global injustices and bring about necessary reforms. (For more information about resistance, do a Google search for

Instructor Resource: *TA's Guide*
"Managing Sensitive Topics" (pp. 50–51) in *The Teaching Assistant's Guide to the Basic Course* provides advice on how to deal with emotionally charged discussions, such as those that some of the topics in this chapter might provoke.

Teaching Tip
Use clips from movies such as *The Breakfast Club, Remember the Titans,* and *School Daze* as examples of college students encountering diversity.

Student Learning: Workbook
Students can complete Activity 3.1, "Explore Your Personal Values," in the Student Workbook.

resisting response to diversity in which you refuse to change and you defend your own positions or attack others

Maximum

Western/Asian

Italian/Saudi Arabian

U.S. American/Greek

U.S. American/German

U.S. American/French-Canadian

White Anglo-American/Reservation Indian

White Anglo-American/African American, Asian American, Mexican American, or Urban Indian

U.S. American/British

U.S. American/English-Canadian

Urban American/Rural American

Catholic/Baptist

Male Dominance/Female Equality

Heterosexual/Homosexual

Environmentalist/Developer

Minimum

Figure 3.1
Minimum-Maximum Differences Scale
Each point along the minimum-maximum scale of sociocultural differences indicates more pervasive and more pronounced differences between the people or groups involved.

assimilating response to diversity in which you surrender some or most of your ways and adopt cultural patterns of another group

accommodate response to diversity in which you listen and evaluate the views of others; both sides adapt, modify, and bargain to reach mutual agreements

multivocal society society that actively seeks expression of a variety of voices or viewpoints

"protest movement," and read about two or three movements that interest you.)

Assimilating groups or individuals reject or surrender their beliefs and values and embrace those of another group.[10] At the turn of the 20th century, the United States was often called a "melting pot" in which millions of immigrants were "Americanized." A century later, however, we know that assimilation is rarely total, so updated metaphors such as "tossed salad" (a whole comprising distinct entities) or "stew" (distinguishable entities, changed and merged into a whole) were used to describe this country's multiethnic reality.

Because choice is a dominant U.S. value, we can freely change aspects of our lives. Immigrants might change language and clothing and adopt American ways; some may convert to another religion. However, such decisions have ethical implications if people passively allow themselves to be coerced or manipulated into changing without thinking critically or using careful reasoning.

In contrast, groups or individuals who **accommodate** diversity are willing to hear diverse ideas and evaluate them with an open mind. (To *accommodate* means to adjust or adapt.) Accommodating individuals rethink their ideas and surrender some, modify others, but hold still others relatively intact. Accommodation helps create a **multivocal society** in which a variety of ideas, opinions, and visions are sought out and voiced openly and formally. Henry Louis Gates, Jr., Chair of African and African American Studies at Harvard University, believes that an ideal society consists of co-cultural groups, or groups that diverge from the mainstream, that recognize their diversity of opinions yet work together to forge a civic culture that accommodates

© AP/Wide World Photos

In an "argument culture," a war of words is a common form of resistance by those who are unwilling to accommodate diverse ideas.

both differences and commonalities.[11] Barnett Pearce[12] uses the term **cosmopolitan communicators** to describe people who judge another group based on the group's own standards, not in terms of "superior" or "inferior." Pearce and Pearce[13] say:

> Participating in this form of communication requires a set of abilities, the most important of which is remaining in the tension between holding your own perspective, being profoundly open to others who are unlike you, and enabling others to act similarly.

Resistance, assimilation, and accommodation all have ethical implications. You probably label extreme forms of resistance (terrorist attacks, for example) or even taunting as unethical, but what about simply ignoring people who differ from you? Is assimilation ethical if you have allowed yourself to go along with cultural norms unquestioningly? Your decision to resist new ideas or to embrace them with relatively few questions, to block voices from being heard or to invite dialogue have ethical implications for both speaking and listening in a diverse society. Let's now turn to specific cultural resources that can help you be a more ethical speaker.

> ### ✓ STOP AND CHECK
> #### YOUR RESPONSES TO DIVERSITY
>
> Examine your personal responses to diversity. Where do you resist diverse ways of believing and behaving? When, if ever, do you march or openly protest differences? What perspectives, if any, do you ignore or put down? What *wars* or *battles* do you wage? In what areas, if any, have you changed your beliefs or behaviors and assimilated diverse perspectives into your personal life? When and how have you made an effort to be accommodating?

Speaking Ethically

The emphasis on ethical speaking has a long history. Centuries ago, Roman educators used the Latin motto *vir bonum, dicendi peritus* (the good person, skilled in speaking) to inspire students to combine good character with knowledge about the world and skill in speaking. They understood the power of words and the ethical implications of persuasive speaking: You can urge your listeners to behave abominably, or you can inspire them to noble pursuits.

Your concern with ethics should begin as soon as you receive your speech assignment. Think about your responsibilities to your audience, your topic, and yourself by considering some guidelines that scholars have proposed for ethical speaking. These principles fall into two major categories: dialogical and democratic.

Use Dialogical Principles

Chapter 1 points out the importance of dialogue as foundational to all communication. Many communication scholars think of public speaking as a form of public dialogue, which is not a set of communication rules, but rather a mindset that is linked to cultural values of honesty, openness, and freedom of choice.[14] In *The Magic of Dialogue: Transforming Conflict into Cooperation*, Daniel Yankelovich[15] identifies equality, empathy, and examination as three essential components of dialogue.

▶ *Equality* means that all parties involved respect each other and regard each other's opinions as important enough for consideration. This contrasts with the belief that

---

Instructor Resource: PowerPoint
The *Multimedia Manager with Instructor Resources* CD-ROM includes a Power-Point slide of Figure 3.1.

Classroom Discussion/Activity
Discuss metaphors about the United States and the meanings of each (e.g., melting pot and assimilation; tossed salad and accommodation).

Student Learning: Workbook
Students can complete Activity 3.2, "Explore Your Responses to Diversity," in the Student Workbook.

cosmopolitan communicators communicators who don't think in terms of superior or inferior, but who judge others on the standards of the other

vir bonum, dicendi peritus "the good person, skilled in speaking"

your opinions are the most important and that you have the right or obligation to impose them on others, even if this requires trickery or manipulation.

▶ *Empathy* means you attempt to understand other perspectives. You show compassion and a willingness to identify emotionally with others. Empathy contrasts with self-centered absorption with your own needs and perspectives.

▶ *Examination* means that you put aside a know-it-all attitude and willingly scrutinize your own and others' assumptions with an open mind. Examination doesn't mean you must abandon your personal biases or strong beliefs; in fact, you may *never* agree with some people, and you might eventually persuade them to adopt your views. But, in the process, you challenge your own ideas as well.

Barnett Pearce and Kimberly Pearce summarize three skills required for a dialogical perspective: (1) the ability to engage in dialogue in response to another's invitation; (2) the ability to invite others into dialogue; and (3) the ability to create contexts that facilitate dialogue.[16] (Chapter 18 develops in more detail the principles of "invitational rhetoric," a dialogical concept developed by communication professors Sonja Foss and Cindy Griffin.[17])

Finally, Amitai Etzioni[18] has set up several rules of engagement to make dialogue more productive when people have major differences:

1. Don't demonize the other side or depict it as completely negative.
2. Don't insult or offend the deepest moral commitments of diverse groups; don't bring up dark moments from the group's history.
3. Talk less about non-negotiable "rights" and more about negotiable needs, wants, and interests.
4. Don't feel you must deal with every issue.
5. Don't abandon your convictions, but balance your beliefs and passions against those strongly held by others. (The speech "Lay Your Hammer Down: Defend Your Convictions," challenges an audience of graduating seniors to do just this. You'll find the transcript of an excerpt from it at the end of this chapter and on the book's website. On the website you'll also find a video of it being delivered.)

Dialogue is considered so important that the United Nations designated the year 2001 as the Year of Dialogue Among Civilizations. U.N. Secretary General Kofi Annan[19] explained:

> The United Nations itself was created in the belief that dialogue can triumph over discord, that diversity is a universal virtue, and that peoples of the world are far more united by their common fate than they are divided by their separate identities.

In the past, dialogue has been credited with bringing about international changes. For instance, Mikhail Gorbachev, head of the former Soviet Union, said the turning point in the Cold War came during a conversation in which he and President Reagan respectfully discussed their values and aspirations for their respective countries.[20] The Seeds of Peace project described in the Diversity in Practice box is an example of people with very divergent opinions who come together for honest discussions of their prejudices and conflicts and refuse to settle for stereotyping, name calling, or violence.

Dialogue helps resolve problems at campus, state, and national levels. For example, Bruce Mallory and Nancy Thomas facilitate campus dialogues by developing "intentionally designed, permanent spaces on campuses for identifying, studying, deliberating, and planning action regarding pressing issues with ethical or social implications."[21]

Class Discussion/Activity
Ask students to conduct a search on the Internet for the phrase "hate speech," and then come to class prepared to share an example that they found. Use this to stimulate a discussion on whether hate speech violates the criteria for ethical speaking discussed in this chapter.

Student Learning: Speech Videos on the Website
A video of this speech is available on the book website for viewing and guided critical analysis. The video segment is also available on the *Multimedia Manager with Instructor Resources* CD-ROM.

Classroom Discussion/Activity
With their long history of hatred and miscommunication, Israelis and Palestinians provide an example for discussion about the need for dialogue. Discuss ways that dialogue might increase common understanding between these two groups.

Seeds of Peace is dedicated to dialogue among young people from mutually hostile groups. Former President Bill Clinton said, "The success of Seeds of Peace will mean a brighter future for the region and the world" (quoted on the organization's home page at www.seedsof peace.org).

Courtesy of Seeds of Peace Organization, www.seedsofpeace.org

Student Learning: Book Website
All URLs mentioned in the text are available as live, regularly maintained links on the book's website, located in the "Chapter Resources" list under "Web Links."

FOUNDED IN 1993, Seeds of Peace first brought together 43 young people from Egypt, Palestine, and Israel to communicate in face-to-face dialogues held at a camp in Maine. Since then, its mission has expanded to include young leaders from three additional regions of conflict: South Asia, Cyprus, and the Balkans. The goal remains the same: to empower future leaders with the communication, negotiation, and leadership skills they need to advance co-existence and reconciliation between combative groups in their home regions. Empathy and respect are fundamental to the program, which aims to reach youth "before fear, mistrust, and prejudice blind them from seeing the human face of the enemy."[22]

Two additional programs have been developed: "Maine Seeds" focuses on ethnic and racial issues within the state of Maine, and "Beyond Borders" brings students from Arab countries such as Kuwait and Iraq to interact with students from the United States.

Seeds of Peace founders might not be familiar with specific Arab customs relating to dialogue. Traditionally, Arabs met in tents to discuss socially important issues; participants were required to respect other's opinions, to listen carefully, to speak their minds, and to negotiate divisive social issues. So knowingly or not, Seeds of Peace is perpetuating longstanding cultural traditions.[23]

To learn more about Seeds of Peace, visit the organization's website at **www.seeds ofpeace.org**.

Practice Democratic Principles

Whereas dialogical principles focus on your relationship with your audience, democratic guidelines focus more on the ethical issues you face when you create the speech itself.[24] Events over the last several decades have highlighted tensions in the United States between free speech and responsible expression. McCarthyism in the 1950s, antiwar and civil rights protests in the 1960s, disputes over music lyrics in the 1980s, rancorous presidential campaigns in 2000 and 2004—all these controversies have brought into focus freedom of speech versus responsibility. The National Communication Association (NCA) has responded with a credo that summarizes widely accepted principles for ethical communication; you'll find the latest version in the Diversity in Practice box.

DIVERSITY IN PRACTICE

NCA CREDO FOR ETHICAL COMMUNICATION

QUESTIONS OF RIGHT AND WRONG arise whenever people communicate. Ethical communication is fundamental to responsible thinking, decision making, and the development of relationships and communities within and across contexts, cultures, channels, and media. Moreover, ethical communication enhances human worth and dignity by fostering truthfulness, fairness, responsibility, personal integrity, and respect for self and others. We believe that unethical communication threatens the quality of all communication and consequently the well-being of individuals and the society in which we live. Therefore we, the members of the National Communication Association, endorse and are committed to practicing the following principles of ethical communication:

▶ We advocate truthfulness, accuracy, honesty, and reason as essential to the integrity of communication.

▶ We endorse freedom of expression, diversity of perspective, and tolerance of dissent to achieve the informed and responsible decision making fundamental to a civil society.

▶ We strive to understand and respect other communicators before evaluating and responding to their messages.

▶ We promote access to communication resources and opportunities as necessary to fulfill human potential and contribute to the well-being of families, communities, and society.

▶ We promote communication climates of caring and mutual understanding that respect the unique needs and characteristics of individual communicators.

▶ We condemn communication that degrades individuals and humanity through distortion, intimidation, coercion, and violence, and through the expression of intolerance and hatred.

▶ We are committed to the courageous expression of personal convictions in pursuit of fairness and justice.

▶ We advocate sharing information, opinions, and feelings when facing significant choices while also respecting privacy and confidentiality.

▶ We accept responsibility for the short- and long-term consequences for our own communication and expect the same of others.

For more on the National Communication Association's position on ethical communication, visit the organization's website at **www.natcom.org**.

Source: Endorsed by the National Communication Association, November 1999. Reprinted by permission of the National Communication Association.

Develop a Habit of Research

During your speech, you are your listeners' primary source of information. You owe it to them to know what you're talking about, so you should do your homework before you speak. Let's say you decide to discuss a complicated issue such as immigration reform. Don't just settle for a surface understanding; instead, examine several sources and search for diverse perspectives. Find the positions taken by major political parties and by typical border state governments. Seek out immigrants' perspectives, and identify relevant social class issues. When you present a wide variety of perspectives, you give your audience the breadth of information they need to form reasoned conclusions. Deborah

Tannen believes that, in contrast, an argumentative mentality "obscures the complexity of research"[25] and creates oversimplification of ideas, which leads to disinformation and distortion.

Be Honest and Fair

Honest speaking means that you present your information as truthfully as you can. Don't exaggerate a problem and make it seem greater than it actually is. Don't distort or twist evidence. Statistics can be particularly misleading, so find out as much as you can about the numbers you present. For instance, you might find statistics showing that wine can be healthy when used in moderation, but your statistics may come from studies funded by the wine industry. Does this mean they are inaccurate? Not necessarily, but probe further and see if impartial sources produce similar statistics.

Strive for fairness, balance, and evenhandedness rather than presenting one side— the one that favors your position. Do not give in to the slanted, unfair approach of some talk radio hosts, political spinmeisters, and Internet advocacy websites or blogs that only provide a lopsided view of a specific topic. For example, contrast the ways www.handgun control.org (the Brady Campaign to Prevent Gun Violence), www.handguncontrol.net (Second Amendment Sisters, Inc.), and www.nra.org (the National Rifle Association) present gun control issues.

Practice Civility

Talk-show host Jerry Springer's guests yell insults and attack one another; talking heads on all-news channels interrupt and shout each other down; politicians use negative ads against their opponents. The common lack of civility in public discourse has led one commentator to coin the term *drive-by debating* to describe this phenomenon.[26]

Civility is a social virtue that involves self-control or moderation, not pride, insolence, or arrogance. Civil speakers and listeners are more than simply polite; they choose persuasion, consultation, advising, bargaining, compromising, and coalition building. Civility is related to accommodation and dialogical public speaking. Both require the communicators to understand, appreciate opposing perspectives, and accept the outcome when their own position loses. Cultures from the ancient Greeks to modern Asia have promoted civility as an ethical principle.[27]

An example of civility comes after each election in the United States. At local, state, and national levels both the winning and the losing candidates are expected to deliver a civil speech. The loser concedes; the winner thanks voters for their ballots. Both winners and losers pledge to support democratic ideals, even as they continue to work for the causes they hold dear.

This is by no means a complete list of democratic principles. However, you have a beginning point for thinking about ethical speaking in a pluralistic culture. Since diversity is pervasive, you must decide how you can best respect (and live comfortably with) it.[28]

Student Learning: Book Website
This Stop and Check activity can also be found on the book's website, where it's located under "Chapter Resources."

Teaching Tip
If you have not already created a class code of conduct, now would be a good time to do so, using the NCA credo as a guide.

civility self-control or moderation, in contrast to pride or arrogance; civil speakers persuade, consult, and compromise rather than coerce and manipulate

STOP AND CHECK

CIVILITY IN PUBLIC LIFE

To learn more about civility, go to InfoTrac College Edition and search for the article "In Legislating and in Life, Long May Civility Reign." It describes the 2004 inauguration ceremony that installed Bart Peterson as mayor of Indianapolis. Discuss with your classmates the recommendations for both dialogical and democratic principles that you find in this article.

Open forum sessions provide the public with opportunities to deliberate about important issues. Speakers should enact dialogical and democratic principles; participants should be mindful of their ethical responsibilities to each speaker, to other audience members, and to themselves.

Listening Ethically

Student Learning: Workbook
Activity 3.3 in the Student Workbook gives students practice with ethical listening skills.

The dialogical attitude applies to listening as well as speaking. Obviously, you do not have time to listen to everyone, but respectful listening is a way to empower others. Although you don't have to agree someone else's ideas, polite listening affirms the speaker as significant and the ideas as important enough to hear. Think about how positive you feel when someone who disagrees with you still takes time to ask what you believe and how you came to your conclusions. Sincere questions, not meant as personal attacks, show that listeners really are trying to understand your viewpoint.

In contrast, it is easy to silence others. Someone who walks away from a conversation, saying, "I don't want to hear this," leaves the other person frustrated. A similar thing can happen in public speaking settings. As the case study at the beginning of this chapter illustrates, hecklers can silence speakers by shouting them down in an attempt to keep others from hearing the speech. Someone who leaves in the middle of a speech or audience members who whisper and laugh during a speech are doing two things: (1) disrespecting the speaker and his or her ideas; and (2) disrespecting other listeners who want to hear the speech.

You face additional ethical dilemmas as a listener. When you hear a speaker saying something you know is false or arguing for a viewpoint that runs counter to yours, what do you do? Do you confront the speaker in front of others? Do you prepare a speech to present more accurate information or provide a different perspective? Do you ask questions that help other listeners detect the misinformation or bias? Do you write a letter to the editor? These are all possible responses. To think about your ethical responsibilities as a listener, ask yourself these questions:

▶ Do I keep myself informed about significant issues by exposing myself to a number of arguments, or do I listen only to the side with which I already agree? In short, do I listen with an open mind?

▶ Do I fulfill my ethical responsibilities to other listeners by not distracting them and their audience?

▶ Do I fulfill my responsibilities to speakers by letting them know they are being heard?

> Do I encourage speakers to meet ethical standards? This may mean that I ask for further information about their sources or that I point out relevant information they omit.

Academic Honesty

Tom's speech started dramatically:

> How would you react if I told you that inside this box there was a snake? Would you frantically jump up on top of your desk? Would you panic and let out a shrill scream? Would you run hysterically from the room? If you answered yes to one or more of these questions, chances are you have a phobia of snakes.

Students listened intently, but the professor frowned. This opening scenario sounded too familiar, and a quick check of department speech files turned up an identical outline submitted in a previous term. Tom's speech was plagiarized, which is a specific ethical breach. In a speech about drug cartels, Aaron made up a statistic—an act of fabrication. To avoid ethical problems such as plagiarism and fabrication, it is important that you understand just what they are.

Avoid Plagiarism

Your college or university degree is the school's official recognition and certification that you have personally grappled with important ideas and learned practical skills.[29] **Plagiarism,** on the other hand, occurs if you present the ideas, words, or works of others as if they were your own, without giving credit to the originators. It is somewhat like sending your roommate to the weight room to do your weight training; you do not benefit from the exercise.[30]

According to plagiarism.org,[31] plagiarism is increasingly common in the age of the Internet; in fact, this site states that as many as 54 percent of students surveyed admitted that they plagiarize from Internet sources by downloading textual material, pictures, diagrams, and other information that they fail to cite.

Purdue University's Online Writing Lab recognizes that even well-intentioned students may be confused about the many rules regarding plagiarism. That site explains, "While other cultures may not insist so heavily on documenting sources, American institutions do."[32] (For more information, see Diversity in Practice: Plagiarism and Culture.)

There are several types of plagiarism:[33]

> **Deliberate fraud.** Students who borrow, buy, or steal another person's speech or written outline and present it as if it were their own work plagiarize knowingly and intentionally. Because Tom's speech on phobias, mentioned above, was deliberately copied, he would be subject to his university's penalties for plagiarism, which can range from a failing grade to expulsion.

> **Cut-and-paste plagiarism.** This type of plagiarist copies entire paragraphs word-for-word from various articles and pieces them together into a paper or speech without using quotation marks or giving credit to the specific sources. To avoid this, read the material carefully and then paraphrase it in your own words. (Chapter 7 suggests you write your summaries on note cards.) Give credit to the sources, and identify direct quotations.

> **Improper paraphrase.** This type of plagiarism occurs if you don't put the selection in your own words; instead, you change or translate a few words but keep the basic structure and ideas of the original intact. For example, a professor at MIT made

Teaching Tip
This would be a good time to go over your school, departmental, or classroom standards and the consequences for plagiarism.

Instructor Resource:
TA's Guide
"Plagiarism" (p. 51) provides teachers with advice on how to decrease the likelihood of plagiarism and on how to deal with it if it occurs.

plagiarism presenting the words, images, or ideas of others as if they were your own

deliberate fraud knowing, intentional plagiarism

cut-and-paste plagiarism copying material word-for-word and then patching it together without quotation marks or citations

improper paraphrase changing some words of a source but keeping the basic structure and ideas intact without citing it

Dun Dun Drum

http://media.dickinson.edu/gallery/Sect5.html

Some students accidentally plagiarize because they don't know they must include the source of a downloaded image on the slide itself.

national news for his book about the poet E. E. Cummings; a literary magazine argued that the following paraphrase was actually plagiarism:[34]

> *From a 1980 biography of Cummings:* "Esther Lanman organized a cocktail party for Cummings with as many of the old Cambridge crowd as she could locate. Amy Gozzaldi was there, her jet-black hair now grey. She and [Cummings] looked at each other and grinned self-consciously, feeling what the years had done to them. He raised his hand to his bald head."[35]
>
> *From a 2004 biography about Cummings:* "Lanman even organized a cocktail party for Cummings, inviting every member of the 'old gang' she could round up, including Cummings's first crush, Amy de Gozzaldi. Her hair, once jet black, was now gray and Cummings, now fifty-eight, had finally gone bald. They looked at each other self-consciously, then grinned."[36]

The professor hadn't thought he plagiarized, because he credited the first book throughout. However, he failed to cite the source for this section.

Plagiarism can be intentional or accidental. **Accidental plagiarists** don't know the rules about plagiarism, so they innocently fail to properly paraphrase or give credit to their sources. For example, Allison created a series of PowerPoint slides with pictures of Mia Hamm that she'd downloaded from the Internet. She omitted the URLs of the websites where she found the pictures, which is a form of cut-and-paste plagiarism. However, it never occurred to Allison that she was supposed to credit the source of a photograph. Intentional or not, she had plagiarized, and plagiarism is comparable to stealing.

Because your school's policies are easily available in student handbooks and library and writing lab resources, you are held responsible for knowing the rules relating to plagiarism. Thus, you have no basis for pleading ignorance.

Here are some guidelines for citing sources, according to Purdue University's Online Writing Lab:[37]

Classroom Discussion / Activity
Ask students to conduct a search on the Internet for the word *plagiarism* and then come to class prepared to share from their research a strategy for avoiding plagiarism.

- Give credit when you use somebody else's words, ideas, or creative works—whether you found them in library resources, the Internet, films or television shows, audio recordings, advertisements, letters from friends, or elsewhere.
- Provide sources for information taken from interviews, conversations, or email.
- Tell the audience the source of the unique words and phrases that were not your own.
- Name your sources of diagrams, illustrations, charts, photographs, and figures.

You do not need to document:

- Personal experiences, observations, conclusions, or insights.
- Common knowledge, such as folklore or traditions within your cultural group.
- Generally accepted facts—the kind of information you find in five or more sources or information you think your audience already knows or could easily find in reference material.
- Results of experiments you personally conduct.

accidental plagiarism
plagiarism due to lack of knowledge about the rules

sources published or unpublished speech materials

Sources can be published or unpublished works. Books, magazines, newspapers, paintings, journal articles, websites, films, or sound recordings are considered published. Lecture notes, handouts, papers you've submitted for another class, sermons, most speeches, and personal interviews, photographs, and letters are unpublished.[38]

Within your speech, name your sources. For example, when you use a direct quotation, introduce it as such. When you paraphrase someone else's ideas, cite the originator. When you present a diagram or chart on a PowerPoint slide or an overhead transparency, write the source somewhere on the slide. Here are some specific examples:

▶ *Published source, newspaper.* The *Boston Globe* reported on January 24, 2002, that some adult stem cell lines have grown in cultures for two years and show no signs of aging.[39]

▶ *Published source, Internet.* Citation in small font at the bottom of the PowerPoint slide showing a photograph of *dun dun* drummers and featuring a sound clip downloaded from the Internet: Source: Yoruba drums from Benin, West Africa: The world's musical traditions 8. [online]. Accessed April 25, 2002. www.eyeneer.com/Labels/Smithsonian/Sounds/yoruba.aiff[40]

▶ *Unpublished source, personal interview.* Today I checked in with the hospital's Chief of Staff, Dr. Callari. He said the situation has worsened. Though he has never been sued, his liability insurance has doubled. He couldn't afford it and had to drop it.[41]

Chapter 11 describes ways to document sources on your outline. Be sure to list your references at the end using a standard format such as MLA (Modern Language Association) style or APA (American Psychological Association) style. These style manuals are available on the Internet or in the reference section of the library, and they show you how to cite just about any source, from a book to a personal letter, from a CD to a website.

Plagiarists, accidental or intentional, are subject to severe penalties. Typically, those guilty of fraud receive an "F" for the assignment. More serious breaches may result in temporary suspension, permanent expulsion, and/or a notation on the student's permanent record, which can seriously affect his or her life. Accidental plagiarists may be asked to redo the assignment or may lose points.

DIVERSITY IN PRACTICE
PLAGIARISM AND CULTURE

IN THE UNITED STATES, plagiarism is considered a serious intellectual breach because of three important cultural notions.[42] Here, writing something down is a concrete way to demonstrate your knowledge and skills; as a result, instructors expect you to complete assignments on your own. Turning in someone else's work does not show what *you* know.

A second concept is linked to the cultural value of individuality. You should develop yourself to your highest potential and do creative, original thinking. Turning in someone else's work does not demonstrate your originality.

Third is the cultural notion that ownership of personal property includes ownership of intellectual property. You can patent, copyright, or sell your ideas, creations, musical works, unique words, and writings. They are legally yours. Consequently, if someone else uses your original work or even a portion thereof without crediting you, you can charge them with "stealing" your intellectual property.

In other cultures, intellectual property is seen differently. Consider a society that values the group over the individual, one in which words and ideas belong to the culture as a whole, not to any one person. Would stealing or pirating works be viewed with the same perspective? What might happen when U.S. businesses move into such a culture? Also, consider the impact of the Internet on notions of "ownership" of words and ideas. For example, hypertext allows people to "write collaboratively and use non-linear connections; the product shows few indications of who said what";[43] Wikipedia, the online encyclopedia, is just one example of a jointly created resource. (See Chapter 7.)

For more information about academic honesty and culture, read "Confessions of an Academic Honesty Lady," by Judy Hunter, available at www.grinnell.edu/academic/writinglab/forum/con_hj.pdf.

Student Learning: Book Website
All URLs mentioned in the text are available as live, regularly maintained links on the book's website, located in the "Chapter Resources" list under "Web Links."

Avoid Fabrication

Student Learning: Book Website
All URLs mentioned in the text are available as live, regularly maintained links on the book's website, located in the "Chapter Resources" list under "Web Links."

Plagiarism is not the only form of academic dishonesty. If you make up information or guess at numbers but present them as factual, you are guilty of **fabrication.** Citing a reference that you have not actually read or passing along rumors or other unsubstantiated information are additional types of fabrication. For instance, after the deadly tsunami of December 26, 2004, hundreds of stories about victims and survivors circulated on the Internet. You could easily research the topic of tsunami relief, discover one of these rumors or false statistics, and use it as an example; however, doing so without checking its accuracy puts you at risk for perpetuating the falsehood. (A hypothetical example, described in Chapter 8, is in a different category because the audience understands that the example is not real.)

The best ways to avoid fabrication are to use a number of sources and be alert for conflicting information. Thoroughly check any discrepancies before you present information as factual. If your information seems suspicious, check it out on a site that uncovers hoaxes and false claims such as www.hoaxbusters.org, or visit www.snopes.com, an excellent site that exposes urban legends of all kinds, from food to computers, holidays to weddings.

✓ STOP AND CHECK

WOULD YOU USE QUESTIONABLE STATISTICS?

Student Learning: Book Website
This Stop and Check activity can also be found on the book's website, where it's located under "Chapter Resources."

Kilolo is researching the topic of breast cancer. Many sources say women have a 1-in-8 chance of developing the disease. However, as she does more extensive research, Kilolo discovers that this figure applies over the course of a lengthy life. According to a *New York Times* article, a woman who lives to be 110 has a cumulative 1-in-8 chance of contracting the disease, but the risk is 1 in 10 for 80-year-olds and about 1 in 1,000 for women under 50. A spokesperson for the American Cancer Society admitted that the 1-in-8 figure is more metaphor than fact but said it's used for good ends: It increases awareness of the disease and makes women concerned enough to seek early detection. Some physicians, however, point to an "epidemic of fear" created by the inflated numbers.[44] Furthermore, many women focus on detection and prevention of breast cancer but remain in the dark about their much higher risk of heart disease.[45]

QUESTIONS

1. Should Kilolo use the 1-in-8 figure because she's seen it in five or six sources?
2. Why or why not?
3. What do you think of the American Cancer Society's decision to continue using the figure when they know it is inaccurate? Is this ethical?
4. How might hyped information about one disease help or harm women's overall health?

Student Learning: Book Website
Under "Chapter Resources," students will find several tools for reviewing the information in this chapter, including a "Tutorial Quiz." You can have them email the results of this quiz to you as a participation or extra-credit activity.

Summary

People in pluralistic cultures differ in beliefs, values, attitudes, and behaviors to degrees that range from superficial to fundamental. You can respond to diversity in a number of ways.

If you choose to defy or resist, you will bolster your position and (perhaps) attack or ignore diverse perspectives. If you choose to assimilate, you will surrender some aspect of your own belief or cultural tradition and replace it with something new. Finally, when you accommodate diversity, you accept differences and work with others to create a society in which all can live together.

fabrication making up information or repeating a rumor without sufficiently checking its accuracy

Our culture provides both dialogical and democratic resources that you can use to speak and listen ethically. Choose a dialogical relationship with your listeners. Respect them as equals, have empathy with their perspectives, and examine both your own and your listeners' assumptions in an honest, open manner. Democratic principles remind you to develop a habit of research, to present your materials honestly and fairly, and to respond to diversity with civility.

Listening also calls for ethically responsible actions. Allowing people to speak empowers them, giving them a voice and enabling others to hear their ideas. However, when speakers present incorrect or misleading information, you are faced with an ethical decision, in which you need to balance your rights and responsibilities against the rights and responsibilities of the speaker and other listeners. Vernon Jensen coined the term *rightsabilities* to highlight this tension.

As you present your materials, be sure to cite your references and check a variety of sources to avoid the ethical problems of plagiarism or fabrication. Plagiarism occurs when you present the ideas or words of another person as your own without giving credit to the original source. Fabrication occurs when you make up material or present something as factual when it is not.

STUDY AND REVIEW

The premium website for *Public Speaking* offers a broad range of resources that will help you better understand the material in this chapter, complete assignments, and succeed on tests. The website features

▶ Speech videos with critical viewing questions, speech outlines, and transcripts, and
▶ Interactive practice activities, self quizzes, and a sample final exam.

For more information about this text's electronic learning resources, consult your **Guide to Online Resources for Public Speaking** or visit http://communication.wadsworth.com/jaffe5.

KEY TERMS

The terms below are defined in the margins throughout this chapter. The book's website also provides interactive flashcards and crossword puzzles to help you learn these terms and the concepts they represent.

ethical communication 34	civility 41
"rightsabilities" 34	plagiarism 43
heckling 34	deliberate fraud 43
resisting 35	cut-and-paste plagiarism 43
assimilating 36	improper paraphrase 43
accommodate 36	accidental plagiarism 44
multivocal society 36	sources 44
cosmopolitan communicators 37	fabrication 46
vir bonum, dicendi peritus 37	

APPLICATION AND CRITICAL THINKING EXERCISES

The exercises below are among the practice activities on the book's website.

1. Draw a minimum-maximum scale that represents diversity on your campus. Identify differences at the minimum end of the range. Work your way up the scale and identify increasingly greater areas of diversity that create conflicts. When and how do campus speakers address this diversity?

2. With a small group of your classmates, use the scale you made in Exercise 1 to decide what diversity issues on your campus provide opportunities for people with different beliefs, values, or behaviors to encounter one another. Which of the three ways of dealing with differences— resistance, assimilation, or accommodation— do members of your student body most commonly use? Assess the ethics of their responses.

3. With a small group in your classroom, discuss ways that people who hold diverse perspectives on a controversial topic might engage in dialogue (for example, pro-choice advocates meeting with pro-life activists; born-again Christians talking with committed Muslims; animal rights activists meeting with research scientists; leaders of NATO meeting with leaders of the African Union). How can each group listen to the other and explore their perspectives with an open mind?

4. Form small groups and choose a controversial issue about which you have moderate to strong disagreement. Discuss the topic within the group, and put into practice the principles for speaking and listening in this chapter.

5. With a small group of your classmates, discuss speakers who demonstrate opposite characteristics of one of the elements depicted in the Latin phrase *vir bonum, dicendi peritus:*

   ▶ *A person lacking in character who is a skilled speaker.* Make a list of people skilled in speaking but who are not "good" persons. (Hitler tops most people's list.) What problems can these skilled orators bring about in the world?

   ▶ *A person of excellent character who is unskilled in speaking.* Identify situations, real or hypothetical, in which good people want to do something that will better their world but lack the skills needed to present their ideas effectively.

6. For an example of a famous speech that addresses religious diversity, read or listen to streaming video of John F. Kennedy's Address to the Greater Houston Ministerial Association in June, 1960, available at www.jfklibrary.org/j091260.htm. Kennedy became the first Catholic president in November 1960, but five months before the election, some voters worried that his allegiance might be to the Pope, not the American people. Notice how JFK lays out his views on religious diversity and how he affirms core American values.

7. Use your own values and beliefs as well as the guidelines described in this chapter to write an ethical code that states the principles by which you want to speak and listen.

8. Evaluate yourself as a responsible listener. How do you avoid silencing speakers? Use the questions in the section on Listening Ethically on page 42 to guide your self-evaluation.

9. Look up your campus's guidelines regarding academic honesty. What guidelines do they provide to help students learn and practice ethical research procedures? What are the penalties for plagiarism?

Student Learning: Speech Videos on the Website
A video of this speech is available on the book website for viewing and guided critical analysis. The video segment is also available on the *Multimedia Manager with Instructor Resources* CD-ROM.

SPEECH VIDEO

Log on to the book's website to watch and critique a commencement address by Edwin J. Feulner, president of the Heritage Foundation. A transcript of the speech appears below and is also available on the book's website.

Professional Speaker's Speech with Commentary

LAY YOUR HAMMER DOWN: DEFEND YOUR CONVICTIONS
Edwin J. Feulner

In 1969 a Stanford University psychologist named Philip Zimbardo set up an experiment. He arranged for two cars to be abandoned— one on the mean streets of the Bronx, New York; the other in an affluent neighborhood near Stanford in Palo Alto, California. The license plates had been removed, and the hoods were left open. Zimbardo wanted to see what would happen to the cars.

In the Bronx, he soon found out. Ten minutes after the car was abandoned, people began stealing parts from it. Within three days the car was stripped. When there was nothing useful left to take, people smashed windows and ripped out upholstery, until the car was trashed.

In Palo Alto, something quite different happened: nothing. For more than a week the car sat there unmolested. Zimbardo was puzzled, but he had a hunch about human nature. To test it, he went out and, in full view of everyone, took a sledgehammer and smashed part of the car.

Soon, passersby were taking turns with the hammer, delivering blow after satisfying blow. Within a few hours, the vehicle was resting on its roof, demolished.

Now at this point, you might be wondering what all this has to do with your graduation . . . ? I promise I'll try to make that story relevant to this happy occasion. . . .

Among the scholars who took note of Zimbardo's experiment were two criminologists, James Q. Wilson . . . and George Kelling. The experiment gave rise to their "broken windows" theory of crime, which is illustrated by a common experience: When a broken window in a building is left unrepaired, the rest of the windows are soon broken by vandals. But why . . . does the broken window invite further vandalism? . . . The broken window is their metaphor for a whole host of ways that behavioral norms can break down in a community. If one person scrawls graffiti on a wall, others will soon be at it with their spray cans. If one aggressive panhandler begins working a block, others will soon follow.

In short, once people begin disregarding the norms that keep order in a community, both order and community unravel, sometimes with astonishing speed. . . . Now all this is a preface. My topic is not crime on city streets; rather, I want to speak about incivility in the marketplace of ideas. The broken windows theory is what links the two.

As the head of a think tank in Washington, I work exclusively in the marketplace of ideas. . . . What we're seeing . . . today is a disturbing growth of incivility that follows and confirms the broken windows theory. Alas, this breakdown of civil norms is not a failing of either the political left or the right exclusively. It spreads across the political spectrum from one end to the other.

A few examples:

▶ A liberal writes a book calling Rush Limbaugh a "big fat idiot." A conservative writes a book calling liberals "useful idiots."

▶ A liberal writes a book titled *The Lies of George W. Bush*. A conservative writes a book subtitled *Liberal Lies about the American Right*.

▶ A liberal publishes a detailed "case for Bush-hatred." A conservative declares "even Islamic terrorists don't hate America like liberals do."

Those few examples— and unfortunately there are many, many more— come from elites in the marketplace of ideas. All are highly educated people who write nationally syndicated columns, publish best-selling books, and are hot tickets on radio and television talk shows.

Further down the food chain, lesser lights take up smaller hammers, but they commit even more degrading incivilities. The Internet, with its easy access and worldwide reach, is a breeding ground for websites with names like

▶ Bushbodycount.com;
▶ Toostupidtobepresident.com.

Feulner opens with a story that leads into the metaphor he will use throughout the speech.

He recognizes that his listeners might be thinking, "Nice story, but how is it relevant?"

Feulner explains the metaphor; throughout, he will compare incivility to a hammer.

He works in politics, so he uses politics as an example, but he could be talking about other controversial subjects such as music lyrics or workplace policies toward gays and lesbians.

Although he is a conservative, Feulner shows how people from many perspectives are not civil.

This is how the broken windows theory plays out in the marketplace of ideas. If you want to see it working in real time, try the following: Log on to AOL, and go to one of the live chat rooms reserved for political chat. Someone will post a civil comment on some political topic. Almost immediately, someone else will swing the verbal hammer of incivility, and from there the chat degrades into a food fight, with invective and insult as the main course.

This illustrates the first aspect of the broken windows theory, which we saw with the car in Palo Alto. Once someone wields the hammer— once the incivility starts— others will take it as an invitation to join in, and pretty soon there's no limit to the incivility.

Now if you watch closely in that chat room, you'll see something else happening. Watch the screen names of people who make civil comments. Some— a few— will join in the food fight. But most will log off. Their screen names just disappear. They leave because the atmosphere has turned hostile to anything approaching a civil exchange or a real dialogue.

This illustrates the second aspect of the broken windows theory: Once the insults begin flying, many will opt out. Wilson and Kelling describe this response when the visible signs of order deteriorate in a neighborhood: "Many residents will think that crime, especially violent crime, is on the rise, and they will modify their behavior accordingly. They will use the streets less often, and when on the streets will stay apart from their fellows, moving with averted eyes, silent lips, and hurried steps. Don't get involved. . . ."

The chat room shows us that a similar response occurs when civility breaks down in the marketplace of ideas. Many people withdraw and tune out . . . This is the real danger of incivility. Our free, self-governing society requires an open exchange of ideas, which in turn requires a certain level of civility rooted in mutual respect for each other's opinions and viewpoints.

What we see today, I am afraid, is an accelerating competition between the left and the right to see which side can inflict the most damage with the hammer of incivility. Increasingly, those who take part in public debates appear to be exchanging ideas when, in fact, they are trading insults: idiot, liar, moron, traitor. . . .

Incivility is not a social blunder to be compared with using the wrong fork. Rather, it betrays a defect of character. Incivility is dangerous graffiti, regardless of whether it is spray-painted on a subway car, or embossed on the title page of a book. The broken windows theory shows us the dangers in both cases.

But those cases aren't parallel in every way, and in closing I want to call your attention to an important difference. When behavioral norms break down in a community, police can restore order. But when civility breaks down in the marketplace of ideas, the law is powerless to set things right.

And properly so. Our right to speak freely— and to speak with incivility, if we choose— is guaranteed by those five glorious words in the First Amendment: "Congress shall make no law. . . ."

And yet, the need for civility has never been greater. Our nation is divided as never before between the left and the right. We are at loggerheads on profoundly important political and social questions. . . . .Sadly, too many of us are not rising to these challenges as a democratic people. On the contrary, we've seen a 40-year decline in voter participation in national elections. In the last two presidential elections, fewer than half of eligible voters even bothered to vote.

Rather than helping to reverse this decline, the rising chorus of incivility is driving out citizens of honest intent and encouraging those who trade in jeering and mockery.

Fortunately, this is not the stuff of [this college].

If we are to prevail as a free, self-governing people, we must first govern our tongues and our pens. Restoring civility to public discourse is not an option. It is a necessity.

Who will begin the restoration of civility?

I hope you will. Your graduation today is proof that you're up to the job, and I urge you to take it on as a serious, lifelong commitment. . . . After four years of study [here], you know the difference between attacking a person's argument and attacking a person's character.

Here, the examples move closer to home— to personal computers and the Internet where people hammer one another in chat rooms.

The consequences of incivility are that good people drop out.

Feulner emphasizes the cultural value of and necessity for open dialogue.

Here's another metaphor. This is not table manners that show a lack of polish; it's a deeper flaw.

Here he uses a contrast to show how incivility differs from vandalism or other crimes, and he praises free speech.

What do you think causes low turnouts for elections?

Respect that difference.

Your education here has taught you how to engage in rational debate and either hold your own or lose with grace and civility.

Take that lesson with you.

Your professors . . . have shown you, by their example, that you don't need the hammer of incivility to make your point.

Follow their example.

Defend your convictions— those virtues— with all the spirit you can. But do it with all the civility that you ought. . . . So, as you leave this special place,

Lay your hammer down. . . .

Thank you and congratulations to the Class of 2004.

Feulner, E. J. (2004, July 15). Lay Your Hammer Down. *Vital Speeches of the Day*, 70 (19), 595–598 (adapted).

He has pointed out the *why* of civility; now he points to the *who*. In the rest of the speech he challenges his listeners to apply their educational learning to contribute to civil dialogues in society.

CHAPTER 4

EFFECTIVE LISTENING

THIS CHAPTER WILL HELP YOU

▶ Appreciate the importance of listening skills

▶ Name two linguistic barriers to listening

▶ Describe cultural factors that hinder listening

▶ Explain how personal barriers affect your listening

▶ Draw and explain four thought patterns that are common during listening

▶ Use cultural schema to improve your listening

▶ Discuss diverse cultural listening styles

▶ Identify strategies to improve your comprehensive listening

▶ Improve your critical listening skills

▶ Practice dialogical listening through nonverbal feedback

▶ Give appropriate verbal feedback

"Learning Wall" Mural © 1989 by Keith Sklar. (SFSUD Headquarters, Franklin and Hayes Streets, SF, CA)

T HINK ABOUT ALL your communication activities during a typical week. Then rank the following activities—reading, writing, listening, and speaking—in order according to the amount of waking time you normally spend doing each one:

_____ reading   _____ writing   _____ listening   _____ speaking

Chapter-at-a-Glance
Listening is an essential skill for personal and professional success. This chapter begins by discussing the importance of listening. Next, linguistic, cultural, and personal barriers to listening are identified, and thought patterns that are common during listening are described. The second half of the chapter focuses on strategies for improving listening. The chapter ends by discussing the importance of dialogical listening: nonverbal, verbal, and written feedback.

If you ranked listening first, you're like the average person, who spends about 50 percent of the time listening and less than 18 percent each reading, writing, and speaking. An ancient proverb, attributed to Zeno of Citium, emphasizes the comparative importance of listening: "We have been given two ears and but a single mouth in order that we may hear more and talk less."

If we listen so much, we should be pretty good at it. Right? Unfortunately, we often fail to give this vital skill as much attention as we give other communication skills. Compare the number of reading, writing, and speaking courses to the number of *listening* courses your college or university offers. Most schools offer many writing, literature, and speech courses, but few offer courses in listening to comprehend or in critical listening. Instead, instructors incorporate listening into other courses.

Because listening is so vital, this chapter begins by stressing its importance. Then it looks at areas you may need to improve in. Finally, you will learn some strategies to help you become a more effective listener.

CASE STUDY: SERVICE ADVISERS WHO LISTEN

Because of their excellent listening skills, many women are being hired as automobile service advisers.

© Jack Jaffe

Mike Lazarus had a problem in his car dealership.[1] Customers were complaining about botched repair jobs. An examination of his service department pointed blame at the service advisers. Thinking that they knew more about cars than the customers did, they stopped listening a few moments into the customer's description of the problem and hastily wrote up a repair order, diagnosing the problem themselves instead of simply writing down the issues. Lazarus decided that good listening skills were essential for service advisers, but technical expertise was optional. He figured it was easier to teach a novice some automobile terminology than it was to teach professionals some listening skills.

So he set about hiring good listeners and discovered that women often had the skills he sought. They listened to the entire complaint and took it seriously; they took careful notes to make sure they understood the facts; they dealt patiently with customers who brought along young children; and they empathized with each customer's feelings. Eventually, 64 percent of his service advisers and 50 percent of his service managers were women. Lazarus confessed, "I just wanted someone who could listen to customers." He added, "Women listen, men tell."

Questions for Discussion

▹ Listening skills are important in thousands of jobs, ranging from your advisor or the financial aid officer on campus to your haircutter and physician. Tell of a time when someone really listened to you, and then tell of a time when someone failed to listen well. What was the outcome in each case?
▹ Describe how good listening skills will help you in your chosen career.
▹ What is your response to Lazarus's statement, "Women listen and men tell"?

Listening Skills Are Valuable

If you do a Google search for "listening skills," you will get more than 800,000 hits. Obviously, many people understand the importance of good listening; however, many are overconfident, thinking that they remember 75 to 80 percent of what they hear, when, in fact, after 48 hours, average listeners recall only about 25 percent.[2] Listening skills are worth developing because they are so essential:

▹ *We listen most.* Listening is the most commonly used skill in the workplace; understanding and following instructions (skills linked to listening) come in second.[3] Similarly, you must listen for information and directions if you want to succeed in college. Thus, in work and in school, you are more productive when you listen well.
▹ *Good listening skills are good job skills.* The most successful people are effective listeners. One study reports that 80 percent of executives rank listening as the most important work skill.[4] And Madelyn Burley-Allen, author of *Listening: The Forgotten Skill*, says the most common comment about well-liked bosses is: "he or she really listens to me."[5] Barbers, doctors, journalists, automobile service advisers—even politicians—understand the need to listen; in fact, "listening tours" are now indispensable in political campaigns.
▹ *Listening and being heard empowers people and aids personal relationships.* Sheila Bentley, past president of the International Listening Association, says, "Most people would agree that having someone listen to you makes you feel better—mentally and physically. In fact, according to Ralph G. Nichols, . . . 'The most basic of all human needs is to understand and to be understood. . . . The best way to understand people is to listen to them.' Thus, being listened to is one of our most basic needs."[6]

These are only a few reasons that listening is important; you can probably think of many other situations in which good listening habits make life easier. Pause now, and ask yourself how your listening habits help or hinder your comprehension of course work. What personal relationships benefit or suffer as a result of your listening behaviors? How are listening skills used in a job you currently hold or plan to hold someday? Keep these questions in mind as you study the remainder of the chapter.

Figure 4.1

Listening in Chinese
The Chinese character that translates as "listening" emphasizes its holistic nature by combining the symbols for ears, eyes, and heart.

Instructor Resource: PowerPoint
The *Multimedia Manager with Instructor Resources* CD-ROM includes a PowerPoint slide of Figure 4.1.

Instructor's Resource Manual
"Application and Critical Thinking Exercises" 1 and 2 in Chapter 4 of the Instructor's Resource Manual (available in print, online, and on the Multimedia Manager CD-ROM) give advice on how to lead discussions about Figure 4.1.

Teaching Tip
The movie *Nell* can be used to illustrate vocabulary differences that cause communication difficulty.

Barriers to Listening

The Chinese character for listening (Figure 4.1) combines the symbols for ears, eyes, and heart; it reinforces the idea that good listeners are wholly involved in listening. Most of us don't begin the day thinking, "I'm going to be a terrible listener today." We intend to listen well, but we face linguistic, cultural, and personal barriers. Understanding these barriers and planning strategies to deal with them will help you listen more effectively.

Linguistic Barriers

Diversity shows up in language variations. Visit a large city in the United States, and you'll hear many languages and accents; for example, more than one hundred languages are spoken in New York City alone. Then contrast the slang that teenagers invent with the phrases their grandparents use, or the terminology that skateboarders use with the legalese that only lawyers understand. Clearly, the potential for linguistic misunderstandings is great. Linguistic barriers show up in language and vocabulary differences.

▶ *Language differences.* If you don't share a speaker's language, you will need an interpreter in order to understand the speech. Even then, you will probably miss some concepts, because languages and the ideas they embody are so different. In addition, you may have a hard time understanding someone who speaks your language with a heavy accent, whether it be a regional or ethnic accent, or an accent influenced by a first language.

▶ *Vocabulary differences.* Speakers whose vocabulary is more extensive than yours may talk over your head much of the time. In addition, speakers who use technical jargon that is associated with a specific topic such as medicine will probably lose their audience unless they translate the jargon. Finally, speakers who use slang or other specialized linguistic codes will reach some people, but not others.

Chapter 13 provides more information on how language differences affect comprehension.

Cultural Barriers

Comprehension also depends upon your ability to understand **cultural allusions,** or references to specific historical, literary, and religious sources. You can probably think of many things that are familiar in your culture or co-culture that might confuse someone from a different group. Here are a few examples:

cultural allusions references to historical, literary, and religious sources that are familiar in a specific culture

Nelson Mandela speaks English with British and South African syllable stress and pronunciation patterns; you may have to listen closely to understand his message.

- An opera lover might be more familiar with Wagner's Ring Cycle than with Beyoncé or Los Lonely Boys.
- Allusions to the classic Japanese novel *The Tale of Genji* would need to be explained to most people outside of Japan.
- A philosophy major may understand Kant's Categorical Imperative, but many of his public speaking classmates won't.

In our pluralistic society and multicultural world, each group draws from different historical events, cultural heroes, literary or oral traditions, and religious resources. In pluralistic settings, you may be unfamiliar with these culture-specific references. It is up to each speaker to be sensitive to differences and explain allusions or choose areas of common knowledge.

Personal Barriers

Personal distractions can obstruct your listening. For example, William identified a number of listening problems:

> Sometimes I become aggressive; sometimes I get defensive when I feel attacked. I have attention deficit disorder; at times I am easily distracted by others around me. I let my feelings for people get in the way.

Many personal factors can hinder your listening. *Physical factors* (hearing loss, sleep deprivation, hunger pangs, the flu) can affect your ability or your desire to focus on a speech. *Psychological factors* can also keep you from listening closely: You just had an argument with a friend; you have a huge test coming up in your next class; your bank account is overdrawn. The worries that accompany psychological stressors can take your energy away from listening.

Stereotypes and prejudices can also hinder listening. When you put people into a category and then assume they will fit the characteristics of the category, you are **stereotyping** them. When you listen with pre-formed judgments about the speaker, either negative or positive, you are being **prejudiced** or biased. To illustrate, several students who support abortion rights listened approvingly to a speaker from Planned Parenthood, but they blocked one representing National Right to Life, and vice versa. Perhaps this helps explain why Mike Lazarus's original service advisors (in Case Study 4) failed to listen well. Because most service customers are women,[7] the male service advisers may have listened in a biased way. In contrast, his new hires took customer complaints seriously and empathized with the frustration involved.

Paying attention is another major factor in listening. Here Gail discusses some of her struggles to focus on a speech:

> I'm easily distracted. . . . It's easy for me to either focus on one particular thing that has been said, and then sort of drift off, exploring it further in my own mind, or—and this applies more specifically to someone whose speaking style or subject does not impress me—float off on unrelated topics ("I wonder where she gets her hair cut?"). Also, depending on the subject, I can get easily bored.

Listening is often hard work. For one thing, you can think far more rapidly (about 500 words per minute) than the fastest speaker can talk (about 300 words per minute). Most speakers average about 150 words per minute, leaving you with 350 words per minute of a **speech-thought differential,** also called "**leftover thinking space.**"[8] The following four thought patterns, illustrated in Figure 4.2, are common during listening:[9]

- *Taking small departures from the communication line.* Small departures can hinder your comprehension, but they can also help you follow a message if, during them, you produce your own examples, relate the material to your personal experiences, answer the

stereotyping placing someone in a category, and then assuming the person fits the characteristics of that category

prejudiced having pre-formed biases or judgments, whether negative or positive

speech-thought differential the difference between the rate you think (about 500 words per minute) and the rate you speak (about 150 words per minute)

leftover thinking space another term for the difference between your thinking rate and your speaking rate

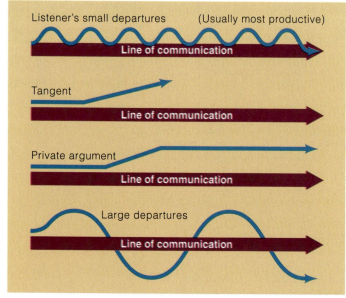

Figure 4.2

Listening Thought Patterns
These four thought patterns are typical during listening. The first can be productive, but the rest characterize poor listening.

speakers' rhetorical questions, and otherwise interact with the ideas.

▶ *Going off on a tangent.* When you depart from the speakers' line of thinking and seize on one of their ideas, taking it in your own direction, you stop listening. One idea leads to another, and before you know it, you're in a daydream, several subjects removed from the topic at hand.

▶ *Engaging in a private argument.* When you carry on a running debate or mental argument that parallels the speech, you close your mind and stop trying to understand the speaker's reasoning. In contrast, effective critical listeners identify arguments that don't make sense, but they withhold final judgment until they have heard the entire speech.

▶ *Taking large departures from the communication line.* Your attention wanders off into unrelated areas; you bring it back and focus on the speech for a while; then, off it goes again, and you find yourself thinking about a totally unrelated topic. This cycle repeats indefinitely.

As you can see, linguistic, cultural, and personal factors can make listening difficult. To assess your listening skills, complete the test in the Stop and Check box. In the remainder of the chapter, you will discover some strategies you can use to become a better listener.

 STOP AND CHECK

LISTENING SKILLS SELF-ASSESSMENT

Evaluate your listening by taking this test. First, write the letter that most accurately indicates how often you exhibit the specific behavior; then tabulate your listening score using the key that follows the questions.

A = Almost always	C = Sometimes	E = Almost never
B = Usually	D = Rarely	

How often do you:

_____ 1. Get lost in a speech because of your small vocabulary?

_____ 2. Tune out a speaker whose position is different from one you hold?

_____ 3. Feel angry, defensive, or fearful when you disagree with the speaker?

_____ 4. Become distracted by external factors, such as noises outside the room?

_____ 5. Let internal preoccupations, such as personal worries or stresses, distract you?

_____ 6. Carry on a running argument with a speaker instead of hearing her or him out?

_____ 7. Go off on a tangent?

_____ 8. Give in to your short attention span and lose your place in a long speech?

_____ 9. Stereotype a speaker and let that affect how you listen?

_____ 10. Give up trying to understand a speaker's accent and tune the speaker out?

Key

For every A give yourself 2 points.
For every B give yourself 4 points.
For every C give yourself 6 points.
For every D give yourself 8 points.
For every E give yourself 10 points.

Total score _____

More than 90	Your listening skills are exceptional.
Between 76 and 90	You are above average.
Between 60 and 75	Your skills are about average.
Below 60	You are probably not as effective a listener as you could be.

If you scored below 80, identify specific strategies from the rest of this chapter that will help you improve your listening.

Strategies to Improve Listening

Being mindful of your thought patterns during the listening process can lead you to develop strategies for understanding and retaining material. Use a combination of resources from within your culture, along with nonverbal and note-taking skills.

Use Cultural Schemas

Listening schemas are sets of cultural expectations that can help you organize and understand messages (Figure 4.3). **Schemas** are mental plans, blueprints, or models you use to perceive information and then interpret, store, and recall it.[10] Think of how you listen to a story. You have a mental model of what a good story is like, and you use this

schemas mental plans or models that guide your perception, interpretation, storage, and recollection of a speech

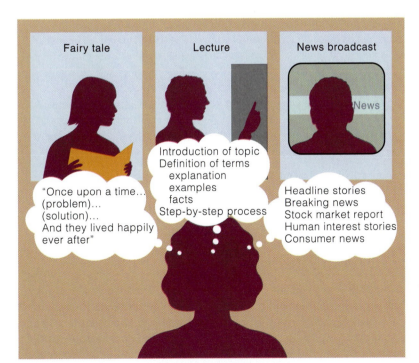

Figure 4.3
Listening Schemas
Our minds contain a number of schemas, or models, that help us listen and respond to specific types of speeches.

model to interpret a specific story—your schema tells you whether to take it seriously, how to draw lessons from it, what parts are worth remembering, and so on.

You formulate schemas through listening to many speeches of various types. For instance, you've heard lots of announcements, and you have a pretty good idea of what they are like, because they follow a fairly predictable pattern. Similarly, you've learned what to expect from a how-to speech, a news report, a funeral eulogy, or an award presentation because you've heard many speeches in each category. (The Diversity in Practice box on Cultural Listening Styles identifies some listening expectations that are common in other cultural and co-cultural groups.)

DIVERSITY IN PRACTICE
CULTURAL LISTENING STYLES

THE WAYS LISTENERS APPROACH public speeches reflect differences in worldviews and behaviors among cultural groups. Knowing some cultural variations will make you more mindful of listening diversity. Here are a few examples:

▸ *A Javanese listening schema:* On the Indonesian island of Java, listeners turn to their neighbors and repeat phrases they like. The resulting buzz of voices throughout the speech signals the speaker that the audience is receiving it well.[11]

▸ *Additional listening traditions found in several Asian cultures:* In cultures that emphasize unity, listeners often expect speakers to develop oneness with them rather than present divisive ideas. Both the speakers and their audiences share responsibility for making the speech successful.[12] In some groups, audiences listen in silence, thinking that noise breaks their concentration and diverts their attention. Applause signals suspicion, similar to booing by United States audiences; some cultures do not applaud at the end of the speech so that the speaker can remain modest.[13]

▸ *An African American schema:* The entire audience participates in a "call and response" pattern, which reflects African traditions. The speaker's statements (calls) are punctuated by the listeners' reactions to them (response), and in a real sense, the audience is talking back to the speaker. No sharp line distinguishes speakers and listeners, and both cooperate to create the message.[14]

▸ *Various student preferences:* A cross-cultural study of student listening preferences[15] showed that American students like messages that are short and to the point. They tend to prefer speakers with whom they can identify (women more so than men). German students prefer precise, error-free messages; disorganized presentations frustrate and annoy them. They are much less concerned about identifying personally with the speaker. Israeli students prefer complex and challenging information that they can ponder and evaluate before they form judgments and opinions. The length of the speech is relatively unimportant.

Log on to InfoTrac College Edition to read Christian Kiewitz's entire study of cross-cultural student listening preferences, "Cultural Differences in Listening Style Preferences: A Comparison of Young Adults in Germany, Israel, and the United States."

Know Your Listening Purpose

Just as you have speaking goals, you also have listening goals. You turn on the radio for entertainment but, when a commercial comes on, you tune out, or you critically evaluate the claims, deciding whether or not the product interests you. You listen to a lecture for information, and then you eat lunch with friends and listen empathetically to their frustrations. For each type of listening, you shift strategies to meet your listening goals. This section focuses on listening to comprehend and listening to evaluate messages.

Improve Your Comprehension

Think of all the times you listen for information: Your boss gives directions for your next project; a friend directs you to the financial aid office; a radio reporter tells where an accident blocks traffic. According to the student handbook of the University of Minnesota, Duluth,[16] average students spend 14 hours each week in class listening. Listening to learn, or **comprehensive listening,** is a vital skill in many areas of life.

Several strategies can help you increase your comprehension. Jot down vocabulary words, and look up unfamiliar terms and concepts. Develop skills for identifying major ideas and important supporting materials by studying Chapter 8 (supporting information) and Chapters 9 through 11 (organization) in this text. Use these tips to overcome the listening departures discussed earlier and shown in Figure 4.2:

Effective note taking is one way you can improve your comprehensive listening skills.

▶ *Prepare in advance.* Before class, read the related material in the text or look up background information. Study the list of concepts found at the chapter opening; skim the chapter, and notice headings and boldfaced terminology; read the summary. Look at the pictures and diagrams, or look for supplementary information on the Internet.

▶ *Use attention-directing strategies.* To overcome listening departures and tangents from the speech, both large and small, take notes. Direct your attention to specific areas of the message; for example, listen for and write down the main ideas, focus on practical "things I can use," or listen for examples that will help you remember concepts.

▶ *Enhance the meaning.* Use small departures productively by asking yourself questions that link the material to your personal experiences and ideas. For example: "Who do I know who is like that?" "Isn't that what happened to my grandmother?" "How does that work?" "What will the next step be?" "Does this match what I learned in another class?" Elaborate on the ideas by creating mental images or by referring to what you already know or have experienced.

▶ *Look for organizational patterns.* Use organizational skills from the canon of disposition to help you remember material. For instance, identify the main points and watch for signals such as "first," "next," or "finally" that will help you understand a series of steps. Be alert for words like "therefore" or "in contrast" that connect ideas.[17]

▶ *Use strategies that complement your personal learning style.* For instance, if you are an auditory learner, get permission to record the lecture or speech and replay it later. If you are a linear learner, outline the main points and the important supporting information. If you are more graphically oriented, make a mind map and draw connections between ideas. Draw useful illustrations in the margins of your notes. I include the lecturer's examples in my notes, because I learn and remember abstract ideas best when I tie them to real-life situations.

▶ *Take note of the speaker's manner.* Confident enthusiasm about the subject adds a dimension that says "this is important, pay attention" or "I care about this topic and so should you." In contrast, a tentative, apologetic, or apathetic manner suggests "this is not very important material" or "this speaker seems unsure about this material, so how can I trust it?"

comprehensive listening
listening to learn, understand, or get information

In summary, comprehensive listening requires you to understand words and ideas, to identify major ideas and supporting materials, to connect new material with old, and to recall information. Comprehensive listening corresponds with the general speech purpose of informing. We now turn to critical listening skills that you'll employ when you hear a persuasive speaker.

Improve Your Critical Listening Skills

Persuasive messages surround you, urging you to buy something, sign a petition, donate time or money, accept a religious belief, or use a particular product. You need to develop critical listening skills to sort out competing claims for your allegiance, your beliefs, your money, and your time.

Taking a critical approach means that you ponder and weigh the merits of various appeals rather than accepting them without reflection. **Critical listening** skills build on comprehensive listening skills but add questions such as these:

▶ What is this speaker's goal?
▶ Does this message make sense?
▶ Where does this information come from?
▶ What are the benefits of adopting the speaker's ideas?
▶ What problems, if any, go along with this position?
▶ Am I being swayed by my emotions?
▶ Should I trust this speaker?

**Classroom Discussion/
Activity**
Do audience members have
ethical responsibilities as
listeners? Refer back to
Chapter 3.

Critical listening is one way to live out the cultural saying "Don't believe everything you hear." Sharpening these skills will guide you as you sift through all the persuasive appeals each day brings. Chapters 8 and 18 provide tests you can use to evaluate evidence and reasoning. In a diverse culture, as I note in Chapter 3, you may seek out speakers who bolster and affirm your ideas, especially if the dominant society challenges them. The following examples may clarify this listening purpose:

▶ People who give money to support needy children attend a banquet where they hear narratives describing how their gift literally saved lives. These stories convince them to continue their donations.
▶ Members of synagogues, churches, mosques, and temples gather regularly to reaffirm their spiritual beliefs.
▶ Members of neo-Nazi groups organize gatherings in which speakers passionately argue for the merits of white supremacy.
▶ Every year on the anniversary of the Supreme Court decision of *Roe v. Wade*, supporters on both sides of the abortion issue attend rallies where speakers reaffirm their position.

In similar contexts, you may find yourself reacting enthusiastically by clapping, nodding, or verbally encouraging the speaker. Because of your biases, you may accept questionable arguments or emotional appeals that support your cause. However, you should test these messages as you would any other persuasive speech. Think how different history would be if more of Hitler's listeners had evaluated his messages critically.[18]

To practice the skills presented here, listen to two political convention speeches from the 2004 Republican and Democratic national conventions. Go to http://www.c-span .org and search for speech videos archived from each convention. If you prefer the Republican Party, practice your comprehensive listening skills on a Democrat's speech. Be able to summarize it and show that you understand it. Then listen to a Republican's speech critically and analytically, using the guidelines described above. If you prefer the Democratic Party, do the opposite: Make sure you understand a Republican's speech, and then critically evaluate a speech given by a Democrat.

critical listening listening
that requires you to reflect
and weigh the merits of persuasive messages before you
accept them

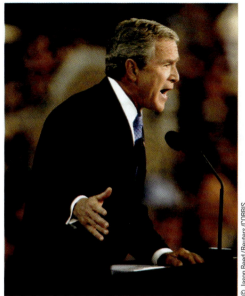

Strong loyalty to one political party leads some voters to listen uncritically to their side but critically to the opposition. In contrast, dialogical listeners— even those who prefer one party to the other— try to understand the issues on both sides and critique the reasoning of both parties.

STOP AND CHECK

DEVELOP STRATEGIES TO LISTEN MORE EFFECTIVELY

Return to the Listening Skills Self-Assessment (pages 58–59 or on the book's website), and note each question you answered with an "A" or a "B." Using materials from this section, develop a Listening Skills Development Plan that will help you overcome the listening barrier implied in each question.

For additional effective listening tips, log on to InfoTrac College Edition and search for Arleen Richman's article "Listen Up!"

Practice Dialogical Listening

Remember the communication model and the dialogical theory described in Chapter 1? Because dialogue involves active participation from listeners and speakers alike, your feedback helps co-create the meanings that ultimately come out of the presentation. Feedback can be nonverbal, verbal, or written. As you read the suggestions that follow, remember that cultural expectations influence appropriate feedback behaviors.

Give Appropriate Nonverbal Feedback

Your posture, your movements, even the distance you sit from the speaker are all ways to provide meaningful feedback.

▶ *Posture.* Posture communicates involvement and helps focus your attention. Face the speaker squarely and lean forward slightly. When you are thoroughly engrossed, being "on the edge of your seat" is natural. Even if you sit in a corner or off to the side, you can still turn toward the speaker. Let your body assume a relaxed, open position.

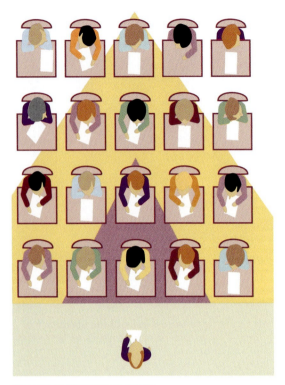

Figure 4.4

Classroom Seating Zones

"In the formal classroom seating arrangement depicted here, the "action zone" is shaded red. Students who sit in this zone interact more with the instructor. Those
in the area shaded yellow interact less frequently, and those in the unshaded area have the fewest number of

loaded questions questions containing implications intended to put the speaker on the defensive

closed questions requests for brief, specific answers

open questions requests for more lengthy responses

clarification questions requests to clear up confusing ideas

requests for elaboration questions asking for more information

comment information from personal experience or research

▶ *Distance.* Think about the difference in your attentiveness when you sit in the far corner of the back row with people passing by an open door versus when you sit front and center with fewer outside distractions. Which seat contributes more to your learning? One study, illustrated in Figure 4.4, found that instructors interact more regularly with students who sit in the first two or three rows, toward the center.[19] It makes sense that the more you interact with the speaker, the more you will understand and remember.

▶ *Movements.* Avoid distracting behaviors such as fidgeting, shuffling papers, or playing with your pen. Instead, look at the speaker, which helps focus your attention. Smile at amusing anecdotes, nod in support of a major point, or applaud when appropriate to further increase your involvement and provide additional feedback.

When listeners are attentive, the speaker may actually become more interesting. One campus legend relates that a boring professor always stood at the lectern and read from his notes. His students decided to act *as if* he were fascinating. Whenever he moved away from his notes, ever so slightly, they all leaned forward a bit, made eye contact, and used supportive motions. According to the legend, the professor eventually was walking back and forth across the front of the room, lecturing animatedly!

Give Verbal Feedback

"Where can I get more information?" "How is he defining that word?" Questions and comments such as these arise as you listen. Question-and-answer periods provide opportunities to co-create meanings. Here are a few of the most common types of questions:[20]

▶ **Loaded questions** put a speaker on the defensive because of what they imply. Try to avoid them. "When will you begin to look at both sides of the issue?" is loaded; it implies that the speaker was one-sided, and *when* is not really asking for a time. In other words, you wouldn't expect to hear, "I am going to research the other side tomorrow afternoon at 3:00."

▶ **Closed questions** ask for brief, specific answers. Use them to gain precise information or to verify your understanding. Here are some examples: Are you a member of the NRA? When did Ronald Reagan die? What website do you use most? Who wrote *Ivanhoe?*

▶ **Open questions** invite longer answers, as these examples show: What do you think are the best methods to help grieving students deal with the death of a classmate? What suggestions do you have for getting rid of unwanted email? How will your spending habits change now that you've destroyed your credit cards?

▶ When you are confused, ask **clarification questions** to gain more information, such as: Could you explain the difference between the Russian Old Believers and the Molokan Russians? How are you defining the word "rational"?

▶ To get a speaker to expand on an idea, make a **request for elaboration:** You said that some of the Founding Fathers grew hemp; could you elaborate? Can you provide more information about the cost and availability of the eye chip?

▶ Instead of questions, you can **comment** or add information from your own experience or research. For instance, after a speech on bullying, Tiffany shared statistics she had heard on a television show. Jon told a story about a coach who bullied his team. If you know that data in the speech is incorrect (for example, the statistics were out-dated), you can provide supplementary information.

Although question-and-answer periods are common in the United States, not all cultures participate equally in a co-creation of meaning process, as the Diversity in Practice box titled Saving Face explains.

DIVERSITY IN PRACTICE
SAVING FACE

Question-and-answer periods are rare in some cultural groups. For instance, in the context of traditional Chinese or Japanese public speaking, listeners are supposed to understand the speaker. Asking questions means admitting that they're not intelligent enough to unravel the speaker's shades of meaning. Furthermore, questions reflect on the speaker's communication abilities; that is, if listeners are left confused, the speaker failed to communicate. Finally, to preserve the speaker's "face," it's considered inappropriate to publicly question a speaker's information and, thus, his or her character.[21]

Provide Written Feedback

Your instructor will probably ask you to respond in writing to some of your classmates' speeches. The most effective comments focus on two or three specific elements of the presentation, using the **D-R-E method: D**escribe-**R**espond-**E**valuate.[22] Describe what you heard; respond with your personal interpretations and reactions; and evaluate by critiquing what you found effective and what could be improved. Phrase your comments objectively and positively. Here are some examples:

- Description: "I noticed that you quoted *Newsweek*, the *Jerusalem Post*, and *National Review*." [content] Or, "You looked out the window during your introduction, but you looked more directly at us as the speech progressed." [delivery]
- Response: "I really connected emotionally with the story about the grandfather and the little boy." [content] Or, "Because your tone was so conversational, I found myself wanting to hear what you had to say." [delivery]
- Evaluation: "Using a variety of sources was good, because it showed you sought out opinions from national, international, conservative, and less conservative sources. Your use of examples balanced the statistics well. I think your speech would be even stronger if you added a map to your PowerPoint slides." [content] Or, "Your ability to remember your ideas was impressive, but try to eliminate the phrase 'you know.' It became distracting." [delivery]

Comments such as these are both specific and helpful, because they give the speaker an idea of the overall impression the speech made on you and why. On the other hand, writing "good job" is not helpful at all because it is so vague. In general, write out as many positive things as you can, and then evaluate the performance by identifying a few things that could be improved.

✓ STOP AND CHECK
WRITE A CRITIQUE

Log on to the book's website to watch a speech video of your choice. As you listen, take notes on the content and jot down some personal responses and observations on the effectiveness of the speech. Then write a critique that (1) describes, (2) responds to, and (3) evaluates the speech. Discuss this critique with a group of classmates.

D-R-E method a feedback method that describes content, shares personal responses, and gives evaluation

Summary

Listening is the communication activity that we do most and study least. Listening is important in your personal and work life. However, listeners often face some cultural as well as personal barriers that impede effective listening. Different languages, vocabularies, and cultural allusions all make comprehension difficult. In addition, personal and psychological factors, such as fatigue, stresses and worries, stereotypes and prejudices, and wandering attention, can hinder listening.

Fortunately, you can devise strategies to listen more effectively. Use cultural schemas or mental blueprints to guide your perception, interpretation, storage, and recollection of what you hear. Know your listening purpose, and identify strategies to help you comprehend information or critically evaluate persuasive messages.

Finally, practice dialogical listening by contributing appropriate nonverbal, verbal, and written feedback. Nonverbal actions communicate that you are interested in the speech; they also help you pay attention. Useful nonverbal elements include a posture that communicates involvement, a distance that helps focus your attention, and movements that support rather than disrupt the speech. When you have an opportunity to interact verbally with a speaker, ask questions or provide comments that elaborate on the topic. However, be aware that after-speech questions and comments are inappropriate in some cultures. Finally, write out comments using the D-R-E method to describe what you heard, respond personally, and evaluate the overall presentation.

STUDY AND REVIEW

The premium website for *Public Speaking* offers a broad range of resources that will help you better understand the material in this chapter, complete assignments, and succeed on tests. The website features

▶ Speech videos with critical viewing questions, speech outlines, and transcripts, and
▶ Interactive practice activities, self quizzes, and a sample final exam.

For more information about this text's electronic learning resources, consult your **Guide to Online Resources for Public Speaking** or visit **http://communication.wadsworth.com/jaffe5**.

KEY TERMS

The terms below are defined in the margins throughout this chapter. The book's website also provides interactive flashcards and crossword puzzles to help you learn these terms and the concepts they represent.

cultural allusions 56
stereotyping 57
prejudiced 57
speech-thought differential 57
leftover thinking space 57
schemas 59
comprehensive listening 61
critical listening 62

loaded questions 64
closed questions 64
open questions 64
clarification questions 64
requests for elaboration 64
comment 64
D-R-E method 65

APPLICATION AND CRITICAL THINKING EXERCISES

The exercises below are also among the practice activities on the book's website.

1. Automotive columnist Tom Torbjornsen wrote more about female service managers. Read his vivid narrative, which describes bad listening, on his website, America's Car Show, at **www.americascarshow.com/tc/?article~Women_Enter_the_Auto_Industry**. What additional information does he provide about women, listening, and service?

2. Think about the Chinese symbol that stands for listening (see Figure 4.1). In what way do you use your ears, eyes, and heart when you listen to your classmates? Your professors? A speaker whose ideas support your own opinions? A speaker with whom you fundamentally disagree?

3. Using the diagrams in Figure 4.2 as models, draw a diagram that depicts your listening pattern during the most recent lecture you heard. Next, draw a diagram that depicts your listening pattern during the last conversation you had with your best friend. Draw a third diagram that shows your listening pattern during your last major conversation with a family member. Compare the three. What conclusions can you draw about your listening patterns in various contexts?

4. Go to **www.usu.edu/arc/**, a Utah State University website that provides many student aids. Link to "Idea Sheets," where you'll find two especially helpful worksheets: (1) "listening skills for lectures," and (2) "active listening skills." Use the suggestions you find there to create your Listening Skills Development Plan under Activities for Chapter 4 at the Jaffe Connection website.

5. Practice the nonverbal skills of active listening in one of your courses. That is, use posture, space, and movement to help focus your attention on the lecture. Afterward, evaluate whether your nonverbal behaviors helped you pay attention and recall the class material.

6. Verbally interact with one of the speakers in the next round of classroom speeches. During the speech, jot down several comments or questions to ask during the question-and-answer period.

7. Use the Describe-Respond-Evaluate method to give written feedback after one of your classmates' speeches.

8. Listen to a speaker who takes a position that differs dramatically from your views; you may find such a speaker on radio or television (for example, a person whose lifestyle differs from yours, one whose views on a social issue such as capital punishment diverge from yours, or a person with different religious beliefs). Describe, respond to, and evaluate the content and delivery, and then assess how well you listened.

SPEECH VIDEO

Log on to the book's website to watch and critique speeches of your choice, and to link to additional sites that offer speech videos, such as **www.c-span.org**.

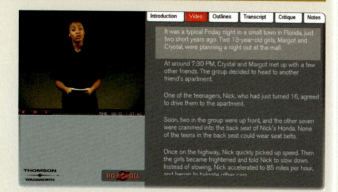

AUDIENCE ANALYSIS

THIS CHAPTER WILL HELP YOU

▶ Describe various audience motivations

▶ Tell how demographic audience analysis helps you adapt your speech to the audience

▶ Develop a questionnaire to assess your listeners' psychological profile

▶ Explain how the situation affects your audience

▶ Analyze your audience's perception of your credibility

"Educate to Liberate" Mural ©1988 by Miranda Bergman, Jane Norling, Maria Ramos, Vicky Hamlin, Arch Williams. (Hayes Street and Masonic, SF, CA)

EVERY YEAR, colleges and universities recognize and honor outstanding instructors. The University of Washington, for example, commended the following professors and listed some characteristics that set them apart:

▶ Senior lecturer, James Green (anthropology) says, "I try to tailor my presentations to what I think is on the minds of people 18 to 20 years old . . . you make yourself sensitive to what people are saying and how they're responding to you."

▶ Professor Priti Ramamurthy (women's studies) says, "I try to get [students] to see how the headlines are connected to their own lives."

▶ David Domke (communication) has the ability "to connect with students one-to-one, even though they sit among hundreds of others in the classroom."[1]

All these teachers understand the importance of sensitivity to students at every step of lecture preparation. They use **audience analysis** skills to think carefully about a specific class and find resources to communicate most effectively with the students in it. This is an example of a dialogical perspective; they become **listening speakers,**[2] who hear audience interests and concerns before, during, and after their presentations. Because your relationship with your audience is complex, this chapter examines your perception of your audience and the situation as well as their perception of you.

CASE STUDY: POPE JOHN PAUL II

Pope John Paul II was sensitive to his audiences, and listeners, in turn, viewed him favorably.

© AP/Wide World Photos

When Pope John Paul II died in April 2005, millions flocked to Rome to pay their respects. Because this charismatic leader reached out to people throughout his life, people reached out to him in his death. During his 27-year papacy, the pope communicated effectively with various groups—from wealthy French and American youth to rock stars to poor families in Morocco and Burkina Faso to Communists and capitalists. He was the first pope to visit both a synagogue and a mosque.

John Paul II's ability to adapt to his audiences was evident from the very beginning. Although Popes for 455 years were Italian born, John Paul II was Polish—the first ever Slavic pope. In his first appearance, the new Pope addressed the crowd in Italian, "I don't know if I can express myself well in your—our—Italian language. If I make a mistake, correct me."[3] The crowd roared its approval, and the tone of his papacy was set.

Over the course of the next 27 years, John Paul II's appeal was broad. He spoke with diverse ethnic groups, with rich and poor, educated and uneducated, men and women, the young and the aged. Even non-Catholics and non-Christians responded favorably. (Representatives of the Taliban sent condolences at his death!)

His obituary writers called him humble, authentic, tolerant, compassionate, and caring.

audience analysis identifying audience characteristics to communicate more effectively

listening speaker dialogical speaker who hears audience interests and concerns before, during, and after a speech

Questions for Discussion

▶ Why do you think John Paul II had such global appeal?

▶ What lasting impression do you have of this pope?

▶ Why did audiences like him?

▶ What lessons could an ordinary speaker learn from his ability to reach a variety of listeners?

Analyze Who Is Listening

A good speech is one that's prepared for a particular group at a particular time; even politicians, salespersons, or university recruiters, who present the same material repeatedly, adapt their material to each audience and each setting. Pope John Paul II was a good example of someone who could adapt the same basic message to a variety of audiences and settings. This section explores ways you can think about a specific audience and a specific speaking situation.

Consider Audience Motivations

Why do audiences gather? What attracts them? What holds them? Answering these questions provides clues about your audience's motivations and helps you prepare each speech more effectively. H. L. Hollingsworth[4] identified the following six types of audiences:

1. **Pedestrian audiences** randomly and temporarily come together because something grabs their attention—perhaps a salesman's flashy demonstration of a food processor, the impassioned voice of an activist in an outdoor forum, or the humorous stories of a sidewalk entertainer. Your challenge with these audiences? To attract attention and keep listeners interested long enough for you to present your message.

2. **Passive audiences** listen to speeches in order to accomplish other goals. For instance, some teachers attend job-related workshops not because they're fascinated by the topics but because their principal insists they attend. Most speech classes consist of passive listeners who attend class not just to hear speeches but to receive academic credit. For these audiences, you should select an interesting topic and help your listeners understand its relevance to their lives.

3. **Selected audiences** voluntarily and intentionally gather to hear about a topic (for example, windsurfing) or to hear a particular speaker (such as a famous author). A **homogeneous audience** is composed of members who share an attitude, whether positive or negative. Speaking to an audience with a positive attitude can be fun, but you must develop your ideas clearly so that listeners understand and accept them. Facing a negative or **hostile audience** presents an entirely different set of challenges. (Chapter 17 discusses ways to address hostile audiences.)

4. **Concerted audiences** voluntarily listen because they basically agree that the subject is important but don't know what to do about it. They need someone to motivate them and provide specific directions. For example, students, parents, and educators gather at the state capitol to protest cutbacks in education funding. There, speakers urge them to organize letter-writing campaigns, coordinate additional protests, and so on.

5. **Organized audiences** already know about the topic and are motivated and committed to act but need specific "how-to" instructions. Students at my university participate in overseas service trips. At meetings before each trip, they learn how to get their passports, what type of clothing to pack, how to say a few basic phrases in the language, and what cultural differences they can expect.

6. **Absent audiences** are separated from the speaker. They listen through radio, telephone conferencing, television, the Internet, videotapes, or videoconferences, either live or days (even years!) later. Our technological resources make this type of audience common. If you speak to absent audiences, remember that they can easily

pedestrian audiences random, temporary, and accidental audiences who were not intending to hear a speech

passive audiences groups that listen to accomplish other goals

selected audiences groups that choose to listen to a selected subject or speaker

homogeneous audiences listeners who are similar in attitude

hostile audiences listeners who are negative toward the topic or the speaker

concerted audiences listeners who are positive toward a topic but don't act; they need motivation and a plan

organized audiences motivated listeners who need specific instructions

absent audiences intentional listeners separated in distance and time who are reached through various media

change channels or tune you out. Focus on being interesting and relevant, and use conversational delivery as if you were speaking to one listener at a time.

An individual's motivation varies from meeting to meeting. Let's follow a student through several sessions that precede a service trip. She first hears about the trip during an announcement in her social work class (passive); she shows up at an informational meeting (selected) to learn more about the country they'll visit. Next, she gets additional information about various service possibilities in that country (concerted). After she is accepted for a specific trip, she attends meetings to get specific details for the trip (organized). She may even check out websites or a video about Romania (absent).

As you might imagine, audiences are not entirely homogeneous. For instance, a mostly passive audience such as your class may have several students who select both the topic and the instructor; a mostly organized audience may include passive listeners who are just tagging along with friends. Regardless, you'll be more effective if you consider the fundamental motivation of your audiences and plan speeches that are sensitive to their interests and needs.

Analyze Audience Demographics

In **demographic audience analysis,** you analyze listeners according to the groups or populations they represent. In some situations, demographic factors help you specifically tailor your remarks. However, it is easy to classify listeners into categories and then stereotype them. So keep in mind that each person belongs to many groups, and membership in a specific group is more **salient** (significant or relevant) in some situations than in others.[5] Rothenberg[6] summarizes the complexity of demographic analysis:

> When we engage in [demographic analysis], we should never lose sight of the fact that (1) any particular woman or man has an ethnic background, class location, age, sexual orientation, religious orientation, gender, and so forth, and (2) all these characteristics are inseparable from the person and from each other. . . . It is also true that . . . we may have to make generalizations about the experience of different groups of people, even as we affirm that each individual is unique.

demographic audience analysis identifying audiences by populations they represent, such as age or ethnicity

salient relevant or significant

When you do a demographic audience analysis, you consider the groups or populations your listeners represent. These students represent a variety of ethnic and socioeconomic backgrounds; they are affiliated with different religions and interest groups.

In short, because no one is simply a "lawyer" or a "Latina" or a "senior citizen," analyze your listeners' identification with various groups *in light of your specific speaking situation.* The following categories are common in demographic analysis: ethnicity, race, religion, gender, marital status, age, group affiliation, occupation and socioeconomic status, and region. Let's look at each of them in more detail.

Ethnicity

Ethnicity refers to a group's common heritage and cultural traditions, usually national or religious in origin.[7] For example the Russian Old Believers in rural Oregon are a distinct ethnic group, distinguished from their European American and Mexican American neighbors by language, clothing, cultural heroes, and religious traditions.[8] Urban America is especially diverse. For example, students at LaGuardia University in Queens, New York, speak 110 languages.[9] Ethnicity is complex, in part because many people have ancestors from more than one group.

Ethnic identity assumes more or less salience depending on the context. One's Norwegian heritage is salient in a context such as a Scandinavian festival; however, being Norwegian may be less relevant in a speech class, where educational and occupational goals count more than ancestry.

Race

Ethnicity is often linked to **race,** but the two are different. Racial categories are generally based on physical traits such as skin color or facial features, but races are not clearly distinct, and characteristics that supposedly identify one race are found in other populations as well. For example, Africa, India, Australia, and New Guinea all have brown-skinned populations, but the populations are unrelated.[10] Moreover, millions of people have mixed racial backgrounds that blur the lines between groups.[11] In his final State of the Union Address, President Clinton[12] cited scientists such as Alan Templeton, an evolutionary and population biologist, who argue that there is no genetic basis for distinct racial categories; instead, we are "99.9 percent the same." However, because race is a "social category," it is, unfortunately, easy to stereotype people by race. If you assume that a person or group has specific abilities, skills, or behaviors associated with racial stereotypes, you are being **racist.** Read the first-person account of one woman's ethnic and racial identity at http://mapage.noos.fr/dardelf/Race.html. Identify the various labels the author has been tagged with. What conclusions has she drawn?

Religion

It's an old saying that you should avoid both religion and politics in social conversation. This reflects the deep feelings these topics evoke in many people. Of course, it is permissible to speak publicly on religion, but it is essential be sensitive to the possible range and intensity of religious beliefs within your audience. For instance, a student who says, "when we all go home to celebrate Christmas" is oblivious to her Jewish and Muslim classmates. Some listeners align themselves with a particular faith, but their religion is peripheral to their identity. Others consider religion a central factor in their daily lives. Religious traditions are often linked to ethnicity, and disparagement or dismissal of a group's sacred texts, heroes, or rituals often creates intense emotional reactions—even among people who hold them loosely.

Sex and Gender

Don't confuse sexual differences—being biologically male or female—with gender differences, which are cultural. **Gender** is a cluster of traits culturally labeled as masculine, feminine, or androgynous (neither specifically masculine or feminine). To illustrate, some cultural groups consider changing diapers to be a woman's task; however, nothing in a man's biological makeup prevents him from cleaning up a baby, and diaper changing

Teaching Tip
http://www.census.gov/
The website of the U.S. Census Bureau has a wealth of information about U.S. demographics. The section American FactFinder has a look-up tool that provides demographic information about your city or zip code.

Instructor's Resource Manual
Teaching Idea 5.2 in the *Instructor's Resource Manual* (available in print, online, and on the Multimedia Manager CD-ROM) describes a classroom activity for introducing audience demographics by comparing ads targeted to different audiences.

Student Learning: InfoTrac College Edition
Have students use InfoTrac College Edition to find and read the article "How Demographics Shape Development," from *National Real Estate Investor,* September 1, 2002. The article discusses ways that demographic analysis can be used, with a specific emphasis upon minorities.

Teaching Tip
This would be a good time to go over any class or university policies regarding proselytizing or religious discrimination.

ethnicity heritage and cultural traditions, usually stemming from national and religious backgrounds

race categories, often associated with stereotypes, based on physical characteristics

racist assuming that someone has certain traits or behaviors because of race

gender clusters of traits culturally labeled as masculine, feminine, or androgynous

can be classified as androgynous. In our rapidly changing society, we continually examine and negotiate gender-associated ideas, and we change our notions of "proper" behaviors for men and for women. **Sexism** is the assumption that a man or a woman will think or act in a certain way because of his or her sex.

One's identity as male or female is salient at events like a Million Man March, a Promise Keepers rally, a conference of the Association for Women in Science, or a mother-daughter banquet. However, all-male or all-female audiences can be drawn to a speech for other reasons. For example, engineers at a workshop on disaster preparedness may all be women, but their interest in safety motivated them to attend, not their biological sex.

Marital Status/Sexual Expression

Keep in mind the interests and perspectives of married, divorced, or never married listeners. In addition, don't make assumptions about sexual orientation and sexual activity. One student on a campus with an active fraternity system assumed that his listeners were heterosexual and sexually active. He advised them to attend a fraternity party, scope out interesting women, persuade one to drink heavily, and then invite her to an upstairs bedroom to "look at the goldfish." Some listeners laughed, but many were offended by his unwarranted assumptions. Married students were amused at his immaturity but bored with his speech.

Age

Not surprisingly, age influences listeners' motivations and concerns. Globally, cultures distinguish between generational groups, and market researchers in the United States identify and then target age cohorts because different generations were brought up differently, experienced different events, and pursue different social missions.[13] The following are common labels for, and descriptions of, these generations:

- *Mature Americans* include people born before 1924; these seniors have adapted to enormous cultural changes. As young people, they lived through the Great Depression and World War II, listened to the radio but not television, and drove Model Ts instead of SUVs. Also in this category are people born between 1925 and 1945; they tend to be adventurous and determined to remain youthful. Their teachers read the Bible and prayed in school and fretted about students who chewed gum!
- *Baby boomers*, 77 million of them, were born between the end of World War II and the early 1960s. Older boomers remember the assassinations of President Kennedy and Martin Luther King, Jr. They tend to be individualistic, driven, and "me"-centered. Some avoided the draft, fought in Vietnam, marched for social change, or experimented with drugs. Boomers grew up with television, but they went off to college with typewriters, not computers.
- *Generation Xers*, the first latchkey generation, are racially and culturally diverse; between 1963 and 1981 44.5 million of them were born. They came of age in a media-dominated culture with high divorce rates, legal abortion, a huge national deficit, and a series of political scandals.[14] Some researchers describe them as fun-loving and routine-hating, reactive and angry. Younger Gen Xers began using personal computers when they were in first grade, so their outlook on life and their view of technology is vastly different from that of mature Americans.[15]
- *The millennium generation*, born after 1981, inherited many social and environmental problems; they tend to be more civic-minded (and less angry) than Gen Xers. The millennium generation was born into the "twitch speed" era of MTV and personal computers, in which technology makes everything seem to move faster.[16] They are sometimes called Generation Y, the "I-generation," or the Internet generation.[17]

sexism assuming someone will act or think a certain way because of gender

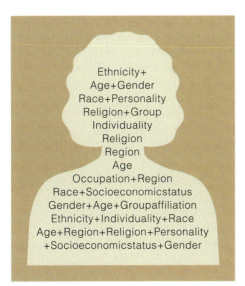

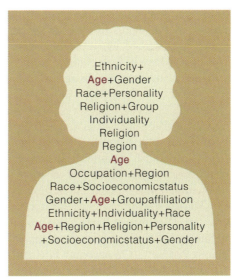

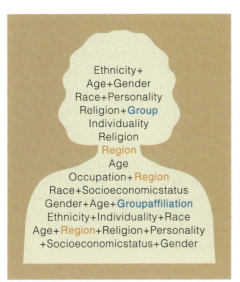

Instructor Resource: PowerPoint
The *Multimedia Manager with Instructor Resources* CD-ROM includes a Power-Point slide of Figure 5.1.

Figure 5.1
Demographic Silhouettes
These silhouettes represent a single audience member who is influenced by many demographic factors that are interwoven with individual traits and personality characteristics. In one situation, the listener's age is the salient factor; in another, her region and group affiliation matter more.

Although individuals within each group are different, members of a generational cohort tend to be moved by appeals and allusions that another generation might not understand. Age differences also play out in the classroom. Graduating seniors in the audience will differ in several ways from first-year students. Figure 5.1 illustrates the complicated nature of demographic analysis.

Group Affiliation

People create groups to share interests, experiences, or hobbies. Veterans of Foreign Wars, wheelchair athletes, Alcoholics Anonymous, and members of fraternities or sororities are examples. Often these groups invite guest speakers to meetings. Because group identity is highly salient in these situations, you should draw on common experiences and shared beliefs and values. For instance, if you're giving a speech to the Young Democrats, find heroes within that party that you can praise, even if your political loyalties lie elsewhere.

Occupation/Socioeconomic Status

Differences in educational level, income, occupational choice, and social class status can all be salient in particular situations. Knowing your classmates' job experiences and their academic majors can help you adapt more specifically to your unique classroom context.

Classroom Discussion/ Activity
Randomly assign group affiliations to small groups of students. Have them discuss what topics would and would not be appropriate for each group and share their conclusions with the class.

In the world of work, computer engineers or physicians may differ in other demographic categories, but similar interests and experiences give them commonalities you can draw upon. Furthermore, when the topic is investment bonds, comfortably middle-class individuals may have little in common with those who struggle to make ends meet; however, a topic such as cheating cuts across many economic lines.

Regions

You know that audiences in different countries require different speaking strategies, but what if you move from one state or region to another? Although people in the United States share much in common, people in different regions tend to have somewhat varied characteristics due to climate, history, language, economic base, politics, and so on. These differences influence their interests and perspectives.[18]

You can see this principle in practice if you follow presidential candidates around the country. They discuss hurricane damage in Florida but not in Oregon. Their emphases in Silicon Valley differ from their emphases in the ranchlands of the West. Issues important in Vermont (97.6 percent white) and in Hawaii (29 percent white, non-Latino) vary. Candidates recognize that Bostonians probably have more in common with Manhattan residents than they do with people in rural Massachusetts.[19]

In summary, demographic audience analysis provides insights into your listeners' ethnicity, religion, gender, age, group affiliation, and regional identity. Keep these identities in mind when you select a topic, choose supporting materials, and organize your speeches. However, don't stereotype your listeners; instead, try to use the more inclusive model depicted in Figure 5.1.

✓ STOP AND CHECK

ANALYZE YOUR AUDIENCE

Log on to the book's website to complete an interactive Audience Motivations and Demographics form that will help you to analyze your classmates.

To further investigate the topic of demographic audience analysis, search InfoTrac College Edition for the journal *Marketing to Women*. Select three articles (most are very short and address topics such as acupuncture, vacation tours, self-employment, and investment clubs), and tell how you could prepare to speak to the group of women presented in each article.

Analyze the Audience's Psychological Profile

Amara was a pre-med student who wanted to inform her audience about the biological makeup of food, but she didn't want to repeat widely known information. So during the week before she spoke, she created a **psychological profile** of her classmates by distributing a questionnaire and analyzing their answers. She wanted to know what they already knew about nutritional components, how they felt, what they considered important, and how they actually ate. In other words, she assessed their psychological approach to her topic. To determine your audience's psychological profile, analyze their beliefs, values, and attitudes regarding your subject. (These concepts are briefly defined in Chapter 1.)

Beliefs

A **belief** is a mental acceptance of something as true or false, correct or incorrect, valid or invalid.[20] Beliefs are based on study or investigation, as well as on conviction without much factual information or knowledge; misconceptions are common. A series of open questions such as these allowed Amara's audience to respond in a variety of ways:

psychological profile assessment of an audience's beliefs, values, and attitudes

belief mental acceptance that something is true or false, correct or incorrect, valid or invalid

> What do you think are the benefits of a healthy diet?
> If you eat a healthy diet, why? In not, why not?
> What do you typically eat for lunch?
> How do fats function in our bodies?

She added some closed questions such as these:

Are fats essential to your health?

_____ yes

_____ no

_____ I'm not sure

Do you eat a healthy diet?

_____ yes

_____ no

_____ I'm not sure

List the four kinds of macromolecules that make up our food:

_____, _____,

_____, _____

She discovered that all her classmates knew that fats were essential in a healthy diet, but half of them did not understand why. Most couldn't name all four types of macromolecules in food. Overall, a few people had a fairly good understanding of macromolecules and the biology of food, but most had some gaps in their knowledge, and quite a few considered their diets to be unhealthy.

Attitudes

Attitudes are our tendencies to like or dislike something or to have positive or negative feelings about it. Attitudes have an emotional component that involves feelings and values, a mental component that involves beliefs, and a behavioral component that influences actions. For instance, Americans tend to _feel_ positively toward work because they _believe_ it's linked to success, which they _value_, so they _act_ by setting personal goals and striving to accomplish them. **Scaled questions** typically measure attitudes along a range or continuum, from highly positive to neutral to highly negative. Listeners with neutral attitudes probably have not thought about the subject enough to form an opinion. Here are typical scaled questions related to healthy eating:

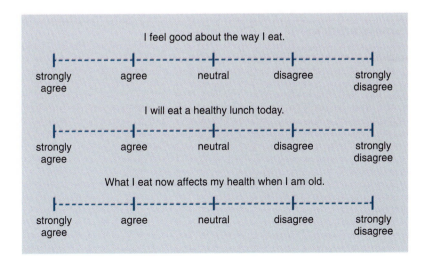

attitudes preferences, likes and dislikes, that involve beliefs, feelings, and behaviors

scaled questions questions asking for responses along a continuum; used to assess attitudes

Notice that the first statement identifies feelings, the second looks at a predisposition to act, and the third assesses beliefs. This combination of feelings, behaviors, and beliefs comprises our attitudes. When listeners share your attitude toward your topic, whether it's negative or positive, your speaking task is usually easier than it is when audience attitudes are diverse. Amara found that most classmates were positive about healthy eating. Several were neutral; no one was downright hostile toward her topic. Knowing her audience's range of attitudes helped her plan an effective speech.

Values

Values are the standards we use to make judgments such as good or bad, beautiful or ugly, kind or cruel, appropriate or inappropriate. U.S. cultural values include choice, individualism, fair play, progress, freedom, and equality. Almost every topic you choose touches on your values because you at least consider the subject significant enough to discuss. However, when you use words such as *right* or *wrong, moral* or *immoral, important* or *insignificant*, you are directly addressing value questions. Scaled questions work well for value questions such as this:

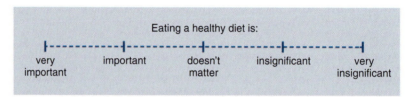

Amara found that most classmates considered nutritious diets to be important, which allowed her to build her speech around the fundamental value of health. Because values are our assumptions about what is good, we usually respond positively when they are supported.

Throughout her speech, Amara wove together the insights she gleaned from her questionnaire, which increased her sensitivity to her audience. (Read her outline at the end of the chapter or on the book's website, where you can also watch Amara deliver her speech.)

Each listener's psychological profile affects her or his interest in your topic. Take a listener who doesn't know much about writing a résumé but has a positive attitude about a speech on résumé writing because a good résumé can help him get a good job, which he values. Contrast him to a woman who understands the need to wear seatbelts, who values safety, and who buckles up automatically. Her interest in a seatbelt speech is minimal.

STOP AND CHECK

CONSTRUCT A QUESTIONNAIRE

With your topic in mind, construct a questionnaire that you can use to analyze your classmates' psychological profile. An interactive questionnaire is available on the book's website. You may also want to use the sample Combination Questionnaire here; it combines closed questions, open questions, and scaled questions on the topic of road rage.

(continued)

values ideals by which we judge what is important and, consequently, how we should behave

A Combination Questionnaire

Name (optional) _____

Age _____   Sex _____   Major _____

Have you experienced road rage?   _____ yes   _____ no   _____ not sure

Have you been the object of road rage?   _____ yes   _____ no   _____ not sure

Place an X on the point of the scale that best indicates your response to the sentence.
Use the following codes:

SA	=	strongly agree
A	=	agree
MA	=	mildly agree
N	=	no opinion
MD	=	mildly disagree
D	=	disagree
SD	=	strongly disagree

Sometimes I get so angry at other drivers, that I feel
I could do something that might endanger their safety.

SA   A   MA   N   MD   D   SD

Angry drivers in other cars pose threats to my safety.

SA   A   MA   N   MD   D   SD

Road rage is a serious national problem.

SA   A   MA   N   MD   D   SD

How would you define road rage?

What effect do you think it has on its victims?

What is the best way to deal with this phenomenon?

What kinds of road rage, if any, are worse than others?

To learn more about how to design effective questionnaires, go to the "Questionnaire Design" page at **www.quickmba.com/marketing/research/qdesign**. Pay particular attention to the advice on content, wording, and sequencing of questions.

Assess the Situation

After you consider your listeners' demographic categories and their psychological profile, assess the specific situation in which you will speak. Many situational features, including time and environment, affect your audience.

Consider the Time

Two aspects of time affect public speaking: the time of day and cultural time norms. First, consider when your class is held and the effect that may have on your audience. For instance, what problems might listeners face in an early morning class? What about a

Student Learning: Workbook
Students can complete Activity 5.3, "Case Study: Time Violations," in the *Student Workbook* for a better understanding of the effect of time on a public speaking event.

class just before lunch, when they are hungry? Or another just after lunch, when they're sleepy? What challenges might an evening class pose? Evaluate these questions, and adapt your talk appropriately. For instance, you might be more animated when listeners are sleepy, or you might shorten your speech when it's very late.

Also, consider the *cultural* time system. In the United States, time is commonly seen as a line divided into segments, each lasting a specific duration, with distinct activities assigned to each segment.[21] Take your speech class, for example. You chose it partly because it fills a time slot you had available. The clock tells you when class starts and when it is over. In this setting, both the date and length of your speech are important. (You may be graded down if you don't appear on the assigned date or give a speech of the assigned length.) Your listeners expect you to work within this time pattern.

In contrast, listeners from a culture or co-culture with a more relaxed sense of time often focus less on starting precisely on time or on fitting their remarks into a rigid time frame, as Robert Levine's story illustrates. Professor Levine, who grew up in fast-paced Brooklyn, went to Brazil to teach psychology in a class that was scheduled from 10:00 A.M. to noon.[22] Because he carried his cultural expectations with him, he thought the class would begin at 10:00 and end at 12:00. However, students arrived as late as 11:00, showing few signs of concern. At 12:15, almost everyone was still there, asking questions. Finally, at 12:30, Levine himself ended the class and left. The students, however, seemed willing to stay even longer.

Consider the Environment

I once taught in a small college theater that was painted black. Floors, ceiling, chairs—everything was black. The few small windows all had heavy black shades. We met there twice before I called the schedule desk and begged for a different room. The black theater is just one type of room that can work against you. Windowless spaces, those too small or too large, or rooms located by a noisy stairwell may all affect your audience, whether or not they realize it.

Other environmental considerations such as the temperature inside (too hot, too cold), the weather outside (sunny and beautiful, stormy and icy), or noise (an air conditioner or radiator) might affect your listeners' comfort or distract their attention. You'll be a better speaker if you adapt to the overall environment.

In summary, you form perceptions of your listeners and can better address them by analyzing demographic, psychological, and situational factors.

Take into account the effect of the situation on your listeners. Distractions they encounter in an informal outdoor situation like this are different from distractions in a cold, noisy indoor classroom.

© Jack Jaffe

STOP AND CHECK

DO A SITUATIONAL ANALYSIS

Log on to the book's website to complete an interactive situational analysis of your audience.

For more information on situational analysis, read the article "One Speaker's Pet Peeves" on InfoTrac College Edition. What similarities and differences do you find when analyzing a classroom versus a business situation?

Classroom Discussion / Activity
Experienced speakers always try to check out the physical setting for a speech in advance. Ask students to develop a checklist of what to look for in any physical setting and then discuss how obstacles to the speaker's effectiveness might be handled.

Student Learning: Book Website
This Stop and Check activity can also be found on the book's website, where it's located under "Chapter Resources."

Consider Your Audience's Perception of You

Professional speechwriter Larry Tracy says you actually deliver four speeches: "(1) the one you plan, (2) the one you actually give, (3) the one your audience hears, and (4) the one you wish you had given."[23] This section focuses on the third type of speech: what your audience hears. While you are forming impressions of your listeners, they are busily forming perceptions about your character, your intentions, and your abilities—in short, your **credibility,** and their impressions affect what they think you are saying. The evaluation begins before your speech, it's modified while you speak, and it leads to a lasting impression after you finish.[24]

Be Aware of Prior Credibility

Let's say a former senator comes to your campus to speak on foreign policy. You go to the speech assuming that she will know her subject well. Or one of your classmates is on the fencing team, so when he arrives on his speech day with fencing equipment in hand, you expect him to have an insider's perspective on the topic. This type of credibility, the speaker's reputation or expertise that makes the speaker believable even before he or she says a word, is called **prior** or **extrinsic credibility.** Pope John Paul II, for example, had prior credibility whenever he spoke. Practically speaking, you probably won't have prior credibility in your class, because most students lack the credentials or reputations that cause others to consider them experts. Therefore, you should establish some link between yourself and your topic in the introduction. Chapter 10 describes how to do this, and the Diversity in Practice box on page 82 provides some cross-cultural information on this topic.

To further your understanding of prior credibility, log on to InfoTrac College Edition and read the article titled "Marquee Speaker Adds Prestige to Engagement." Work with several classmates to identify a campus event such as a commencement ceremony, an alcohol abuse workshop for dormitory residents, or a sports recognition banquet for athletes and their parents. Using information from this article, choose a local, regional, or nationally known figure who would make a good speaker for the event.

Demonstrate Credibility in Your Speech

Regardless of your reputation, you must demonstrate credibility as you speak. Not surprisingly, this is called **demonstrated** or **intrinsic credibility.** Think of the student on the fencing team. If he couldn't name pieces of equipment or describe a fencing match, you would decide he was no expert.

What does your audience look for as they decide whether you are credible? They look for evidence that you are knowledgeable about the subject. Consequently, it is important to do careful research and cite your sources. Define unfamiliar terminology, give

credibility listeners' impressions of your character, intentions, and abilities that make you more or less believable

prior or extrinsic credibility credibility that speakers bring to the speech because of their experience and reputation

demonstrated or intrinsic credibility obvious knowledge the speaker shows during the speech

© AP/Wide World Photos

Steve Jobs, CEO of Apple Computer and Pixar Animation Studios, brings prior credibility to his speeches because of his expertise in high-tech industries. However, within each speech, he must again demonstrate that he is competent and trustworthy.

terminal credibility final impression listeners have of a speaker

examples, tell your personal experiences with the subject, and otherwise show your thorough understanding of the subject. Finally, be prepared to answer questions afterward.

Your listeners also expect you to be calm and poised. Think of it this way: If you're agitated during a classroom presentation, your audience may wonder why you can't control yourself. In contrast, if you appear confident, they will perceive you more favorably.

Take Terminal Credibility into Account

Relief! Your speech is over and you're through. But wait. Your listeners continue to evaluate you. The overall impression you leave, your **terminal credibility,** is a balance between the reputation you brought to your speech and the expertise you demonstrated as you spoke. Terminal credibility is not fixed. If your listeners eventually discover that some of your information was incorrect, they will lose confidence in you. For example, suppose one of your classmates praises the pharmaceutical product Ritalin that is used to treat attention deficit disorder (ADD). In a previous speech, she mentioned that her little brother had ADD, which gives her some prior credibility for this speech. In the speech itself, she provides facts and figures that describe the prescription drug: what it is, what it does, what doctors say about it. You're impressed. A month later, a physician suggests that your cousin take Ritalin. As you do further research, you learn that your classmate's speech was clearly one-sided; she presented only the positive side of the medication. Your final impression of her credibility plummets.

DIVERSITY IN PRACTICE
PRIOR CREDIBILITY IN OTHER CULTURES

CULTURES VARY in their evaluations of prior credibility. Age and gender loom large in some Native American cultures. When the occasion calls for "saying a few words," younger males and women in these cultures will seek out older men to speak for them. Weider and Pratt relate the story of a young woman who spoke for herself and her husband on a public occasion. Her elders scolded her for not knowing how to act![25]

In Kenya, credibility is linked to wealth, social status, education, age, and ethnicity. Wealth comes in the form of wives, children, cattle, or money, but wealth in itself is not the only criterion. The more credible speakers have used their wealth to help others. Furthermore, unmarried men or men with few children or no sons lack authority, especially in rural areas. In a country made up of 40 distinct groups, members of certain ethnic groups have higher overall credibility.[26]

Your age may affect your audience, either positively or negatively. Because U.S. culture celebrates youth and actively looks for fresh ideas, young people often receive as much or more attention than older speakers. In contrast, listeners in cultures that respect the wisdom and experience that come with age may pay less attention to youth and more attention to their elders. Consider this potential difference whenever you adapt to a culturally diverse audience.

Summary

You and your audiences are involved in an interactive process in which you form impressions of one another. You assess your listeners' motivations as well as their demographic characteristics such as age, ethnicity, race, religion, gender, marital status, group affiliation, occupation and socioeconomic status, and region; however, you also realize that these characteristics are only salient at specific times and in specific circumstances.

Analyze your audience's psychological profile as it relates to your topic. What do they already know or believe? How do they feel about your subject? What attitudes and underlying values influence their interest? Developing a questionnaire with various types of questions will help you identify their responses to specific aspects of your subject.

Finally, situational characteristics affect your audience. The time of day, the length of your speech, and the noise level or temperature in the room influence their interest and attention. Do what you can to minimize environmental distractions.

Your listeners actively evaluate you as well. Before your speech, they assess your reputation. During your speech, they form impressions of your credibility and your overall trustworthiness based on cultural criteria such as sound evidence, source citation, overall knowledge, and composure. After you've finished, your listeners continue to assess your credibility, either positively or negatively.

This is one of the most important chapters in this text. As award-winning teachers and great speakers like the Pope know, sensitivity to a specific audience is not an option. It is essential to good speechmaking.

STUDY AND REVIEW

The premium website for *Public Speaking* offers a broad range of resources that will help you better understand the material in this chapter, complete assignments, and succeed on tests. The website features

▶ Speech videos with critical viewing questions, speech outlines, and transcripts, and
▶ Interactive practice activities, self quizzes, and a sample final exam.

For more information about this text's electronic learning resources, consult your **Guide to Online Resources for Public Speaking** or visit http://communication.wadsworth.com/jaffe5.

KEY TERMS

The terms below are defined in the margins throughout this chapter. The book's website also provides interactive flashcards and crossword puzzles to help you learn these terms and the concepts they represent.

audience analysis 70
listening speaker 70
pedestrian audiences 71
passive audiences 71

selected audiences 71
homogeneous audiences 71
hostile audiences 71
concerted audiences 71

organized audiences 71
absent audiences 71
demographic audience analysis 72
salient 72
ethnicity 73
race 73
racist 73
gender 73
sexism 74

psychological profile 76
beliefs 76
attitudes 77
scaled questions 77
values 78
credibility 81
prior or extrinsic credibility 81
demonstrated or intrinsic credibility 81
terminal credibility 82

APPLICATION AND CRITICAL THINKING EXERCISES

The exercises below are among the practice activities on the book's website.

1. Identify times when you have been a member of each type of audience: pedestrian, passive, voluntary, concerted, organized, and absent.

2. What occupation(s) most interest you? Think of opportunities you might have to address each type of audience listed in Exercise 1 within your chosen occupational field. Which type of audience is most common in that occupation? Which is least common?

3. Choose one of these topics, and talk with a small group of your classmates about the different ways you would develop a speech for each of the following audiences:

Topic: Your school's administrators are discussing a policy that will abolish all competitive sports on campus.

Audiences
▶ Your classmates
▶ A group of prospective students
▶ Alumni who are consistent donors to the school
▶ Basketball team members

Topic: The United States should double its foreign aid budget.

Audiences
▶ Senior citizens
▶ A high school government class
▶ The local chapter of the League of Women Voters

4. Try to see yourself as your classmates see you. At this point in the term, what credibility do you bring to each speech? How can you demonstrate credibility in your next speech? How do you think your audience sees you after you're finished?

5. In 1981 *Washington Post* reporter Joel Garreau wrote *The Nine Nations of North America*. You can find a summary of his ideas online at **www.harpercollege.edu/~mhealy/g101ilec/ namer/nac/nacnine/na9intro/nacninfr.htm**. Follow the link to your region and see if you agree with his description of the area in which you live. Then link to another region. Do you think the regions have changed in the last 25 years? If so, how? How might a speaker from your region adapt to an audience in the second region?

6. For a somewhat different perspective on audience analysis, read artist Dan Brady's essay describing the characteristics he considers when he shows a piece of art work, hoping for a positive audience response. The essay can be found at **www.creativeideas foryou.com/essofprf.html**.

Student Learning: Workbook
Students can use Activity 5.1, "Audience Motivations Worksheet," in the *Student Workbook* to complete Question 3 in small groups.

SPEECH VIDEO

Log on to the book's website to watch and critique Amara Sheppard's speech. An outline of her speech appears below and also is available on the website.

Student Speech with Commentary

THE BIOLOGY OF YOUR LUNCH: YOU ARE WHAT YOU EAT
Amara Sheppard

General Purpose: To inform

Specific Purpose: To inform my audience about the biological explanation of the phrase "you are what you eat."

Thesis Statement: The human body breaks down four major macromolecules in food to provide many bodily functions.

Introduction

I. In a short skit, I will discuss lunch and take a phone call from my body calling to remind me that "you are what you eat."

II. By understanding how it is that you are what you eat, you can make more informed choices about the food you eat.

III. As a biology/pre-med major, I have studied the human body for five of the last six years, and I am interested in how it works on a daily basis.

IV. The human body breaks down four major macromolecules in food to provide many bodily functions.

   A. Today, we will see how our bodies use carbohydrates, lipids, proteins, and nucleic acids, the four molecules I asked you about on the questionnaire you filled out.

   B. You can remember these components by learning the acronym: Can Lucy Play Now?

Body

I. First, carbohydrates are complex sugars that are found in a variety of foods.

   A. Carbohydrates are found in a variety of foods.

     1. They are in breads and fruits.

     2. The majority of you claimed to include carbohydrates in your lunches in the forms of fruits and sandwiches.

   B. You may eat the grape, which symbolizes carbohydrates.

     1. Even now, the carbs are breaking down to become simple sugars that your body uses for energy.

     2. Carbs give you the energy you need to provide energy to stay awake in class.

In a late-morning class, Amara gains attention by referring to lunch.

She has no prior credibility, so she shows her qualification to speak on the topic.

She states her thesis and previews her points.

Here, she incorporates specific results from the questionnaire her audience previously completed.

Each person has a small cup with a grape, a Goldfish cracker, and a small carrot.

Again, she refers to the questionnaire results and invites them to eat the cracker. In this point, she cites several credible sources.

II. Lipids, better known as fats, are the second category.
   A. All 22 of you correctly answered on the questionnaire that some fat is needed, but only 11 could tell why.
   B. Like carbohydrates, lipids are found in many foods, including dairy products, meats, nuts, oils, and dressings.
      1. You can eat the fish as an example of lipids because it's made of cheese.
      2. About.com's online biology resource explains that fats store energy, help insulate the body, and cushion and protect organs.
      3. In an article entitled "Human Nutrition," Encyclopedia.com adds that fats form important portions of cell membranes and aid in the absorption of important fat-soluble vitamins.

She continues to build intrinsic credibility by citing credible sources.

III. Third are proteins, which are probably the most familiar.
   A. Proteins, made of twenty building blocks called amino acids, exist in several types of lunch food.
      1. Associate professor of biology Dwight Kimberly said that eight proteins cannot be made by the body.
      2. They must all come from our foods, such as the fish you previously ate.
      3. A 1997 issue of the *Harvard Health Newsletter* says that complete proteins are found in seafood, meat, eggs, and soy.
   B. Proteins are all over your body, skin, hair, and nails.
      1. Proteins provide structural support and aid in muscle contraction.
      2. Proteins do most of the work in your body.

IV. The final component are the nucleic acids DNA and RNA.
   A. They are found in the vegetables you say you include in your lunch, such as the carrot (which you may now eat).
   B. Raven and Jones's 6th edition of *Biology* says nucleic acids are information-storage devices.
      1. *Biology* uses an analogy, comparing nucleic acids to blueprints.
      2. These acids instruct the body's cells on how to build proteins.

She displays their questionnaire responses on a pie graph on an overhead transparency.

V. According to the questionnaire, 62% of you said you were healthy eaters; 24% said you were not; 14% were neutral; perhaps after this speech, you're better able to be a better eater.

Conclusion

I. In conclusion, the foods we eat can largely be placed into four categories of substances our bodies can use.
   A. Carbohydrates are the energy providers.
   B. Lipids or fats repair damaged tissue, keep you warm, and absorb vitamins.
   C. Proteins made up of amino acids are the body's "workers."
   D. Nucleic acids are the "blueprints" or instructions for the body's cells.

II. So as you head off to lunch, be kind to your body and choose foods that will keep your body functioning at its best.

III. Before your body gives you a call, remember, you are what you eat.

After a brief review, Amara concludes with "you" words that reinforce the importance of the topic to the audience.

SELECTING YOUR TOPIC AND PURPOSE

THIS CHAPTER WILL HELP YOU

▶ Choose your speech topic

▶ Narrow your topic to fit the situation

▶ Identify both a general purpose and a specific purpose for your speech

▶ Write a thesis statement that states the main concept of your speech

Detail from "Family Life and Spirit of Mankind" Mural © 1977 by Susan Kelk Cervantes and Judith Knepher Jamerson. (Leonard R. Flynn School, East Wall, Army Street at Harrison, SF, CA)

THERE ARE literally millions of topics in the world; in fact, there are so many possible subjects that selecting just one that's appropriate for a classroom speech may feel daunting. The subject can't be too broad or too complex (after all, most speeches are limited to ten minutes at the most); it should be interesting to you, as well as to your audience; it should be relevant; it should be novel . . . there are numerous factors to consider.

Is there a surefire method you can use to select a topic that fits you, your audience, and the occasion? Probably not, but here are techniques that students have used:

> The way I usually come up with topics is by looking around and noting what things I see that I think are interesting. I evaluate whether or not they would make good speech topics. Also, I will take things that puzzle me or torque me off.
>
> AMY

> When I choose a topic, I analyze the parameters first: time limit, any given topic area, audience . . . then I think of something I'm interested in. If nothing comes to mind, I file the assignment in my thoughts—and often something during the day sparks an interest.
>
> JOY

> I spend a lot of time on the Internet, so I naturally go online and browse for topics. Google and Yahoo provide links to newspapers and magazines that include international and national topics, business and entertainment news. I always find several interesting topics.
>
> TERRENCE

Regardless of method, eventually you will come up with a number of possible subjects. The key—as Amy, Joy, and Terrence point out—is to find something you are comfortable with, something that is significant enough to discuss publicly. This chapter will give you guidelines for choosing your topic, narrowing it to a manageable size, and then selecting your purpose and focus.

CASE STUDY: SPEECH COACH PAUL SOUTHWICK ON TOPIC SELECTION

Paul Southwick works with speech team members to come up with interesting topics that take a unique perspective.

© Jack Jaffe

One of Paul Southwick's major challenges is topic selection—not topics for his personal use, but topics for team members to develop into competitive speeches.[1] Paul is coach of George Fox University's speech team.

Early in the season he asks team members to identify unique interests or distinctive things about themselves, their families, or their cultural backgrounds. Out of these discussions, some general topics emerge, such as "My mother is from Mexico, so I am interested in immigration," or "My parents just informed me that they are getting a divorce." Now, Paul knows that judges look for unique perspectives, so the next step is to focus more narrowly. For example, one might examine immigration from the perspective of elderly Hispanics or from the perspective of schoolchildren whose parents are illegal immigrants. Another might look at divorce from a Jewish, Native American, or Islamic perspective.

The next step is to choose among three competitive speech categories: informative, persuasive, or humorous. The category chosen will further focus the topic.

For example, Ray De Silva is interested in gender issues because his father, a Sri Lankan, comes from a patriarchal culture, and his mother, a Filipino, has a more matriarchal background. Ray considers an informative speech about gender expectations across cultures, but he eventually decides to do a humorous speech. This decision influences the rest of his preparation.

Questions for Discussion

▶ Southwick coaches competitive speakers. How is choosing a topic for a competitive speech similar and different from choosing a topic for a classroom speech?
▶ Given the choice, would you prefer to inform, to persuade, or to entertain?
▶ How, given your experiences and background, might you narrow your focus for a speech about immigration? Divorce? Gender roles?

Choose Your Topic

Finding a topic is comparatively easy in some contexts. Not surprisingly, in the world of work, topics are work related; in ceremonial situations, such as graduations or weddings, the general subject is a given. However, most instructors don't assign specific subjects, so topic choice is up to you. To avoid being overwhelmed at the open-endedness of this challenge, consider the significance, or need to discuss a particular topic, and then look for subjects in four places: your personal interests and experiences, other courses you're taking, current events, and international and cultural subjects.

Teaching Tip
http://www.ku.edu/~coms/
virtual_assistant/vpa/
vpa2.htm
This site, part of the University of Kansas's "Virtual Presentation Assistant," is devoted to topic selection.

Assess Your Audience's Need to Know

Topics are all around you. What kind of car do you drive, and why? Who is your favorite recording artist or group? How many fast-food restaurants are nearby? What's the traffic like in your town? Everyday topics such as these often result in interesting speeches.[2] But look for a significant topic—one that needs to be discussed to bring about change, increase your audience's understanding, or highlight important cultural values and beliefs.[3] Also, evaluate topic possibilities from your audience's perspective (see Figure 6.1). How familiar are they with the subject? What more do they need to know? Does the subject affect their finances? Their future? Their health? Will it appeal to their curiosity?

Provide a measure of novelty. This is a basic element of maintaining interest, so speak about something unfamiliar, or present a familiar topic in a different way.[4] One student demonstrated how to make a peanut butter and jelly sandwich: Take two slices of bread; put peanut butter on one slice and jelly on the other; put them together. This wasted her listeners' time; they had known this recipe since kindergarten. But is her topic completely out of line? Not necessarily. Another student researched the nutrients in

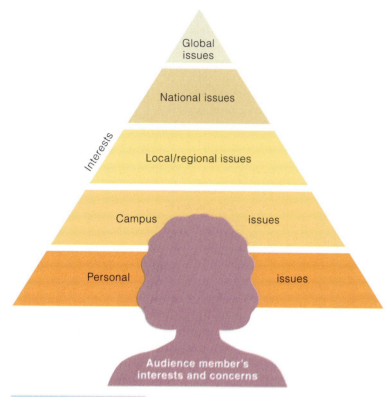

Figure 6.1

Topic Pyramid

Topics range from personal to global in scope. Whatever topic you choose, always evaluate it from your listeners' perspective. They are usually interested in personal topics or ones that are relevant to their daily concerns. Take care to develop your subject in a novel way that connects to their interests.

peanuts, talked about their fat content, and explained how bread complemented the proteins in peanuts. Many of his facts were novel and valuable to listeners who were on a tight food budget.

In short, choosing a topic that meets your audience's need to know and presenting your subject in a novel way are two fundamental principles in speechmaking. When audience members already know a lot about your subject, you'll be more successful if you dig for supplementary information or select another topic that will not waste their time. (Chapter 16 discusses this in more detail.)

Consider Your Personal Interests

Use your natural curiosity and personal interests to generate possible topics.[5] What ideas would you like to explore further? What is your major? Your occupational goals? What pets do you own? What interesting television shows or movies have you seen? What irritates you? What changes would you like to see in society? Here are ways some students worked their personal interests into their speeches:

▶ Philip was curious about the mullet hairstyle. He shared his research findings about the mullet's long history.
▶ Andrea is an art major. She created a speech about Jackson Pollock. (Her outline is in the Student Workbook.)
▶ Chris saw an article in a magazine about making diamonds from cremated human remains. (You can find the text of his speech at the end of Chapter 8.)

Unique life experiences also make good topics. You are who you are because of what you know and what you've experienced.[6] Draw information from your family background, jobs, hobbies, or recreational interests.

▶ Bonita's mother was killed by a driver who fell asleep at the wheel. Bonita's speech on driving while drowsy was powerful because of her firsthand loss. (Her outline appears at the end of Chapter 10 and on the book's website, where you'll also find video of her delivering the speech.)
▶ Because Josh is a drummer; he chose a particular type of drum (the African *dun dun* drum) for his topic. (His outline is included at the end of Chapter 16 and on the book's website, where you'll also find video of the speech being delivered.)
▶ Fadi works with the homeless. He believes they are not receiving enough attention, so his speech advocated increased funding for low-cost housing.

Speaking on a topic that is personally compelling has obvious advantages. When you are truly interested in your subject, you are more enthusiastic about it. Your enthusiasm can help you concentrate on your message rather than focusing on your insecurity as a speaker. Your enthusiasm also will energize your audience—nothing is more boring than a bored speaker!

Look for Topics from Other Courses

Look for speech topics in your academic major or in other courses you are taking. For example, if you're taking anthropology, study your textbook's table of contents for possible topics, such as marriage customs, kinship patterns, or gender differences among cultures. Preparing a speech on an interesting topic from another class has the added advantage of helping you learn the material for that course.

Don't hesitate to use research you have done for a paper in another course if the subject is appropriate. For example, as part of a nursing course, Jack wrote a paper on Cherokee beliefs and practices. He used information from that paper in his classroom speech on Native American medicine. Remember, however, if you adapt a paper, you must tailor the information to your particular audience.

Investigate Current Events

Newspapers, news magazines, and television shows are good topic sources. Skim headlines or surf Internet news sites and blogs, jotting down current issues that interest you. Major newspapers and news magazines, as well as trade and other specialized periodicals, are available on InfoTrac College Edition and on sites such as www.refdesk.com. Here are some topics from a single day's news:

"extinct" woodpecker found in Arkansas	a new mobile music phone
Social security reform	creation of "designer babies" for treatment
Vitamins D and C don't prevent fractures	upright or vertical burials
American Idol	illegal sales of fake drivers' licenses

Topics from current events usually address a need in society. The fact that they are important enough to discuss in the print or broadcast media means that they are significant to many people. And, because they are publicly covered, you should be able to find information easily. For example, Google provided 84 links related to upright burials, which take up less space and have less environmental impact than traditional, horizontal burials.

Consider International and Cultural Topics

You may find it easier to think of personal (time management) or national (medical insurance) topics because these are close to our lives and they regularly appear in the news. However, don't overlook international subjects, especially if you have traveled abroad or if you were born outside the United States. Explore your cultural heritage and experiences; for example, someone of French ancestry could speak about the Huguenots or about French attitudes toward the United States. Another possibility is to consider global aspects of your major. A film studies major might investigate a director or film genre from another country or a different cultural group. Even your job can be a starting point. For instance, a restaurant worker might give a speech about traditional Russian foods. Other sources include newspapers, magazines, and television broadcasts, which regularly report on trade, global investments, and international crime, all topics of increasing importance in the 21st century.

© Steven L Raymer/Getty Images

An international topic such as land mines can be developed in several ways. You could explain their history, their structure, their effects on unsuspecting victims, the process of detonating a mine, and so on. The key is to make the topic relevant to your audience.

Teaching Tip
www.news.co.uk/2/hi/
www.csmonitor.com
BBC News World Edition and
The Christian Science Monitor are good resources for
current events and international news topics.

**Classroom Discussion /
Activity**
Have students bring to class
a list of five topics they are
interested in talking or hearing about from the various
sources suggested here.
Compile the suggestions into
a master "Topics of Interest"
list and provide it to the students to use when choosing
topics.

Instructor's Resource Manual
Teaching Idea 6.1 in the Instructor's Resource Manual
(available in print, online, and
on the Multimedia Manager
CD-ROM) offers several suggestions for classroom activities to help students generate
ideas for their speech topics.

**Classroom Discussion /
Activity**
Ask students to conduct an
Internet search on a topic
they know something about
and look for ways the topic
could be narrowed. Have
them bring the results to
class for discussion.

Teaching Tip
http://www.library.ucla.edu/
libraries/college/help/topic/
This site from the UCLA
College Library offers suggestions on narrowing and
broadening a topic.

Cultural topics are easily found on the Internet. For example, you can find excellent resources on race and ethnicity at **http://lumen.georgetown.edu/projects/asw/**, which is maintained by Georgetown University. Start by searching the American Studies Web and linking to the "Race, Ethnicity, and Identity" resources. Follow additional links that interest you.

A word of caution: If you choose an international or cultural topic, be sure to make connections to your listeners' here-and-now concerns. For example, the subject of land mines might seem pretty far removed from your campus world. How could your classmates identify with the topic? Would they empathize with children and other civilians who lose limbs when they step on a mine? Do any listeners have friends or relatives in the military who might encounter these weapons? Do you have ancestors who immigrated from countries that are heavily mined? What about tax dollars that finance specialists who detonate the mines? Could you link the topic to fundamental values, such as the desire for a world at peace or for freedom and justice for all? Your challenge is to find connections that allow your audience to understand the relevance of your topic.

DIVERSITY IN PRACTICE
DOES REQUIRING ONE SPEECH ON "COMMUNICATION AND CULTURE" INCREASE STUDENTS' EMPATHY?

LORI CARRELL[7] reported the results of research done in a medium-sized Midwestern university. The goal of the study was to determine if student *empathy,* the ability to understand diverse perspectives, increased when diversity issues were incorporated into the course. An underlying assumption was that competent communicators can view issues from multiple perspectives. Four groups participated in the study: The control group had no special treatment; the second group took an entire course in intercultural communication; the third discussed concepts related to diversity at several points during the term; and the fourth group had a one-shot assignment to give a public speech on a "communication and diversity" topic.

Results indicated that students who studied intercultural communication for an entire term significantly increased in empathy. Those who often discussed diversity issues throughout the semester also showed increases. However, students who gave only one diversity speech made no significant gains.

What does this mean to you? How might an increase in empathy make you a more competent communicator? What connections can you see between the ability to understand a variety of perspectives and the diversity concepts presented in this text and in your classroom? How might your topic choices make you more sensitive to issues of diversity?

Narrow Your Topic

Once you have chosen a broad topic, you must narrow it enough to discuss it within a designated time frame. This principle applies across all speaking contexts, from project reports, sales presentations, and town hall meetings to farewell speeches. As a classroom topic, let's consider the general subject of animals. Obviously, you can't discuss "Animals from Aardvark to Zebra" in seven minutes, but you can focus on a single species, on a controversy like wearing fur, or on dangerous pets. Consider using a mind map as a way to let your ideas flow. Figure 6.2 illustrates how to start with a broad subject and narrow

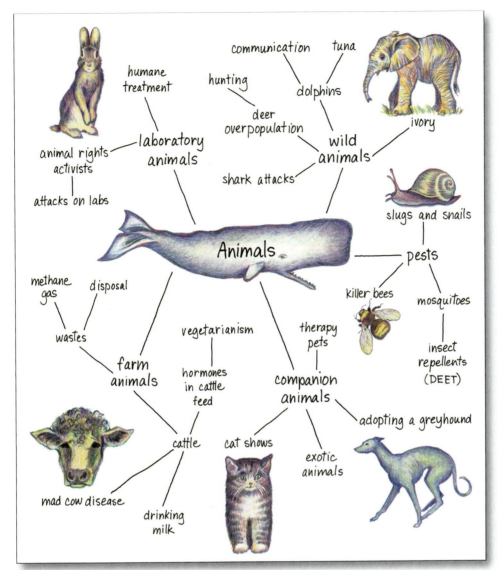

Figure 6.2
Mind Map
This mind map shows
several animal-related
topics.

Instructor Resource:
PowerPoint
The *Multimedia Manager*
with Instructor Resources
CD-ROM includes a Power-
Point slide of Figure 6.2.

Teaching Tip
Students can complete a
mind map similar to the one
in Figure 6.2 and present it to
class. Encourage students to
add to them throughout the
semester.

it to a series of more realistic classroom topics. Use your creativity to approach the topic
from a personal, national, even international level.

Careful work early in the term will produce several subjects you can use throughout
the term. Let's say Figure 6.2 is Katherine's mind map.

▶ Her first presentation, a self-introductory narrative, relates an experience she had
  with her dog when she volunteered him as a therapy animal in a nursing home.
▶ Her informative speech describes how to adopt a retired greyhound.
▶ Later, she reports on the use of hormones in beef production.
▶ Finally, she argues that environmental laws to protect endangered species have gone
  too far.

Student Learning:
Book Website
A sample outline for this topic
is available on the book website as well as in Appendix C
of this textbook.

As you can see, the topic "animals" provides a wealth of subtopics for specific
speeches. You'll find a sample outline on the topic of "Dolphin Communication" in Appendix C and on the book's website.

> ### ✓ STOP AND CHECK
> #### IDENTIFY SEVERAL USABLE TOPICS
>
> List ten to fifteen major topic areas that interest you, and then narrow your list to two or three. Make a mind map for each topic on your narrowed list.
>
> If you select these general areas early in the course, you can be alert throughout the term for information to use in your speeches. Let's say you are looking for material on eating disorders; you might scan weekly TV schedules for shows that feature the topic, or you could take advantage of the "news alerts" feature at Internet sources such as Google (news) or Yahoo (news) that provide updates on relevant stories. For different perspectives, consider blogs related to your topic, and use a blog tracker service that lets you know when a specified blog is updated. You could set up interviews with professionals as well as with people who have experienced eating disorders. Because you have the topic clearly in mind, you have plenty of time to gather materials.
>
> You can also create a file for each speech, photocopying or clipping articles from newspapers or magazines, taking notes on lectures, or videotaping related television programs. At speech time, you will have many resources available for a good presentation, including a number of audiovisual aids that a last-minute scramble might not produce.

Choose Your Purpose and Focus

You don't just "accidentally" give a public speech; instead, you speak to accomplish specific goals or purposes.[8] Before each speech, clarify what you want to achieve by identifying your general purpose and tentatively formulating a specific purpose for that particular speech. (You will continue to refine your specific purpose as you work on the speech.) Writing out a thesis statement helps both you and your listeners understand the central idea that you'll develop.

Identify Your General Purpose

Almost 2,000 years ago, St. Augustine,[9] who taught rhetoric before he became a bishop, identified three public speaking purposes: to teach, to please, and to move. In the 18th century, George Campbell[10] identified four purposes that reflect the psychology of his era:[11] to enlighten the understanding, to please the imagination, to move the passions, and to influence the will. In the 20th century, Alan Monroe[12] said we attempt to inform, to entertain, to stimulate through emotion, or to convince through reasoning. Today, speech instructors commonly identify four **general purposes:**

▶ *To inform,* in which your goal is to explain, teach, describe, announce, introduce, or provide a basis for your audience to have a greater understanding of your topic. Within the broad subject of animals, for example, you might inform your audience about killer bees, methane gas produced by farm animals, or frog deformities caused by environmental pollution.

▶ *To persuade,* in which you hope to convince, motivate, nominate, and reinforce cultural ideals. You might gather evidence to convince listeners that a species is endangered or to persuade them to donate money to their local humane society.

▶ *To entertain,* in which you want listeners to laugh at your humorous portrayal of a subject. For instance, speeches on pet psychiatrists or pet wardrobes can be funny.

▶ *To commemorate,* in which you highlight and reinforce cultural ideals. Tributes, toasts, awards ceremonies, and other special occasion speeches are just a few examples. A famous tribute to a dog extols this animal's faithfulness. An award presented to a hard-

general purposes a speaker's general purpose could be to inform, to persuade, or to entertain

A broad topic such as animals yields subtopics as wide ranging as insect repellents, dolphin communication, and adopting greyhounds that have finished their racing careers.

© Digital Vision/Getty Images

working volunteer at an animal shelter reinforces the cultural slogan "Be kind to animals."

Speech purposes often overlap. Take the case of a university recruiter who attempts to persuade her listeners to attend the school she represents by both informing them about the university and entertaining them with humorous accounts of campus life. She has several purposes, because she has several potential audiences: She persuades prospective students to fill out application forms, informs parents or spouses about financial aid, and entertains alumni (and encourages donations). Although her talk is not specifically commemorative, she does reinforce cultural values on education.

Classroom instructors usually assign the general purpose for each classroom speech. Consequently, when you are assigned an informative speech, focus your research on discovering and presenting factual material that will increase your audience's knowledge or understanding of your topic. When you must persuade, select convincing and motivating materials that will influence your listeners to believe and act in the ways you advocate. (Chapter 17 details ways to narrow persuasive purposes.) If you're asked to be entertaining, choose a ridiculous event or situation and use strategies such as exaggeration and wordplay to highlight humorous aspects of the topic. Although giving a speech to entertain is less common in the classroom, you should strive to be interesting, rather than boring, no matter what kind of speech you give; this will help you accomplish your other speech purposes. Figure 6.3 shows how to come up with a variety of speech purposes for a broad topic such as animals.

STOP AND CHECK

NARROW YOUR PURPOSE

Practice narrowing your purpose by making a diagram similar to the one in Figure 6.3, using one of the subject-area mind maps you made for the Stop and Check exercise on page 96.

Figure 6.3
Speech Purposes
A broad topic such as
animals can generate
informative, entertaining,
persuasive, and commemo-
rative speeches.

Instructor Resource:
PowerPoint
The *Multimedia Manager*
with Instructor Resources
CD-ROM includes a Power-
Point slide of Figure 6.3.

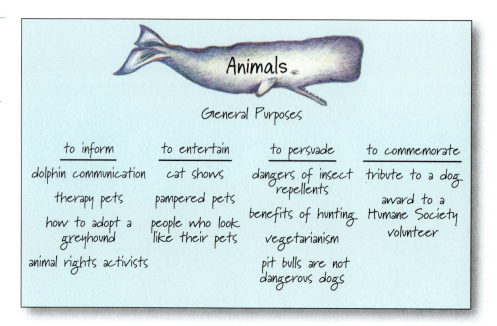

Identify Your Specific Purpose

Jen has become convinced that DEET, a chemical commonly used in insect repellents, is potentially dangerous to humans, so she chooses DEET as her topic. Her next step is to decide exactly what she wants the audience to know or do as a result of her speech. Does she want them to know what DEET is? How it affects the body? Why it's so widely used? Does she want them to stop using insect repellents that contain DEET? How she answers these questions leads her to her **specific purpose** statement, which identifies her desired audience response or her speaking goal.[13] She might concentrate on the effect she wants to have on her listeners' thoughts, emotions, or actions.

- **Cognitive effects** are influences on the audience's beliefs, thoughts, or understandings. Does she want them to think differently about what they might consider a harmless chemical?
- **Affective effects** are the feelings or emotions she wants to arouse in her listeners. Does she want to instill fear or distrust of DEET?
- **Behavioral effects** are the actions she wants audience members to perform as a result of her speech. Does she hope listeners will stop using DEET or, at the very least, use it more sparingly?

In short, Jen must clarify what she wants her listeners to know, feel, or do and combine her topic and goal into a specific purpose statement. One way to keep her desired response in mind is to begin with an infinitive phrase and use the words "my audience" within the statement. Here are some specific purpose statements she might formulate, depending on her general speech purpose:

- To inform my audience about the chemical makeup of DEET and the way our bodies process this chemical, which is common in insect repellents. (Cognitive effect: The audience will know more about DEET.)
- To convince my audience that DEET is a health hazard when it is misused. (Cognitive effect: The audience will believe there is a link between misuse of the chemical and health problems.)

specific purpose the cognitive, affective, or behavioral responses a speaker desires

cognitive effects influences on beliefs, understandings, and other mental processes

affective effects influences on listeners' feelings

behavioral effects influences on audience actions

- To persuade my audience to distrust the chemical DEET. (Affective effect: The audience will have an emotional response and thus develop a negative attitude toward misuse of this chemical.)
- To persuade my audience to use insect repellents containing DEET properly and only when necessary. (Behavioral effect: The audience will be motivated to do something as a result of this speech.)

Although some instructors ask students to begin the specific purpose with the phrase "to inform my audience," others prefer that students write the specific purpose as a statement that specifies the desired audience response:

- As a result of my speech, my audience will *know* the chemical makeup of DEET and understand how our bodies process it.
- As a result of my speech, my audience will *believe* that misusing insect repellents with DEET is potentially dangerous.
- As a result of my speech, my audience will *have a negative attitude* about misuse of DEET.
- As a result of my speech, my audience will *use* insect repellents *that contain DEET properly and with caution.*

At this stage of preparation, Jen has this much of her speech formulated:

Topic:	The dangers of DEET
General purpose:	To persuade
Specific purpose:	As a result of my speech, my audience will be convinced that DEET poses a health hazard when misused.

By formulating her general and specific purpose early on, she can focus her additional research more effectively. Jen needs facts, descriptions, and explanations for all her speeches, but especially for informative ones. If she wants to prove links between DEET and health problems, she should look for scientific research and opinions from experts. She should search out examples and comparisons if her goal is to motivate listeners to care or to act. If her goal is to have listeners restrict their use of DEET, she should find guidelines and substitutes for DEET that will help listeners enact this goal.

After selecting your general purpose and writing out a specific purpose statement, you are ready to begin formulating a statement, known as the central idea or thesis statement, that captures the major idea of your speech.

Write Your Thesis Statement

The **thesis statement** is the most important sentence in your speech because it names your subject and establishes its importance to the audience.[14] It's as if someone asked, "Tell me in one sentence what you're going to speak about. No details, just the bottom line. A complete declarative sentence, not a question." The sentence you come up with is your thesis statement, sometimes called the **central idea.** Robert Gwynne, professor at the University of Tennessee Knoxville, advises you to write this sentence from the audience's point of view. (This contrasts with the *specific purpose*, which you write with your own goals in mind.)[15] Richard Engnell of George Fox University gives his students the following guidelines:[16]

Write a single declarative sentence
    that makes a statement about the subject matter and
        summarizes the content of the speech
            in a reasonable, simple manner
                that is precise enough to guide you and your audience.

thesis statement a single sentence that names the subject and establishes its significance

central idea a synonym for thesis statement

Notice, for example, the contrast between these correctly and incorrectly written thesis statements:

Correct:	DEET, a chemical compound that is found in insect repellents, is dangerous when misused, but you can prevent serious health problems by carefully following directions.
Incorrect:	Why should you use insect repellent with caution? (This is a question, not a declarative sentence.)
Incorrect:	We must first define what DEET is. Then we will find out why Americans have overlooked DEET's damaging effects. Finally, we will look at ways you can protect yourself when using DEET-based insect repellents. (Use one sentence, not three.)
Incorrect:	Why you should be careful about using DEET-based insect repellents. (This is a fragment, not a complete sentence.)

Begin to formulate your thesis statement as soon as you select your topic and decide on your general and specific purposes. Then allow yourself plenty of time to explore and develop your ideas, narrowing the approach, the slant, the point of view you'll develop, and the general direction you'll take.[17] The process of invention takes time and energy. New ideas will emerge and others will seem less important, so don't be afraid to revise your direction as you do additional research, preparation, and organization. As this student explains:

> I tend to have running dialogues in my head, sometimes even out loud. While I talk to myself, I work out particulars. I answer questions I've posed to myself ("Well, really, Gail, if you argue that, where will you go? It's too huge!" or "Now does that really make sense?"). My answers often lead me to modify my central idea as I continue my preparation.
> GAIL

When you actually give your speech, incorporate your thesis statement into your introduction, and follow it with a **preview,** or short summary of the major points you'll use to develop your thesis. (Chapter 10 provides more details about previews.) Here are some additional examples from student speeches that show the relationship between topic, general purpose, specific purpose, thesis statement, and preview.

Topic:	Dolphin communication
General purpose:	To inform
Specific purpose:	To inform my audience about research showing that dolphins engage in intelligent communication.
Thesis statement:	Dolphins are intelligent creatures who communicate with other dolphins and with human researchers.
Preview:	I will first explain the concept of dolphin intelligence; then I'll show examples of dolphin-to-dolphin communication before concluding with a summary of some research on dolphin-to-human communication.

(A complete outline of this speech is included in Appendix C.)

Topic:	Medical misinformation on the Internet
General purpose:	To persuade
Specific purpose:	To convince my audience that medical misinformation on the Internet is a problem that we can solve.

Student Learning: Workbook
The three speech examples given here (dolphin communication, medical misinformation, and driving while tired) can be used in conjunction with Activity 6.4 in the Student Workbook. Have students work with a partner to complete the activity in class or assign it as homework.

Student Learning: Book Website
An outline for this speech is available on the book website as well as at the end of Chapter 7.

preview short summary of the major points you'll develop in the speech

Thesis statement: Medical misinformation is rampant on the Internet, but three major solutions would correct many problems.

Preview: We will first explore the dangerous problem of medical misinformation on the Internet by looking at some causes and by learning how to protect ourselves as consumers through codes of conduct, government regulations, and personal actions.

(This speech outline appears at the end of Chapter 7 and on the book's website, where you'll also find video of the speech being delivered.)

Topic: Driving while tired

General Purpose: To persuade

Specific Purpose: As a result of my speech, my audience will choose not to drive while drowsy.

Thesis statement: Driving while tired is dangerous and potentially affects not only your own life but the lives of others on the road as well.

Preview: Tired drivers are responsible for many road accidents and deaths, and the only real solution lies within our hands. But the benefits of avoiding driving while tired greatly outweigh any sacrifices you make.

(An outline of this speech appears at the end of Chapter 10 and is also available on the book's website, where you can view a video of the speech being delivered.)

In summary, topic and purpose selection are important aspects of speechmaking; however, this process can sometimes seem overwhelming. Focus your preparation by selecting a subject that interests you, narrowing it to a manageable subtopic, formulating general and specific speech purposes, and then synthesizing your main ideas into a thesis statement or central idea that names the subject and alerts the audience to its significance. When you give your speech, state your thesis in the introduction, and add a preview of the main points you will use to develop your central idea.

BUILD YOUR SPEECH
GENERAL PURPOSE, SPECIFIC PURPOSE, AND CENTRAL IDEA

Choose three topics from the list below (or select three topics that you can talk about without doing much research). Then log on to Speech Builder Express to write out the general purpose, a specific purpose statement, and the central idea for an impromptu speech about each topic.

- Online shopping
- Stress relievers for college students
- Simple breakfasts
- Free things to do in this community
- Going to the movies
- Exercising regularly
- Study tips

Student Learning:
Speech Builder Express
Speech Builder Express provides prompts to help students through the process of narrowing a broad topic. You can also ask students to email you a copy of their work for your review or evaluation.

Summary

As you begin the process of choosing a speech topic, look for something your audience needs to know. Then, examine your personal experiences, other courses, current events, and international or cultural possibilities for significant subjects. Be sure to find a topic that interests you! If you do careful work early in the term, you can produce a list or develop a series of files on topics that will interest both you and your listeners.

After selecting your topic, focus on your general intention or purpose for the speech. Then write the specific purpose that names the response you want from your listeners. Focus on the speech content by writing out the thesis statement, a single sentence that summarizes the major ideas of your speech in a way that guides both you and your listeners. Begin to formulate your thesis early in the speech, but revise it if necessary as you proceed in your research and preparation.

STUDY AND REVIEW

The premium website for *Public Speaking* offers a broad range of resources that will help you better understand the material in this chapter, complete assignments, and succeed on tests. The website features

▶ Speech videos with critical viewing questions, speech outlines, and transcripts, and
▶ Interactive practice activities, self quizzes, and a sample final exam.

For more information about this text's electronic learning resources, consult your **Guide to Online Resources for Public Speaking** or visit http://communication.wadsworth.com/jaffe5.

KEY TERMS

The terms below are defined in the margins throughout this chapter. The book's website also provides interactive flashcards and crossword puzzles to help you learn these terms and the concepts they represent.

general purpose 96   behavioral effects 98
specific purpose 98   thesis statement 99
cognitive effects 98   central idea 99
affective effects 98   preview 100

APPLICATION AND CRITICAL THINKING EXERCISES

The exercises below are among the practice activities on the book's website.

1. Design a mind map on the general topic of education after high school.
2. Work with a small group of your classmates to create a mind map based on a very general international topic, such as Japan, world trade, ethnic conflicts, or the United Nations. Record your ideas on a blank transparency or a large piece of paper, and then display it for the entire class.
3. Discuss in a small group some ways you could add the element of novelty to the following common topics: seatbelts, making coffee, television, weddings.
4. For additional information on St. Augustine, one of the great figures of rhetoric, go to http://ccat.sas.upenn.edu/jod/augustine/ddc4.html and read Chapters 2 and 11–13 of his treatise on rhetoric. He gave this advice seventeen centuries ago. Which principles still apply?

5. For each of the following topics, tell how you could create one speech to inform, one to persuade, and one to entertain: Mardi Gras, visiting an aquarium, choosing a college, reality TV, recreational fishing.

6. Choose one of the topics above and write a general purpose statement, specific purpose statement, and a central idea or thesis statement that matches the ideas you had for informative, persuasive, and entertaining speeches.

SPEECH VIDEO

Log on to the book's website and click on the video tab to watch and critique Jill Lacey deliver "The Benefits of Pet Ownership."

Student Speech Outline with Commentary

THE BENEFITS OF PET OWNERSHIP
Jill Lacey

General purpose: To persuade

Specific Purpose: To actuate behavior so that listeners save an animal's life by adopting one slated for death.

Thesis Statement: Millions of animals are euthanized annually, but by adopting one, you can enjoy benefits while you are saving the life of a dependent being.

Preview: If you adopt an animal slated for euthanasia, you can enjoy physical, psychological, and family benefits.

Introduction

I. In her essay "The Longest Walk" (1998), Teri Campbell, a Humane Society worker, describes her trip around rows of cages filled with unwanted animals.
   A. It's Thursday; she must choose 13 animals; the others will be euthanized the following day.
   B. In one cage, a weak, mistreated, pregnant coonhound wags her tail hopefully.
   C. Teri cannot choose the coonhound, her unborn pups, and 50 other animals.

II. Eight to ten million pets are euthanized in a year; ten million equals 192,308 per week or 27,473 per day (Pawprints & Purrs, 2005).

III. As I study to become a vet, my career goal is to save animals; you can help by adopting an animal that would otherwise be killed, which brings many benefits.

IV. After listening to my speech, you should be sold on animal adoption for three reasons: health, psychological, and family benefits.

Jill's topic comes from her interests and career plans.

Because she wants to move her audience to action, she opens with an emotional story and some surprising statistics.

Her thesis statement and preview let the audience know what she wants from them and how she'll develop her ideas.

She goes through her three main points in a straightforward manner. Emphasizing benefits to her listeners gives them many reasons for acting on what she asks them to do.

Facts gleaned from studies help build her argument; quotations from actual people keep her speech grounded in reality.

Her second point is probably the most familiar— pets give psychological benefits.

Jill includes the sources in her outline. She can work them in as she delivers her speech.

Self-confidence, empathy, and responsibility are all characteristics that her listeners value.

Body

I. Pet owners enjoy physical benefits.
  A. Studies show that pet owners are healthier overall than non-pet owners.
    1. They have lower cholesterol and blood pressure (Schulte, 2004).
    2. Older pet owners require fewer doctor visits (Schulte, 2004).
    3. They recover more quickly from surgeries and illnesses.
    4. Children raised in a home with two or more animals may have fewer pet allergies or other allergies (National Institute, 2002).
  B. Pets also need physical activity.
    1. Dog owners (not cat owners) get more exercise than adults without pets (Kale, 2005).
    2. Playing with pets requires physical exertion.
    3. Pet owner Florence Kellog says "When you get older, you try to stay very active, but older people have a tendency to just sit. Because you have the responsibility for the animal, you don't have that tendency" (Kane, 2005).

II. Having a companion animal brings psychological benefits.
  A. Linda Case, animal science professor at the University of Illinois, says, "Pets teach me to love unconditionally. They don't care if I have a bad hair day or put on 5 pounds. They love me just the way I am and I love them for who they are" (Wilkey, 2003).
  B. Owning a pet can help reduce loneliness and depression (BestFriendsPetCare.com, 2002).
    1. Some nursing homes use pets to help their residents.
    2. UCLA researchers found that AIDS patients who owned pets were half as likely to report depression.
    3. South African researchers found that pet ownership can produce the endorphins found in anti-depressants.
  C. Companion animals also can reduce anxiety.
    1. Touching and stroking animals give us something to focus on.
    2. Animals are "sympathetic, supportive and non-judgmental" (Human-animal bond, 2004).
    3. They make us laugh and keep us amused with their antics (Benefits, 2004).
    4. People feel safer with pets in the home or outdoors (Delta Society, 2005).
  D. Mayo Clinic oncologist Dr. Edward Creagan summarizes, "It doesn't really matter what type of pets you have. When you pet a dog, stroke a cat on your lap, or enjoy any animal, something good happens. There's a feeling of contentment and joy from the unconditional love an animal brings into your life" (Benefits, 2004).

III. Pet-owning families also enjoy benefits.
  A. Children become more cognitive and pro-social (Human-animal bond, 2004).
    1. Research on 394 college students showed that those who grew up with pets were more self-confident.
    2. Research on 455 school-aged children showed those with pets could better decode nonverbal communication.
    3. Children with pets scored higher on empathy and pro-social scales (BestFriends PetCare.com, 2002).
  B. Children also learn responsibility at a young age; think of your experiences caring for pets.
  C. Owning pets can minimize interfamily tensions and help families during crises such as illnesses or death (BestFriendsPetCare.com, 2002).

Conclusion

I. In conclusion, pets can help you live longer, ease depression and anxiety, and reap benefits for your family.

II. I hope you consider adopting an unwanted animal when you can.

III. Think about that pregnant coonhound and her unborn pups; if she had been adopted, they would be alive today.

IV. They could have avoided the fate of the 198,203 animals that were euthanized that week.

References

Benefits of pet ownership. (2004). Humane Society of Marathon County, WI. Retrieved November 21, 2004, from http://catsndogs.org/index1.php

BestFriendsPetCare.com. (2002, Spring). Between friends! Pets are good medicine. Newsletter. Retrieved November 21, 2004, from www.bestfriendspetcare.com/bf_feature_14.cfm

Campbell, T. (1998). The longest walk: A day in the life of a humane society employee. Hugs for Homeless Animals. Retrieved July 21, 2005, from www.h4ha.org/roadhouse/longestwalk.html

Delta Society. (2005). Healthy reasons to have a pet. FAQ sheet. Retrieved November 20, 2004, from www.deltasociety.org/dsc020.htm

Human-animal bond. (2004). Pet Owners. Retrieved November 21, 2004, from www.ovma.org/pets/human_animalbond.shtml

Kale, M. (2005). What you already "knew"—Fluffy and Fido are good for you. Delta Society. Retrieved November 20, 2004, from www.deltasociety.org/dsx412.htm (original work published 1992 in *Inter Actions, 10*, 1).

Kane, E. (2005). For seniors: Pets are just plain healthy. Delta Society. Retrieved November 21, 2004, from www.deltasociety.org/dsc102.htm

National Institute of Allergy and Infectious Diseases. (2002, August 27). Multiple pets may decrease children's allergy risk. NIAID News. Retrieved July 21, 2005, from www2.niaid.nih.gov/newsroom/releases/petallergyrisk.htm

Pawprints and Purrs. (2005). Stop—don't litter! Spay and neuter. Retrieved July 21, 2005, from www.sniksnak.com/stop_s-n.html

Schulte, S. (2004). Animals and your health: The benefits of pet ownership. Swedish Medical Center, Seattle. Retrieved July 21, 2005, from www.swedish.org/15309.cfm

Wilkey, Maureen (2003, February 26). UI lecturer teaches importance of pets. *The Daily Illinois.* Retrieved November 21, 2004, from www.illinimedia.com/di/feb03/feb26/news/stories/news_story05.shtml

The brief conclusion restates her thesis and reviews her points.

She ends by referring back to the emotionally powerful story and statistics.

RESEARCHING YOUR SPEECH IN AN ELECTRONIC CULTURE

THIS CHAPTER WILL HELP YOU

▶ Plan your research

▶ Distinguish between primary and secondary sources

▶ Gather materials from personal experience, interviews and lectures

▶ Use the Internet critically

▶ Find library resources and electronically stored resources

▶ Include ethnic and international sources in your research

▶ Record your information in a way that is suited to your learning style and avoids plagiarism

"Time After Time" Mural © 1995 by Betsie Miller-Kusz.
(Collingwood Street near 19th Street, SF, CA)

MBER'S TOPIC WAS HEPATITIS C; Krista chose the Electoral College; Kaliope decided to speak about television violence. However, none of these students was an "expert" on her topic. They all faced the challenge you face—once you have selected and narrowed your topic, you must gather information to support your ideas.

Gathering effective supporting materials is part of the canon the ancient Romans called *invention* (see Chapter 2). Finding information combines several skills that contribute to your developing competence in speechmaking. As you select materials, you must:

▶ Know how to find the data you need to support your ideas
▶ Formulate a research plan
▶ Critically evaluate sources and choose the best materials available
▶ Record your findings in a systematic way that steers clear of plagiarism

This chapter presents information on the research process, with the goal of helping you effectively accomplish these four major tasks.

CASE STUDY: LUKE AND JONATHAN RESEARCH THEIR SPEECHES

Chapter-at-a-Glance
This chapter examines the process of gathering appropriate supporting materials for a speech. Developing a research plan; distinguishing between primary and secondary sources; using personal experience, interviews, and lectures; conducting library research; and using the Internet are discussed. The chapter ends with techniques for recording supporting information and avoiding plagiarism.

When asked to describe his research strategies, Luke listed five steps:

1. I start with a Google search and find basic information about the topic. I figure out the difference between important information and superfluous information.
2. I go to InfoTrac College Edition and find some full-text, primary-source articles about the subject.
3. The library is next. I check out related books for quotations and additional information.
4. Then I outline the speech with information I've collected, looking for gaps in the information. I delete or insert material as necessary.
5. I start typing the outline, doing "spot-research" as needed to fill in gaps.

In contrast, Jonathan used mostly library sources. He described his strategies:

1. First I figure out how much I already know about the subject and try to outline what I might want to write/speak about.
2. Second, I go to the university library or the city library and find credible books on my topic.
3. I flip through and check to see if they will be useful.
4. Usually I check them out or at least take notes and photocopy important pages.
5. I look through and grab the important information for my subject and outline, then start writing and practicing my speech.

Questions for Discussion

▶ What are the strengths and weaknesses of each student's research strategies?
▶ Who do you think has the most effective overall strategies? Why?
▶ Which student's strategies are most like yours?
▶ What suggestions would you give Luke? Jonathan?

Teaching Tip
If most of your students are first years, arrange a tour of your campus library early in the term. Explain to the librarians your students' research tasks so that the tour can include these materials. The tour should include the library's online catalog and holdings as well as its non-electronic sources.

Gather Materials for Your Speech

So you can learn about your subject from a variety of perspectives, your instructor will probably ask you to consult from three to seven sources, including both primary and secondary materials. You should be able to find enormous amounts of information easily; however, selecting the *best* information requires critical thinking. This section discusses effective ways to plan, conduct, and evaluate your research.

Consult a reference librarian if you need help during any stage of your research. These professionals have had specialized training in finding information.

© Indiana University School of Law Library, Bloomington

Plan Your Research

Laurie Lieggi, a **reference librarian** at George Fox University, says students often wait until the last minute, thinking they can pop into the library once, spend a couple of hours in attack mode, get speech materials that are easy to find, and leave—satisfied with whatever they come up with.[1] Many go directly to the Internet, and, because it's so convenient, use it exclusively. Lieggi likens this type of research to only eating at fast-food restaurants. Fast food alone fails to provide the nutrients, variety, and quality of meals you carefully prepare at home.

To make the best use of your research time, sit down and plan a search strategy at the outset. The following tips will help you:

▶ *Budget enough time.* Good research is time consuming, and if you think you'll get wonderful, usable information in one short session, you will be disappointed. Consequently, set aside on your calendar more than one block of time for research.

▶ *Get to know your library.* Because each library is different, visit or tour the one you will use the most. Also, look for how-to pamphlets and brochures your campus librarians have prepared to explain specific features available in your library.

▶ *Include a librarian in your research plan.* Librarians are paid to assist you, so be sure to consult them if you need help. Lieggi said, "I'm a reference librarian because I want to be available to students. That's what I enjoy. Every question is a puzzle, and I get to help a student solve a puzzle." Besides, who knows a library better than the people who work there daily? In large academic libraries, **subject librarians** have a library degree as well as an advanced degree in another discipline.

▶ *Let your topic guide your research.* This chapter suggests a number of research sources, but you probably won't need them all for a single speech. Instead, identify the best sources for your particular subject. For instance, if your topic is a current event, schedule a nightly network or cable news program into your plan. For a speech on pet overpopulation, plan to interview a humane society worker. For whitewater rafting, look to personal experiences, books, articles in sports magazines, and Internet sites.

▶ *Identify key terms for your searches in computerized catalogs, databases, or the Internet.* Think creatively, consult a librarian, or find the Library of Congress subject headings in the reference section of the library. For example, Marcus searched for "disabled"

reference librarian library specialist whose job is to help you find research information

subject librarian librarians who are specialists in a particular subject such as law or medicine; they have an advanced degree in the subject

and "housing" with little success until his librarian suggested he use the word "handicapped." Then he found all the information he needed. (Headings do not always reflect current usage.) Many online databases have thesaurus, index, or browse features you can use to identify specific key terms.

▶ *Identify experts in the field (if possible).* You'll save research time if you learn the names of recognized experts on your topic. Search library databases under "authors," or try to fit an interview with a campus expert into your plan.

▶ *Make critical evaluation a part of your plan from the outset.* So many resources are available that you might think you're drowning in data—some highly credible, some very questionable. Find out as much as you can about every source you use, whether book, article, website, or personal interview. Then compare sources. Some will be OK, some pretty good, and some excellent. Choose the best.

▶ *Keep a running list of all your sources as you search.* This way, you can easily assemble your final bibliography and return to a source if necessary. If you are using the Internet, bookmark each site you use. Carefully noting each source also helps you avoid plagiarism and credit each source appropriately.

▶ *Use a variety of sources.* Remember the fast-food analogy? You wouldn't eat only Big Macs, so don't expect to use only the Internet or newspapers or encyclopedias or any other single type of source. Also, look for diverse perspectives so you can approach the topic from various viewpoints.

This is not an exhaustive list, but these tips will help you focus your search more effectively. Return to the case study on page 108 and evaluate Luke's and Jonathan's research plans in light of these tips. The rest of the chapter will guide you in carrying out your overall plan.

Distinguish Between Primary and Secondary Sources

Primary sources are created by individuals and groups who are directly involved in events as they take place. These sources fall into several categories. **Original documents** are resources such as such as letters, interviews, news footage, autobiographies, and minutes of meetings that were created by a primary source. **Creative works** include books, paintings, poems, and dance performances. **Relics** or **artifacts** are cultural objects such as jewelry, tools, buildings, clothing, and other created items.

Secondary sources are a step away from the events. They have been produced by nonparticipants who have summarized or interpreted original reports. Some are created at the time the events occurred; others are created months, decades, even centuries later. History books or biographies, critical reviews of artistic performances, and scholarly articles are examples.

In your research, distinguish between primary and secondary sources. Although both are useful, there is a difference between a participant's account and an outsider's summary or interpretation of the same event. Let's say you decide to watch the *News-Hour with Jim Lehrer* (PBS) for information on a nationally-discussed current event. Each segment usually begins with factual information about the subject and then Lehrer

---

primary sources information from people actually involved in the event

original documents letters, news footage, minutes of a meeting, and other evidence recorded by a primary source

creative works poems, dances, paintings, writings, and other aesthetic creations

relics or **artifacts** culturally significant creations such as buildings, jewelry, or tools

secondary sources information provided by nonparticipants who summarize and interpret events or people

assembles several guests, who discuss it for up to fifteen minutes. Some guests, like a representative of the Brazilian government, are primary sources who give a participant's perspective. Others, like a U.S. professor of South American studies, are secondary sources who provide opinions and interpretations.

You can find primary and secondary materials in personal experiences, interviews and lectures, print materials, and recorded and electronically stored data.

Draw From Your Personal Experiences

You have probably chosen your topic because it relates in some way to your interests and experiences. Don't overlook personal experience as a source for usable information. In fact, your personal expertise may actually increase your credibility for demonstration or how-to speeches. I've heard speakers describe their own experiences with Ritalin, immigration, beekeeping, cartooning, arranged marriages, and so on.

Interview a Knowledgeable Person

Well-planned interviews can help you gain information and clarify confusing ideas by questioning someone who knows about your subject firsthand. **Experts** are people whose studies, experiences, or occupations make them knowledgeable. For example, I consulted a reference librarian when I wrote this chapter; students have talked with chiropractors, police officers, construction workers, and other similar professionals for their speeches. **Laypeople** or **peers** are individuals who have gained insights and formulated opinions through ordinary living. By interviewing students who use library research tools effectively, for example, I would gain practical information about this topic.

Because most people have full schedules, and potential interviewees are doing you a favor when they agree to be interviewed, keep these factors in mind:

▶ Give the person an idea of your speech topic and the kind of information you need. This is especially important if you interview non-native English speakers. In order to think through and prepare their answers, they may request written questions before the interview.

▶ *Be conscious of the time.* When you make the appointment, estimate the length of time your questions will take, and then respect those limits! Although different cultural groups have different norms regarding punctuality, be on time. If anyone is late, let it be your interviewee. If you absolutely cannot keep your appointment, give the person as much notice as possible.

▶ *Prepare in advance.* Write out your questions so you will remember everything you want to ask. (Written questions also keep the interview focused.)

▶ *Take careful notes.* Make sure you've understood correctly by reading your notes back to the interviewee, who can then make corrections or additions. Ask questions such as "Is this what you mean?" or "Did I understand you correctly when you said . . . ?"

▶ *Aim to understand your topic from your interviewee's perspective.* If you interview people whose ideas and actions clash with yours, practice civility. Listen politely, and try to understand how they came to believe or behave the way they do.

▶ *If you want to record the interview, ask permission* in advance, and place the recorder in full view.

When you cannot meet in person, consider a telephone interview, following the same guidelines regarding questions, advance preparation, and punctuality. Technology also expands your interviewing possibilities. Through email, for instance, you can conduct a written interview with a source by using a question-and-answer format. In fact, thousands of experts in hundreds of subjects permit websites such as **www.askanexpert**

expert person whose knowledge is based on research, experience, or occupation

laypeople or **peers** ordinary people whose knowledge comes from everyday experience

News programs provide interviews from both primary and secondary sources. Here, moderator Tim Russert of *Meet the Press* interviews Egyptian Prime Minister Ahmed Nazif about economic and political reforms in Egypt. What kind of source is Nazif? Explain your answer.

© Getty Images

.com to list their email addresses because they want to share their knowledge.[2] In addition, television and radio programs regularly feature interviews. Some shows allow you to call in or fax your questions to the interviewee.

To investigate this topic further, search InfoTrac College Edition for the article "10 Tips for Top-Notch Interviews." Read the author's tips and identify additional tips you can incorporate into your interviews.

Attend Lectures and Performances

Lectures or performances such as poetry readings can also provide useful information. Take careful notes. If you use a tape recorder, make sure you have advance permission, of course. (Some well-known lecturers are syndicated and their contracts prevent personal recordings; however, they often sell tapes of their most popular talks.) Electronic technologies such as television, DVDs, or streaming feeds allow you to "attend" lectures or performances; in fact, close-up camera angles can make you feel like you're sitting in the front row.

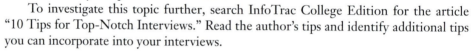

STOP AND CHECK

REVISIT YOUR RESEARCH PLAN

Return to the Practice activities for Chapter 7 on the book website to continue your research plan by completing H to L of the form. You'll be guided through the following steps:

1. Identify personal experiences that can support your ideas. Or identify places such as museums, hospitals, or schools that you might visit.
2. Consider using experts or laypeople for helpful information and plan an interview.
3. Think back on classes you've taken, and identify lecture notes you could use.
4. Look for usable recorded interviews. Public libraries, campus libraries, and media centers usually have taped interviews or lectures on common topics, such as eating disorders. For current topics, look for interviews on television or radio news broadcasts, or search online news outlets such as www.bbc.com or www.cbsnews.com for videos of interviews.

Student Learning: Book Website
This Stop and Check activity can also be found on the book's website, where it's located under "Chapter Resources."

Use Internet Resources

We live in an Information Age in which communication technology—especially the Internet—has multiplied the amount of available information by geometric proportions. In fact, there is so much data online that you could literally spend the rest of your life in front of a computer, skimming a screen full of material every five seconds, and you would never run out of something to read. Rather than either being overwhelmed or simply accepting the available data at face value, you should improve your strategies for doing online research. This section reviews some unique characteristics of the Internet, describes Internet tools, and explores how to evaluate online materials.

Characteristics of the Internet

Hundreds of millions of people log on to this vast communication system that links computers globally. Originally designed for military and scientific purposes, today's Internet can be compared to a road system (the "Information Superhighway") or a huge mall with numerous entrances, information centers, levels, concourses, and specialized areas.[3] Finding credible information online differs from finding reliable resources in a library because the Internet is:

1. *Democratic.* Anyone who can gain access to the Internet can potentially contribute material; however, there's no guarantee the posted information is checked for accuracy. For example, millions of people have their say in online journals called web logs or blogs in which they rant, act as media watchdogs, post opinions, link to related sites, and so on. Thousands of blogs are added daily.[4]
2. *Global.* Documents are available from your town or from around the world.
3. *Up-to-the-minute.* Facts, such as weather information and breaking news, are as close as your computer. In fact, the Internet is especially good for researching current topics.
4. *Interactive.* You can send email messages and join chat groups. If you like, you can play chess at any time of day or night with someone on the other side of the globe.
5. *Free.* Although you may have to pay for Internet access, most of the materials there are free. Fortunately, most public libraries as well as campus libraries and computer centers provide free terminals.[5]

A site with highly screened, reputable material may provide links to unregulated sites. For instance, a serious, well-researched report about a political candidate, accessed at the *Denver Post* online, might have a sidebar link to a forum in which anyone can state an opinion about the same candidate, factually based or not, in complete anonymity. Although the forum may be interesting and even accurate, you'll be more credible if you present data that listeners recognize as coming from quality sources.

Internet Research Tools

If you are new to academic research on the Internet, your best bet is to take an online tutorial. Check at your campus library or writing lab or do a tutorial at a credible, award-winning site such as the University of California Berkeley's Learning Library.[6] Tutorials introduce you to the concepts and skills you need to navigate the Net efficiently. Revisit them whenever you run into a problem.

Of course, an effective Internet search requires some strategies that are not unlike traditional research strategies. The Berkeley Learning Library suggests five search steps:

1. Analyze your topic to decide exactly what you need. Do you want an overview of a subject? Are you looking for specific, specialized words or phrases? Is your topic narrowed and focused?
2. Decide where to start. The Internet provides subject directories (good for overviews), search engines (good for unique words and phrases), and specialized data-

Student Learning: Workbook Activity 7.2, "Internet Research," in the Student Workbook will give students practice using the Internet for research. Activity 7.4 has them evaluate blogs.

bases (good for specialized facts or statistics). Learn the distinctive features of each tool, and plan out where you'll search first. (Each tool is described below.)

3. Jump in. Learn from your successes and your mistakes, and then vary your strategies accordingly.

4. Don't get bogged down or frustrated when your attempts are ineffective. Just try something else.

5. Use what you learn by trial and error to be more effective the next time.

The three general categories of search tools include subject directories, search engines, and searchable databases. A **subject directory** is somewhat like the *Yellow Pages*, where your fingers "walk" to a general category (Health), find a more specific designation (Quacks, Rumors, and Hoaxes), and hone in specifically (Health-Related Hoaxes and Rumors). The Web pages on subject directories are hand-picked by humans, classified by subject, and often annotated. These directories allow you to browse or use fairly broad search terms, because you are searching categories and descriptions; you are not trying to match your terms to specific words on a page. Here are some recommended subject directories:

▌ Librarians' Index to the Internet (**www.lii.org**) links you to websites that librarians carefully select and annotate.

▌ Academic Info (**www.academicinfo.net**) gives you sites chosen primarily for academic research at the undergraduate level.

▌ Yahoo! (**www.yahoo.com**), the biggest and best-known subject directory, differs from the first two in that page authors often supply the annotations themselves.

Search engines are built by computer robot programs (*spiders*), not by human selection. The spiders create a database of full-text Web pages that are linked to other pages already in their database. Information is not categorized by subjects, nor is it rated; there is no "browse" feature. When you type in keywords, the search engine will show you a list of Web pages containing terms that match your search terms. Here are three recommended search engines:

▌ Google (**www.google.com**) is the giant in the field. Its enormous database yields documents according to a popularity ranking, which means the hits are ranked by how many other sites are linked to a particular page. Because Google is so widely used, you should learn to use it well.

▌ Yahoo!Search (**http://search.yahoo.com**) compares favorably to Google in size. This relatively new search engine utilizes up-to-date computer engineering technology that helps block spam from its Web page index.[7]

▌ Teoma (**www.teoma.com**) has a smaller database, but its home page proudly announces, "The Teoma Difference is *Authority*." Teoma ranks the popularity of sites, not simply by the number of links to it, but by the number of links from same-subject pages. Accordingly, it claims to yield hits that are more finely tuned and more precise.

Although search engines can find billions of documents, less than half of the Web documents are searchable on them. The remaining documents, sometimes called the **Invisible Web**, lie in **specialized databases.** Because they are not linked to other Web pages, the spiders can neither "see" nor retrieve them. However, you can use a search engine or subject directory to find databases. For example, search the Librarian's Index to the Internet or Teoma for "Shakespeare database" or "genealogy database" or "searchable database," or explore The Invisible Web Directory (**www.invisible-web.net**), which provides resources that are "informative, of high quality, and contain worthy information from reliable information providers."[8] Most resources on databases are free, but some charge small fees or require you to register before you can access their information.

Hang Gliding at Kitty Hawk

Figure 7.1a and 1b
**Content Differences
by Domain**
The Raven Sky Sports site
is sponsored by a commer-
cial enterprise; compare
that site with the official
United States Hang Gliding
Association site on hang
gliding.

Evaluating Internet Resources

Because powerful search tools can overwhelm you
with information, you might be tempted to take the
material that is easiest to access and get on with your
life; however, it's better to exercise critical judgment
about each source and its content.[9]

Source   Before you even select a document to
open, carefully examine its URL (uniform resource
locator). Does it appear to be someone's personal
page? Is it a page from a commercial provider such
as aol.com? The **domain** suffixes indicate the pro-
vider's primary purpose and tax status. The most common are educational (.edu), commercial (.com), government (.gov), military (.mil), nonprofit organization (.org), and foreign (.ca for Canada, .jp for Japan, and so on). Ask yourself which domain is most reliable
for your particular topic. Ask who or what entity published the page. (For example, **www
.cdc.gov** means the entity is a government website hosted by the CDC or Centers for Disease Control.) Decide if the entity supports your subject well, and choose links that seem
the most appropriate, given your topic. Figures 7.1a and 7.1b show two Web pages about
the same subject that differ by domain; the first is commercial, the second is not.

After you link onto the Web page, look for information about the author, institution, organization, or agency that accepts responsibility for the material on the site. If
this is not immediately apparent, look for a home page or follow links such as "about us,"
"philosophy," or "background" that might provide information about the page's author.
Take care to distinguish between primary or secondary, expert or peer sources.

Content   Look for a site rating. Outside teams often evaluate a site to determine how
complete, current, and thorough its coverage of a topic is. They also look at how the

**Classroom Discussion/
Activity**
http://museumofhoaxes.com/
hoaxsites.html
http://www.snopes.com/
The information on the Internet is not always credible.
How can we determine if a
site on the Internet is an appropriate source of supporting material? Ask students
to visit the Museum of
Hoaxes or the Urban Legends
Reference pages and come
prepared to discuss their
favorite hoax.

domain the type of site such
as .com, .edu, or .org

material is organized to assess whether or not the site is user friendly. However, a rating, although helpful, does not guarantee that the site provides accurate or high-quality materials, and lack of a rating doesn't automatically mean the site is not useful or authoritative. Do your own rating based on these tips:

1. *Determine the intent or purpose of the site.* Pages don't just spring up on the Internet. People put them there intentionally. So ask if the page is designed to inform, to entertain, or to sway opinion. Who is its intended audience?

2. *Look for bias.* Does the material emphasize a particular perspective, or is it relatively objective? Is it free of gender or ethnic stereotyping? Does the creator or sponsor have a personal or commercial goal? Does the source have an established position on the topic?

3. *Check timeliness.* Is the information (especially factual or statistical data) up to date? Is the site maintained regularly? Look for the latest update.

4. *Assess accuracy.* Is the material similar to what you find in other credible sources? Would reputable sources accept the ideas as plausible and accurate? Look for links. Do linked sites appear to be reputable? Does the document list its sources? Its methodology?

5. *Assess originality.* Many sites use material from other sources, and they sometimes plagiarize. For example, the same article from the *Columbia Encyclopedia* about the artist Dante Gabriel Rossetti appears on factmonster.com, answers.com, yahooligans.yahoo.com, and other sites that credit the encyclopedia. However, slider.com and canvas-prints.com both plagiarize by presenting the same article with no source citation.

6. *Finally, consider organization.* If you must decide between two sites that appear to be equal in accuracy and quality of information, choose the one that is better organized and easier to use.[10]

For example, a Google search for the topic "medical misinformation" turned up thousands of documents, including the following:

▶ "Medical Misinformation on the Information Superhighway," by CNN Food and Health News. CNN is well known for its reporting on medical news, but this article is dated August 30, 1995. Millions of Web pages have been added to the Internet since then; still, the report does contain some valid principles for evaluating medical information on the Internet.

▶ "Charlatans, Leeches, and Old Wives: Medical Misinformation," by Susan Detweiler of the Detweiler Group. *Searcher, 9(3),* March 2001. The home site for this journal is Information Today, Inc., a site for users and producers of electronic information services. It provides a great deal of data, including phone numbers, addresses, and email addresses of the organization as well as the author.

▶ "Second Opinions," by Barry Groves, Ph.D. (This site has .uk—United Kingdom—in the URL). A link, "about Barry Groves," provides information that helps you decide if he's credible. He was trained as an electronics engineer and served in the British Royal Air Force. He became interested in food and diets, and earned a Ph.D. in nutritional science. He has been published in some credible journals.

▶ "Doctor in the Mouse," by Natasha Wallace, is a newspaper article in *The Age* (Australia). Wallace uses creative words such as *cyberquackery* (people who pretend to be doctors online) and *cyberchondria* (the "Internet disease" or the "printout syndrome"). Wallace shows that the issue is global in scope. She also provides interesting examples, interviews with experts, and statistics.

▶ Urban Legends and Folklore. This site provides many amusing examples that would add interest to a speech on the topic.

Because Internet research is potentially satisfying and frustrating as well, use your critical thinking abilities whenever you log onto the Internet. More detail about critical analysis is found in Quianna Clay's outline at the end of this chapter; her speech deals with medical misinformation on the Internet.

STOP AND CHECK
CRITICAL THINKING AND THE INTERNET

Although the Internet is wonderful, use it with care. Alongside the verifiable facts and research data, texts of 19th-century British novels, and pictures of Roman architecture, you'll find commercials and papers for sale and rumors and opinions that you cannot verify because many Internet contributors are anonymous and not accountable.

1. Use the guidelines provided above to assess the reliability of the following sites about hang gliding. That is, evaluate the source and the content (the purpose, bias, timeliness, accuracy, and organization) of information you find on an organizational site for hang gliding, available at www.ushga.org, and on a specific commercial site such as www.hanggliding.com.
2. Then go to www.whitehouse.gov, and read the biographical information you find there about the president of the United States. Assess the content. What is the purpose, the bias, the timeliness, and the accuracy of this biographical information? Use a subject directory such as www.yahoo.com and search for the president by name. Follow at least one link and, using the same tests for site content, compare the biographical information you find there with the information the White House presents.
3. Of the sites you reviewed in activities 1 and 2, which materials are more apt to be verifiable? Which features more expert contributions? Which materials were probably not screened or edited? What are the strengths and limitations of each type of material? That is, when would you be likely to use each source effectively?

Sometimes you will find hoax sites that look legitimate, but are really prank Web pages that mimic and poke fun at the real thing. For example, type .net instead of .gov in the White House Internet address and you will find a prank site set up to look official.
You can access these links and answer these questions on the book website.

Use the Library and Online Resources

Libraries contain a variety of materials, including printed matter, pictures, maps, video and audio recordings in various formats, research works such as indexes, and specialized databases. Library resources have academic credibility because of the number of screenings the materials undergo before they are acquired. Book publishers employ editors and reviewers to validate each manuscript. Magazine and newspaper editors screen articles and use fact checkers to catch and correct errors. However, library materials still require critical evaluation. You'd expect to find opinions on editorial pages and in syndicated columns, but you must watch for unsupported statements, wherever they may be. Specific publications often have a bias, which they sometimes state forthrightly: The *New Republic* proclaims its liberal bias, for example, and the *National Review* proudly labels itself conservative. Other publications and books have an unstated bias that you must discern. This is one reason your instructor asks you to consult several sources.

Almost all college libraries have converted to Online Public Access Catalogs (**OPAC**s).[11] Although the catalogs are computerized, they reflect a mindset carried over from the days of card catalogs. For example, the average librarian is a baby boomer, but the average OPAC user comes from the "Google generation."[12] Googlers tend to approach OPACs with tools that they use for Web surfing.[13] On the Internet, they type in a few search terms, and expect the search engine to come up with numerous hits. Google also suggests spelling alternatives, and it adjusts to abbreviations.

OPACs online public access catalogs

© Tom Stewart/CORBIS

Library books, magazines, and newspapers have a measure of academic respectability because of the selection process they undergo before they appear on the shelves.

Online catalogs, however, are less flexible. They use controlled vocabulary, not natural language. Consequently, doing a keyword or author search is usually more effective than doing a subject search, because subject terms are often highly specific.[14] For example, to find material on the Civil War, it seems logical to search for "civil war," but if you do, you'll end up with data about civil conflicts in ancient Greece, 19th-century Bolivia, and 21st-century Sudan. Instead, look for "United States—History—1861—1865—battles." OPACs require correct spelling and typing with no abbreviations.

If you have not done so already, spend some time becoming familiar with your library's cataloging system; however, the research principles discussed next are applicable to many systems.

Books

Each library book is cataloged by subject, author, title, and key words. For example, Sally McClain's book about the Navajo code talkers is found under the author ("McClain, Sally"), the title (*Navajo Weapon: The Navajo Code Talkers*), and the subject ("Native Americans, Navajo"). Key words include *Navajo* and *Code Talkers* and *encryption*.

Look carefully at the copyright date in the front of the book and in the catalog information. For topics such as bicycle helmets or AIDS medications, up-to-date materials are essential. However, a subject such as *honesty* draws from philosophical, religious, and cultural traditions that go back thousands of years, and books written in 1910 may still be useful.

Many free full-text books, especially classics or books in the public domain, are now available online; to access them easily, search for "online books" or browse through sites such as http://digital.library.upenn.edu/books/, www.gutenberg.org, or www.bartleby.com.

The Reference Section

Student Learning: Book Website
All URLs mentioned in the text are available as live, regularly maintained links on the book's website, located in the "Chapter Resources" list under "Web Links."

What was the murder rate in New York City in 2005? Who were the signers of the Declaration of Independence? When was the Taj Mahal built? To help you find specific information quickly, libraries contain hundreds of reference works such as encyclopedias, dictionaries, and sources for statistics.

general encyclopedia text that collects and summarizes information on a wide array of topics

specialized encyclopedia text that summarizes information in specific subject areas

Encyclopedias **General encyclopedias,** such as the *Encyclopedia Americana* and *Collier's Encyclopedia*, review and summarize information on thousands of topics. They provide a helpful overview early in your research. The *Encyclopedia Britannica* is especially useful for international topics. An encyclopedia's index will guide you to related subjects, and bibliographies at the end of articles suggest other sources of information. Many encyclopedias are available online, some for a fee; however, libraries often pay the fees so that you can freely access the information.

In addition to general encyclopedias, hundreds of **specialized encyclopedias** provide information about specific subjects. If you want to know about a particular bird, look in the *Encyclopedia of Birds*. Psychological depression? There is a whole encyclopedia on the topic. How about the *Encyclopedia of American Indian Costume*, or one on world pop music? Use your judgment to evaluate the publication date for specialized encyclopedias.

One about world pop music will be rapidly outdated, but one about birds can remain useful for decades.

Encyclopedias, such as *Grolier's Multimedia Encyclopedia*, are available on CD-ROMs, and some are loaded onto personal computers. In addition to articles, they feature sound clips, speeches, movie segments, and thousands of visuals.

Dictionaries   The most familiar type of **dictionary** provides definitions, historical sources, synonyms, and antonyms for words. If your computer's software program has a built-in dictionary, simply type in a word and the definition and pronunciation will appear on your monitor. In addition, you can find specialized dictionaries in the reference section, including ones devoted only to pianists, psychotherapy, or American slang.

Sources for Statistics   Consult the *Statistical Abstracts of the United States* (a government document) for U.S. statistics on a wide variety of topics, including population, health, education, crime, government finance, employment, elections, the environment, and defense. The *Abstract* shows historical trends as well as current statistics. Almanacs, such as the *World Almanac*, also provide statistical information.

> ### DIVERSITY IN PRACTICE
> ### RESEARCH IN KENYA
>
> DIFFERENT CULTURAL GROUPS have different traditions regarding research. For instance, Kenyan students described typical speech preparation in their culture:
>
> ▶ "Audiences in the African context do not expect researched and memorized speeches, but speeches compiled spontaneously and using the speaker's wisdom."
> ▶ "Public speaking in Africa is not . . . something that someone will spend a week researching."
> ▶ "In the African context there are less rules to follow, or at least the emphasis is not as much as it is in the West."[15]
>
> Kenyan students, however, noted that research and preparation is becoming more common in their country.
>
> Even within the United States, the type of research described in this chapter is not required for every speech. (Examples include the narrative speeches described in Chapter 15 and some of the special occasion speeches described in Appendix B.)

Reference Materials on the Web   Millions of reference materials are available on the Internet. Here are some suggestions for using these resources:

▶ Check out www.refdesk.com, an amazing site with links to hundreds of reference materials.
▶ Link to "reference" under "Web directory" at www.yahoo.com to find encyclopedias, dictionaries, books of quotations, and statistical sources.
▶ Access *Merriam-Webster OnLine* at www.m-w.com/dictionary.htm or link to the *American Heritage Dictionary* at www.bartleby.com/61/.
▶ For statistics, try the site that advertises itself as the "gateway to statistics from over 100 U.S. Federal agencies," www.fedstats.gov.
▶ The U.S. Census Bureau's Web page is located at www.census.gov. This user-friendly, reliable site records each new birth automatically; consequently, population figures are updated regularly.[16]
▶ Be cautious about online reference works. For example, **Wikipedia** is a new style of encyclopedia, launched in 2001, that provides free articles about thousands of topics.

Teaching Tip
http://www.bartelby.com/reference/
Bartleby.com offers many online references, including recent editions of the Columbia Encyclopedia, the World Factbook, and books of quotations.
http://www.ipl.org/div/reading/
The "Reading Room" at the University of Michigan's Internet Public Library provides links to websites of newspapers and magazines around the world.

dictionary text that provides definitions and other information about words or terms

Wikipedia the online encyclopedia created by Internet users

Currently, it's available in 195 languages.[17] Its major innovation is that it features "community-generated knowledge";[18] anyone (you included!) can contribute an original article or correct or add to someone else's work. **Wiktionary** is its dictionary counterpart. The *Wall Street Journal* called this a "free-for-all approach to editing";[19] and, although it is often reliable, accuracy is not guaranteed. As a result, your instructor may insist that you choose other sources with established credibility instead.

Periodicals

Periodicals are issued once per time period—weekly, monthly, quarterly, or annually. They range from popular or general interest magazines like *Time*, *Sports Illustrated*, and *MacLean's* (Canada) to more specialized periodicals such as *Hiker's World* or *Vital Speeches of the Day*. Popular magazines are generally easy to understand, and they contain contemporary examples, up-to-date statistics, illustrations, and quotations from both experts and laypeople.

Libraries also house **trade** and **professional journals,** such as the *Quarterly Journal of Speech* or the *Journal of Nonverbal Behavior*, which contain topics of interest to people in specific occupations and the research findings of scholars writing in academic areas. Some journal articles may be too technical for classroom speeches; others, however, may provide excellent materials.

You'll find current issues of periodicals on file and older issues archived, often on microfiche or microfilm, if not in digital format. These storage devices require specialized machines, but they usually have a print capability so that you can copy useful articles. Currently, most major magazines and many scholarly journals are also on the Internet, and you can easily download and print a hard copy of articles that you need. The Info-Trac College Edition database also provides articles from thousands of magazines and journals.

The *Congressional Digest: The Pro-and-Con Monthly* is an especially helpful periodical for researching controversial topics. Each issue presents multiple viewpoints on a single issue like overtime pay, global warming, or crack cocaine. For example, an issue on highway funding provides a timeline of federal highway legislation, explains the Highway Trust Fund, and assesses the status of U.S. highways and transit systems. It then identifies relevant subtopics and summarizes the proposed highway funding bill. Finally, it presents pro and con arguments about the bill made by members of Congress.

An annual index presents titles and subjects from 1921 to the present. More helpful are the detailed tables of contents for topics covered from 1981 to the present. When you need to understand both sides of an issue, save valuable time by consulting this source early.

Newspapers

Newspapers generally cover current events in greater depth than radio or television news broadcasts. You'll find articles on current issues and events, along with opinion pieces by editors, syndicated columnists, and readers who submit letters to the editor. Newspapers typically print humorous articles, obituaries, human interest pieces, and critical evaluations of movies, plays, books, art exhibits, and musical performances.

Daily, weekly, and monthly newspapers range in size from metropolitan papers with international circulation to small student papers. Some are specifically targeted toward various cultural and ethnic groups (see the Diversity in Practice box for more on this). A few are dubbed the "elite media" because of their reputation for high-quality, detailed reporting; "elite" papers include the *New York Times*, the *Washington Post*, and the *Los Angeles Times*. Papers with smaller circulation often use their stories. Most school libraries carry at least one elite paper, and they are all available over the Internet. The website **www.refdesk.com/paper.html** links to thousands of local, national, and international papers; see if you can find your hometown paper there.

Classroom Discussion/ Activity
Bring examples of several types of periodicals to class. Discuss which would be best for researching various topics. Have small groups practice using periodicals for research.

Wiktionary the online dictionary created by Internet users

periodicals magazines or journals issued at regular intervals

trade or professional journals journals that pertain to specific occupations or areas of academic research

The *New York Times* reprints many primary documents, such as the president's State of the Union address, in part or in whole. Look there for excerpts of testimony given at Senate hearings, presidential remarks made at press conferences, and majority and dissenting opinions on significant Supreme Court decisions. The *Times*, along with many other major newspapers, is included in the InfoTrac College Edition database.

Indexes

An easy way to locate articles from scholarly journals, popular magazines, and newspapers is to use indexes. Look in books or in computerized databases, such as the *ERIC* index for the field of education. The *Readers' Guide to Periodical Literature* is invaluable for locating articles in popular magazines from 1900 to the present; its editors list each article in alphabetical order by subject, author, and title. Also indexed are broad topics with a number of subheadings, as this sample entry found under *Golf* demonstrates:

> *Tournaments—Ethical aspects*
> Quiet, Please [Heckling at golf tournaments] J. Dodson, il *Golf Magazine* v46 no10 p143-4 O 2004.

Each entry gives the title, author's name, magazine, volume, page number, and date. The "il" indicates that the story is illustrated.

Use key words to search a computerized index. Many of the resulting hits will have an *abstract* (brief summary) that helps you decide which articles are worth looking up. For example, while researching his speech on the Promise Keepers (men who publicly pledge to be faithful husbands and fathers), Diego typed in both "Promise Keepers" and "Men's Movement." He skimmed abstracts from more than twenty articles, marked those that seemed suitable, printed the references he'd marked, and then went to the magazines and journals to read the articles.

Major newspapers also provide tools for locating specific articles. The *New York Times Index*, for example, provides the date, page, and column location of almost every news article that has appeared in its pages since 1851. Each annual index lists articles alphabetically under one of four types of headings: subject, geographic name, organization, and personal name. Since 1962, the foreword has summarized each year's important events. The index itself is a source of information for brief answers to questions such as "Is the teenage birth rate rising or falling?" or "How many rhinoceroses are left in the wild?"

Teaching Tip
ERIC, PsyINFO, and ComAbstracts are all very useful indexes for researching speech topics. Find out which indexes your university subscribes to and provide students with information on how to find them and use them.

> DIVERSITY IN PRACTICE
> ## INTERNATIONAL AND ETHNIC PRESSES
>
> MANY LIBRARIES carry newspapers from around the world, and many more are available on the Internet. These papers allow you to gain different perspectives and to hear voices other than those found in local or national sources. Check out *World Press Review*, a monthly magazine that prints excerpts of translated materials from international papers; its editors identify the bias of each source as conservative, liberal, or moderate. Also look for diverse perspectives within the United States, such as organized labor, African Americans, gays and lesbians, Catholics, and Muslims, which all publish periodicals from their perspectives.
>
> If your library doesn't subscribe to the periodicals you need, go to InfoTrac College Edition and check its list of journal names; you'll find a wide variety of diverse perspectives there. Or check out www.refdesk.com or yahoo.com, which provide links to thousands of newspapers and magazines, including alternative, regional, and international periodicals.

(continued)

Teaching Tip
Emphasize to students the importance of having hard copies of all their research findings, both for their protection and for future research. Remind them that websites may be updated daily, and what they find one day might be gone the next. The only proof they have that it was ever there is their printed copy.

Record Your Information

Obviously you won't remember everything you discover during your search, so you need a strategy for recording your findings, avoiding cut-and-paste plagiarism, and citing sources properly. Then, when you sit down to organize your speech, you will have the necessary information at your fingertips and can easily classify your ideas into themes and patterns. There are three common methods for recording information: note cards, photocopies or printouts, and mind maps. Choose the ones that match your learning style or your topic, but always list your sources at the end of your outline, using a standard bibliographic format.

Write Note Cards

With all the technology now available to copy and print materials, why would anyone write information on index cards or note cards? This method actually has several advantages: It is probably the most structured way to do research; the cards are small enough to handle easily; you can cite your sources directly on each card; and you can easily classify your information. Better yet, cards can help you avoid cut-and-paste plagiarism because it's easier to jot down key ideas and summarize the material than to copy long paragraphs. (See Chapter 3.) For this reason, we'll look at this method first. There are two basic kinds of note cards: source cards and information cards.

Source Cards

Begin by making a separate **source card** for each reference, using a standard bibliographic format. Include the author, date, article or chapter title, book or periodical title, place of publication (for books), followed by the page number(s). For Internet sites, add the title of the website, the sponsoring organization, the date you retrieved the information, and the website's URL. It is helpful to **annotate** your bibliography, meaning that you write a brief description of the information you found in the book, article, or website. Make source cards for materials gathered from interviews and films as well. See Figure 7.2 for an example.

Information Cards

Next, write down important data, using a separate **information card** for each idea, statistic, quotation, example, and so on. Use quotation marks around every direct quotation and each uniquely worded phrase, and write down the page number each piece of information is from, whether directly quoted or not. This practice will help you avoid plagiarism.

On the top of each card, create a heading that classifies the information into a category you might later use as a main point. Also, label the card with an abbreviated source citation so that when you use the material in the speech, you can cite its source. Figure 7.3 shows examples of information cards.

The advantage of this method is that you can separate your cards into piles and move them around, placing your major point at the top and arranging your supporting information below. You can easily change the order of your points and your relevant supporting materials before writing your outline.

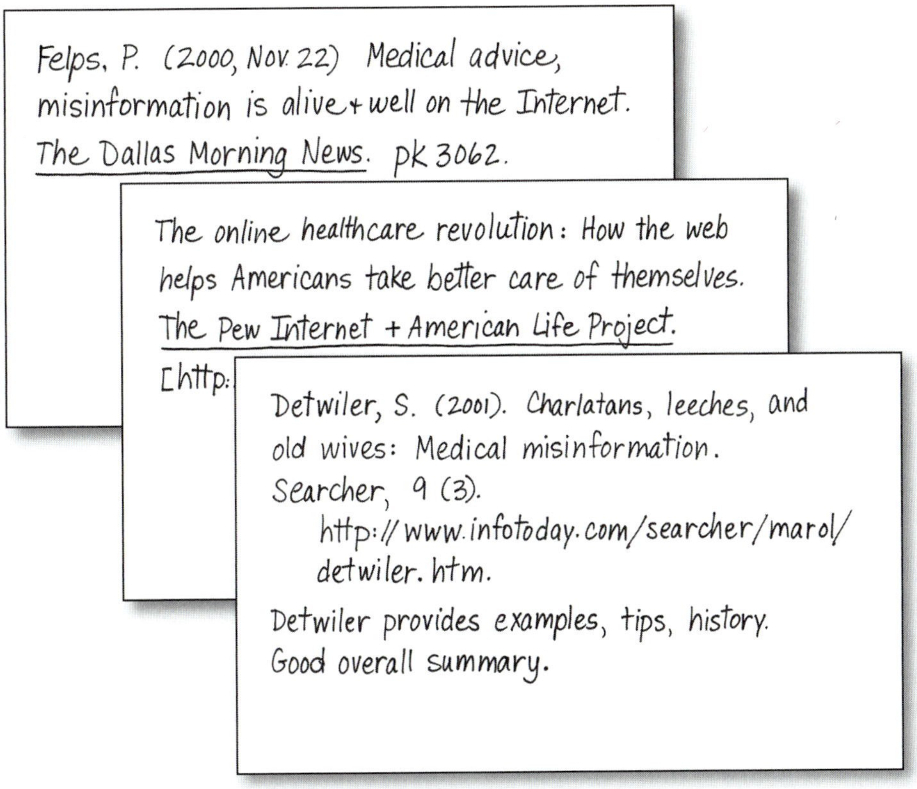

Felps, P. (2000, Nov. 22) Medical advice, misinformation is alive + well on the Internet. The Dallas Morning News. pk 3062.

The online healthcare revolution: How the web helps Americans take better care of themselves. The Pew Internet + American Life Project. [http:

*Detwiler, S. (2001). Charlatans, leeches, and old wives: Medical misinformation. Searcher, 9 (3).
http://www.infotoday.com/searcher/marol/detwiler.htm.
Detwiler provides examples, tips, history. Good overall summary.*

Figure 7.2
Source Cards
Source cards contain bibliographic information. Annotated cards also include a brief summary of the material found in the source.

source cards cards used to record bibliographic information

annotate to summarize a book or article's contents on a source card

information card card for recording and categorizing important data

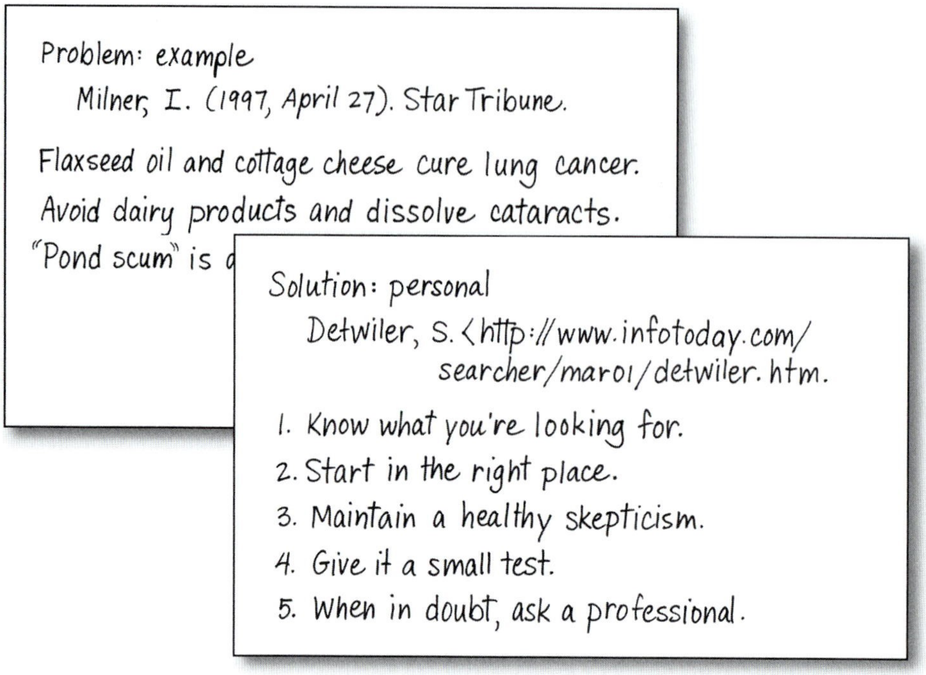

Figure 7.3
Information Cards
Use a different information
card for each source, and
classify each card according to the major idea the
information supports.
Include an abbreviated
source citation, including
the page number, on
each card.

**Instructor Resource:
PowerPoint**
The *Multimedia Manager
with Instructor Resources*
CD-ROM includes PowerPoint
slides of Figures 7.2 and 7.3.

Problem: example
    Milner, I. (1997, April 27). Star Tribune.

Flaxseed oil and cottage cheese cure lung cancer.
Avoid dairy products and dissolve cataracts.
"Pond scum" is

Solution: personal
    Detwiler, S. < http://www.infotoday.com/
                        searcher/mar01/detwiler.htm.

1. Know what you're looking for.
2. Start in the right place.
3. Maintain a healthy skepticism.
4. Give it a small test.
5. When in doubt, ask a professional.

Photocopy or Print Your Materials

There are many advantages of photocopying material or downloading and printing it directly from the Internet. Printing out the Internet article instead of downloading it to an
electronic file makes cut-and-paste plagiarism easier to avoid. Both methods are quick,
easy, and readily available, and you will have the entire resource in front of you when you
sit down to write your outline. Downloaded materials usually have source information
on the printout, but also make sure the source (in standard bibliographic form) is on your
photocopies. Then, use highlighters to mark major ideas and salient information.

For example, consider the speech topic "medical misinformation on the Internet."
Quianna photocopies pages from books and newspapers and supplements them with articles downloaded and printed out from the Internet. She next writes entire reference on
each page. Then, using one color for major points and a second color for examples and
quotations, she highlights the material relevant to her subject. When she is ready to organize and outline her ideas, she spreads out her photocopied and highlighted articles
and weaves the materials together into a coherent speech.

When you copy materials, you are using the intellectual property of another person
who has a right to profit from its use, so you are obligated to credit your sources. Fortunately, the **Fair Use provision** in the federal Copyright Act allows you to print and use
materials for nonprofit educational purposes; therefore, photocopying materials for one-
time speech research is within your legal rights as a student.[20]

Create a Mind Map

Fair Use provision the provision in the federal Copyright Act that allows free use
of materials for educational
and research purposes

If your learning style is more holistic, consider making a mind map. Chapter 6 showed
how to create mind maps to generate speech topics, and you can use a similar process to
record, subdivide, and categorize information. Although there is no single "right" way to
create a mind map, you can follow some general principles. First, identify your subject
in the center of the page, using a diagram or drawing. Write your major points around

the subject, and draw a line from each main point to the center. Identify further subtopics and connect each one to the main point it supports. For example, a mind map of Jill's speech on the benefits of pet ownership (outlined at the end of Chapter 6), might have a dog or cat drawn in the middle of the page, with lines radiating out to three major points: health benefits, psychological benefits, and family benefits. Each point would then have supporting material linked to it. If you have a lot of material, you can make a separate page for each major point. But always list your sources. If there is room, write references directly onto your mind map; however, if space is limited, make source cards or list your references on a separate piece of paper. Figure 7.4 shows a mind map about medical misinformation.

Medical Misinformation

The Problem

- Examples
  - flaxseed oil/cottage cheese cure lung cancer (Beckwith)
  - pond scum = appetite suppressant (Light Force Spirulina)
  - Rhythmic coughing during ♡ attack can keep you alive (Susan Detwiler)

- Statistics
  - Internet global village numbers 888 million
  - 93 million Americans have used Internet to get medical information (Pew Internet + American Life Project)
  - 83% in an international survey used Internet for medical search (Wallace)

- Quotations
  - "The Internet is the greatest collection of misinformation about health the world has ever known." (Professor Branko Cesnik, Monash University quoted in Wallace)

The Solution

- Causes
  - Lack of accountability
  - No editors, other scientists are required to review the findings
  - Clerical staff or PR people may create the web pages — not researchers (Koralage)
  - Many consumers don't critically analyze site
  - Anyone with computer and modem can create them

- Health on the Net Foundation Code HONcode (www.hon.ca)
  1. Transparency of Sponsorship
  2. Authority
  3. Attribution
  4. Justifiability

- Government agencies
  - FDA should develop guidelines similar to FDA standards for regulating pharmaceuticals

- Personal
  1. Determine if credible
  2. Look for names/credentials
  3. Be a "cyberskeptic"
  4. Internet Health Watch site
  5. Confirm with your doctor

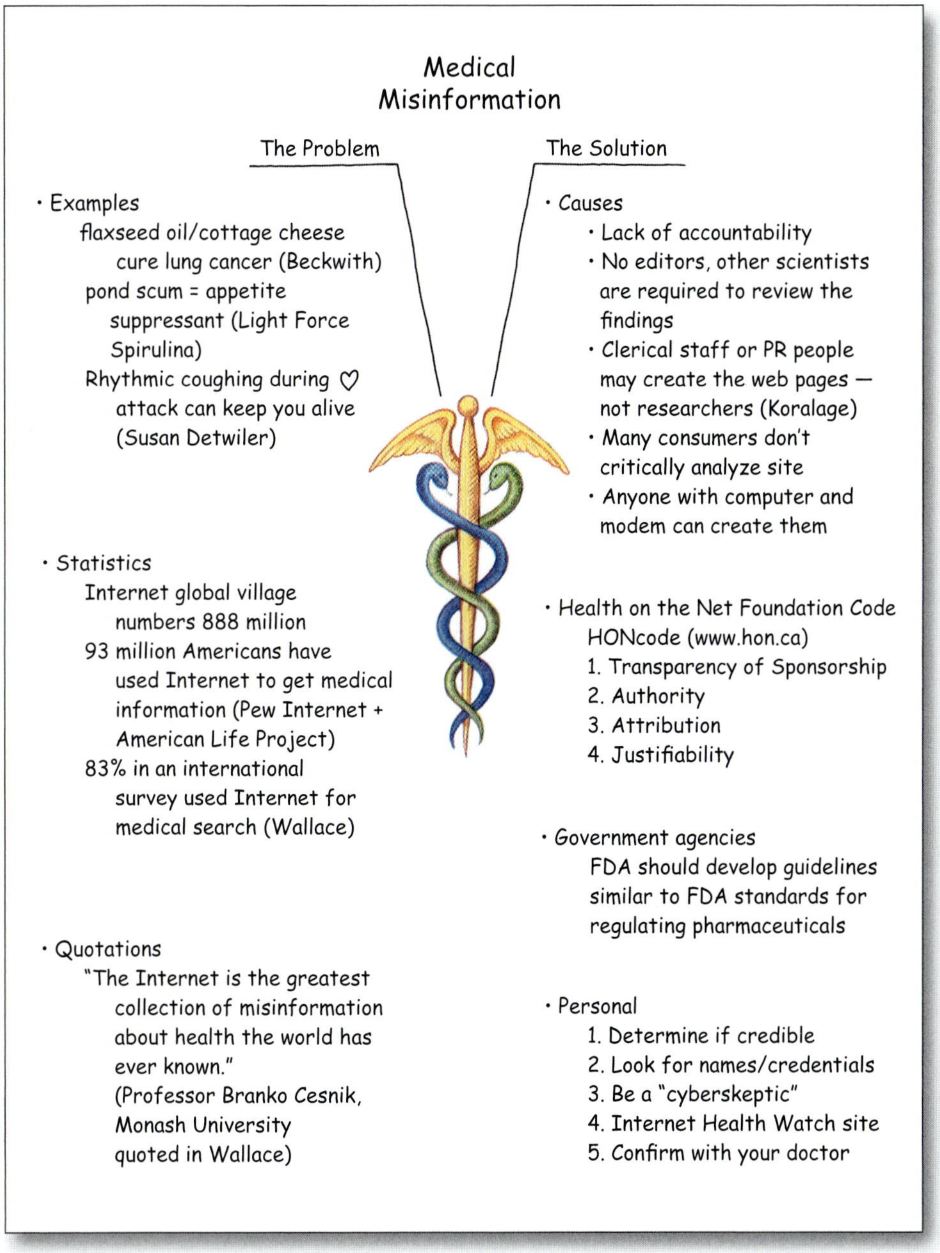

Instructor Resource: PowerPoint
The *Multimedia Manager with Instructor Resources* CD-ROM includes a Power-Point slide of Figure 7.4.

Figure 7.4
Mind Map for Information
If you are a visual thinker, consider creating a mind map to record your information.

Teaching Tip
http://www.wisc.edu/
writetest/Handbook/
Documentation.html
The Writing Center at the
University of Wisconsin–
Madison provides samples of
citations for various kinds of
sources in APA and MLA (as
well as other) styles.

Use a Standard Format to Cite Your Sources

To avoid plagiarism and build and maintain credibility, credit each source by listing it in a bibliography at the end of your outline. Alphabetize your sources using the standard bibliographic format found in the style or publication manual your instructor recommends. The reference section of your library has many popular style manuals, including ones from the American Psychological Association (APA) and the Modern Language Association (MLA). Check your school's library site for guidelines or search online for the APA manual (**www.apastyle.org/pubmanual.html**) or MLA manual (**www.mla.org/style**). They provide excellent examples of all kinds of bibliographic citations, often furnished by professors and librarians. The basic elements of any source citation include the author(s), title, place of publication, and date published.

You can see that an important element of research is recording information so that it is readily available when you put your speech together. If you like a structured, linear method, note cards may be your best choice. If you approach the research task holistically, you might download or photocopy your materials and use highlighters to identify important information. If you are a visual thinker, you could make mind maps, using images as well as words to record your findings. Whatever method you choose, always use a standard bibliographic format to list your sources alphabetically. Return to the case study at the beginning of the chapter and identify the ways Luke and Jonathan recorded their information. What advice could you give that would help each one improve his recording strategies?

STOP AND CHECK

COMPLETE YOUR RESEARCH PLAN

Return to your research plan on the book's website, and complete sections M to P. Make any other alterations that seem justified in light of what you have learned in this chapter.

**Student Learning:
Book Website**
This Stop and Check activity
can also be found on the
book's website, where it's
located under "Chapter
Resources."

Student Workbook
Students can complete "Before You Take the Exam" in
Chapter 7 of the Student
Workbook for a review of the
chapter.

**Student Learning:
Book Website**
Under "Chapter Resources,"
students will find several
tools for reviewing the information in this chapter, including a "Tutorial Quiz." You
could also have them email
the results of this quiz to you
as a participation or extra-
credit activity.

Summary

Part of your competence in speechmaking is your ability to gather information. To be more effective, set aside plenty of time to explore your topic, and use a research plan that is appropriate for the subject. Distinguish between primary sources—original documents and other firsthand information—and secondary sources, which interpret, explain, and evaluate the subject. You can find both primary and secondary materials in interviews and in print sources such as books, periodicals, and newspapers, both in traditional libraries and online. Consider also the wide variety of visual and recorded materials that are available. Throughout your research, seek out diverse perspectives from a variety of viewpoints.

Through the Internet, you can access literally millions of documents from local, national, and global sources—some highly credible, others useless. Use a subject directory to look up general topics. If you need information on specific or unusual topics or if you're looking for specific phrases, use a text index. Sift through the materials you find by evaluating each source and the purpose, bias, timeliness, accuracy, originality, and organization of each site's content. Consistently record your findings, using a method that meets your learning style preferences, such as source and information cards, photocopying, and making a mind map. Whatever your method, avoid plagiarism by crediting your sources in your notes, in your speech, and on the bibliography that accompanies your outline. Use a standard source citation form that you can find in a style manual.

STUDY AND REVIEW

The premium website for *Public Speaking* offers a broad range of resources that will help you better understand the material in this chapter, complete assignments, and succeed on tests. The website features

▶ Speech videos with critical viewing questions, speech outlines, and transcripts, and
▶ Interactive practice activities, self quizzes, and a sample final exam.

For more information about this text's electronic learning resources, consult your **Guide to Online Resources for Public Speaking** or visit http://communication.wadsworth.com/jaffe5.

KEY TERMS

The terms below are defined in the margins throughout this chapter. The book's website also provides interactive flashcards and crossword puzzles to help you learn these terms and the concepts they represent.

reference librarian 109	domain 115
subject librarian 109	OPAC 117
primary sources 110	general encyclopedias 118
original documents 110	specialized encyclopedias 118
creative works 110	dictionary 119
relics or artifacts 110	Wikipedia 119
secondary sources 110	Wiktionary 120
expert 111	periodicals 120
laypeople or peers 111	trade or professional journals 120
subject directory 114	source card 123
search engine 114	annotate 123
Invisible Web 114	information card 123
specialized databases 114	Fair Use provision 124

APPLICATION AND CRITICAL THINKING EXERCISES

The exercises below are among the practice activities on the book's website.

1. Read the cover story from a current magazine like *Time* or *Newsweek*. Make a list of all the experts and laypeople quoted in the article. Compare and contrast the type of information given by each type of source.
2. For more information about the Internet's history and use, explore the information found at www.isoc.org/internet/history, a site sponsored by the Internet Society (ISOC).
3. To learn more about finding credible information on the Internet, do a Google search for "Internet tutorial." Read the material on at least two of the hits. Compare and contrast the two sites in terms of source and content, following the guidelines on pages 115–117. Which site would you recommend to others in your class?
4. If you have not already done so, visit your campus library. Locate and browse the reference books, the newspapers and periodicals, and the indexes and the guides to their use.
5. If your library provides handouts with instructions for using your campus library, make a file containing the ones you'll use most often, and consult these during your research. (Examples: HOW TO: Locate U.S. Government Documents; HOW TO: Cite References According to the APA Manual; Periodicals Collection: A Service Guide.) Or search your library's online resources for information about research and recording information.

6. Make a list of library resources that provide diverse perspectives. That is, discover the resources your library has in international, ethnic, and alternative newspapers and magazines. Read an article in at least one of the resources.

7. To understand the variety and number of specialized encyclopedias and dictionaries on the Internet, do a Google search for "encyclopedia of" and "dictionary of" and list at least 10 titles in each category that may someday be useful to you. Bring your lists to class and discuss your findings with a small group of your classmates.

8. Set aside an hour to explore newspapers and magazines on the Internet. Try www.refdesk.com/paper.html for links to many news sites, or check Google news for information about current events. With your classmates, select an interesting, significant current event and surf around, clicking on links related to that event. Then, discuss the value as well as the drawbacks of doing research over the Internet.

9. Browse several weblogs (www.blogwise.com links you to thousands). Assess the quality and bias of the blog. Why or when might you use a blog? Why or when might you avoid them?

10. As a class, research a current event or an issue. Go to the library and find and photo-copy a print article, or download information from a website. If possible, interview an expert or layperson. Some students should consult mainstream sources and others should seek out diverse perspectives. Bring your information to the next class meeting, and discuss and evaluate the various sources and data by determining the purpose, the source bias, the timeliness, the accuracy, and the organization of the material.

11. Think about the three ways to record information presented in this chapter. Which method— note cards, photocopies, or mind maps— will you most likely use? Which are you least likely to use? When might you combine methods? Discuss your research style with a classmate.

SPEECH VIDEO

Log on the book website to watch and evaluate the sample speeches that are research-based. Also, watch this speech by Quianna Clay and read the accompanying commentary.

Student Outline with Commentary

MEDICAL MISINFORMATION ON THE INTERNET
Quianna Clay

General Purpose: To persuade

Specific Purpose: To persuade my audience that medical information on the Internet is often faulty but they can protect themselves by being critical consumers.

Central Idea: The Internet contains a plethora of medical misinformation that has several causes, but foundations, the government, and consumers can help solve the problem.

Introduction

I. Did you know that flaxseed oil and cottage cheese can cure cancer, that pond scum can suppress your appetite, and that rhythmic coughing during a heart attack can keep you alive (Beckwith, 2001; Light Force Spirulina, 2005; Detwiler, 2001)?

II. We might laugh at these examples, but people can get poor, even deadly, information online.

  A. According to the Pew Internet and American Life Project, ninety-three million Americans have used the Internet to get medical information (Fox & Fallows, 2003).

  B. However, Monash University's Professor Branko Cesnik cautions, "The Internet is the greatest collection of misinformation about health the world has ever known" (Wallace, 2002).

III. Today we will explore the dangerous problem of medical misinformation, we'll look at some causes, and we'll learn how to protect ourselves from being misled.

Body

I. The World Wide Web and the Internet are increasingly accessible here and abroad.

  A. The Pew Internet and American Life Project reported that five million people used the Internet in 1994; however, by January 2005, 77 million Americans were logging on *daily* (Daily Activities, 2005).

  B. Today, more than 888 million people globally have access to the Internet, and predictions are that one billion will be online by 2006 (Internet World Stats, 2005).

  C. The international watchdog group Health on the Net Foundation (HON) found that 83% of users surveyed from the United States, Canada, South America, and Europe said they searched for medical information online (Wallace, 2002).

    1. Many turn to the Internet first.

    2. Users often trust Web pages, but their trust is not always justified.

      a. One study of searches for the term "vaccination" found that 43% of hits told people not to get vaccinated (Gupta, 2004).

      b. In other instances, patients "learn" so much that they consider themselves experts, so they ignore their doctor's advice and make their own, sometimes harmful, treatment decisions (Gupta, 2004).

      c. "Cyberchrondriacs" are people who use the Internet and make incorrect self-diagnoses; their numbers are large and are growing (Wallace, 2002).

      d. Currently, thousands of "cyberquacks" are waiting and willing to make money off of gullible e-patients.

II. There are many causes for the incorrect information that is available online.

  A. The main one is lack of accountability on the Internet.

    1. Print publications are judged by the credibility of the author, the publication's editorial content versus its advertising commitments, its educational value versus product promotion, and the number of scientific facts it presents.

    2. Information on the Internet cannot be regulated, and advertisers and pharmaceutical organizations can get around laws that would otherwise keep them from directly advertising to the public (Koralage, 2004).

  B. Often, there's no medical specialist or researcher who is involved directly in the creation of Web pages.

    1. Clerical staff, or worse yet, public relations people who are unfamiliar with the subject matter often type material onto websites, and they may be unaware of errors (Koralage, 2004).

    2. Anyone with a computer, modem, and twenty dollars can create a Web page.

      a. The pages can have wonderful information, or they can pass on rumors and falsehoods (Gupta, 2004).

Quianna gains attention with amusing examples of misinformation. She then spells out the problem and the need for consumers to be critical thinkers. Throughout she demonstrates credibility by citing respectable sources.

Here she previews the three main ideas she'll develop in the speech.

This section describes aspects of the problem.

The use of creative words such as "cyberchondriacs" and "cyberquacks" adds interest.

Here, she echoes the contrast between print and Internet sources highlighted in this chapter.

Quianna explains that anyone with basic skills and equipment can create a Web page.

b. Anonymous writers may have a personal agenda, no formal medical training, or a profit motive for unsuspecting consumers.

c. Websites, unlike physicians, take no responsibility toward the patient (Koralage, 2004).

C. Internet users also have themselves to blame.

1. Many people trust search engines to lead them to quality sites.

2. However, savvy users know that searches do not distinguish among sites; they just count the times a key word appears within a site and then direct the user to the site with the most matches.

3. Unfortunately, many Internet novices are unaware of the pitfalls awaiting them.

III. Fortunately, several steps can be taken to improve the quality of medical information on the Internet, and we can personally look for correct, reliable information.

A. Some standards should be in place to ensure the safety of those who seek medical information on the Web; the Health on the Net (HON) Foundation has a code of conduct which includes the following principles (2004):

1. *Transparency of sponsorship:* the site should name all supporting organizations, commercial and non-commercial.

2. *Authority:* all authors and contributors as well as their affiliations and credentials should appear.

3. *Attribution:* the site should include all references to source data, with links where possible.

4. *Justifiability:* all claims must be supported by credible evidence.

B. In addition, governmental agencies need to take a more active role in regulating medical information on the Internet.

1. The drug industry asked the Food and Drug Administration (FDA) to quickly develop new guidelines for Internet advertising.

2. The guidelines should be separate but consistent with rules governing other media.

3. However, the FDA prefers first to focus on drug labeling guidelines.

4. The Merck company says research is needed, because consumers seek out websites, but they don't request TV and print ads (iHealthBeat, 2004).

C. We consumers must determine if a site is credible, using suggestions issued by the National Institutes of Health (MedlinePlus, 2004).

1. Determine who maintains the site.

a. Government sites are maintained by agencies such as the National Institutes of Health or the Centers for Disease Control.

b. Private practitioners or organizations may have financial or political agendas that influence their material and their links.

2. Look for a listing of names and credentials of people who contributed to the site; see if you can contact them with questions or inquiries for more information.

a. Look for links to other sites; good sites don't consider themselves the only source of information.

b. Search the "about us" page for an editorial policy or review policy that describes how material is selected and approved for inclusion on the site.

3. Be a "cyberskeptic" and question claims that seem too good to be true.

4. Log on to the Internet Health Watch site, which evaluates other health websites.

a. Reuters Health Information Service sponsors the Internet Health Watch, and Dr. John Renner, founder of the Consumer Health Information Research Institute in Independence, Missouri, maintains it.

b. Renner evaluates three sites each week on their technical content, credibility, usefulness, and linkage characteristics.

5. Most important, remember that the Internet should complement, not replace, the physician–patient relationship, and always have your physician corroborate information you find on the Net (Gupta, 2004).

In this solution section, Quianna points out that many people are concerned about erroneous materials available online and are creating standards and guidelines for website creators.

She describes the work of non-governmental watchdog groups (such as HON) before discussing governmental agencies.

Quianna summarizes the guidelines for assessing Internet information found on pages 115–117.

Conclusion

I. Knowing where cases of inaccurate medical information have been found, knowing the causes of such misinformation, and being armed with tools that can correct the situation allows us to exercise caution.

II. So the next time you are on the Internet and you begin to consider pond scum or cottage cheese as a cure for what ails you, keep these words in mind: *Caveat emptor—* let the buyer beware.

References

Her bibliography is formatted in APA style.

Beckwith, C. (2001, September 7). *Flaxseed oil and cancer. Testimonial, Part 1.* Retrieved April 11, 2005, from www.beckwithfamily.com/Flax1.html

Daily Internet activities. (2005, March 2). In *Pew Internet and American Life Project tracking surveys.* Retrieved April 13, 2005, from www.pewinternet.org/trends/Daily_Activities_3.02.05.htm

Detwiler, S. (2001). Charlatans, leeches, and old wives: Medical misinformation. *Searcher, 9*(3). Retrieved August 21, 2001, from www.infotoday.com/searcher/marol/detwiler.htm

Fox, S. & Fallows, D. (2003, July 16). Internet health resources. In *Pew Internet and American Life Project.* Retrieved April 11, 2005, from www.pewinternet.org/pdfs/Pip_Health_Report_July_2003.pdf

Gupta, S. (2004, November 1). Click to get sick? People who get medical advice from the Web actually get worse, a study shows. *Time, 164,* 102.

Health on the Net Foundation. (2004, May 18). Principles. In *HON Code of Conduct (HONcode) for medical and health-related websites.* Retrieved April 15, 2005, from www.hon.ch/HONcode/Conduct.html

iHealthBeat. (2004, March 16). *FDA to focus on other DTC issues before Web ads.* Retrieved April 15, 2005, from www.ihealthbeat.org/index.cfm?Action=dspItem&itemID=100759

Internet World Stats and Population Statistics. (2005, March 25). *Now 888 million Internet users.* [Blog.] Retrieved April 13, 2005, from www.internetworldstats.com/blog.htm

Koralage, N. (2004, April). Kitemarks won't cure "cyberchondriacs." *Student BMJ, 12,* 175–176. Retrieved April 13, 2005, from InfoTrac College Edition.

MedlinePlus. (2004, May 3). *MedlinePlus guide to healthy Web surfing.* Retrieved April 15, 2005, from U.S. National Library of Medicine and the National Institutes of Health website: www.nlm.nih.gov/medlineplus/healthywebsurfing.html

Light Force Spirulina. (2005). FAQs about RoyalBody care. Retrieved April 15, 2005, from www.usvitamin.com/spirulina-faq.htm

Wallace, N. (2002, September 7). Doctor in the mouse. *The Age* (Australia). Retrieved April 13, 2005, from www.theage.com.au/cgi-bin/common/articles/2002/09/04

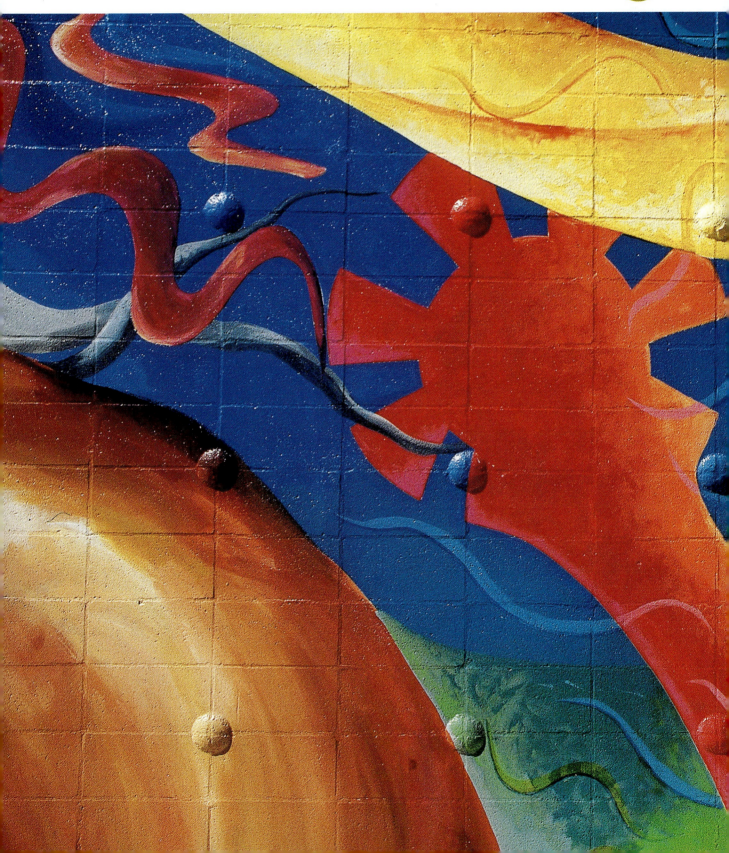

CHOOSING SUPPORTING MATERIALS

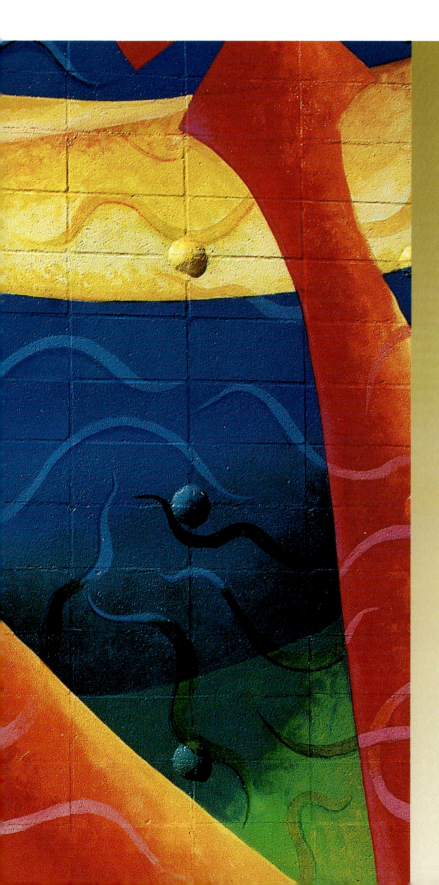

THIS CHAPTER WILL HELP YOU

▶ Distinguish between fact and opinion and learn how to test factual data

▶ Use examples effectively

▶ Quote authoritative sources

▶ Select numerical data carefully

▶ Distinguish between literal and figurative analogies

Detail from "Carnaval" Mural © 1995 by Joshua Sarantitis, Emmanuel Montoya, and Precita Eyes Muralists. (PG&E Yard Wall, 18th Street and Harrison, SF, CA)

T HINK ABOUT YOUR DECISION-MAKING PROCESS. How do you choose a computer, decide on a career, or select a college or university? Do advertisements influence your decisions? Do you consult friends or trusted advisers? Do you turn immediately to the Internet? We usually make decisions after considering questions like these: "Why should I buy that?" "Why this career?" "How much does it cost?" We seek out evidence—facts, figures, examples, and recommendations from knowledgeable people. We compare and contrast before deciding. We want support for the ideas and behaviors we choose. And, not surprisingly, we expect speakers to support their ideas with various types of evidence.

Each culture has its own rules for determining what counts as acceptable evidence. Rather than accept all information at face value, we follow cultural standards for weighing evidence, accepting some as valid and rejecting other data as inadequate, irrelevant, or inaccurate. In the United States, we commonly use facts, examples, quotations, statistics, and analogies to support our ideas. This chapter looks at some typical kinds of evidence used in public speaking. Following the presentation of each type of evidence, you will find a Stop and Check section to help you think critically about the quality of the data or evidence, both when selecting materials for your own speeches and when listening to the speeches of others.

CASE STUDY: IS GLOBAL WARMING A PROBLEM?

Al Gore says "yes" to the question of whether global warming is a problem. Bjorn Lomborg says the problem is overstated and there are more pressing issues to discuss.

© AP/Wide World Photos

© AFP/Getty Images

Former vice president Al Gore and hundreds of other environmental activists regularly warn audiences that, unless we act quickly to save the environment, human-created global warming will change the planet so much that the future will be bleak.[1] They support their claims with information from the National Academy of Sciences and the Intergovernmental Panel on Climate Change. On the other hand, Bjorn Lomborg,[2] author of *The Skeptical Environmentalist* and one-time member of Greenpeace, disagrees with their conclusions. A statistician formerly with a university in Denmark who is now head of the Danish government's Environmental Assessment Institute, Lomborg initially set out to prove global warming was a true danger. He pored over statistical data from the World Bank and United Nations and eventually concluded that "eco-fundamentalists" are overstating the problem. He argues that far worse dangers, such as the global need for pure drinking water, are more urgent concerns.

Lomborg's critics say he manipulates data, discards inconvenient statistics, plagiarizes, is motivated by money, and so on. Environmentalists' critics say similar things about environmentalists' research. The debate continues.

Questions for Discussion

▶ What do you personally believe about global warming?
▶ Why?
▶ What actual research have you done on the subject?
▶ What kind of information would you trust on an issue such as this?
▶ How do you evaluate conflicting data?

Provide Facts

Most of the information you discover about your subject probably will be factual, because in U.S. culture people typically demand facts before they accept an idea or proposal. **Empirical facts** are data that can be verified by observation, and **established facts** are those consistently validated by many observers. Generally accepted definitions and descriptions are considered facts. You judge factual information as true or false. Facts derive from a variety of sources, as these examples reveal:

▶ The origin of the word *coffee* is disputed. (Some say it derives from the Arabic word *qahwah;* others say it comes from Kaffa, the province in southwest Ethiopia that is considered coffee's birthplace.) [source: dictionary]
▶ N'Djamena is the capital city of the Republic of Chad. [source: almanac]
▶ Fetal alcohol syndrome, a condition caused by consuming substantial amounts of alcohol while pregnant, is one source of mental retardation in children. [source: empirical research studies conducted by scientists]

Use Definitions

You can **define,** or give the meaning of a term, in several ways. Dictionaries provide the meaning generally accepted in common usage, but speakers also give definitions derived from traditions, philosophers, and so on. In his speech on the root causes of terrorism, Tariq Karim,[3] Ambassador of Bangladesh to the United States, cited two dictionaries:

> What is terrorism? The *Chambers Twentieth Century Dictionary* (1976 edition) defines it as an "organized system of intimidation." The *Merriam-Webster Collegiate Dictionary* (current edition) defines it as "the systematic use of terror especially as a means of coercion." The word "terror" is derived from Middle English, inspired by middle French, Latin, and Greek, from words which mean to frighten, to cause one to tremble or be afraid, or to flee; or to arouse a state of intense fear.

Because his sources are well known, most people would agree that, yes, this is what terrorism is. However, Karim also added his personal interpretation:

> To my mind, terrorism is Terrorism (with a capital "T"). It recognizes no caste, creed, religion, race, ethnicity, or physical and political boundaries. It stalks a global theatre. Its specter will haunt us everywhere, in all societies, unless we stand up against it, unitedly, and indict its perpetrators.

Here, Karim interjects his personal **opinions** or interpretations into his definition. Stating personal opinion, either yours or someone else's, adds a subjective interpretation

Student Learning: Workbook
Have students work in small groups on Activity 8.1, "Fact-Opinion Worksheet," in the *Student Workbook.* This exercise provides practice distinguishing between facts and opinions in research.

empirical facts data verifiable by observation

established facts data verified consistently by many observers

define to give the meaning of a word

opinions subjective interpretations of facts; can be questioned

that is open to question. For instance, some listeners might disagree with this personal definition of terrorism.

Provide Vivid Descriptions

Descriptions provide details about a subject, such as size, shape, sound, and color. This description of a tsunami-ravaged area was given by a journalist/photographer covering the story:[4]

> On Sumatra two days later, we clambered aboard a Cessna carrying dried fish to Meulaboh, a shattered coastal town southeast of Aceh province. From the air, we could see the devastation was far worse this close to the fault line. Huge swaths of land were flattened, houses exploded as if by a hurricane. Yet here and there, just as in California during the fires, a single house remained by some fluke.

The details (dried fish, a coastal town, destroyed homes, a single house left standing) give facts; the choice of words (*shattered, swaths, exploded*) makes these facts easy to visualize.

When a fact looks suspicious, double-check it, because it is easy to pass on unverified or inaccurate material. For instance, Camilla quoted from the speech "Brother Earth, Sister Sky," which she attributed to Chief Seattle from over 100 years ago. Had she searched further, she would have discovered that the speech was actually written in 1972 by a screenwriter named Ted Parry for a film about ecology.

With the current explosion of available information, especially through the Internet and other electronic sources, distinguishing facts from opinions is now more important than ever. As Chapter 3 points out, http://hoaxbusters.ciac.org/ and www.snopes.com/ are two good sources for checking suspicious "facts."

STOP AND CHECK
THINK CRITICALLY ABOUT FACTS

© Ed Kashi/CORBIS

"Facts" about Arab culture are often inaccurate and misleading.

Arab Americans often say they are stereotyped and that simplistic or just plain incorrect information about them circulates widely. A fact sheet from the *Detroit Free Press* ex-

(continued)

description an image or impression created through vivid words

plains, "Although the Arab culture is one of the oldest on Earth, it is, in many parts of the United States, misunderstood. There are no easy, one-size-fits-all answers. Culture, language and religion are distinct qualities that act in different ways to connect Arabs, and to distinguish them from one another."[5] To avoid passing along misinformation on any topic, apply the following three tests:

1. *Check for accuracy or validity.* By definition, Arab Americans have ancestors in Arabic-speaking countries in the Middle East (including northern Africa). This definition excludes Iranians, who originate from the Farsi-speaking Persian Empire. The Arabic language is a unifying factor among Arabs; however Arabic has many dialects, and third- or fourth-generation Arab Americans often only speak English.

2. *Are the facts up to date?* Recently, the Associated Press began substituting *Qur'an* for *Koran. Muslim* designates a follower of Islam; the term *Mohammedan* is outdated. Census 2000 says about 1.25 million people in the United States identified themselves as Arab Americans. However, the Arab American Institute puts the number as at least 3.5 million, based on Zogby Poll data showing that people of Arab descent often fail to self-identify. According to the Arab American Institute, the majority of Arabs in the United States are Christians.[6]

3. *Consider the source.* The *Detroit Free Press* prepared a fact sheet for journalists called "100 Questions and Answers about Arab Americans." It is available online at **www .freep.com/jobspage/arabs/index.htm**. What credibility does a major newspaper have? How would you assess the credibility of sources such as the U.S. Census, the Zogby Poll, and the Arab American Institute? What other sources might provide information?

In short, test facts by asking three questions: Is this true? Is this true now? Who says so? Log onto the *Detroit Free Press* site or another source mentioned here and identify some common misconceptions about Arab Americans that are debunked there.

Use Examples

Have you ever listened to a speech that seemed abstract and irrelevant until the speaker used an example that showed how the topic affected someone like you? Most likely, your interest increased because of the illustration. **Examples,** or specific illustrations, can be short or long, real or hypothetical. David explains their usefulness:

> The speeches that are interesting usually start with an example—often from that person's life. It shows the communicator is human. The story adds credibility . . . and leads the audience into the speech, almost like a conversation; this lets the speaker earn the audience's trust.

Examples also attract and maintain attention. Narrative theorists argue that we listen for examples and stories that make abstract concepts and ideas more concrete and relevant.[7] In addition, illustrations help listeners identify emotionally with the subject. When an example rings true, your listeners' internal dialogue runs something like this: "Yes, I've known someone like that" or "I've seen that happen—this seems real." Finally, as David pointed out, examples can enhance your personal credibility. They let listeners know that you understand real-world experiences and the practical implications of your theories and ideas.

Examples fall into two major types: real and hypothetical. Both types can range from very brief to longer and quite detailed.

examples specific instances used to support ideas

Use Real Examples

Real examples, those that actually happened, provide concrete, real-life illustrations of your concepts. For instance, John's topic was culture shock. He defined the term and began his discussion of the first stage, the honeymoon stage. His audience listened politely, but their attention perked up and they more clearly understood the emotional impact of the stage when he described Sara's experiences during her first few weeks as a nanny in Belgium. (An outline of this speech appears in Chapter 11.)

As you gather materials, look for people's experiences, as well as actual events, to illustrate your ideas. Because real examples actually occurred, you are able to provide specific names, dates, and places. For instance:

**Classroom Discussion/
Activity**
Review the defense's closing
arguments at the end of *A
Time to Kill*. Discuss whether
the "hypothetical example"
used there was effective or
ineffective and why.

▶ To illustrate a speech about the downside of winning the lottery, Maria told about William, a lottery winner whose brother hired a hit man to kill him; Daisy, whose friend sued for half her winnings (because he had prayed that she'd win and she did); and Debbie, whose sisters no longer spoke to her after she won because she refused to pay their bills. (You can find an outline of this speech at the end of Chapter 9 and on the book's website, where you can also watch a video of the speech being delivered.)

▶ Examples of prominent Americans who claim Arab ancestry include Doug Flutie (NFL quarterback), J. M. Haggar (founder of Haggar clothing), Candy Lightner (founder of Mothers Against Drunk Driving), Ralph Nader (presidential candidate), John Zogby (pollster), Paula Abdul, Shakira, and Salma Hayek (entertainers).

▶ For his speech on LifeGems, diamonds created out of cremated human remains, Chris listed some additional creative approaches to death. Ed Headrick's remains were made into flying discs. (He created the Frisbee.) Ashes from Gene Rodenberry (the Star Trek creator) were launched into space. Others have had their remains mixed with concrete and formed into artificial coastal reefs. (A transcript of this speech is printed at the end of this chapter and the video is available on the book's website.)

Personal examples often bolster your credibility. John's personal stories from his semester in Ghana illustrated his progress through the stages of culture shock, and showed listeners that he not only had book learning, he also knew firsthand what culture shock was like.

Personal stories are indispensable in some cultures. In Kenya, for example, focus group participants rated personal stories as the most convincing type of example. One Kenyan said, "We believe you only really know about something if you've experienced it."[8] In fact, some Kenyans thought personal narratives should be placed in a separate category because their impact is so different from other types of narratives.

Consider Hypothetical Examples for Sensitive Topics

A **hypothetical example,** one that did not actually occur but seems plausible, usually contains elements of several different stories woven together to create a typical person who has experiences relevant to the topic. So in a speech about teens who injure themselves, instead of revealing details about a specific person you actually knew, you might combine elements from the experiences of various teenagers to create a typical person. To distinguish hypothetical examples from fabricated stories, introduce them something like this: "Let's say there's a sixteen-year-old girl named Carly; let's put her in a close-knit family in rural Oregon. . . ."

Our cultural value of privacy can make hypothetical examples more appropriate than real ones for sensitive topics like mental illness or sexual behaviors, so speakers whose work involves confidentiality, such as physicians, ministers, counselors, and teachers, often use them. Family counselors who present parenting workshops, for instance, tell hy-

**Classroom Discussion/
Activity**
Have students discuss the
difference between a hypothetical example and one that
is fabricated. What, if any,
ethical concerns should a
speaker have when using
hypothetical examples? For
homework, ask students to
construct a hypothetical example that would be appropriate in their next speech.
Have volunteers share their
example in class and explain
what makes the example hypothetical rather than real.

real examples actual happenings

hypothetical example not a real incident or person, but true to life

pothetical stories of bad parenting skills without revealing confidential information about specific, identifiable clients.

Creating an imaginary scenario that invites your listeners to personalize your topic can also be effective at attracting attention and helping audience members become emotionally involved. Here's the opening illustration that Maria used for her speech on the problems that lottery winners face:

> Imagine that you just won the lottery. You can't sleep; you're so excited! You call everyone you know, and for a few days you bask in the joy of being an instant millionaire. Notice I said a few days. A week after you win, relatives you've never seen start asking for loans. A few days later, a friend sues for half the money, arguing that she encouraged you to buy the ticket, and without her urging, you'd still be poor. . . . The demands and the expectations pile up— so much so that you may almost wish you'd never bought that ticket!

Although hypothetical examples and imaginary scenarios can work well in informative speeches, real examples are better for persuasive speeches. Think of it this way: Your listeners are probably more persuaded by something that *did* happen than by something that *might* happen.

Combine Brief Examples

Examples don't have to be long; in fact, you may prefer short illustrations. However, a single example is easily missed or disregarded, so it's better to string together two or three—especially when gaining attention in your introduction. Layering example upon example gives your listeners a number of images they can use to visualize and personalize your subject. The following vivid examples of self-injury could effectively introduce the topic of self-mutilation among teens:

> Brianna began cutting herself when she was 14; now 17, her arms reveal numerous scars that mark out the past three years of emotional pain. Brooke started etching words she couldn't say to others on her stomach, which she called her "billboard." Marissa's cutting began after her father left. She substituted self-mutilation for suppressed feelings, which she withheld so as not to be a burden on her already-grieving family.[9]

Create Emotional Connections with Extended Examples

Extended examples include many details; each one gives your listeners an opportunity to identify emotionally with the subject of the story. Use them to clarify, to explain in depth, and to motivate your listeners. Look at how each detail in this illustration makes the story more engaging. The subject is gastric bypass surgery for teens:

> At 7, Nikki weighed 160 pounds. At 9, she was a veteran dieter whose weight was 250 pounds. By 14, she was up to 363 pounds; her heart was enlarged, her liver inflamed, and her face turned blue when she exercised. Finally, her mother agreed to let her have gastric-bypass surgery—an extreme procedure that costs about $30,000 and sometimes has deadly consequences. Today, Nikki feels "like a whole other person;" she is 6-foot-1, and she is down to 207 pounds.[10]

Speakers whose work involves confidentiality, such as police officers, often describe hypothetical characters whose predicaments typify the problems that officers encounter.

extended examples longer incidents whose many details make them more compelling

Listeners can identify with one or more of the details: health and money concerns; self-esteem issues during childhood and the teen years. These facts help them become interested in Nikki and this topic. Because extended examples provide multiple points that engage listeners, they are generally more compelling. In fact, narratives or well-developed stories can function as the entire speech. (Chapter 15 gives detailed information about organizing and evaluating narrative speeches.)

STOP AND CHECK

THINK CRITICALLY ABOUT EXAMPLES

Let's say you're researching a speech about social anxiety and you come across the example of Grace Daily, who experienced panic attacks so severe that she often had to leave college lectures. To help her complete her college degree, her professors agreed to leave the classroom door open during lectures, and they let her take tests alone.[11] To evaluate the usefulness of such an example, ask yourself the following questions:

▶ *Is this example representative or typical?* That is, does Grace represent typical a college student with social anxiety? Or does her case seem extreme? This test relates to the probability of occurrence. Although the example may be possible, how *probable* is it?

▶ *Do you have a sufficient number of examples?* Are enough cases presented to support the major idea adequately? How many people like Grace are attending college? Your listeners should be able to see that the issue you discuss is extensive, affecting a significant number of people.

▶ *Is the example true?* Did Grace actually leave lectures? How often? How did such a shy woman convince her professors to work with her? If Grace is a hypothetical character, does her experience ring true with what you know about the world and how it operates?

Quote Culturally Acceptable Authorities

Teaching Tip
Remind students that not giving the source of a quotation is plagiarism.

Remember this childhood challenge?

You make a statement.

Your friend responds, "Who says?"

"My dad says!"

"Your dad? What does he know?"

Mentally reactivate this question-and-answer scenario as you gather speech materials. Whatever your subject, think of your audience as asking, "Who says?" Then identify the authorities you think listeners would believe given your topic and purpose. Would they accept opinions of scholars or scientists? Laypeople? Medical practitioners? Literary or scriptural texts? Quoting authorities bolsters your ideas if, and only if, your audience views them as credible on the topic.

Patrick Wilson,[12] author of *Secondhand Knowledge: An Inquiry into Cognitive Authority,* says that we learn a few things directly, but most of our information is hearsay; that is, we get it secondhand, from people, books, institutions, and so on. Consequently, we must decide who we consider reliable and who we will allow to influence our beliefs. Authoritative sources differ in degree (some have little credibility, others have a lot), and their sphere of influence varies (an authority in Eastern European economics will have less authority in matters of Central American economics).

Every culture identifies authoritative sources such as teachers, elders, scientists, religious leaders, seers, and written texts. Recognized authorities vary among cultures and co-cultural groups. Quoting culturally accepted sources can be valuable, especially when your expertise on the topic is limited. This shows that knowledgeable, experienced people support your conclusions. Stating the source's exact words is a **direct quotation,** but it's often better to **paraphrase** or summarize long quotations.

Chapter 7 points out two basic types of authorities: (1) experts and (2) peers or laypersons. To show that your sources are credible, tell who they are, why you believe their testimony, and why your audience should believe them.

DIVERSITY IN PRACTICE
VISUAL EVIDENCE: CHICANO MURALS

WORDS ARE NOT the only type of possible information; pictures, images, and symbols can provide evidence in visual forms. For example, Margaret LaWare[13] examined Chicano/a murals in Chicago. She says murals— like those reproduced in this text— make statements or arguments about ethnic pride, community activism, and cultural re-vitalization. Study some of the murals used to open each chapter. Look for images such as mythical beasts or a pink rose (associated with the Virgin of Guadalupe); find possible portraits of community members. Then think of ways these images combine to define identity, reflect people's needs, and celebrate their histories. LaWare believes "the murals argue that Mexican American people need not assimilate or give up their culture to survive in an urban center that is both geographically and socially distant from Mexico and from the Southwest." (LaWare's article is available on InfoTrac College Edition.)

Quote Culturally Accepted Experts

According to Patrick Wilson,[14] we look to people whose occupational or educational expertise, career success, and reputation in their field make them **experts.** Thus, testimony from scholars, elected officials, practitioners such as doctors or other professionals, and so on is generally good supporting material. Here is expert testimony that fits well in a speech about self-mutilation in teens taken from an article that was published in *Time* magazine:[15]

> ▶ "Girls have a more conflicted relationship with their bodies," says Wendy Lader, clinical director of Self Abuse Finally Ends, a treatment program in Naperville, Ill. "They go after it and hurt it when they're angry."
> ▶ "Every clinician says it's increasing," reports psychologist Michael Hollander, a director at Two Brattle Center in Cambridge, Massachusetts, an outpatient clinic that treats cutters. "I've been practicing for 30 years, and I think it's gone up dramatically."
> ▶ Cutting provides a high, but kids get addicted to the high, so the longer they cut, the more they need it, says psychologist Jennifer Hartstein of the Montefiore Medical Center in the Bronx, N.Y.

Notice that the third example paraphrases rather than directly quotes the expert. Because most people in the audience have probably never heard of any of these people, it's up to the speaker to provide information that will help listeners decide whether or not they are credible. Telling the expert's institutional affiliation or explaining the person's credentials helps.

We commonly expect people to agree with the general beliefs of others who are like them in some way. However, well-known people sometimes hold surprising opinions. Consider these examples:

> ▶ William F. Buckley, Jr., a well-known conservative writer and journalist, supports legalization of drugs, a position not generally associated with conservatives.
> ▶ Nat Hentoff, a writer and editor associated for many years with the liberal New York newspaper *The Village Voice*, holds a pro-life position, which many readers of the *Voice* disagree with.

Classroom Discussion / Activity
Have the class discuss what criteria determine whether someone is an expert on a particular topic. Can students be experts on the topics of their speeches? How can speakers communicate their expertise to listeners?

Teaching Tip
Remind students that experts can be biased. In fact, as a person's expertise increases so does his or her potential for bias.

direct quotation presenting the exact words of the source

paraphrase to summarize the source's ideas in your own words

expert person considered an authority because of study or work-related experience

Quoting a proverb, literary quotation, or scriptural text is meaningful to people who accept the cultural beliefs and values it stands for.

Using unexpected testimony like this can be especially powerful in persuasive speeches. Why? Because your listeners will reason that someone willing to go against his peers has probably thought through his opinions carefully.

Quote Credible Peers or Laypeople

Because U.S. cultural values include individual expression and equality, we use the opinions of "regular people" who have firsthand knowledge about a subject to influence our thinking. These **peer** or **lay sources** may not know scientific facts and related theories, but they can tell you how it feels to be involved as a participant. What do lay people report about self-injury? The *Time* magazine article mentioned above[16] gives several examples:

- Thirteen-year-old Michelle, who is being treated at a clinic in Vista Del Mar said, "Cutting grew into a huge fad at school. In seventh grade it seemed every single girl had tried it—except the really smart ones."
- "When I would cut myself deliberately, I didn't even feel it," says Emily, 16, now in her third week at a treatment center. "But if I got a paper cut I didn't want, that would hurt."
- After successful treatment, one father of a 20-year-old reported on her progress. "When Melanie wanted to cut, she learned to find something else to do. She'd be stressed, and the next thing we'd know, she'd be cleaning her closet."

Put simply, the young women in treatment and the father who watched his daughter go through the process of conquering the problem all give a participant's perspective that adds important details. (A self-injury speech outline is in Appendix C.)

> ### DIVERSITY IN PRACTICE
> ### PROVERBS IN A WEST AFRICAN CULTURE
>
> AN ARTICLE ENTITLED "YOUR MOTHER IS STILL YOUR MOTHER"[17] describes the importance of proverb usage among the Igbo people of Nigeria, where proverbs both contain and transmit cultural wisdom. Chinua Achebe, a famous Nigerian author, calls them the Igbo's "horse of conversation." Adults who are considered wise conversationalists invariably use proverbs effectively, and every functioning adult in the village community learned to use them properly during childhood. Each competent user understands each proverb's meaning and discerns the situations in which a specific proverb fits.
>
> You can find the full article on InfoTrac College Edition.

Teaching Tip
Quotations, proverbs, and words of wisdom are great attention getters for speeches. If possible, show examples of student speeches that open with quotations.

---

peer or lay sources people considered credible because of firsthand experiences with a topic

Quote Sayings, Proverbs, and Words of Wisdom

Every culture provides a store of sayings, proverbs, phrases, and other words of wisdom that encapsulates culturally important ideas, beliefs, and values. Words of wisdom come from literature and oral traditions, from well-known and anonymous sources, from philosophical and political treatises. Here are a few examples:

- This, above all, to thine own self be true. (literature)
- It takes a village to raise a child. (proverb)
- You shall know the truth, and the truth shall set you free. (religious text)

▶ Ask not what your country can do for you; ask what you can do for your country. (political speech)

▶ The greatest good for the greatest number [of people]. (philosophy)

Sayings do not always originate in well-known sources. You can quote figures of authority in your own life, as long as your audience respects the source. Farah Walters' speech illustrates this:

> My parents — and especially my father — taught me to draw an invisible line. He said to me, "Farah, you decide how you want other people to treat you, and if somebody crosses that line and it's unacceptable to you, just walk away from it. Don't let people treat you the way that they feel you should be treated. Have people treat you the way *you* feel you should be treated." That was good advice then. It is good advice now.[18]

Walters expects her audience to accept her father as a credible source of wisdom because this culture respects (although we sometimes reject!) the advice of friends and families.

Religious writings also provide rich sources of material when the audience accepts the text as valid. The evangelist Billy Graham, for example, commonly uses the phrase "The Bible says . . ." when he invokes his ultimate authority, God. Listeners who are not affiliated with the Christian faith, however, will likely discount Graham's source to at least some degree.

To find usable sayings, proverbs, and wise words, go to www.bartleby.com/100. (The Diversity in Practice box on page 142 provides additional details about the importance of proverbs in some African cultures.)

STOP AND CHECK

THINK CRITICALLY ABOUT QUOTING AUTHORITIES

Look back at the quotations from experts and laypeople relating to self-mutilation. Ask yourself these questions about each source cited.

1. *What is the person's expertise?* Wendy Lader's? Michael Hollander's? Jennifer Hartstein's? Is it relevant to the subject under discussion?

2. *Is the person recognized as an expert by others?* How could you determine his or her reputation?

3. *Is the layperson stating an opinion commonly held by others like him or her?* In other words, is it a typical or representative view? Do Emily and Melanie typify people who have sought treatment for self-injury? Do you think Michelle's school was typical? Or is this an extreme situation?

4. Because you don't have the entire article, you cannot assess the context for the person's words. However, whenever possible, *ask if the words are taken out of context.* That is, do they fairly represent the speaker's intended meaning? Words can be distorted so that the quoted person appears to hold a position not actually held.

5. *Is the quotation accurate?* One speaker said, "I was reminded of DeTocqueville, who wrote about [America] in the late eighteenth century, 'America is great because America is good, and when America ceases to be good, America will cease to be great.'"[19] Although this quotation has been used by hundreds of speakers and writers, including Bill Clinton and Pat Buchanan, it's, unfortunately, nowhere to be found in any of DeTocqueville's writings — although he did say nice things about America.

To investigate quotations further, do an Internet search for the exact words "taken out of context," and read several of the hits to identify the effect of misleading quotations.

Classroom Discussion/ Activity
Often students remember a quotation they would like to use but can't remember its source. As an exercise in finding the sources of quotations, have students find the source of each quotation listed in this section. Suggest that they use a reference book, such as *Bartlett's Quotations,* or the Internet.

Student Learning: Book Website
This Stop and Check activity can also be found on the book's website, where it's located under "Chapter Resources."

Use Statistics Carefully

People in U.S. society tend to like numbers. We begin measuring and counting in preschool. We study opinion polls and statistical research. Many of us consider numbers and measurements to be credible and trustworthy hard facts. Consequently, using numerical support well may increase your credibility and cause you to appear more competent and knowledgeable. Numerical information commonly helps us understand the extent of an issue or predict the probability of some future happening.

Although numerical data can be useful, it has unique drawbacks. In general, statistics are short on emotional appeal because they don't involve listeners' feelings, and too many in a speech may bore your audience. Furthermore, numerical information is often misleading, and if you present biased information, your listeners may distrust you. Consequently, take extra care to use enumeration and statistics both accurately and sparingly.

Provide a Count

Enumeration means counting. A count helps your listeners understand the extent of a problem or issue: the number of people injured in accidents annually, those diagnosed with a particular disease, the number of older child adoptions, and so on. Two tips will help you use enumeration more effectively.

1. *Round your numbers up or down.* There are two good reasons for doing this. First, listeners find it hard to remember exact numbers. In addition, numbers related to current topics can change rapidly. By the time they're published, they're probably outdated in some way. Consequently, instead of saying, "The 2000 Census showed that 17,969 people lived on the Nez Perce reservation in Idaho," you're better off rounding the number up to "almost 18,000" individuals.
2. *Make numbers come alive by comparing them to something already in your listeners' experience.* Let's take hot dogs. In 2000, baseball stadiums sold about 26.5 million hot dogs during the season, but just how many *is* that? If you were to lay that many hot dogs end-to-end, they'd stretch from Dodger Stadium in Los Angeles to the Baseball Hall of Fame in Cooperstown, New York.[20]

Regina Lewis used specific details to explain how much information is available on Google's database:

> Within two seconds, the search engine Google provides you with enough information that, if it were printed out, would create a stack of paper 140 miles high.[21]

These specific, meaningful details help clarify her numbers.

Unfortunately, numerical information can be misleading, as almost every political campaign demonstrates. For example, several 2004 election ads stated, "Under this president, two million jobs have been lost. That's the worst record since Herbert Hoover." Now, the "two million" figure may be factual (although the ads didn't say how many jobs had been *gained*), but calling this the "worst record" since Hoover is questionable. The job situation in 2004 (when the population was approximately 290 million) was quite different from the situation in 1930 (when the population was about 122 million). Read the article at **www.FactCheck.org/article101.html** to see how the ads exaggerated the economic downturn.

Choose Statistics with a Critical Eye

The statistics most commonly used in speeches include means, medians, modes, percentages, and ratios (see Figure 8.1).

enumeration a count

Figure 8.1
Mean, Median, and Mode
This pictograph shows lottery winnings of twenty-five participants. The mean or average winning was $5,700; the median or midpoint was $3,000. However, most people won $2,000 — the mode. When a few extreme instances lead to unrealistic conclusions, the median or the mode is often more useful than the mean.

Instructor Resource: PowerPoint
The *Multimedia Manager with Instructor Resources* CD-ROM includes PowerPoint slides of Figures 8.1, 8. 2, and 8.3.

Mean

The **mean** is the *average* of a group of numbers. To calculate the mean, add up all the specific measurements and divide by the total number of units measured. Here are some examples:

▶ Mean age in 2000 for a Massachusetts woman having her first child was 27.8 (up from 22.5 in 1970); for a woman in Utah it was 23.3 (up from 21.4 in 1970).[22]
▶ Mean credit card debt per U.S. family is $8,000.[23]
▶ Mean number of hours of television viewing per week is 19 (U.S.), 13.3 (India), and 11.6 (Mexico); mean number of hours spent reading is 5.7 (U.S.), 10.7 (India), and 5.5 (Mexico).[24]

The mean is skewed when extreme figures at either end of the range make the comparison less useful. Just average the annual incomes of nine people who work for minimum wage and one billionaire to understand the limitations of the mean.

Median

The **median** is the middle number in a set of numbers that have been arranged into a ranked order: Half the numbers are above it and half below it. For example, home prices in a particular area are typically stated as a median, which balances the very expensive mansions against the inexpensive fixer-uppers.

Mode

The **mode** is the number that appears most commonly. For example, on some college campuses, a few first-year students are sixteen years old, more are seventeen, some are in

mean average of a group of numbers

median middle number in a set of numbers arranged in a ranked order

mode most frequently occurring number

their twenties, thirties, or forties, but most are eighteen—the mode. A few nurses in one hospital might earn $30 an hour; a few might earn only $18; but the mode for nurses' pay in that particular hospital is $23 per hour.

Percentages

Percentages show the relationship of a part to the whole; the whole is represented by the number 100. Public speakers commonly use percentages, as the following information about student credit cards shows:[25]

- In 2004, 76% of undergraduates carried credit cards; in 2001, the figure was 83%.
- In 2004; 43% of undergrads had at least four cards; in 2001, the figure was 47%.
- 56% of students said they obtained their first card at age 18.

Often you'll find percentages stated as **rates of increase** or **decrease,** which compare growth or decline during a specific period of time to a baseline figure from an earlier period. Treat these rates cautiously, for unless you know the baseline number the rate of increase or decrease is almost meaningless. Case in point: A company that employs two people in the year 2005 and adds an additional employee in 2006 will increase hiring at a rate of 50%. However, a company that employs 100 people in 2005 and adds one additional employee in 2006 will increase hiring by 1%. The actual number of additional employees hired for the two companies is the same, but the rates of increase are dramatically different. The reverse is also true: The two-person company that loses one employee decreases by half, or 50%; the larger company hardly notices a loss of one. As you can see, when baseline numbers are initially very low, the rate of increase is potentially astounding!

Ratios

You can present relationships between numbers as a **ratio,** instead of using a percentage. This is because 10% and 1 in 10 are interchangeable, as are 25% and 1 in 4. Ratios are especially helpful when the percentage is very small; for example, .000001 percent equals 1 case in 100,000. So it's more effective to say, "18 out of 100,000 teens died of gunshot injuries in 1989, up from the 12 per 100,000 recorded in 1979," instead of "one-hundred-thousandth of one percent of teens. . . ."

Use Visual Aids to Clarify Numerical Data

Because numerical data are sometimes complex, present them in visual form whenever you can. Elizabeth Winslea, shown in the photograph, used drops of water to illustrate her point. The pictograph (Figure 8.1) is another visual aid that clarifies the statistics.

Figure 8.2 shows the value of a table to help your audience visualize complex numbers. Imagine trying to understand a speaker who simply says:

Child care workers are underpaid.
Men who graduate from college

Presenting numerical information creatively can help your audience understand it better. Elizabeth Winslea, Portland State University campus pastor, could have simply stated the number of lives lost in the December 26, 2004, tsunami disaster. Instead, she poured water from a pitcher, nine quarts' worth; each drop of water represented a person.

Courtesy Deirdre Steinberg

percentage figure that shows the relationship of the part to the whole, which is represented by the number 100

rate of increase or decrease a percentage that uses an earlier baseline figure to compare growth or decline

ratio a relationship shown by numbers, such as 1 in 10

Comparative Salaries of Child Care Workers		
	Average for all men	Average for all women
College graduates	$51,804	$33,615
Some college	$33,161	$22,445
High school diploma	$27,865	$19,309
Highest paid child care worker	$15,488	

Figure 8.2
Tables
A table such as this one presenting salary information effectively depicts complex numerical data in a way that listeners can easily grasp.

average more than $51,804 annually; female graduates average $33,615. Men who have some college earn an average of $33,161 versus women in the same category, who average $22,445. Even men with a high school diploma average $27,665, and women who have graduated from high school earn on the average $19,309. Compare all these salaries to the average of $15,488 that the highest-paid child care workers earn.

Is your head spinning? Do you remember any of this data? Now, imagine that the speaker either gives you a handout or projects a transparency with Figure 8.2 on it. How is your response different? In what ways does the visual help you grasp the material more easily?

You can see that different types of data call for different types of visual aids. Because visual aids are vital in American culture, this text devotes Chapter 12 to the topic of creating and displaying visual materials.

STOP AND CHECK

CRITICALLY ANALYZE NUMERICAL DATA

Because numbers are easy to manipulate, evaluate them carefully with these questions before you use them.

1. *What is the source of the numbers?* Does the source have an interest such as a possibility of financial gain that would make high or low numbers more desirable?
2. *Are the numbers up to date?* Using a count or a percentage that is old is generally not applicable to current conditions.
3. Before you use startling rates of increase, *look at the baseline figures of the percentages.* Note any other relevant factors that might affect this rate. For example, one source said the rate of U.S. children and teens killed by gunfire is 120% higher than in the other 25 industrialized countries combined. (Any deaths are lamentable, but what if the other countries only have 10 such deaths? What if they have 20,000?) [26]
4. *Be careful of combined statistics.* The same source said that males experience violent crime at rates 28 percent greater than females; however, females are raped and sexually assaulted at 7.5 times the rate of males. (Why do you think the authors reported the figure relating to males as a percentage but the figure relating to females as a multiple? What is 7.5 when stated as a percentage?)

For further information about testing your numbers, search InfoTrac College Edition for "statistics." Click on "subdivisions," and then link to the articles in the "analysis" subdivision. Read one that interests you, noting the guidelines for statistical interpretation.

Classroom Discussion/ Activity
Bring in several news articles (newspaper, periodical, Internet). Have students evaluate them in groups, using the questions in the Stop and Check as a guide.

Find Compelling Comparisons

A **comparison** or **analogy** points out similarities between things. We understand new information or unfamiliar ideas better when we find points of comparison to something that's already in our experience. Comparisons can be literal or figurative.

Use Literal Analogies

Literal analogies compare actual things that are similar in important ways. For example, a Pakistani speaker, Liaquat Ali Khan,[27] explained to the U.S. Senate how his country was founded:

> Pakistan was founded so that millions of Muslims should be enabled to live according to their opinions and to worship God in freedom. . . . Like some of the earlier founders of your great country, these Muslims, though not Pilgrims, nevertheless embarked upon an undertaking, which, in aim and achievement, represented the triumph of an idea. That idea was the idea of liberty, which has had its ardent followers in all climates and all countries. When our time came, its call summoned us, too, and we could not hold back.

By showing the similarities of his country's founding to that of the United States and by linking both countries in their shared values, Khan helped his listeners understand why Muslims broke away from India's Hindu population to create Pakistan.

In a classroom speech about the pros and cons of fetal-cell transplantation, Chris Patti showed how proponents on both sides of this controversial issue literally compare the dead fetus to other dead bodies:

> Supporters of transplantation believe that the fetus is essentially a cadaver. They reason that adult cadavers are used in research with the consent of their families. So why shouldn't fetal cadavers be used to develop more effective methods of treating debilitating diseases? John Robertson, a law professor at the University of Texas, says that the dead fetus is essentially an organ donor and that its usable organs should be used to treat horrible diseases.
>
> . . . Critics of fetal tissue research and transplantation believe that the fetus is essentially a victim. They ask, "Should we do harm so that good may come?" Their answer is no. Arthur Caplan, Director of the Center for Biomedical Ethics at the University of Minnesota, argues against using a victim to save the lives of others. "Society will not tolerate killing one life for another," he asserts.

Sometimes pointing out *differences*, or showing **contrasts** between a new concept and a more familiar one, is a good strategy. For example, Andres explained lacrosse by contrasting it with the more familiar games of baseball and football.

comparison or analogy stating similarities between two things

literal analogies comparisons between two actual things that are alike in important ways

contrasts stating differences between two things

figurative analogies stated similarities between two otherwise dissimilar things; requires an imaginative connection

Create Vivid Figurative Analogies

When you highlight similarities between otherwise *dissimilar* things, you're using **figurative analogies.** These analogies require your listeners to apply their imagination and integrate likenesses between two otherwise different things or ideas. In a convocation speech at Queens College in North Carolina, a music professor compared personalities to various melodies:

> . . . each of us has a unique melody. . . . Some of you are quiet, soft, and lyrical. Others are rhythmic and energetic. Some are majestic and somber. Yet others may be whimsical and funny. Still others are cool and mellow. And truthfully, some of you are like the new styles of music, you are just way out there. Regardless, your melody is your own sound, your own style, your essence, your identity.[28]

Fouling out, having a game plan, scoring a slam dunk— all these are figurative analogies that compare life to a sporting event. Can you identify other common examples?

© George Tarbay, NIU Media Services

In short, figurative analogies connect familiar images with those less known. Many of the students in the audience could identify characteristics of musical genres—hip-hop, soft rock, jazz, heavy metal—that resemble different people.

STOP AND CHECK

THINK CRITICALLY ABOUT ANALOGIES

Evaluate your use of comparisons and contrasts. To test literal analogies, make sure the two items are alike in essential details. For instance, you could mislead your audience by comparing the work of a police officer in Houston, Texas, with one in Sioux Falls, South Dakota. Although their duties are alike in many ways, they have significant differences. Comparing the Houston officer to one in Los Angeles or Miami is more appropriate because all three operate in large metropolitan settings with diverse populations. Sioux Falls officers, on the other hand, have more in common with police officers in smaller cities in Michigan and Nebraska.

To test figurative analogies, be sure the comparison is clear and makes sense. Can your listeners make the necessary connection of ideas?

To learn more about both literal and figurative analogies, log on to InfoTrac College Edition and do a subject search for "analogies."

Summary

It is vital to support your ideas with evidence that listeners can understand so they can see reasons for your major ideas. Select facts, including definitions and descriptions, that you can verify in a number of sources. In addition, select facts that are up to date.

Further, during your research, distinguish factual material from opinions and take care to not pass on distorted or incorrect information.

Most listeners respond to examples, and using specific incidents as supporting material helps make abstract concepts more concrete and relevant. Whether real or hypothetical, brief or extended, illustrations also help listeners identify emotionally with your topic. To be effective, examples should be representative, sufficient in number, and plausible.

The use of quotations can enhance your credibility if you are not considered an expert on the topic. Directly quote or paraphrase the opinions of experts and lay or peer sources. In addition, quote cultural proverbs, written texts, and even words of wisdom from relatively unknown sources that your audience will accept as credible.

In a society that tends to place value on quantification, the judicious use of enumeration and statistics may increase your audience's acceptance of your ideas. However, be sure that your numerical support is understandable, up to date, and used in ways that do not create misleading impressions. Visual aids are often helpful in clarifying complex numerical data.

Finally, comparisons or analogies are an additional means of support. Literal analogies compare or contrast two actual things; figurative analogies compare two things that are generally considered different but share one specific likeness. Both types add vividness to your speeches.

As you interweave facts, examples, numbers, testimony, and analogies, you give your listeners more reasons to accept the conclusions you present.

STUDY AND REVIEW

The premium website for *Public Speaking* offers a broad range of resources that will help you better understand the material in this chapter, complete assignments, and succeed on tests. The website features

▶ Speech videos with critical viewing questions, speech outlines and transcripts, and
▶ Interactive practice activities (including most of the chapter's Stop and Check exercises), self quizzes, and a sample final exam.

For more information about this text's electronic learning resources, consult your **Guide to Online Resources for Public Speaking** or visit http://communication.wadsworth.com/jaffe5.

KEY TERMS

The terms below are defined in the margins throughout this chapter. The book's website also provides interactive flashcards and crossword puzzles to help you learn these terms and the concepts they represent.

empirical facts 135	peer or lay sources 142
established facts 135	enumeration 144
define 135	mean 145
opinions 135	median 145
description 136	mode 145
examples 137	percentage 146
real examples 138	rate of increase or decrease 146
hypothetical example 138	ratio 146
extended examples 139	comparison or analogy 148
direct quotation 141	literal analogies 148
paraphrase 141	contrasts 148
expert 141	figurative analogies 148

APPLICATION AND CRITICAL THINKING EXERCISES

The exercises below are among the practice activities on the book's website.

1. Bring to class a current edition of a news magazine or newspaper. With your class-mates, choose a topic from the week's news. Collect and display information by dividing the board into five sections, one for each kind of evidence: facts, examples, quota-tions, numerical data, and analogies. Contribute information from your magazine or paper, cooperating with your classmates to fill the board. Evaluate the evidence using the tests presented in this chapter.

2. Go to the online edition of *Time* (www.time.com) or *U.S. News & World Report* (www.usnews.com). Read the cover story and find examples of a fact, expert and peer testi-mony, a statistic, and an analogy.

3. With a small group of your classmates, evaluate the effectiveness of the following pieces of evidence taken from student speeches. What kind (or kinds) of evidence does each excerpt represent? Is the evidence specific or vague? Does the speaker cite the source of the evidence adequately? Does it meet the tests for the type of evidence it represents?

   ▶ A recent study showed that at least three out of four black children who were placed in white homes are happy and have been successfully incorporated into their families and communities.

   ▶ According to the *Natural History of Whales and Dolphins,* dolphins communicate through a system of whistles, clicks, rattles, and squeaks. These clicking sounds are not only used for navigation in the deep waters but they may also be used to convey messages. Pulsed squeaks can indicate distress, while buzzing clicks may indicate aggression.

   ▶ As far as deaths [from killer bees] are concerned, Mexican officials report that only sixteen people have died in the last three years as a result of their stings. That num-ber is similar to the number who die of shark bite. As one Texan put it, "The killer bee will be no more a threat to us than the rattlesnake."

   ▶ According to New Jersey congressman Frank Guarini, "American families play amuse-ment ride roulette every time they go on an outing to an amusement park."

   ▶ As reported by the *World Press Review Magazine,* the Japanese use of disposable chopsticks has resulted in the destruction of half of the hardwood forests in the Philippines and one-third of the forests in Indonesia. This trend will likely continue as long as the Japanese use twelve billion pairs of throwaway chopsticks a year, which is enough wood to build 12,000 average-sized family homes.

   ▶ In 1988, fetal brain cells were implanted deep into the brain of a fifty-two-year-old Parkinson's victim. Traditional treatments all failed this person. Now, he reports that his voice is much stronger, his mind is sharper and not confused, and he can walk without cane or crutches.

SPEECH VIDEO

Log on to the book's web-site to watch and critique Chris Russie's use of sup-porting materials.

Student Speech with Questions

The following is a speech Chris Russie gave at competitive speech meets throughout the Northwest. Read it, and identify the types of support he uses; then, using the tests in the text, evaluate the effectiveness of his support. This transcript of Chris's speech is also available on the book's website, where you can watch video of Chris's delivery.

LIFEGEMS: CREMAINS INTO DIAMONDS

Do you know that with use of modern technology you can be made into a perfect and permanent object of incredible beauty? There is one down side, however—first you have to die.

What am I talking about? you may ask yourself. Well, I'll tell you. A new company called LifeGem can take your cremated ashes and make diamonds out of you. Creepy? Perhaps, but before passing judgment, we should examine the company and their diamonds, the process for making these diamonds, and finally the need that such a service fulfills in our society. LifeGem allows people in the search for immortality to find it in some degree, in innovation.

What is LifeGem? LifeGem is a company, but more than that, it is a product and an idea that helps people deal with the loss of the recently departed. According to their website, LifeGem.com, this company was founded after three years of intensive research and development. They produce certified, high-quality diamonds from the cremated ashes of people— or their pets.

LifeGem believes that it is important to honor the dead, but that the experience of the survivors is equally important. They hope to be able to provide for families' distinct and individual needs, in producing a memorial to the ones they have lost.

Major type of support? Effectiveness?

Since the *Chicago Tribune* ran a front-page article about LifeGem on August 20th, the company's website has received approximately 20,000 hits daily, according to the September 13th *The Vista* Online.

Major type of support? Effectiveness?

In their product line, LifeGem carries between .25 carat diamonds for about $2,000— minimum order of two— and 1.0 carat diamonds, which cost about $14,000. Presently the diamonds come in three colors: blue, yellow, and red; in the future, they plan to create clear diamonds as well.

Major type(s) of support? Effectiveness?

In order to assure customers of the quality of their diamonds and to avoid any bias, LifeGem anonymously sent diamonds to be certified for quality by the European Gemological Laboratory before going public. . . . Greg Herro, head of LifeGem Memorials, claims that an August 21st news release by Reuters reported the diamonds are of the same quality "you would find at Tiffany's." The European Gemological Laboratory, according to the August 22nd *Milwaukee Journal Sentinel,* has since been certifying all of LifeGem's diamonds.

Major type of support? Effectiveness?

The idea for LifeGem started in 2001, according to the August 20th *Chicago Tribune,* when its creator and current chief operating officer, Rusty VandenBiesen, decided that he didn't want his final resting place to be in a cemetery or in an urn left on a fireplace mantle. He didn't know much about biochemistry or synthetic diamonds, but given that the body is in large part carbon, he figured that it should be possible to make diamonds, if he could find some way to extract a person's carbon.

Major type of support? Effectiveness?

This might lead one to ask, how are LifeGems made? LifeGem clients take a posthumous trip around the world. This trip has five stages: a European lab, a crematorium in Chicago, another lab in Pennsylvania, back to Europe, and finally, home. After several years of trial and error, an American-owned lab outside of Munich successfully produced diamonds out of a cadaver, claiming that one body could yield up to 50 stones of varying sizes. That number has now been increased to over 100 stones, according to LifeGem.com. This trip is of course the first and most important step, for without it the rest of our journey would be impossible.

Major type of support? Effectiveness?

Just after her death, the client is transported to a cremation facility— let's say in Chicago— that has an arrangement with LifeGem. She is then stored for one or two days, according to state law.

After that, she undergoes a special cremation where technicians control oxygen levels in order to minimize the conversion of the carbon into carbon dioxide. Before the incineration has been completed, the technicians halt the process long enough to collect the carbon. The cremation process then continues normally, according to the *Chicago Tribune*. Afterwards, the remains are removed from the chamber. Any foreign material such as shrapnel or bridgework is removed and typically discarded, according to LifeGem.com.

The remains are then processed to a consistent size and shape and placed in an urn of the family's choosing. If there is no urn, the remains are sent home in a cardboard or plastic container.

According to the *Journal Sentinel,* the carbon powder that was extracted during the cremation process is sent to Pennsylvania, where it is heated in a vacuum at 3,000 degrees Celsius or 5,400 degrees Fahrenheit, which turns it into graphite.

This graphite, in turn, is sent to the lab in Germany or to the Technological Institute for Superhard and Novel Carbon Materials near Moscow. There it will be placed around a diamond a few thousandths of a millimeter across to aid the crystallization process. Next, it is subjected to intense heat and pressure, roughly 80 thousand times the atmospheric pressure, replicating the forces involved in making a naturally occurring diamond, according to the September 3rd edition of the *Boston Globe*. This whole process takes about 16 weeks, according to Reuters.

The last and final step of this journey, as I am sure you have all suspected, is returning home. LifeGem will now send the client, in her new diamond form, back home to her family.

What possible function can this procedure serve? Our society has a growing demand for non-traditional funerals. According to *USA Today,* last year 26% of Americans who died were cremated, triple the number from 1973. By the year 2010 the Cremation Association of North America expects that number will jump to nearly 40%.

Major type of support? Effectiveness?

A primary reason for this change in American behavior is the rising cost of traditional funerals. Embalming and high-end coffins have raised the cost of the average funeral to $6,500 (and burial costs are extra). In contrast, cremations can cost less than $1,000, according to the National Funeral Directors Association. LifeGem can produce a single, quarter-carat diamond for $2,000. Even with the requirement of purchasing at least half a carat of diamonds, there is still a significant price difference.

This behavior is not isolated to America. One of LifeGem's goals is to break into the Japanese market, where, according to the *Chicago Tribune,* the national cremation rate is more than 98%. This is due, in large part, to the exorbitantly high property values.

Another important feature of American society that such an industry cannot ignore is the way that people shower their pets with love, attention, and, perhaps most importantly for this discussion, money. LifeGem plans to market their services in veterinarians' offices across the U.S. "People would wear a LifeGem to show off the love, light, and energy that came from their animals, too," states Herro. The pet market might in fact turn out to be significant, according to the *Boston Globe*. The company has had about 100 inquires from people who were interested in the process for a person and more than 100 inquires about using this process to immortalize a pet.

Major type of support? Effectiveness?

It seems logical to assume that price is not the only reason for this increase. People want to do something original with themselves, not only in life, but in death as well. This is clearly illustrated in the growing number of new forms of funerals. According to *USA Today,* the remains of Frisbee inventor Ed Headrick are being made into flying discs. Eternal Reefs in Atlanta will mix human ashes and concrete to produce artificial coastal reefs. According to the September 29th *Independent on Sunday* (London), Celestius, Inc. of the U.S. will launch your cremated ashes into space, an option that Gene Rodenberry chose. As you can see, people are being encouraged to be creative with their deaths. LifeGem provides another way they can do so.

Major type of support? Effectiveness?

One of Rusty VandenBiesen's hopes was that people could have something very personal to remember their loved ones with. He thought that urns and cemetery plots fail to inspire memories and discussions about loved ones who have passed away. He didn't like the idea of being forgotten.

Major type of support? Effectiveness?

So as you can see, you can be made into a perfect and permanent object of incredible beauty. LifeGem uses an extensive process to produces high-quality diamonds that do fulfill an actual societal demand. LifeGems provide people with a connection to those who have passed on, and a measure of immortality for those who never want to disappear.

Major type of support? Effectiveness?

CHAPTER 9

ORGANIZING YOUR SPEECH

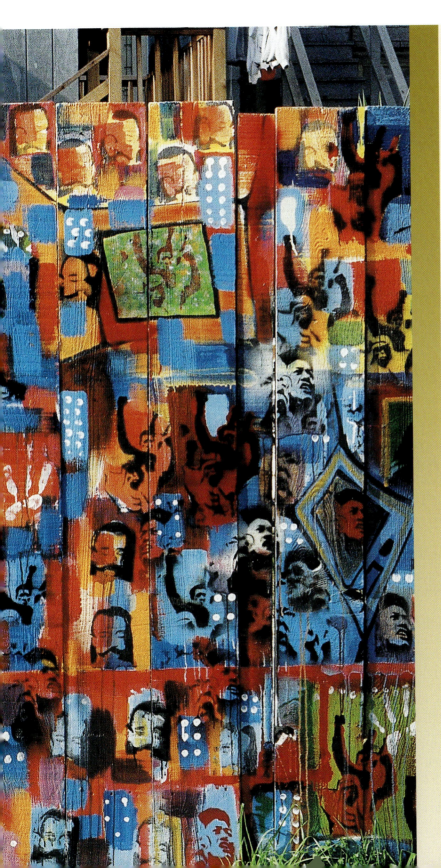

THIS CHAPTER WILL HELP YOU

▶ Organize your main points

▶ Identify and use a number of linear patterns, including chronological, spatial, causal, problem-solution, pro-con, and topical

▶ Identify and use more holistic, alternative patterns when they are appropriate, including the wave, the spiral, and the star

"Desaparecidos Pero no Olvidados" Mural © 1999 by Carlos Madriz, Josh Short, and Mabel Negrette. (Balmy Alley, Balmy and 24th Street, SF, CA)

BY NOW, you have chosen and carefully focused your topic. Even so, your research probably has produced so much information that you feel overwhelmed. How do you sort through it all to make an understandable speech—one that hangs together with a number of main points that have some sort of logical connection? Good speakers find ways to organize their thoughts and present their ideas in patterns that audiences can follow and remember. Otherwise, they frustrate their listeners, as Heidi and Gail point out:

> If an audience is confused or overwhelmed with disarrayed information, not only is the speech difficult to understand but the whole underlying credibility of the rhetor is diminished.
>
> HEIDI

> Organization is everything. . . . I consider it being kind to your audience as well as yourself.
>
> GAIL

Guidelines for organization fall into what the Romans called the *canon of disposition.* (See Chapter 2.) This chapter begins with general tips for identifying and organizing main points, moves on to explain some linear organizational patterns, and concludes with holistic, alternative methods of arranging the body of your speech.

CASE STUDY: CAREER ADVICE

The website **www.winningthejob.com** is an online career resource center from Impact Publications that gives advice for getting and keeping a job. One "secret" related to making presentations is not really so secret: Organized ideas are easier to understand.[1] Audiences are more likely pay attention, understand, accept, and remember your speech if it's well-organized. Put yourself in the listener's place: "Are you apt to be interested in something you don't understand? How hard will you work to make sense out of a speech that is hard to follow? If you don't see the speaker's point, you will probably soon take a mental exit." The "secret" concludes, "Some speeches are nothing more than a lot of thoughts on a given topic strung together. These 'stream of consciousness' presentations are an affront to the audience."

Questions for Discussion

▶ Is it true that you are more interested in well-organized speeches?
▶ What is the relationship between speech organization and your ability to remember ideas?
▶ How hard do you work to understand a speech that is disorganized?
▶ Do you consider a "stream of consciousness" speech to be an affront or insult when you are an audience member?
▶ Why is speech organization discussed in terms of "winning the job"?

Organize Your Main Points

Although the body is the middle part of your speech, you should plan it before you plan the introduction. Throughout your research, you probably have identified several subcategories of information such as causes, proposed solutions, or a sequence in which events occurred. Identifying these patterns can help you determine major points and supporting materials under each one. Here are a few general organizational tips.

Limit the Number of Points

Cognitive psychologists say we learn better when we portion blocks of information into three to seven major units (which explains why your telephone number is divided into three- and four-digit segments).[2] Consequently, listeners will remember your speech better if you develop a limited number of main points; three to five are common.

At this point in your preparation, return to the thesis statement you developed in Chapter 6. There you clearly identified the goal and direction of your speech; now you can start fleshing it out.

For instance, Maria wants to convince her classmates that the lottery winners are often unhappy, and people who want to be wealthy should spend their money elsewhere. So she initially set out this thesis:

> The lottery is a form of gambling that should be avoided because it often leads to unhappiness.

During her research, she finds material that clusters into three major points: (1) the lottery and its history, (2) the problems that winners encounter, and (3) alternatives to buying lottery tickets. She then revises her thesis statement to read like this:

> Lottery participants can avoid the financial and personal problems that often accompany lottery winnings by finding alternatives to this form of gambling.

Her major points are now easy to identify:

> I. Lotteries are a form of gambling.
> II. Lottery winners often have financial and personal problems as a result of winning.
> III. Most people would be happier if they found an alternative to playing the lottery.

She can now refine the preview of her major points:

> The lottery is a form of gambling that raises money for good causes; however, winning often creates financial and personal problems for winners, who would be better off spending their money elsewhere.

Support Each Point with Evidence

Chapter 8 describes numerous ways to support the major ideas of a speech, among them facts, examples, quotations, numerical information, and analogies. At this stage, Maria sits down with her articles about lottery winners and arranges specific pieces of data under each main point. Here's an example of her first major point:

> I. Lotteries are a form of gambling that raise money for good causes.
>   A. *Webster's Dictionary* identifies the lottery as a popular form of gambling.
>   1. Winners pay to participate, generally by purchasing tickets at a uniform price.
>   2. Winners are determined by chance.
>   B. Lotteries generate revenues for good causes.
>   1. The earliest lottery, organized in London in 1680, raised money for a municipal water supply.
>   2. A French lottery helped pay for the Statue of Liberty.
>   3. Lotteries helped support the colonial Jamestown colony and the American Revolution.
>   4. They provided funds for Harvard, Princeton, and Dartmouth colleges.
>   5. Current lotteries in New Hampshire and Oregon, among other states, provide educational funding.

(Maria's entire outline can be found at the end of the chapter and on the book's website, where you can also watch a video of the speech being delivered.)

Instructor's Resource Manual
Students sometimes have difficulty planning the middle of their speech before the introduction or conclusion. "Principles for Organizing Points" under "Discussion Topics" in Chapter 9 of the *Instructor's Resource Manual* (available in print, online, and on the Multimedia Manager CD-ROM) offers some suggestions for helping students with this problem.

Teaching Tip
Beginning speakers often try to incorporate too many points in their speech. Advise students to thoroughly develop two to five points well rather than mention all the points they can think of.

Classroom Discussion/ Activity
Have the class to generate a list of ways that organization helps speakers be more effective. Answers include increasing the speaker's confidence, helping audience members follow and understand the main points, maintaining audience interest, enhancing the speaker's credibility and persuasiveness, and ensuring that the speech does not last longer than the time allotted for it.

Order Your Points Effectively

For some topics, the ordering of points flows logically. Obviously, explaining lotteries in general before moving to the problems that winners encounter and suggesting alternatives is more logically satisfying than if Maria were to suggest alternatives, discuss the problems, then explain what lotteries are. For other speeches, the natural flow is less obvious. A topic such as recreational opportunities available in your state might have the following organization:

    I. Bungee jumping
   II. Hang gliding
  III. Hot air ballooning
  IV. Windsurfing

No logical reason dictates that bungee jumping is first and windsurfing last. In fact, the speaker might start with windsurfing, which happens on a river, and then describe the airborne sports. Or he might move from the least expensive to the most costly, depending on the audience. If these sports are centered in specific places, he could move from the nearest to the most distant options.

With these principles in mind, we now turn to a number of common organizational patterns.

Traditional Patterns

From listening to speakers throughout the years, you have developed some schema for organizational patterns. Some patterns work especially well for presenting facts and information; others are better for persuasive messages. (Chapter 17 presents additional persuasive patterns.) Here, we look at six traditional patterns that can help you organize a wide variety of topics: chronological, spatial, causal, problem-solution, pro-con, and topical.

Chronological Organization

In a **chronological pattern,** the sequencing—what comes first and what follows—must occur in a given order. This pattern is useful for biographical and historical speeches and for those that explain processes, stages, or cycles. It stands to reason that biographical speeches are often developed chronologically, because an individual's life unfolds across a period of years. Here is a sketch of the main points of a speech about a person's life:

James Nahkai, Jr. was a Navajo Code talker.
    I. He grew up on the Navajo reservation.
   II. He served his country as a code talker in the U.S. Marine Corps during
       World War II.
  III. He later participated in the Navajo Tribal Council.

Chronological organizational patterns also function effectively for describing historical happenings:

Horse racing, the second-most watched sport in the U.S., has a long history.
    I. The ancients, including Greeks and Romans, raced horses.
   II. In the 12th century, Crusaders brought swift Arabian horses to Europe.
  III. Racing became a professional English sport during Queen Anne's reign
       (1702–1714).
  IV. British settlers brought thoroughbreds to America, where a racetrack was built
       in 1665.
   V. Today there are 119 race tracks in 33 states.

chronological pattern a
pattern that presents points
in time or sequential order

Process speeches generally feature a chronological pattern, in which several steps or stages follow one another in fairly predictable sequences. You can speak about natural as well as social processes. This outline shows the chronological organization of a natural process:

> Tsunamis are enormous waves that have destructive potential.
>   I. They are triggered by landslides, volcanic actions, or most commonly, undersea earthquakes.
>   II. The trigger generates enormous waves that can move at speeds of 500 miles per hour.
>   III. As they approach land, the waves slow down and become higher.
>   IV. They hit land in an enormous wall of water.[3]

TSUNAMI!

A chronological pattern is useful for topics that describe ordered sequences. For example, a natural process such as a tsunami unfolds in stages or steps.

Many social, psychological, or personal processes also occur in patterned sequences or cycles. Norma summarized Professor Steve Duck's "theory of relational dissolution" in this brief outline:

> Four phases are typical when a relationship dissolves.
>   I. Intrapsychic phase: one or both partners ponder what to do about the relationship.
>   II. Dyadic phase: they discuss the possibility of breaking up.
>   III. Social phase: they tell other people about their breakup.
>   IV. Grave-dressing phase: they rationalize the breakup.

The key with chronological speeches is that events *must* occur in a sequence and follow a clear "first, next, finally" pattern. Occasionally, however, speakers vary the pattern by beginning with the final point before showing the events that led up to it. For instance, the speaker could first describe a divorced person rationalizing the divorce ("grave-dressing phase"), then flash back and provide details about the first three phases.

Spatial Organization

A less common way to organize points is spatially—by location or place. The **spatial pattern** is useful for speeches about places or things made up of several parts. For example, a campus guide showing a group how to use the library usually provides a map and describes what is located on each floor. Beginning on the ground floor, she works her way up to higher floors. The order in which you present your points doesn't matter with some topics, as this speech outline (which is divided geographically) demonstrates:

> New York City is made up of five boroughs.
>   I. Manhattan, located on Manhattan Island, is commonly thought of as "The City."
>   II. Brooklyn comprises King County on Long Island.
>   III. Queens, also on Long Island, is the most diverse county in the U.S.
>   IV. Staten Island is closer to New Jersey than to Manhattan.
>   V. The Bronx is on the mainland, just north of Manhattan.

Objects that you describe from top to bottom, bottom to top, or side to side are suitable for this pattern. For example, a brick pathway in a garden is constructed in four layers: gravel, heavy-duty weed-barrier fabric, sand, and bricks. A speech on the effects of alcohol on the human body could move from the brain down to the heart and other

process speech a speech that describes a sequence of steps or stages that follow one another in a fairly predictable pattern

spatial pattern presents points by place or location

© NOAA Tsunami Warning Sign

organs. Similarly, an exercise instructor might begin at the top with the head and neck and then work his way down the body spatially.

Causal Organization

Teaching Tip
http://web.utk.edu/~gwynne/
organizing.html
This site, developed by
Robert Gwynne at University
of Tennessee at Knoxville,
reinforces the importance
of organization. It defines
types of organization and
challenges students to
answer basic questions
about various methods of
organization.

Because Euro-American thought patterns emphasize causes and effects, many people in the U.S. look for reasons behind events. Consequently, **cause-effect patterns** are useful for organizing speeches on problems. You examine the reasons underlying the problem (the causes) and then look at implications of the problem for individuals or for society at large (the effects). There are two basic causal patterns: cause to effect and effect to cause. Here is a cause-to-effect outline for a speech on amusement park tragedies:

Amusement park tragedies injure thousands of people annually.
  I. Tragedies have three major causes.
    A. Equipment sometimes fails.
    B. Operators make mistakes.
    C. Riders' behaviors cause accidents.
  II. The effects are both personal and corporate.
    A. Riders suffer death or dismemberment.
    B. The industry becomes defensive and stonewalls the problem.

For some topics, you might decide it is more effective to first examine the problem's effects on an individual or group before you explore its causes. This is an effects-to-cause organization pattern.

People in the United States consume too much sugar.
  I. Effects include obesity, even in young children.
    A. Obesity is linked to cancer.
    B. Obesity is linked to heart disease.
    C. Obesity is linked to Type II diabetes in children.
  II. There are several causes of overconsumption of sugar.
    A. People lack awareness about the presence of sugar in common foods.
    B. Consumption of carbonated drinks is a major source of sugar.

Instructor's Resource Manual
European-American students
sometimes have difficulty following the speaking patterns
of students from other cultures. "Looking at Diversity:
Some African Organizational
Patterns" under "Discussion
Topics" in Chapter 9 of the *Instructor's Resource Manual*
(available in print, online, and
on the Multimedia Manager
CD-ROM) provides ideas
about discussing this issue.

> ### DIVERSITY IN PRACTICE
> ## SOME AFRICAN ORGANIZATIONAL PATTERNS
>
> IN MANY AREAS OF THE WORLD, speakers choose patterns markedly different from those presented in this text. Two such examples come from Africa.
>
> ### Madagascar
>
> Elders in the Merina tribe use a four-part organizational pattern when they speak:[4]
>
> 1. First is a period of excuses in which the speaker expresses his humility and reluctance to speak. He uses standard phrases such as "I am a child, a younger brother." He sometimes relates well-known stories and proverbs.
> 2. He follows this by thanking the authorities for letting him speak at all. He uses a formula that thanks God, the president of the republic, government ministers, the village headman, major elders, and finally the people in the audience.
> 3. In the third section, he uses proverbs, illustrations, and short poems as he makes his proposal.
> 4. He closes by thanking and blessing his listeners.
>
> *(continued)*

cause-effect pattern presents reasons (causes) and implications (effects) of a topic

Kenya

The body of the speech is not necessarily linear. In fact, a circular pattern, somewhat like a bicycle wheel, is more typical. The hub or center of the wheel is the single main point that ties the entire speech together. The speaker then wanders out repeatedly from the central point, telling stories and providing other supporting materials and stories that tie back to the main idea. To an outsider, the speech might seem boring or illogical, but Kenyan listeners are able to follow the logic that ties the points together.[5]

Problem-Solution Organization

In line with core beliefs that life is full of problems to be solved, we often approach global and national issues, as well as personal problems, as challenges to understand and solve through knowledge and effort. (In contrast, some cultures believe it is futile to fight fate.) Thus, you may find yourself using a **problem-solution pattern.** Not surprisingly, you'll first look at the problem—sometimes examining its causes and effects—and then you'll propose solutions. Here is an outline for an informative speech on the cost of prescription drugs and senior citizens that uses this pattern:

The high cost of prescription drugs is affecting the health of many senior citizens.
  I. Prescription drugs are increasingly costly.
    A. The problem is caused by higher demand for drugs and higher research costs.
    B. Effects include rising health-care costs and seniors who cannot pay for prescriptions.
  II. Several solutions have been proposed.
    A. Government solutions include Medicare prescription drug coverage and relaxed laws on drug imports.
    B. Individuals can comparison shop, get prescriptions by mail, and look for discounts.

Some speakers present problem-solution approaches to personal as well as national or global topics. This outline shows the major points in a speech about a personal issue:

Hair loss affects millions of people.
  I. Women as well as men experience hair loss.
    A. Hair loss is triggered by hormones, genetic factors, disease, drugs, or stressors.
    B. Hair loss effects are both psychological and social.
  II. There are several solutions on the market.
    A. Hairpieces or "rugs" vary in price and quality.
    B. Bonding requires glue that fixes hair fibers to the scalp.
    C. Certain medications have proved effective in hair regrowth.
    D. Transplanting is a surgical process done by a doctor.

When your purpose is to inform, introduce your listeners to a variety of solutions. In persuasive speeches, however, propose several solutions and then focus on the one solution you believe should be implemented. (Chapter 17 gives more information on the problem-solution pattern and explains additional organizational plans commonly used for persuasive speeches.)

problem-solution pattern describes a problem and a possible solution to it

The major points of a speech on sovereignty for the Hawaiian Islands can be organized in a number of ways, including pro-con, topical, chronological, and spatial.

Pro-Con Organization

In the United States, we commonly explore arguments on both sides of controversial issues. Consequently, for speeches that summarize both sides of an issue, the **pro-con arrangement** is very useful. Classify all the arguments in favor of the issue under the *pro* label, and then list the arguments against it under the *con* label. Here is an example of pro-con organization:

> The Hawaiian sovereignty movement has both proponents and opponents.
> I. There are four major arguments for an independent nation of Hawaii.
>   A. The 1898 annexation was illegal because the Senate never approved it.
>   B. Promises to return lands to Native Hawaiians made in the 1920s are still unkept.
>   C. The 1959 statehood vote is meaningless because independence was not a ballot option.
>   D. In 1993, President Clinton apologized for the illegal overthrow of 1898.
> II. There are three basic arguments against an independent nation of Hawaii.
>   A. Most residents of Hawaii are not native Hawaiians.
>   B. Changing the current legal, economic, and political systems would be difficult.
>   C. Other less drastic solutions would solve the problems.

This organizational pattern works best for informative speeches, when your goal is to explain the nature of an issue. By hearing both sides, your listeners can weigh the evidence and evaluate the arguments for themselves. When your purpose is persuasive (you advocate one set of arguments over another), a different pattern is usually more appropriate.

Topical Organization

When your material doesn't really fit into any of these organizational patterns, arrange your points with the most common pattern: topical organization. This arrangement classifies the major points into subdivisions, each of which is part of the whole. Although every point contributes to an overall understanding of the subject, the points themselves can be ordered in different ways. For instance, Jenn used the following **topical arrangement** for her classroom speech on animal communication:

> Animals communicate for four purposes:
> I. *Aggression* communicates their fierceness.
> II. *Appeasement* shows submission to another animal's aggressiveness.
> III. *Courtship* communicates attraction to a potential mate.
> IV. *Identification* provides information about themselves.

Perhaps she did so accidentally, but Jenn arranged her points in alphabetical order. She could have changed the order in several ways. For example, making identification the first point and then discussing appeasement, courtship, and aggression proceeds from calm, more social behaviors to more intense, antisocial animal behaviors.

pro-con arrangement presents arguments in favor of and arguments against an issue

topical arrangement a pattern that divides a subject into subtopics, each of which is part of the whole

Choosing the Best Pattern

Because you can organize the same topic in a number of ways, choose the pattern that works best given your purposes and your supporting materials. For instance, Hawaiian sovereignty could be effectively developed by using three other patterns:

Chronological: The Hawaiian sovereignty movement has made rapid gains in recent years.

I. In 1993, President Clinton apologized for the U.S. treatment of Hawaii.
II. In 1994, the Ohana Council members, led by "Bumpy" Kanahele, declared Hawaiian independence.
III. In 1998 and 1999, sovereignty supporters led an Aloha March in Washington, D.C. and held a sovereignty convention.
IV. In 2003, Hawaiian politicians submitted the Native Hawaiian Federal Recognition Bill.
V. In 2005, the U.S. Senate voted on the Native Hawaiian Government Reorganization Act which gives legal recognition to and a governing body for native Hawaiians.

Spatial: Four Hawaiian regions are so different that each one would experience sovereignty uniquely.

I. Ceded lands include 1.5 million acres of crown lands.
II. Homesteaded lands comprise 200 thousand acres promised to homesteaders in the 1920s.
III. Privately owned islands were purchased and developed by individuals such as Bill Gates.
IV. Developed islands are used for tourism and other industries.

Topical: Supporters of sovereignty have three general demands.

I. Independence: desires international recognition as a sovereign nation.
II. Nation-within-a-nation status: makes Hawaiians similar to Native American tribes in the United States.
III. Status quo: asks for reparations and full control of Hawaiian trust assets granted to Native Hawaiians.

BUILD YOUR SPEECH
DEVELOPING YOUR MAIN POINTS

Write your topic here: _____

Begin the process of organizing your material into main points. Study the evidence you found in your research, and then check all that apply.

The topic unfolds in *stages*.
The topic unfolds in *steps*.
Ordered dates are important to this topic.
There is a *before, during, and after* pattern.
The topic takes place in *distinct locations* or *places*.
Several *causes* are mentioned.
Several *effects* are present.
The topic describes a *problem*.
There is a *solution* or *solutions* to a problem.
There are *pro arguments* for a particular position.
There are *con arguments* against a particular position.
There are several *topical points* that don't really fit into one of these patterns.

(continued)

Teaching Tip
Most topics can be organized into more than one pattern. One criterion for choosing a particular pattern is the purpose of the speech. Which organizational pattern will best help the speaker accomplish that goal? A second criterion is the supporting material that the speaker has gathered. Organizational patterns can naturally emerge from these materials.

Student Learning: Workbook
Activity 9.1, "Using Traditional Patterns," in the *Student Workbook* helps students practice using traditional patterns for speeches with different purpose statements. This activity can be used with small groups or in a class discussion.

Teaching Tip
Effective speakers incorporate variety into their speeches, including variety in organizational patterns. They may use one pattern for the main points and a different pattern for subpoints. A speech on the history of the Internet might use a chronological pattern for the main points and a topical pattern for each subpoint. Remind students that they can combine organizational pattern to add variety to their speeches.

Student Learning: Speech Builder Express
Students often find it difficult to distinguish main points from subpoints, and they try to include too many main points for the typical brief classroom speech. Speech Builder Express provides customized prompts to help students develop a set of main points. Remember, you can ask students to email you a copy of their work for your review or evaluation.

Write your tentative thesis statement here: _____
_____
_____
_____

In light of the boxes you checked and your tentative central idea, select the organizational pattern that would work best with your speech:
_____
_____

Revise your thesis statement, if necessary: _____
_____
_____

Once you know which organizational pattern will work best for your speech and have confirmed your central idea, log on to Speech Builder Express for help developing the main points of your speech.

Alternative Patterns

In addition to the traditional patterns we've just examined, researchers have identified several alternative organizational patterns that allow speakers to visualize their speeches in a less linear way. For example, Cheryl Jorgensen-Earp[6] points out a number of alternative patterns that women have used historically. She believes that many speakers are uncomfortable with the standard organizational patterns due to cultural backgrounds or personal inclinations. As alternatives, she proposes several less direct and more **organic patterns** that provide a clear structure for a speech but have a less linear form. Jorgensen-Earp uses visual images to describe these patterns, comparing them to a wave, a spiral, and a star.[7]

organic pattern alternative pattern that provides a clear speech structure in a less linear form

wave pattern a repetitive pattern that presents variations of themes and ideas, with major points presented at the crests

The Wave Pattern

This pattern, illustrated in Figure 9.1, consists of repetitions and variations of themes and ideas. Major points come at the crests of the waves, which are developed with a variety of examples leading up to another crest, which repeats the theme or makes another major point. Conclusions wind down and lead the audience gradually from your topic; or they begin with a transition and then rebuild, so that your final statement is a dramatic peak. Women and members of various ethnic groups often choose the **wave pattern.**[8]

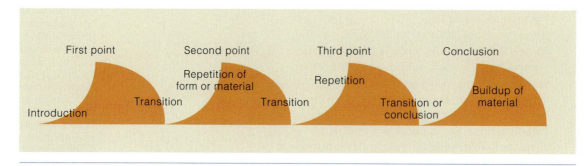

Figure 9.1
The Wave Pattern
Wave patterns are built around a repetitive theme such as "When I think of Ramadan" or "I have a dream."

Perhaps the most famous wave pattern speech is Martin Luther King, Jr.'s "I Have a Dream." King used this memorable line as the crest of a wave that he followed with examples of what he dreamed; then he repeated the line. He concluded with a dramatic peak that emerged from the final wave in the speech—the repetition and variation of the phrase "Let freedom ring." (Dr. King's entire speech is reprinted at the end of Chapter 13.)

An excerpt from Sojourner Truth's "Ain't I a Woman?" speech illustrates this pattern:[9]

> That man over there says that women need to be helped into carriages, and lifted over ditches, and to have the best place everywhere. Nobody ever helps me into carriages, or over mud-puddles, or gives me any best place!
>
> And ain't I a woman?
>
> Look at me! Look at my arm! I have ploughed and planted, and gathered into barns, and no man could head me!
>
> And ain't I a woman?
>
> I could work as much and eat as much as a man—when I could get it—and bear the lash as well!
>
> And ain't I a woman?
>
> I have borne thirteen children, and seen them most all sold off to slavery, and when I cried out with my mother's grief, none but Jesus heard me!
>
> And ain't I a woman?

As you can see, this can be a very powerful technique to stir audience emotions.

Another example comes from McGill University's Professor Fahri Karakas, a Muslim who is a native of Turkey, in an address to an interfaith dialogue dinner in Canada.[10]

> Ramadan is commonly called the "Lord of Eleven Months." It is a very special month for Muslims, filled with lots of blessings, happiness, love, and sharing.
>   When I think of Ramadan, I remember Turkey . . . [followed by details]
>   When I think of Ramadan, I remember special *iftar* (dinner) tents built on every corner in Istanbul . . . [details]
>   When I think of Ramadan, I remember my dear mother . . . [details]
>   When I think of Ramadan, I remember fasting . . . [details]

(An excerpt from this speech is printed in Appendix C.)

In summary, between the major points or crests of your speech, use a barrage of specific and general examples to illustrate and support them. Employ repetition and variation throughout. Although the examples in this section repeated a phrase, this is not a requirement. You can use a similar style by stating main points that are similar in intensity but differently phrased.

The Spiral Pattern

When Shanna was asked to talk to high school students about selecting a college, she decided to create a hypothetical student, Todd, and have him appear in three scenarios, each one costing more money and taking him further from home. She visualized a **spiral pattern** as she framed her speech using the three scenarios. In the first loop of the spiral, she described his choices and experiences at a local community college. In the next one, she described sending Todd out of town but kept him at a public institution within the state. In the third and final loop, she described placing Todd at a private university across the continent from his hometown.

Instructor Resource: PowerPoint
The *Multimedia Manager with Instructor Resources* CD-ROM includes a PowerPoint slide of Figure 9.1.

spiral pattern a repetitive pattern with a series of points that increase in drama or intensity

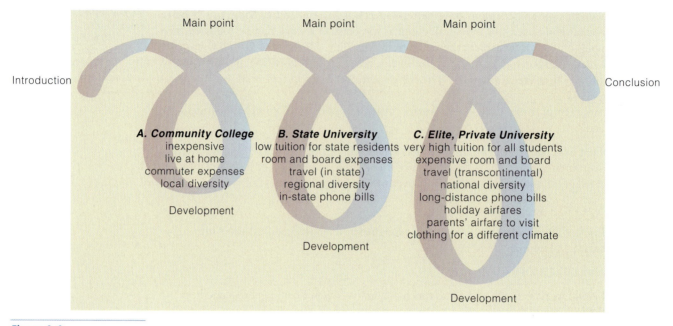

Main point   Main point   Main point

Introduction   Conclusion

A. Community College
inexpensive
live at home
commuter expenses
local diversity

Development

B. State University
low tuition for state residents
room and board expenses
travel (in state)
regional diversity
in-state phone bills

Development

C. Elite, Private University
very high tuition for all students
expensive room and board
travel (transcontinental)
national diversity
long-distance phone bills
holiday airfares
parents' airfare to visit
clothing for a different climate

Development

Figure 9.2
The Spiral Pattern
Shanna uses this pattern to show Todd's progress through increasingly dramatic situations and levels of adjustment.

star pattern presents relatively equally weighted speech points within a thematic circle that binds them together; order of points may vary

Because each major scenario was more difficult or more dramatic than the preceding one, her speech depicted Todd moving from smaller to larger adjustments. Figure 9.2 illustrates the spiral pattern and how Shanna how might sketch and write out her points using it. Notice the increasing sizes of the loops used to represent each scenario.

The spiral pattern is often useful for speeches on topics such as battered men that can build in dramatic intensity. A series of narratives might revolve around a hypothetical character named Dan who lives with an abusive partner. In the first scenario, Dan is abused verbally. In the second, he receives a black eye and a broken nose. In the final scenario, his partner rams him with her car and he is hospitalized with life-threatening injuries. Each scene builds in tension, with the most controversial scenario reserved for the final spiral.

The Star Pattern

Each point in a **star pattern** speech, illustrated in Figure 9.3, is more or less equally weighted within a theme that ties the whole together. This variation on the topical pattern is useful if you present the same basic speech to a number of audiences. By visualizing your major points as a star, you have the flexibility of choosing where to start and what to emphasize, depending on what's relevant for a specific audience. For example, you could begin with a point your audience understands or agrees with and then progressively move to points that challenge their understanding and agreement. For inattentive audiences, begin with your most dramatic point. For hostile audiences, begin with your most conciliatory point. This gives you the advantage of quickly making audience adaptations and still having your speech work effectively.

There are two ways to develop the points of the speech. One way is to state the point, support or develop it, and then provide a transition to the next point. Alternatively, you could develop each point fully and then state it. Base your decisions on the type of audience and the nature of your message.

The final element in the pattern is the thematic circle that binds your points together. By the close of the speech, listeners should feel that the circle is completed and the theme is fulfilled. For instance, Jan presents seminars on investment management around the general theme of financial security, with points on retirement plans, medical insurance, growth investments, and global funds. With some audiences, she begins with retirement plans and ends with global investments; with others, she begins with growth and global funds and ends with medical insurance and retirement plans. Either way, her points show how listeners can create financial security.

We commonly hear this pattern during election years. The underlying theme is "Vote for me!" Then the candidates stake out their positions on various issues. However, instead of giving an identical "stump speech" to every group, they rearrange the issues and target specific points to specific audiences. For soccer moms, a candidate might begin with education and end with crime issues; for elders, the same candidate might begin with Social Security and end with educational policies.

Repetition patterns are common in songwriting. Each verse develops the song's theme, while the chorus lyrics are repeated unchanged. Although they might appear to be easier to use than a linear format, these patterns require just as much organizational planning.

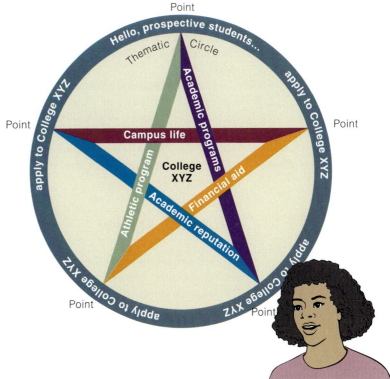

Figure 9.3
The Star Pattern
This college recruiter visualizes her speeches as points of a star enclosed by the overall theme "Apply to this college." The order of her points depends on her specific audience— sometimes she starts with the sports program, sometimes with campus life, sometimes with the academic reputation of the college.

✓ **STOP AND CHECK**

DEVELOP YOUR SPEECH USING AN ALTERNATIVE PATTERN

Write your topic here: _____

For a wave pattern:
Draw out a diagram similar to Figure 9.1, and then identify each wave crest that you will develop with supporting evidence. Write the repetitive phrase or idea at the crest of the wave and then list your supporting material below it.

For a spiral pattern:
Draw a diagram similar to Figure 9.2. Write out the main point at the bottom of each loop. Then jot down the supporting material you will use to develop each loop.

For a star pattern:
Sketch out a star within a circle. (Your star does not have to have five points.) Write your major ideas on the points of the star, one idea per point. In the circle that connects your points, write out your speech's central theme.

Summary

After you've gathered speech materials, you must organize them into a pattern. Begin with the body of the speech, and choose from among several linear patterns to organize your major points. Common organizational frameworks include chronological, spatial,

Instructor's Resource Manual
Teaching Ideas 9.1 and 9.2 in the *Instructor's Resource Manual* (available in print, online, and on the Multimedia Manager CD-ROM) provide ways to help students practice identifying organizational patterns.

Student Learning: Workbook
Students can complete "Before You Take the Exam" in Chapter 9 of the *Student Workbook* for a review of the chapter.

causal, pro-con, problem-solution, and topical patterns. These patterns are appropriate for many types of speeches; causal and pro-con are especially good for informative purposes. However, the six patterns discussed here are not the only ways to organize materials; Chapter 17 presents several additional methods typically used in persuasive speeches.

Furthermore, nonlinear patterns are typical in diverse settings, as the examples from Madagascar and Kenya and the alternative patterns show. Women and various ethnic speakers, for example, might prefer holistic or organic patterns such as the repetitive wave or the spiral. Speakers who want flexible points within a major theme pattern can visualize their ideas in the form of a star. Regardless of the pattern, traditional or alternative, you must carefully identify your main points and then develop them with appropriate supporting materials.

STUDY AND REVIEW

The premium website for *Public Speaking* offers a broad range of resources that will help you better understand the material in this chapter, complete assignments, and succeed on tests. The website features

▶ Speech videos with critical viewing questions, speech outlines, and transcripts, and
▶ Interactive practice activities, self quizzes, and a sample final exam.

For more information about this text's electronic learning resources, consult your **Guide to Online Resources for Public Speaking** or visit http://communication.wadsworth.com/jaffe5.

KEY TERMS

The terms below are defined in the margins throughout this chapter. The book's website also provides interactive flashcards and crossword puzzles to help you learn these terms and the concepts they represent.

chronological pattern 158
process speech 159
spatial pattern 159
cause-effect pattern 160
problem-solution pattern 161
pro-con arrangement 162

topical arrangement 162
organic pattern 164
wave pattern 164
spiral pattern 165
star pattern 166

Student Learning: Book Website
Under "Chapter Resources," students will find several tools for reviewing the information in this chapter, including a "Tutorial Quiz." You could also have them email you the results of this quiz as a participation or extra-credit activity.

APPLICATION AND CRITICAL THINKING EXERCISES

The exercises below are among the practice activities on the book's website.

1. Outline one of the speeches available on the book's website. (Don't use a Speech of Introduction; they usually have a slightly different organizational pattern.) Is the organizational pattern easy to discern? What suggestions, if any, could you give the speaker about arranging the points of the speech?

2. With a small group of your classmates, take a topic such as abortion, divorce, alcohol on campus, or immigration, and organize major points in as many of the following patterns as you can: topical, chronological, spatial, cause-effect, pro-con, problem-solution, spiral.

3. Read or listen to a recording of a speech by an African American such as Vernon Jordan, Malcolm X, or Martin Luther King, Jr. You can find several good examples on www.AmericanRhetoric.com. What basic organizational pattern does the speaker use? Can you find examples of alternative patterns within the speech?

4. Do an Internet search for "I have a dream" or "Ain't I a woman?" How many hits do you get? Both of these speeches have inspired groups as well as individuals, which shows the power of rhetoric to influence a culture. Follow one of the links to find out more about King's or Truth's vision.

5. Take the theme of creativity or the theme of perseverance. Then work with two or three classmates and discuss how you might create a speech organized around the wave, the spiral, or the star pattern. For example, think of three famous people who persevered . . . each one in a more dramatic way. Or use examples from your school's sports teams, your personal lives, lives of entertainers, and so on.

SPEECH VIDEO

After reading and analyzing Maria DiMaggio's speech outline below, log on to the book's website to watch video of her speech being delivered. You may also want to watch Hans Erian's speech "The Overconsumption of Sugar." Then determine the organizational pattern he used.

Student Learning: Book Website
Video clips of these speeches are available on the book website for viewing and evaluation or guided critical analysis. The clips are also available on the Multimedia Manager CD-ROM.

Student Outline with Commentary

YOU HAVE MY DEEPEST SYMPATHY: YOU JUST WON THE LOTTERY
Maria DiMaggio

General Purpose:	To persuade
Specific Purpose:	To persuade my audience that winning the lottery is not as great as it's perceived to be and that they should invest their money in alternative ways.
Thesis statement:	Lottery participants could avoid the financial and personal problems that often accompany lottery winnings by finding alternatives to this form of gambling.
Preview:	The lottery, a form of gambling, raises money for good causes; however, winning often creates financial and personal problems for the winners, and participants are better off spending their money elsewhere.

Introduction

I. You have my deepest sympathy; you just won the lottery.

II. Most of us would be shocked if someone said we'd won $20 million and then offered us condolences; however, hundreds of lottery winners have discovered the downside of winning big.

III. I used to think I'd be the happiest person in Brooklyn if I could just win a million dollars, but my research about lottery winners convinced me to spend my money elsewhere— and I hope you'll follow my example.

IV. Lottery participants can avoid problems that often accompany lottery winnings by finding alternatives to this form of gambling.

Maria's introduction starts dramatically. She follows with her thesis statement and previews the major points she'll develop.

Maria uses a problem-solution organizational pattern.

V. Today, I'll explain that the lottery is a form of gambling that raises money for good causes; however, winners often end up with financial and personal problems, and you are better off spending your money elsewhere.

Body

I. Lotteries are a form of gambling that raise money for good causes.

A. *The World Book Encyclopedia* (Chuman, 2000) identifies lotteries as a popular form of gambling.

1. Winners pay to participate, generally by purchasing tickets at a uniform price.
2. Winners are determined by random drawings; unfortunately, you are 16 times more likely to get killed driving to buy the ticket than you are to win a record amount (Associated Press 2002).
3. Lotteries were popular in the United States in the 1700s.
4. However, several states made them unconstitutional in the 1880s due to fraud by lottery companies and pressure from social reformers (von Herrmann 2002).
5. New Hampshire reinstated the lottery in 1963; now, more than half the states have state-run lotteries.

B. Lotteries generate revenues for good causes.

1. The earliest lottery, organized in London in 1680, raised money for a municipal water supply.
2. A French lottery helped pay for the Statue of Liberty.
3. Closer to home, a national lottery helped support the American Revolutionary War (Findlay 1986).
4. In 1772, one lottery's proceeds were divided among a Presbyterian church, a German Lutheran church, the Newark Academy, and three Philadelphia schoolmasters (Findlay 1986).
5. Current lotteries in New Hampshire and Oregon, among other states, provide educational funding.

Transition: Now that we know a bit about the history of lotteries, you'd think your life would be great if you could only win big. Right? Well, there can be major problems for winners and their heirs.

II. Unexpected problems arise for lottery winners.

A. First, their dreams of instant riches are not always fulfilled.

1. Unless winners take a much lower lump sum, funds are distributed over twenty to twenty-five years.
2. A lottery "millionaire" is really a "thousandair" who gets about $50,000 annually before taxes, delinquent taxes, past-due child support, and student loans are taken out (Sanford 1996).
3. Winners cannot draw cash from winnings, use them as collateral for loans, or liquidate future payments.

B. In addition, many suffer personal loss and rejection.

1. William "Bud" Post won $16.2 million but watched his brother go to jail, convicted of hiring a hit man to kill him (Goodman 2004).
2. Debbie won $6.85 million but lost contact with her sisters, who stopped speaking to her when she declined to pay their debts.
3. Bernice took a day off work to claim her $1 million; her job was given to someone else.
4. Daisy won $2.8 million but went through a painful lawsuit.
   a. Her son's friend sued for half the winnings because she asked the friend to pray that she'd win.
   b. He prayed, she won, so he thought he was entitled to some of her money.
   c. The court ruled against him, saying he couldn't prove his prayers caused her to win.

The problem section comes in two main points; first she gives some background information.

The transition tells where she's been and where she's going.

In this, her second major point, Maria describes problems not only for the winners but also for their heirs.

C. Lottery winnings don't necessarily bring happiness.
1. A study of people with the best of luck and those with the worst of luck supported this conclusion (Brickman, Coates, and Janoff-Bulman 1978).
2. Accident victims weren't as unhappy as expected; however, lottery winners were more unhappy and took less pleasure in life than expected.

D. Finally, heaven help the heirs if a lottery-winning relative dies and leaves them a fortune.
1. They must immediately pay estate taxes on the unpaid total, with monthly penalties added after nine months.
2. Johnny Ray Brewster won $12.8 million, taking it in annual payments. His sister Peggy inherited the payments, but upon inheritance she immediately owed $3.5 million in taxes (Beyer and Petrini 2000).

Given the low probability of winning and the many problems winners face, there surely must be other solutions if you have money to burn.

The solution section is relatively brief. Maria focuses on personal solutions, not more top-down regulations.

III. Use your extra money in far more profitable expenditures.
A. Invest in the stock market; investing just $10 to $20 monthly can pay off immensely by the time you retire.
B. Donate your extra money to a charitable organization and claim a tax deduction.
C. Indulge yourself: buy cable, eat lobster occasionally, buy season tickets to a sporting or a cultural event, or get an exotic pet.
D. Finally, if you like to think your lottery money supports education, you can donate to my college fund!

Her final suggestion adds humor.

Conclusion

I. I hope I've convinced you that playing the lottery is not all it's advertised to be.
II. I've explained what the lottery is, the problems it can cause, and some alternative ways to get rid of money.
III. So the next time you see a new lottery multimillionaire, consider sending your sympathies rather than your congratulations.

References

Associated Press. (2002). Compare the odds. *The Detroit News.* [Electronic version]. Retrieved June 2, 2005, from **www.detnews.com/2002/metro/0204/16/b01-446437.htm**

Beyer, G. W. & Petrini, J. (2000). *Lottery players and winners: Estate planning for the optimistic and the lucky.* Retrieved June 2, 2005, from **www.professorbeyer.com/Articles/Lottery.htm**

Brickman, P., Coates, D. & Janoff-Bulman, R. (1978). Lottery winners and accident victims: Is happiness relative? *Journal of Personality and Social Psychology, 36*(8), 917–927.

Findlay, J. M. (1986). *People of chance.* New York: Oxford University Press.

Goodman, E. (2004, November 18). *8 lottery winners who lost their millions.* Retrieved June 2, 2005, from **http://moneycentral.msn.com/content/Savinganddebt/Savemoney/P99649.asp**

Sanford, R. (1996). *Jackpot! What to do before and after you win the lottery.* Retrieved June 2, 2005, from **www.note.com/note/pp.jackpot.html**

Von Herrmann, D. (2002). *The big gamble: The politics of lottery and casino expansion.* Westport, CT: Praeger.

COMPLETING YOUR SPEECH

THIS CHAPTER WILL HELP YOU

▶ Develop an introduction for your speech that gains attention, motivates the audience to listen, establishes your credibility, and previews the speech

▶ Develop a conclusion that signals the end, summarizes, provides psychological closure, and ends with impact

▶ Link the parts of the speech to one another through skillful use of connectives such as signposts and transitions, internal previews, and internal summaries

"The Chant of the Earth, The Voice of the Land"
Mural © 1991 by Betsie Miller-Kusz.
(Market Street and 19th Street, SF, CA)

OR SOME TIME NOW, you've immersed yourself in your topic. You've worked hard to gather material and organize it into major points, and you've selected interesting supporting data. But your audience is so far unaware of all the interesting information you have discovered. Your task now is to create an introduction that functions to take listeners from their everyday concerns into the carefully crafted world of your speech. Then, plan a brief conclusion that brings your audience back to the here-and-now of the classroom, but leaves them with something to remember.

This chapter will help you skillfully lead your listeners into your subject and, at the end, conclude in a way that summarizes your thoughts and leaves a memorable impression. You will also learn how to connect your ideas to one another and to the speech as a whole.

CASE STUDY: TWO INTRODUCTIONS

Chapter-at-a-Glance

This chapter presents the fundamentals of effective introductions, conclusions, and connectives. It begins with four major purposes of an introduction: gaining audience attention, providing a reason to listen, establishing credibility, and previewing the speech's main points. Next, it presents four major functions of a conclusion: signaling the end, summarizing, providing psychological closure, and ending with impact. The chapter ends with a discussion of four techniques to connect the parts of a speech into a coherent whole: signposts, transitions, internal previews, and internal summaries.

Instructor Resource: Video Clip

The Multimedia Manager CD-ROM (and the book website) includes several short clips that provide examples of effective beginnings and endings. Each segment begins with an attention-getting device. Have students identify each device or combination of devices.

Teaching Tip

Emphasize that an effective introduction achieves all four of the major purposes: gaining attention, providing a reason to listen, establishing credibility, and previewing the main points. An introduction that fails to accomplish any of the four is less effective.

Imagine that you're listening to these two introductions for a speech about televised executions of criminals.

> Introduction #1: Would you watch an execution? Today, I'll enlighten you with some information about television coverage of live executions.

> Introduction #2: On May 16, 2001, three hundred people solemnly filed into a Midwest auditorium to participate in a unique American experience: the telecast of a live execution. In order to watch Timothy McVeigh die, he must have tried to kill you or murdered a member of your family on April 19, 1995. . . . No one will really know the tangle of competing motives in that remote viewing room. After all, we see death on TV every day — in the news, in the coverage of auto races and in virtually all television dramas. Why would anyone expend so much time, effort, and anguish simply to watch another human die on television?[1]

Questions for Discussion

- What impression does each speaker initially create?
- Which introduction best gains your attention? Arouses your curiosity? Why?
- Which speaker seems more prepared? More credible? Why?
- How would you introduce a speech on the same topic?

Plan Your Introduction

Work on your introduction after you have planned the body of the speech. As Chapter 2 points out, the Roman educator Quintilian identified four purposes for an introduction[2]:

1. To draw the listeners' attention to the topic
2. To motivate the audience to listen
3. To establish yourself as knowledgeable about the topic
4. To preview the major ideas of the speech

In addition, include definitions or background information that listeners must know if they are to understand your subject. By including these elements in your introduction, you'll answer four basic questions that listeners ask up front: What's this all about? Why should I listen? Why should I listen to you? What will you cover? Figure 10.1 depicts the four introductory functions that this section covers.

Figure 10.1
The Audience's Four Questions
The introduction functions to answer these four questions that your listeners have.

Teaching Tip
Effective introductions and conclusions must be carefully researched, planned, written, and practiced. Speakers who start strong are more likely to be forgiven for minor slips later. Speakers who begin poorly rarely regain the audience's confidence. Speakers rarely get a second chance to make a positive first impression.

Instructor Resource: PowerPoint
The *Multimedia Manager with Instructor Resources* CD-ROM includes a PowerPoint slide of Figure 10.1.

Teaching Tip
Advise students to look for appropriate material for the introduction and conclusion while they are doing research for their main points. A quotation that is too dramatic for supporting material might be perfect for the introduction. Speakers should keep their eyes open for usable stories, examples, statistics, anecdotes, humor, and quotations.

Instructor's Resource Manual
Teaching Idea 10.1 in the *Instructor's Resource Manual* (available in print, online, and on the Multimedia Manager CD-ROM) suggests three ways to help your students understand and practice gaining attention in their introductions.

Gain Attention

Gaining attention is the first step in the listening process, so it's important to answer immediately your audience's question, "What's this speech about?" Avoid the temptation to simply announce: "Today, my speech is about the mullet hairstyle." True, this introduces your subject, but it's not very creative, so look for a more effective attention-gaining strategy from among the ideas discussed in this section.

Ask a Question

Choose either a rhetorical or a participatory question. **Rhetorical questions** are the kind listeners answer in their mind; **participatory questions,** in contrast, call for an overt response, such as a show of hands or a verbal answer. Quianna Clay's speech (outlined at the end of Chapter 7) began with two rhetorical questions:

> Did you know that flaxseed oil and cottage cheese can now cure lung cancer? Or that avoiding dairy products will dissolve cataracts? Well, neither did registered dietician Ira Milner, until he spent 60 hours online and found a plethora of such medical misinformation.

Her listeners could respond internally to these rhetorical questions; many probably know someone with lung cancer or with cataracts, and they are aware of typical medical procedures for these conditions. Most listeners can conjure up a mental picture of a scoop of cottage cheese or a glass of milk. The incongruity of these "cures" draws the audience into the topic.

In contrast, for a participatory question, let the audience know the response you want. For instance, ask for a show of hands or call on a member of the audience to answer a specific question you pose. One professional speaker[3] asked listeners to take out a pen or pencil and write down the age to which they expected to live; he then asked these questions:

> By a show of hands please, how many put in at least age 70? Just about everyone in the room. How many put in at least age 80? How many put at least age 90? Still

rhetorical questions
questions that listeners answer in their minds

participatory questions
questions that listeners answer overtly

Student Learning: Workbook
Activity 10.1, "Gaining Attention," in the Student Workbook asks students to choose the most and least effective attention-gaining choices from several examples.

Classroom Discussion/ Activity
Ask students to describe ineffective questions they have heard speakers use as attention-getters. If you have access to previous student speeches or outlines with examples of effective and ineffective questions, share them with the class and have students suggest alternatives that would be more interesting.

a healthy number, isn't there? And how many put at least age 100? How about 105? . . . The people who raised their hands for 90 or 100 are likely to be accurate . . . but the paradox of living to 100 or 105 is that it's wasted if each day flies by quickly.

To capture attention, a question must be sufficiently intriguing. Return to the chapter-opening case study; both speakers ask a question, but the second speaker makes his question more engaging. Now look at these three questions from student speeches:

How many of you have ever purchased an album, cassette, or compact disc?

Have you ever had your finger almost sliced off and left hanging by a small piece of skin?

Have you ever visited a nudist colony?

They are not very effective: The first is too broad; the second too specific; the third too remote for most people to relate to. In contrast, good rhetorical and participatory questions can establish dialogue between you and your listeners because they invite audience responses, whether mental or physical.

Provide a Vivid Description

Draw attention to your subject by describing a scene so vividly that your listeners are compelled to visualize it. The scene can be either real or imaginary. The second introduction in the opening case study is one example; here is another: Danae's opening for her classroom speech on arachnophobia (fear of spiders):

Imagine yourself just hanging out one morning, minding your own business, when a large, monstrous body, fifty times your size, casually approaches you, then, suddenly, lets out a blood-curdling scream, hurls a giant bowl your way, and takes off running. Sound familiar? It would if you were the spider that had the misfortune of getting just a little too close to Little Miss Muffet of nursery rhyme fame. I venture to say that we all have had to deal with spiders at some time in our lives. They seem to be everywhere, especially at this time of year. What causes this Muffet-type reaction? It just may be arachnophobia—the irrational fear of spiders.[4]

Begin with a Quotation

Teaching Tip
Quotations used to gain audience attention should be brief. Whenever possible, quotations that may be familiar to some audience members are particularly effective.

Classroom Discussion/ Activity
http://www.bartelby.com/ quotations/
The website Bartleby.com provides access to a 1919 edition of the best-known collection of quotations, Bartlett's Familiar Quotations, as well as three more contemporary collections, but there are other online sources. Ask students to conduct an Internet search for the word "quotations" and bring to class information about a site they found particularly useful along with an interesting quotation.

Beginning with a quotation or a familiar cultural proverb, either *about* a subject or, for a biographical speech, *by* the subject, is a good way to gain attention. Choose a saying that captures your overall theme, and cite its source. For example, Thomas Martin[5] began his speech, with a quotation from the *Hobbit*:

Yesterday morning I rose at 3 a.m. to drive 200 miles to Omaha, Nebraska, in order to fly to Hartford, Connecticut. When the alarm went off at 3, I was immediately reminded of Bilbo Baggins's response to Gandalf, who had asked him to leave his hobbit hole and venture forth with him into the world.

Gandalf: "I am looking for someone to share in an adventure that I am arranging, and it's very difficult to find anyone."

Bilbo: "I should think so in these parts! We are plain, quiet folk and have no use for adventure. Nasty, disturbing uncomfortable things! Make you late for dinner! I can't think what anybody sees in them."

I, like Bilbo, wanted to stay in my hobbit hole. . . . Gandalf, as you might remember, did not allow Bilbo to stay home.

When Harold Tinkler[6] spoke on accounting ethics at Texas A&M, he used a quotation that was familiar to his audience:

This afternoon, I took a few minutes to see the monument to the Aggie Code of Honor, and I was impressed by the message it sends to the university community. "Aggies don't lie, cheat or steal, or tolerate those who do." That just about says it all. It's straightforward and direct. I admire that.

Search for quotations in song lyrics, poems, or scriptural texts. Or use family sayings or memorable words spoken by someone such as a coach or teacher. For instance, a speech on perseverance might open with "My immigrant grandmother used to say, 'It's a great life if you don't weaken.'" The Internet contains sources for thousands of quotations on sites like www.quoteland.com, www.bartleby.com/100/, or www.quotesandsayings.com.

Use an Audio or Visual Aid

Posters, charts, tape recordings, and other visual and audio materials can successfully draw attention to your topic. For example, Tom displayed a large poster of an automobile as he began his speech explaining how to buy a car overseas. Denise began her speech on artist Dale Chihuly with a photograph of one of his blown glass pieces. Yesenia, who spoke about the composer Hector Berlioz, opened with a short cut from a Berlioz symphony:

© Josh Nauman

> [Play a 20-second clip of Berlioz's music during points I & II of the introduction.] (Voice over, pausing between words) unearthly sounds . . . nighttime . . . distant horn calls . . . summoning . . .

Tell a Joke or Funny Story

Professional speakers often begin with a joke that immediately creates an informal, humorous atmosphere. If you have good comedic skills, you might try this strategy; however, you can easily embarrass yourself if the joke flops. To avoid humiliation, test your attempt at humor in advance on some friends and let them decide if it's really funny. Make sure your joke relates to your topic. Otherwise, although you might gain attention, it won't focus on your subject. Here is a riddle that could start a speech on learning a second language:

Draw listeners' attention to your topic at the outset of your speech. One effective attention-gaining strategy is to use a visual aid like this Navajo rug.

> You know the word for a person who knows three languages? It's trilingual.
> What's the word for a person who knows two languages? Right, it's bilingual.
> What do you call a person who knows only one language?
> The correct answer is: "An American!"

Although most students in the rest of the world study English as well as their own languages, most high school graduates in the United States know only English.

You can include humor without having to tell a joke by displaying a relevant cartoon that you have transferred to a transparency or scanned into a PowerPoint presentation (giving proper credit to the source, of course).

Refer to a Current Event

One way to identify with your listeners and establish common ground is to begin with well-known current happenings—airplane crashes, campus controversies, weather disasters, well-publicized trials, elections, and the like. In late 2004, many speakers referred to the Boston Red Sox's amazing win in the 2004 World Series; in late December of that year, others incorporated the tsunami disaster into their introductions. Here's how Richard Abdoo incorporated election ads into his October 2004 speech titled "Lessons in Doing the Right Thing":[7]

> Ladies and Gentlemen: My name is Richard Abdoo and I approve this message!

Search InfoTrac College Edition for the journal *Vital Speeches,* and look for examples of other speakers who have used current events in their speech openings.

Begin with an Example

As Chapter 8 pointed out, examples give your listeners an opportunity to become emotionally involved with your topic. Everyone likes a good story, and stories of real people involved in real situations generally makes us more attentive. Bonita began her speech on the dangers of driving drowsy with this example:

> On July 3, 2003, a man and his family are driving their van down the road as it is getting light. An oncoming driver has been driving since midnight; he tries to pass a bus, but fails to see the van coming toward him. Because he is tired, the would-be passer cannot react quickly enough to slide back into his own lane, and his car collides head-on with the van, killing the woman in the passenger seat.

 (This entire speech is found at the end of this chapter and on the book's website.) This example introduced a speech about the process of marriage annulment:

> After twenty-three years of marriage, four children, a year of separation, and fifteen years of divorce, a man tells his ex-wife that he has decided to get an annulment in the Catholic Church.

Start with Startling Numbers

Numbers and statistics can be dry; however, they can also capture and hold your listeners' attention if they are shocking enough or if they are put into an understandable context, as this example illustrates:

> According to the Centers for Disease Control, 72 percent of young adults eat too much fat, and fewer than one in five follow recommended dietary guidelines. That means that, in this classroom with twenty-five students enrolled, we might predict that eighteen people indulge in too many hamburgers and milkshakes and that twenty people routinely ignore their physicians' nutritional recommendations. I confess, I'm talking about myself here.

Although this is not an exhaustive list of successful opening strategies, it gives you examples of common means used in a variety of settings. Remember that your opening should not simply gain attention; it must also draw attention to your topic. James ignored this rule and slapped the podium loudly; when listeners jumped to attention, he said, "Now that I have your attention, I am going to talk about animal overpopulation." His introduction failed because, even though it attracted attention, it was irrelevant to the topic.

DIVERSITY IN PRACTICE
CONSIDERING ORGANIZATIONAL CULTURE

CHAPTER 1 POINTS OUT THAT culture includes the visible, stated aspects of a group's way of life as well as the more embedded beliefs and assumptions that guide group members. The concept of **organizational culture** extends this definition by recognizing that organizations and institutions also have histories, traditions, hierarchies, rituals, folklore, and so on, which makes them function as small cultures within the larger society. Insiders know the group's culture; newcomers must learn it. For example, Microsoft differs from IBM; St. John's University (Catholic sponsored) is unlike George Fox University (Quaker sponsored) in many ways.

Before you speak within an organization, learn whatever you can about its culture—even expectations for speech introductions change from setting to setting. For example, a community leader recently addressed graduates at my university. She introduced her remarks by referring to the occasion, congratulating the graduates, expressing respect for the university, and acknowledging the cultural event (graduation). The graduates and their families would think it abrupt and strange if she immediately launched into her speech on this special occasion.

organizational culture the way of life of a specific organization, which includes its history, traditions, heroes, folklore, vocabulary, rituals, and ways of doing things

To see how speakers adapt their introductions to specific organizations, look at several issues of *Vital Speeches of the Day* at your campus library or accessed through InfoTrac College Edition. Read the introductions of three or four talks given at ritual events, and analyze how the guest speakers recognize elements of the organization's culture in their opening remarks.

Give Your Audience a Reason to Listen

After you gain attention, answer your listeners' second question, "Why should I listen to this speech?" You may consider your topic important and interesting, but your listeners may think it boring or irrelevant. Jill, from Hawaii, faced this challenge when she spoke about Hawaiian sovereignty for one of her classes at Oregon State University. Most OSU students had never heard of the controversy about returning Hawaii to Hawaiian rule, and the issue seemed pretty remote. Jill related the topic to her Oregon audience as follows:

> Although you may not be aware of the issue of Hawaiian sovereignty, your senators are voting on the issue soon, and you may someday vote on whether or not to allow Hawaiians to again be a sovereign nation instead of a state.

You can frame your topic within a larger issue; for instance, childhood obesity is health related, elder abuse is part of a nationwide problem of violence. A speech on polar bears does not directly relate to listeners in most classrooms; however, the treatment of polar bears is linked to larger issues such as animal rights and animal overpopulation. Here's one way to relate this topic to an urban audience:

> At this point, you may be curious about polar bears, but you may not think much about them. After all, the only polar bears in New York are in the zoo. However, the polar bear problem in Canada is similar to problems here on Long Island with a deer population that is getting out of control. What do we do with animals that live close to humans?

Two important human characteristics are curiosity and the ability to learn new things, so you sometimes will speak to increase your audience's knowledge or to satisfy their curiosity. For instance, few people in the classroom will ever annul their marriages, but 58,000 annulments are granted annually to U.S. Catholics—and about 25 percent of the U.S. population claims affiliation with the Catholic Church. Here's how Maureen related her topic, "The Annulment Process," to her audience:

> Since at least two people in this classroom are Catholic, this subject should be of interest to you. For you who are non-Catholics, I hope this information will help you better understand one aspect of the Catholic religion.

Many issues that don't seem to directly concern your listeners may actually affect their pocketbooks, whether or not they know it. National issues that rely on tax dollars for support are in this category, such as funding for public broadcasting, weapons development, and Medicare increases. Chapter 18 provides more details about the needs, wants, emotions, and values that motivate people to listen to speeches.

Establish Your Credibility

After you have the audience's attention and they have a reason to listen to your topic, give them a reason to listen *to you* by linking yourself to your subject. Typically, speakers briefly tell about subject-related experiences, interests, and research findings. If relevant, you can mention your major, courses you have taken, television shows that first interested you, and so on. Maureen linked herself to the topic of annulment through her personal experiences:

Teaching Tip
Remind your students that convincing their classmates of the relevance of a topic is particularly difficult because they are usually a random sample who share only their status as college public-speaking students.

Classroom Discussion / Activity
Have small groups of students brainstorm different ways to motivate diverse audiences to listen. Examples could be business executives in a meeting, activists at a rally, politicians at a convention, parents at a PTA meeting, residents of a retirement home, or students in a public-speaking classroom. (Use these same audiences for a suggested activity in the next section, "Establish Your Credibility.")

Student Learning: Workbook
Activity 10.2, "Relating to the Audience," in the Student Workbook asks for ways to relate each of several topics to a classroom audience.

Classroom Discussion / Activity
Have your students brainstorm ways of establishing their credibility with each of the sample audiences from the previous section's classroom activity.

© Kevin Winter/Getty Images

Audiences instantly recognize Bethany Hamilton's credibility when she speaks about both surfing and sharks, because of her celebrity as a 13-year-old surfing champion who lost an arm to a tiger shark. However, your link to your topic is probably not as well known, so you must explain your interest in and experiences with your subject.

The annulment process is of particular interest to me since I am a divorced Catholic who is engaged to be married to a Catholic man.

Here are some additional ways students have linked themselves to their topics:

I support pet adoption because I am studying to be a veterinarian, and my career goals are to save animals, not euthanize them.

As a musician trained in piano, clarinet, and guitar, I attended Fiorello H. La Guardia High School of Music and Art, where I was required to study music history and research the lives of musicians and composers.

I became interested in the topic of antioxidants because of my childhood. I always begged for Cocoa Puffs, but I got oatmeal and bananas instead. So I developed my health consciousness from my mother who fed me fruits and vegetables and other good foods.

Establishing your credibility is optional if another person introduces you and connects you with the topic or if your expertise is well established. However, even professionals who speak on topics outside their area should link themselves with the topic. Let's say an engineer urges her local school board to adopt a district-wide sex education program. Her experiences as a parent are more salient in this context than her engineering expertise.

DIVERSITY IN PRACTICE
A NAVAJO (*DINÉ*) SPEECH INTRODUCTION

NOT EVERY CULTURAL GROUP begins a speech by first gaining attention, next relating to audience interests, and then establishing credibility. Speakers at Diné College (formerly Navajo Community College) first answer the question, "Who are you and what is your clan affiliation?" They give their names (who they are) and identify their clan affiliation before moving into their topic. This helps listeners understand the roots of their life. Until they share this personal, identifying information, neither the speakers nor the listeners can feel comfortable.[8]

Preview Your Ideas

You may have heard the old saying, "Tell them what you're going to say; say it; then tell them what you said." The **preview** serves the first of these functions. It is a short statement that provides the transition between the introduction and the body of your speech, in which you state some form of your thesis statement and indicate how you will develop it. Previews aid listeners who are taking notes or outlining the talk. Heidi explains the importance of a preview for listeners:

> It obviously helps to have an idea of where the speaker is headed. The preview provides a brief synopsis of what key points will be expanded upon. The speech then should continue in the order first declared.

Here are three student previews that alert their audiences to the speaker's organizational pattern:

> Before we can drift off for a good night's sleep, we must first wake up to some of the alarming effects of sleep debt. Then we can open our eyes to better understand their causes, and finally we'll cozy up to some solutions at both the personal and the societal levels.

> Today, I'll retell the story of the boy who cried "wolf," with a few character changes. The boy who cries "wolf" is the American government, and the wolf we are to fear is industrial hemp.

> I will share with you some aspects of Hector Berlioz's fascinating biography and explain the important contributions he made in music composition.

In short, a good introduction draws attention to your topic, relates the subject to your listeners, links you to the subject, and previews your major ideas.

STOP AND CHECK

CREATE AN INTERESTING INTRODUCTION

Select one or two of the following previews. Then work with a classmate to create an introduction that answers the four questions your listeners ask regarding any subject.

- Childhood obesity is an increasing problem in our society, but several solutions have been proposed.
- Arachnophobia, the irrational fear of spiders, has three major causes and two basic treatments.
- Many women, as well as men, experience hair loss, and they try medications, hairpieces, bonding techniques, and transplants to solve the problem.
- You can save money at the market on produce, meat, cereal, and baked goods.
- Thousands of students default on federal student loans every year, leaving taxpayers with their school tabs.

The listener's questions are:

1. What's this about? (Identify several strategies to gain attention to the topics you choose. Which do you think are more effective?)
2. Why should I listen? (How could you relate the topics to audience interests or experiences?)
3. Why should I listen to you? (How might a speaker establish credibility on each subject?)
4. What will you cover? (How would you preview the main ideas of each topic?)

To learn more about introductions, do an Internet search for "speech introductions" and skim several results for tips you can incorporate into your speeches. Alternatively, watch the introductions of several speech videos on the book's website. Evaluate how well each one fulfills the criteria described here.

Teaching Tip
Students often have difficulty developing a preview. Usually, however, the thesis statement that the student crafts for the preparation outline can be used as a preview in the introduction if it is well crafted.

Student Learning: Book Website
This Stop and Check activity can also be found on the book's website, where it's located under "Chapter Resources."

preview the transition from the introduction to the speech body; some form of the central idea

Conclude with Impact

A conclusion leaves listeners with their final impression of both you and your topic. This is the place to provide closure through a summary and a satisfying or challenging closing statement without adding new information. Appearing disorganized at the end can lessen the positive impressions your audience gained during the speech. Like the introduction, the conclusion has several important functions: to signal the end, to summarize the main points, to provide psychological closure (often by a reference to the introduction), and to end with impact.

Signal the Ending

Just as your preview provides a transition to the speech body, your ending signal lets the audience know that you're concluding. Both beginning speakers and professionals use common phrases such as "in conclusion" or "finally." However, the following transitions are more creative:

> We now know that when we feel the need to escape from our world and enter into the zones of biting insects, dousing ourselves too liberally with DEET for protection carries some risks.

> Today we've taken a look at our National Debt . . . our national sleep debt, that is.

Don't overlook nonverbal actions as a way to signal to your conclusion. For instance, pause and shift your posture, or take a step away from the podium. You can also slow down a bit and speak more softly. Combining both verbal and nonverbal transitions generally works well.

Review Your Main Ideas

Teaching Tip
All of the devices for gaining audience attention are equally effective at achieving impact in the conclusion. Recommend that students use parallel construction. That is, if they begin with a quotation, end with a quotation. If they begin with a story, end with a story. If they begin with a rhetorical question, end with a rhetorical question. In addition to being effective, parallel construction helps signal closure.

Briefly summarize or recap your main points to fulfill the "Tell them what you said" axiom, but make the review brief. The audience already heard your speech, so you don't have to repeat supporting material. The following brief summaries are examples:

> We've explored ways that sleep deprivation affects us in three areas: in our personal lives, in our relationships, and in our workplaces.

> I hope that I have increased your knowledge about oxidation and convinced you that antioxidants help prevent heart disease, arteriosclerosis, strokes, chronic illnesses, and even cancer.

Many speakers combine their transition statement with their summary, as this example shows:

> Now that we have looked at the shark as it really is [transition phrase] I hope you realize that its reputation is really inaccurate and that humans present a greater threat to sharks than sharks present to humans [restatement of the central idea].

Provide Psychological Closure

Looping back to something from your introduction—which some writing instructors call an "**echo**"—provides your audience with a sense of psychological closure. One professor explains:

> The echo is the inside joke of writing. By repeating or suggesting a previous detail—a description, word, question, quote, topic or whatever—you make a point with that which is already familiar to your reader. It's a way of putting your arm around the reader and sharing a bit of information that only the two of you can appreciate.[9]

echo repeating something from the introduction in the conclusion

The echo principle similarly applies to speaking. Look in your introduction for something that you could echo at the end. For instance, if you begin with an example, you might address it again in the conclusion. Or you can refer to startling statistics or to quotations you presented in the opening. Here are some examples:

> I will personally avoid driving while I am tired, because the woman who died in the van that July morning was my mom.

> The woman whose twenty-three-year marriage ended in annulment is more common than you might think. Although she considered an annulment inconceivable, she did not contest her ex-husband's request for one. She realized that the annulment did not erase the existence of her marriage, but it allowed her ex to have good standing within the Catholic Church.

> For those eighteen of us in this classroom who eat too much fat and the twenty of us who regularly ignore our doctor's nutritional advice, there's hope.

End Memorably

Finally, plan to leave a positive and memorable impression. During the few minutes you speak, the audience is focusing on your subject. When you finish, however, each listener will return to his or her thoughts, moving away from the mental images you co-created throughout the speech. So end with impact by choosing similar strategies to those used to gain attention in the beginning:

© Bettmann /CORBIS

- End with humor.
- Ask a thought-provoking question.
- Use a quotation.
- Issue a challenge.
- Tie the subject to a larger cultural theme or value.

Using humor and using quotations are two memorable ways to end a speech. Quoting a well-known humorist such as Mark Twain is one way to combine the two.

Study some of the speeches and outlines provided in the text and notice the different and creative ways that students memorably end their speeches. Here are two effective endings:

> So, next time you are on the Internet and you begin to consider pond scum or cottage cheese as a cure for what ails you, you may want to keep this Latin phrase in mind: *Caveat emptor*— let the buyer beware.

> Next time you drive, consider those in the cars around you and think of whose friend, mother, sister, brother they are. Do you really want others to go through pain and suffering simply so you can get to your destination a little earlier?

In summary, a good conclusion provides a transition to your conclusion, summarizes your major points, gains psychological closure, and finishes with a thought-provoking closing statement.

STOP AND CHECK

EVALUATING INTRODUCTIONS AND CONCLUSIONS

Here you'll find an introduction and conclusion for two different speeches. Read through each set and then answer the questions that follow it.

Introduction: Four of the six leading causes of death among Americans are diet related: heart disease, cancer, stroke, and diabetes mellitus, as stated by the

Teaching Tip
Emphasize that an effective conclusion achieves all four major purposes: signaling the end, summarizing, providing psychological closure, and ending with impact. A conclusion that fails to accomplish any one of these purposes is less effective.

Vegetarian Times magazine. Everyone here would like to live a healthy life, right? Today, I will explain the advantages of being a vegetarian to your health and to the environment.

Conclusion: Because I have this information, I have reduced my consumption of meat lately, and I ask you to do the same thing. Being a vegetarian is not that bad; you're improving your health and, at the same time, saving the environment. Don't forget, once you're old and suffering from a heart ailment or cancer, it will be too late. Take precautions now.

- ▶ Does this introduction make you want to hear this speech? Why or why not?
- ▶ How does the speaker gain attention?
- ▶ How does he relate to the audience? Is this effective?
- ▶ Do you think he is credible on the topic?
- ▶ Could you write a brief outline of his major points from his preview?
- ▶ Is his conclusion as effective as his introduction? Why or why not?

Introduction: What is the easiest way to raise $125,000 for research for multiple sclerosis? That's right. Swim 1,550 miles down the Mississippi River like Nick Irons did. Nick, a 25-year-old, swam the murky waters to raise money for a disease his father has. Many people would think this was crazy, because they don't know about the disease. Only one in ten George Fox students surveyed had the slightest idea of what MS was. My dad has had this disease for eight years, and I really didn't know a lot about it until I researched MS and found a lot more than I expected. Because most people are unclear about multiple sclerosis, I will first define the disease, describe some of its effects, and tell you what is known about the cause, the cure, and the current treatments.

Conclusion: In conclusion, little is known about the causes and cures of MS, a disease that attacks the central nervous system, impairing many senses. Next time you question why a person might swim over 1,500 miles down a dirty river, you will have a clearer understanding of the reason. A lot is being done to find a cure for this debilitating disease. It will be found.

- ▶ What is the most effective part of her introduction?
- ▶ What's the most effective element of her conclusion?
- ▶ Which is better: her introduction or her conclusion? Why?
- ▶ What improvements, if any, should she make?

To learn more about conclusions, do an Internet search for "speech conclusions" and skim several results for tips you can incorporate into your speeches. Alternatively, watch the conclusions of several speech videos on the book's website. Evaluate how well each speaker signals the ending of the speech, reviews main ideas, provides psychological closure, and ends memorably.

Connect Your Ideas

After you plan the body of your speech and formulate your introduction and conclusion, you're ready to add final touches in the form of **connectives**—the words, phrases, and sentences that lead from one idea to another and unify the various elements of the speech. They function somewhat like tendons or ligaments by holding your speech together. You can also think of them as bridges that link one idea to another or relate one major point to the whole. Use them to emphasize significant points, show relationships between ideas, and help your listeners keep their place as you talk. The most common connectives are signposts and transitions, internal previews, and internal summaries.

connectives words, phrases, and sentences used to lead from idea to idea and tie the parts of the speech together smoothly

Signposts and Transitions

Signposts are similar to highway signs, those posted markers that help you know your location as you drive along. Verbal signposts help your listeners orient themselves to their place in your speech. Words such as *first, next,* and *finally* introduce new points and help your listeners identify the flow of your ideas. Other words and phrases such as *in addition, for example, therefore,* and *as a result* connect one idea to another. Signposts like *the main thing to remember* or *most importantly* highlight ideas you want to emphasize. Here are some examples of signposts from student speeches:

▶ *The final step* occurs when the case is submitted to the judge for a decision.
▶ *On the other hand,* the computer does have a lot of things going for it.
▶ *In addition,* brain wave patterns can be measured and analyzed.
▶ *Not surprisingly,* people who carry high sleep debts are also more susceptible to disease and micro-sleep.
▶ *However,* this idea seems a bit far-fetched.

Transitions summarize where you have been and where you are going in the speech. You can use them both between points and within a single point. Here are some simple transitions *between* major points:

> We have looked at what oxidation is [where we've been]; now let's examine what antioxidants are and what they can do to help prevent oxidation in the arteries [where we're going].

> The problem, as you can see, is complex, because both the people and the polar bears need protection [a summary of the last point]; however, two solutions have been proposed [a preview of the next main idea].

> Although the glass ceiling is widespread [where we've been], it is not shatterproof [where we're going].

Transitions can also lead from subpoint to subpoint *within* a major point. For example, Tamara's major point "There are several causes of amusement park tragedies" has three subpoints: equipment failure, operator failure, and rider behavior. After she describes the first two causes, she transitions to the final one by saying this:

> While both equipment and operator failure cause accidents [first and second subpoint], a number of tragedies are additionally caused by rider behavior [third subpoint].

Here's another example. Jenny's speech about goldenseal root has as one of its major points that people use this herb both internally and externally. She first describes internal uses and then transitions to the second use by saying:

> Not only do people use goldenseal root internally [first use], they also apply the herb externally [lead-in to second use].

Internal Previews and Internal Summaries

Internal previews occur within the body of your speech and briefly summarize the subpoints you will develop under a major point. For instance, Tamara might say:

> Experts agree that there are three main causes of amusement park tragedies: equipment failure, operator failure, and rider behavior.

This internal preview helps her audience see the framework she'll use as she develops her major point, the causes of accidents.

If you summarize subpoints after you've made them but before you move to another major point, you're using an **internal summary.** Thus, this sentence summarizes the causes before moving on to the effects of amusement park accidents:

> In short, we have seen that equipment failure, operator failure, and rider behavior combine to create thousands of tragedies annually.

signpost connective such as *first, most importantly, however,* and *consequently* that links ideas, lends emphasis, and helps listeners keep their place in the speech

transition summary of where you've been and where you're going in your speech

internal preview brief in-speech summary that foretells the subpoints you'll develop under a major point

internal summary restatement of the ideas within a subpoint

After she discusses the uses of goldenseal root, Jenny could summarize her entire point by saying:

In summary, people use goldenseal root both internally and externally.

Connectives, then, are words, phrases, and complete sentences you use to connect your ideas to one another and to your speech as a whole. They serve to introduce your points, to show the relationship of one point to another, to preview and summarize material within a point, and to help your listeners keep their place in your speech.

Summary

After you've organized the body of your speech, plan an introduction that will take your listeners from their various internal worlds and move them into the world of your speech. Do this by gaining their attention, relating your topic to their concerns, establishing your credibility on the subject, and previewing your main points. Finally, plan a conclusion that provides a transition from the body, summarizes your major points, gives a sense of closure by referring back to the introduction, and leaves your listeners with a challenge or memorable saying. Throughout your speech, use connectives to weave together your points and subpoints into a coherent whole.

STUDY AND REVIEW

The premium website for *Public Speaking* offers a broad range of resources that will help you better understand the material in this chapter, complete assignments, and succeed on tests. The website features

▶ Speech videos with critical viewing questions, various types of outlines, transcripts, and note cards
▶ Interactive practice activities, self quizzes, and a sample final exam

For more information about this text's electronic learning resources, consult your **Guide to Online Resources for Public Speaking** or visit http://communication.wadsworth.com/jaffe5.

KEY TERMS

The terms below are defined in the margins throughout this chapter. The book website also provides interactive flashcards and crossword puzzles to help you learn these terms and the concepts they represent.

rhetorical questions 175	connectives 184
participatory questions 175	signpost 185
organizational culture 178	transition 185
preview 181	internal preview 185
echo 182	internal summary 185

APPLICATION AND CRITICAL THINKING EXERCISES

The exercises below are among the practice activities on the book's website.

1. Before your next speech, trade outlines with someone in your class. Use the guidelines in this chapter to evaluate your classmate's introduction, conclusion, and connectives, and advise her or him on what you think is effective and what could be improved. When

you get your own outline and suggestions back, make adjustments that would improve these sections of your speech.

2. Outline a speech given by one of your classmates. Evaluate the effectiveness of the introduction and conclusion. What suggestions, if any, would you give the speaker to improve the beginning or the ending?

3. Review the section on credibility—what your audience thinks of you—in Chapter 5. How and why does a good introduction and conclusion affect the audience's perception of you? How and why does a poor start or finish influence their perception?

4. Read the introductions and conclusions of some speeches you find on www.american rhetoric.com. Evaluate them using the criteria in the text. Does the introduction gain attention, link to the audience, establish credibility, and preview the major points? Does the speaker provide a transition to the conclusion? Review the major points? Provide psychological closure? End memorably? What improvements, if any, would you suggest?

5. Search the Internet for the exact phrase "introductions and conclusions." You should find many sites that were created by both writing and speech instructors. Go to a site for writers, and compare and contrast the guidelines there with those for speakers that you find in this text. What are the similarities? The differences? How do you account for the differences?

Instructor's Resource Manual
Chapter 10 of the *Instructor's Resource Manual* (available in print, online, and on the Multimedia Manager CD-ROM) suggests ways to use Application and Critical Thinking Questions 1–3.

Instructor's Resource Manual
For an alternative to Question 3 that also looks at credibility, see Teaching Idea 10.2 in the *Instructor's Resource Manual* (available in print, online, and on the Multimedia Manager CD-ROM).

SPEECH VIDEO

Log on to the book's website and click on the video tab to watch and critique the clip of Hillary Carter-Liggett's introduction to her informative speech titled "Shakespeare." Then watch Bonita Persons deliver her speech "Driving While Drowsy."

Student Speech with Commentary

To complete her persuasive speech assignment, Bonita Persons chose a topic that she cared deeply about. After she finished, her fellow students commented on the effectiveness of her introduction and conclusion. Read her speech, and evaluate the way she begins and ends it. This transcript of Bonita's speech is also available on the book's website.

DRIVING WHILE DROWSY
Bonita Persons

Introduction

July 3, 2003, a man and his family drive their van down the road as it is getting light. Another driver has been driving since midnight. He tries to pass a bus, but fails to see the van coming toward him. Because he is tired, the driver cannot react quickly enough to slide back into his own lane, and his car collides with the van, killing the woman in the passenger seat.

How well does Bonita fulfill the four major elements of a good introduction? Does her overall introduction make you want to hear more?

Almost everyone will drive while tired at some point in their lives, especially worn out, stressed college students and workers.

I'm guilty of this. I drove tired just last summer when I went to visit my brother in Kansas.

However, drowsy driving is not a good idea. A lot of people are killed because of tired drivers, and the only real solution lies within our hands, but the benefits of avoiding tired driving definitely outweigh the sacrifices one must make.

Underline all the connectives you can find in the body of this outline. Where could she effectively add a transition, internal preview, or internal summary?

Body

Many people have died because of accidents related to tired driving. According to the American Academy of Otolaryngology, driving with sleep apnea is just as bad as driving with an alcohol content of 0.08 percent. In addition, the Pennsylvania Department of Transportation says statistics show that 1,500 people die each year because of drowsy driving accidents. Finally, the Queensland Transport website on road safety tells us that 1 in 6 fatal crashes in Queensland, Australia, are caused by driving tired. However, these statistics do not include the damage done to cars and other property. All over the world, sleep-related accidents happen.

The consequences for driving while tired can be fatal, so precautions are important. According to David Jamieson, Road Safety Minister in the United Kingdom, most sleep-related accidents happen on Mondays, although most *accidents* occur on Fridays.

Dr. Mercola, author of *The Total Health Problem,* says that "After 17–19 hours without sleep, performance on some tests was equivalent or worse than that at a blood alcohol content of 0.05%." This may sound like a long time to be up, but consider that if a college student woke up at 7 for this class and did not get to bed until midnight, that is 17 hours without sleep right there. Going to bed at midnight, for many, is early.

Because sleepiness can be a problem, we need to be able to tell when we are getting sleepy. Signs warning that you are tired are fairly obvious and should not be ignored. Queensland's road safety website outlines several signs of fatigue: sore or heavy eyes, dim or fuzzy vision, "seeing" things, droning and humming in the ears, general tiredness, stiffness and cramps, aches and pains, daydreaming, delayed reaction times, unintentional increases or decreases in speed, fumbling for gear changes, and a car that wanders across the road.

Consequently, if you feel yourself getting tired, PULL OFF THE ROAD! The Pennsylvania Department of Transportation says to pull off and take a 15–25 minute nap when you feel tired and to switch drivers every few hours if the drive is going to be long. Make sure the driver has a good night's rest before driving.

Coffee is a stimulant, but the effects, according to PENNDOT, do not come into play for half an hour after you drink it, and the effects do not last long, so it should not be relied on. Interestingly enough, the Driving While Tired Advice and Checklists from the UK states that certain foods such as turkey, warm milk, and bananas induce sleepiness and therefore should NOT be eaten before or during a drive!

Is there a government solution to this problem? According to ABC News, New Jersey is the first state to make driving tired a crime if a deadly accident occurs when there are signs that it is a tired-related accident. But this still does not cure driving while tired. The solution is a decision each person must make as an individual.

The benefits for driving when one is NOT tired are obvious: Lives are saved. The downsides are that one may take a bit longer getting somewhere or may not be able to stay at that place for quite as long. However, when one considers the good versus the bad, the good obviously outweighs the negative.

Conclusion

If we ourselves don't want to become a statistic of tired driving, then we need to take steps to protect ourselves and others. Know when you are tired and do your best to prevent driving then. Longer road trips may be inevitable because you avoid tired driving, but it is worth it if you want to live. I myself will avoid driving while tired, because the woman who was killed in the van that July morning was my mom. So next time you consider driving while tired, consider those in the cars around you and think of whose friend, mother, sister, or brother they are. Do you really want others to go through pain and suffering simply so you can get to your destination a little bit earlier?

Identify the ways this conclusion signals the end and reviews the main points. How effectively does she create psychological closure? What other ending choices could she have made?

CHAPTER 11

PUTTING IT ALL TOGETHER: OUTLINING YOUR SPEECH

THIS CHAPTER WILL HELP YOU

▌ Outline the contents of your speech in a linear form

▌ Prepare note cards or a speaking outline

▌ Record your ideas in a more organic pattern

"Family Life and Spirit of Mankind" Mural © 1977 by Susan Kelk Cervantes and Judith Knepher Jamerson. (Leonard R. Flynn School, East Wall, Army Street at Harrison, SF, CA)

LTHOUGH YOU may wonder, "Why should I write an outline? I'm preparing a speech, not writing an essay," your instructor has good reasons for requiring you to outline your ideas. An outline is to a speech as a skeleton is to the body or steel girders are to a skyscraper. A good outline highlights your speech's framework and displays your ideas and their relationships to one another.

By now you've done much of the work for creating an outline. That is, you've researched your topic (Chapter 7), selected supporting materials (Chapter 8), and identified ways to organize the speech body, introduction, and conclusion (Chapters 9 and 10). You've already seen the value of clearly identified points, each one supported by carefully chosen data. In fact, you may have made a **rough draft outline** of your main points and supporting materials. This chapter will help you tie all these efforts together and complete a formal content outline that will function as the framework or skeleton for your thoughts.

Outlines differ from a **script** or **text,** which includes every word you say. And both differ from the **speaking notes** you actually take to the podium. Compare and contrast the script at the end of Chapter 2 with the outline at the end of Chapter 9 and in the middle of this chapter and with the speaker's notes presented later in this chapter.

Experienced speakers know that there's no single way to outline a speech correctly; the more speeches you give, the more you'll find a way that works best for you and your individual learning style. This chapter presents tips for making full-sentence content outlines, followed by a description of how to prepare speaking notes. It concludes with ideas for more holistic methods of pulling together a speech that take into account diversity in individual thinking styles.

Chapter-at-a-Glance
This chapter explains how to write a full-sentence content outline and an abbreviated speaking outline. It begins with a discussion of the principles of an effective content outline: coordination, indentation, parallel structure, and subordination. Next, it describes more abbreviated speaking outline. Use of notes and tips for creating the speaking outline are presented. The chapter ends with a discussion of outlining for less conventional organizational patterns.

CASE STUDY: THE BENEFITS OF OUTLINING

I noticed her from the very first moment of class. She sat in the front row with arms folded, looking grim. After I took roll, I asked students what they hoped to get out of the class. She said, "Credit." She was a pharmacy major, and she saw no reason for the public speaking requirement. Every day, she similarly sat and scowled; she even refused to give the first speech.

Then something began to change. She eventually started to relax and turn in outlines and give speeches. One day near the end of the semester, she stayed behind after others left the classroom. "I want to thank you for this class. I was really mad that I was forced to take it, but I found out how useful it turned out to be—especially learning how to outline," she said. "Choosing ideas and supporting materials, organizing my ideas—I have been able to use these skills in many other classes. I just want you to know."

rough draft outline a preliminary outline that's not yet formatted formally

script or text writing down every word of the speech

speaking notes the key words and phrases you take to the platform when you speak

content outline also called a preparation outline or full-sentence outline; formal record of your major ideas and their relationship to one another in your speech

Questions for Discussion

▶ What do you see as the advantages of outlining?
▶ What do you think are disadvantages?
▶ How might outlining skills help you in other classes? In your chosen profession?

How to Prepare a Content Outline

Most instructors require a **content outline,** also called a *preparation outline* or a *full-sentence outline.* A written outline is a record of your major ideas and speech materials and their relationship to one another. Although specific details may vary, several general guidelines can help you prepare your outlines.

Begin with a Heading

Give your speech a title and then include the general purpose, the specific purpose, your finalized thesis statement, and the organizational pattern you've developed using principles found in Chapters 6 through 9. The heading is a nutshell look at what you plan to accomplish. Here is John's heading for his speech on culture shock:

Topic:	The Five Stages of Culture Shock
General Purpose:	To inform
Specific Purpose:	To explain to my audience of the stages of culture shock and to demonstrate these with real-life examples.
Thesis Statement:	Culture shock is a psychological process that typically progresses through five stages.
Organizational Pattern:	Chronological

Use a Standard Format

Three formatting features—alternation, coordination, and indentation—combine to make visible the structure and interrelationships of your various speech elements.

Alternate Numbers and Letters

Show the relationships among your ideas by alternating numbers and letters in a consistent pattern. Identify your major points using one of the patterns described in Chapter 9, and then designate each major point with a Roman numeral. Under each main point, identify first-level supporting points and give each one a capital letter head (A, B, C, . . .). Second-level supporting points get Arabic numerals (1, 2, 3, . . .), and third-level points are identified by lowercase letters (a, b, c, . . .). The following system is typical:

    I. Major point
       A. First-level supporting point
          1. Second-level supporting point
          2. Second-level supporting point
             a. Third-level supporting point
             b. Third-level supporting point
       B. First-level supporting point
    II. Major point
       A. First-level supporting point
       B. First-level supporting point

Coordinate Points

The principle of **coordination** means that your major points have basically the same value or weight, your second-level points are similar in value, and so on. In the following outline, the problem and the solution are major points. First-level points—causes and effects—are coordinated approximately equally. Each first-level point is further supported by coordinated second-level points.

    I. Problem
       A. Causes
          1. First Cause
          2. Second Cause
          3. Third Cause

coordination points arranged into various levels, with the points on a specific level having basically the same value or weight

© Peter Chapman Photography

       B. Effects
          1. First Effect
          2. Second Effect
    II. Solution
       A. The plan
       B. Cost
       C. Benefits

Indent

Indentation means you space some text further to the right to visually separate it from surrounding text. Outlines indent various levels of supporting points to show interrelationships between materials. For example, I and II level points begin at the left margin, but A and B headings are indented to the right. Third-level supporting points begin even further right and so on, as this example illustrates:

     I. Sleep deprivation affects safety in our work environments.
        A. Volunteers in a sleep-deprivation study became listless, serious, and grim; they did poorly on tasks of vigilance, reaction time, and simple arithmetic.
           1. Imagine a truck driver or firefighter with lowered vigilance and reaction time.
           2. Or visualize a teacher or bank officer who is listless and grim and who makes simple math mistakes.
        B. Work accidents related to sleep deprivation include the *Challenger* space shuttle disaster and the Exxon *Valdez* oil spill.

Use a computerized word processing program to autoformat your outline; you can then save time and energy when you actually sit down to write out your outline.

Write Your Points in Sentence Form

Complete sentences allow you to see the content included in each point. In contrast, John's introduction to his speech on culture shock *could* use only phrases, like this:

     I. *Craik* in Ireland
    II. Travelers abroad
   III. My Kenyan experiences
    IV. Five stages

Obviously, someone reading his outline could not tell what each point actually covers, and his phrases would function better as a speaking outline. Both John and his professor will have a clearer idea of his speech content if he uses full sentences to outline his major points, as his introduction illustrates:

     I. If a man offers you some *craik* (pronounced "crack") in Ireland, should you be surprised or offended?
    II. Whenever you enter another culture, you can expect to go through culture shock.
   III. I experienced this process during my summer in Kenya.
    IV. Culture shock progresses through five stages: honeymoon, disintegration, reintegration, autonomy, and interdependence.

Another key is to construct **parallel points.** That is, don't write out some points as declarative sentences and others as questions. Avoid mixing phrases and complete

Student Learning: InfoTrac College Edition
At this point in outline development, many students realize they do not have enough supporting material. Direct them to InfoTrac College Edition to research additional supporting material.

indentation formatting by spacing inward various levels of points

parallel points making the points similar in construction

sentences, and don't put two sentences in a single point. This student originally made all these mistakes:

    I. What is multiple sclerosis (MS)? [a complete sentence in question form]
   II. The big mystery! [a sentence fragment or phrase]
  III. Who? [a single word in question form]
  IV. Effects . . . symptoms of MS. [an incomplete sentence]
   V. There are three prominent medications being used right now to treat MS. These are talked about in the magazine *Inside MS*. [two declarative sentences]

Here's how her rewritten points should look:

    I. Multiple sclerosis (MS) is a disease of the central nervous system.
   II. The causes remain a mystery.
  III. Its victims tend to be similar in age, gender, and regional characteristics.
  IV. The condition affects eyesight and bodily coordination.
   V. Most physicians prescribe one of three major medications.

Use the Principle of Subordination

The word **subordination** comes from two Latin root words: *sub* (under) and *ordinare* (to place in order). This means that all first-level points support and are placed under major points; all second-level points support first-level points and are put under them, and so on. Return to the above example and think critically about the speaker's points. Are all her first-level points equal? Do some seem more logically to follow others? What would happen if she used a problem–solution pattern for first-level points, and then subordinated the other material to the second level of support? Her new outline would look like this:

    I. Multiple sclerosis (MS) is a disease of the central nervous system. [problem]
       A. Its causes remain a mystery. [causes of the problem]
       B. Victims tend to be similar in age, gender, and regional characteristics. [extent of the problem]
       C. It affects eyesight and bodily coordination. [effects of the problem]
   II. Most physicians prescribe one of three major medications. [solution]

Coordinating her major points into a problem–solution pattern is a much more effective way to organize this speech. And subordinating three points—the causes, the extent, and the effects of MS—under the problem section of this speech creates a more logical flow of ideas.

In summary, good content outlines begin with a heading and use a standard format that includes coordinated points arranged by alternating letters and numbers and by indenting material in a way that shows the relationship of ideas to one another. They are written in complete sentences that are parallel in construction, and they contain supporting materials arranged underneath the major ideas.

John Streicher's outline, below with commentary, pulls these elements together and provides a good model and an explanation of John's speechmaking strategies. His professor requires a list of references at the end of the outline. Although John outlines his introduction and conclusion, some instructors ask students to write out these sections of the speech. Here is John's complete content outline. Notice that it does not read like a script or text of the speech. Instead of putting in each word he'll say, he writes one sentence that summarizes the contents of each point.

Teaching Tip
http://www.ku.edu/~coms/
virtual_assistant/vpa/vpa6
.htm
The Virtual Presentation Assistant at the University of Kansas offers tips on outlining.

Classroom Discussion/ Activity
Have students develop a "how to outline" list using John Streicher's outline as a guide. Write the basic principles on the board or on an overhead transparency. After developing this list, have students break into groups and use these principles to begin their own outlines. Alternatively, provide each group with the text of an actual speech (one with clear previews and signposting) and have them to outline this speech using the "how to outline" principles.

subordination placement of supporting points under major points

By writing out his heading, John made sure the focus of his speech is clear and that his outline accomplishes his stated purposes.

Specifically identify your introduction, your body, and your conclusion. This introduction gains attention, relates to the audience, establishes credibility, and previews the major points.

Each element is assigned a separate Roman numeral.

Point IV, the preview, functions as the transition between the introduction and the speech body. It tells the audience to listen for chronologically organized information about the stages of culture shock.

John labels the body of his speech. He uses the principle of coordination; each point identifies a single stage. In his first major point, he sets up a pattern he'll modify and use to develop each point. He defines the stage, explains typical responses, provides examples, and ends with helpful tips for navigating the stage.

Subpoints B and C are first-level points that are made up of both second- and third-level supporting materials.

Student Outline with Commentary

THE FIVE STAGES OF CULTURE SHOCK
John Streicher

General Purpose: To inform
Specific Purpose: To explain to my audience of the stages of culture shock and to demonstrate them with real-life examples.
Thesis Statement: Culture shock is a psychological process that typically progresses through five stages.
Organizational Pattern: Chronological

I. If a man offers you some *craik* (pronounced "crack") in Ireland, should you be surprised or offended?
II. Whenever you enter another culture, you can expect to go through culture shock.
   A. In *The Five Stages of Culture Shock,* Paul Pedersen (1995) defines culture shock as "an internalized construct or perspective developed in reaction or response to a new or unfamiliar situation."
   B. Culture shock typically involves several stages of adjustment.
III. I experienced this process during my summer in Kenya, but I learned coping strategies that make me more sensitive to newcomers to our culture.
IV. I will identify and describe five stages of culture shock: honeymoon, disintegration, reintegration, autonomy, and interdependence.

Body

I. The Honeymoon stage represents your initial contact with the culture.
   A. Your cultural identity isolates you from belonging in that culture.
      1. You are surrounded by strange sights, sounds, and smells.
      2. You do not understand what others expect.
   B. But you typically feel like a tourist—excited, adventuresome, even confident.
      1. People in the host culture may be kind and helpful.
      2. You may be oblivious to your errors.
         a. Students in a Venezuelan airport made unintentional errors.
         b. A Western businessman was naïve about doing business in China (Sinclair & Po-yee, 1999).
   C. Steps you take during this stage can help you later.
      1. Begin a journal to record positive and negative experiences.
      2. Act like a tourist and find things you enjoy doing.
         a. Look for cultural offerings in the area.
         b. Find areas of natural beauty that you can retreat to, both now and later.
      3. Plan a vacation for six months down the road.
      4. Build a support system with contacts in the area or with people back home.
      5. Keep your sense of humor; lighten up and laugh at yourself (Bellini, 2005).
II. About two to eight weeks later, the Disintegration stage arrives when the novelty has worn off, and unexpected things happen.
   A. You're no longer a spectator, and you must solve practical problems.
   B. Typically, you experience confusion (Help! What do I do now?), failure (I'm inadequate), and self-blame (It's all my fault).
   C. Several steps can help your through this stage.
      1. Take care of yourself physically.
      2. Continue learning the language and the nonverbal communication system.
         a. As a nanny in Belgium, Sara Reamy (personal communication, October 12, 2001) spoke French with the children's family, but she also took a French course at a nearby university.

b. Look for cues to nonverbal expectations.

c. Record your insights in your journal (Guanipa, 1998).

III. Two to three months later, the Reintegration stage allows you to shed your self-blame and interact within the culture.

A. You might reject the "overwhelmed feeling" and stand up for yourself.

B. However, you might feel anger and rejection toward the host culture.

1. One anthropologist in Africa opposed perceived injustice in the legal system.

2. Some exchange stereotypes about their hosts with others like themselves.

3. Some give up and go home, which can cost thousands of dollars in relocation funds.

C. Plan ways to get through this stage positively.

1. Go on the vacation you planned during the Honeymoon stage.

2. Avoid talking negatively about your hosts.

3. Record your frustrations in your journal.

(Transition: You've adjusted to the Honeymoon, Disintegration, and Reintegration stages; next you either regress or move toward greater understanding in the Autonomy and Interdependence stages.)

IV. After three to six months, you find balance at the Autonomy stage.

A. You can relax and understand rather than criticize the host culture.

B. You negotiate effectively in the foreign setting.

C. Some tips will help you through this stage.

1. Don't overestimate your abilities and commit a blunder.

2. Do some serious shopping, because you're less likely to be "taken."

V. Finally, after about nine months, you come to the final stage — Interdependence.

A. You feel bicultural or multicultural.

1. You're not controlled or dominated by cultural differences.

2. You can demonstrate trust and sensitivity.

3. This stage is best demonstrated by the experience of an American in Kenya.

B. You begin to assume responsibilities and privileges in your new culture.

Conclusion

I. I hope this helps you understand the process of integrating into a new culture.

II. Culture shock has five stages: honeymoon, disintegration, reintegration, autonomy, and interdependence.

III. Even if you never go abroad, you can better understand immigrants.

IV. And go ahead, have some *craik*— it's the Irish slang word for a good time!

References

Bellini, M. A. S. (2005). *Coping with culture shock*. Retrieved April 22, 2005, from www.hthtravelinsurance.com/travel_center/stud_international/020.cfm

Culture shock. (2005, January 30). Retrieved April 22, 2005, from Comox Valley International College, School of English Language website: www.cvic.bc.ca/c_shock.htm

Furnham, A., & Bochner, S. (1986). *Culture shock*. New York: Methuen.

Guanipa, C. (1998). *Culture shock*. Retrieved April 22, 2005, from San Diego State University, College of Education website: http://edweb.sdsu.edu/people/CGuanipa/cultshok.htm

Jordan, P. (1992). *Re-entry*. Seattle: Youth with a Mission.

Loss, M. (1983). *Culture shock*. Winona Lake, IN: Light and Life Press.

Pedersen, P. (1995). *The five stages of culture shock*. Westport, CT: Greenwood.

Sinclair, K., & Po-yee, I. W. (1999). *Culture shock!: A guide to customs and etiquette in China*. Portland, OR: Graphic Arts Center Publishing Company.

Storti, C. (1990). *The art of crossing cultures*. Yarmouth, ME: Intercultural Press.

His first-, second-, and third-level supporting points are subordinated by indentation and alternating numbers and letters.

All his points are phrased as declarative sentences and that he includes only one sentence per point.

Frustration climaxes the third point, so here is a good place to write out a transition statement rather than use a signpost. John separates his transition from the lettering and numbering system. A signpost leads to his last point.

By setting apart the conclusion, he makes sure that he's crafted a memorable ending that summarizes the speech and is both purposeful and brief.

John formats his references in the American Psychological Association (APA) style. Ask your instructor which format he or she prefers, but always list the references you consulted during your speech preparation.

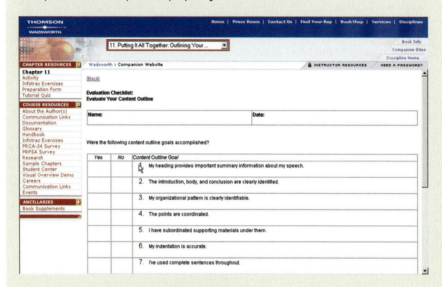

BUILD YOUR SPEECH
EVALUATE YOUR CONTENT OUTLINE

Use Speech Builder Express to prepare your content outline.

When you have finished your outline, evaluate it using the Evaluate Your Content Outline checklist available on the book's website.

How to Create Speaking Notes

Content or full-sentence outlines help you organize your ideas and visualize your points in relationship to one another, but they differ from speaking notes—what you actually use when you're delivering the speech. In speaking notes, use sentences in only two places: transition statements and direct quotations. Otherwise, use **key words** for your points, including just enough phrases or words to jog your memory as you speak. This section describes two major formats for speaking notes: note cards and speaking outlines.

Use Note Cards

Writing key words out on note cards and using them in delivery offers several advantages. For one thing, cards are smaller, less noticeable, and easier to handle than standard sheets of paper. They are sturdy enough not to waver if your hand trembles. And if you deliver your speech without a podium, you can hold your cards in one hand and still use the other to gesture. Here are some tips for creating note cards:

◗ Use index cards.
◗ Write legibly; print or type key words in capital letters; double- or triple-space your lines.
◗ Number your cards so that you can quickly put them in place if they get out of order.
◗ Write on only one side of each card because turning note cards over can be distracting.
◗ Delete nonessential words—use only key words and short phrases.
◗ Use no more than five or six lines per card, and space your lines so that you can find your place instantly. For longer speeches, use more cards instead of crowding additional information onto your cards.
◗ Highlight important ideas; circle or underline words you want to emphasize during delivery.

key words important words and phrases that will jog the speaker's memory

© Peter Chapman Photography

Avoid this speaker's mistake by keeping your speaking notes largely invisible. Make smooth transitions between cards or pages. Don't wave them around or tap your cards on the podium. However, do let listeners see you refer to your notes when you're giving direct quotations or complicated statistics.

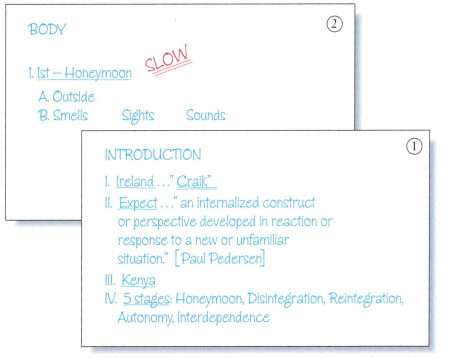

Figure 11.1
Speaking Note Cards
Your note cards are highly individualized. Make a personalized set of key term cards that will jog *your* memory.

Instructor Resource: Power-Point
The *Multimedia Manager with Instructor Resources* CD-ROM includes PowerPoint slides of Figures 11.1 and 11.2.

Teaching Tip
Decide early about form of notes you will allow your students to use while speaking: the content outline, a manuscript, three 4 × 6 note cards, or speaking notes? Remind students that the type of notes they use is less important than their ability to deliver the message effectively. A memorized speech can sound extemporaneous. A manuscript speech can sound conversational. No one type works equally well for every speaker in every situation, although most public speaking classes require that every speech be delivered extemporaneously with limited use of notes.

◗ Put delivery reminders such as *pause* or *slow down* on your cards.
◗ Practice in front of a mirror using your note cards. Revise them if they are not as helpful as you would like.
◗ When you actually give your speech, use your cards unobtrusively. Never wave them around. However, when you read a direct quotation or give complicated statistics, hold up a card and look at it frequently to show your audience that you are being as accurate as possible.[1]

Figure 11.1 shows two of the note cards for John's speech on culture shock.

Teaching Tip
A key to teaching outlining is to have lots of models, both good and bad. Make sure the models you provide are accurate and that they are consistent with the models provided in the text. Variations between the text and supplemental models may confuse students and lead to errors.

Create a Speaking Outline

A second strategy is to create a speaking outline by typing out key terms on a standard sheet of paper. Many of the tips for creating note cards apply to key term outlines, but there are some minor differences:

▶ Use plenty of space to distinguish between the various sections of your speech.

▶ Use highlighter pens to distinguish the sections easily. For example, you might underline signposts and transition statements in orange, and use yellow for the introduction, the body, and the conclusion.

▶ Use different font sizes and formatting features to break up visual monotony and to direct your eyes to specific places as you go along. For example, in Figure 11.2, the preview alternates lowercase and capitalized words.

Figure 11.2
Speaking Outline
Speaking outlines contain key words to remind you of your ideas and advice words to remind you of your delivery.

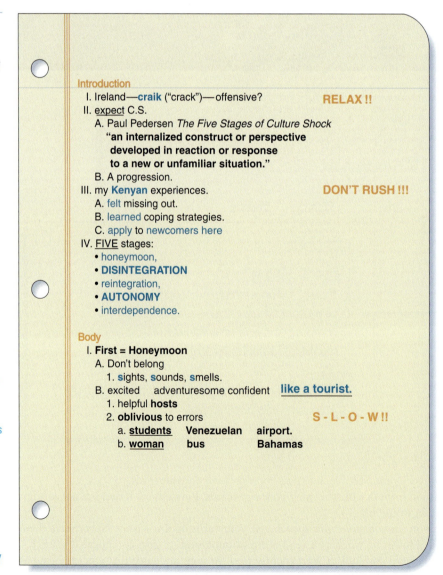

Classroom Discussion/ Activity
Going from a full sentence content outline to a speaking outline is often difficult for students. Have the class complete John Streicher's speaking outline based on his content outline. Discuss delivery cues he might find useful. Alternatively, have groups of students develop speaking outlines from their own content outlines. Discuss the importance of rehearsing with speaking outlines until the speaker is comfortable with the delivery cues and organization.

◗ If you have several sheets of notes, spread them across the lectern in such a way that you can still see the side edges of the lower pages. Then when you move from one page to another, slip the top sheet off unobtrusively and tuck it at the bottom of the pile.

◗ If a lectern is unavailable, place your pages in a dark-colored notebook or folder that you hold with one hand while gesturing with the other. (Angle your notebook so that the audience doesn't see your pages.)

Figure 11.2 shows the first page of a speaking outline for the culture shock speech. If you use brief notes, rather than reading from an outline or trying to memorize your speeches, you can remember your major ideas and supporting materials. Moreover, you can still maintain eye contact with the audience, secure in the knowledge that if you lose your train of thought you can easily glance at these notes to regain your place.

BUILD YOUR SPEECH
EVALUATE YOUR SPEAKING OUTLINE

Return to Speech Builder Express and select Completing the Speech Outline to preview your content outline. Using this complete outline, you can easily prepare your speaking outline or note cards.

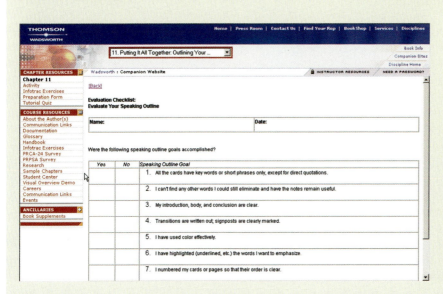

When you have finished your outline, evaluate it using the Evaluate Your Speaking Outline checklist available on the book's website.

How to Work with an Alternative Pattern

Diversity in Practice: Individual Cognitive Style (on page 204) discusses thinking styles and their influence on outlining. If your cognitive style leans toward more global or imagistic thinking, you might prefer an alternative pattern, such as the wave, spiral, or

Student Learning: Workbook
Activity 11.5 in the Student Workbook provides practice in creating an outline for the spiral pattern.

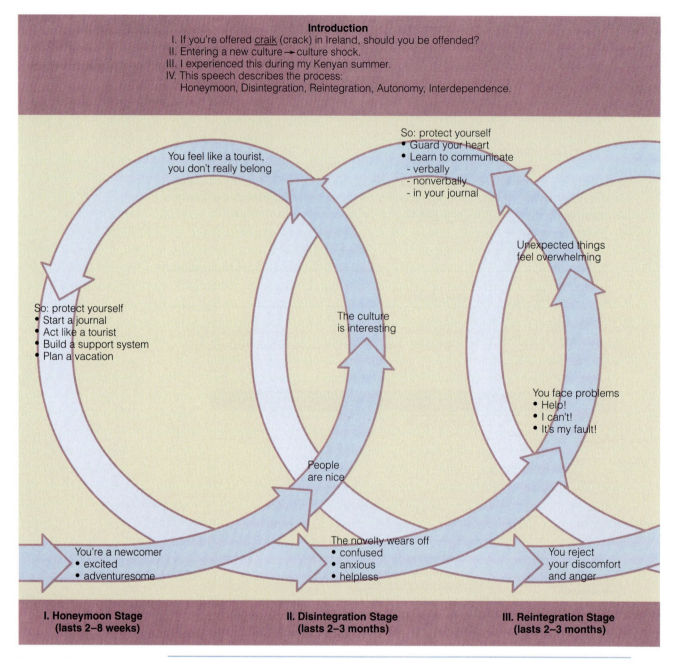

Introduction
I. If you're offered craik (crack) in Ireland, should you be offended?
II. Entering a new culture → culture shock.
III. I experienced this during my Kenyan summer.
IV. This speech describes the process:
Honeymoon, Disintegration, Reintegration, Autonomy, Interdependence.

You feel like a tourist, you don't really belong

So: protect yourself
• Guard your heart
• Learn to communicate
- verbally
- nonverbally
- in your journal

Unexpected things feel overwhelming

So: protect yourself
• Start a journal
• Act like a tourist
• Build a support system
• Plan a vacation

The culture is interesting

You face problems
• Help!
• I can't!
• It's my fault!

People are nice

You're a newcomer
• excited
• adventuresome

The novelty wears off
• confused
• anxious
• helpless

You reject your discomfort and anger

I. Honeymoon Stage
(lasts 2–8 weeks)

II. Disintegration Stage
(lasts 2–3 months)

III. Reintegration Stage
(lasts 2–3 months)

Figure 11.3
Using an Alternate Pattern
This figure depicts the contents of the culture shock speech as visualized in a spiral form.

star, described in Chapter 9. Although your depiction of your speech's content will be less conventional, you can still design an appropriate representation of your ideas and their relationship to one another by using the tips provided here:[2]

◗ First, select an appropriate pattern; you may find it useful to sketch the diagram.
◗ Then write out your main points.

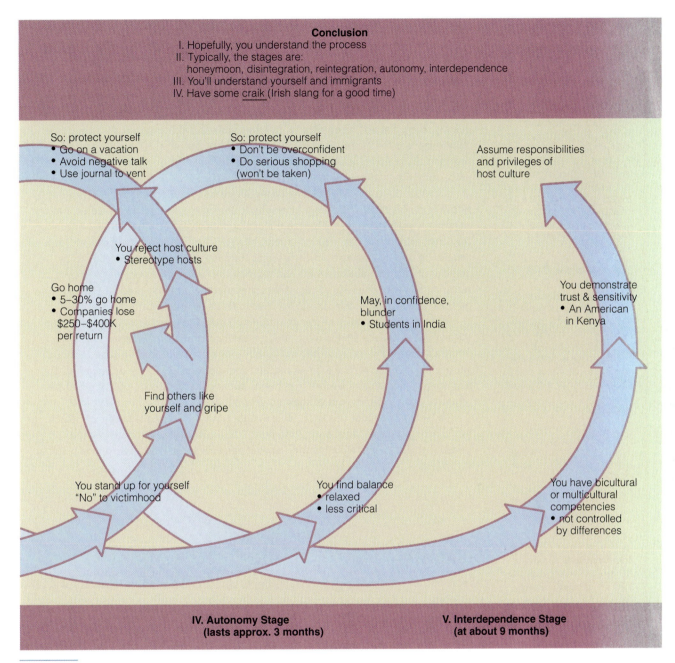

Conclusion
I. Hopefully, you understand the process
II. Typically, the stages are:
honeymoon, disintegration, reintegration, autonomy, interdependence
III. You'll understand yourself and immigrants
IV. Have some craik (Irish slang for a good time)

So: protect yourself
• Go on a vacation
• Avoid negative talk
• Use journal to vent

So: protect yourself
• Don't be overconfident
• Do serious shopping
(won't be taken)

Assume responsibilities
and privileges of
host culture

You reject host culture
• Stereotype hosts

Go home
• 5–30% go home
• Companies lose
$250–$400K
per return

May, in confidence,
blunder
• Students in India

You demonstrate
trust & sensitivity
• An American
in Kenya

Find others like
yourself and gripe

You stand up for yourself
"No" to victimhood

You find balance
• relaxed
• less critical

You have bicultural
or multicultural
competencies
• not controlled
by differences

IV. Autonomy Stage
(lasts approx. 3 months)

V. Interdependence Stage
(at about 9 months)

Figure 11.3
(continued)

⟩ With your pattern in mind, indicate what you'll use for developmental material and subordinate this material under the points it supports.

⟩ Indicate how you plan to begin and end your speech, and then write out key transition statements.

⟩ Use standard indentation and numbering only if it's helpful.

Figure 11.3 provides an example of John's culture shock speech formatted into a spiral pattern.

cognitive style comprises the modes you typically use to think, perceive, remember, and solve problems; it's influenced by your culture but unique to you

---

DIVERSITY IN PRACTICE
INDIVIDUAL COGNITIVE STYLE

ANY DISCUSSION OF DIVERSITY IS INCOMPLETE without a mention of individual differences, and in a chapter on outlining, it's important to note that each person's **cognitive style** (sometimes called thinking style or learning style) is unique. Consequently, every classroom contains "a diverse population of learners."[3] Your cognitive style comprises the modes you typically use to think, perceive, remember, and solve problems. Our cultures influence our styles to an extent, but your particular way of processing information is unique to you.[4]

In 1981, the cognitive scientist Roger Sperry won the Nobel Prize in Physiology or Medicine for his research in brain hemispheric dominance. His studies revealed that the right brain processes information more globally, intuitively, and artistically; in contrast, left-brain processes are more linear, analytic, logical, and computational. Most people use both hemispheres of their brains, but one side or the other tends to be dominant.[5] This text obviously will not describe the finer points of cognitive science research; however, diversity of cognitive styles and the fact that they reflect both a personal and a cultural orientation fits the emphasis of this text.

Why is this topic in a chapter on outlining? Well, the linear form of outlining described in this chapter and in most public speaking texts is a more left-brained way to frame a speech, which may or may not match your preferred cognitive style. Although you are required to produce a linear outline, your personal style may be more holistic, and when you organize speeches in contexts outside the classroom, you may prefer alternative, more organic ways of showing your points.

To learn more about this topic, do a Google or an InfoTrac College Edition search for "thinking styles," "right-brain/left-brain," "learning styles," or other related terms. If you're interested in identifying your personal style, look for an online learning styles test.

Summary

As part of the speechmaking process, it's important to understand and show the ways that your points and subpoints relate to one another. Consequently, your instructor may ask you to outline your ideas in a linear form, using alternating letters and numbers and careful indentation. Coordinate your main points, and subordinate supporting materials under them. Write your content outline in full sentences, and include a list of references at the end.

However, don't take this content outline to the podium with you. Instead, use a key word outline that helps you remember your main points but prevents you from reading your speech verbatim.

A linear outline is not the only way to record your ideas; in fact, one way to recognize diversity is to admit that people with various learning styles may actually benefit from using an alternative, more visual way to record speech content. If you choose an alternative pattern, you may find it helpful to sketch out a simple diagram and then arrange your major ideas and supporting materials on it.

STUDY AND REVIEW

The premium website for *Public Speaking* offers a broad range of resources that will help you better understand the material in this chapter, complete assignments, and succeed on tests. The website features

▶ Speech videos with critical viewing questions, various types of outlines, transcripts, and note cards
▶ Interactive practice activities, self quizzes, and a sample final exam

For more information about this text's electronic learning resources, consult your **Guide to Online Resources for Public Speaking** or visit http://communication.wadsworth.com/jaffe5.

KEY TERMS

The terms below are defined in the margins throughout this chapter. The book website also provides interactive flashcards and crossword puzzles to help you learn these terms and the concepts they represent.

rough draft outline 192
script or text 192
speaking notes 192
content, preparation, or
   full-sentence outline 192
coordination 193

indentation 194
parallel points 194
subordination 195
key words 198
cognitive style 204

APPLICATION AND CRITICAL THINKING EXERCISES

The exercises below are also among the practice activities on the book's website.

1. Outline an in-class speech while it is being given by one of your classmates. After the speech, give the outline to the speaker, and ask him or her to check its contents for completeness and faithfulness to the speech.
2. Using the same outline, ask another student to evaluate your formatting— use of indentation, alternating numbers and letters, complete sentences, and the like.
3. Before you give your next speech, work from your content outline to prepare a speaking outline. Let a classmate evaluate both outlines and make revisions that would improve either one or both.
4. Dr. John Bourhis at Missouri State University has created an excellent website that provides additional information about outlining. You'll find it at www.smsu.edu/com/com115/outlines.htm. What additional tips did you find at this site?
5. Using the website in Exercise 4, find the sample student preparation outline "Buying a Baseball Bat" and critique it.

Instructor's Resource Manual
The Application and Critical Thinking Questions in Chapter 11 of the *Instructor's Resource Manual* (available in print, online, and on the Multimedia Manager CD-ROM) suggest a way of using peer grading for Questions 1 and 2.

Student Learning: Book Website
Many video clips are available on the book website for viewing and evaluation or guided critical analysis. Many clips are also available on the Multimedia Manager CD-ROM.

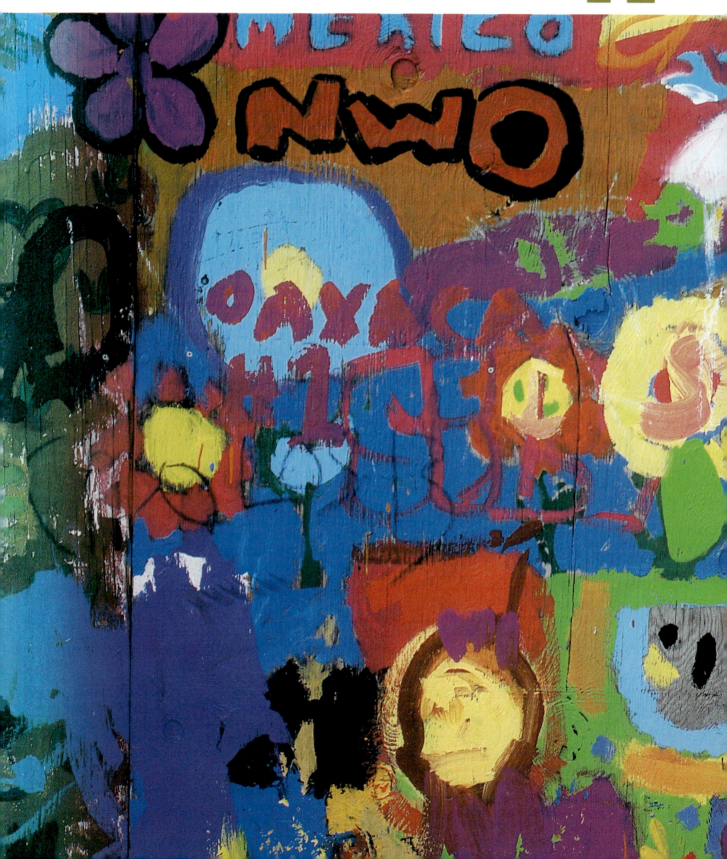

CHAPTER 12

VISUAL AIDS: FROM CHALKBOARD TO COMPUTER

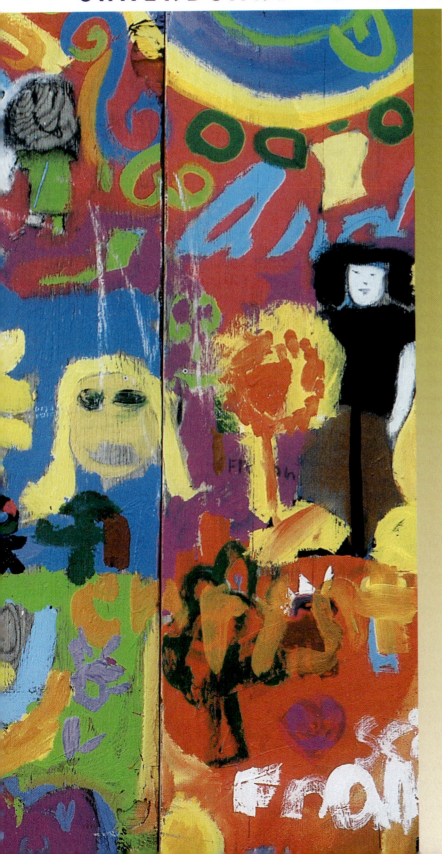

THIS CHAPTER WILL HELP YOU

▶ Explain the value of visual aids

▶ Create your personal visual presentation plan

▶ Choose specific visual aids, including objects, models, people, lists, charts, graphs, photographs, drawings and maps, and audio and video resources

▶ Determine the advantages and disadvantages of using various presentation technologies, including overhead projectors, slide projectors, LCD projectors, document cameras, classroom boards, poster boards and flip charts, and handouts

▶ Explain some principles of visual design

▶ Give guidelines for using visual aids

"Immigrant Pride Day Community Mural"
Mural © 1998 by Precita Eyes Muralists.
(Mission District, SF, CA)

OME VISUAL AIDS are legendary—as horror stories:

One student killed, skinned, and cleaned a live fish in front of her stunned classmates.[1] Another thought it would be creative and dramatic to open his speech on terrorism with a role-play scenario. He arranged for a couple of friends dressed in fatigues and carrying realistic but fake automatic weapons to burst into the classroom just as he got up to speak, and order everyone to hit the floor. He didn't anticipate his classmates' reactions: Some screamed, others cried. One began hyperventilating and had to go to the emergency room. (She had immigrated from a country in which terrorist incidents were common.) Someone called 911. As you might imagine, class ended immediately.

Other visuals are memorable for positive reasons:

One speaker gave an inspirational message on shedding bad habits and replacing them with positive behaviors. He began his speech in ragged, dirty clothing, but as he talked, he removed one item after another and replaced each with a clean, new garment.

In this era of advanced technology, many visual and audio aids are available. Clearly, this type of support can be memorable—either positively or negatively—and the most competent speakers understand how to create and use visual and audio aids well. Most of this chapter focuses on visual aids, but it also suggests ways you can use audio resources to enhance your message and create positive impressions about you.

CASE STUDY: NEIL WOLKODOFF, FITNESS SPECIALIST

You may not immediately think of a personal trainer as a public speaker who has mastered the use of visual aids, but Neil Wolkodoff, Ph.D., fitness trainer and owner of Physical Golf, is just such a person. In his more than 15 years of fitness workshops and seminars, he has used a variety of visual aids. For example:

▶ *Objects.* Golf clubs and an exercise ball help him demonstrate how to use equipment.
▶ *Himself.* His own body illustrates how to stretch and strengthen core muscles.
▶ *Transparencies and slides.* Overhead transparencies or PowerPoint slides supplement his demonstrations.
▶ *Handouts.* Wolkodoff creates handouts with plenty of room for note taking, which helps some listeners learn the material better.

His advice regarding transparencies and slides is, "Keep the visual points very simple, and elaborate verbally."[2] If you provide handouts for subsequent reading, distribute them at the end of the speech so that audience members are not tempted to read them instead of listening to you.

Questions for Discussion

▶ What other specific visual aids might a fitness trainer incorporate into a workshop?
▶ Name some other occupations that rely heavily on the use of actual objects in seminar or workshop presentations.
▶ What types of visual aids are most commonly used in the occupation you hope to enter?

Visual Aids Transcend Culture

Although the technology has changed, visual aids have a long tradition. In oral cultures, speakers used objects to clarify their ideas and help their listeners better understand abstract concepts. For instance, in the sixth century B.C., the prophet Jeremiah used a ruined linen belt as an object lesson to symbolize the decay that disobedience to God would bring upon the kingdom of Judah.[3]

In addition to clarifying ideas, people learn and remember better when they use more than one sense to take in information, and in an image-saturated culture, audiences expect visual support. Think of your own listening experiences. Don't you learn more and remember more from speakers who use posters, charts, models, maps, objects, and graphs than from those who don't even use the chalkboard?

Visual support also enhances communication in pluralistic settings. They are a valuable tool for international marketers[4] and for presenters who must speak in a second language, as the Diversity in Practice box below explains.

Visuals are not new, but the available number and types differ from those used even a decade ago. And the future promises greater technological diversity. To use visual aids effectively, separate the parts of your speech you can easily express in words (and don't need visual support for) from the parts you find difficult to express in words alone (and would benefit from visual or audio support).[5] Then select the best type of support and the best technology to display that support.

Planning Your Visual or Audio Aids

Visual or audio aids are important for at least four reasons:

1. You can best clarify some types of information by using the right support.
2. Visuals can emphasize important ideas.
3. They relieve monotony and help keep audience attention.
4. Visuals appeal to a variety of learning styles.[6]

Consequently, plan your visual and audio support carefully. After you prepare your speech, go over your outline and identify the places where such support would clarify, emphasize, add interest, or help listeners learn and remember your material. But don't overdo it. In short speeches (six to ten minutes), some consultants suggest a maximum of three visuals, each selected because it shows your speech structure, supports your concepts, or shows relationships between ideas.[7]

First, ask where you *need* additional support because a particular concept is difficult to describe only in words. Speeches about artists or composers come to mind. For

Classroom Discussion / Activity
Have students do an equipment assessment of the room where they will be speaking. Is there an overhead in the room? Is there a table or podium? Where are the electrical outlets? Do the lights have variable control so they can be dimmed? What adjustments would need to be made to accommodate different kinds of audio and visual equipment?

Teaching Tip
http://www.presenters
university.com/visuals.php
These articles from Presenters University discuss
choosing, designing, and
using a large variety of
visual aids.
http://louisville.bizjournals
.com/louisville/stories/
1999/11/29/editorial2.html
"Success in the Workplace:
How to Kill a Presentation
with Visual Aids," an article
from Louisville's Business
First gives five ways of
"killing a presentation" with
poor use of visual aids and
offers tips on how to use
them correctly.
http://www.sasked.gov.sk
.ca/docs/comm20/mod10
.html
This site created by Regina
Saskatchewan Education
describes a teaching module
about visual aids. It includes
classroom exercises and a
design checklist.
http://www.ku.edu/~coms/
virtual_assistant/vpa/vpa7
.htm
The Virtual Presentation
Assistant at the University of
Kansas offers tips on using
visual aids.

**Classroom Discussion/
Activity**
Break students into small
groups and assign one or
more types of visual aid to
each group. Have each group
create visual aids for a
speech based on a former
student's speech outline. The
groups can present their
visuals to the class, who can
discuss which visual aids
were the most effective and
why. Alternatively, if having
groups create visual aids will
take too much time, assign
each group a type of visual,
give them several speech
topics, and have them assess
the appropriateness of their
visual for each topic. Have
the groups present their
findings to the class.

instance, images of Jackson Pollock's paintings were almost essential for Andrea's biographical speech about the artist. Ysenia's audience better understood Hector Berlioz's music because she played clips from his symphonies. Technical topics often need visual support. A math concept is more easily understood by a formula written out on a white-board; the results of a campus survey make sense when shown on a pie graph; and the facial expressions of gorillas come to life in photographs. Demonstrations, similarly, are best understood with visuals. How well could you explain how to fold a flag in words alone?

Next, ask where support would illustrate an idea but is not essential. The mullet hairstyle is familiar enough that Philip could probably get by just describing it; however, pictures of mullets throughout history added greatly to his presentation.

Look, also, for places where supporting materials could gain or maintain attention. A photograph of Lance Armstrong pedaling up a grueling hill would nicely illustrate a story about his final race. Or a cartoon that illustrates a point, inserted well into the speech, could break the monotony of words alone.

Keep in mind that diversity includes diverse learning styles. Some people learn best by seeing, others by doing. Incorporating more sensory support into your speech will meet a wider variety of listeners' styles.

Finally, identify the purpose of each visual by asking: Is it necessary? Is it interesting but not essential? Is it chosen because it's memorable? Is it included because it will help maintain attention? Which learning styles do these visuals support?

Choosing the Right Type of Aid

After you have identified places where support is helpful, look through your options. Several visual or audio aids could potentially make your ideas more understandable, although one type is often better than another. The key is to choose the *best* support, not the kind that's easiest to create. This section will discuss a variety of aids:

- Three-dimensional objects, models, and people
- Lists, charts, and graphs
- Photographs, drawings, and maps
- Audio- and videotaped resources

Objects

What soccer coach would even try to convey the finer points of passing without using a ball? What music instructor would explain how to play the drums without demonstrating on an actual drum? These examples illustrate that some subjects require seeing as well as hearing and that actual three-dimensional objects are useful, especially in speeches that demonstrate a process.

Your topic and the setting determine whether or not an object is a realistic visual aid. For example, what object could you use for a speech about bankruptcy reform? The Kyoto Protocol? Media bias? It's difficult to think of an appropriate *thing*. However, a little creative thinking applied to other topics can result in ideas for communicating through objects, touch, smell, or taste. Here are some examples:

- Luke brought in samples of melons, asparagus, tomatoes, and avocados for his speech on how to select produce.
- Shelly gave each listener a tuft of unprocessed wool and a piece of yarn to touch as she discussed yarn making.
- Melissa provided small samples of freshly ground coffee beans for her talk on coffee roasting procedures.

▶ Nutritionist Joanne Lichten uses items such as a glob of fat or a fast-food bag to gain attention when she speaks.[8]

Objects often have limitations. For instance, firearms are illegal in classrooms, and it's unwise to use live animals, as Denis discovered. His nervous wolf dog detracted from his speech because wary listeners focused on the size of the animal's teeth, not Denis's words! Furthermore, some objects are impractical. Marko couldn't think of a way to bring his motorcycle into the classroom. (Fortunately, his classmates walked to a nearby parking lot where he spoke from the seat of his bike.) Overall, objects must be legal, accessible, and practical. You will use them well if you follow these guidelines:

▶ Be sure the object is large enough for everyone to see, or provide each listener with an individual object.
▶ Don't pass an object around. Some listeners will focus on the visual instead of your speech, and by the time everyone actually holds the object you may be finished speaking.

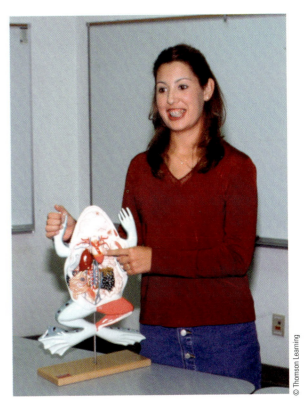

Models are good choices for visuals when an actual object is too large or too small or otherwise too difficult to bring into the speaking situation.

Models

When an object won't work, look for a **model** or realistic facsimile instead. Scaled-down models depict larger objects, such as buildings, dinosaurs, or cars; enlarged models increase the size of small objects such as atoms, ants, or eyeballs. Teachers often use models such as an enlarged human cell or a scaled-down solar system. You can make your own model, or you might be able to borrow one from a professional.

One student's topic was his summer job as a pyrotechnician, or fireworks display technician. Because federal regulations (and common sense) prevented him from bringing explosives into the classroom, he made a model of the spherical explosive device, complete with a fuse. He supplemented the model with several objects: the actual cylinder into which he dropped lit explosives while on the job and the jumpsuit and the safety helmet he wore at work.

People

Use friends, volunteers from the audience, even your own body to demonstrate a concept. For example, to point out the inherent problems in judging people by their looks, Nancy introduced her friend to the class. Then, during the course of the speech, she used makeup, hair gel, and black clothing to transform her friend from a "preppy" into a "Goth." Consider ways to incorporate the audience as a whole; for example, you might ask fellow students to stand and participate in an exercise of some sort. And don't overlook yourself as a visual aid. Jacinda, an Alaskan of Eskimo origin, used two volunteers from the audience to demonstrate a native sport called the "stick pull." Her tee-shirt was adorned with the letters W-E-I-O, which stands for "World Eskimo-Indian Olympics." Neil Wolkodoff, the subject of the chapter's opening case study, uses himself and volunteers from the audience to demonstrate techniques and concepts.

In short, an object, a model, or a person is almost indispensable in certain types of speeches, especially demonstration speeches. However, when it's unrealistic to use them, many other types of visuals are available.

model a facsimile of an object that you can't easily bring to the speech

Lists

Lists are **text-based visuals** that rely on written words more than on visual images. Lists can incorporate art in a minor way, but their value depends on the words or numerical information they display. Without the art, the message would still come through, but without the words or numbers, it would not.

Lists are popular for chronological speeches because stages or steps lend themselves to listing. Lists can also summarize in words or phrases the key points of topically arranged speeches. For example, a list of the kinds of animal communication, as shown in Figure 12.1(a), helps listeners identify and remember the main subpoints. Lists are most effective when you remember the following guidelines:

▶ Don't put too much information in the list. With too many details, your listeners may simply read the material and stop listening to you.
▶ Follow the **six-by-six rule:** Use no more than six lines, no more than six words per line.[9]
▶ Use phrases or short sentences instead of long sentences or paragraphs.

Charts

The two basic types of charts are flowcharts and organizational charts. **Flowcharts** show the order in which processes occur. You can often recognize them by the use of arrows indicating directional movement. Flowcharts can include drawings (pictorial flowcharts), or they may simply be a series of labeled shapes and arrows. Figure 12.1(b) illustrates a portion of a flowchart.

Organizational charts show hierarchies and relationships. A family tree, for example, depicts relationships among family members. The organizational chart in Figure 12.1(c) shows relationships among various individuals involved in television production.

Photographs

Although photographs actually show an object, a person, or a scene, the saying "A picture is worth a thousand words" is not necessarily true. Pictures are of little value if your audience can't see them. Fortunately, many students have successfully used photographs in their speeches, and the next section of this chapter describes several ways you can enlarge your visuals. For her speech on Harry Truman, Tricia showed four pictures of him at various stages of his life. Alene used black-and-white fetal sonograms for her speech on fetal development. Namky found photographs of Hanoi to illustrate his speech on the capital of his country, Vietnam. (Each student cited sources in a small font below each picture.) To be successful, you should avoid two common mistakes with photographs:

▶ Don't pass them around. As with objects, the person closest to the speaker sees all the pictures and hears them explained, but the last person sees them long after they have been described.
▶ Don't show pictures from a book. John walked back and forth across the front of the room, displaying several photographs in a book that didn't fully open. Students craned their necks to see the pictures, and John was put into an awkward posture trying to keep the book open. He also wasted time flipping from one page to another. Overall, his visuals were a distraction, not an aid.

Graphs

Have you ever felt bombarded with statistics? Speeches full of numerical data are often boring, difficult to follow, and impossible to remember without a graph that represents

text-based visual carry meaning in the written words rather than in visual images

six-by-six rule limit information to six lines, six words per line

flowcharts show the order or directional flow in which processes occur; may simply be a series of labeled shapes and arrows

organizational charts show hierarchies and relationships

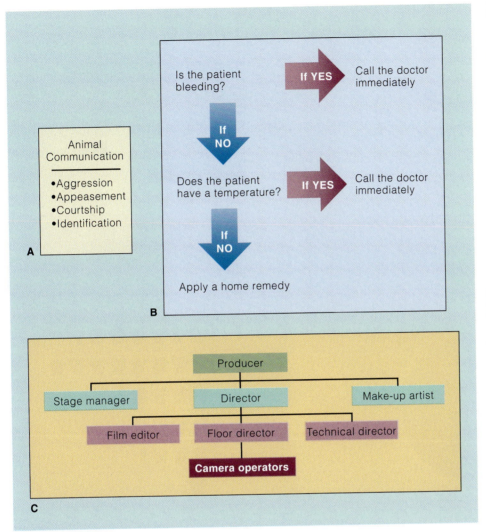

Figure 12.1
Lists and Charts
Common visuals include
(a) a list, (b) a flowchart,
and (c) an organizational
chart.

**Instructor Resource:
PowerPoint**
The *Multimedia Manager
with Instructor Resources*
CD-ROM includes PowerPoint
slides of Figures 12.1
and 12.2.

the numbers in diagram form. Graphs are a type of **image-based visual** that communicate via a figure of some sort. Depicting your material in one of four types of graphs allows your listeners to see how your numbers relate to one another.

1. **Line graphs** present information in linear form; they are best for showing variables that fluctuate over time, such as changes in college enrollment over two decades. They are also good for showing the relationship of two or more variables, for instance, comparing the number of male and female students during the same period. (Figure 12.2a shows fluctuation in the funding of three projects over a six-year period.)
2. **Bar graphs** are useful for comparing data from several groups. For instance, numerical information comparing the salaries of men and women with differing educational levels is displayed on the bar graph in Figure 12.2b.
3. **Pie graphs** are circular graphs that are especially good for showing divisions of a population or parts of the whole. The pie graph in Figure 12.2c depicts ways typical Americans get to work; you could use it to speak about carpooling or public transportation.
4. **Picture graphs** or **pictographs,** the least common of the four types, are especially effective for data related to objects or people. Each picture represents a certain number of individual cases, as Figure 12.2d demonstrates.

image-based visual carries meaning in visual images; written words are secondary

line graphs display in a linear form one or more variables that fluctuate over a time period

bar graphs compare data from several groups by using bands of various lengths

pie graphs represent parts of the whole or divisions of a population by circles divided into portions

picture graphs or pictographs present data in pictures, each representing a certain number of individual cases

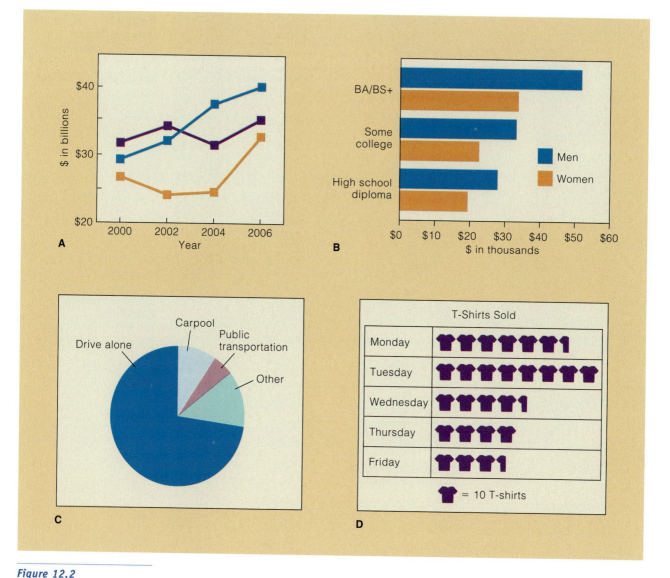

Figure 12.2
Graphs
Major types of graphs:
(a) a line graph, (b) a bar graph, (c) a pie graph, and (d) a pictograph.

Drawings, Diagrams, and Maps

Drawings can stand alone or be added to lists or other visuals as decorative or supplementary support. **Diagrams** are line drawings or graphic designs that explain, rather than realistically depict, an object or a process.

If you can't draw even stick figures, you can at least trace or photocopy a commercial drawing onto a transparency or a handout. Or your computer can come to your rescue. Many software packages have clip art files of drawings and diagrams that you can easily add to your visuals. The Internet is another source for thousands of drawings, diagrams, and maps. When you use a published or downloaded drawing, diagram, cartoon, or map, always avoid plagiarism by crediting your source on the visual.

This partial list gives you some ideas of how to use drawings effectively:

▶ Substitute drawings for illegal firearms, nervous wolf dogs, inaccessible motorcycles, buildings that are too large, or insects that are too small to bring into your classroom.

diagram drawing or design that serves to explain, rather than realistically depict, an object or process

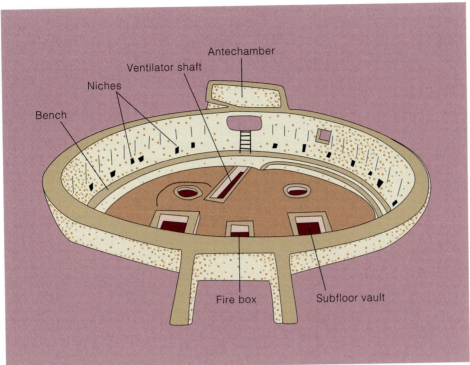

Bench • **Niches** • **Ventilator shaft** • **Antechamber** • **Fire box** • **Subfloor vault**

Figure 12.3
Map
A floor plan of a building is a type of map. This Native American kiva is one example.

Instructor Resource: PowerPoint
The *Multimedia Manager with Instructor Resources* CD-ROM includes a Power-Point slide of Figure 12.3.

▶ Show a cartoon that perfectly illustrates your point and adds humor to your talk. But be sure to read the caption to the audience.

▶ Use a diagram to illustrate the acid rain cycle or the circulatory system.

Maps are drawings that visually represent spaces. We map the heavens as well as the Earth; we map weather; and we even talk about mind maps—maps of information. Choose from the following kinds of maps:

▶ **Political maps** show borders between nations and states. However such maps can be quickly outdated. For instance, any world map dated before 1990 is obsolete; since then, a number of countries, including the Soviet Union and Yugoslavia, have been dismantled, and new political boundaries have been drawn.

▶ **Geographic maps,** showing mountains, deserts, lowlands, and other natural features, do not go out of date.

▶ Blueprints and floor plans of buildings, maps of routes between two points, city maps, campus maps—the list goes on. Figure 12.3 depicts a map of a Native American kiva.

To draw your listeners' attention to specific features on a map, mark them with a letter or number. Then, during your speech, ask listeners to focus on each feature.

The wide variety of visuals available for speeches can illuminate ideas, clarify concepts, help audiences organize and remember material, and present abstract concepts more concretely. Three-dimensional objects and text- or image-based visuals are useful in visually oriented cultures. However, in some cases, recordings of sounds or images are even more effective support.

political maps show current borders for states and nations; rapidly outdated in fast-changing world

geographic maps show mountains, deserts, and other natural features; not easily outdated

Video and Audio Recordings

Think of the difference between hearing a speech about *dun dun* drums and actually hearing the drums. Although audio and video recording require extra preparation and planning, they can help you better convey certain types of information.

Audio Resources

Audio support is particularly important with music- or sound-related topics. Portable electronic keyboards, other musical instruments, tapes, CDs, MP3 players, and so on can add to your speech. They all let your audience hear the sounds you are explaining, ranging from reggae music to the music of a particular composer (as demonstrated in the speech about *dun dun* drums, outlined at the end of Chapter 16 and available on the book's website).

Although less common, you can effectively use sounds other than music. Before her speech on whales, for instance, Mary Beth played a recording of a whale song and asked her listeners to identify the source of the sound. Use your creativity to think of other ways to incorporate short sound clips, such as sounds from nature, traffic noises, or conversations, to enhance your presentation.

Video Resources

College recruiters visit high schools, bringing along videotapes or DVDs showing their institutions, complete with campus images, background music, and interviews with administration, faculty, and students. In many cases, the images themselves provide most of the message. The recruiter simply introduces the video and then fields questions afterward.

In the classroom, your goal is to let video recordings supplement, not replace, your ideas. There are massive amounts of recorded resources available to you, including clips from television shows, feature films, advertisements, and home movies. By carefully selecting short segments to illustrate your points, you can clarify your ideas dramatically and memorably, as these examples demonstrate:

- Lisa made the *Guinness Book of Records* for being part of the largest tap dancing group ever assembled at one time for a performance. As she explained ways to get listed in the famous record book, Lisa used a fifteen-second video clip that her mother had recorded.
- Mary Beth's whale speech ended with a ten-second clip taken from a television program, showing a number of whales playfully leaping in and out of the water.
- Effie used a scene from the film "The Importance of Being Ernest" to illustrate a particular type of territory violation.
- Andrew discussed the differences between men's and women's gestures. He brought a fifteen-second commercial showing a male and a female interacting. He played the tape as he introduced the topic. Then, as he discussed each point, he again played the tape, this time with the sound turned off, pausing at various places to illustrate a specific point.

All these students succeeded because they preplanned carefully. The short clips they selected *illustrated*, rather than substituted for, their words; they cued up their tapes or selected the scene in advance; and they planned exactly when to start and stop the clip.

Enabling listeners to see or hear your topic is important in many public speaking settings today. Indeed, it's almost essential in some presentations, such as demonstrations. Skillful construction and use of visuals distinguish good speakers from adequate ones, and as you learn to work with visuals, your competence will increase.

STOP AND CHECK

CONTINUE YOUR AUDIOVISUAL PRESENTATION AID PLAN

Review your speech outline, and decide which ideas must be supplemented by a visual or audio aid. Decide which specific types are best suited, and then fill in section C of the plan. Using a separate sheet for each visual, make a preliminary sketch of the material you plan to use.

You may want to use Speech Builder Express to complete this step of the process, as its prompts include lists of possible visual aids that you can select. Click on "Visual Aids" in the left-hand navigation bar.

Student Learning: Book Website
This Stop and Check activity can also be found on the book's website, where it's located under "Chapter Resources."

Choosing the Right Type of Presentation Technology

You can probably list several ways to display visuals; in fact, giant corporations exist solely to provide machines and materials for creating and displaying visual aids. The 3M Company, for example, makes transparencies, plastic envelopes for storing them, frames for holding them, machines for projecting them, and so on. This section covers a number of common ways to display visual aids, along with their advantages as well as disadvantages.

Overhead Projectors

Overhead projectors are everywhere; they're in classrooms, businesses, and other organizations, nationally and globally. Using them, you can enlarge and display an image on a wall or a screen so that everyone can see it, even in a large auditorium. Using an overhead projector has other advantages. Transparencies are simple and inexpensive to make; they are easy to store and transport; the film is widely available; and it comes in colors. You can overlap transparencies to show a progression of related content by simply placing one on top of another.

You can draw freehand directly onto the transparency or trace a cartoon, map, or other drawing from any printed copy (giving source credit, of course). For a more professional look, photocopy a printed image onto the transparency. Or insert a transparency into your printer and print directly from your computer. I personally like to write on a blank transparency instead of using the chalkboard; this eliminates the need to turn my back to the audience.

Skillful use of an overhead projector adds to your audience's perception of your competence. However, poor skills can have the opposite effect. For best results, follow these guidelines:

▶ Before you begin speaking, turn the machine on and adjust the focus. Then turn the machine off until you're ready to use your visual.

▶ You can "build" a list by using a cover sheet and revealing each point as you discuss it, or by cutting your transparency into strips and displaying the strips one by one.[10]

▶ To draw your listeners' attention to some part of your visual, point to the transparency, not the screen. If your hand is trembling, place a pointed object where you want listeners to focus, and then move your hand away from the projector.

▶ If you use a transparency several times but you want to highlight or comment on the material each time, place a blank transparency on top and underline, mark, or write comments on the blank one. This ensures that your originals remain clean.

Slide Projectors

Slide projectors, like overhead projectors, show images on a screen so fairly large audiences can see them. You can make slides from photographs or special film. They are good for projecting high-quality images with excellent color reproduction. One drawback is that slides are hard to see in well-lit rooms, and you may thus find yourself speaking in the dark when you use them.

Common slide projectors have a carousel-type tray in which you place ordered slides. For each new slide, simply press a button on your hand-held control. To enhance your professionalism, put a black slide between sections of content so that you can pause to talk while avoiding a blast of white light or leaving a picture or diagram up so long that it's distracting or boring.[11]

Presentation Software and LCD Projectors

LCD projectors connect directly to a computer and project what appears on the monitor onto a screen. If you create your visuals using PowerPoint or another **presentation software program,** you'll need one of these projectors. Transfer your slides to a diskette, CD-ROM, or USB data storage device (also referred to as a flash memory or removable hard drive, among other names). When you present, simply insert the storage device into the computer and launch your presentation. A click of the mouse changes the slide. The "b" key brings up a blank slide; use it when you discuss material with no visual support, and then click the mouse again to display your next slide.

Unfortunately, this technology is not always used well. For example, in an article in *Technical Communication,* Jean-Luc Doumont says, "Several hundred million copies of Microsoft PowerPoint are turning out trillions of slides each year."[12] Most of these are ineffective and detract from the message—but the problem lies in the creators, not the technology. To improve your skills with PowerPoint or a similar program, follow these guidelines from Doumont:

▸ Write out the words you'll use, and sketch the illustrations before you make the slide. Identify the purpose for everything you include on the slide.
▸ While still in the planning stage, go back and remove every unnecessary word or figure. In other words: simplify, simplify, simplify.
▸ Avoid the temptation to write out your entire speech and read it to your hapless audience.
▸ Develop your slides in black and white, and then add color sparingly to emphasize ideas.
▸ Rehearse at least once without the slides to make sure that they don't substitute for your message.

Document Cameras

One website calls **document cameras** (also known as *visual presenters* and *visualizers*) "the 21st-century overhead projector,"[13] because they are like a projector, scanner, microscope, whiteboard, and computer rolled into one. Some units are compact enough to fold into a notebook-sized carrying case.

These high-resolution cameras let you project photographs, slides, three-dimensional objects, a document you've created, material from a book, and so on. You can zoom in on a painting or enlarge a small object, such as a dime, or even a microscopic object, so that small details are visible. Document cameras are becoming more common in classrooms and businesses nationwide.[14]

presentation software programs computer software to create a package of lists, tables, graphs, and clip art

document cameras high-resolution cameras that display documents and three-dimensional objects

Chalkboards or Whiteboards

Chalkboards or whiteboards are standard equipment in most educational settings. They have several advantages. They're widely available. They're great for explaining unfolding processes, such as math problems. They also encourage informality, which is appropriate in some contexts. Finally, they are useful in settings that include speaker-audience interactions, such as brainstorming sessions.[15] Unfortunately, boards have three major drawbacks:

▶ You can't prepare your visual beforehand. An unprepared visual creates additional anxiety if you like to have everything, including the visuals, ready and rehearsed in advance.
▶ Most people don't write well on boards, so the visuals look unprofessional.
▶ You must turn your back to your audience while you write on the board. This is probably the major drawback of boards in general.

Boards continue to evolve. Although **interactive whiteboards** are often used in educational settings, businesses are recognizing their advantages. They allow you to connect the board to a document camera or to a computer with markup software. You can then use "electronic markers" or even your finger, to overwrite material on the board. Finally, you can save your markups to files and later retrieve, email, or print them out.[16]

Poster Boards and Flip Charts

For convenience and economy, consider a lower-tech option: poster board. It's readily available in a variety of weights and colors at campus bookstores and art supply stores. However, you'll need some sort of easel to hold the posters. On C-SPAN, you can see members of Congress display charts and graphs on poster board. People who deliver the same speech over and over, such as financial planners, for example, also use professionally prepared posters. Posters are effective with relatively small audiences, but at greater distances they're difficult to see. These tips will help you make professional-looking posters:

▶ Use rulers or yardsticks to ensure straight lines and avoid a "loving-hands-at-home" look.
▶ Use more than one color to attract and hold interest.
▶ For a more professional look, use adhesive letters.
▶ To protect your posters from becoming bent or soiled, carry them in a portfolio, or cover them with plastic when you transport them.

Flip charts are oversized tablets, lined or unlined; they are common in businesses and other organizations but rare in college classrooms. Their name reflects the fact that pages can be turned, or "flipped," from one to another. They are made of paper that varies from tablet thickness to stiffer weights. Larger flip charts work well in conference rooms; smaller ones work well for presentations to just a few listeners.

Flip charts can function like a chalkboard or whiteboard, especially in brainstorming-type situations where you interact with your audience. For example, you might ask listeners to contribute ideas that you later incorporate into your talk. Tear off the lists you create with your listeners, and pin or tape them to the wall. When you use a flip chart this way, you must overcome disadvantages similar to those you faced with a classroom board. As you write on the chart, you turn your back on the audience. In addition, your writing may be messy.

Instructor Resource: Video Clip
The Multimedia Manager CD-ROM (and the book website) includes several videos of speakers using visual aids. Show or assign Anna Riedl's speech, "Pumpkins." What does the speaker do well? What could the speaker do to improve the use of visual aids? Ask students to suggest two additional visual aids that could be used in this speech.

interactive whiteboards connect to other technology; you can overwrite material and then save your markups

flip charts tablets you prepare in advance or create on the spot; turn to a new page or tear off and display pages as you finish them

Document cameras are more versatile than many other types of presentation technology, because they can easily display written material, photographs, drawings, objects, and so on.

Use flip charts to "build" a diagram in front of the audience. In advance, lightly draw the entire visual in pencil. Then, during your presentation, trace over the lines for a professional-looking diagram that appears to be done on the spot. This way, you can be sure that all the words are spelled correctly beforehand, and you can use the chart as a giant prompt card.

If you repeat the same presentation for different audiences, prepare your visuals in advance on heavier-weight tablets. Then use the flip chart much as you would use a series of posters, exposing each new visual as you discuss it. The separate visuals will stay in order. In addition, because the cover is stiff, the tablet can stand alone on a table. This makes it a useful display method when other equipment is unavailable.[17]

DIVERSITY IN PRACTICE
TRAVELING AND TALKING

TODAY, THOUSANDS OF PROFESSIONALS use visuals abroad. Engineers, marketers, physicians, and computer specialists, who may have once taken a required college speech course, are surprised to find themselves speaking internationally. Someday you may join their numbers. Taking along visual aids presents some challenges.

Jeff Radel,[18] from the University of Kansas Medical Center, emphasizes that the United States is not the center of the technological universe, and that the size of slides here is not globally uniform. Slots in slide projectors and carousels differ in size, and the number of slots varies in some countries to accommodate thicker or thinner slides. Consequently, a speaker who plans to use slides overseas should assess in advance any potential equipment problems.

Dave Zielinski[19] describes "secrets and strategies of speakers on the go." In the light of post—September 11 security regulations, experienced on-the-road presenters consider customs agents' or security guards' perspectives on their equipment. Even a collapsible presentation pointer can look suspicious in carry-on luggage. In addition, expensive equipment tempts thieves in some places. Customs regulations also vary. One sales representative had to post a bond equaling 30 percent of her equipment's cost as a guarantee that she would return with it and not sell it in the country. Overall, Zielinski's advice is: don't assume anything, and have a contingency plan.

Handouts

Brochures, pamphlets, photocopies, or other handouts free audiences from having to take extensive notes and give them details they can study later.[20] Handouts can also provide supplementary information you don't have time to cover in your speech. One student who chose a health-related topic distributed professionally made brochures from his campus health services; another distributed a photocopied diagram illustrating an origami project. Handouts are common in business settings; for example, sales representatives commonly give brochures to potential customers. Committee members, such as a university's board of trustees, often receive an entire book of supplementary handouts.

Your primary challenge with handouts is to make sure they supplement, not replace, your message. To use them more effectively, do the following:

▶ Distribute the handout, face down, before you begin speaking; then, when you discuss the material on it, ask your listeners to turn it over.

▶ Mark the points you want to emphasize with a letter or number so you can easily direct listeners to specific places on the handout. Let's say you distribute a diagram showing how to groom a dog, and you want to highlight three potential trouble spots. Mark the first with an "A," the second with a "B," and the third with a "C." Then, draw your listeners' attention to each place as you discuss it.

▶ Put identical material onto a transparency and project it as you speak. Highlight on the transparency the information you want them to find on their handout.

Read more tips for effective handouts at http://buffalo.bizjournals.com/buffalo/stories/1997/10/13/smallb3.html.

STOP AND CHECK

CONTINUE YOUR AUDIOVISUAL AID PLAN

With your audiovisual aid plan in mind, assess the equipment that is available for your classroom speech by filling in sections D—F on your Audiovisual Aid Plan. Try to imagine yourself using the various types of visual display technology during your speech.

Using Proven Design Principles to Create Visuals

Create your visuals by hand, or use a presentation programs, such as Microsoft's PowerPoint or Adobe Persuasion, that lets you produce visuals with varied backgrounds, fonts, colors, bullets, and border options. Add some clip art or images scanned into the program or downloaded from Internet sources; throw in a video clip, some animation or music, and in a few moments you have a multimedia presentation that your grandparents could only dream about. Transfer your creations to slides, transparencies, or computer disks, and you

Teaching Tip
http://www.kumc.edu/SAH/OTEd/jradel/Effective_visuals/105.html
"Four Important Design Concepts" from Jeff Radel of the University of Kansas summarizes key design principles for visual aids.

are off to a successful presentation. Or are you? Perhaps—if you remember that the best package is helpful only insofar as it helps listeners understand your ideas, and if you create your visuals with some design principles in mind.

A plethora of design features may tempt you to overdo things—and impress but fail to enlighten your audience. For example, you can create transitions between slides, progressive builds on slides, lines of text flying in from the left, the corner, flashing on and off, one letter appearing at a time with clicking sound effects, and so on, creating a mishmash of movement that has nothing to do with your *ideas*. Experiment with a presentation program for fun, but in the end follow some basic guidelines for simple, well-designed visuals described in the following sections.

Choose a Readable Font

Whether you create your visuals on poster board or rely on a computer to produce your materials, make readability your primary concern. One key is to choose a **font**—a complete set of letters and numbers of a given design—that enables your audience to read it easily. Here are some readability tips that are illustrated in Figure 12.4.

1. Choose title case or sentence case, and avoid using only capital letters.
   ▶ USING ALL CAPITAL LETTERS IS MORE DIFFICULT TO READ— BESIDES, YOU'RE NOT SHOUTING, SO WHY CAPITALIZE?
   ▶ Title Case (Capitalizing the First Letter of Main Words) Is Easier to Read.
   ▶ Sentence case (capitalizing only what you'd capitalize in a sentence) is also readable.
2. On handouts, use a **serif font** (with cross lines at the top and bottom of letters) rather than a **sans serif font** (with no cross lines). A serif font is easier to read because the serifs lead your eyes from letter to letter,[21] but sans serif fonts are well suited to smaller chunks of text.
3. Adapt your font to the formality or informality of the topic and the occasion. Generally, serif fonts are more formal; sans serif are less so.[22]
4. Determine whether the visual contains display or content material. If you display only a series of photographs, for instance, you might choose a fancier display font, such as a script or handwriting font, to catch attention.[23] However, for slides containing a lot of content, choose a simple font such as Bookman, Garamond, or Arial. When you handwrite your visuals, use plain, legible lowercase letters.
5. Maintain consistency from one visual to another. That is, if you use Helvetica for your title on the first visual, use it on every visual. Do likewise for the subtitle and text fonts. And limit yourself to just a couple of fonts.
6. It goes without saying that letters should be large enough to be visible and that titles and first-level material should be larger than second-level material, which in turn should be larger than third-level material.

For more information about fonts in general, search InfoTrac College Edition for "fonts." For instance, an article in the *PR Newsletter* (December 8, 2003) says that fonts fall under copyright laws, and although you can usually download them for free, they are considered to be the creator's property and can be licensed.[24]

Use Formatting Features Wisely

A variety of formatting features add visual appeal. For example, centering the title, underlining the subtitle, and bulleting the points can help your audience better see the relationships among ideas. Also, balance the information by spreading it across the visual rather than bunching all the text into the upper left quadrant. **Attributes** such as boldfacing, underlining, or italicizing can highlight and emphasize specific ideas. But use them sparingly, or the impact will be lost.

---

font a complete set of letters and numbers of a given design

serif font a font with cross lines at the top and bottom of letters

sans serif font a simple font with no cross lines on each letter

attributes features such as boldface, italics, and underlining

Figure 12.4
Fonts
Both serif and sans serif fonts have their place in classroom and other presentation visuals. Readability is the major issue: Make fonts large enough to be read easily, and avoid any fancy display font that is difficult to read.

Instructor Resource:
PowerPoint
The *Multimedia Manager with Instructor Resources* CD-ROM includes a PowerPoint slide of Figure 12.4.

Serif fonts such as these are easier to read; using boldface makes them even more visible.

Palatino	**Palatino (bold)**
Times New Roman	**Times New Roman (bold)**
Bookman	**Bookman (bold)**

Sans serif fonts are useful for titles and headings.

Helvetica	**Helvetica (bold)**
Optima	**Optima (bold)**
Avant Garde	**Avant Garde (bold)**

Tempting as they may be, you're wise to avoid fancy display fonts that are difficult to read.

Zapf Chancery	***Zapf Chancery (bold)***
COPPERPLATE	**COPPERPLATE (BOLD)**
𝔚𝔦𝔱𝔱𝔢𝔫𝔟𝔢𝔯𝔤𝔢𝔯 𝔉𝔯𝔞𝔱𝔱𝔲𝔯	**𝔚𝔦𝔱𝔱𝔢𝔫𝔟𝔢𝔯𝔤𝔢𝔯 𝔉𝔯𝔞𝔱𝔱𝔲𝔯 (bold)**

Don't cram too much information on each visual. Limit yourself to one idea per visual, and leave plenty of white space so that the audience can find their place easily. The *maximum* amount of material recommended is six lines, with no more than 40 or 45 characters per line.

Color and Emphasis

Use color to add interest and emphasis and to attract and hold attention. However, carefully plan your color scheme. Colors have a variety of associations that vary culturally. For example, red can be a good emphasis color when used sparingly, but it is "culturally loaded"; in the United States it symbolizes anger ("seeing red") or danger (being "in the red");[25] in China, it symbolizes luck and celebration; in India, it is associated with purity. It is the most common color found on national flags.[26]

For words and images, choose colors that contrast dramatically with the background color. White or ivory-colored posters and clear transparencies are best with text material in high-contrasting black or dark blue, not yellows or oranges.

Experiment until you find a color combination you like. Try yellow lettering, followed by white then lime green, on a dark blue background. Notice the difference when you try red or green on the same dark blue. To avoid a cluttered look, use a maximum of three colors on all of your visuals.

To emphasize ideas with color, use brightly colored bullets to draw attention to a list. Or vary the color of a word or phrase you want to stand out.

The most pleasing visuals follow principles of good design: the fonts, sizing and spacing, and color combinations aim at readability and balance. These principles will help you remember that your aids are just that—aids. They aren't your message, and they aren't a display of your personal artistic or computer skills.

STOP AND CHECK

COMPLETE YOUR AUDIOVISUAL AID PLAN

Return to your Audiovisual Aid Plan and make any revisions you'd like; next, sketch out each visual, paying attention to the size and spacing of your words and images. Select appropriate colors and decide which words or phrases you want to emphasize. Then go to work on your text- or image-based visuals. If you plan to use audio or video support, make arrangements now for the equipment you'll need. And have fun!

General Guidelines for Using Visual and Audio Aids

As noted throughout this chapter, each type of visual or audio aid has specific techniques for successful use. You can build your skills by reviewing and applying these general guidelines:

- Whatever type of audio or visual aid you choose, make sure it can be seen or heard by everyone in the room where you will speak.
- Don't create a visual for its own sake. For example, a presenter who says, "Today, I'll talk about 'character,'" and shows the word "CHARACTER" on a slide is not clarifying a complex point or strengthening a bond with the audience. She's created what professional presenter Joan Detz[27] calls a "dreaded" word slide that doesn't really add to a message.
- Display visuals only when you discuss them. If you use posters, include a cover sheet. As noted earlier, if you use PowerPoint, press the "b" key on your computer and you will get a blank screen between slides.
- Talk to your audience, not to your visual.
- Rehearse using your aids. If you don't have access to a projector during your practices, use a table as a "projector." Or visualize yourself using your posters or transparencies or playing your tape—where you'll stand in relation to the equipment, how you'll point out specific features, what you'll do when they're not in use.
- Don't violate your audience's norms or expectations to the point where you shock, offend, revolt, or anger them. One student showed pornographic photographs to illustrate her speech about pornography. When you shock or violate expectations so severely, you may never regain attention, and your credibility—especially in the area of good sense—suffers as a result.[28]
- Whenever machines are involved, have a Plan B in case the technology fails. Imagine what will happen if the slide projector jams, the light on the overhead projector burns out, or the VCR eats your tape. An alternate plan, usually in the form of a handout, saves your speech. Demonstrating your composure in case of equipment failure will enhance your credibility.[29]

Now that you have read the chapter, go back to the opening case study. From the information provided, how effective do you think Wolkodoff's visuals were overall? Give a reason for your answer.

Summary

As a speaker in a visually oriented culture, it is to your advantage to use visual and audio support effectively. Visuals illustrate your ideas, keep your audience focused on your speech, and make abstract ideas more concrete. Although they are not new, the amount and kind of support available today is unprecedented.

Before you make a single visual, sit down with your outline and determine where support is essential, where it would be useful, where variety is needed, and where audio or visuals would accommodate for a variety of learning styles. If you can state the purpose for every item of support you use, you will have a meaningful package.

Choose from several types of visuals. Objects, people, and models compose three-dimensional visuals. In addition, you can sometimes incorporate touch, smell, and taste into your presentation. Text-based lists or image-based charts, graphs, photographs, drawings, or maps are other options. Finally, select audio or video clips when they would best clarify your ideas.

To display your visuals, choose a means that suits your topic and the room in which you will speak. Various projectors—overhead, slide, LCD, and document cameras—chalkboards or whiteboards, and interactive boards combine with poster boards, flip charts, and handouts as high-tech and low-tech ways to present visual aids. All have advantages and disadvantages, and you should take care to have a Plan B in case your equipment fails.

Emerging technologies have led to a variety of sophisticated presentational packages that can help you create professional-appearing visuals and multimedia presentations. However, visual support should enhance, not replace, your speech. So use principles of design, including readability, formatting, and color, to their best advantage. And follow a few rules: Display visuals only when you are discussing them, and talk to the audience, not to the visuals. Don't create a visual just to have one. Carefully edit your tapes and videos, and make sure they are visible and audible to everyone. And rehearse with your visual in advance of your speech.

In conclusion, don't overlook the importance of competent use of visual materials as a way to enhance your credibility. Keep in mind that professional-looking resources create more positive impressions than those that appear to be scribbled out just minutes before your presentation. Further, the disastrous case of equipment failure may actually increase your credibility if your listeners see you handle the stressful situation with composure. Finally, demonstrate your good sense by selecting and presenting only visual support that does not violate your listeners' expectations.

Student Learning: Workbook
Students can complete "Before You Take the Exam" in Chapter 12 of the Student Workbook for a review of this chapter.

Instructor Resource: Video Clip
Show clip "Self-Injury." Ask students if this speech would have been more effective with visual aids. The answer will probably be "no." Discuss why. This should lead into Chapter 13 and the importance of choosing effective language.

STUDY AND REVIEW

The premium website for *Public Speaking* offers a broad range of resources that will help you better understand the material in this chapter, complete assignments, and succeed on tests. The website features

▸ Speech videos with critical viewing questions, various types of outlines, transcripts, and note cards
▸ Interactive practice activities, self quizzes, and a sample final exam

For more information about this text's electronic learning resources, consult your **Guide to Online Resources for Public Speaking** or visit http://communication.wadsworth.com/jaffe5.

KEY TERMS

The terms below are defined in the margins throughout this chapter. The book website also provides interactive flashcards and crossword puzzles to help you learn these terms and the concepts they represent.

model 211
text-based visual 212
six-by-six rule 212
flowcharts 212
organizational charts 212
image-based visual 213
line graphs 213
bar graphs 213
pie graphs 213
picture graphs or pictographs 213
diagram 214

political maps 215
geographic maps 215
presentation software programs 218
document cameras 218
interactive whiteboards 219
flip charts 219
font 222
serif font 222
sans serif font 222
attributes 222

APPLICATION AND CRITICAL THINKING EXERCISES

The exercises below are also among the practice activities on the book's website.

1. Observe public speakers, such as professors in various courses, who regularly use visuals. What kind(s) of visual displays are most common? Which do you see used least? Evaluate the speakers' use of the visuals; that is, do they use them well, or should they follow some tips in this chapter? Explain.

2. Which technology for displaying visuals will you probably use for your classroom speeches? Which would you not consider? In your future employment, what equipment do you think you'll use the most? The least? Why?

3. Think about speeches you've heard during the last week. What kinds of visuals, if any, did the speakers use? When would visuals have made it easier for you to understand the material? When would visual or audio support have helped you pay better attention?

4. Discuss with a small group of your classmates how you would best display a drawing in (1) a large auditorium, (2) a classroom, (3) a speech given outdoors, and (4) a presentation in someone's living room. (Several means may be appropriate.)

5. What kind of visual might work most appropriately for a speech on each of these topics:
   ▶ The circulatory system
   ▶ The physical effects on the lungs of smoking
   ▶ The fabled Silk Road in Asia
   ▶ Ozone depletion
   ▶ Changes in mortgage interest rates over two decades

6. Make a visual using a presentation software program. Experiment with fonts. Use your software's print preview function to look at the overall balance of the visual; adjust line spacing and font size as necessary.

7. Browse the Internet using your favorite search engine, and find and read material on several sites about visual aids. Analyze the credibility of each site. (That is, does the URL contain an .edu or a .com? Why might that make a difference? Who wrote the materials? When? What links can you find? With this information, assess the overall usefulness of each site.) Take notes as you work and bring them to class so you can discuss your findings with a small group of your classmates.

SPEECH VIDEO

Log onto the book's website to watch the informative speech *Pumpkins* by Anna Riedl, answer questions for analysis, and evaluate the speech. An outline of the speech appears below and is also available on the book's website.

Student Outline with Visual Aids with Commentary

PUMPKINS
Anna Riedl

General Purpose:	To inform
Specific Purpose:	To inform the audience about characteristics and facts about pumpkins.
Thesis Statement:	Although the pumpkin is well known by name, there are facts that many people may not know about pumpkins.
Preview:	Many facts about pumpkins are not well known, including their anatomy, variety, health benefits, and other interesting trivia.

Introduction

I. Did you know that pumpkins are 90% water?
   [Display title slide.]
II. Although I've seen pumpkins all my life, I've never really thought much about them, and I'm sure many of you have not as well.
III. After going through pages of information on the Internet about pumpkins, I discovered many things I did not know about this squash.
IV. Today, I will share what I now know about their anatomy, variety, nutrients, and other interesting facts, so that we can all go into the festive October and November months with a little more knowledge of pumpkins.

Body

[Display "Anatomy of the Pumpkin" slide. Throughout this point, click the mouse to build the slide as each point is discussed.]
I. There are several parts of a pumpkin.
   A. The stem is like the umbilical cord of the plant, so when it is attached to the vine, the plant gains nutrients and grows.
   B. Leaves— The leaves are only on the vine, not the stem.

In this speech, Anna uses PowerPoint-generated slides throughout. The LCD display is on standby before she begins. She reactivates it and brings up each slide and each build by clicking the mouse.

Slides act as a transition between points. Each slide has a point-by-point build programmed in.

Each slide has beautiful photographs or clip art.

The words and images are artistically balanced.

C. Skin— Also known as the "rind," the skin is not to be eaten.

D. Pulp— This is the "meat" of the pumpkin, the part commonly made into desserts, ice cream, and so on.

E. Ribs— These are the ridges on the outside shell of the pumpkin.

F. Fibrous strands— This part is also known as the "brains," because it is basically composed of strings and seeds.

[Display "Varieties" slide. As each point is discussed, build the slide by clicking the mouse.]

II. These are four major varieties of pumpkins (*curcurbita*).

A. *Curcurbita moschata*— These types of pumpkins are used commercially, such as canned pumpkin, baking, and making other food products.

B. *Curcurbita pepo*— These are the teeny pumpkins that we can hold in one hand and that are very difficult to carve!

C. *Curcurbita maxima*— These are recognized as the huge pumpkins that are often entered into contests or put on display, such as the one in the cafeteria.

D. *Curcurbita mixta*— This group is consists of the genetically modified pumpkins. They can be white, blue, green, or even seedless.

[Display "Pumpkins are Nutritious" slide; and build with each new point.]

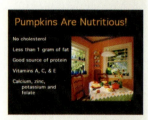

III. Health Benefits of Pumpkins

A. Pumpkins contain no cholesterol and less than one gram of fat; they are a good source of protein.

B. Pumpkins are high in vitamins A, C, and E.

C. Calcium, zinc, potassium, and folate are all important nutrients found in pumpkins.

[Display "Interesting facts about pumpkins" and build with each point.]

IV. There are many interesting facts about pumpkins.

A. Morton, Illinois, is the pumpkin capital of the world: Illinois produces more pumpkins than any other state.

B. Pumpkins are very versatile; they can be grown on any continent other than Antarctica; their origin is unknown, but they probably originated in Central America.

C. The largest pumpkin ever grown weighed 1,440 pounds.

She includes a photograph of herself on this slide.

[Display "Pumpkins Around the World" slide, and build with each point.]

D. Pumpkins appear throughout the world.

1. In South Wales, they are used in pies along with meat, apples, rhubarb, or pears.

2. French cooks make pumpkin soup and mix pumpkins with other vegetables.

3. The Jack-o-lantern tradition originated in Ireland.

4. In Switzerland, pumpkin seeds are mixed with chocolate.

Anna uses the "b" key so that a blank screen shows when she is not discussing a particular slide.

Conclusion

[Press "b" key for a blank slide.]

I. There is so much more to learn about pumpkins; if only there was more time!

II. But at least we now know the parts of a pumpkin, the varieties there are, their health benefits, and a few interesting facts.

[Display final slide.]

III. Now we can go into this festive month with a little more knowledge about how great pumpkins truly are.

References (formatted in MLA style)

The Pumpkin Patch. 1999. <www.pumpkin-patch.com/facts.html>

"Pumpkins Around the World." *Pumpkin Nook*. 1998–2000. <www.pumpkinnook.com/commune/world.htm>

Williamson, Joseph F. *Sunset Western Garden Book*. Menlo, CA: Lane, 1988.

Wise, William H. *The Wise Encyclopedia of Cookery*. New York: Grosset and Dunlap, 1978.

Wolford, Ron. "Pumpkins and More." 24 Oct. 2004. University of Illinois Extension, University of Illinois at Urbana-Champaign. <www.urbanext.uiuc.edu/pumpkins/history.html>

©1997 GRETCHEN ROSENBLATT

CHOOSING EFFECTIVE LANGUAGE

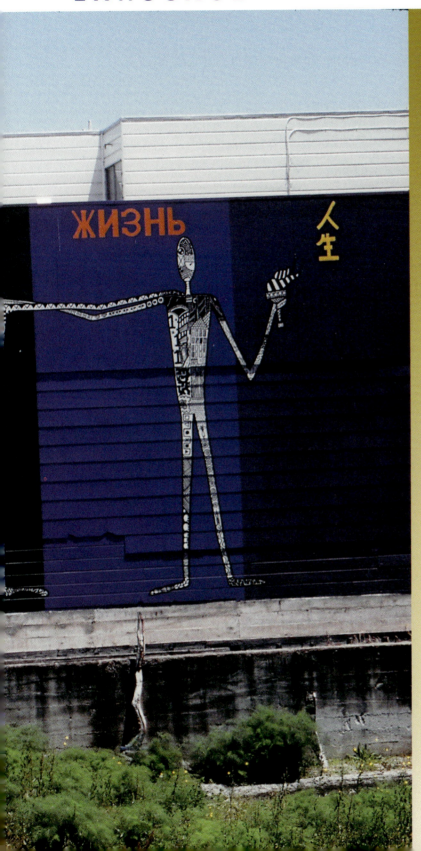

"Life" Mural © 1997 by Gretchen Rosenblatt.
(16th Street and Market, SF, CA)

THIS CHAPTER WILL HELP YOU

▶ Explain how words are linked to culture and meaning

▶ Distinguish between the denotative and connotative meanings of words

▶ Define dialect and jargon, and explain when they are appropriate in public speaking

▶ Recognize examples of epithets, euphemisms, and ageist and sexist language

▶ List six guidelines for effective language in public speaking

▶ Understand how alliteration, rhyme, repetition, personification, hyperbole, metaphor, and simile can make a speech more interesting

▶ Give guidelines for listening and speaking in linguistically diverse contexts

ANGUAGE DOESN'T JUST convey ideas. Your word choices also provide clues about your region of origin, age, educational level, income level, sex, ethnicity, and occupation. Here are a few examples:

▸ Regional distinctions: Oregonians might purchase a can of *pop*; New Yorkers would call it *soda*; in much of the South, it's a *coke* (meaning any brand of soda pop). Oregonians wonder what a *frappe* is, but they understand *milkshake* immediately.

▸ Male-female distinctions: The same color that a man calls *green* a woman might call *lime* or *sage* or *jade*.

▸ Occupational distinctions: Communication professors say things like, "the exclusions that characterize the historical practice of the bourgeois public sphere are constitutive of the concept itself. . . ."[1] Stockbrokers, barbers, and dentists don't talk like this.

In the study of rhetoric, language falls within the canon of style, which is the focus of this chapter. First, this chapter looks at some aspects of language and examines how our vocabularies both reveal and express cultural assumptions. Next, it provides tips for effective language choices in your classroom. Finally, it discusses language issues in linguistically diverse settings.

CASE STUDY: PAY ATTENTION TO WORDS

Chapter-at-a-Glance
This chapter emphasizes the importance of language choices in effective public speaking. It opens with a case study illustrating language choices in a business situation and follows with an explanation of how words and meaning are linked to culture. Next is a discussion of denotative and connotative meanings, including epithets, euphemisms, dialects, and jargon. Emphasis then shifts to issues of language and power—including ageist, sexist, and racist language—and strategies for inclusive language. Students are introduced to six guidelines for effective language in public speaking. Linguistic techniques to hold audience interest include alliteration, rhyme, repetition, personification, hyperbole, metaphor, and simile. The chapter ends with guidelines for listening and speaking in a linguistically diverse society.

What image does a businesswoman have in mind when she "launches" a new product?

Design Week columnist David Berstein gives consultants the following advice: Listen to the client, and write down her exact words (with the possible exception of "good morning"). At first, specific words may not seem all that important, but the client has carefully prepared for the consultation; she's eager to communicate her ideas. So listen. Attentively. Then examine your notes carefully. Ask, "Why this [word] rather than another?

© Reuters./CORBIS

A specific word should fix a specific meaning. No two words convey the exact same meaning. Synonyms aren't identical."[2]

For example, does the client call other businesses *competitors? Rivals? Enemies?* Her word choice reveals something about her mindset. What metaphors does she use? If she discusses product launch, does she continue with naval launch metaphors (dockside, smooth sailing, navigating)? Or does she follow with space launch details (countdown, three-stage rocket, soaring to new heights)? In the words of Noam Chomsky, "Language is a mirror of the mind."[3]

Whether you are the speaker or the listener, David Berstein's advice is sound: Words matter. Pay attention to them.

Questions for Discussion

▶ What other images do you associate with the word *launch?*
▶ How do Berstein's principles apply to audience members listening to a public speaker?
▶ How might his advice help you prepare a classroom speech? A presentation in your chosen career?

Language Reflects Culture

Languages are verbal codes made up of a system of symbols that a community of language speakers uses to share their ideas. **Symbols** represent or stand for objects and concepts the community shares. To be meaningful, the persons who use them must understand them in the same way. For example, we sometimes use symbols in the form of simple drawings to convey ideas such as those depicted in Figure 13.1.

If you're familiar with these symbols, you know them as (a) recycle, (b) health professionals, (c) love, and (d) New Mexico. Some, like the Cupid that represents love or the Hippocratic staff that represents medicine, are well known because they are so widely

Instructor's Resource Manual
Chapter 13 of the *Instructor's Resource Manual* (available in print, online, and on the Multimedia Manager CD-ROM) offers several suggested videos for use throughout this chapter; they are an ideal way to demonstrate the power of language.

languages verbal codes consisting of symbols that a speech community uses for communication

symbols signs that represent or stand for objects and concepts

Figure 13.1
Signs or Symbols Stand for Ideas
Knowing the association between the symbol and the idea is essential to
understanding the concept it represents.

Instructor Resource:
PowerPoint
The *Multimedia Manager*
with Instructor Resources
CD-ROM includes a Power-
Point slide of Figure 13.1.

used. Less familiar is the *zia*, or sun symbol, which represents my home state of New
Mexico. Obviously, when you're unfamiliar with a sign, you can't decipher its meaning.

Although we can represent some ideas by pictograms or drawings, a picture cannot
communicate every concept. So each society has developed a language system made up
of **words**—verbal symbols that stand for or represent cultural ideas. Each member of the
culture learns the language in order to communicate and interact within the group.

Words and Meaning

In *New Words and a Changing American Culture*, Raymond Gozzi[4] explains that words are
the names we give to our "cultural memories." They serve as "markers of cultural attention" or shared experiences that we consider significant enough to name. Put another
way, one or more people in a culture notice a phenomenon, formulate an idea about it,
and label it, encoding their idea into a word. The process looks something like this.

Long ago humans:

Teaching Tip
On the website The Word Spy
(http://www.wordspy.com/
index/subjects.asp), technical writer Paul McFedries
shares his sizable collection
of new words in a variety of
subjects, from gadgets and
appliances to marriage and
relationships. All URLs mentioned in the text are available as live, regularly maintained links on the book's
website, located in the
"Chapter Resources" list
under "Web Links."

1.   Noticed a phenomenon—some creatures can fly.
2.   Formed a concept—all these creatures have two legs, two wings, a beak, and feathers.
3.   Created a label for this category of flying animals—the label *bird* (English), *oiseau*
     (French), *pájaro* or *ave* (Spanish).

According to this theory, our vocabulary names what our society identifies as
significant, and our labels carve out the ways we interpret our world, forming our social
realities. An example might help. How many camel-related words do you know? One?
Two? If you lived in Somalia, you could distinguish between a male pack camel (*awr*), dairy
camels (*irmaan*), a female camel kept away from her young (*kareeb*), a camel loaded with
water vessels (*dhaan*), and so on, more than forty different categories. You would also know
dozens of words for camel diseases, things camels do, things made from camels, and so on.
Obviously, language shows that camels aren't important in U.S. culture, but they are very
significant in Somalia.[5]

It's easy to see how humans create words for objects such as birds, camels, buildings,
or chairs. However, words also label less tangible experiences, actions, feelings, and ideas;
language is, in Owen Barfield's words, "the storehouse of imagination."[6] To understand
this better, think of the meanings (if any) you attach to the word *Watergate*.

Before Richard Nixon's presidency, a small number of people associated the word
with an apartment complex in Washington, D.C. However, after the famous break-
in and subsequent presidential resignation, along with the movie (*All the President's*

words verbal symbols that
stand for or represent ideas

Men), books, interviews, and articles that surrounded those events, the word *Watergate* came to symbolize scandal. Even today, reporters coin terms like *Enron-gate* to refer to scandals.

DIVERSITY IN PRACTICE

DIALECTS

A **DIALECT** IS A VARIANT FORM OF A LANGUAGE that differs in pronunciation, vocabulary, and/or grammar. English dialects include British English, American English, Black English (ebonics or African American Vernacular English, AAVE), international English, and a variety of other regional and ethnic group variations.[7] **Standard English** is the dialect most common in institutions such as education, business, and broadcasting in the U.S.; it is the language of print, and the version of English generally used in classroom speeches.

Dialects other than Standard English function effectively in many settings. If you speak one, you may choose to be bi-dialectical, meaning that you use your dialect around family and friends and use Standard English in public contexts. This is called **code switching.** Bank officer Pauline Jefferson, for instance, uses Standard English to transact business with customers in her bank and to make public presentations for her coworkers. However, in front of a small female audience in her local church, she switches codes and alternates between Standard English and AAVE.

For more information, go to **www.slanguage.com** for a look at English slang terms that vary by city. Or log on to InfoTrac College Edition and read Jeanette Gisldorf's article "Standard Englishes and World Englishes." For fun, take the test or watch the videoclips at **www.pbs.org/speak/seatosea/americanvarieties/map/map.html.**

Languages change to reflect cultural transformations. Among the thousands of words added to English in the last few decades are *gridlock, serial killer, microchip, junk food,* and *minivan.* Sportscaster Chick Hearn added *slam dunk* and *air ball.* More recent are *carb-friendly, phish,* and *blue state/red state.* When your grandparents were growing up, there were no microchips or junk food, no carb-friendly foods or slam dunks. They either didn't exist or they weren't important enough to name.[8] English often adopts words from other languages, including *giraffe* (Arabic), *ambiance* (French), and *kamikaze* (Japanese). Meanings also change over time, as you notice whenever you read Shakespeare; Renaissance English is very different from contemporary English.

Denotative Meaning

Words denote or "point" to an object or abstract idea; thus, the **denotative meaning** is what the word names or identifies. The following list might clarify this further. You'll find several categories, followed by examples of words that denote or stand for objects or ideas within each:

Real objects: rock, building, necklace, tea

Imaginary things: unicorn, Martian, elf, Superman

Qualities of objects: softness, generosity, width, height

Feelings: anger, envy, peace, love

States of being: happiness, depression, contentment, gratitude

Abstractions: justice, beauty, conscience, success

Actions: exercise, sing, eat, study

dialect a variant form of a language

Standard English the English dialect most commonly used in public speaking and in U.S. institutions

code switching changing from one dialect to another

denotative meaning what a word names or identifies

The dictionary provides denotative meanings; for instance, *police officer* denotes "a member of a police force" and *principal* denotes "a person who has controlling authority or is in a leading position as (a) a chief or head man or woman, or (b) the chief executive officer of an educational institution."[9]

Some words are **ambiguous,** which means they have more than one meaning and the context determines their meaning. For instance, the word *pot* has at least five meanings:

- A rounded container used chiefly for domestic purposes
- A sum of money, as in the total amount of bets at stake at one time (the jackpot)
- An enclosed frame of wire, wood, or wicker used to catch fish or lobsters
- Slang for marijuana
- Ruin, as in "her business went to pot"[10]

You know that when you cook in a pot, you're thinking of the first meaning. But when you discuss legalization of pot, you're not talking about laws regulating cooking containers or poker. Thus, *pot* is an ambiguous word and you must rely on the context to discern the meaning. As you plan language for your speech, make sure you use the correct word in the correct context to denote your intended meaning. Consult a dictionary or thesaurus if necessary.

Increasing your vocabulary and discriminating among shades of meaning between words are valuable skills, for the greater your vocabulary, the more power you have to communicate your thoughts precisely. Check your vocabulary by looking on the Internet for the list of 100 words that every high school students—and their parents—should know.

Connotative Meaning

Although words denote objects and concepts, they also carry emotional overtones or **connotative meanings.** That is, words not only stand for ideas; they also represent feelings and associations related to the concepts. Thus, *police officer* and *principal* have different connotations for different individuals depending on their experiences. Some people like police officers because of relatives or friends who are officers; others fear or mistrust law enforcement professionals because of negative experiences with them. Similarly, a person's school experiences influence his or her view of principals. Each person's reactions form the connotative meanings of the words for that individual.

Because language can be emotionally charged, either positively or negatively, we commonly substitute a more neutral word for one with negative connotations. To discuss this further, we now turn to epithets and euphemisms.

Classroom Discussion/ Activity
Ask students to offer examples where using the wrong word led to misunderstanding or an embarrassing situation.

Epithets

Epithets are words or phrases, often with negative connotations, that describe some quality of a person or group. For example, one political party calls the other *extremists* because opinion polls show that voters respond negatively to "extremists." Within hours, the attacked party counters with the term *big government spenders*, another negative term. Words like *nerd*, *pig* (for police officers), and *fag* are negative epithets that function to frame perceptions about specific groups. Calling anti-abortion advocates *anti-choice* creates a negative image, whereas the group's self-chosen title, *pro-life*, has positive connotations.

Members of labeled groups often try to lessen the negative power of the epithet by accepting and using the term themselves. Police officers take the letters of the word *pig* and reinterpret them to form the slogan *P*ride, *I*ntegrity, *G*uts. Similarly, some homosexuals transform the epithet *queer* in slogans such as "We're here, we're queer, get used to it" or in group names such as Queer Nation. One activist explained, "We have to take the power out of these words."[11]

ambiguous word that identifies more than one object or idea; its meaning depends on the context

connotative meaning emotional overtones, related feelings, and associations that cluster around a word

epithets words or phrases with powerful negative connotations, used to describe some quality of a person or group

"SAY, ISN'T THAT THE GUY WHO USED TO DRAFT LEGAL DOCUMENTS AT OUR LAW FIRM?"

www.CartoonStock.com. Used with permission.

Use of jargon— a set of technical words associated with a topic or field— is appropriate in contexts where everyone knows the terms. However, undefined jargon in a speech to a lay audience is generally more confusing than enlightening.

Euphemisms

Euphemisms, in contrast, are words or phrases that substitute an agreeable or inoffensive term for a more offensive, embarrassing, or unpleasant word. We regularly use euphemisms for things we hesitate to speak of, such as bodily functions (*go to the powder room*), religion (*the Man Upstairs*), and death (*passed away*). Euphemisms also mask unpleasant situations, like corporate layoffs. It's supposedly easier to be *dehired* or *downsized* rather than *fired*.

Public speakers, especially in politics, often use euphemisms for controversial actions, ideas, and policies. Consequently, planned tax increases become *revenue enhancement* or *investments in America*. Similarly, *shell shock* (World War I) became *combat fatigue* (after World War II) which became *post-traumatic stress syndrome* (Vietnam War). Each subsequent term further removes the condition from its cause.[12] Learn more about this subject by doing an Internet search for the word *euphemisms*.

Be alert for connotative language in your research, especially when the issue is controversial. For example, a military leader calls an opponent a *warlord* rather than an *influential leader*. Politicians label their opponents *obstructionists* who *attack* and *destroy* legislation, whereas they, of course, *stand up for the rights of ordinary people*. By carefully choosing their words, these speakers hope to create perceptions that produce the spin or interpretation they want.

Jargon

Jargon is a specialized, technical vocabulary and style that serves special groups (doctors, lawyers), interests (feminism, education), and activities (football, gardening). For example, football has specialized meanings for *drive*, *down*, and *safety*. When everyone in your audience knows the meaning of the jargon, it's appropriate to use it. However, when you're communicating with nonspecialists, you must define and clarify technical terms to avoid excluding listeners. Translating jargon is one way to demonstrate your rhetorical sensitivity.

In summary, languages are systems of symbols—words that denote or stand for ideas and evoke feelings or connotative meanings that differ from person to person. Carefully choose your words, making sure you use the correct word in context. Pay attention to connotative meanings—either positive or negative—that listeners might attach to your words. And demonstrate that you are rhetorically sensitive by adapting your dialect and your jargon to your audience and the occasion. As you do this, you take into account the cultural implications of your language choices.

Classroom Discussion / Activity
Show the clip from the movie *Patch Adams* in which Patch Adams attempts to cheer up a dying man by dressing as an angel and reading a list of epithets and euphemisms. Ask students to identify each type.

Classroom Discussion / Activity
Show a video clip of a highly jargoned speech or photocopy an article from an academic journal in a scientific field. How could the material be made more salient to a lay audience?

euphemism word or phrase that substitutes an inoffensive term for a potentially offensive, embarrassing, or unpleasant thing

jargon a specialized, technical vocabulary that serves the interests and activities of a particular group

STOP AND CHECK

THINK CRITICALLY ABOUT DENOTATIVE AND CONNOTATIVE WORDS

Test your understanding of meanings with these exercises.

1. Whenever they launch a new product, marketers carefully select terminology that will have positive connotations for consumers. Look up two or three advertisements in your favorite magazines, and then list some of the words you find in each ad. What is the denotative meaning of each word on your list? Now jot down some of your personal connotations for each term. Evaluate the overall marketability of the term itself.

2. Work with your classmates to make a list of the car models owned by class members (Mustang, Explorer, Sport, and so on). Within a small group, identify the denotative meaning of each word. Then discuss the connotative associations you think the manufacturers hope will sell the car.

For additional information about connotative meanings, visit **www.washburn.edu/services/zzcwwctr/connotation.txt**. The book's website provides additional exercises about denotative and connotative words.

Student Learning: Book Website
This Stop and Check activity can also be found on the book's website, where it's located under "Chapter Resources."

Instructor's Resource Manual
Teaching Idea 13.1, "Gender Differences in Speaking," in the *Instructor's Resource Manual* (available in print, online, and on the Multimedia Manager CD-ROM) offers an example of sexist language as well as some suggestions on how to discuss it and avoid it.

Use Language Ethically: Inclusive Language

Language choices have ethical implications because words and phrases can include or exclude, affirm or dismiss individuals or entire groups.[13] The University of Tasmania's publication *Just Talk: Guide to Inclusive Language*[14] defines discriminatory language as words that create or reinforce a hierarchy of difference between people. It is both a symptom of and contributor to the unequal social status of women, people with disabilities, and people from various ethnic and social backgrounds. Consequently, it's important to use nondiscriminatory, inclusive language.

Emory University's Statement on **Inclusive Language** recommends, "A recognition of the full humanity of all peoples should prompt an attempt to speak and think in ways which include all human beings and degrade none."[15] Using inclusive language can increase your credibility. For example, a recent study[16] found that speakers who put down persons with disabilities or focus on the disability rather than on the individual lose credibility, likeability, and persuasiveness. Here are several guidelines for sensitive use of language.

inclusive language ethical terminology that affirms and includes, rather than excludes, persons or groups of people

sexist language language that negatively influences the way listeners see men or women

ageist language language that negatively influences the way listeners see older people

racist language language that privileges one racial group over another

nonparallel language language that does not treat the two sexes equally

Avoid Language That Privileges One Group Over Another

Sexist language subtly influences the way we view the sexes by giving priority to males, their activities, and their interests. **Ageist language** portrays older people in ways that privilege youthfulness and demean or devalue age. (To illustrate, phrases like *feel younger* or *look ten years younger* subtly reinforce the notion that youth is better than age.) **Racist language,** similarly, favors one racial or ethnic group and degrades or devalues others. Nonsensitive language also highlights physical conditions, demeans sexual orientation, puts down a particular religion or social class, and so on.

Nonparallel language treats women and men differently and reinforces gender differences in ways that privilege males. It's nonparallel to designate a female by adding a suffix to a male term, as in *actor/actress* and *steward/stewardess*. It's also nonparallel to mark job titles, as in a *male nurse* or a *female judge*. (Would you ever say a *female nurse* or a *male judge?*) Differing terms of address are also nonparallel; a woman may be called *Mrs. Alberto Sanchez*, but you won't hear *Mr. Jane Andrews*. Similarly, couples might be called *man and wife* but never *woman and husband*.

Avoid Stereotyping

Try to recognize and avoid stereotypes. For instance, common misconceptions are that older people are closed minded, less capable mentally, unhealthy, physically unattractive, lonely, and poor. This shows up in language that perpetuates these stereotypes: *set in her ways, losing his marbles, ready for a nursing home*, or *well-preserved* (to describe an attractive elderly person).[17] Stereotypes of gay men as effeminate, athletes as stupid, Native Americans as alcoholics, welfare recipients as lazy or as unmarried women of color are common. That Democrats are pro-choice (at least 40 states have Democrats for Life chapters), and Chinese Americans are Buddhists (most are Christian) are two additional stereotypes.

Avoid Creating Invisibility

Language can render people and groups invisible. The "generic he" is a good example. People who are now your grandparents' age used *he* to designate a person of either sex, as this illustration from an outdated speech text shows:

> When one has settled upon a subject and has some notion of what *he* wishes to do with it, *his* immediate concern is with the materials, the stuff out of which *his* speech is to be woven. *He* must have ideas and data with which to hold attention and to make and impress *his* point [italics added].[18]

Such language subtly implies that only males speak in public. The use of the suffix *man* creates similar problems. Replace words like *chairman, mailman, caveman*, and *policeman* with the inclusive labels *chair, mail carrier, cave dweller*, and *police officer*.

Other examples include language that assumes relationships are all heterosexual or that *Americans* equals *U.S. residents*. (Canadians, Brazilians, and Guatemalans are also *Americans*.)

Avoid Demeaning Epithets or Slurs

Avoid epithets that frame negative perceptions of a group. Think about negative labels commonly applied to the elderly: *old duffer, little old lady* (in tennis shoes), *granny, gramps* or *pop, old biddy, old hag*, and *dirty old man*. These all create mental images that demean seniors. Other examples of slurs include *woman driver, sissy, dumb jock, dumb blonde, welfare queen*, and *dyke*.

Avoid Dismissive Language

Dismissive language is applied to people in ways that discount the importance of their ideas, as these examples show: elderly people are *too old, senile, no longer in the thick of things, over the hill*. Phrases like *just a secretary, white trash*, and *typical female* are dismissive put-downs.

© JoelSimonImages.com

In cultures where elderly citizens are highly respected, ageist language is not the issue that it is in the United States, where youth is valued. Ageist language can demean older people by subtly influencing listeners to perceive them negatively.

Instructor Resource: Service Learning Handbook
Chapter 9, "Intercultural Communication in Service-Learning," (pp. 152–165) in *The Art and Strategy of Service-Learning Presentations*, 2e, provides information on cultural variety and how understanding it and avoiding ethnocentrism can enhance our lives and the lives of those we help through service learning.

Avoid Undue Emphasis on Differences

Don't mention differences unless they matter in the context of the speech. For instance, replace "the *Latina* nurse" or "my *African American* physics professor," with "the nurse" or "my physics professor." Don't mention someone's competency as if it were unusual for that group: Instead of "an *intelligent* welfare recipient," simply say "a welfare recipient." Don't describe the disabled as helpless victims to be pitied and aided. Also, don't suggest that they are more heroic, courageous, patient, or special than others, and avoid contrasting them to *normal* people.[19]

In short, terminology is not neutral. The words you select have the power to influence audience perceptions regarding issues as well as individuals and groups. The fact that some language choices demean or put down others raises ethical questions and colors your listeners' impressions about you. Choosing words that are inclusive is one way to show respect for diversity, and will likely enhance your personal credibility.

Student Learning: Book Website
This Stop and Check activity can also be found on the book's website, where it's located under "Chapter Resources."

✓ STOP AND CHECK

AVOIDING DISCRIMINATORY LANGUAGE

With a small group of your classmates, select a group that has been put down or demeaned by language use. This may include women, specific ethnic groups, religious groups, or groups with alternative lifestyles.

1. Make a list of some terms that outsiders have used to label group members.
2. Then list some labels the group places on itself.
3. Assess the connotative meanings associated with the words on each list.

With a few classmates, talk about ways you can select language that respects the group you've chosen.

To investigate this topic further, do an Internet search for an exact term such as *sexist language, ageist language,* or *racist language.*

Teaching Tip
The History Channel's archive of speeches at http://www.historychannel.com/speeches/ gives your students the opportunity to listen to the greatest words ever spoken in the English language. Speeches include Lou Gehrig's 1939 farewell to baseball, Douglas McArthur's farewell to Congress, John Kennedy's 1961 Inaugural Address, and Neil Armstrong's 1969 walk on the moon speech. These historic examples illustrate language, delivery, argument, supporting material, and persuasion. This URL can be found in Chapter 13's Helpful Links in the Student Workbook. All URLs mentioned in the text are also available as live, regularly maintained links on the website.

Use Language Effectively

Six principles in the canon of style will help you choose language more effectively for your speeches: accuracy, appropriateness, conciseness, clarity, concreteness, and vividness.

Be Accurate

Accuracy involves three areas: meaning, context, and grammar. Check meaning by looking up the word in your dictionary. However, it's also important to know the context in which the word is used. For example, a Japanese student described a wreck that "*distorted* the car door." Her Japanese–English dictionary came up with *distort* to convey the idea that the car was *bent, caved in,* or *dented.* Although *distort* does mean *crooked, deformed,* or *contorted,* no native speaker of English would use it in the context of a dented fender. For an excellent article about Japanese speakers whose dictionaries misled them, log on to InfoTrac College Edition and read the article titled "Say What You Mean / Denotation and Connotation.")

Finally, use standard grammar when the situation calls for Standard English. Non-standard forms such as *me and him* (instead of *he and I*) or *they was* (instead of *they were*) or *it don't* (for *it doesn't*) create negative impressions in public presentations. The key is to adapt your grammar to fit the occasion. (Check grammatical forms by using the grammar-checking feature on your word processor.)

Be Appropriate

Match your language to the topic, the audience, the situation, and yourself as an individual. Generally, language appropriate in public settings is more formal, with less slang than you'd use in everyday life; however, your audience and the situation should be the final influence over your linguistic choices. For example, you would use different words and different levels of formality to speak to homeless people gathered in a park than you would to address members of an alumni association at a formal banquet, even for the same topic. Similarly, language in a lecture differs from language in a eulogy.

A dialect can be appropriate for some speakers, but not others. An African American, for instance, might use African American Vernacular English (AAVE) when it's expected and appropriate; however, a Euro-American or an Asian American who used AAVE, even in the same setting, would almost certainly be out of line.

Be Concise

Because directness is valued in the United States, we commonly eliminate unnecessary words, called **verbiage.** However, verbiage often shows up in speeches, especially demonstration speeches where it's easy to lapse into this form: "What you want to do next is you want to take the coffee and pour it over the cake. . . ." It would be more concise to say, "Next, pour the coffee over the cake." Students often clutter their speeches with too many words. This excerpt from a student speech on the value of learning a second language contrasts how he actually gave the speech with how he could have given it:

> *As he gave it:*
>
> I became interested in this topic *upon the constant hounding of my father urging me* to take a foreign language, preferably Japanese, *the reason being is because* my major is business, and the Japanese are dominating the international business scene.
>
> *As he might have given it:*
>
> I became interested in this topic because my father constantly hounded me to take a foreign language— preferably Japanese, because my major is business, and the Japanese are dominating the international business scene.

Although brevity or conciseness is valued in the United States, many other cultures value flowery words and language. Consequently, what we may consider verbiage, other groups may regard as good verbal skills, as Diversity in Practice: Understanding Aristide explains.

Student Learning: Workbook Activity 13.3, "Eliminate Clutter," in the Student Workbook helps students recognize and eliminate wordiness by having them edit a speech filled with verbiage.

DIVERSITY IN PRACTICE
UNDERSTANDING ARISTIDE

Haitian President Jean-Bertrand Aristide's Speaking Style often confuses American congressional leaders and administration officials. A *U.S. News & World Report* article argues that Aristide "speaks a cultural tongue Americans don't understand."[20] He is a master of competitive oratory, a type of speechmaking that features indirect language laced with proverbs and metaphors, and he commonly uses a stylistic device called "throwing pwent" that is intentionally indirect and ambiguous. Contrast this with the public speaking tradition explained in this chapter, which emphasizes clarity, concrete wording, and elimination of vague terminology, and you can see the potential for misunderstandings on both sides.

This article, "The Mind of Aristide," is available on InfoTrac College Edition.

verbiage nonessential words

© James L Stanfield/Getty Images

Create vivid images by using concrete words. Saying "she owns an *Arabian*" is more specific than saying she owns a *horse;* but that is more specific than calling her an *animal owner.*

Be Clear

The purpose of public speaking is to clarify ideas, not to make them harder to understand. One of the best ways to be clear is to avoid jargon, but because many topics involve technical terms, you may have to look up jargon words to translate them into understandable English. Jesse failed to do this in his discussion of how AIDS is transmitted:

> We've all been taught that AIDS is perinatal and that it is transmitted through sexual contact.

When asked what *perinatal* meant, Jesse couldn't answer; the word came from an article he had read, and he had not bothered to look it up. (*Perinatal* actually means "associated with the birth process, the period immediately before, during, or just after the time of birth.") If he'd taken the time to look up the word, he could have said instead:

> We've been taught that AIDS is transmitted from mother to child perinatally—that is, during the birth process—and that it is transmitted through sexual activity.

This brief definition clarifies the word's meaning and makes the speech more understandable.

Be Concrete

Another important aspect of style, one that can help your listeners form precise understandings, is to choose **concrete words** that are specific rather than abstract, particular rather than general. Words range along a scale of abstraction such as this:

abstract/general	plant
	tree
	evergreen
	fir
concrete/particular	Douglas fir

When you say, "She put in a Douglas fir," your ideas are much more concrete than when you say, "She put in an evergreen." But "She put in a tree" is more concrete than "She put in a plant." The more distinct and specific your word choices, the more vivid your images and the more precise your meanings.

Here is an excerpt from Bob Pettit's speech on electronic drums,[21] which is exceptional for its use of concrete language:

> Picture your stereotypical rock drummer: shaggy, smells, looks, and sometimes acts like a lower primate, body type—lean and wiry, definitely the fast-twitch kind of muscles, and they aren't in the head. And it always seems that they're the first in the band to OD. On the *Muppets* TV show, the drummer's name was "Animal," and they kept him chained to his set of drums.

Bob's concrete language is made up of sensory imagery that help you picture the sights, movements—even the smells—of drummers.

Vague words have indefinite boundaries and, consequently, are imprecise. For example, what is a *hill?* When does it become a *mountain?* Who is *young?* An eighty-year-old thinks a fifty-year-old is young, but the fifty-year-old thinks young is thirty-five.

concrete words specific, rather than general or abstract, terms

vague words imprecise terms that have indefinite boundaries

What is *large? Small?* Compared to what? A *large* root beer is not on the same scale as a large barn. You can minimize your use of vague words by choosing specific details to define or illustrate what you mean. Let's say you're speaking of a *small* inheritance. Give a dollar figure that shows what you consider *small.* One listener may think $2,500 is *small* whereas another has $25,000 in mind.

STOP AND CHECK

CHOOSING MORE PRECISE WORDING

The purpose of this exercise is to raise your awareness of vague words that we typically use in place of more precise ones. For example, *get* is an ambiguous verb that you can often replace with a more concrete term. In the blank that follows each sentence, replace *get* (or a form thereof) with more precise wording.

Can you *get* the telephone, please? _____

What did you *get* for your birthday? _____

Why did you *get* angry about that? _____

I'm *getting* ready to outline my speech. _____

He *got* a thousand dollars just for giving one speech! _____

It *got* cold last night. _____

He *gets* nervous just before he speaks. _____

After I studied the calculus problem for over an hour, I finally *got* it! _____

You can *get* information 24 hours a day on the Internet. _____

After he *gets* here, we can leave. _____

Student Learning:
Book Website
This Stop and Check activity can also be found on the book's website, where it's located under "Chapter Resources."

Be Interesting

A major speaking goal is to help your listeners see, feel, and remember the information you present. Use colorful, vivid language to keep listeners' attention and interest. You can make the language of your speech more memorable by incorporating alliteration, rhyming, repetition, personification, hyperbole, metaphors, and similes.

Alliteration

Alliteration is the use of words that have the same recurring initial sounds. For instance, one environmental activist wondered, "What *t*raits, *t*enacity, and *t*alents does it *t*ake" to be a good environmentalist?[22] Another speaker referred to author Harriet Beecher Stowe as "very *p*roper, *p*rimly dressed, and *p*recisely spoken."[23] You can borrow phrases such as "*d*oughnuts in the *d*ark" to describe nighttime eating disorders,[24] if you cite the source. One way to help listeners remember your main ideas is to alliterate the main points. For example:

A good team has three essential qualities:

Commitment

Communication

Competitiveness

Rhyming

As you know, **rhymes,** whether rhymed words, phrases, or entire lines, end in the same sounds. Although rap artists rhyme their entire presentations, most people use rhymes in more limited ways. In his speech about electronic drums, Bob rhymed three words

Classroom Discussion/ Activity
 A speech can be very informative without being interesting. Provide the class with a list of not-so-interesting topics and have students offer examples of alliteration, rhyming, repetition, personification, hyperbole, metaphors, and similes that could make the topics more interesting. This could be done as a class discussion or in small groups.

---

alliteration words with recurring initial sounds

rhymes words that end in the same sound

within one sentence: "So I want to examine this new world of the push-button beat and pose the question to you: What or who would you rather have in your band, a *mean* and *clean* drum *machine* or a stereotypical rock drummer?"

Rhymes are also effective for wording the main points of your speeches. Here are two examples:

> We are faced with two choices:
> Retreat
> Compete

> Workplaces typically have three generations of employees.[25]
> Boomers
> Bloomers
> Zoomers

As you might imagine, rhymed main points often help listeners remember them more easily.

Repetition

Technically, there are two ways to use **repetition.** One is to repeat the same word or phrase at the beginning of clauses or sentences. For example, Ronald Reagan's tribute[26] to the space shuttle Challenger astronauts who lost their lives when their spacecraft exploded included these repetitive phrases: "We will cherish each of their stories, *stories of* triumph and bravery, *stories of* true American heroes." Another type of repetition restates the same phrase at the end of a clause or a sentence. Lincoln's famous phrase "government of *the people*, by *the people*, for *the people*" is an example. This speech excerpt, which shows two repeated phrases, comes from a talk by a Native American speaker:[27]

> This idea is not original with me. It was taught to us by a great leader of the Lakota people—my people—Chief Sitting Bull. *He taught us* that Indian children could succeed in modern society and yet retain the values of their culture, *values such as* respect for the earth, for wildlife, for rivers and streams, for plants and trees; and *values such as* caring for each other and for family and community. *He taught us* that we must leave behind more hope than we found.

Sometimes a speaker repeats, but reverses, in a second phrase, some words from the first phrase. (The technical term for this is **antimetabole.**) Some examples from www .americanrhetoric.com include:

> *The absence of evidence* is not *the evidence of absence.* (Carl Sagan)

> We say *to our children, "Be like grownups,"* but Jesus said *to us grownups, "Be like children."* (Rev. Billy Graham)

> Whether we *bring our enemies to justice,* or *bring justice to our enemies,* justice will be done. (President George W. Bush)

President Kennedy's inaugural address, printed in Appendix C, includes several famous examples of antimetabole.

Personification

Personification means giving human characteristics to nonhuman entities such as animals, countries, natural objects and processes, and social processes. Native American Chief Seattle[28] used personification in an 1853 speech before the governor of the Washington Territory:

> Yonder sky that has wept tears of compassion upon my people for centuries untold, and which to us appears changeless and eternal, may change.

Teaching Tip
This URL can be found in Chapter 13's Helpful Links in the Student Workbook. All URLs mentioned in the text are also available as live, regularly maintained links on the book's website.

repetition saying the same word or phrase at the beginning or at the end of clauses or sentences

antimetabole saying words in one phrase, and reversing them in the next phrase

personification giving human characteristics to nonhuman entities

Hyperbole

Hyperbole (hype) is the use of exaggeration for effect. I've heard politicians say, "If we don't do something about health care, there will be *no more* jobs" or "If we don't do something about AIDS, there will be *no more* people." They use these exaggerations to indicate that the problems are serious and deserve government attention.

Although hyperbole can be effective, excessive hype can lessen the speaker's credibility. Some exaggerations border on the ridiculous, and listeners think the speaker is overreacting or lying. Moreover, instead of focusing on the policy, the discussion often focuses on the hyperbole itself. *No* jobs? Really? *No* more people? At all? In the classroom, Zack's use of hyperbole created a negative impression:

> Imagine a world where you have *no* trees, *total* pollution, and a landfill in *every* neighborhood. This is where we are heading because of our abuse of the land and lack of concern for ways to replenish the earth and her resources. There is a way where each person . . . could help, maybe even solve the problem. It's called recycling.

His point that recycling will contribute to the preservation of natural resources is a good one. However, *no* trees, *total* pollution, and landfills in *every* neighborhood is overstating the case; furthermore, although recycling may help, it will not *solve the problem* of environmental pollution in and of itself. Thus, Zack's exaggerations might lead listeners to question his reasoning in general and, because this hype was in his introduction, to discount his ideas from the very beginning.

Metaphor

A **metaphor** is a comparison between two dissimilar things; the words *like* and *as* are not used. To Professor Michael Osborn,[29] speech students are builders who frame and craft their speeches; or they are weavers who intertwine verbal and nonverbal elements into a successful performance; or they're climbers who scramble over barriers or obstacles such as speech anxiety on their way to a successful speech. As with the word "launch" in this chapter's case study, each metaphor provides a different perspective on the subject. Which comparison best describes you as a speech student? Can you come up with a better metaphor for speechmaking?

One danger in using metaphors is the possibility of beginning with one comparison and ending with another, creating a **mixed metaphor**. To illustrate, a panelist on a news broadcast said:

> We must solve the root problem, or the line will be drawn in the sand, and we'll be back in the soup again.

Unfortunately, he combined three images: *root* compares the problem to a plant; the *line drawn in the sand*, an uncrossable boundary; and *soup*, a food. By going in three directions with his comparison, he left his listeners with no clear image of the problem.

Simile

Similes are similar to metaphors in that they compare two items that are unlike in most ways but alike in one essential detail. However, similes explicitly state the connection by using *like* or *as*. These examples come from **www.americanrhetoric.com**:

> Don't worry about the future; or worry—but know that worrying is as effective as trying to solve an algebra equation by chewing bubble gum. (Baz Luhrmann)

> It is a curious thing, the death of a loved one. It's like walking up the stairs to your bedroom in the dark and thinking that there's one more stair than there is. Your foot falls down through the air and there's a sickly moment of dark surprise. (Jude Law's character in the 2004 film *Lemony Snicket's A Series of Unfortunate Events*)

hyperbole using exaggeration for effect

metaphors comparison of two dissimilar things

mixed metaphor combining metaphors from two or more sources, starting with one comparison and ending with another

similes short comparisons that use the word *like* or *as* to compare two items that are alike in one essential detail

Archetypal symbols, such as sunrise and sunset, sickness and health, parent and child, are widely used as metaphors by people all over the globe.

© Kyle Krause/Index Stock Imagery/PictureQuest

Similarly, Chief Seattle[30] used vivid similes, as this excerpt indicates:

> [The white] people are many. They are *like* the grass that covers vast prairies. My people are few. They resemble the scattering trees of a storm-swept plain. . . . There was a time when our people covered the land *as* the waves of a wind-ruffled sea cover its shell-paved floor, but that time long since passed away with the greatness of tribes that are now but a mournful memory.

Some metaphors and similes emerge and reemerge, because they arise from our experiences of being human. For instance, all human groups experience day and night, sickness and health, seasonal changes, and family relationships. Michael Osborne[31] calls these **archetypal symbols,** because all humankind understands them. Other common comparisons relate to cultural modes of transportation (*the ship of state*) and sports (*the game of life*) and, as the culture changes, new metaphors linked to electronic technology are emerging (*experiencing static, feeling wired*).

Language and Pluralistic Audiences

Students enter classrooms across the country with many types of linguistic diversity:

- Monolingual (speaking one language only)
- Bi-dialectical (speaking two dialects)
- Multidialectical (speaking three or more dialects)
- Bilingual (speaking two languages)
- Multilingual (speaking three or more languages).

Communicating in a linguistically diverse setting is often complicated and frustrating. However, you can plan ways to adapt to multilingual situations that will be beneficial to everyone involved.

archetypal symbols
recurring metaphors and similes that arise from shared human and natural experiences

Adapt to Multilingual Situations

When you speak to a linguistically diverse audience, don't assume you'll be instantly understood.

Take a hypothetical student, Ryan, whose only language is Standard English. His classmates include people who speak Spanish and English, Japanese and English, AAVE and Standard English, and Russian, Spanish, and English. Because he wants to speak effectively, he adapts his speech by using a few simple strategies:

▶ Before preparing his outline, he tries to "hear" the terminology and jargon related to his topic in the way a non-native speaker of English might hear it.
▶ When possible, he chooses simple words that most people understand; however, he avoids talking down to his audience.
▶ He identifies words that might be confusing and puts them on visual aids, which he displays as he talks.
▶ He defines difficult words and jargon as he goes along.
▶ He builds in redundancy by saying the same idea in a number of different ways. If listeners don't comprehend the concept the first time around, they may understand it when it's expressed another way.

Being mindful of linguistic diversity allows Ryan to strategically select language that communicates effectively with listeners from various linguistic backgrounds.

When you are listening to a nonfluent speaker, you must make a more-than-normal effort to make the experience satisfying, both for the speaker and for yourself. Remember that the major goal of any speech is communication of ideas, not perfection of language skills. So concentrate on the ideas rather than on each specific word. Use patience and **perspective taking.** This means that you put yourself in the speaker's shoes and try to imagine what it would be like to give a speech in a foreign language to a group of native speakers of that language. Also, remember that nonfluency is linked to inexperience in English, not to lack of intelligence or education.[32] These additional tips can help you listen more effectively:

▶ Approach the speech with a positive attitude, expecting to understand.
▶ Listen all the way through. Make special efforts to keep your mind from wandering in the middle of the speech. It may help to take notes.
▶ Practice *respons*-ibility in co-creating meaning. Plan to give appropriate nonverbal feedback to demonstrate your interest, patience, and support for the speaker.
▶ Control your negative emotional responses. Let's face it, it is difficult to deal with linguistic barriers, and people often get frustrated or bored when faced with language differences.
▶ Don't laugh, even if the speakers do, at their language skills. Often they laugh nervously to relieve tension.[33]

Adapt to an Interpreter

Although using an interpreter may seem remote right now, you may eventually communicate through someone who translates your words into another language, including sign language. If you must use an interpreter, here are a few things to remember:

▶ Keep your language simple. Avoid overly technical or uncommon words.
▶ In advance of the speech, give your interpreter an outline so she can check the meaning of any unfamiliar words. She may also refer to it during your speech as a guide to what you will say next.
▶ When your interpreter translates into another language, speak in short units, not entire paragraphs. After a sentence or two, allow the interpreter to speak.

perspective taking putting yourself in another person's shoes

Kelly Bilinski and Uriel Plascencia teamed up for a classroom speech. He spoke in Spanish, and she interpreted into English.

> Look at the interpreter while she speaks. This encourages the audience to look at the interpreter instead of at you.

> Because it takes two to three times longer to speak this way, shorten your speech accordingly.

Remember that using interpreters is not easy, but without them, you could not communicate effectively. Consequently, work on maintaining a positive attitude throughout the speaking event. (Appendix C provides an example of a classroom speech, delivered in Spanish and interpreted into English by a fellow student. Video of this speech is also available on the book's website.) Here is an excerpt:

> *Cuando estaba en mi último año de Preparatoria, yo tuve buenos amigos. Nuestra amistad era muy fuerte que estábamos juntos mucho tiempo.* (When I was a senior in high school, I had some very good friends. Our friendship was so strong that we spent a lot of time together.) *Nosotros éramos como un equipo en todos los aspectos porque estábamos en las mismas clases, hacíamos juntos nuestra tarea, practicábamos deportes y platicábamos mucho. Nosotros nunca tuvimos problemas serios.* (We were like a team in all aspects because we spent time in classes doing our homework, playing sports, and talking. We never seemed to have any serious problems.)
>
> *En el principio del segundo semestre, se abrió un campeonato de vóleibol.* (In the beginning of the second semester, there were openings for intramural volleyball.) *Yo no pensaba estar en estos juegos porque yo estaba muy ocupado con mis estudios.* (I didn't think about being in those games because I was very busy with my studies.) *Dos de mis amigos hicieron un equipo y me invitaron a formar parte del equipo, yo acepté estar en el equipo.* (Two of my friends made a team and they invited me to be a part of the team; I decided to play with them.) *Ellos me dijeron la hora y el día de nuestros partidos.* (They told me the time and the days that we were supposed to play.) *Un día, ellos me llamaron por teléfono para saber si yo iba a venir al partido y yo les dije que sí.* (One day, they called me to find out if I was coming to the game, and I said yes.)

Summary

Language is a tool that humans use to communicate with one another and build complex societies. We use words to name our cultural memories, meaning that we label those things we notice and need to know in order to survive. In short, we name the events, people, and things we find important. Languages are dynamic, with words being added, borrowed, and discontinued in response to social changes.

Words denote or stand for objects, actions, and ideas; jargon, a technical vocabulary common to members of an occupation, can confuse outsiders who don't know its meaning. More importantly, words have connotative meanings that consist of the feelings and associations that they imply. Epithets generally carry negative connotations, whereas euphemisms put negative things more positively. In recent years, people have become concerned about the power of words—especially those used in discriminatory ways—and have worked to eliminate sexist, ageist, racist, and other non-inclusive language from acceptable vocabulary.

Your speaking effectiveness depends largely on how well you can put your ideas into words. Thus, there are several guidelines for using language effectively in public speaking. First, be accurate in both your vocabulary and grammar. Further, use language that is appropriate to the audience and occasion, and to you. Eliminate extra words and phrases that make your speech less concise. Define jargon in an effort to be clear, and select concrete words that will enable your listeners to form more precise meanings. In addition, choose interesting strategies, such as alliteration, rhyme, repetition, personification, hyperbole, metaphors, and similes that draw from shared cultural references.

Finally, you will most likely be in a public speaking situation where you either speak in a second language, necessitating the use of an interpreter, or listen to a speaker who is not a native speaker of English. In these situations, it is most important to communicate ideas rather than have linguistic precision. When you listen to a speaker from another linguistic background, take the responsibility of listening with an open mind in a supportive manner.

Student Learning: Book Website Under "Chapter Resources," students will find several tools for reviewing the information in this chapter, including a "Tutorial Quiz." You can also have them email the results of this quiz to you as a participation or extra-credit activity.

STUDY AND REVIEW

The premium website for *Public Speaking* offers a broad range of resources that will help you better understand the material in this chapter, complete assignments, and succeed on tests. The website features

- Speech videos with critical viewing questions, various types of outlines, transcripts, and note cards
- Interactive practice activities, self quizzes, and a sample final exam

For more information about this text's electronic learning resources, consult your **Guide to Online Resources for Public Speaking** or visit http://communication.wadsworth.com/jaffe5.

Student Learning: Workbook Students can also complete "Before You Take the Exam" in Chapter 13 of the Student Workbook to review this chapter.

KEY TERMS

The terms below are defined in the margins throughout this chapter. The book website also provides interactive flashcards and crossword puzzles to help you learn these terms and the concepts they represent.

languages 233　　　　　　　words 234
symbols 233　　　　　　　　dialect 235

APPLICATION AND CRITICAL THINKING EXERCISES

The exercises below are among the practice activities on the book's website.

1. A web page by Phil Simborg titled "Incredible Facts" (http://bg-info.com/humor1.html) claims that the English word with the most dictionary meanings is *set*. First, come up with all the meanings of *set* that you can, and then use a dictionary to look it up. Do you agree with Simborg, or can prove him wrong? Thumb through a print edition instead of an online dictionary, and look for other ambiguous words with more than ten meanings.

2. Do an Internet search for the word *ebonics* or *African American Vernacular English*. Print out at least two articles and bring them to class. In a small group, discuss one of the following questions; then share your group's conclusions with the entire class.
   ▶ Identify some ways that ebonics (AAVE) differs from Standard English.
   ▶ What controversies swirl around ebonics? Why do you think the dialect is controversial?
   ▶ What do linguists say about the dialect?
   ▶ What are some arguments in favor of instruction in ebonics?
   ▶ What are some arguments against instruction in ebonics?

3. Interview a member of a specific occupation, and make a list of jargon terms associated with the job (for example, carpenters, waiters, foresters, pharmacists, truckers, bankers). Discuss your list with a classmate. How many terms do you know? Which terms are unfamiliar? If you were listening to a speaker from that occupation, how might the speaker translate the jargon so that you would better understand?

4. Find a speech by a speaker who represents a different culture than your own on www.americanrhetoric.com. Locate the metaphors and similes in the speech. Note the differences, if any, between the metaphors of that culture and your own.

5. When (if ever) might you use an interpreter in the future? When might you listen to a speech delivered with the help of an interpreter? (Include televised speeches.) When (if ever) might you give a speech in a second language? When might you listen to a nonnative speaker of English?

6. If you know a second language, prepare a short speech in that language, and then work with an interpreter who will present your speech in English as you give it in your language. For example, Maria prepared and gave her speech in Italian; an Italian-speaking classmate interpreted when she gave it to the class. Paula prepared her speech in Romanian and brought her cousin to class to translate because all her classmates were monolingual.

SPEECH VIDEO

Log on to the book's website to watch and critique Uriel Plascencia and Kelly Bilinski deliver Uriel's speech, which Kelly interprets for the audience. Also log onto **www.american rhetoric.com** to watch President John F. Kennedy's inaugural speech, focusing especially on his skillful use of language. A transcript of Kennedy's speech appears in Appendix C, and transcripts for both speeches are available on the book's website.

PROFESSIONAL SPEECH WITH COMMENTARY

I HAVE A DREAM
Reverend Martin Luther King Jr.

This speech was delivered on the steps of the Lincoln Memorial on August 28, 1963, to an audience that numbered about 250,000 people. The occasion was a March on Washington for Jobs and Freedom. It was televised and reprinted in newspapers. The *Seattle Times,* April 4, 1993, calls it "the most famous public address of 20th Century America." King was famous for his skillful use of language, especially repetition and metaphor.[34]

I am happy to join with you today in what will go down in history as the greatest demonstration for freedom in the history of our nation.

Five score years ago, a great American in whose symbolic shadow we stand today signed the Emancipation Proclamation. This momentous decree came as a great beacon light of hope to millions of Negro slaves who had been seared in the flames of withering injustice. It came as a joyous daybreak to end the long night of their captivity.

But one hundred years later, the Negro still is not free. One hundred years later, the life of the Negro is still sadly crippled by the manacles of segregation and the chains of discrimination. One hundred years later, the Negro lives on a lonely island of poverty in the midst of a vast ocean of material prosperity. One hundred years later, the Negro is still languished in the corners of American society and finds himself an exile in his own land. So we have come here today to dramatize a shameful condition.

In a sense we have come to our nation's capital to cask a check. When the architects of our republic wrote the magnificent words of the Constitution and the Declaration of Independence, they were signing a promissory note to which every American was to fall heir. This note was a promise that all men, yes, black men as well as white men, would be guaranteed the inalienable rights of life, liberty, and the pursuit of happiness. It is obvious today that America has defaulted on this promissory note insofar as her citizens of color are concerned. Instead of honoring this sacred obligation, America has given the Negro people a bad check, a check which has come back marked "insufficient funds."

But we refuse to believe that the bank of justice is bankrupt. We refuse to believe that there are insufficient funds in the great vaults of opportunity of this nation. So we have come to cash this check— a check that will give us upon demand the riches of freedom and the security of justice. We have also come to this hallowed spot to remind America of the fierce urgency of now. This is no time to engage in the luxury of cooling off or to take the tranquilizing drug of gradualism. Now is the time to make real the promises of democracy.

Teaching Tip
A complete audio recording of this speech is available from Stanford University's King Research and Education Institute speech archive at http://www.stanford.edu/group/King/. Ask students to listen to the speech before coming to class.

President Abraham Lincoln signed the Emancipation Proclamation on January 1, 1863. In this special occasion speech, King is framed by the giant statue of Lincoln.

King opens with metaphors of light and darkness. See how many you can find throughout the speech. Look for additional archetypal metaphors of seasons, thirst, weather, or mountains.

Here is the first series of repetitions: "one hundred years later . . ."

The Bank of Justice is King's second major metaphor.

Language changes over time. In 1963, the term "Negro" was common; today, it is rarely used. King refers to black and white children later in the speech, but he never uses the term "blacks," which came later in the 1960s. Today, "African American" is commonly used.

Now is the time to rise from the dark and desolate valley of segregation to the sunlit path of racial justice. Now is the time to lift our nation from the quicksands of racial injustice to the solid rock of brotherhood. Now is the time to make justice a reality for all of God's children.

It would be fatal for the nation to overlook the urgency of the moment. This sweltering summer of the Negro's legitimate discontent will not pass until there is an invigorating autumn of freedom and equality. Nineteen sixty-three is not an end, but a beginning. Those who hope that the Negro needed to blow off steam and will now be content will have a rude awakening if the nation returns to business as usual. There will be neither rest nor tranquility in America until the Negro is granted his citizenship rights. The whirlwinds of revolt will continue to shake the foundations of our nation until the bright day of justice emerges.

But there is something that I must say to my people who stand on the warm threshold which leads into the palace of justice: In the process of gaining our rightful place we must not be guilty of wrongful deeds. Let us not seek to satisfy our thirst for freedom by drinking from the cup of bitterness and hatred. We must forever conduct our struggle on the high plane of dignity and discipline. We must not allow our creative protest to degenerate into physical violence. Again and again, we must rise to the majestic heights of meeting physical force with soul force. The marvelous new militancy which has engulfed the Negro community must not lead us to distrust of all white people, for many of our white brothers, as evidenced by their presence here today, have come to realize that their destiny is tied up with our destiny. And they have come to realize that their freedom is inextricably bound to our freedom. We cannot walk alone.

And as we walk, we must make the pledge that we shall march ahead. We cannot turn back. There are those who are asking the devotees of civil rights, "When will you be satisfied?" We can never be satisfied as long as the Negro is the victim of the unspeakable horrors of police brutality. We can never be satisfied as long as our bodies, heavy with the fatigue of travel, cannot gain lodging in the motels of the highways and the hotels of the cities. We cannot be satisfied as long as the Negro's basic mobility is from a smaller ghetto to a larger one. We can never be satisfied as long as a Negro in Mississippi cannot vote and a Negro in New York believes he has nothing for which to vote. No, no, we are not satisfied, and we will not be satisfied until justice rolls down like waters and righteousness like a mighty stream.

King, a clergyman, refers to the Biblical passage of Amos 5:24.

I am not unmindful that some of you have come here out of great trials and tribulations. Some of you have come fresh from narrow jail cells. And some of you have come from areas where your quest— quest for freedom left you battered by the storms of persecution and staggered by the winds of police brutality. You have been the veterans of creative suffering. Continue to work with the faith that unearned suffering is redemptive. Go back to Mississippi, go back to Alabama, go back to South Carolina, go back to Georgia, go back to Louisiana, go back to the slums and ghettos of our northern cities, knowing that somehow this situation can and will be changed. Let us not wallow in the valley of despair, I say to you today, my friends. And so, even though we face the difficulties of today and tomorrow, I still have a dream. It is a dream deeply rooted in the American dream.

This short repetitive phrase ("Go back to . . .") is almost dwarfed by the more famous phrases in the speech.

I have a dream that one day this nation will rise up and live out the true meaning of its creed: "We hold these truths to be self-evident, that all men are created equal."

I have a dream that one day on the red hills of Georgia, the sons of former slaves and the sons of former slave owners will be able to sit down together at the table of brotherhood.

I have a dream that one day even the state of Mississippi, a state sweltering with the heat of injustice, sweltering with the heat of oppression, will be transformed into an oasis of freedom and justice.

This is King's most famous repetitive sequence, the one that gave the speech its title. Notice that he follows it with two additional repetitions: "with this faith . . ." and "let freedom ring. . . ."

I have a dream that my four little children will one day live in a nation where they will not be judged by the color of their skin but by the content of their character.

I have a *dream* today!

I have a dream that one day, down in Alabama, with its vicious racists, with its governor having his lips dripping with the words of "interposition" and "nullification" —one day right there in Alabama little black boys and black girls will be able to join hands with little white boys and white girls as sisters and brothers.

I have a *dream* today!

I have a dream that one day every valley shall be exalted, and every hill and mountain shall be made low, the rough places will be made plain, and the crooked places will be made straight; "and the glory of the Lord shall be revealed and all flesh shall see it together."

This is our hope, and this is the faith that I go back to the South with.

With this faith, we will be able to hew out of the mountain of despair a stone of hope. With this faith, we will be able to transform the jangling discords of our nation into a beautiful symphony of brotherhood. With this faith, we will be able to work together, to pray together, to struggle together, to go to jail together, to stand up for freedom together, knowing that we will be free one day.

And this will be the day— this will be the day when all of God's children will be able to sing with new meaning: *"My country 'tis of thee, sweet land of liberty, of thee I sing. Land where my fathers died, land of the Pilgrim's pride, From every mountainside, let freedom ring!*

And if America is to be a great nation, this must become true.

And so let freedom ring from the prodigious hilltops of New Hampshire.

Let freedom ring from the mighty mountains of New York.

Let freedom ring from the heightening Alleghenies of Pennsylvania.

Let freedom ring from the snow-capped Rockies of Colorado.

Let freedom ring from the curvaceous slopes of California.

But not only that:

Let freedom ring from Stone Mountain of Georgia.

Let freedom ring from Lookout Mountain of Tennessee.

Let freedom ring from every hill and molehill of Mississippi.

From every mountainside, let freedom ring.

And when this happens, when we allow freedom ring, when we let it ring from every village and every hamlet, from every state and every city, we will be able to speed up that day when *all* of God's children, black men and white men, Jews and Gentiles, Protestants and Catholics, will be able to join hands and sing in the words of the old Negro spiritual:

Free at last! free at last!

Thank God Almighty, we are free at last!

He is quoting from the Bible, Isaiah 40:4–5.

This is a well-known patriotic song.

This repetitive series, which recognizes geographical diversity but emphasizes the unity that comes with freedom, brought roars of approval from the crowd.

CHAPTER 14

DELIVERING YOUR SPEECH

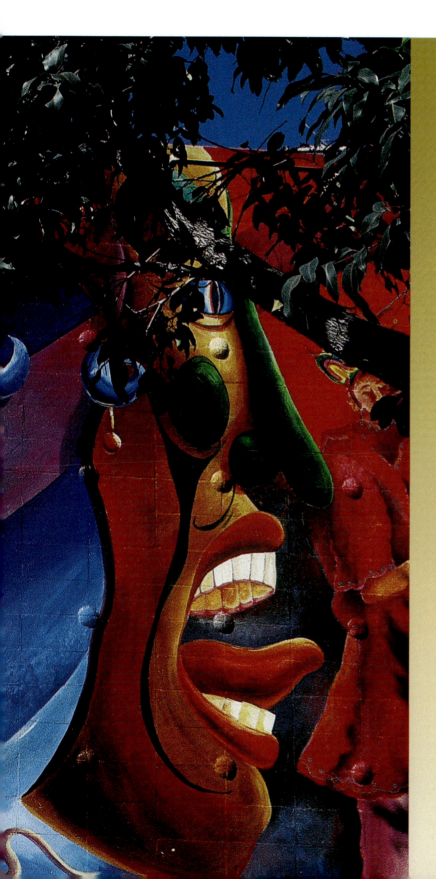

THIS CHAPTER WILL HELP YOU

▶ Describe how personal appearance, clothing, and accessories can affect public speaking

▶ List five functions of gestures, and explain how each can be used in public speaking

▶ Understand the role of eye contact in delivery

▶ Describe vocal elements that affect your presentation

▶ List four methods of delivery

▶ Discuss ways to use technology effectively in speech delivery

"Carnaval" Mural © 1995 by Joshua Sarantitis, Emmanuel Montoya, and Precita Eyes Muralists. (PG&E Yard Wall, 18th and Harrison, SF, CA)

OMPARE POLITICIANS you're familiar with—George W. Bush, Hillary Rodham Clinton, Arnold Schwarzenegger, or Barack Obama. Although they all discuss policy issues, each one creates a different impression based on personal appearance, manner, and vocal quality—in short, delivery.

Delivery is how you perform your speech or how you present your words and ideas. It requires nonverbal communication skills of appearance, gestures, and vocal variety that combine to create a positive impression. In the last few decades researchers have learned a great deal about nonverbal communication, and fortunately, you can apply their insights when you speak.

The chapter discusses personal appearance, movements or mannerisms, and vocal variations that can enhance or detract from your words. It elaborates on the four major types of delivery introduced in Chapter 2 and concludes with ways to adapt your delivery when you use technology.

CASE STUDY: WINSTON CHURCHILL'S ORATORY

© Hulton-Deutsch Collection /CORBIS

Sir Winston Churchill, British Prime Minister during World War II, is known as one of the 20th century's most effective orators. He was not a natural speaker. His voice was raspy; he lisped and stammered. He was often compared to a bulldog in looks, with his snub nose and his jutting lower lip; he was also short, overweight, and stoop-shouldered.[1] But he spent hours polishing his speeches and perfecting his delivery, and in 1953 he was awarded the Nobel Prize "for his mastery of historical and biographical description as well as for brilliant oratory in defending exalted human values."[2]

As a young man, Churchill knew that he could write well, but he also knew that he needed help if he were to speak as effectively. So he adopted several strategies to improve his delivery:[3]

▶ Churchill highlighted specific words and phrases for emphasis, and he rehearsed them aloud, complete with supporting gestures.

delivery the verbal and nonverbal behaviors you use to perform your speech

◗ He kept his audience in mind. Once when he was rehearsing in the bathtub, his valet heard him through the door and asked, "Were you speaking to me, sir?" Churchill replied, "No, I was addressing the House of Commons."

◗ He mastered the dramatic pause. This gave listeners time to digest what he said and to prepare for what was next. Pauses also drew restless members back to attention.

◗ Churchill worked on his weaknesses; because of his lisp, he carefully rehearsed words that began with /s/.

◗ He let his personality and emotions show through. For example, his voice dripped with contempt when he spoke about Hitler and the British Empire's other enemies.

◗ His timing was excellent; even his "gar-rumphs" and throat clearings came just at the right moment.

◗ Churchill varied his volume, going from loud and roaring to soft and conversational, and he matched his volume with gestures and facial expressions.

Questions for Discussion:

◗ Who is on your list of great speakers?

◗ Describe some nonverbal characteristics of the speakers on your list. That is, how do they use appearance, gestures, facial expressions, and vocal variation effectively?

◗ Churchill is famous for speeches he gave during World War II. Listen to an audio of one of his speeches at **www.molloy.edu/academic/philosophy/sophia/audio/speeches.htm**. Do you think his type of oratory would be as effective nowadays? Why or why not?

◗ What other speakers can you name who are effective, despite their less-than-perfect appearance or vocal qualities?

◗ In 2005, the opening of the Churchill Museum marked the 40th anniversary of his death. Search InfoTrac College Edition for "Winston Churchill," and read an article that summarizes his legacy. What is your overall impression of him?

Maximize Your Personal Appearance

Erving Goffman[4] develops the concept of **impression management** in his influential book, *The Presentation of Self in Everyday Life*. Goffman compares our self-presentation to a dramatic performance in which we attempt to create and maintain impressions of ourselves as if we were on stage, using a combination of props and personal mannerisms. Your physical appearance, your clothing, and your accessories all give your audience an initial impression of you.

Make the Most of Your Physical Appearance

Several relatively permanent physical features disclose information about you. For example, just by looking at you, others can figure out your sex, general age range, racial background, height, weight, and body type. Unfortunately, some audiences may stereotype you based on your personal appearance. As Chapter 5 pointed out, audiences sometimes discount younger speakers or pay less attention to women or minority speakers.

Because images of physically perfect bodies are pervasive in the media, less-than-perfect skin, crooked teeth, visible birthmarks, above-average or below-average weight or height, poor eyesight, or use of a cane or wheelchair can cause reluctance to speak publicly; you may feel as if you're in the limelight, being scrutinized.[5] Remember, however, that although people do see your features, they generally don't focus on them throughout your entire speech. If you worry about your appearance, a good strategy is to have an interesting topic and a good opening statement that draws listeners' attention to your subject rather than to you.

impression management
self-presentation, using the metaphor of a staged drama in which we use props and personal mannerisms to create and maintain impressions of ourselves

Regardless of physical features, you should pay special attention to grooming, which is important in this culture.[6] The proverb "Cleanliness is next to godliness" shows that neatness can be even more important than attractiveness. Furthermore, appropriate facial expressions, posture, and gestures add to your overall appearance. However, your listeners don't just see your physical characteristics; your clothing and accessories are an important part of the total impression you create.

Choose Appropriate Clothing and Accessories

Dirk always wore black—typically a black T-shirt with an image of a creature with fangs dripping blood emblazoned across the front. However, on speech days his attire was still all black, although it was more conservative. Some authors, notably John Molloy[7] of *Dress for Success* fame, have made millions telling people that their clothing choices influence the way they are perceived. Apply this principle to your classroom, where a good general rule is to select clothing that is slightly more formal and doesn't draw attention to itself.

Before you speak anywhere, check out clothing expectations for the particular occasion. For instance, Seana was embarrassed when she spoke at a staff retreat at her university. She dressed as if she were going to an interview, but she later reported, "I was overdressed! I didn't realize it was a retreat setting, and everyone was dressed very casually."

Accessories—the objects you carry or add to your clothing—include jewelry, glasses, briefcases, notebooks, or folders. The basic principles are to choose simple, appropriate accessories of the best quality you can afford. Avoid accessories that distract or draw attention to themselves.

There are ethical implications in impression management. If we try to create an impression that truly reflects who we are or if we try to deceive our audiences to one degree or another, we are making ethical choices. When you present verbal and nonverbal messages that you actually believe, you are **sincere.** In contrast, if you intentionally choose to create false or misleading impressions, you are being **cynical,** because you don't believe your own messages.

STOP AND CHECK
MANAGING IMPRESSIONS

You can probably think of public personalities who try to appear genuinely interested in people only when they want their money, time, or votes. How about lawyers who hire consultants to advise and coach their clients in selecting clothing, mannerisms, and nonverbal techniques to create an impression of innocence in jury members' minds? What about Ivy League–educated politicians who wear flannel shirts to "connect" with the working class? Using the following questions, discuss with a small group of your classmates the ethical appropriateness of these and similar actions.

1. Is it wrong to imply that the politician, a Harvard Law School graduate, is very similar to the blue-collar workers in his audience?
2. Are lawyers and consultants acting ethically if they believe their client is guilty?
3. What if they believe in their client's innocence?
4. How do sincere lawyers and politicians contribute to the judicial or political process?
5. How do cynical lawyers and politicians contribute to the judicial or political process?

accessories objects you carry or add to your clothing

sincere speakers presenting verbal and nonverbal messages they themselves believe

cynical speakers presenting verbal or nonverbal messages they don't believe in an attempt to create a false image

Develop Effective Mannerisms

To a significant degree, you can control your manner, or the way you speak, move, and look at the audience. Mannerisms discussed in this section include gestures and eye contact.

Control Your Gestures

Body movements range from large motions such as posture, walking, and gesturing, to very small movements such as raising one eyebrow. Ekman and Friesen[8] classified **gestures** into five functional categories: emblems, illustrators, affect display, regulators, and adaptors.

Emblems

Emblems take the place of words or ideas. They're comparatively rare in public speaking, but holding up a hand to ask for quiet or putting your forefinger to your lips in a "sh-h-h-h" gesture are some possibilities. Not surprisingly, emblems vary across cultures. For instance, Ethiopians put one forefinger to their lips when silencing a child, but they use four fingers to silence an adult. The sign that stands for "A-OK" in the United States refers to money in Japan[9] and is an obscene gesture in some Latin American countries. U.S. President Richard Nixon discovered this only after he exited a plane in Latin America, smiled broadly, and signaled a huge "A-OK!"

Illustrators

Illustrators illustrate or add emphasis to your words. They are very common in speeches and function in a variety of ways, including the following:

- To accent words and phrases. For example, "He was *guilty!*" (hit the lectern to emphasize *guilty*)
- To show spatial relationships. For example, "It's about *this* wide." (extend your hands to show the distance)
- To point out something. For instance, "Look at this part of the ocean." (point to the area on the map)

Make sure that your illustrators are purposeful. It's easy to wave your arms about randomly or to repeat an annoying or distracting gesture. Watch two or three speech videos on the book's website; turn the sound down and focus on how the speakers use their hands and arms to make effective points, or notice if they simply make meaningless movements.

Affect Display

Affect display occurs when bodily movements show emotion (affect). In the case study that opens this chapter, Churchill famously displayed his emotions. For example, he scowled when he discussed Nazi soldiers. He used other facial expressions to convey anger, disgust, and contempt for England's enemies.[10] If you frown to show displeasure or give "thumbs up" to indicate victory, you are using gestures to communicate your feelings.

Regulators

Regulators manage or help mediate interactions. They are useful as transitions between points or parts of a speech; for example, when you begin the conclusion, you might step back slightly and drop your hands from the lectern. Or you might change your posture between the problem and solution sections of your speech. Some professors walk

Student Learning: Workbook Activity 14.2, "Evaluating Videotaped Delivery Worksheet," viewing a speech with the sound off, gives students the opportunity to see the effect of nonverbal communication on the audience.

gestures body movements or motions, whether large or barely noticeable

emblems gestures that stand for words or ideas; a head nod means *yes*

illustrators gestures that add emphasis to or illustrate verbal messages

affect display showing emotion through bodily movements

regulators bodily movements that manage or help mediate interactions

across the front of the room as they lecture, moving closer to a student whose attention is wandering or moving to the lectern and looking at notes when they come to a new point.

Adaptors

Using too many **adaptors,** a third kind of gesture, is an indication of nervousness, because adaptors often betray stress or fear. There are three kinds of adaptors:

- **Self-adaptors** include fidgeting with your hair, biting your lip, scratching yourself, rubbing your hands together during your speech, and so on.
- **Object adaptors** involve touching things, such as playing with your keys, jingling change in your pocket, twisting a ring, or tapping your pencil or note cards.
- **Alter-adaptors** are gestures used in relationship to the audience. For instance, if you fold your arms across your chest during intense questioning, you may be subconsciously protecting yourself against the perceived psychological threat of the questioner.

Because adaptors indicate anxiety or other stresses, especially when they appear to be nervous mannerisms, strive to eliminate them.

Make Eye Contact

> I find it hard to listen to speakers who look down, not giving full attention to the audience.
>
> LARISA

Direct eye contact communicates honesty and trustworthiness in the U.S., so it's important to look at the audience. The phrase "Look me in the eye and say that" is partly premised on the cultural notion that people won't lie if they're looking at you. **Eye contact** also communicates friendliness. In contrast, a person who purposely avoids another's gaze in interpersonal relationships generally signals a lack of interest.

Making eye contact is often difficult at first, because it is tempting to look at your notes, the desktops in the front row, the back wall, or out the window, all gazes that communicate your discomfort. Instead, look around the room in at least three general directions: at the listeners directly in front of you, those to the left, and those to the right. Because of your peripheral vision, you can generally keep most listeners within your vision as your gaze changes direction.

Finally, look at various people within the room—not just at one or two. And resist the urge to make more eye contact with audience members you perceive as more powerful. For example, students sometimes look more at their instructors rather than at their classmates or at men more than at women, but try to avoid these behaviors. During a guest lecture, one job applicant addressed the faculty members; unfortunately, he made noticeably more eye contact with the male professors—largely ignoring the female department chair. Needless to say, he wasn't hired!

Expectations common in the United States are not universally applicable. For instance, Japanese communicators use less direct eye contact. Thus, it is not unusual to see downcast or closed eyes at a meeting or a conference, because within Japanese culture this demonstrates attentiveness and agreement rather than rejection, disinterest, or disagreement. Additionally, Nigerians, Puerto Ricans, and other cultural groups consider it disrespectful to make prolonged eye contact with superiors.[11]

For additional information on gestures and eye contact, search InfoTrac College Edition for the key words *eye contact, nonverbal gestures,* or *body language.* What additional principles can you learn from the articles you read?

Teaching Tip
"The Most Important Interview Nonverbals," at http://www.collegegrad.com/ezine/21nonver.shtml from CollegeGrad.com's E-Zine discusses nonverbal behaviors in ranked order: eye contact, facial expressions, posture, gestures, and space. All URLs mentioned in the text are available as live, regularly maintained links on the book's website, located in the "Chapter Resources" list under "Web Links."

adaptors gestures that betray stress or fear

self-adaptors nervously touching yourself (like biting your lip) when you're stressed

object adaptors nervously touching or playing with items like pens or jewelry

alter-adaptors gestures, like folding your arms protectively, that betray nervousness about the audience

eye contact looking audiences in the eye; communicates friendliness in the United States

© Thomson Learning

© Thomson Learning

Vary Your Vocal Behaviors

When you answer your phone, you recognize a friend's voice instantly because of his or her distinctive vocal features. Even without seeing someone, as when you listen to the radio, you can distinguish between young or old, males or females, Southerners or New Yorkers, native or non-native speakers of English. Moreover, you can often detect moods such as boredom, hostility, or enthusiasm. This section discusses two important aspects of vocal behaviors that will help you become a better public speaker: pronunciation and vocal variation.

Pronounce Your Words Clearly

Pronunciation, the way you actually say words, includes articulation and stress or accenting. Your pronunciation can reveal your regional origin, ethnicity, or social status.

Articulation and Stress

Articulation is the way you say individual sounds, such as *this* or *dis*, *bird* or *beerd*. Some speakers reverse sounds, saying *aks* instead of *ask*, for example, or *nuculer* for *nuclear*. **Stress** is the way you accent syllables or whole words—*poe-LEESE* (police) or *POE-leese*, for example. Some people alter both articulation and stress, for instance, comparable (*COM-purr-uh-bul*) becomes *come-PARE-uh-bul*; potpourri (*poe-per-EE*) becomes *pot-PORE-ee*. When you're in doubt about a pronunciation, consult a dictionary. You'll find that some words, such as *data* have two acceptable pronunciations—*DAY-tuh* or *DATT-uh*. When the dictionary provides two variations, the first is preferable.

Regional Origin

Variations in pronunciation and articulation are associated with regional dialects. The following list illustrates just a few differences:

▶ There are differences in the *extent* to which sounds are held. Southern speakers typically draw out vowel sounds, resulting in the "southern drawl."
▶ Many Bostonians add an *r* at the end of a word such as *tuba*. President John Kennedy, a Massachusetts native, typically said *Cuber* for *Cuba*.
▶ Speakers from different regions often articulate sounds differently. Go to Brooklyn and you'll hear *oi* instead of *er* (*thoity* for *thirty*).

Ethnicity

Ethnicity can affect pronunciation. Dialects such as Appalachian or African American Vernacular English have distinctive articulation and stress patterns. Furthermore,

articulation the way you enunciate or say specific sounds

stress accenting syllables or words

non-native speakers of English use accents that reflect articulation and stress patterns from their first language. In a multilingual world and in pluralistic classrooms, there are bound to be accents, and as travel and immigration continue to shrink the world, you'll hear even more in the future.

Social Status

Classroom Discussion/ Activity
If possible, show a few clips from *My Fair Lady* to illustrate this point. Other movies that illustrate social class and regional origin's influence on dialect are *My Cousin Vinny* and *Sweet Home Alabama*. Do people still judge others on the basis of their dialect or pronunciation? Could your dialect or pronunciation impact your persuasiveness? How?

Pronunciation differences often indicate social status. This is the premise for the classic movie *My Fair Lady*. Although Eliza Doolittle *says* the same words as Professor Higgins, her pronunciation marks her as a member of the lower class. By changing her pronunciation (as well as her dress and grooming), she eventually passes as a Hungarian princess.

Unfortunately, we tend to judge one another on the basis of accents that reflect ethnicity or social class; however, the letter in Diversity in Practice: Immigrants, Don't Be in Such a Hurry to Shed Your Accents presents a good argument for affirming a variety of accents.

DIVERSITY IN PRACTICE

IMMIGRANTS, DON'T BE IN SUCH A HURRY TO SHED YOUR ACCENTS

THIS LETTER TO THE EDITOR appeared in the *New York Times*.

To the Editor:

You report that immigrants in New York City are turning to speech classes to reduce the sting of discrimination against them based on accent. . . . I'd like to tell all my fellow immigrants taking accent-reduction classes: As long as you speak fluent and comprehensible English, don't waste your money on artificially removing your accent.

I am fortunate enough to be one of the linguistically gifted. I even acquired an American accent before I left China for the United States five years ago. From the day I set foot on this continent till now, the praise of my English has never ceased. What most people single out is that I have no, or very little accent. However, I know I do have an accent. . . . I intend to keep it because it belongs to me. I want to speak and write grammatically flawless English, but I have no desire to equip myself with a perfect American accent. . . .

America is probably the largest place for accents in English because the entire nation is composed of immigrants from different areas of the world. This country is built on accents. Accent is one of the most conspicuous symbols of what makes America the free and prosperous land its own people are proud of and other people long to live in.

I work in an urban institution where accents are an integral part of my job: students, faculty and staff come from ethnically diverse backgrounds. Hearing accents confirms for me every day that the college is fulfilling its goal to offer education to a multicultural population. I wonder what accent my fellow immigrants should obtain after getting rid of their own: a New York accent? a Boston accent? Brooklyn? Texas? California? . . . Fellow immigrants, don't worry about the way you speak. . . .

YanHong Krompacky

Instructor's Resource Manual
Teaching Idea 14.1, "Vocal Variation and Meaning," in the *Instructor's Resource Manual* (available in print, online, and on the Multimedia Manager CD-ROM) suggests a way of teaching students how to use vocal variety to match the intended message.

Use Vocal Variation

Around 330 BC, Aristotle discussed three important vocal components in his text *Rhetoric:*[12] volume, pitch, rate, and the variations in each.

It is not enough to know what we ought to say; we must also say it as we ought. . . .
It is, essentially, a matter of the right management of the voice to express the

various emotions—of speaking loudly, softly, or between the two; of high, low, or intermediate pitch; of the various rhythms that suit various subjects. These are the three things—volume of sound, modulation of pitch, and rhythm—that a speaker bears in mind.

What kinds of impressions do **vocal variations** create? For one thing, listeners enjoy hearing pleasing vocal variations. David summarized delivery skills that leave him with positive impressions:

> An audience stays in tune when the speaker's voice changes, adding life to the message. An animated speaker is also more interesting than a "block" of ice. The speaker must be interested in what he/she is saying in order to be convincing.

In addition, several studies[13] conclude that audiences typically associate vocal characteristics with personality traits such as these:

Loud and fast speakers: self-sufficient, resourceful, dynamic

Loud and slow speakers: aggressive, competitive, confident

Soft and fast speakers: enthusiastic, adventuresome, confident, composed

Soft and slow speakers: competitive, enthusiastic, benevolent

Is there a relationship between your voice and your credibility? Various studies indicate that audiences make a number of associations about your trustworthiness based on your voice. Speak quickly and you may be considered intelligent, objective, and knowledgeable. Males may be seen as dominant, dynamic, and sociable. Speak with a moderate rate and you may be perceived as composed, honest, oriented toward people, and compassionate.[14]

Make vocal variations work for you. For example, use a slower rate when you're giving key points, and speed up for background material.[15] Change your vocal inflections if your audience appears to be losing interest; add pitch variation and slightly increased

Student Learning: Workbook Activity 14.3, "Vary Your Vocalics," is a fun group activity that helps students understand the effects of different "voices."

vocal variations changes in volume, rate, and pitch that combine to create impressions of the speaker

© AP/Wide World Photos

Whoopi Goldberg uses her distinctive vocal features along with variations in rate, volume, and pauses to create a style that's uniquely her own.

volume and rate to communicate enthusiasm.[16] Use your tone of voice, rising or falling inflection, and stress on specific words to vary your meanings. Again, Winston Churchill provides a model:

> "What kind of people do they think we are?" he asked of the enemy. The incisive, intense, affronted tone of his voice as he said those words told eloquently of his anger, disgust and determination to fight on. In a stern but stimulating manner he growled, "I have nothing to offer but blood, toil, tears and sweat."[17]

For additional tips on vocal variation, log on to the Internet site provided by the Birmingham, Alabama, Toastmasters at **www.angelfire.com/tn/bektoastmasters/Toast masters5.html**. Practice some of the suggested exercises you find there.

Pause for Effect

Finally, consider your use of pauses. Pauses can be effective, or they can be embarrassing—to both you and your listeners. Effective pauses are intentional; that is, you purposely pause between major ideas, or you give your audience a few seconds to contemplate a difficult concept. In a speech to corporate executives, Judith Humphrey[18] advised:

> [C]onsider this: when does the audience think? Not while you're speaking, because they can't think about an idea until it's delivered. They think during the pauses. But if there are no pauses, they won't think. They won't be moved. They won't act upon what you say. The degree to which you want to involve the audience is reflected in the length of your pauses.

Humphrey's article is available on InfoTrac College Edition. Look for the title "Executive Eloquence"; step 7 describes effective delivery.

Pauses can also function as punctuation marks. For example, at the end of the body of the speech, you could pause, move one step backward, and then say, "In conclusion . . ." Your pause functions as a period that signals a separation in your thoughts.

In contrast, ineffective pauses or hesitations disrupt your fluency and signal that you've lost your train of thought. **Unfilled pauses** are silent; **filled** or **vocalized pauses** include *uh* or *um*, *like*, *OK?* and *you know*. Beginning public speakers, as well as many professionals, use *um*s. However, too many can be distracting, so work to minimize them.

Put It All Together

unfilled pauses silent pauses

filled (vocalized) pauses saying *um* or *uh* or other sounds during a pause

confident style a way of speaking characterized by effective vocal variety, fluency, gestures, and eye contact

conversational style speaking that's comparatively calmer, slower, and less intense, but maintains good eye contact and gestures

Chapter 1 defines communicative competence as the ability to communicate in a personally effective and socially appropriate manner.[19] The key is to find what delivery works best for you in a given situation. A **confident style** incorporates vocal variety, fluency, good use of gestures, and eye contact to create an impression of dynamism as well as credibility. If you're naturally outgoing, this style may best fit your personality. However, in some situations—somber occasions, for example—you should choose a more **conversational style,** one that's calmer, slower, softer, and less intense, but still maintains good eye contact and gestures.[20] Listeners associate this style with trustworthiness, honesty, sociability, likableness, and professionalism, and it may actually fit you better if your personality is more laid back. But more conversational speakers can adapt for an occasion, such as a rally, where excitement runs high and people expect a more enthusiastic delivery. Both styles are persuasive.

Don't worry if you are not yet dynamic or confident. Instead, begin to develop your personal delivery style, using your appearance, mannerisms, and vocal variations to your advantage. Then, choose a mode of delivery that fits the specific context.

STOP AND CHECK

THINK CRITICALLY ABOUT DELIVERY

Political candidates often illustrate the link between delivery and effectiveness. For example, President Reagan was called the "Great Communicator," and President Clinton's speaking skills were praised. In contrast, however, many candidates fail the "charismatic challenge." One presidential candidate's voice was described as "somewhere between that of a dentist's drill and the hum of a refrigerator. . . ."[21] Another's delivery was wooden, earnest, solemn, and uptight, focused more on content than on delivery. Enter the consultants. Some spun their candidate's delivery as *authentic*. In contrast, other handlers sat beside their candidate, watching and rewatching videotaped speeches, analyzing volume, rate, gestures, facial expressions. Their advice was to loosen up— leave the podium, gesture widely, smile, wear cowboy boots, trade in his blue suit for warmer brown, more casual clothing. The candidate finally admitted what good public speakers know: No matter how wonderful his ideas, his message would be unheard if his delivery put the audience to sleep.

    In small groups, discuss the following questions:

1. What qualities are important in a president? How does presidential image matter? What do you think of the handlers' decision to spin unremarkable delivery as "authentic"?
2. Should a candidate undergo a makeover or "be herself," regardless?
3. On MTV's campaign coverage, a young person responded that a specific candidate was, "Uh, uh, old." What difference does it make if a president looks old?
4. President William Taft (1909–1914) weighed around 300 pounds. Would he be elected president today? Why or why not? Is this good or bad?
5. Why have no women yet been elected to the presidency? When do you predict that the United States will elect its first female president?
6. Could Abraham Lincoln— with his looks and awkward mannerisms— be elected in this television-dominated society? Why or why not?
7. How do you judge your classmates' abilities based on the way they present themselves?

Select the Appropriate Type of Delivery

Tim forgot that his classroom speech was due until his name was called, so he just stood up and "winged" his talk. Quianna memorized her speech (see the outline at the end of Chapter 7) because, as a member of the University of Alaska's speech team, she presented this speech more than twenty-five times in competition. The U.S. Secretary of State read her prepared commencement address to the Ivy League graduating class, and excerpts of it were reprinted in the *New York Times*. Prosecutor Juan prepared his closing arguments carefully, but when he actually faced the jury, he delivered his final appeal using only his legal pad with a few scrawled notes. These speakers illustrate the four major types of delivery, introduced briefly in Chapter 2: impromptu, memorized, manuscript, and extemporaneous.

Impromptu Delivery

Use **impromptu delivery** when you must think on your feet. This mode requires the least amount of preparation and rehearsal, because impromptu speeches are given on the spur of the moment. In other words, you don't prepare what you'll say in advance. However, in a sense, your entire life—your knowledge and experience—prepares you for the speech. Let's say you attend a wedding reception, and you're asked to speak spontaneously

impromptu delivery
delivering the speech as you create it

about the bride and groom. You don't have time to prepare. Instead, you think quickly and draw from your experience with the couple to find material for your speech.

You may shudder at the thought of speaking without preparation and rehearsal, especially if your performance will be rewarded or punished in some way, a grade or a job evaluation, for example. However, a few students give an impromptu speech when the professor has assigned a carefully prepared one. Bad strategy!

Memorized Delivery

Memorized delivery used to be common. Orators in ancient Rome, for example, memorized their speeches word for word. As a result, they could give the same oration repeatedly. In oral cultures, orators memorize the stories and legends of the tribe, a tradition that ensures that the exact stories continue throughout succeeding generations.

College students who successfully memorize speeches are generally speech team members who repeat each speech dozens of times in intercollegiate tournaments. However, memorized speeches are rare in classrooms, offices, boardrooms, churches, and clubs. Consequently, you're better off not to rely on this method. Regardless of this advice, some students think memorizing will help them overcome their fears. One international student confided:

> I think if I memorize the entire speech including the pauses, gestures, posture, etc., I will feel more comfortable delivering the speech and I will be less nervous.
>
> LAMBROS

Unfortunately, the opposite often happens. Standing in front of an audience, a beginning speaker's mind can easily go blank. Some pause (ineffectively), look toward the ceiling, repeat the last phrase in a whisper, repeat it aloud, and then look hopelessly at the instructor. When this happens, they end up embarrassed. Recently, I met an elderly lady who vividly remembered her college speech class. She said she was scared to death to give her speech on the topic of spanking, so she decided to memorize it. Unfortunately, memory failed her, and her resulting embarrassment has stayed with her for more than fifty years!

Another drawback is that memorized speeches are often not delivered conversationally. They simply don't sound natural. Rather than engaging in a dialogue with the audience, the speaker appears to be speech centered.

Manuscript Delivery

Manuscript delivery means you write your speech out and read it. In general, this is not recommended in the classroom because it's the most inactive delivery method,[22] one that lets you impart a lot of information—most of which the audience soon forgets. More active speaker-listener interactions, in contrast, keep participants' attention longer, involve them mentally, and make the speech more enjoyable.

Despite the disadvantages, on some occasions—especially formal ones such as commencement addresses—manuscript delivery is acceptable, even necessary. Further, a manuscript is useful if you speak on radio or television, where exact timing is essential. For competent manuscript delivery, type your entire script in a large font (20 points) and use double or triple spacing. Then go over your manuscript, using a highlighter or underlining the words you wish to accent. Make slashes where you plan to pause. Finally, practice until you can read your speech in a natural manner, with as much eye contact as possible. Conversational delivery is essential, because most people don't like to be read to, especially if you never pause or look up.

If you ever speak on television, you'll probably use a **teleprompter** screen, located just beneath the camera lens, that projects your manuscript line by line so that you can read it while looking directly at the camera. It is somewhat like reading the credit lines that unroll on a movie screen at the end of the film. During rehearsal, work with a technician who controls the speed of the lines so that the text unrolls at your speaking rate. The technician can circle key words or underline phrases that you want to emphasize.

memorized delivery
delivering a speech you've learned word for word

manuscript delivery
reading a speech

teleprompter screen, located beneath the camera lens, on which the words of the speech scroll up during a filmed speech

A video of former First Lady Barbara Bush delivering a speech is available on the book's website; it is an example of effective manuscript delivery. A transcript of it is also available in Appendix C. Representative Barack Obama's speech at the Democratic National Convention, available at **www.c-span.org**, provides another good example.

Although manuscript delivery is occasionally appropriate, the fourth delivery mode, extemporaneous, is generally preferred in most situations.

Extemporaneous Delivery

In contrast to impromptu speeches, you prepare extemporaneous speeches carefully in advance, but you don't plan every single word. Instead, you outline your major ideas and use note cards with cue words during your delivery. Extemporaneous speeches begin with the process of topic selection, research, organization, and outlining. Give yourself plenty of time to let your ideas jell. Finally, put your main ideas on note cards and jot down key words for the evidence you'll use. (See Chapter 11.) Then, practice, practice, practice—aloud, in the shower, to your friends, as you drive. On speech day, review your outline and your notes and go to class with the confidence that comes from thorough preparation.

Of the four types of delivery, three—impromptu, manuscript, and extemporaneous—are used with some regularity in the United States. Each has its strengths and weaknesses. In general, **extemporaneous delivery** is most commonly used in public presentations, and it is the one most common in your classroom speeches.

Summary

By increasing your knowledge of nonverbal communication, you can create a positive impression as you deliver your speech. The idea of managing nonverbal aspects of delivery to affect listeners' impressions is at least as old as Aristotle—and he surely didn't invent the idea. Modern scholars continue to explore specific aspects of appearance, mannerisms, and vocal variations that create positive or negative impressions in audiences.

How you dress, your grooming, and your accessories communicate your competence; your mannerisms—gestures, eye contact, and vocal variation—are also important in creating impressions of dynamism, honesty, and other characteristics of credibility. As your nonverbal skills increase, your competence in public speaking will increase correspondingly.

Of the four major types of delivery, memorization is common in oral cultures and in competitive speech tournaments, but it is less frequently used elsewhere. You may speak spontaneously in the impromptu style, or you may read from a manuscript. More commonly, you'll join the ranks of extemporaneous speakers—preparing in advance but choosing your exact wording as you actually speak.

As with all attempts to influence others, the attempt to manage impressions has ethical implications. Speakers who believe in both the verbal and nonverbal messages they are sending are said to be sincere, but those who try to create false or misleading impressions are termed cynical.

Teaching Tip
If possible, videotape at least one speech for each student. Have students use their tape to complete Exercises 3 and 4 in the Application and Critical Thinking Exercises at the end of the chapter (and on the book's website).

Student Learning: Book Website
Under "Chapter Resources," students will find several tools for reviewing the information in this chapter, including a "Tutorial Quiz." You can also have them email the results of this quiz to you as a participation or extra-credit activity.

extemporaneous delivery preparing and rehearsing a speech carefully in advance, but choosing the exact wording as you deliver the speech

STUDY AND REVIEW

The premium website for *Public Speaking* offers a broad range of resources that will help you better understand the material in this chapter, complete assignments, and succeed on tests. The website features

▶ Speech videos with critical viewing questions, various types of outlines, transcripts, and note cards
▶ Interactive practice activities, self quizzes, and a sample final exam

For more information about this text's electronic learning resources, consult your **Guide to Online Resources for Public Speaking** or visit http://communication.wadsworth.com/jaffe5.

KEY TERMS

The terms below are defined in the margins throughout this chapter. The book website also provides interactive flashcards and crossword puzzles to help you learn these terms and the concepts they represent.

Student Learning: Workbook
Students can also complete "Before You Take the Exam" in Chapter 14 of the *Student Workbook* to review this chapter.

delivery 256	eye contact 260
impression management 257	articulation 261
accessories 258	stress 261
sincere 258	vocal variations 263
cynical 258	unfilled pauses 264
gestures 259	filled (vocalized) pauses 264
emblems 259	confident style 264
illustrators 259	conversational style 264
affect display 259	impromptu delivery 265
regulators 259	memorized delivery 266
adaptors 260	manuscript delivery 266
self-adaptors 260	teleprompter 266
object adaptors 260	extemporaneous delivery 267
alter-adaptors 260	

APPLICATION AND CRITICAL THINKING EXERCISES

The exercises below are among the practice activities on the book's website.

1. The combination of environment, appearance, and mannerisms forms a "front." Whether intentional or unwitting, the front influences the way observers define and interpret the situation. With this in mind, why do some people appear to be something they're not? Why do some speakers appear to be competent or trustworthy, and you later discover they aren't? Have you ever tried to put on a front?[23] If so, when? Why? What are the ethical implications of fronts?

2. Write a script for an ad selling one of these products:

   ▶ Used-car dealership
   ▶ Perfume
   ▶ Vacation to South America
   ▶ Brand of cola

   Bring your script to class and exchange it with a classmate. Demonstrate the type of vocal variation you would use if you were delivering the ad.

3. If possible, videorecord one of your speeches and then watch it. Specifically pay attention to your gestures, noting your use of emblems, illustrators, or adaptors. Plan specific strategies to improve your gestures, eliminating those that create negative impressions and strengthening those that produce favorable impressions.

4. Watch the recording again. This time, evaluate your eye contact. Throughout your speech, notice the way you use your voice. Check for appropriate rate and volume; be alert for pauses, and count the number of "ums" you use, if any. Discuss with a classmate how you can improve these nonverbal aspects of delivery.

5. If you can't videorecord a speech, create a worksheet that identifies the elements of delivery mentioned in the chapter. Give it to a classmate just before your speech, and have him or her specifically note nonverbal aspects of your delivery; afterwards, discuss with that person strategies you can use to improve problem areas.

6. With a small group of your classmates, make a set of guidelines for delivery that's appropriate to your classroom's unique culture. For example, would you change the advice about clothing or accessories presented in this chapter? What might you add that's not covered here?

7. Some colleges and universities offer public speaking courses online. With a group of your classmates, discuss the pros and cons of this practice. How do the courses work? What are the drawbacks? Would you take one? Why or why not? (Prepare for this discussion by doing an Internet search for all the words *public speaking course online*.)

SPEECH VIDEO

Log on to the book's website to watch and critique examples of memorized, extemporaneous, manuscript, and impromptu speeches.

CHAPTER 15

TELLING NARRATIVES

THIS CHAPTER WILL HELP YOU

▶ Explain how narratives function to explain, to persuade, and to entertain

▶ List elements of narratives

▶ Give guidelines for using language effectively in narratives

▶ Identify five parts of an exemplum

▶ Apply three tests for narrative reasoning

Detail from "Culture of the Crossroads" Mural © 1998 by Precita Eyes Muralists. Directed by Susan Kelk Cervantes. (McDonald's Building, 24th Street at Mission, SF, CA)

T'S A WARM FALL DAY in Jonesborough, Tennessee. You're in a tent with hundreds of people listening to a man dressed in overalls tell stories from his boyhood in Mississippi; you hear occasional bursts of laughter and applause from the "Tall Tales Tent" down the street and the "Family Tales Tent" next door. You are just one of some 8,000 visitors who annually trek to the storytelling festival in Jonesborough, Tennessee's oldest town and "epicenter of a worldwide revival in storytelling."[1] In fact, more than 225 storytelling organizations nationwide host similar festivals.[2]

Storytelling has existed in every culture during every era; as a result, we live in a "story-shaped world."[3] Lawyers frame their arguments as narratives, and politicians present their political visions in story form. Coaches, teachers, members of the clergy, and comedians all routinely tell stories. Everyone uses narrative reasoning, especially women and speakers from ethnic groups such as African Americans and Native Americans.[4] Stories are so much a part of every culture that Professor Walter Fisher[5] refers to humans as **homo narrans,** the storytelling animal. The scholar Roland Barthes summarizes:

> The narratives of the world are numberless. . . . Narrative is present in every age, in every place, in every society; it begins with the very history of [humankind] and there nowhere is nor has been a people without narrative. All classes, all human groups, have their narratives, enjoyment of which is very often shared by [others] with different, even opposing, cultural backgrounds. . . . Narrative is international, transhistorical, transcultural: it is simply there, like life itself.[6]

This chapter discusses narrative functions, tests for narrative reasoning or merit, and narrative organizational patterns. It concludes by discussing tests for narrative reasoning.

Chapter-at-a-Glance
This chapter focuses on the narrative as an alternative form of speech making. It begins with a case study about applied storytelling and then explains how the narrative form can function to inform, persuade, and entertain. This is followed by a discussion of the key elements of narratives and techniques for using vivid language. Next come patterns for organizing narratives, including the exemplum pattern. Finally, students are presented with three tests to assess the effectiveness of narrative reasoning.

CASE STUDY: STORYTELLING FOR HEALING AND PEACE

Professional storyteller Laura Simms, who founded the "Gaindeh Project," an international storytelling venture, addresses the needs of children and adults who are victims of trauma.

Laura Simms

Applied storytellers use narratives for practical reasons—to promote social action, to better the world—not just to entertain an audience.[7] They show up in prisons, homeless shelters, battered women's shelters, hospitals, negotiating sessions, houses of worship, and so on.

Laura Simms, pictured here, uses narratives to help children who are trapped in war and conflict situations. She chooses stories from many cultures as "metaphors for redemption, to help children overcome overwhelming feelings of fear or powerlessness."[8] Taking inspiration from centuries-old oral traditions passed on in villages and families across the globe, she reports:

> I have gathered traditional stories from many different cultures that hopefully can provide an internal place of peace and inner nourishment for children who are dealing with tremendously overpowering feelings and images. This is what stories have done through the ages.[9]

Other applied storytellers work to build peace, one story at a time. They believe that conflict arises when our stories diverge from the stories of other people and other

homo narrans a Latin phrase that identifies humans as storytelling animals

applied storytelling using stories for practical purposes, not just for entertainment

groups. Although we might try to avoid or discount divergent stories, we can actually learn and grow by sharing stories, questioning other narratives and ours, and reconsidering our stories and encouraging others to do likewise. Exchanging competing narratives lets us look for commonalities that can help us understand and examine our differences and together create new, shared narratives. Peacemakers use personal stories, as well as folktales about peace and reconciliation from many cultures to offer insights about transforming conflict into peace.[10]

Questions for Discussion

▶ Laura Simms tells stories to heal emotional traumas. Can you give an example of someone who was helped emotionally through a story?
▶ How might storytelling function to help a person heal physically?
▶ Describe a time you resolved a conflict by sharing stories with the person with whom you disagreed.
▶ What conflicts on your campus result from divergent, competing stories? What opportunities, if any, are provided for sharing conflicting stories? How effective are they?
▶ How might storytelling promote civility and dialogue?

Narrative Functions

Storytelling preserves and transmits "ideas, images, motives and emotions with which everyone can identify."[11] Stories tell about the past, highlight human emotions and drives, illuminate cultural ideals, and illustrate facets of a culture by identifying its themes and showing cultural differences. Through stories, audiences become more self-aware and more aware of cross-cultural issues.[12] Stories inform, persuade, and entertain.

Informative Narratives

What's it like to attend that college? How is my charitable donation used? What happened during the *Titanic*'s last hours? Often, we find our answers in a story. Before you chose a college, did you ask students to explain campus life by telling stories about classes, professors, registration, and social events? Both their positive and negative tales helped you anticipate the good as well as the bad of college life. A story about a single mother whose child received medicine because you gave money lets you know that your gift was used wisely. And the fate of the *Titanic*—whether presented in oral, written, or filmed versions—still fascinates millions. The scholar Didier Coste[13] says that our narratives tell our culture's understandings of natural, social, and ultimate things.

Explaining Natural Phenomena

Why do cats and dogs fight? The Kaluli tribe from Papua New Guinea explains this in a myth. Where do babies come from? Parents dust off the "birds and the bees" story for each new generation. How did the world come into being? Scientists weave together facts and ideas into narrative accounts such as the big bang theory, which, along with evolutionary narratives, profoundly affect our perceptions of the natural world.[14] Of course, conflict arises because many people or groups modify or reject outright these stories, offering, instead, alternative explanations. How did the victim die? Who killed her? Prosecutors and defense lawyers offer competing explanations that jury members must weigh and compare, finally accepting the story that makes the most sense to them.

storytelling an oral art form we use to preserve and transmit commonly held ideas, images, motives, and emotions

Explaining Society and Institutions

Stories also explain cultural institutions or structures. Your history texts are peopled with characters facing dramatic choices, overcoming hardships, inventing useful as well as harmful machines, and making mistakes. Stories explain the country's founding, its wars, blameworthy scenes (slavery), and praiseworthy scenes (the Constitutional Convention). Naturally, history books from other countries relate some of the same events quite differently. Often, myths obscure historical facts, and other historians—"Afrocentric" or feminist "her-storians," for example—tell narratives that differ from "malestream" stories.

To read another culture's explanation of its history, search InfoTrac College Edition for "Stone Camels and Clear Springs" in the journal *Asian Folklore Studies.* This drama features audience participation and feedback in the retelling of the history of the Salar people.

Organizations and groups also have unique explanatory stories. Your college has a story, as does your family. Couples even describe their relationships in story form—a journey, a war, an addiction, and so on.[15] Corporate trainers emphasize the importance of storytelling within organizational cultures. Jim Endicott says that a good presentation has a strong underlying story that connects with personal interests, characters, and issues that matter to the audience.[16] Annette Simmons says you should have a variety of stories—one to explain who you are, another to tell why you are speaking, a third to describe your vision; you should also have teaching stories (with both positive and negative lessons) and values-in-action stories.[17]

Explaining Ultimate Things

Philosophical and religious stories attempt to explain ultimate realities, to answer questions such as "Who are we?" "What is our purpose on Earth?" "What happens after death?" "How should I live a moral life?" Many of these stories explain religious rituals that are usually based in historical events. Jewish people, for instance, narrate the story of the Maccabees as they light Hanukkah candles. Muslims tell of the Prophet's flight to Medina during the fast of Ramadan. Christians remember the death and resurrection of Jesus as they celebrate Easter. In short, religious beliefs and practices are grounded in

Storytelling is universally used to pass on important cultural ideas. Here, Kitbidin Atamkulov recounts the epic tale of Manas, the Kirghiz hero, to his entranced listeners, both young and old.

© Franz Lanting/Minden Pictures

stories that followers have preserved over generations, stories that give ultimate meaning to the lives of adherents.

WHO SHOULD TELL NATIVE STORIES?

LENORE KEESHIG-TOBIAS, an Ojibway poet, argues that non-native writers and filmmakers should not borrow native stories. To do so is to commit "cultural theft, the theft of voice." She argues:

> Stories, you see, are not just entertainment. Stories are power. They reflect the deepest, the most intimate perceptions, relationships, and attitudes of a people. Stories show how a people, a culture, thinks. Such wonderful offerings are seldom reproduced by outsiders.[18]

Within Ojibway culture, stories are considered so potent that one storyteller must ask permission to tell another's story. Consequently, Keeshig-Tobias believes that someone who wants to use a native story should come live with the storytellers for more than a few months.

> Hear the voice of the wilderness. Be there with the Labicon, the Inmu. Be there on the Red Squirrel Road. . . . If you want these stories, fight for them. I dare you.[19]

Consider these questions for discussion:

▶ What do you think? Should non-natives tell a native story? Why or why not?
▶ Does this apply to other groups? For example, can only Muslims tell stories about Islam or only Christians tell New Testament stories? Can a heterosexual tell the story of someone who's gay or lesbian? Why or why not?
▶ What is "cultural theft?" Explain your answer.

Persuasive Narratives

We commonly tell stories to reinforce values and influence listeners' beliefs, actions, or attitudes. In fact, narrative reasoning is so effective that Aristotle classified it as a type of **deliberative speaking,** the kind of speaking that gives people information and motivates them to make wise decisions regarding future courses of action.[20] Stories sometimes provide a rationale *for* a particular course of action, a proof of its necessity. At other times, they provide good arguments *against* a particular course of action. For example, narratives that serve as models or examples of successful people (those who behave in certain ways or hold specific values) contrast with failure narratives or horror stories (characters who suffer the consequences of socially unacceptable actions).

A Rationale *for* a Belief, Attitude, or Action

Does a low-carbohydrate diet help people lose weight?

> Yes. My mother's been on one for three months and she's lost 35 pounds; let me tell you about her lifelong struggle to control her weight . . .

Do UFOs exist?

> Well, one day the most interesting thing happened to me! It was like this . . .

Can one person make a difference?

> Yes. Clara "Mother" Hale opened Hale House in Harlem to care for babies of drug addicts and babies with AIDS. This ordinary person helped a lot of at-risk children by . . .

Classroom Discussion / Activity
What functions do classic children's stories play in our culture? What do we teach our children when we tell them the fable of the tortoise and the hare? What is the moral of "The Three Little Pigs"? Does *The Cat in the Hat* simply entertain or does it serve another function?

Teaching Tip
To illustrate the power of persuasive narratives, have students visit the Urban Legends Reference Pages at http://www.snopes.com. Did they find any legends they had heard and believed to be true? What makes urban legends so compelling?

deliberative speaking a form of speaking that gives people the information and motivation they need to make wise decisions regarding future courses of action

© Kenji Kawano

The late James Nahkai Jr., a Navajo Code Talker, inspired listeners with stories of his World War II adventures. Navajo Code Talkers were Navajo Marines who created an unbreakable code based on their native language. Their dedication and patriotism helped win the war in the Pacific. The 2002 movie *Wind Talkers* tells a fictionalized (and sometimes inaccurate) version of their story.

These stories provide a rationale to believe in something such as the value of a diet, UFOs, or the power of the individual.

Other persuasive stories provide a rationale for attitudes and actions, some personal, some on a wider scale. (For example, every war is justified by stories.) The following examples urge listeners toward positive goals:

Be honest.

> Look at what happened to Pinocchio when he told a lie.

Be courageous in the face of adversity.

> In the prime of his baseball career, Dave Dravecky lost his pitching arm and shoulder to cancer. He struggled through a period of depression and an identity crisis, and found a meaningful life as a writer and speaker. Follow his example.

Wage peace; peacemaking begins with concerned, committed individuals.

> Israeli storyteller Noa Baum entered into a dialogue with a Palestinian woman when both were living in the U.S. Her one-woman show, "A Land Twice Promised," weaves together their personal memories and their mothers' stories, providing multiple perspectives on the same places and events.[21]

Some stories are unpleasant to hear because they expose a societal wrong. However, emotionally involving narratives can motivate others to intervene, to make a difference, to improve the lives of people in need. Ganga Stone, founder of God's Love, We Deliver, a volunteer network that has delivered more than six million meals to needy people, often told this persuasive narrative:

> I hugged the heavy bag of donated groceries and began to climb the five long flights of stairs to Richard's studio apartment. I remember feeling a strong sense of satisfaction knowing that I was bringing help to a dying man who was all alone. That satisfied glow disappeared the instant I saw him.
>
> Richard lay propped up in a bed, his swollen features all distorted by AIDS-related disease. He hadn't eaten in two days, so when I approached his bedside he eagerly grabbed the grocery bag. I watched him reach again and again in the bag to find something, anything, that he could eat . . . now. Bread mix, oatmeal, canned beans, a box of macaroni and cheese—there was nothing ready to eat and no way he could get out of bed to cook. He finally gave up.
>
> Then he looked up at me still clutching the empty bag, the useless assortment of ingredients strewn across the bed and floor. For a moment we just stared at one another. Then I made a promise I wasn't sure how I would keep. But I promised to bring him meals for as long as he needed, and I vowed that no one else in the same situation would ever have to face the unthinkable combination of AIDS and starvation. That was [many] years and [millions of] meals ago.[22]

Ms. Stone clearly hopes listeners will identify with both Richard and herself, a woman determined to change a bad situation. If they become concerned enough, they might also seek ways to become personally involved with people like Richard, and they might tell her story to others, inviting even more people to attack such problems.

A Rationale Against an Action, Belief, or Attitude

Not all stories are positive models of how we should live. Some tell a cautionary message or show what policy *not* to enact, how *not* to behave, or what *not* to believe.

Don't drink and drive.

> Police officers tell young drivers a number of horror stories about teens whose careless driving killed innocent people, including their friends. . . .

Practice safe sex.

> Health professionals tell tales of people who practiced unsafe sex, with dire consequences. . . .

Avoid credit card debt.

> Your personal story about problems that resulted from a credit card spending spree can motivate your listeners to use their credit cards wisely.

The United States should stay out of another military conflict.

> Remember Vietnam . . .

The motivational power of cautionary tales lies in their emotional appeal. They typically appeal to fear, shame, anger, or other strong emotions.

Not only do persuasive stories change individuals, they also contribute to wider policy changes. For instance, on the campus level, stories about a series of muggings convinced administrators to establish corrective security policies. National stories about oil spills led to tighter regulations for oil tankers. International tales of tsunami victims led millions across the globe to respond with money and muscle.

Visionary Narratives

Although many stories are told in the past or present tense, some provide a vision of the future. Science fiction is well known for painting bleak scenarios of out-of-control technology or for depicting a bright future where machines are harnessed and controlled, allowing humans to do superhuman things. On a more mundane level, investors have poured millions of dollars into stocks based not on past earnings but on visions of future wealth. Healing stories about a healthy future can give hope to a family in crisis; a physician who comforts parents with an "after-surgery-another-child-just-like-this-walked-again" story is one example.

Visionary narratives sometimes suggest ideals that go beyond your listeners' current beliefs and experiences, confronting them with possibilities, expanding their understandings of themselves and their lives. Through this, the **rhetoric of possibility,**[23] you narrate what might be, and you help others envision a future that they can make real. A famous example is Martin Luther King, Jr.'s 1963 call to be a nation in which all are judged "not by the color of their skin, but by the content of their character." His vision still inspires us, but it's not yet a universal reality. (This chapter's case study describes some ways that applied storytelling can contribute to social change.)

Persuasive stories can influence one person or millions. They provide examples of both wise and unwise behaviors; they provide a rationale *for* or *against* a policy, belief, or behavior; and they present a vision of what might be.

Entertaining Narratives

Let's face it: Not all stories are deeply profound. We often tell a story just to relax or have a good time. For instance, storyteller Jackie Torrence[24] identifies "Jump Tales" that end

rhetoric of possibility
points out what can be, not what is

with a "BOO!" We tell them because we love the shivers they give. Children's stories, urban legends, and television sitcoms are examples of narratives that feature unusual or quirky characters in unusual or quirky situations. Humorous stories also come in the form of extended jokes or exaggerated situations carried to the extreme.[25]

You've probably told your share of entertaining stories. Friends tell friends the funny things they saw or did during the day. Parents and grandparents tell silly stories to bored kids during road trips; campers entertain one another as the campfire dies down. Do an Internet search for *silly stories* or *jokes*, for *scary stories*, *urban legends*, or *campfire tales*. The number of hits you get in each category should give you some idea of the popularity of entertaining stories. (A Google search turned up millions and millions of hits for *jokes!*)

The great rhetoric scholar Kenneth Burke summarizes types of narratives as "the imaginative, the visionary, the sublime, the ridiculous, the eschatological (as with . . . Purgatory . . . [or] the Transmigration of Souls), the satirical, every detail of every single science or speculation, even every bit of gossip . . ."[26] We are indeed storytelling animals.

Student Learning:
Book Website
This Stop and Check activity can also be found on the book's website, where it's located under "Chapter Resources."

STOP AND CHECK

YOUR NARRATIVE PURPOSES

Of all the stories you've told within the last twenty-four-hour period, estimate the percentage you told for the following purposes:

_____ to inform
_____ to persuade
_____ to entertain

Do you think these percentages will change when you're working full time in your chosen career? If so, what kind(s) of stories will you probably tell more? What kind(s) will you tell less frequently? Discuss with a small group of your classmates how you will probably use narratives to do the following in your choice of career:

- Explain natural things
- Explain organizational or social realities
- Explain ultimate things
- Motivate people to believe or act in specific ways
- Provide a rationale not to believe or do certain things
- Present a vision of the future
- Entertain an audience

Guidelines for Narratives

Because you have been hearing and telling stories all your life, narrative elements are probably quite familiar. This section covers five important elements of a good story: purpose, characters, sequence, plot, and language.

Identify Your Purpose

Whether you give a narrative speech or tell a story as part of a larger speech, consider your purpose carefully. What function do you want the narrative to fulfill? Do you hope to inform, persuade, or entertain? Will you present a vision of possibilities that your audience has not yet considered? Remember that even when a story is mainly told for entertainment purposes, it should convey a lesson or point; otherwise, it's pointless.

Animals are sometimes the characters in stories, especially in children's tales where they inform, entertain, or persuade children to act in culturally appropriate ways.

Develop the Characters

It almost goes without saying that stories contain characters, whether real or imaginary. Fictional characters include animals or natural objects (like a talking tree) that are personified or given human traits. Clearly imaginary characters (dragons, talking trains, genies in bottles, and other fanciful characters) commonly convey important cultural values. For almost 2,500 years, Aesop's fables have used animals to communicate western cultural wisdom. Coyote stories, similarly, communicate the wisdom of various Native American groups. Depending on your purpose, realistic stories about people who act, move, speak, form relationships, and interact with others often may be more effective. To be believable, these characters will be motivated by distinctive personality traits, ethnic and religious backgrounds, educational experiences, and social backgrounds.

Develop the Plot

The **plot** is the challenge or conflict that tests the characters' assumptions, values, or actions. The way they respond to the challenges and the resulting changes in their lives form the plot, or action of the narrative. During this period of change, natural processes occur, such as growing up. The characters meet physical, psychological, and economic challenges. They have accidents; they begin and end relationships; they lose their possessions in a tragic manner, and so on. How they deal with these challenges provides the point of the story.

Select Vivid Language

Narrative speaking requires careful attention to language. Vivid word choices and details bring the story to life and let your listeners feel as if they are in the story. Detailed

plot the story's action

descriptions convey information, help create the scene, and provide a sense of authenticity by giving specific names, places, and times to listeners who psychologically prefer to set events in space and time.[27] Language includes details, constructed dialogue, and listing.

Provide Detailed Descriptions

Details are important in several places. When you first orient the audience to the plot, include enough descriptive material to give your audience a sense of the context. When you come to the key action, give listeners important details they can use to clearly understand the changes taking place within the characters. Finally, use a cluster of details in the climax of the story to drive home your main point.

The opening details function to set the story in a time and a place. Mythical stories often begin with the formulaic phrase, "Once upon a time in a faraway land." Listeners immediately pull up their mental "fairy tale schema" and listen to the story through that filter. Setting a true-life narrative in a specific place and time draws listeners into the world of the story. A student who starts her narrative, "When I was a junior in high school, I was enrolled in a very small private school in the mountain country of Montana," immediately activates her listeners' "personal experiences" schema. Regardless of the type of story, details about the setting help listeners place themselves psychologically in the story's space.

Take care to include just the right amount of detail. Certain details are vital, but others are irrelevant. First, you may have *too many details*. Just ask a child to describe a movie he saw, and he'll probably get bogged down in details. He might even miss the movie's point entirely, because children don't always separate *relevant* details from *interesting* ones. Details also can be inappropriate when they reveal more than listeners want to know. For instance, narrators who disclose intimate or shocking information sometimes cause listeners to focus on the details and miss the story's point. For these reasons, be rhetorically sensitive and evaluate details carefully in light of your specific audience, then edit out irrelevant or inappropriate material.

Construct Dialogue

Created or **constructed dialogue** between characters adds realism. By using vocal variety that conveys your characters' personalities and emotions, you further increase not only your involvement but also your listener's involvement in the story. For example, here is one way to report a scene:

> He told me to move my car, but I didn't, because I was only going to park for a moment. The next thing I knew, he threatened me.

Contrast the different effect it would have on your audience if you create a dialogue, then use different "voices," volume, and rate for each character, like this:

> He rolled down his car window and yelled, "Hey, kid, move your pile of junk!" I turned down my radio and explained through my open window, "I'll just be here a minute. I'm waiting for my mother." He jerked open his car door, stomped over to my car, leaned into my window and said slowly through clenched teeth, "I said, (pause) 'Move . . . your . . . pile . . . of . . . junk, *kid!*'"

As you can see, the scene with vivid, memorable dialogue is far more likely to involve listeners, helping them imagine themselves in the scene. By increasing their emotional involvement in the story, you keep their attention and have greater potential for communicating your point.

Create Lists

constructed dialogue
created conversation between characters that adds realism to a story

Lists increase rapport with an audience because they introduce specific areas of commonality with the storyteller. If you said "I packed my bags and checked twice to see if I had forgotten anything" you would get across the message, but adding specific details that are familiar to travelers enliven it, as this example illustrates:

As I packed for my trip to China, I was afraid I would forget something vital. I looked through my bag for the seventh time. Toothpaste? Check. Toothbrush? Check. Toilet paper? (I like being prepared.) Check. Deodorant? Yep. Yet something seemed to be missing — as I was to discover in an isolated village in Shanxi Province.

Again, the details involve listeners actively, inviting them to create mental images for each item you list. As you can see, the language you choose makes a difference. Because narratives appeal to emotions, it is vital that your audience become involved in the story, and word choices that increase audience involvement make your story more powerful and memorable.

STOP AND CHECK
ANALYZING A FOLKTALE

Do an Internet search for the exact phrase *folklore and mythology electronic texts*. Download a folktale from another culture. Compare the way it's constructed with the guidelines presented here. What is the purpose of the story? Are the characters real or imaginary? What details provide clues to their personality and motivations? What is the plot of the story? How does the storyteller incorporate vivid language, use of details, dialogue, and lists? How is the story similar to one that's typical of narratives from your culture? If it's different, tell how. Jot down your analysis and prepare to discuss your conclusions with a small group of your classmates.

**Student Learning:
Book Website**
This Stop and Check activity can also be found on the book's website, where it's located under "Chapter Resources."

Organizing Your Narrative Speech

Although the various elements in the speech could be arranged by importance, interest value, or recency,[28] the chronological pattern is probably used most frequently in narrative speeches. Storytellers typically begin at the beginning, lead to the middle section, and wrap up the action in the conclusion, bringing in relevant information that contributes to the overall main point and editing out irrelevant facts. Often, they state the point or moral of the story explicitly at the beginning, at the end, or both.

Another useful pattern, used by speech teachers for hundreds of years, is called the **exemplum**.[29] Exemplum speeches have five elements that follow one another, as Paul Lee's personal experience speech about immigrating to the U.S. illustrates:

1. *State a quotation or proverb.* "Ask not what your country can do for you; ask rather what you can do for your country."
2. *Identify and explain the author or source of the proverb or the quotation.* President John Kennedy, the thirty-fifth President of the United States, said this in his Inaugural Address.
3. *Rephrase the proverb in your own words.* In other words, instead of taking for granted the things our country has to offer, we should actively seek opportunities to improve our country.
4. *Tell a story that illustrates the quotation or proverb.* Immigrating to the United States from Hong Kong posed many challenges and hardships as the family learned a new language and customs. Eventually, family members proudly took the oath of citizenship—with all the rights and privileges that it brought—before a presiding judge who welcomed the new citizens with Kennedy's challenging words.
5. *Apply the quotation or proverb to the audience.* Everyone—both native-born and immigrants—should reflect on the privilege of being in the United States; each listener should think of some way to make the country better for all.

Select your narrative from personal experiences, from historical events, or from episodes in the life of someone else. Choose one that represents, illustrates, or explains

exemplum an organizational pattern in which a narrative is used to illustrate a quotation

something important to you, perhaps a turning point in your life. Identify a lesson or point to your story, then find a quotation that supports this point. You can use a common saying, such as "silence is golden," or you can consult sources of quotations (listed topically and by author) in the reference section of the library or online. As Chapter 8 points out, **www.bartleby.com/100/** is a good place to start. The book's website includes videos of two narrative speeches: Angela Bolin's "Overdose" and Gail Grobey's persuasive narrative. A transcript of Gail's speech appears at the end of this chapter.

Evaluating Narrative Reasoning

Stories aren't equally valuable, so we should test our narratives to see if they are sensible and worthy of being told. Some are true and honest; others are false, mistaken, or downright lies.[30] But how do we judge narratives? And when faced with competing stories, how do we weigh and decide which is best? To answer these questions, narrative theorists offer three major tests of narrative logic.[31]

1. Does the story have **narrative coherence**? That is, is it understandable? Does it hang together logically? Do the events in the story follow one another in a predictable sequence? Do the characters act and interact in ways that are probable, given their personalities and cultural backgrounds? Or do some things seem out of character or out of order?

2. Does the story truly or faithfully represent what you know about the world and the way it works? In other words, does the story make sense within the larger cultural framework? If it is a myth, folktale, or hypothetical story, does it contain important truths that demonstrate appropriate ways to live? Walter Fisher[32] terms this **narrative fidelity.**

3. Does the **narrative** have **merit**? Should it be told because the message is important or worthwhile? Does it draw conclusions or motivate people to behave in ways that result in ethical outcomes for individuals and for society as a whole? Does it serve as a cautionary tale? Before passing along a story, it is important to evaluate the desirability of doing so.

We weigh priorities and make ethical decisions when we choose whether or not to repeat a particular story. A narrative that creates problems for the individuals involved or their families can provide a good cautionary example, but the harm to innocent people may outweigh the benefits. Gossip, such as information about a political candidate's shaky marriage or the suicide attempt of a public figure's child, poses questions of narrative merit. If sensational details of the characters' private lives are merely entertaining, examine your motives. Why disclose them? However, if a story uncovers a public figure's character flaws or tendencies to behave badly; then it *might* be appropriate to tell.

Good stories aren't necessarily true—fiction does have its place. But stories that are blatantly false and result in harm are wrong to tell. History provides examples of leaders who spread lies with disastrous consequences. Here's one: In the Middle Ages, people circulated false narratives about Jews poisoning the water supply of villages, stories that resulted in the murder of many Jewish people and produced irreversible negative consequences on individuals and on society in general.

narrative coherence deciding if a narrative is understandable or sensible

narrative fidelity testing if the narrative faithfully represents how the world works

narrative merit testing whether or not a narrative is worth telling

Summary

In every society, narrative exists as a form of reasoning or sense making. Narratives both reflect and shape cultural beliefs and values, and hearing narratives from other cultures highlights commonalities and differences between groups. Narratives in all cultures function to inform, to persuade, and to entertain. Explanatory narratives provide answers for why and how things are the way they are. Persuasive narratives provide reasons for or against a belief or course of action. Visionary narratives help us see possibilities that we had not imagined before. Finally, some narratives are just plain fun, and we tell them for entertainment purposes.

Stories have five major elements: purpose, characters, sequence, plot, and language. Vivid language is especially important because it brings characters to life and makes the action more compelling, causing listeners to identify with more elements of the story.

Organize your story in a chronological pattern or use the exemplum pattern, an excellent pattern that begins with a quotation, provides information about the source, and paraphrases the saying. An illustrative story forms most of the speech, which concludes with a stated lesson or moral.

Some stories are better than others, but every good story should be coherent, it should have fidelity, meaning that it represents some aspect of the real world, and it should be worthy of being told. To evaluate a story's merit, consider its effect on society, its effect on individuals, and its overall truthfulness about life.

Student Learning: Book Website
Under "Chapter Resources," students will find several tools for reviewing the information in this chapter, including a "Tutorial Quiz." You can also have them email the results of this quiz to you as a participation or extra-credit activity.

STUDY AND REVIEW

The premium website for *Public Speaking* offers a broad range of resources that will help you better understand the material in this chapter, complete assignments, and succeed on tests. The website features

- ▶ Speech videos with critical viewing questions, various types of outlines, transcripts, and note cards
- ▶ Interactive practice activities, self quizzes, and a sample final exam

For more information about this text's electronic learning resources, consult your **Guide to Online Resources for Public Speaking** or visit http://communication.wadsworth.com/jaffe5.

KEY TERMS

The terms below are defined in the margins throughout this chapter. The book website also provides interactive flashcards and crossword puzzles to help you learn these terms and the concepts they represent.

homo narrans 272	constructed dialogue 280
applied storytelling 272	exemplum 281
storytelling 273	narrative coherence 282
deliberative speaking 275	narrative fidelity 282
rhetoric of possibility 277	narrative merit 282
plot 279	

Student Learning: Workbook
Students can also complete "Before You Take the Exam" in Chapter 15 of the Student Workbook to review this chapter.

APPLICATION AND CRITICAL THINKING EXERCISES

The exercises below are among the practice activities on the book's website.

1. Search InfoTrac College Edition for the words "healing AND storytelling." Read an article you find there and discuss it with a small group of your classmates.
2. What narratives do you use to explain the world of nature? The social world? Your family? Other groups to which you belong? The ultimate meanings in life? Do your stories ever clash with the narratives of others? If so, what do you do about these differences?

Instructor's Resource Manual
Advice on how to use these critical thinking exercises is presented in Chapter 15 of the *Instructor's Resource Manual* (available in print, online, and on the Multimedia Manager CD-ROM).

3. Share with a group of classmates a few examples of persuasive narratives you heard while you were growing up. In what ways were they intended to influence your behaviors? How successful were they?

4. In what settings have you heard inspiring life stories? Have you ever shared your personal saga of overcoming some challenge? If so, describe the occasion. Where might you give an inspirational personal story in the future? What would be your purpose?

5. Think of stories that you have only heard orally. Who are the "legends" in your family, your sports team, your religious group, living group, or university? What lessons do their stories provide? What values or actions do they help you remember and perpetuate?

6. Many speeches are given in narrative form; in others, an extended narrative takes up a significant part of the speech. Chief Joseph's speech in Appendix C is one example. Read through it and describe how he uses a story to drive home his point.

7. The exemplum pattern is useful in a variety of settings. With a small group of your classmates, sketch out themes and suggest the types of supporting narratives that would be appropriate on each of the following occasions:

   ▶ A sports award banquet
   ▶ A luncheon meeting of a club such as Rotary or Kiwanis
   ▶ A religious youth group meeting
   ▶ A scholarship presentation ceremony
   ▶ A Fourth of July celebration
   ▶ A keynote address to a conference focusing on issues relevant to female physicians

8. Go to the National Storytelling Festival's home page, **www.storytellingfestival.net**, and follow the link to Featured Tellers. Choose the three storytellers you'd most prefer to hear. Why those choices?

SPEECH VIDEO

Log on to the book's website to watch and critique Gail Grobey's narrative speech. A transcript of the speech appears below and is also available on the book's website.

STUDENT SPEECH WITH COMMENTARY

Gail gave this narrative speech in an argumentation class. Besides being a narrative speech, it's an example of invitational rhetoric (see Chapter 18); she invited her classmates, many of whom disagreed with her claim that spanking is wrong, to understand her perspective by telling this story.

SPANKING? THERE'S GOTTA BE A BETTER WAY
Gail Grobey

Gail puts a picture of Celeste on the table she's standing behind and introduces the characters, her

My daughter Celeste [displaying the photograph] has always been a rather precocious child. She's picked up all kinds of concepts and language from listening to her future-English-teacher mom talk and has learned how to apply them. When given the opportunity, she'll wax lyrical in her piping four-year-old voice at some length about the Joker's role as antagonist in *Batman* and how Robin functions as a foil or why the conflict between the villain and the hero is necessary. She's constantly telling me when I'm stressed about school or work or the mess in the kitchen, "Mom, just breathe. Just find your center and relax in it."

Yes, she's a precocious child, but this time let me place the emphasis on child. Her temper is fierce and daunting, like her mother's! She can get very physical in her anger, striking out destructively at anything she can get her hands on. She can also be manipulative (which is really more like her father)!

At times, my patience is driven to the very end, and so I can understand why some parents turn to spanking. There are times when there seems to be no other alternative, when I can't think of any other way to get through to this completely irrational being. And there are a lot of things about me that would make me the ideal spanking parent: my temper, my impatience, my obsessive need to control. And after all, I was a spanked child. But when she was born, and I saw that tiny body and the light in her eyes, I made a conscious commitment never to strike my child.

As she's grown, that commitment has been challenged. About a year ago, she pranced into my room chanting in the universal language of preschoolers, "Look what I found! You can't have it." I looked down and in her hand was a large, inviting, bright red pill with irresistible yellow writing on it. I recognized it at once as one of my mother's blood pressure pills, and quite naturally, my first impulse was to snatch it.

I also recognized, however, that she was looking for just such a reaction from me. She had lately begun establishing clear patterns of button-pushing. I would say, "Give it to me." To which she would naturally reply, "No!"

And so it would begin. She was prepared to throw and fully enjoy the temper tantrum that would inevitably follow and tax me to the end of my patience. I repressed my impulse to aggressively take command and instead, bent down on one knee and asked her with casual awe, "Wow. Where'd you find it?"

She eyed me suspiciously, backing up. She said, "On the kitchen floor. It's mine. I'm keeping it."

All I could think of was how easy it would be to tip her over the edge into a major fight. (The big ones always begin over something small and silly— me attempting to exercise control over something and her asserting that this is not acceptable. We both get lost in our rage.) It would have been so easy to just grab the pill and move into fight mode. But I held firm to creativity over violence.

"Oh, Celeste," I said, "thank you so much. You are a real hero. You found that dangerous pill and picked it up before the dogs could eat it and make themselves sick. You saved them! What a hero!"

The change on her face was instant. She voluntarily and proudly relinquished the pill and dashed off to tell her grandma what a noble deed she'd just done. I remember saying out loud, "Whew. That was close!" It seems like such a small thing, but I see it as representative of the greater whole.

It's one of my proudest moments as a parent: Celeste and I both walked away with the feeling that we had accomplished something important. She experienced a boost in self-esteem, and I ended up holding firm to my commitment and reinforcing to myself my belief that there is always an alternative way to deal with children, no matter how small the situation or problem. One never needs to resort to violence.

daughter Celeste and herself, using vivid details. Listeners have mental images of the child and her relationship to her mother early in the speech.

Because she knows her audience pretty much disagrees with her position, she shows that she understands their frustration and their desire to deal with children who are angry and obnoxious.

Here is the point of climax, and Gail again clusters vivid details that enliven the scene. Her use of constructed dialogue, delivered with the vocal variations that would actually occur in the scene, keep the audience's attention.

Celeste "frames" the issue in terms of ownership and control, and Gail tries to see things from her child's perspective.

Here is an excellent example of re-sourcement (see Chapter 18) in which Gail reframes the discovery of the pill as a safety issue.

Gail's narrative provides an excellent example that others can use as a model for nonviolent childrearing.

Choosing to tell a narrative, rather than building a case with examples, statistics, and other evidence, was probably more effective with her specific audience.

CHAPTER 16

INFORMATIVE SPEAKING

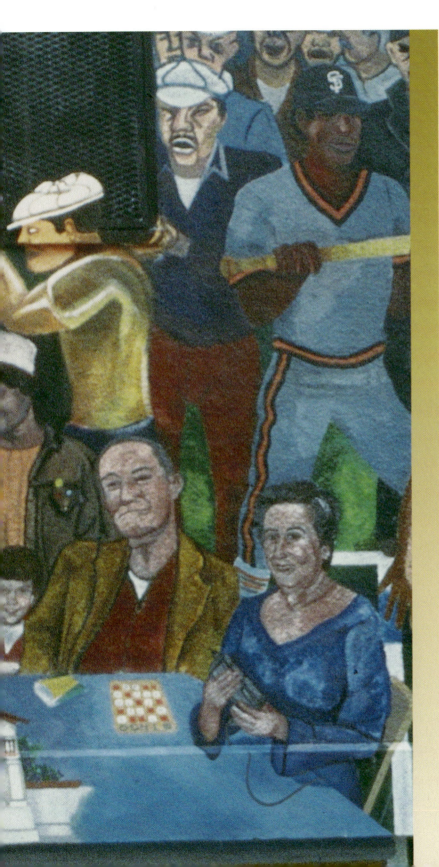

THIS CHAPTER WILL HELP YOU

▌ Describe the global importance of information

▌ Analyze an audience's knowledge of your subject

▌ Create several types of informative speeches including demonstrations and instructions, descriptions, reports, and explanations

▌ Use guidelines to make your informative speeches more effective

"Balance of Power" Mural © 1996 by Susan Kelk Cervantes, Juana Alicia, and Raul Martinez. (Mission Street Playground, Swimming Pool, Linda at 19th Street, SF, CA)

WALK INTO A thriving corporation and you will hear employees giving reports, providing instructions, demonstrating techniques and products, and updating their coworkers on the latest information related to their organization. Enter a school and you'll hear students and teachers making announcements, discussing facts, defining terms, and explaining complex concepts. Now, take a moment and picture yourself fifteen years down the road. Where are you working? What instructions or directions are vital to your success? What information will you give your coworkers or the public? What information will you need to be healthier, more productive, or happier? Informative speeches, the "speech to teach," are all around, as these examples show:

▶ A member of the student government reports a committee's findings about the possibility of bringing a well-known entertainer to campus.

▶ A nurse demonstrates how to wash a newborn to first-time fathers.

▶ A teen explains to younger students some strategies for saying no to sex.

▶ An accountant presents the annual audit to a client company's board of directors.

This chapter first examines the global importance of information. It then turns to audience analysis and distinguishes four levels of audience knowledge you should consider before you speak. Next, it describes several types of speeches, including demonstrations and instructions, descriptions, reports, and explanations, and includes skeletal outlines of speeches in these categories. General guidelines for informative speaking conclude the chapter.

CASE STUDY: BACK-UP SPEAKER AT THE SPRING FLING

Representatives from a variety of business ventures, even wind farms, can present informative speeches that draw positive attention to their enterprises.

Chapter-at-a-Glance
This chapter introduces students to informative speaking. It begins with examples of informative speaking and discusses the global importance of information. The chapter then moves to the first step in informative speaking: analyzing what the audience already knows about the subject. It describes strategies for presenting new, supplemental, and updated information and for countering misinformation. Next, several types of informative speeches are described—demonstrations and instructions, descriptions, reports, and explanations. The chapter ends with seven guidelines students can use to insure that their informative speeches are effective.

© Glen Allison/Getty Images

An article in InfoTrac College Edition reported that William Moore, the project manager of a planned 190-turbine wind farm in upstate New York, was invited to be the keynote speaker at a local Chamber of Commerce's "spring fling" dinner.

Moore knew that he was not the Chamber's first choice as speaker. In fact, a local newspaper announced that organizers really had wanted a local politician but he turned them down for the second year in a row, so they invited Moore instead. The Chamber director said, "We're looking forward to [Mr. Moore's speech]. This is a great project." He added, "We were just looking for someone who has a positive feel for the economy."[1]

In another InfoTrac College Edition article,[2] speech coach Victoria Chorbajian advises representatives of businesses or organizations to take up public speaking as a way to increase visibility for their enterprises. However, she urges them to educate or inform listeners on something of interest to the audience, rather than simply promote their ventures.

Questions for Discussion

▶ How might the wind farm project manager approach this speech assignment?

▶ How would you respond if you came into a speech situation knowing that you were not the organizers' first choice for speaker?

▶ How might Moore educate or inform his Chamber of Commerce audience about something of interest to them, given the circumstances of his speech?

▶ With a small group of your classmates, discuss ways that speakers who represent a career that interests you educate or inform the public.

Information Is Important Globally

We live in an **information age** in which more people, nationally and globally, have access to more information than ever before. Enormous industries exist to distribute information through print and electronic channels with data storage and cable linkages that connect televisions, telephones, and computers into **electronic superhighways.**[3] This daily bombardment with fragments of disconnected, irrelevant facts leaves many of us feeling that we are actually in an Over-Information Age,[4] where **information overload** is a burden, not a blessing.

For example, in one five-minute newscast, you can learn about marchers gathered at the White House, a bridge collapse in the Philippines, and a child abduction in Virginia—but do any of these facts affect you personally? What's really important, and what's trivial? What must you know to live better, and what's simply interesting or distracting?

Similarly, your listeners can feel overwhelmed with disparate facts and ideas unless you relate the material to their lives and help them integrate new information with old. When you do this successfully, you not only help listeners make sense of their world but also provide them with basic information they can use to make wise decisions.[5] A clear description or explanation of new developments in genetically modified foods, effective strategies for studying, or wind power as an renewable energy source can furnish meaningful information for various audiences.

Having access to information is so important that Article 19 of the Universal Declaration of Human Rights (1948) states:

> Everyone has the right to freedom of opinion and expression; this right includes freedom to hold opinions without interference and to seek and impart information and ideas through any media and regardless of frontiers.[6]

Article 19 recognizes the potential dangers of an **information imbalance,** where some people and groups have lots of information and others have very little. People kept in ignorance may lack fundamental understandings of the world. Democratic countries often try to adjust this imbalance; for example, during the Cold War, Radio Free Europe provided otherwise unavailable information to people living in Communist-controlled countries. Today, a number of governments attempt to restrict Internet access. North Korea is the most notorious; leader Kim Jong Il limits email privileges to society's elites, walling off most average citizens from free access to the Internet.[7]

In summary, information is a valuable resource or commodity. It's abundant in the U.S. and many countries; it's more restricted in other nations. Some groups and social classes have access to information essential to success and health; others have limited access to the same knowledge. Finally, some individuals know how to take advantage of the available information; others do not.[8] (You can find the entire U.N. declaration at **www.un.org/Overview/rights.html**.)

information age an era with vast amounts of available information

electronic superhighways television, telephones, and computers linked together through networks

information overload feeling overwhelmed by the sheer amount of available data

information imbalance some people or groups having very little access to information while others have it in abundance

Figure 16.1
Knowledge Bubbles
Early in your planning, assess your audience's current levels of knowledge about your topic and identify misconceptions or outdated information they may have. Doing so will help you devise strategies that will make your information more useful to your listeners.

Analyze Your Audience's Current Knowledge

Dwight saw an article in the *World Press Review* about harems. His curiosity was piqued because he knew little about harems, and the article confronted his stereotypes. Dwight assumed that his classmates were similarly misinformed, so he decided to provide accurate information. First, however, he first had to discover what the audience already knew and believed about harems so that he could adjust his speech accordingly.[9] Listeners may have no information, a minimum of information, forgotten or outdated information, or misinformation (see Figure 16.1). Each level of understanding calls for different strategies.

Presenting New Information

Some audiences will be unfamiliar with your subject; they've never even heard of it, so your information will be novel. Your task is to provide a basic overview of the topic. For instance, what do you know about music thanatology? Emmaline Pankhurst? The Vietnamese alphabet? I've heard speeches on each of these topics, and each speaker succeeded by following these guidelines:

1. Provide basic, introductory facts—the "who," "what," "when," "where," and "how" information.
2. Clearly define unfamiliar terminology and jargon.
3. Give detailed, vivid explanations and descriptions.
4. Make as many links as you can to the audience's knowledge by using literal and figurative analogies and by comparing and contrasting the concept with something familiar.

Presenting Supplemental Information

The great inventor Thomas Edison said, "We don't know a millionth of one percent about anything."[10] This means that listeners often have vague or superficial knowledge about a topic but lack detailed, in-depth understanding. They don't want a rehash of basic information; they want supplemental information. An audience somewhat familiar with Bono, the lead singer for U2, will be more impressed if you provide little-known information that gives additional insight into his character or his music. Another example: Most people learned in elementary school to select foods from several food groups, so presenting the major groups is redundant. However, audiences may lack information about specific nutritional elements such as nucleic acids. Use these guidelines with audiences whose information is limited:

1. Dig into your research sources to discover less familiar details and facts.
2. Go beyond the obvious; add in-depth descriptions, details, and explanations.

Narrow a broad topic and provide interesting and novel information about just one aspect of it. For example, explore only Bono's childhood or focus on his educational background instead of his musical career.

Presenting Review or Updated Information

Listeners once knew about your subject, but they've forgotten some or most of what they learned, or they lack current, updated information. Your speech can function as a review that refreshes the audience's memories, reinforces their knowledge, and keeps their information current. Reviews and updates are common in schools or job settings. For instance, students may have once studied the five canons of rhetoric, but they need to review them before taking the test; workers may have read or heard about privacy laws a decade ago, but a workshop on new regulations keeps them updated. With these audiences, you'll be more effective using these guidelines:

1. Review material by approaching the subject from different angles and different perspectives.
2. Be creative; use vivid supporting materials that capture and hold attention.
3. Use humor when appropriate, and strive to make the review interesting.
4. For both reviews and updates, present the most recent available information. Educator Dennis Mills[11] reports that our current proliferation of information results in 100 percent new knowledge every five years (at least in high-tech areas); consequently, what we learn can quickly become outdated. Overstated? Perhaps. But people who want to stay current must be lifelong learners.

Countering Misinformation

A third type of audience has misconceptions or misunderstandings that you can clarify by providing definitions and facts and by countering misinformation. For instance, the saying, "A dog is a human's best friend," is widely accepted in the United States. However, Stephen Budiansky[12] presents scientific evidence suggesting that dogs don't really adore their owners; instead, they fake devotion to manipulate humans. If this is true, many or most people in your audience misunderstand dog behavior!

In other examples, students from different ethnic backgrounds sometimes counter misconceptions about their culture, or politicians sometimes clarify policy positions that their opponents have distorted. When you counter misunderstandings, you are presenting material that is inconsistent or contradictory to what listeners "know," so consider the following:

1. Prepare for emotional responses—often negative ones. (Think about it. Who wants to hear that her beloved Fido is really a con artist?) Consequently, present the most credible facts you can find, and tone down the emotional aspect.
2. Look for information derived from scientific studies, especially quantification, when statistical or numerical support would be best.

3. Define your terms carefully; consider explaining the origin of specific words or ideas.
4. Counter negative prejudices against and stereotypes about a topic (such as a particular culture) by highlighting positive aspects of the subject.

In summary, the amount of information your audience brings to your speech should make a difference in the way you select and present meaningful information. By assessing listeners' knowledge about your subject in advance, you can more effectively prepare a speech that meets their need to know.

STOP AND CHECK

ANALYZE YOUR AUDIENCE'S KNOWLEDGE

To determine your audience's prior knowledge— or lack thereof— regarding your topic, complete the preparation form titled Assess the Knowledge Level of Your Audience, which is provided on the book's website. The form presents a series of questions for you to answer. (Refer to Chapter 5 if you need to construct a questionnaire to determine your audience's knowledge about your topic.)

Types of Informative Speeches

Informative speeches fall into several categories. Demonstrations and instructions, descriptions, reports, and explanations are some broad categories of informative speaking common in college classrooms and in many careers. This section gives specific guidelines for these types of speeches.

Doing Demonstrations and Providing Instructions

Instructions answer the question, "How do you do that?" On the day her company went public, Martha Stewart became a billionaire. What's her line of work? She demonstrates how to do things and creates instructional books and magazines. She's like thousands of teachers, coaches, and salespeople who both *show* and *tell* others how to do a procedure, how to use a specific object, or how to complete a task. Successful instructors understand and use several principles that can help you succeed in your "how-to" speeches. (Unfortunately, no one can guarantee that you'll earn millions!)

In **demonstration speeches,** you both show and explain how to do a process or how to use an item. The following tips will help you.

1. First, think through all the required stages or steps by asking the following questions: What comes first? What's absolutely essential? Which step is easiest? Which is hardest? What does the audience already know how to do? Where will the audience most likely be confused? Which step takes the most time? Which take practically no time at all?[13]
2. Next, work on speech content. Organize the essential steps sequentially, and concentrate on clarifying and simplifying those that may be difficult or confusing. Carefully preplan the environment to facilitate learning—this may mean your audience must move chairs or stand up and spread out around the room. Or you may have to furnish supplies if you want them to do the project along with you.
3. Plan your visual support. Ask yourself if actual objects are practical (see Chapter 12); if not, plan videotapes or other supplementary visuals. Then practice working with your props so you can use them and still maintain rapport with your audience.[14]

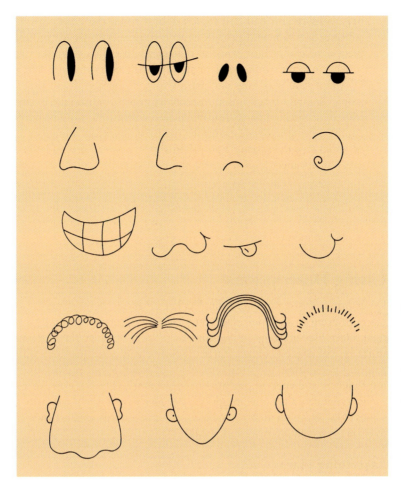

Figure 16.2
Cartoon Faces
For his speech on drawing cartoon faces, one speaker put a number of facial features on a transparency. He uncovered each row as he discussed the separate elements, and his listeners created personal cartoons, feature by feature, as he went along.

Visual aids are vital during some demonstrations. For example, if this speaker simply tried to describe how to create a cartoon face, he'd have surely failed! However, he drew cartoon features onto a transparency as shown in Figure 16.2, and then he uncovered lines of features as he progressed through his speech.

Instructor Resource:
PowerPoint
The *Multimedia Manager with Instructor Resources* CD-ROM includes a Power-Point slide of Figure 16.2.

> Specific Purpose: To inform my audience about simple features they can draw to create a cartoon character.
>
> Central Idea: By drawing simple shapes for eyes, noses, mouths, hair, and facial outlines, almost anyone can easily draw a cartoon.
>
>   I. First, select the eyes.
>   II. Then draw a nose.
> III. Choose a mouth.
> IV. Add hair.
>   V. Outline your character's face.

Before he started, he had each student take out a pencil or pen and a blank sheet of paper. (He'd brought along some blank paper and extra pencils, just in case.) Then, as he spoke, each student created a cartoon.

4. Time the entire process. If it takes too long to accomplish in the allotted time, a better strategy is to demonstrate the process and provide handouts with step-by-step instructions for listeners to take home. One student failed in her attempt to have each listener fold an origami crane in a seven-minute speech; twenty-two minutes later,

her audience still had half-folded cranes when the class period ran out! Demonstrating the crane and providing each student with an instructional handout and a piece of origami paper would have been a better plan. Another strategy for a lengthy process is to prepare several versions of the item, stopping each at a different point of completion. Cooking and art instructors commonly do this. The cook, for example, begins a complicated casserole, but rather than take twenty minutes on each step, he sets aside a partly finished pan, reaches for a second pan that contains a more complete version of the casserole and then proceeds. Similarly, a sculptor shows an essential step in creating a pot; then she leaves it to dry and takes up a pot she prepared in advance that's ready for the next step.

Not all "how-to" speeches require a demonstration. You can give tips on topics like how to resolve conflict, listen more effectively, select a caterer for a major celebration, or manage time effectively. In these cases, you focus on instructions or pointers that will help audience members accomplish the goal.

Giving Descriptions

Descriptions answer the question, "What's it like?" Before you can describe an object, place, or event to someone else, you must first observe it carefully. Look for details and then select vivid imagery and sensory words that help people understand the look, taste, smell, or feel of your subject. An art museum guide, for example, walks her group from painting to painting, pointing out details of color, form, and texture within each painting that her audience might miss at first glance. Descriptions of places, objects, and events range from personal to global. Because listeners are generally more interested in topics close to their daily lives in location, time, and relevance, explicitly relate each topic to their perceived interests and needs.

Describing Places

People often seek information about places. A prospective student visiting a campus, for example, wants to know how it is laid out, so a college guide describes campus sites as he shows the visitor around. Descriptions of different countries or places such as national parks or tourist attractions similarly attract audiences, and travel agents or park rangers are just two types of professionals who describe places.

In describing a place, provide vivid details so your listeners can form precise images. Take advantage of visual aids including maps, drawings, slides, brochures, or enlarged photographs, and consider spatial or topical organizational patterns. Here are the main points of a speech about Ha Noi, given by a student from Vietnam: [15]

Specific Purpose: To inform my audience about Ha Noi and how it communicates.

Central Idea: Ha Noi is a thousand-year-old city, and its many scenic attractions reveal a lot about Vietnamese culture.

    I. *Ho Hoan Kiem,* Sword Lake, reminds us of the holy sword the gods gave to protect our country.

    II. *Van Mieu— Quoc Tu Giam,* the Temple of Literature, is Vietnam's first university, which was built in 1076.

    III. *Lang Bac,* Ho Chi Minh's Mausoleum, honors "Uncle Ho," who brought independence to Vietnam.

    IV. *Chua Mot Cot,* the One Pillar Pagoda, which honors the Buddhist goddess of mercy, was built in 1049.

If you are searching for an international topic, consider places such as buildings (the Taj Mahal), geographical features (the Sahara desert), or sites (Vatican City).

Describing Objects

Descriptions of objects, including natural objects (glaciers), human constructions (the Vietnam War Memorial), huge things (the planet Jupiter), or microscopic matter (carbohydrates), are common. Students have described inanimate (wind generators) or animate (brown recluse spiders) objects by providing information such as their origin, how they are made, identifying characteristics, how they work, how they're used, and so on.

Topic choices range from personal to international. On the personal level, students describe body features such as skin or fingernails. They talk about campus objects like a historical tree or a memorial plaque and explain cultural artifacts such as the Golden Gate Bridge, CD players, and guitars. International topics have included the Great Wall of China and London's Big Ben.

Describing Events

Events or occurrences range from personal (birthday customs), community (local festivals), national (holidays), to international (the bombing of Hiroshima). Chronological, narrative, and topical organizational patterns are most common. The first two patterns work well for step-by-step events such as the bombing of Hiroshima. The topical pattern is useful for happenings that consist of several different components (birthday customs, for instance). Here is an example of major subtopics for a speech describing a sporting event.

> Specific Purpose: To inform my audience about different rodeo events.
>
> Central Idea: Rodeos are athletic contests with people and animals competing in a variety of events.
>
> > I. Bull riding
> > II. Barrel racing
> > III. Bronco busting
> > IV. Calf roping

When you describe events in concrete detail and vivid language, your listeners can place themselves at the happening; your speech lets them participate vicariously.

Presenting Reports

Reports answer the question, "What have we learned about this subject?" Reporting is a global business that employs millions; around the clock, reporters collect and organize news and information about people and issues of public interest. For example, investigative reporters search for answers to questions such as "What are scientists learning about the causes of attention deficit disorder?" And campus reporters pass along conclusions reached by university task forces. In classrooms and boardrooms, here and abroad, people give reports. This section discusses two common topic areas: people and issues.

Buildings such as Chua Mot Cot, the One Pillar Pagoda, or cities such as Ha Noi, Vietnam, are good topics for informative speeches.

© Charles Marden Fitch/SuperStock

Reporting about People

What individuals have shaped our world? What did they accomplish? How did they live? You can answer such questions by providing sketches of influential historical or contemporary characters. Biographical reports can be about philosophers (Descartes), military men and women (Mongol warriors, Bodiecia), artists (Mary Cassatt), writers (Toni Morrison), and so on. Don't overlook villains (Machiavelli) as well as heroes (Mother Teresa) for biographical subjects.

Generally, chronological, topical, or narrative patterns best fit a biographical report. Fei Fei's topical outline has two major points: (1) Confucius's (*Kongfuzi*) life and (2) his influence. She then uses chronological sub-points to develop her first section—Confucius's life.

Specific Purpose: To inform my audience of the life and ideas of the Chinese philosopher whose teachings influence more than a billion people globally.

Central Idea: Confucius, who lived in China about 2,500 years ago, developed a life-affirming philosophy that has influenced many Asian cultures.

I. The evidence for his life is scanty, based mostly on the *Analects* (sayings) of Confucius.
  A. He was probably born in the feudal state of Lu, in northern China.
  B. He was concerned about war and bad rulers, and he began to gather disciples.
  C. He journeyed as a wandering scholar.
  D. He may have been a minister of state at one time.
II. Confucius's influence is widespread.
  A. His teaching method focused on growth in moral judgment and self-realization as well as skills.
  B. The concepts of *li* (maintaining proper relationships and rituals) and *jen* (benevolent, humanitarian attitudes) permeate many Asian cultures.
  C. The five vital relationships include: king-subject, father-son, husband-wife, older-younger brother, and friend-friend.

Speeches about groups such as thugs, the Mafia, Australian aborigines, or Motown musicians are also interesting. Here are subtopics from a student speech on the Amish that is organized topically:

Specific Purpose: To inform my audience about the Amish by describing their beliefs and explaining challenges facing their group.

Central Idea: The Amish are a religious group with written and unwritten rules for living that are being challenged by education and tourism.

I. The Amish people
  A. Number and location
  B. Historical information
II. Amish beliefs
  A. Written ordinances—Dortrecht Confession of Faith (1632)
  B. Unwritten rules of local congregations—*Ordnung*
III. Challenges to Amish culture
  A. Education and teacher certification
  B. Tourism attention

As you develop your major points, keep in mind your audience's questions: "Why should I listen to a speech about this person or group?" "What impact has this subject had on society?" "How does knowing about this individual or group tie into my concerns?" Answering these questions will help your listeners better understand the relevance of the person or group. For links to biographical information on thousands of individuals, both contemporary and historical, visit **www.libraryspot.com/biographies/**.

Reporting about Issues

Newspapers and magazines are good sources for issues currently being discussed in our communities, our nation, and our world. We deliberate about wars, welfare reform, immigration policies, medical marijuana, local issues, and campus problems that are complex and controversial. Here are a few examples of questions regarding issues:

▶ What have we learned about the effects of marijuana on the body?
▶ What do we know about the effectiveness of various programs for rehabilitating juvenile offenders?
▶ What issues does each side emphasize in their support of or opposition to taxing sales over the Internet?

Think of your speech as an investigative report, where you research the facts surrounding an issue and then present your findings. Your major purpose is to provide your listeners with a factual foundation they can use in formulating their own conclusions. Consequently, reports do not advocate one position or another. (However, you may decide to follow up a report with a persuasive speech on the same topic.)

Periodicals databases like InfoTrac College Edition can help you access up-to-date newspapers and magazines like the *New York Times*, *Time*, and *Newsweek*. Such sources provide answers to questions about current events like these: What exactly is the issue? What are the current beliefs or theories commonly held about the issue? What is the extent of the problem (how many people does it affect)? How did this situation develop? What solutions are proposed? What are the arguments on both sides of the issue? Generally, pro-con, cause-effect, problem-solution(s), narrative, and topical patterns are effective for investigative reports. The following is a pro-con outline for a speech on legalizing small amounts of marijuana. It includes major points taken from articles found on InfoTrac College Edition.

Specific Purpose: To inform my audience about supporters' and opponents' views about legalizing small amounts of marijuana.

Central Idea: There are several arguments both for and against the legalization of up to three ounces of marijuana for private use and possession.

I. Many argue for the legalization of marijuana.
   A. Former Republican Governor Gary Johnson of New Mexico called the war on drugs ineffective; legalizing marijuana would make it a controlled substance that the government could tax and regulate.
   B. A lot of tax money is wasted on arrests for minor drug possessions.
   C. According to Jack Herer's book *The Emperor Wears No Clothes,* the hemp plant is good for food, fuel, and fiber, and those who oppose legalization give inaccurate "facts."
   D. Some religious groups, like Rastafarians, use marijuana in their religious practices.
   E. Decriminalizing "soft" drugs like marijuana hasn't led to an increase in hard drug usage in the Netherlands.
II. In contrast, many people support current drug laws.
   A. Marijuana is a Schedule I drug, whose negative physical effects include impaired memory, inability to perform complex tasks, and a depressed immune system.
   B. Eighty-five percent of people in the United States disapprove of legalizing drugs.
   C. The campaign of misinformation, including the "medical marijuana" hoax, about legalizing drugs is financed by billionaire George Soros.
   D. Smoking marijuana for medical reasons is unnecessary; the active ingredient, TCH, has long been available under the name "marinol," which controls quality and dosage.
   E. Vermont State Senator Susan Streetser says legalizing marijuana sends the wrong message to children, and a major study shows that marijuana is a gateway drug for school-aged experimenters.

F. In 2005, the Supreme Court ruled that medical marijuana patients who violate federal drug laws can be prosecuted, even if medical marijuana is legal in their home states.

Issues can be personal (eating disorders), campus (parking problems), local (potholes), national (teens and guns), or global (free trade) in scope. Many global decisions, such as what to do with nuclear waste, have broad implications. Others, although less significant, are related to larger problems. For example, cosmetic surgery on teenaged women is linked to issues of women's rights and stereotypes of female beauty.

DIVERSITY IN PRACTICE
INFORMATIVE SPEAKING IN AFRICA

THROUGHOUT PARTS OF AFRICA, public health educators give people information that may save their lives. For example, women in central Africa empower one another with facts they can use to protect themselves against sexually transmitted diseases. In remote areas of Kenya, where less than 10 percent of tribal people can read and televisions and radios are not available, a few individuals travel from their villages to larger urban centers, where they learn news of the world to bring back to their villages. At other times, members of the community come together to advise newlyweds by giving the young couple practical "how-to" information they can use to build an effective marriage.[16]

"Knowledge is power" could be the motto of these educators, who provide health and child care information to mothers in Kenya.

© Sean Sprague/PANOS Pictures

Explaining Concepts

The explanatory or **expository speech** is known more simply as the "speech to teach." Expository speakers set forth, disclose, unmask, or explain an idea in detail.[17] Science and history teachers regularly define terms and explain concepts; parents also answer the endless "whys" of four-year-olds with explanations. Good expository speakers can identify the hurdles listeners are likely to encounter in their attempt to comprehend the concept. They then plan ways to overcome those barriers and make meanings clear.

expository speech the "speech to teach" that sets forth, discloses, unmasks, or explains an idea in detail so that listeners understand it

Defining Terms

Definitions answer the questions "What is it?" or "What does it mean?" Definition speeches are common in educational institutions and workplaces—for example, a philosophy professor defines *justice*, a speech professor clarifies the concept of *confirmation* as it's used in that academic discipline, and an employer defines *sexual harassment* for new employees. Inspirational speakers also define words: a priest defines *peace making*; a commencement speaker defines *integrity*; a coach defines *commitment*. In short, we see people act in ways we classify as just or as sexual harassment, but we can neither see nor touch justice or harassment; defining those terms helps us as a society to discriminate between appropriate and inappropriate behaviors.

One effective organizational pattern for a speech of definition [18] presents first the denotative and then the connotative meaning of a word. (Chapter 13 discusses denotation and connotation in detail.)

1. **Denotative Meaning:** Focus on the *denotation* of the word as found in reference books such as thesauruses or etymological dictionaries. The *Oxford English Dictionary* or another unabridged dictionary provides the most thorough definitions. Books in a specific academic discipline show how scholars in that field define the term; for example, the definition of *confirmation* found in a dictionary is not identical to the definition you'd find in a book on interpersonal communication. Develop the denotative point of your speech by selecting some of the following ideas:

    ▶ Provide synonyms and antonyms that are familiar to your audience.
    ▶ Explain the use or function of something you're defining.
    ▶ Give the etymology of the word. What's its historical source? How has the concept developed over time?
    ▶ Compare an unknown concept or item to one that your audience already knows.

    For example, "an Allen wrench" might be unfamiliar to some listeners, but "a wrench that looks like a hockey stick" or "an L-shaped wrench" helps them select the specific tool, given a line-up of wrenches. [19]

2. **Connotative Meaning:** Focus on *connotative* meanings by using realistic life experiences as creatively as you can. Here, draw from whatever you can think of that will add emotional elements to your explanation.

    ▶ Relate a personal experience that demonstrates the idea.
    ▶ Quote other people telling what the term means to them.
    ▶ Tell a narrative or give a series of short examples that illustrate the concept.
    ▶ Refer to an exemplar—a person or thing that exemplifies the term.
    ▶ Connect the term to a familiar political, social, or moral issue.

    For example, in the denotative section of her student speech on *destiny*, Terez Czapp first provided the dictionary definition and then explained the etymology of the word like this:

    > The Roman saying *Destinatum est mihi* meant "I have made up my mind." In Rome, *destiny* meant a decision was fixed or determined. Later the word reappeared in both Old and Middle French in the feminine form *destiné*. Finally, from the Middle English word *destinee,* we get the modern form of the word.

    Next, a transition led to the connotative section, which consisted of an extended example of a near-fatal car wreck that devastated her family.

    > However, it isn't the word's etymological history that is meaningful to me. You see, destiny is a depressing reminder of a car accident. . . .

    Terez concluded with the following quotation by William Jennings Bryan:

    > Destiny is not a matter of chance; it is a matter of choice. It is not a thing to be waited for; it is a thing to be achieved.

Including both denotative and connotative meanings provided a fuller picture of the concept of *destiny*.

Giving Explanations

Think of explanations as translations: You take a complex or information-dense concept and put it into common words and images that make it understandable. Explanations commonly answer questions about processes ("How does it work?") or about concepts. ("What's the theory behind that?" or "Why?")

How does a telephone work? How do Koreans greet one another? To answer questions like these, you'll describe stages, ordered sequences, or procedures involved in processes, both natural and cultural. You can explain how something is done (bungee jumping, resolving conflict), how things work (elevators, cuckoo clocks, microwave ovens), or how they're made (mountain bikes, a pair of shoes). Not surprisingly, chronological patterns are common, as this outline of Marietta's speech about international adoption demonstrates.

Specific Purpose: To inform my audience about the process of international adoption.

Central Idea: The four parts of the adoption process are application, selection, child arrival, and postplacement.

I. Application: the family and a social worker evaluate the adoptive home.
II. Selection: the agency provides pictures and histories of available children.
III. Child arrival: the child arrives with an "Orphan Visa."
IV. Postplacement: for up to a year, the family and a social worker evaluate the placement, after which time the adoption is finalized.

Concepts also provide good, but challenging, topics. What do we know about intelligence? What's in the mind of a serial killer? What is Johari's Window? These questions relate to concepts or abstractions—the mental principles, theories, and ideas we form to explain both natural and social realities. For example, although we may not know for certain what causes some people to kill repeatedly, we formulate theories or explanations for serial killers' behaviors.

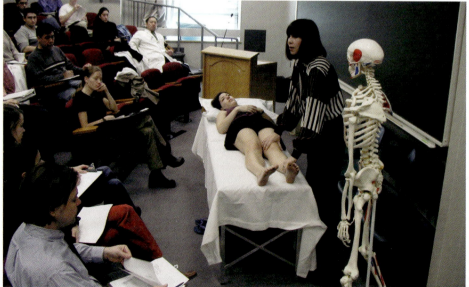

Every speaker who explains complex concepts or processes faces the challenge of making the subject understandable, relevant, and interesting.

Because concepts are sometimes difficult to define and explain, you must make the complex ideas and theories understandable and relevant to your listeners. Here are some guidelines for speeches about concepts:

▶ Simplify complex ideas by breaking them down into their component parts. For example, subdivide intelligence into categories that include social intelligence, spatial intelligence, and musical intelligence.[20]

▶ Carefully define your terminology, avoiding technical jargon. Exactly what falls into the category of spatial intelligence? Use examples that clarify this component of intelligence, or show the items from the tests that measure spatial intelligence.

▶ Clarify confusing details by using analogies, both figurative and literal, to compare the concept to something that listeners already understand. In this case, you might compare spatial intelligence to running a maze.

▶ Use detailed examples of concrete situations that illustrate the actions of people who test high in various kinds of intelligence.

The following example demonstrates major points for an explanatory outline about African music:

Specific Purpose: To inform my audience about important characteristics of sub-Saharan African music.[21]

Central Idea: Sub-Saharan African music features several major variations in pitch and rhythm.

    I. The music is interlocking; pitches and beats fit into the spaces between other parts.

   II. It features dense, overlapping textures and buzz sounds.

  III. It is cyclical and open-ended, with repeated melodies and patterns.

  IV. Complex rhythms may feature double and triple patterns.

   V. The music features a core foundation, often rhythmic, with improvised elaborations.

We sometimes clash over theories, concepts, and ideas. For instance, exactly what does compassionate conservatism mean? People's ideas differ. What caused the dinosaurs to become extinct? Theories vary. What constitutes a date rape? Few people give the same answer. The purpose of explanatory speaking is not to argue for one definition or another but to clarify the concept, sometimes by comparing and contrasting differing definitions and theories regarding it.

Guidelines for Informative Speaking

A common complaint about informational speaking is that it's not interesting.[22] To keep your audience's attention and to be both understandable and relevant, remember these guidelines for producing comprehensible messages:[23]

1. **Do an "obstacle analysis" of the audience.** Think from your audience's perspective. Identify the parts of the message that are hard to understand, and then work on specific ways to make those sections clear. Next, identify internal barriers that might prevent your audience from learning your material. Choosing a scientific topic for an audience who thinks science is difficult and boring or challenging an audience's current misconceptions about a subject they hold dear are examples of topics that meet with psychological resistance. Plan ways to deal with each obstacle.[24]

2. **Organize the material carefully.** Be kind to your listeners by stating your major points clearly and building in transition statements and signposts such as "next" and "in addition" that enable them to identify the flow of ideas. Use structures such as

lists, comparisons-contrasts, or cause-effect patterns. Provide internal previews and summaries along with connectives that show how your material is linked—words and phrases such as *because, for example, therefore,* and *as a result* (see Chapter 10). **Discourse consistency** also helps. This means you use a repetitive style such as beginning every section with a question or alliterating or rhyming your main points throughout the entire speech.[25]

3. **Personalize your material for your audience.** Help listeners see the connection between your topic and their experiences, goals, beliefs, and actions. When they see the information as relevant to their personal lives, they're more likely to listen and learn effectively.

4. **Compare the known to the unknown.** Be audience centered. Start with what's familiar to your listeners and then build on this foundation, showing similarities and differences between what they already know and your topic.

5. **Choose your vocabulary carefully.** You have probably heard lectures or reports that were full of technical information given in incomprehensible jargon that left you more confused than before. To avoid bewildering your audience, define your terms and explain them in everyday, concrete images. Avoid trigger words with negative connotations that might set off negative reactions in your audience.

6. **Build in repetition and redundancy. Repetition** means that you say the same thing more than once. **Redundancy** means that you repeat the same *idea* several times, but you develop it somewhat differently each time. Phrases such as *in other words* or *put simply* are ways to build in redundancy. Repeat and redefine the critical parts of the message to reinforce these crucial points in your listeners' minds.[26]

7. **Strive to be interesting.** In your preparation, occasionally try to distance yourself from the speech and hear it as if it were being delivered by someone else. Do you find yourself drifting off? If so, where? Search for ways to enliven your factual material. Providing examples or detailed descriptions, for instance, engages your audience dialogically, because descriptions and examples invite your listeners to form mental images as you talk.

If you follow these guidelines, you will increase your listeners' motivation and interest in the topic. And your careful attention to details will help them understand the material more clearly.

STOP AND CHECK

DO AN OBSTACLE ANALYSIS AND STRATEGIC PLAN

As you prepare your speech, ask yourself the following questions:

▶ What concepts or steps may be obstacles for this audience?
▶ What psychological barriers are likely?
▶ What is the best way to overcome these obstacles?
▶ Are the steps in order? Are my main ideas clear?
▶ Where might I use alliteration, rhyming, or another form of discourse consistency?
▶ Where are my signposts and transitions? Should I use more?
▶ How, specifically, have I connected this material to the lives of my classmates?
▶ What does my audience already know that I'm building upon?
▶ Is my language clear?
▶ Where should I repeat an idea verbatim?
▶ Which ideas have I presented in a number of different ways?
▶ Would I be interested in listening to my speech if someone else were giving it? If not, how could I make it more interesting?

---

discourse consistency using a repetitive style such as alliteration of main points throughout the speech

repetition saying the same thing more than once

redundancy repeating the same idea more than once, but developing it differently each time

Summary

The ability to give and receive information has always been empowering; this is especially so in the Information Age. Those who lack information do not have the basic knowledge they need to perform competently in complex societies. As a result, a variety of people in a variety of settings give informative speeches. Their goals are to present new information, to supplement what's already known, to review or update material, or to correct misinformation.

There are several categories for informative speaking that answer listeners' questions such as "How do you do that?" or "What does that mean?" These include demonstrations and instructions, descriptions, reports, and explanations.

Finally, remember seven keys to informative speaking. Do an obstacle analysis that identifies elements within the topic or within the listeners that might prove to be barriers, and then work to overcome those obstacles. Organize the speech, and provide links that connect the material. Relate your topic to your listeners, and make vocabulary choices that clarify your ideas. Think of creative ways to present your information, and throughout your talk, tie abstract concepts to concrete experiences that are familiar to your listeners. Finally, include repetition and redundancy to reinforce the critical points of the message.

Student Learning: Workbook
To review this chapter, students can complete "Before You Take the Exam" in Chapter 16 of the *Student Workbook*.

Student Learning: Book Website
Under "Chapter Resources," students will find several tools for reviewing the information in this chapter, including a "Tutorial Quiz." You can also have them email you the results of this quiz as a participation or extra-credit activity.

STUDY AND REVIEW

The premium website for *Public Speaking* offers a broad range of resources that will help you better understand the material in this chapter, complete assignments, and succeed on tests. The website features

- Speech videos with critical viewing questions, various types of outlines, transcripts, and note cards
- Interactive practice activities, self quizzes, and a sample final exam

For more information about this text's electronic learning resources, consult your **Guide to Online Resources for Public Speaking** or visit http://communication.wadsworth.com/jaffe5.

KEY TERMS

The terms below are defined in the margins throughout this chapter. The book website also provides interactive flashcards and crossword puzzles to help you learn these terms and the concepts they represent.

Information Age 289
electronic superhighways 289
information overload 289
information imbalance 289
demonstration speech 292

expository speech 298
discourse consistency 302
repetition 302
redundancy 302

Instructor's Resource Manual
The *Instructor's Resource Manual* provides suggestions on how to use these critical thinking exercises.

APPLICATION AND CRITICAL THINKING EXERCISES

The exercises below are among the practice activities on the book's website.

1. For your classroom speech, consider a topic from the field of communication. Look for information that could help your classmates communicate better. For example, topics such as how to work through conflict, how to become independent from parents, or how to successfully navigate the early stages of a romantic relationship are

useful in interpersonal communication. Speeches about makeovers or the types of touch address nonverbal communication. For mass communication, you could explain how camera angles communicate meaning or how other countries regulate the Internet.

2. Within a small group in your classroom, discuss implications of the unequal distribution of information. For example: What if only some societies knew how to make sophisticated weaponry? What if only some cultures had information that benefits them economically? What if only some individuals or groups knew their cultural history? What if only women had access to health information and men were excluded? What if only people under thirty-five years of age, with incomes over $80,000 a year, knew how to use computers to advantage?

3. Working with a small group, generate a list of speech topics for each of these categories. The audience:

   ▶ Is totally unfamiliar with the topic (medieval manuscripts, an unfamiliar composer).
   ▶ Has some knowledge of the topic, but not a lot (Singapore, the history of MTV).
   ▶ Has studied the topic, but needs a review (the five canons of rhetoric).
   ▶ Has outdated information (an updated computer program).
   ▶ Has major misconceptions regarding the topics (tarantulas, the Roma culture— also known as gypsies).

   Select a subject in two different categories and discuss how you would modify your speech plans to accomplish your general purpose with each topic.

4. In a small group, think of creative ways to present an informative speech that reviews audience knowledge about one of these familiar topics:

   ▶ Good nutrition
   ▶ What to do in case of fire
   ▶ How to read a textbook

5. Descriptions can be speeches in themselves, or good descriptions can be elements of larger speeches. To improve your descriptive skills, identify a place, an object, or an event and then make a list of vivid words that provide information about the look, the feel, the smell, the taste, or the sound of the item or place. Share your description with a small group of your classmates.

6. Search the Internet for the exact term *informative speaking*. Read the material on a site from either a speech team (also called a forensics team) or from a university professor that provides additional information about speaking to inform.

SPEECH VIDEO

Log on to the book's website to watch and critique Josh Valentine's speech "The *Dun Dun* Drum." An outline of the speech is available here and on the book's website.

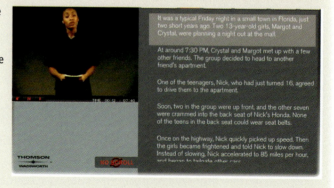

Student Outline with Commentary

Josh's assignment was to research, outline, and deliver an informative speech using a visual aid. He chose the *dun dun* drum, and created a multimedia presentation that showed pictures of the drum and played actual recordings downloaded from the Internet for this one-time use. His audience was unfamiliar with the topic.

THE *DUN DUN* DRUM
Joshua Valentine

General Purpose: To inform
Specific Purpose: To inform my audience about the *dun dun* (which most will not have
                     heard of), and to describe how and why it is used.
Central Idea: The *dun dun* is an African drum with an interesting history that is used
                     both musically and linguistically.

Introduction

I. Imagine that your friend asks you what you did over the weekend, but instead of using words, your friend beats a drum.
II. You will probably never have such an encounter, but in some cultures, music is used for purposes that are different from those we are accustomed to.
   A. *Webster's Dictionary* defines language as "any system of symbols, sounds, or gestures used for communication."
   B. Our culture does not have instrumental sounds that represent English words, but in other cultures around the world, sounds have meaning.
III. I have been playing percussion since junior high, and I first learned about the *dun dun* while attending a percussion workshop two years ago.
IV. Today, I will explain the history of the *dun dun* as well as its linguistic use and its musical use.

Body

I. The Nigerian talking drum, *dun dun* (pronounced *doon-doon*), actually does talk, in the Yoruba language.
   [Display photograph of *dun dun* drum, downloaded and used with permission from http://media.dickinson.edu/gallery/Sect5.html]
   A. The *dun dun* originated during the Oyo Empire of Yoruba-land in the fifteenth century AD for the purpose of worship.
   B. Drums are constructed from trees located near roads where many people pass, which allows the tree to hear human speech (DeSilva).
   C. The Yoruba language is easily communicated on the *dun dun*.
      1. Yoruba is a tonal language.
      2. Yoruba speakers use three basic pitches or tones, connected by glides, as an essential element of pronunciation (How bata drums talk . . .).
         a. Listen to this sound clip and try to identify the three main tones.
         [Play a sound clip downloaded for one-time use from the Internet.]
         b. If you have a sharp ear, you may also be able to pick out some slides essential to the Yoruba language.
      3. Melody is the basis for the Yoruba language since the same word pronounced with a different melody means something different.

Josh, a drummer, takes his topic from his interest in music. He chooses to explain a cultural variation.

Because Josh's audience is unfamiliar with the topic, he must provide basic, introductory information about the drums.

The visual helps his listeners "see" what he is talking about.

Audio support lets audience members "hear" what is complicated to explain in words alone.

D. The *dun dun* functions by changing the tension of two skin heads using the leather straps that hold the heads in place.
[Point out the straps on the PowerPoint slide]

II. The *dun dun* was originally created to communicate.

A. The Yoruba from southwestern Nigeria have used drums for spiritual communication throughout their history.
[Show carved drum downloaded from **www.hamillgallery.com. . . YorubaDrum01 .html**]

The photograph of the carving on a drum suggests its use in worship.

1. The *dun dun* was originally created as a tool for worship of the gods.
2. Songs and hymns of praise were created entirely on *dun dun* drums and are still recited today.
3. Listen to the intensity of this spiritual worship song played on talking drums.
[Play example, downloaded for one-time use from the Internet from **www .world-beats.com/instruments/dundun.htm**]

Point II.B provides details that listeners can relate to.

B. The Yoruba also use drums for social communication.
1. The *dun dun* has been a part of day-to-day casual conversation.
a. "A master drummer can maintain a regular monologue on a talking drum, saying 'hi' to different people, cracking jokes, and telling stories" (Plunkett).
b. *Dun dun* drummers are often heard speaking the names of friends and family on their drums as a greeting and sign of respect.

C. The *dun dun*'s secondary, yet most obvious, use is as a musical instrument.
1. It became a musical instrument because of its use in worship.
a. At first it was used mainly to communicate ideas, but since worship in the Yoruba culture is a corporate activity, people began coming together and music on the *dun dun* was born.
b. Religious songs are still recited today, although often only for their musical value.

2. Even everyday speech becomes song when the Yoruba use the *dun dun*.
a. The word *kabo,* which means *welcome,* is only a two-syllable word, so a more common phrase "spoken" on a *dun dun* is, "Welcome, we are happy that you arrived safely" (Drum Talk, Ltd.).
b. "Speech" on the *dun dun* is always made rhythmic, even when the spoken word would not be rhythmic.

Josh continues to provide factual information in this, his "speech to teach."

3. The *dun dun*'s use as a musical instrument has spread far beyond Nigeria.
a. Next to the *djembe,* the *dun dun* is the most well-known and recognizable African drum used in America.
b. "[It] fares well in jazz blues, R&B, rock and roll, reggae, classical music, even choral music" (Awe).
c. This clip comes from a song by African American musician Francis Awe.
[Play sample clip downloaded from the Internet from **www.nitade.com/html/ cd1.html**]

A final clip acts as a summary of the speech body.

Conclusion

I. Whether in language or in song, the *dun dun*'s sound is always unusually beautiful.
II. Today, we have seen the origins of the Nigerian talking drum (*dun dun*), its uses as a linguistic tool, and its uses as a musical instrument.
III. So next time you hear music as simple as a beating drum, you might remember that the drummer may be communicating much more than you think.

References

Awe, Francis. (1999). *Talking drum drum clinic by Francis Awe.* Retrieved March 20, 2002, from **www.after- science.com/awe/clinic.html**

BataDrum.com. (2002). How Bata drums talk and what they say. In *Understanding the purpose and meaning behind the rhythms*. Retrieved March 21, 2002, from **www.batadrums.com/understanding_rhythms/talk.htm**

DeSilva, Tamara. (1997). Lying at the crossroads of everything: Towards a social history of the African drum. *Research, writing, and culture: The best undergraduate thesis essays, 1998-2000 (No. 2)*. Retrieved March 20, 2002, from **www.artic.edu/saic/programs/depts/undergrad/Best_Thesis_Essay.pdf**

Drum Talk Ltd. (2000). *Background information*. Retrieved March 20, 2002, from **www.drumtalk.co.uk/drum _background.html**

Plunkett, A. (2002). Nigeria (Africa) Dun dun. *World Beats*. Retrieved March 21, 2002, from **www.world-beats.com/ instruments/dundun.htm**

CHAPTER 17

PERSUASIVE SPEAKING

THIS CHAPTER WILL HELP YOU

▶ Find a subject for a persuasive speech

▶ Decide on a claim of fact, definition, value, or policy

▶ Narrow the focus of your speech in light of your listeners' beliefs, attitudes, actions, and values

▶ Identify organizational patterns for your speeches, including problem-solution, direct method, comparative advantages, criteria satisfaction, negative method, and Monroe's Motivated Sequence

Detail from "Desaparecidos Pero no Olvidados" Mural
© 1999 by Carlos Madriz, Josh Short, and Mabel Negrette.
(Balmy Alley, Balmy at 24th Street, SF, CA)

N ANCIENT GREECE, Aristotle identified three areas of a healthy democracy in which rhetoric, the art of persuasion, functioned: law courts, governing assemblies, and ceremonial and ritual occasions that reinforce cultural beliefs and values.[1] Today, speakers continue to present divergent viewpoints in courtrooms and legislatures, and ceremonial speakers still reinforce and emphasize cultural values on ritual occasions. We are fortunate to live in a culture that places value on citizen participation and free speech. (In contrast, the role of persuasive speaking varies cross-culturally, as the Diversity in Practice feature below illustrates.)

This chapter focuses specifically on persuasive purposes and types of speeches. It provides information about selecting a topic and narrowing your speaking purpose, building on your listeners' resources of belief and behavior, values, and attitudes. It closes with several organizational patterns that are especially effective for persuasive speeches.

CASE STUDY: A TEENAGE ACTIVIST

© Mary Clay/Getty Images

When Brittany Farrer was four years old, her father was killed by a drunk driver. Growing up fatherless made her so passionate about alcohol abuse that she joined alcohol awareness clubs and committees and began to devote her spare time to doing research about this legal drug, focusing eventually on its effects on teens. It was only natural that she chose the topic for her classroom speech. However, because students commonly hear "don't drink and drive" or "underage drinking is illegal," Brittany decided to focus more uniquely on a solution that looked at corporate responsibility, not just individual responsibility. She concentrated on alcohol ads targeted at young people. She argued that they contributed to underage drinking and that they should be restricted on television and on billboards.

When is a frog not a frog? When it's the spokes-frog for a beer advertisement targeted toward youth.

Questions for Discussion

▶ Make a list of people who passionately argue for a specific point of view. What impetus compelled each person to speak out?
▶ How does a speaker's passion influence the persuasiveness of her message?
▶ When, if ever, have you spoken out on behalf of something you cared deeply about? If you've never done so, why not?
▶ What effect does a hearing unique slant on the topic have on you as a listener?

(An outline of Brittany's speech is printed at the end of this chapter and available on the book website, where you can also watch a video of Brittany delivering it.)

DIVERSITY IN PRACTICE
PERSUASION IN OTHER CULTURES

DIFFERENT CULTURES place different emphasis on persuasion as a means of publicly discussing issues and coming to reasoned conclusions. Here are a few historical and contemporary examples.

Rome

When Rome was a republic, orators publicly debated issues that affected the entire community. However, emperors such as Nero and Caligula eventually gained power. They made binding decisions and pronouncements regardless of Senate disapproval; dissenters often met with torture or death. In one notorious incident, the emperor Caligula mocked the Senate's power by making his horse a senator!

The Soviet Union

When the Communists ruled the Soviet Union, party leaders made decisions and spoke for the people. They strongly discouraged citizens from dissenting from the "party line," often by using coercive force that could land a nonconformist in a Siberian work camp.

Athabaskan Speakers

Speakers in this oral-based society of native Alaskans think it rude to explicitly state the conclusions they want listeners to draw. It is enough for them to present facts as they understand them, and let audience members draw their own conclusions. This emphasis on information instead of persuasion distinguishes their norms from those found in this text.[2]

International Negotiation

Many cultures recognize the benefits of argumentation in their dealings with representatives of the West. Because of trade negotiations, United Nations deliberations, peace talks, and other international exchanges, speakers with different persuasive traditions sometimes adopt aspects of Western rhetoric to communicate with international audiences. For example, Takakazu Kuriyama, former Japanese Ambassador to the United States, studied at Amherst College (Massachusetts) and Lawrence University (Wisconsin). He intentionally incorporated various Western rhetorical strategies when speaking with members of Congress and U.S. media representatives.[3]

Select Your Persuasive Topic

Choosing a persuasive topic can be challenging. Even if you have some ideas for subjects, you may not know how to focus clearly on one specific purpose and one central idea. This section will describe ways you can find a subject. Then, it will explain how you can select your claim and formulate your central idea.

Finding Your Subject

It is important to find a need that you can address by speaking out, so select a topic that is significant to others and matters to you. It is especially hard to influence others if you yourself are neutral or apathetic. Begin by considering your strong beliefs and feelings; then ask yourself what would improve society in general or people's lives in particular. Here are several categories of questions you can ask yourself as you search for an appropriate topic.[4]

▶ My strong beliefs: What ideas and issues would I argue for? What ideas and issues would I argue against?

▶ My strong feelings: What makes me angry? What are my pet peeves? What arouses my pity? What makes me sad? What do I fear?

Chapter-At-A-Glance
This is the first of two chapters on persuasive speaking; it introduces the basics of persuasive speaking and the next chapter examines persuasive reasoning methods. This chapter begins with advice on how to find a subject for a persuasive speech. Next is a discussion of claims of fact, definition, value, and policy. Then, suggestions are provided for narrowing a topic based on listener beliefs, attitudes, and actions related to the topic. The chapter ends with a discussion of the organizational patterns that are commonly associated with persuasive speaking.

Instructor Resource: *Art and Strategy of Service-Learning Presentations*
Chapter 5 of this handbook offers information on developing persuasive service-learning presentations, including information on resources for evidence. Having students develop such a presentation is an excellent speaking assignment.

Teaching Tip
Saskatchewan Education offers tools for teaching persuasive communication, including learning objectives, a brief overview, suggested activities, and two templates for assessing persuasive speeches: http://www.sasked.gov.sk.ca/docs/comm20/mod6.html.

Classroom Discussion/Activity
Have students provide examples of persuasion in their everyday lives. Ask them to suggest differences between informative and persuasive speaking.

Student Learning: Workbook
Activity 17.1, "Finding a Topic You Care About," can help students choose a topic for a persuasive speech.

▶ My social ideals: What changes would I like to see in society? What current problems or conditions could improve if we believe there is a problem, that there are solutions, and that we can be part of those solutions? Are there any causes for which I would sign a petition or join a protest?

▶ My personal ideals: What can make life more meaningful for others and for me? What activities will expand our horizons? What improves our health? What leads to more fulfilling personal relationships?

Classroom topics have included censorship, high insurance rates, downloading music from the Internet, affordable housing, international child sponsorship programs, the joys of skydiving, learning another language, and so on. Like Brittany's topic of limiting alcohol ads, classroom speech topics often reflect strong beliefs and feelings about issues related to social or personal needs.

✓ **STOP AND CHECK**

SELECT YOUR TOPIC

Fold a piece of paper into fourths, and label each quarter with one of the following categories:

▶ My strong beliefs
▶ My strong feelings
▶ My social ideals
▶ My personal ideals

Next, make a list of possible topics within each section.

Now consider your classroom audience. Circle topics in each section that would be appropriate for this particular group.

Analyze the circled topics, and put an X by those you could discuss within the allotted time.

Finally, select the best topic, given your audience and the time constraints.

Making Persuasive Claims

Selecting your subject is only the first step. Next, ask yourself what claim you want to make. A **claim** is an assertion that is disputable or open to challenge—a conclusion or generalization that some people won't accept, a statement that requires some sort of evidence or backing to be believed. We commonly make four types of claims: fact, definition, value, and policy.

Factual Claims

Here you argue what exists or does not exist, what has led to a current situation, or what will or will not happen; we assess the validity of these claims using terms such as *true* or *false, correct* or *incorrect, yes* or *no.* Three types of **factual claims** are common:

1. *Debatable points* are things that either are or are not true, that did or did not happen (for example, there is life on other planets; Lee Harvey Oswald acted alone to assassinate President Kennedy; angels exist)

2. *Causal relationships* argue that a particular phenomenon is the result of something that preceded it and led to it (for example, secondhand smoke causes health problems in pets; alcohol ads lead to underage drinking; aliens create crop circles)

3. *Predictions* contend that something will happen in the future (for example, a particular stock will gain in value; a deadly strain of flu is inevitable; the Mariners will win the World Series this year)

claim an assertion that's disputable or open to challenge

factual claim argument about existence, causation, or predictions

All these claims generate differences of opinion. Is there life on other planets? Science fiction writers may think so, but no one really knows for sure. If there are space aliens, did they create crop circles? Nobody can prove they did. What, if anything, links smoking to disease in pets? Or alcohol ads to teenage drinking? Studies often find correlations between two things, but correlation is not synonymous with causation. That is, two things may appear together, but this does not necessarily mean that one leads to the other.

Finally, claims about the future are open to debate. People lose huge sums of money in the stock market when their predictions prove wrong. Epidemics may be prevented. And, of course, arguments about sports teams fuel many a conversation.

Definition or Classification Claims

A woman shoots a man. How should she be tried? The answer depends on the category prosecutors decide fits the crime: Was the killing *premeditated murder?* Was it unpremeditated *homicide?* Was it *self-defense?* Was she *insane*, incapable of making responsible decisions? The classification of the crime leads to different charges and different sentencing possibilities.

Claims of **definition** or **classification** are necessary when we must decide what kind of entity or phenomenon we have, in other words, when we must categorize it. For example, people argue over definitions of *pornography*, of *anti-Semitic*, of *family*, of *cruel and unusual punishment*. Because the definitions they eventually select influence the policies they propose, it is important to define terminology early in the discussion of issues. First, set the parameters of the category and then show why the specific entity fits into that category. The abortion issue is a good example. It is so contentious partly because people classify or categorize the fetus differently. Someone who defines an embryo as a *person* (deserving the rights accorded to persons) from the point of conception will think of an eight-celled embryo differently than one who believes a fetus is a *person* only after brain waves are present (usually about six weeks into a pregnancy). Still others classify the fetus as a *person* only when it is capable of living outside the womb. The accepted definition of *personhood* influences the kinds of decisions considered proper regarding abortion, frozen embryos, and related concerns.

Value Claims

When you judge or evaluate something using terms such as *right* or *wrong* (it's morally *wrong* for the U.S. to have hungry children), *good* or *better* or *best* (that restaurant serves the city's *best* chili), *beautiful* or *ugly* (hybrid cars are *ugly*), you're making a **value claim.** Here is a value claim: "It's unfair for airlines to charge obese persons for two seats instead of one." Other examples include "It's better to have loved and lost than never to have loved at all" and "Environmental protection is more important than economic development." Value conflicts are hard to resolve without agreement on the **criteria,** or standards, for deciding whether something is right or wrong, fair or unfair, humane or inhumane.

Consider a movie you liked and your friend thought was a waste of time. Why did you reach different conclusions about its merit? Because you each had different criteria for judging a movie. Let's say your friend's criteria include romance, beginning-to-end action, and stunning visual effects, which this movie lacked. However, you like movies only when the characters are realistic and the plot is unpredictable, and this one met your standards. You can argue for hours about the merits of the movie, but unless one (or both) of you adjusts your criteria, you'll never agree.

Policy Claims

These claims consider whether individuals or groups should act, and, if so, how they should proceed. In short, **policy claims** often deal with problems and solutions,

definition or classification claim determining which category an item belongs in

value claim argument about right or wrong, moral or immoral, beautiful or ugly

criteria the standards used for making evaluations or judgments

policy claim argument about the need or the plan for taking action

Teaching Tip
For examples of policy claims, visit the History Channel's audio archive of great speeches from politics and government at http://www .historychannel.com/ speeches/poligovt1.html. All URLs mentioned in the text are available as live, regularly maintained links on the book's website, located in the "Chapter Resources" list under "Web Links."

assessed by terms such as *should* and *would*. Two major types of policy arguments are common:

▶ **Arguments against the *status quo*** (a Latin phrase that means *the existing state of affairs*) are arguments for change, whether in policies or individual behaviors. (Congress should adopt a flat tax system; you should write your senator and urge a vote on the flat tax.)

▶ **Arguments supporting the *status quo*** are arguments for the current situation and against change. (The university should not raise tuition; the current sales tax rate is adequate.)

For an example from the field of education, many reformers believe that education within the United States needs improvement, and they argue against the status quo by first identifying problem areas and then proposing solutions that will truly improve schools and be workable. Various reformers argue for better teacher training, for smaller classes, or for vouchers as ways to solve some of the problems.

In short, within a single topic area, you can argue facts, show how an issue should be defined or classified, defend a value question, or formulate a policy to solve a problem related to the topic. Whatever you decide on as your major claim will be the tentative formulation of your thesis statement.

Let's say you decide to speak about ocean pollution—specifically, dumping garbage in the ocean. You have the option of focusing on facts, definitions, values, or policies surrounding the issue, as this table illustrates.

Claim		Tentative Thesis Statement
Fact	Argue a debatable point	The amount of garbage dumped in our oceans is not excessive.
	Attempt to prove a cause-effect relationship	Dumping waste products in the ocean poses health risks to seaboard residents.
	Make a prediction	If we do not stop dumping so much garbage in the ocean, our beaches will become too contaminated to use.
Definition	Clarify denotative meaning or classification of a term	Dumped garbage falls into the category of Non-Point Source (NPS) pollution or "people pollution."
Value	Argue something is right or wrong, good or bad, beautiful or ugly	It is wrong to dump garbage in the ocean.
Policy	Propose a policy change	We should stop dumping garbage in ocean waters.
	Propose a behavioral change	Write your representative and voice your concern about garbage being dumped in ocean waters.
	Argue against a policy change	There is no good reason to stop disposing of garbage in oceans.

In summary, select your speech subject from topics and issues that concern you, at the personal to the international level. Then, tentatively formulate your central idea by deciding if you want to argue a factual claim, a definition or classification claim, a value claim, or a policy claim.

status quo a Latin phrase that means "the existing state of affairs"

Student Learning: Book Website
This Stop and Check activity can also be found on the book's website, where it's located under "Chapter Resources."

STOP AND CHECK

MAKE FACT, DEFINITION, VALUE, AND POLICY CLAIMS

To better understand that discussions surrounding a controversial topic contain a mixture of factual, value, and policy claims, work alone or with a small group of classmates and choose a controversial topic such as euthanasia, gay marriage, affirmative action, environmental protection, or sex education. Then write out a factual claim, a value claim, a definition, and a policy claim relating to your topic. Afterward, share your claims with the class as a whole.

▶ Write a factual claim dealing with a debatable fact, causation, or prediction.
▶ Define an essential term.
▶ Assess questions of good or bad, and develop criteria for a decision.
▶ Decide whether or not the status quo needs to be changed, and frame your policy claim accordingly.

Narrow Your Persuasive Purpose

Although your general purpose will be to persuade, narrow it more specifically in light of what your listeners already know and do, how they feel, and what they value. Remember that a single speech may touch on multiple claims. For instance, while you try *to convince* your listeners about hazards of dumping garbage in the ocean—focusing on factual claims—you may also be *reinforcing* their health-related values and their current attitudes against pollution.

This section will present a number of ideas you can use when you concentrate on beliefs and actions, values, or attitudes. (Chapter 18 provides additional information on creating persuasive appeals.)

Focus on Beliefs and Actions

What we accept as true affects how we act. Our beliefs and actions, in turn, spring out of our values and attitudes. To illustrate, you spend time studying because you believe your hard work actually benefits your learning and your grades. You value education and dislike wasting your tuition dollars, and you have a positive attitude toward getting a college degree. Your combination of beliefs, values, and attitudes leads you to schedule time for reading textbooks, working on class projects, and joining study groups. Figure 17.1 shows some possible combinations of belief and action that you should consider as you narrow your speech focus.

Unconvinced

Unconvinced audience members neither believe your claim nor act on it. Take a topic like acupuncture. Some listeners know nothing about it; others have some information, but they don't believe it will help them. Still others have misconceptions about what this Chinese medical treatment entails. They all need enough evidence **to convince** them to believe your factual claims before you ask them to act. The following general guidelines are useful when listeners are unconvinced:

▶ Begin with logical appeals. Build a factual case carefully, using only evidence that passes the test for credible supporting material.
▶ Prove your competence by being knowledgeable about the facts. Further, show respect for your listeners' intelligence and divergent beliefs.
▶ Use comparatively fewer emotional appeals.

to convince a persuasive purpose that targets audience beliefs

	Don't Believe	Believe
Don't Act	unconvinced	unmotivated, unfocused
Act	inconsistent	consistent

Figure 17.1

Sample Belief and Action Combinations
Your audience members approach your topic with various combinations of beliefs and actions.

Inconsistency between belief and action is one of the best motivators for change. For example, these people may know that binge drinking is harmful, but they still go on binges. Highlighting this dissonance is a good way to persuade them to make some effort to moderate their alcohol consumption.

apathy indifference due to lack of motivation

cognitive dissonance theory theory that humans seek stability or equilibrium; when faced with inconsistency they seek psychological balance that may motivate them to change in order to be consistent

dissonance inconsistency or clash

Unmotivated or Unfocused

Some audiences are already convinced by what they know about your subject. However, they fail to act on their beliefs due to **apathy** or indifference (unmotivated listeners) or lack of specific know-how (unfocused listeners). Topics such as donating blood or improving cardiovascular fitness are in this category. Your purpose here is *to actuate*, or move listeners to behave in ways consistent with their beliefs, using two different persuasive strategies.

▶ When your audience is unmotivated, provide good reasons to act. Use emotional appeals to show that what you propose will fulfill their needs and satisfy them emotionally.
▶ When they lack focus, provide a detailed plan that spells out specific steps they can take to implement your proposals.

In both instances, show listeners that you have their best interests in mind as you appeal for action.

Inconsistent

Often we hold contradictory beliefs, or we behave in ways that are inconsistent with our ideals. Leon Festinger[5] developed the **cognitive dissonance theory** to explain the resulting inconsistency or **dissonance** we experience. Humans, like other living organisms, seek balance or equilibrium. When challenged with inconsistency, we seek to return to a balanced psychological state. When our foundational beliefs are undermined or directly challenged, we typically experience discomfort until we either reinforce our faltering beliefs or make some adjustments to accommodate the challenge to our belief systems. Inconsistency between actions and beliefs is one of the best motivators for change. For example, if you become disillusioned with your job, it is easier to persuade you to consult an employment counselor than if you love everything about your current workplace.

With inconsistent audiences, either strengthen or reinforce wavering beliefs or persuade listeners to modify their actions to match their beliefs. Here are a few specific things to do when your listeners' actions and beliefs are out of sync.

▶ Support faltering beliefs by concentrating on logical appeals, using as much persuasive evidence as you can muster to help them resolve their doubts. Include emotional appeals as well, giving listeners reasons to *want* to strengthen their wavering beliefs.
▶ When you hope behaviors will change, appeal to emotions such as honesty and sincerity. Use narratives or testimonials that exemplify how you or someone else changed in a similar situation.

For additional information, do an Internet search for "cognitive dissonance theory" and read a couple of hits that have .edu in their URL.

Consistent

Even when people act consistently with their beliefs, they may need encouragement to "keep on keeping on." Consistent audiences are common in service clubs, religious organizations, and at political rallies. Here, your narrowed purpose is to reinforce both their beliefs and actions by following these guidelines.

> Help listeners maintain a positive attitude about their accomplishments. Use examples and testimony that illustrate how their efforts are making a difference in the world.
> Relate personally to their fundamental beliefs and values.

Throughout this section, we have explored ways that audience beliefs and actions influence both your persuasive purposes and the methods you use to present your ideas. Although you will use a variety of appeals in every speech, each type of audience requires somewhat different emphases and strategies.

Focusing on Values

As noted earlier, value claims contend that something should be judged or evaluated as moral or immoral, beautiful or ugly, right or wrong, important or insignificant, and so on. Here are two value claims: (1) embryonic stem cell research is wrong; (2) finding cures for people who are now living is more important than preserving an embryo. The first makes a judgment about an issue; the second argues that both values are important, but one supersedes the other.

To make an evaluation, first establish the criteria or standards on which to judge the issue by answering questions such as these:

> How do we make and apply judgments regarding this issue?
> What criteria do we use?
> Where do these criteria come from?
> Why should we accept these sources?

When listeners accept your criteria, it's easier for them to accept your evaluation. However, value questions are often conflict laden, for the standards used to make value judgments are sometimes contested.

For a variety of reasons, value judgments within a single audience may vary so widely that some judge a topic as unethical whereas others consider it highly ethical. Furthermore, because values are assumptions about what is good, value questions often generate deeply held emotional responses. It is nearly impossible to move listeners from judging a topic as unethical to evaluating it as highly ethical because of a single speech, but here are some tips for arguing value claims:

> Establish the criteria you are using to make your evaluation.
> Use emotional appeals such as examples that help listeners identify with the issue and link it to related values that you can agree upon (such as fairness or freedom).
> Appeal to authority if your audience accepts your source as authoritative. (See Chapter 8.) Some audiences will be moved by appeals to cultural traditions, words of poets, philosophers, scientists, or scriptures; others will discount those same authorities.

Keisha Walkes's speech, outlined in Appendix C and available on the book website, argues that Barbara Jordan is worthy of being named "Woman of the Century." Some criteria she identifies are authenticity, integrity, initiative, courage, and the ability to motivate others.

Focusing on Attitudes

Generations of scholars have explored how we become influenced or persuaded to believe or act in certain ways. Many recent persuasion-related studies focus on **attitudes,** which,

Instructor Resource: PowerPoint
The *Multimedia Manager with Instructor Resources* CD-ROM includes a Power-Point slide of Figure 17.1.

Instructor's Resource Manual
For more information on theories of persuasion, see Research Note 17.1, "Theories of Persuasion," in the *Instructor's Resource Manual.*

Video of Keisha Walkes delivering her speech is also available on the book website.

attitudes complex mental states that involve beliefs, emotions, and actions

according to the Princeton University Cognitive Science website, are complex mental states "involving beliefs and feelings and values and dispositions to act in certain ways."[6]

One theory, the **Theory of Reasoned Action** (TRA),[7] links behavioral intentions with attitudes, subjective norms, and perceived behavioral control. It assumes that we are rational and that we systematically weigh the costs and benefits of acting on the information we have, given an opportunity to do so.[8] According to this theory:

▸ *Attitudes* are our positive or negative evaluations of the behavior in question; they include both a mental and an emotional component. Typically, we measure attitudes along a scale ranging from strong agreement to strong disagreement. (See Chapter 5.)

▸ *Subjective norms* are our perceptions of what the people who are important to us think we should do.

▸ *Perceived behavioral control* is our opinion about our ability to accomplish the behavior.

These three factors influence our intentions to act, although our attitudes generally carry more weight. For instance, let's say a speaker urges listeners to donate blood, and she wants them to perceive that this is something they can easily do. Consequently, in addition to motivational appeals, she includes specific information about the Bloodmobile's presence on campus. One audience member reasons like this:

> I think I'll donate blood this afternoon (intention) at the Bloodmobile on campus (opportunity). I dislike needles (negative attitude/cost), but I like the overall idea of helping others more (positive attitude/benefits). My friends and family think donating blood is a good thing (subjective norms), and they'd admire me for donating (benefits). Therefore, sign me up.

In contrast, some listeners might respond another way:

> I don't intend to donate blood any time in the near future (intention). I hate needles (negative attitude/cost) and I do a lot of other things to help people. None of my friends or family cares a bit (subjective norms) if I visit the Bloodmobile (opportunity). So don't ask again.

 (You can read more about TRA by searching the Internet or looking on InfoTrac College Edition for "theory AND reasoned AND action.")

In general, the following guidelines will help you plan effective speeches to influence attitudes:

▸ Strengthen positive attitudes about your topic by using examples, connotative words, and appeals to needs and values that evoke emotional responses. Establish common ground throughout (see Chapter 18).

▸ With uninformed audiences, present factual information early so listeners have a basis to form an opinion. Then use emotional appeals to create either a positive or negative attitude toward the topic.

▸ When you face listeners who are neutral toward your claim, ask why. Do they lack information? Are they apathetic? If they are uninformed, present factual information early so listeners have a basis for an opinion. Then use emotional appeals to create either a positive or negative attitude toward the topic. With apathetic audiences, use emotional appeals by linking the topic to listeners in as many ways as you can, and appeal to values such as fairness and justice.

▸ When your audience is mildly different from you, approach the discussion directly. Use objective data to make a clear case; present the positive facets of your subject; and make links to personal and community values your audience accepts. This way, although they might still disagree with you, they can understand why you hold your position.

Theory of Reasoned Action theory that links behavioral intentions with attitudes, subjective norms, and perceived behavioral control; assumes we rationally weigh costs and benefits of acting

▶ When your listeners are negative toward your proposal because they are attached to the status quo, rethink your options. With mildly or moderately negative audiences, try to lessen the negative so listeners can see positive aspects of your proposal. If they're strongly opposed, you face a hostile audience. So set modest goals and aim for small attitudinal changes. Clearly present your points so that they will at least understand how you came to your conclusions.

▶ With audiences that reject your proposals, approach the subject indirectly by establishing common ground on which you can all agree. For instance, begin with a statement with which everyone agrees, and explain why there is agreement. Then make a statement that most would accept, and explain why this is so. Move gradually to the point about which they disagree. By this time, they will have already seen that they agree with you on many points, and as a result, they may be less negative toward your ideas.[9]

Generally, attitudes change incrementally, meaning that listeners change gradually. Each new encounter with the subject may bring about a slight change, but eventually, the small changes can add up.

Perhaps the most distressing speaking situation arises when your audience is hostile toward you personally. Then, it's important to emphasize common ground between yourself and your listeners. Barbara Bush faced hostility when she spoke at Wellesley College's graduation ceremonies. The class wanted a different speaker, not a woman whose fame was linked to her husband. Mrs. Bush used humor to turn a negative situation into a positive one. (Her address is printed in Appendix C and available on the book website, where you can also watch it on video.)

Although we have discussed beliefs and actions, attitudes, and values separately, they are, in fact, intertwined. Keep this in mind as you analyze your audience, select the specific purpose for your speech, and choose supporting material that will be persuasive.

STOP AND CHECK

ADAPT TO THE AUDIENCE'S ATTITUDE

Analyze the following public speaking situation: An anthropology major prepares a speech on government funding for archaeological digs. Her claim is that the study of archaeology is important enough to receive government funding because knowledge of other human cultures helps us to better understand our own.

Divide into three groups within the classroom. Each group will discuss how the speaker should prepare for one of the following audiences:

1. A group of anthropology majors who agree with her and are highly positive toward her topic.
2. An audience that knows nothing about anthropology but expresses concern about how their tax money is spent.
3. Listeners who consider archaeology to be a waste of time.

Questions
1. How will the speaker analyze the particular audience?
2. What purpose should she select for that group?
3. What specific strategies will she use to make her points?
4. What kinds of reasoning and evidence should she use?
5. What should she emphasize, and why?

Choose a Persuasive Pattern

After you analyze your audience's positions regarding your issue, look for an organizational pattern that will best communicate your ideas. This section presents several common persuasive patterns.

Problem-Solution Pattern

The problem-solution pattern (Chapter 9) is common for both informative and persuasive speaking. Informative speakers try to increase the audience's understanding of the issue and the proposed solution or solutions. Persuasive speakers aim to convince or to advocate for a specific policy. When the intent is to convince listeners that there is indeed a problem, the outline looks like this:

Specific Purpose: To persuade my audience that there are too many air disasters but the problem can be solved by concentrating efforts in three areas.

Thesis Statement: Global air traffic has too many disasters and near-disasters that could be minimized by working to eliminate the sources of the problems.

  I. There are too many air disasters and near-disasters around the globe.
  - A. The problem involves near-misses and crashes.
    1. The problem is extensive (statistics).
    2. This has negative implications for travelers.
  - B. There are several causes of this problem.
    1. There are communication problems between crews and air traffic controllers.
    2. Weather is a consideration.
    3. Mechanical and maintenance failures cause disasters.
  II. The problem can be minimized.
  - A. Airplanes should be more carefully inspected and maintained.
  - B. Both crew members and air traffic controllers should continue to receive on-the-job training in communication and in understanding the effects of weather.
  - C. Engineers and researchers should continue to develop state-of-the-art equipment to prevent some of these disasters.

When you argue for a particular solution, a good method is to present several possible solutions first and then advocate or argue for the best one. This adds a third point to the outline.

  I. Problem and need
  II. Possible solutions
  III. The one best solution

This is how a more complete outline looks:

Specific Purpose: To persuade my audience that incineration is the best solution to the problem of medical waste.

Thesis Statement: Of the three methods of medical waste disposal— steam sterilization, ocean dumping, and incineration— incineration is the best.

  I. So much medical waste is being generated that we need a safe method of disposal.
  - A. Several waste products result from medical procedures.
  - B. The problem is extensive (statistics).
  - C. Some waste products pose risks.

Because the health care system in the United States contains many problems, citizens and lawmakers alike must persuade others to enact plausible solutions.

© Paul Conklin/PhotoEdit

   II. There are three ways to dispose of medical waste.
      A. One is the steam-sterilization process.
      B. The second is ocean dumping.
      C. The third is incineration.
   III. Incineration is the best solution.
      A. It completely destroys the product.
      B. Fire purifies.

Monroe's Motivated Sequence

Alan Monroe, legendary speech professor at Purdue University, developed and refined a commonly used persuasive pattern, especially good for speeches intended to actuate behavior. **Monroe's Motivated Sequence** is a modified problem-solution format.

Before people act, they must be motivated to do what they know they should do. Consequently, it's important to provide emotional as well as logical reasons. Monroe's pattern includes the word *motivated*, because it has several built-in steps to increase motivational appeals. (Note that this pattern is not a formula in the sense that you must include each element. Rather, Monroe suggests various ways to develop your points.) Here are the five easily remembered steps in the sequence, as explained by Monroe himself.[10]

1. **Attention Step:** As with any other speech, you begin by gaining the audience's attention and drawing it to your topic.
2. **Need Step:** This step is similar to the problem part of a problem-solution speech. Monroe suggests four elements: (a) *statement*—tell the nature of the problem; (b) *illustration*—give a relevant detailed example or examples; (c) *ramifications*—provide additional support such as statistics or testimony that show the extent of the problem; and (d) *pointing*—show the direct relationship between the audience and the problem.
3. **Satisfaction Step:** After you demonstrate the problem or need, show its extent and its effects on the audience, and then propose a solution that will satisfy the need. This step can have as many as five parts: (a) *statement*—briefly state the attitude, belief, or action you want the audience to adopt; (b) *explanation*—make your proposal understandable (visual aids may help at this point); (c) *theoretical demonstration*—show the logical connection between the need and its satisfaction; (d) *practicality*—use facts, figures, and testimony to show that the proposal has worked effectively or

Monroe's Motivated Sequence a call to action in five steps: attention, need, satisfaction, visualization, and action that the belief has been proved correct; and (e) *meeting objections*—show that your proposal can overcome your listeners' potential objections.

4. **Visualization Step:** This step is unique. Here, you ask listeners to imagine the future, both if they enact the proposal and if they fail to do so. (a) *Positive*—describe a positive future if your plan is put into action. Create a realistic scenario showing good things your solution provides. Appeal to emotions such as safety needs, pride, and pleasure. (b) *Negative*—have listeners imagine themselves in an unpleasant situation if they fail to put your solution into effect. (c) *Contrast*—compare the negative results of not enacting your plan with the positive results your plan will produce.

5. **Action:** In the final step, call for a specific action: (a) name the specific, overt action, attitude, or belief you are advocating; (b) state your personal intention to act; and (c) end with impact.

As you might imagine, this pattern is good for sales speeches. It is also effective in policy speeches that include a "should" or an "ought."

Student Learning:
Book Website
This Stop and Check activity can also be found on the book's website, where it's located under "Chapter Resources."

✓ **STOP AND CHECK**

USE MONROE'S MOTIVATED SEQUENCE

Working alone or with a small group, plan a short outline for a speech intended to motivate your audience to action. Choose one of these general topic categories:

▶ Sales: Convince your classmates to buy a specific product.
▶ Public service: Ask your listeners to donate time or money to a worthy cause.

Direct Method Pattern

In the **direct method,** also called the **statement of reasons pattern,** you make a claim and then state several reasons to support it. Each point provides an additional rationale for accepting your views. It's a good pattern to use when listeners are apathetic or neutral, or when they mildly favor or mildly oppose your claim. Consider it when your goal is to convince, although you can also use it to organize a speech to **actuate** (or motivate the audience to do something).

This outline for a speech on therapy dogs states four reasons these animals are helpful in health facilities, prisons, and shelter homes.[11]

Specific Purpose: To persuade my listeners that therapy dogs provide psychological and physical benefits to people in distressing circumstances.

Thesis Statement: Therapy dogs promote well-being, affection, communication, and movement.

I. They promote a general feeling of well-being (children, the elderly).
II. They provide unconditional affection to those who lack it (prisoners, people in shelters).
III. They interact with those who have trouble communicating (Alzheimer's patients, some psychiatric patients, stroke patients).
IV. They motivate simple activities (patting, brushing) for patients with physical limitations.

As you can see, this pattern is a variant of the topical pattern. It's easy to use, both in speeches to convince and speeches to actuate.

Comparative Advantages Pattern

The **comparative advantages pattern** is good for policy speeches arguing that a particular proposal is superior to competing proposals by comparing its advantages to those of

direct method or statement of reasons pattern a method that makes a claim and then states reasons that provide a rationale for the ideas

actuate motivate the audience to do something

comparative advantages pattern a method that shows the superiority of a proposal by comparing its advantages to those of the competition the competition. Study the following outline from a speech to convince an audience of the superiority of osteopathic doctors:

Specific Purpose: To persuade my audience that a Doctor of Osteopathic Medicine (D.O.) is superior to a chiropractor for many reasons.

Thesis Statement: D.O.s are better than chiropractors because of their training and their ability to do surgery.

Doctors of Osteopathic Medicine (D.O.s) are superior to chiropractors.

  I. They can do everything chiropractors do, and more.
  II. Their training is superior because it includes courses comparable to those in medical schools.
  III. Many D.O.s perform surgeries in hospitals with which they are affiliated.

You can also use the comparative advantages method when you want your listeners to act. For instance, in hopes of recruiting students, a representative of a small private college compares the advantages of her institution over larger state schools. Look for this pattern in advertisements, sales speeches, and campaign speeches, as this outline demonstrates:

Specific Purpose: To persuade my audience to purchase a specific brand of DVD player.

Thesis Statement: This DVD brand is superior to the competition in cost, features, and design.

Buy [a specific DVD player].

  I. It costs less but provides the same features as the best-selling brand.
  II. It is code free, meaning it's not limited to specific regions like the other brand is.
  III. It has a cleaner, more usable front when compared to the more cluttered competitor.

It's easy to see that this pattern is related to reasoning by comparison and contrast, for you continually compare and contrast your proposal or product to other proposals and products the audience already knows.

Criteria Satisfaction Pattern

As defined earlier, criteria are standards that form a basis for judgments; the **criteria satisfaction pattern** first sets forth the standards for judgment and then shows how the solution, candidate, or product meets or exceeds these standards. Because it describes the criteria or standards at the outset, it is useful in speeches that argue value claims.

The cardinals in the Catholic Church go through this process whenever they select a new pope. They first identify specific qualities they want the new pope to have and then they look for a cardinal who has those qualities. A similar procedure takes place during any job search. Whenever you apply for a job, you first read the criteria spelled out in the job announcement and then you show how you meet those criteria.

The following outline demonstrates the criteria satisfaction pattern for the argument that community service is a workable punishment for some criminals.

Specific Purpose: To persuade my audience that community service meets all the criteria for a good punishment for nonviolent criminals.

Thesis Statement: Community service is a punishment that fits the crime, reduces recidivism, and is cost effective.

What does a good punishment for nonviolent felons look like?

  I. The punishment fits the crime.
  II. It reduces recidivism.
  III. It is cost effective.

criteria satisfaction pattern good for value speeches; sets forth the standards for judgment and then shows how the proposed solution meets or exceeds these standards

Community service is the best punishment for nonviolent crimes.

    I. The punishment can be tailored to fit the crime.
    II. It keeps felons out of prison where they can be influenced by career criminals.
    III. It is far less costly to administer than incarceration.

The criteria satisfaction pattern is especially useful for controversial issues, because you initially establish common ground with your audience by setting up criteria on which you all agree. As in the direct methods pattern, it is effective to build to a climax and develop your most persuasive criteria last.

Negative Method Pattern

The **negative method pattern** lets you concentrate on the shortcomings of every other proposal before you show why your proposal is the one logical solution. In other words, you point out the negative aspects in competing proposals; then, after you've dismantled or undermined the other plans, you propose your own. This pattern is often used when a policy claim is just one among many.

Specific Purpose: To persuade my audience that global legalization of drugs is the only way to control the supply and demand of illicit drugs.

Thesis Statement: Because of the failures of drug enforcement agencies and education, we should regulate drugs through legalization.

We need a solution to the global problem of drugs.

    I. More drug enforcement agencies are not the answer.
    II. Better education is not the answer.
    III. Global legalization of drugs is the only way we will regulate supply and demand.

As you can see, there are many useful persuasive patterns. Plan your speech using the pattern that is most appropriate for both your material and your audience. These patterns are not exhaustive, but they are among the most common you'll find in public speeches, advertisements, and other persuasive messages.

Summary

Student Learning: Workbook
To review this chapter, students can complete "Before You Take the Exam" in Chapter 17 of the *Student Workbook.*

The best subjects for persuasive speeches come from the things that matter most to you personally. For this reason, ask yourself questions such as "What do I believe strongly?" "What arouses strong feelings within me?" "What would I like to see changed?" "What enriches my life?" Your answers will generally provide you with topics that you're willing to defend. Choosing your subject is only the first part of topic selection. You then decide whether you will argue a claim of fact, value, definition, or policy.

We consistently argue for our ideas in an attempt to influence one another's beliefs, actions, values, and attitudes, and we strategically organize our speeches and adapt our ideas to different types of audiences. However, assumptions and actions are always interwoven because, while you are motivating listeners to act, you are also trying to reinforce their positive attitudes and beliefs. Throughout the entire time, you rely on underlying values to support your calls to action.

Several common persuasive patterns are available. The problem-solution pattern and its variant, Monroe's Motivated Sequence, both define a problem and identify a solution. The direct method, also called the statement of reasons pattern, directly lists arguments that support your claim. The criteria satisfaction pattern is good for value speeches because you first set up criteria or standards for judgment before you show how

negative method pattern points out shortcomings of other proposals and then demonstrates why your proposal is the one logical solution remaining

your proposal meets these standards. The comparative advantages method gives the advantage of your proposal over similar proposals; the negative method, in contrast, shows the disadvantages of every proposal but your own.

STUDY AND REVIEW

The premium website for *Public Speaking* offers a broad range of resources that will help you better understand the material in this chapter, complete assignments, and succeed on tests. The website features

- ▶ Speech videos with critical viewing questions, various types of outlines, transcripts, and note cards
- ▶ Interactive practice activities, self quizzes, and a sample final exam

For more information about this text's electronic learning resources, consult your **Guide to Online Resources for Public Speaking** or visit http://communication.wadsworth.com/jaffe5.

KEY TERMS

The terms below are defined in the margins throughout this chapter. The book website also provides interactive flashcards and crossword puzzles to help you learn these terms and the concepts they represent.

claim 312
factual claim 312
definition or classification claim 313
value claim 313
criteria 313
policy claim 313
status quo 314
to convince 315
apathy 316
cognitive dissonance theory 316

dissonance 316
attitudes 317
Theory of Reasoned Action 318
Monroe's Motivated Sequence 321
direct method or statement of reasons pattern 322
actuate 322
comparative advantages pattern 322
criteria satisfaction pattern 323
negative method pattern 324

APPLICATION AND CRITICAL THINKING EXERCISES

The exercises below are among the practice activities on the book website.

1. Consider the relationship between beliefs and actions, and identify topics that might fall into each category. For instance, in the "unfocused" category, people often believe they should learn to study more effectively, but they don't know how to proceed. In the "unconvinced" category, people don't know enough about investing wisely, so they don't invest at all.
2. Listen to at least one persuasive speech on television, taking notes on the speaker's arguments. (C-SPAN is a good source for such speeches.) What kinds of claims does the speaker make? How does she or he support the claims? Who are the intended audiences? How effectively does the speaker adapt to audience beliefs, actions, attitudes, and values?
3. To explore hostile speaking in greater depth, go to www.richspeaking.com/articles/ Difficult_Audience.html. Compare the author's list of ten typical ways to respond to hostile audiences with his six positive alternative strategies.

4. With a small group in your classroom, identify areas in which national attitudes have changed, or areas in which your personal attitudes have changed. How did persuasive public speaking contribute to those changes?

SPEECH VIDEO

Student Learning:
Book Website
A video clip of this speech is available on the book website for viewing and guided critical analysis. The clip is also available on the Multimedia Manager CD-ROM.

Log on to the book website to watch and critique Brittany Farrer's speech titled "Limiting Alcohol Ads," the outline of which also appears below. For your further study, see Bonita Persons' policy speech "Don't Drive Drowsy" (printed at the end of Chapter 10 and available on the book website), and watch the video of Paul Southwick's value speech "Embryo Adoption" on the book website.

Student Outline with Commentary

LIMITING ALCOHOL ADS
Brittany Farrer

Topic:	Restricting Alcohol Advertising
Specific purpose:	To convince my audience that alcohol advertising should be restricted because it leads children to view alcohol favorably.
Central idea:	The advertising of alcoholic beverages needs to be curtailed because it leads to children supporting alcoholic lifestyles.

Brittany's dramatic, emotional, and personal narrative draws listeners into her topic.

Introduction

I. In June 1988, a 27-year-old man was killed when a car left the street and slammed into his shop.
   A. He left behind a 25-year-old widow, a 4-year old girl, and a 9-month-old baby.
   B. He did not die instantly, but had he lived, he would have been a paraplegic, restricted to a wheelchair for the rest of his life.
   C. This happened because a drunken woman decided to get behind the wheel.
II. Through this story, I have become committed to sharing the "gospel" about alcohol abuse and prevention.
   A. I was that 4-year-old.
   B. When my dad was killed, we weren't even in a car; my sister, mom, and I were all in the back room of our business, a mere 25 feet away.
   C. I have spent many years on committees, in clubs, and doing research about this subject.
III. I realize that alcohol has not negatively affected everyone's life like it has mine, but everyone should be aware of the influence of alcohol on future generations.
IV. I will now demonstrate through statistics and studies that advertising alcoholic beverages leads children to view alcohol favorably, and this should be curtailed.

Body

I. Alcohol abuse is caused in part because people, beginning in childhood, have positive attitudes toward alcohol consumption.

A. Alcohol ads contribute to such attitudes in children.
   1. When you were 8, could you recite the slogan from a Budweiser commercial (Alcohol Policy Solutions [APS], 2002)?
      a. One study found that fifth- and sixth-graders had good dispositions towards drinking, which mean they will be more likely to drink as adults (APS).
      b. Another study found that kids believed alcohol was fun, relaxing, attractive, and romantic, with no negative effects; they learned this from watching televised ads (APS).
      c. An American Medical Association Office of Alcohol survey revealed that 70 percent of people believe alcohol advertising is targeted at people under the age of 21 (APS).
   2. Products such as alcopop attract young consumers.
      a. According to Lynne Goodwin, who lost her daughter in a drunk driving accident, "[Beer companies] are getting away with grooming children to be customers before they are of legal age" (Hagens, Berman, Sobol, Shapiro [HBSS], 2004).
      b. The average age to start drinking is now 12 (APS) and 13 for girls (Join Together, 2004).
      c. The alcohol industry earns about $22.5 billion annually from underage drinkers (HBSS).
   3. Such factors may have led that woman to start drinking.
B. There are many important statistics to consider when thinking about how many children witness alcohol advertising.
   1. Television is a major source for alcohol ads.
      a. 1 out of every 4 families has put a TV in their children's bedroom (APS).
      b. Children and teens view over 1,000 hours of TV every year— about 2.7 hours of TV per day, 7 days a week, for 365 days straight (APS).
      c. 58 percent of children in one report say that a TV is on during meals (APS).
      d. In 1996, compared to Tony the Tiger, Smokey the Bear, or Power Rangers, children could better recall the Budweiser frogs' slogan (APS).
   2. Children also see ads in public spaces on billboards and buses, at community festivals and sports events, in store windows, and on store displays (University of Minnesota, 2002).
C. The effects of underage abuse of alcohol are staggering.
   1. The *Journal of the American Medical Association* reports that children who started drinking by age 12 will be three times more likely to have serious alcohol dependency than adults who wait until they are 21 (APS).
   2. The University of Pittsburgh Medical Center discovered that the hippocampus (the area of the brain that controls learning and memory) is 10 percent smaller in people who abuse alcohol (particularly teens) than those who don't drink at all (APS).
   3. Many adults worry about blood pressure, and teens aged 12 to 16 who drink alcohol have higher blood pressure than those who don't.
      a. High blood pressure is usually a lifelong condition (National Heart, Lung, and Blood Institute [NHLBI], 2004).
      b. It puts people more at risk for heart disease, kidney disease, or a stroke (NHLBI).
   4. According to the National Academy of Science, underage alcohol usage costs $53 billion annually, including $19 billion from traffic accidents and $29 billion from violent crime (The Marin Institute, 2005).
II. There are several ways to minimize the effect of alcohol ads on children.
   A. One simple solution is parental control of TV.
      1. Of course, families can minimize a child's TV viewing.

The body is organized into a problem-solution pattern. The problem section is further subdivided into causes and effects.

She builds this section with statistics, testimony, and results of studies. Do you find her evidence convincing? Explain your answer.

Statistics dominate in this section. The references to advertising characters establish common ground with listeners.

The effects section presents social, physical, and financial reasons to avoid alcohol abuse, especially among the young.

2. A family can watch TV together; that way if an ad comes on, parents can discuss the consequences of drinking.

B. On a lighter note, one organization has started selling subliminal stickers to parents across the country (PRNewswire [PRN], 1998).

1. You place the sticker in the upper left-hand corner of the TV screen where the child will subliminally absorb the sticker's message of "I do not smoke. I do not use drugs. I do not drink alcohol" (PRN).

2. Drug Smart America, the distributing organization, says that up every time the child blinks (850 blinks per hour or 14 blinks per minutes, and .25 blinks per second), he or she picks up the message (PRN).

3. DSA hopes that a child, when confronted with alcohol in a social situation, will automatically recall the sticker and say "NO" (PRN).

C. Probably the best solution is for networks and the alcohol industry to limit alcohol ads on television.

1. Up until 2001, major networks ABC, CBS, NBC, and FOX decided not to accept advertising from hard liquor companies.

a. However, facing money loss, NBC made the choice to cross the line and start accepting such advertising.

b. Facing criticism, NBC retracted its decision months later (APS).

1) Even after 11 p.m., "Saturday Night Live" attracts a more youthful audience (APS).

2) Networks that refuse hard liquor advertising lose $300 million annually, which is pocket change compared to the $12 billion they make (APS).

2. The alcohol industry has set up self-regulatory guidelines.

a. Companies should not advertise on programs with more than 50 percent underage viewers; unfortunately, some companies continue to violate this regulation.

b. Companies should not use symbols, language, characters, or other tools that violate the rule; unfortunately, lizards, talking frogs, and Spuds MacKenzie violate this rule.

c. New regulations call for companies to advertise only to audiences that are 70 percent or more of drinking age; time will tell how well companies keep this rule.

D. However, because many ads are in public spaces, one California community decided to restrict visual advertising in areas where children were most likely to congregate (Alcohol Epidemiology Program [AEP]).

1. Of the 1,450 billboards in the city, only 70 were left for any type of advertising (AEP).

2. A judge ruled this ban was constitutional, because it is "a reasonable fit with the goal of decreasing youth demand for alcoholic beverages" (AEP).

Conclusion

I. I often wonder how the woman who killed my father ever got started drinking.

A. Was she exposed as a child?

B. I have been told that she was known as the town drunk, and a person does not usually become the town drunk by starting to drink at the age of 21.

II. I hope that by examining the troubling statistics, knowing what children think about alcohol and what parents, networks, the industry, and communities are doing, people will start raising awareness.

III. This may prevent other children from growing up fatherless.

The solution section presents personal, corporate, and municipal attempts to lessen the problem of alcohol abuse among young people.

Brittany's conclusion refers back to the emotional story that she used to begin her speech. She briefly reviews and reminds listeners of the personal impact caused by alcohol abuse.

References

Alcohol advertising and youth. (2005). AlcoholPolicyMD.com. Retrieved April 16, 2003, from www
.alcoholpolicysolutions.net/alcohol_and_health/alcohol_ads.htm

Hagens, Berman, Sobol, Shapiro, LLP. (2004, February 4). *Anheuser-Busch and Miller Brewing litigation.* Retrieved
September 17, 2005, from www.hagens-berman.com/busch_miller_lawsuit

Join Together. (2004, December 21). *AMA warns that more teen girls are drinking.* Retrieved September 17, 2005,
from www.jointogether.org/plugin.jtml?siteID=GRANTHELP&p=1&Tab=News&Object_ID=575457

The Marin Institute. (2005). *Underage drinking: National report details problems and solutions.* Retrieved September 17, 2005, from www.marininstitute.org/alcohol_policy/nas.htm

National Heart, Lung, and Blood Institute. (2004, August, last updated). What is high blood pressure? In *Diseases
and conditions index.* Retrieved June 30, 2005, from www.nhlbi.nih.gov/health/dci/Diseases/Hbp/HBP
_WhatIs.html

PRNewswire. (1998, December 10). *Drug Smart America distributes free TV sticker to keep children from using drugs,
cigarettes.* Retrieved April 15, 2003, from http://forces.org/articles/files/drugsmar.htm

University of Minnesota, Alcohol Epidemiology Program. (2002). *Alcohol advertising restrictions.* Retrieved
September 17, 2005, from www.epi.umn.edu/alcohol/policy/adrstrct.shtm

Her references came from online sources. Look up some of her sources and compare and contrast them. Which are most credible? Least credible?

PERSUASIVE REASONING METHODS

THIS CHAPTER WILL HELP YOU

▶ Describe the elements of Toulmin's model of reasoning

▶ Define logos, or rational proofs

▶ Explain these types of reasoning and identify tests for each: analogy (metaphor and parallel case), inductive, deductive, and causal

▶ Recognize fallacious reasoning

▶ Define pathos, or emotional proofs

▶ Understand how appeals to emotions and needs are aspects of pathos

▶ Define ethos, or speaker credibility

▶ Identify ways ethos functions as a reason to believe

▶ Explain how reasoning strategies vary across cultural groups

▶ Identify elements of invitational rhetoric

"For the Roses/Para las Rosas" Mural © 1985 by Juana Alicia. (Treat Street at 21st Street, SF, CA)

Is that true? Maybe there's something to what she just said. Let me think about it. That's interesting. Maybe I should change my mind.

WITH THESE WORDS from his commencement address, Columbia University's president, Lee Bollinger, challenged students to continue to deliberate about important issues[1] as they graduate into a "Red" and "Blue" society, where contentious issues are often reduced to bumper sticker slogans or talking points. Deliberation involves making arguments and weighing the arguments of others. However, if we define *argument* as a "war of words" or a verbal fight, we only add to the problems; in contrast, if we consider an **argument** to be "an intentional, purposeful activity involving reason and judgment,"[2] we can work toward mutually productive decisions.

Every day you use reasoning to make sense of the world and to make decisions that affect your life. Based on your observations, you form conclusions that seem sensible. You may not think much about how you reason; you just "know" if something makes sense or not. However, you probably find that not everyone shares your conclusions, and you may feel compelled to explain them.[3] You build a case or create an argument to support your conclusions.

This chapter will help you think about several elements of reasoning that are in the canon of invention. It first describes three types of reasoning that Aristotle identified centuries ago:[4]

> Of the modes of persuasion furnished by the spoken word there are three kinds. The first kind depends on the personal character of the speaker [*ethos*]; the second on putting the audience into a certain frame of mind [*pathos*]; the third on the proof, or apparent proof, provided by the words of the speech itself [*logos*].

Ethos, *pathos*, and *logos* overlap to form a totality of "good reasons." In other words, emotion can be reasonable; reason has emotional underpinnings; and it is both reasonable and emotionally satisfying to hear a credible speaker. In specific situations, however, you may emphasize one reasoning type over the others. For instance, when you propose a campus policy change, you'll use different kinds of proofs than when you must explain to middle school students the accidental death of a classmate.

Creating and evaluating arguments by using logos, pathos, and ethos effectively will empower you to be a more effective speaker and listener. However, "winning" an argument is neither desirable nor possible in many cases, and this chapter concludes with principles and forms of invitational rhetoric.

CASE STUDY: QUINTILIAN

As chief educator of Rome, Quintilian wrote a treatise on the education of orators (males, in those days).[5] He argued that evil persons cannot be effective persuasive speakers. They will be so bound up in greed, evil deeds, and concern over being caught in their deceits that they will neglect the tools of invention; consequently, audiences will reject them.

In contrast, he urged orators to cultivate justice, honor, and truth seeking. Before they take to the public stage, they should form moral and intellectual character by studying philosophy, seeking wisdom, and pursuing sincerity and goodness. In fact, Quintilian believed that the study of other subjects should lead up to the study of public speaking, the culmination of a pupil's education. Quintilian was realistic enough to recognize that no orator could be perfect, but he urged each one to be both good and sensible.

Quintilian distinguished rhetoric from oratory. Rhetoric is an amoral activity, meaning that it can function for both good and bad ends. However, oratory should be a moral activity—a means to defend the innocent, repress crime, support truth over falsehood, persuade listeners toward right actions, and promote positive civic action.

argument intentional, purposeful speaking that involves reason and judgment

Questions for Discussion

▶ What is your response to Quintilian's claim: "I do not merely assert that the ideal orator should be a good man, but I affirm that no man can be a good orator unless he is a good man"?[6]

▶ How might our culture be changed if the study of public speaking came at the end of your education and all your other studies were considered foundational to public speaking?

▶ How might the world be different if every speaker met Quintilian's ideals of being both good and sensible, speaking only to promote moral ends?

Use Toulmin's Reasoning Model

Professor Stephen Toulmin[7] diagrammed the elements of an argument, based on interchanges typically found in courtrooms. His linear model, shown in Figure 18.1, illustrates important aspects of reasoning and clarifies the relationships among claims, evidence or data, warrants, backing, qualifiers, and conditions for rebuttal characteristic of traditional reasoning in U.S. culture. Learning to qualify your claim, justifying it with evidence, and planning ways to deal with counterarguments will make your speeches more persuasive.

Vir bonum, dicendi peritus (Cato). The first-century Roman educator Quintilian popularized Cato's saying, which translates as "the good person, speaking well."

Claims

As Chapter 17 points out, claims are disputable assertions that require evidence or backing to be accepted. Factual claims argue about what exists, what causes something else, or what the future will bring. Definition or classification claims determine in which category a phenomenon belongs. Value claims deal with the rightness, the goodness, or the worth of a thing. Finally, policy claims argue over actions or proposals for change.

Grounds, Data, or Evidence

To support your claims, select facts, examples, narratives, quotations, statistics, and literal and figurative comparisons, as described in Chapter 8. Providing your listeners with **evidence**, also called **data** or **grounds**, enables them to weigh your argument and decide

evidence, data, or grounds evidence offered to support a claim

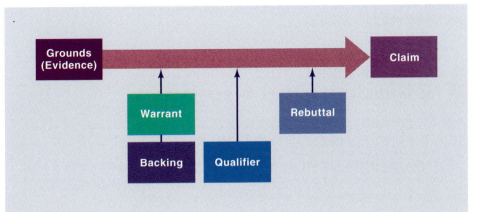

Figure 18.1
Toulmin Model of Argument
Stephen Toulmin developed this model as a way to visualize the reasoning process.

assertions claims put forth without any supporting evidence

warrant justification or reasoning that connects the claim and the evidence

backing reasons given to support the warrant

qualifiers words and phrases that limit or narrow the scope of a claim

rebuttal arguments that counter or disagree with a claim

whether or not your conclusions make sense. Without sufficient and credible data, your claims are simply unsupported **assertions.**

Warrants

The justification or reasoning that you and your listeners use to connect your evidence with your claim is called a **warrant.** Switch your TV on to a police drama and watch how officers justify an arrest. They produce a warrant, which they can only get if they have sufficient data or grounds to connect the suspect to the crime. So, if the fingerprint on the gun (evidence) matches the suspect's print (additional evidence), it is logical to conclude that the suspect fired the gun (claim of fact), because our fingerprints are all unique (the warrant that connects or links the evidence to the claim).

Backing

When a warrant is not broadly understood or broadly accepted, you can give reasons, called **backing,** to support or defend it. For example, think of a trial in which blood was found on a defendant's jacket (evidence). In case the jury doesn't understand the link between the blood evidence and the perpetrator (warrant), the prosecution brings in several experts who explain the science of DNA (backing) and testify that the blood must belong to the victim (backing).

Qualifiers

Avoid words such as *always* or *never* when you make claims. Instead, use **qualifiers,** which are words and phrases that limit or narrow the scope of your claim. Examples include *in most cases, in males between the ages of seven and nine, among voters with a college degree,* and *usually.*

Rebuttal

Not all listeners will agree with your claim. So, as a "listening speaker," try to hear the arguments your audience will raise in opposition, and then prepare to deal with them directly. This is the **rebuttal** part of the model. It might help if you think of rebuttals as your listeners' questions that begin with the phrase, "*But* what about . . . ?" Demonstrating that you've considered these counterarguments and that you still have good reasons for your claim enhances your persuasiveness.

In summary, if you learn to recognize the type of claim you are making, qualify it, provide evidence and backing to warrant it, and then confront potential audience rebuttals, you will be more effective in presenting your ideas to others and having them recognize your views as reasonable.

> DIVERSITY IN PRACTICE
> ### THE INFLUENCE OF CULTURE ON REASONING
>
> CULTURE INFLUENCES OUR REASONING RESOURCES in a number of ways that can easily lead to misunderstandings between cultural groups.[8]
>
> ▸ **Topics considered appropriate for discussion vary across cultures.** Some groups, for instance, would not debate such issues as gay rights, day care, or euthanasia. Openly speaking about sex is unthinkable in some cultures.

- **Cultures conceptualize issues differently.** Many in the United States think of issues as problems and solutions they can define, propose, test and then eliminate or enact; others believe problems result from fate, a bad relationship with the deity or deities, or people who are out of harmony.
- **The norms for structuring and framing a discussion vary.** Rather than seek causes and effects or pro and con arguments, then making claims and counterclaims, some cultures ground their discussions in the historical perspectives of the various participants. Still others rely on narrative structures to frame their speeches. In the United States, we typical ask, "Who won the argument?" But other cultures see themselves as a community of equals who must cooperate to reach consensus.
- **Levels of explicitness differ across cultures.** In the United States, we commonly hear conclusions stated explicitly and concretely. However, other cultures tolerate much more ambiguity; their speakers exert influence through subtlety and indirectness.
- **Forms of proof are often dissimilar.** What's considered rational or irrational, what counts as evidence, and what constitutes a good reason varies across cultures. Here, facts, statistics, and studies by experts are typically used, but elsewhere, cultures find good reasons in narratives, analogies, traditional sayings, authoritative texts, and the words of wise, experienced elders.
- **Communication styles vary.** Mainstream U.S. culture is biased toward linear, analytical models of reasoning, as depicted in the Toulmin model. Other cultural groups reason more holistically through drama, intuition, and emotional expressiveness.

An article on InfoTrac College Edition has the formidable title, "Microcultural analysis of variation in sharing of causal reasoning about behavior." It reports on a study done in a natural foods cooperative store that compares and contrasts the ways a "health food guru" and an animal rights activist make reasonable decisions about foods. Read the introduction and other parts of the article that interest you. Which type of reasoning makes more sense to you?

Teaching Tip
For a quick comparison of the three kinds of persuasion defined by Aristotle (logos, pathos, and ethos), see this page from the University Writing Center at California State University, Los Angeles: http://www.calstatela.edu/centers/write_cn/3waypers.htm. All URLs mentioned in the text are available as live, regularly maintained links on the book's website, located in the "Chapter Resources" list under "Web Links."

Student Learning: Workbook
For practice using and understanding analogies, students can complete Activity 18.1, "Reasoning by Analogy," in the *Student Workbook*.

Classroom Discussion/ Activity
Break the class into small groups, and give each group a list of metaphors to decipher. Ask students to explain the meaning of the metaphors and to come up with alternate metaphors for the same topics. Discuss how changing the metaphor changes the meaning.

Use Logos or Rational Proofs

Logos, often called rational proofs, refers to the verbal arguments you make relating to your subject—arguments such as analogy, inductive, deductive, and causal reasoning. Of course, these are not the only methods of sense making, as the Diversity in Practice feature on cultural reasoning explained.

Reasoning by Analogy: Figurative and Literal

Chapter 8 describes an **analogy** as a comparison between one item that is unknown or less familiar and something already familiar to the audience. Analogies can be either figurative (metaphor) or literal (parallel case).

Figurative Analogies (Metaphors)

When **reasoning by metaphor,** you figuratively compare two things that are generally different but share a recognizable similarity. Metaphors are fundamentally dialogical, for they require your listeners to participate actively and make sensible connections between the two things you compare. For example, what images do these metaphors evoke in you?

- Good news is *music to our ears*; insecurity causes us to *play it by ear*; when we are getting along, we are *in harmony* or *in tune* with one another.[9]

logos verbal arguments; arguments from the words of the speech itself

analogy comparison of one item that's less familiar or unknown to something concrete and familiar

reasoning by metaphor comparing two things that are generally different but share a recognizable similarity

- ▶ The separation between church and state is a *wall* or a *dance* or a *two-way street*.[10]
- ▶ A teacher can see herself as a *police officer* or a *gardener* or a *ship's captain* in the classroom.[11]

Our metaphors often guide our actions. For example, what is the role of the United States in the world? Is it more like a police officer, a kindly big brother, a bystander, or an onlooker? The metaphor we embrace affects U.S. global policies. If we choose "police," our foreign policy is different than if we embrace "onlooker."

Use of analogy is a fundamental, universal form of reasoning. Brian Wicker,[12] author of *A Story-Shaped World*, explains that metaphor is an older, more poetic way of seeing the world, related to the modes of thinking of poets and storytellers. It is a continuation of our oral heritage. Aristotle associated metaphor with mental brilliance, as seen in this quotation from *Poetics*.[13]

> . . . the greatest thing by far is to be a master of metaphor. It is the one thing that cannot be learnt from others, and it is also a sign of genius, since a good metaphor implies an intuitive perception of the similarity in dissimilars.

Asa Hilliard[14] claims that metaphorical reasoning is typical of African and African American speakers.

> Early use was made of proverbs, song, and stories. Direct or symbolic lessons were taught through these. . . . Parenthetically, it is interesting that racist psychologists claim that Black people are not capable of "Level II Thinking," the kind of abstract thinking which is reflected in proverbs and analogies. To the contrary, this is our strong suit. . . . Psychologists . . . miss the extensive use of proverbs and analogies among us.

The images inherent in metaphors can arouse emotional responses. Contrast your feelings about a *harvest of justice* or the *moneyed scales of justice*; a *flood of compassion* or a *trickle of compassion*; a *turkey of a deal* or a *gem of a deal*.

Literal Analogies (Parallel Cases)

Whereas metaphors highlight similarities between two *different* things, reasoning by **parallel case** or **literal analogy** points out likenesses between two *similar* things. We often use this type of reasoning to formulate policies by asking what another person or group decided to do when faced with a problem similar to our own. Here are some examples.

- ▶ How should your school solve parking problems on campus? Look at case studies of schools that solved similar parking problems, and then infer whether the other schools' experiences will be a good predictor of what might or might not work for yours.
- ▶ How should a local hospital keep health care costs under control? Look at cost-saving measures instituted by a hospital in a similar location.
- ▶ How should the U.S. solve health care problems? Well, which countries are most like ours? What do they do? How well do those programs work?

In summary, we commonly use actual cases based on real experiences to formulate policies and make predictions about the future. Then we predict that what happened in a known case will happen in a similar case that we project.

parallel case or literal analogy comparing likenesses between two similar things; arguing that what happened in a known case will likely happen in a similar case

Testing Analogies

Reasoning by metaphor is not generally considered a "hard" proof, so make sure your listeners can sensibly connect your concept with the comparison. Check that the comparison does, in fact, illuminate, clarify, and illustrate your idea.

Parallel case reasoning is different; test it more directly by considering the following two questions.

1. Are the cases really alike? Or are you "comparing apples to oranges"?
2. Are they alike in essential details?

Reasoning Inductively

In **inductive reasoning,** you take specific instances or examples and formulate a reasonable generalization or conclusion from them. In other words, inductive reasoning moves from the particular to the general; it is characteristic of women and many ethnic speakers who ground their knowing and reasoning in personal experiences that arise out of their relationship with others. Patricia Sullivan,[15] for instance, explains that African American leaders tie knowledge to human experiences, human actions, and the human life world. Knowledge is grounded in human experience; it does not exist for its own sake or in the abstract. What is relevant is considered relevant because it makes a difference in people's lives.

Here is an example of induction from a *U.S. News and World Report* feature about inner-city debate teams:[16]

▶ Darinka Maldonado got so involved in debate in her Bronx high school that she avoided negative peer pressure and earned a full scholarship to the University of Pittsburgh.
▶ Reena Rani, an immigrant from India who debates in the South Bronx, uses skills she's learned to counter her father's and brother's arguments that, as a female, she shouldn't aspire to a job.
▶ Urban debaters, who are predominately poor, minority, and female, are excelling against opponents from wealthier schools with longer-established debate programs.
▶ LaTonya Starks, a former Chicago urban school debater who went on to Northwestern University, says that successful debate competition improves the self-images of urban debaters.
▶ Angelo Brooks, who coaches a Baltimore high school team, seeks students who are struggling academically, not overachievers. Debate tools (research, listening, outlining arguments) have helped many improve their grades an average of ten to fifteen points.

Generalization: Urban debate has had remarkable success in diverting at-risk kids from poverty, drugs, and violence.

Because you can only be sure of a conclusion only if you can observe 100 percent of a population, it is ideal to look at every example before you form a conclusion. However, 100 percent samples are rare. (Imagine trying to survey every student who's participated in an urban debate league!) Instead, select a representative sample, survey the characteristics of that sample, formulate conclusions, and then generalize your findings to the larger population it represents. But take care: If you only study inner-city debate programs in Atlanta or New York, don't assume that your conclusions apply to all urban debaters.

The three major tests for inductive reasoning are all linked to the tests you used to evaluate examples (see guidelines in Chapter 8 for evaluating examples).

1. Are enough cases represented to justify the conclusion? Or are you forming a conclusion based on only a few cases?
2. Are the cases typical? That is, do they represent the average members of the population to which the generalizations are applied? Or are they extreme cases that may show what could happen, but not what usually happens?
3. Are the examples from the time under discussion, or are they out of date?

Reasoning Deductively

Inductive reasoning moves from specific examples to conclusions or generalizations, but **deductive reasoning** goes in the other direction. It begins with a generalization or

Instructor's Resource Manual
For a sample lecture on inductive and deductive reasoning, including example, see Teaching Idea 18.1.

inductive reasoning starting with specific instances or examples then formulating a reasonable conclusion

deductive reasoning starting with a principle (the premise) and applying it to a specific case

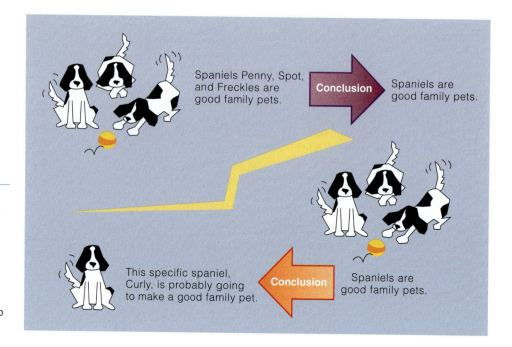

Figure 18.2
Inductive and Deductive Reasoning
You observe a number of spaniels and inductively reason that they make good pets. Using that premise, you deduce that Curly, the dog you want to buy, will be a good pet.

principle, called the premise, and moves logically to an application in a specific case. (See Figure 18.2 for an example of the relationship between inductive and deductive reasoning.) In formal logic, the deductive reasoning process is often shown in a syllogism such as this:

Major premise: All Catholic bishops are unmarried.

Minor premise: He is a Catholic bishop.

Conclusion: Therefore, he is not married.

When you're sure of the major premise, you can state your conclusion with confidence. Because it is a rule that members of the Catholic clergy cannot marry and stay in the priesthood, you can be fairly sure that a Catholic priest who has risen to the level of bishop is unmarried. In contrast, many premises are less certain. Although some, such as "all men are mortal," are 100 percent true, others, such as "urban high school debaters get better grades," are not valid in every case. So it's wise to qualify both your premises and your conclusions. Here is one example:

Many students who participate in urban debate leagues get better grades.

Yolanda Baylor is a debater at an inner-city high school in the South Bronx.

She will *probably* improve her grades.

When you reason deductively, you rarely state the entire syllogism, so your listeners must fill in the unstated premises. Aristotle called this an **enthymeme.** For example, you might say, "Married? He's a Catholic bishop!" and let your audience make the necessary connections. Or (sitting with friends, discussing Yolanda's decision to join the urban debate team), "What a great opportunity! Her grade point needs that boost!" Your friends use their generalizations about urban debating to make sense of what you've just said.

Using enthymemes is inherently dialogical, for listeners must form conclusions based on their knowledge of what you *don't* say. However, if they know nothing about your subject (the rules regarding the Catholic clergy or the connection between debating and grades, for example), they'll miss your meaning.

enthymeme omitting part of the syllogism in an argument and letting listeners supply what's missing; inherently dialogical

There are two major tests for deductive reasoning:

1. For the conclusion to be valid, the premises must be true or highly probable.
2. To be reasonable, the conclusion must follow from the premise.

Reasoning Causally

One speaker stated: "There were nine million immigrants last year, and there were nine million Americans out of work." Both facts could be verified by counting. However, if the speaker linked the two, stating or implying that one resulted in or led to the other, he would be using **causal reasoning,** and his statement would sound like this: "There were nine million Americans out of work last year *because* there were nine million immigrants." In the first statement, the two conditions exist together in time, perhaps by chance; in the second statement, the second condition *results from* the first and would not exist without it.

Because the belief in causation is a fundamental Euro-American belief, this type of reasoning is common. However, to be a cause, one factor must precede another and be linked in such a way *that the second factor follows as a matter of rule.* It is evident that the lack of oxygen to the brain (first factor) causes death (second factor)—this link is observed time after time. But other causal links are less well proved, sometimes because many other variables may be linked to the effects. The causes of unemployment are much more complex than an influx of immigrants. With causal reasoning, the key is to produce enough reasons to warrant the link or connection between the two factors.

Test causation by asking a series of questions to assess whether the reasoning is valid.

1. Is there a real connection? Does one follow as a result of the first, or do the two events simply exist together in time?
2. Is this the only cause? The most important cause? Or are there other factors?
3. Is the cause strong enough for the effect?

In summary, you use a variety of reasons to warrant your claims, including figurative and literal analogies, inductive and deductive reasoning, and causal links. All of these types of reasoning fall under the category of logos, or rational proofs. (The Diversity in Practice feature provides additional information on men's and women's patterns in reasoning.)

DIVERSITY IN PRACTICE
REASONING AND THE SEXES

ALTHOUGH both men and women reason inductively, some feminist philosophers argue that inductive reasoning is a *major* way that women draw conclusions. Women typically describe specific experiences of real people, such as the rape survivor, the family without medical insurance, the student athlete whose sport was eliminated, and then generalize from these examples. This means that their reasoning is characteristically grounded in personal experiences that arise out of their interpersonal relationships.[17]

Women are commonly stereotyped as reasoning with their hearts rather than their heads— an overgeneralization that may have some factual basis. Studies of women's patterns of thinking show the importance of emotion in their reasoning process.[18] Although obviously different from "dispassionate investigation," emotions complement logic, and they intertwine with rational proofs. Feelings are not inferior to reason, and they are *not* something women must overcome if they are to think clearly. Instead,

causal reasoning linking two factors in such as way that the first factor occurs before the second and leads to the second as a matter of rule

emotions can be a source of knowledge, and "truth" or "knowledge" without emotion is distorted.[19]

Some scholars argue against fundamental differences between men and women. They believe that both men and women use evidence, linear thinking, and deductive logic; these are not inherently masculine. Further, intuitive and emotional arguments are not inherently feminine; men often reason through experiences, emotions, and empathy.[20]

The Laboratory for Complex Thinking and Scientific Reasoning at McGill University,[21] studied male and female scientists. They found no major differences in use of inductive, deductive, or causal reasoning processes. However, they discovered that, given an unexpected finding, men tended to assume they knew the cause, whereas women tracked it down.

Whatever differences there may be, the "difference must be viewed as a *resource for*— not an *impediment to*— meaningful dialogue."[22]

To learn more about gender and reasoning, read Professor David Frank's 1997 article or related articles in the journal *Argumentation and Advocacy*, available on InfoTrac College Edition.

Classroom Discussion/ Activity
Ask students to bring to class the most recent edition of the student newspaper. Have small groups search the newspaper for examples of the logical fallacies. Letters to the editor and editorials are especially likely sources.

Teaching Tip
For descriptions and additional examples of the various kinds of fallacies, see Gary Curtis's collection in The Fallacy Files at http://www .fallacyfiles.org/index.html. All URLs mentioned in the text are available as live, regularly maintained links on the book's website, located in the "Chapter Resources" list under "Web Links."

fallacy failure in logical reasoning that leads to unsound or misleading arguments

unsupported assertion a claim presented without evidence

ad populum an appeal to popular opinion

ad hominem an attack on the messenger rather than the message

post hoc a fallacy of causation; a false cause

Recognizing Logical Fallacies

A **fallacy** is a failure in logical reasoning that leads to unsound or misleading arguments. They've been around for thousands of years, as you can tell by the Latin names given to some of them. As a speaker or critical listener, examine the arguments you hear to avoid being taken in by the following common fallacies.

Unsupported Assertion

In the **unsupported assertion** fallacy, the claim is offered without supporting evidence. Have you ever argued for a grade ("I deserve an A, so why did I get a B?")? If you really want to achieve a grade change, you'll have to produce some pretty convincing data to show that you earned the A. Otherwise, your record stays the same.

Ad Populum or Bandwagon

The Latin phrase **ad populum** literally translates "to the people." It's an appeal to popular reason, another failure of evidence. Instead of providing sound rational arguments, the speaker justifies a proposal by phrases such as "Everyone's doing it" or "We all think this way." But ask yourself: How often is the majority wrong?

Ad Hominem (Personal Attack)

Rather than evaluate the claim, the evidence, and the warrant or reasoning behind it, an **ad hominem** (literally, "against the person") attack discounts or demeans the messenger. For instance, one person might present good reasons against physician-assisted suicide, to which the listener replies, "You're just a fundamentalist Christian." This focuses not on the arguments but on the speaker's background. Or a woman who presents good reasons to report an incident of sexual harassment in the workplace is dismissed as a "frustrated feminist."

Post Hoc

Also called **post hoc**, *ergo propter hoc* (literally: "after this, therefore because of this"), this fallacy of causation argues that because one event follows the other, the first must be the cause of the second. For instance, Maria's speech on lottery winners (Chapter 9) told of Daisy, who was sued for half of her $2.8 million winnings because prior to buying the

You don't have to go far to hear analogies comparing speakers and ideas to Nazi-era events. Sometimes it's an *ad hominem* attack on a speaker; sometimes it's a false analogy because the current issue is not comparable to the Nazi atrocities; the comparison often evokes unwarranted negative emotions.

© CORBIS

ticket, Daisy asked for prayers that she'd win. Her son's friend prayed; she won. The teen sued, saying his prayer had caused her fortune. (The judge, however, ruled that there is no way to prove a link.)

Overgeneralization

This fallacy of inductive reasoning extends the conclusion further than the evidence warrants. For example, you might have a bad experience with a specific brand of computer and you judge the whole line of computers (or worse, the entire company) negatively based on your one bad experience. People overgeneralize about blind dates, crooked politicians, student cheating, members of ethnic groups, and so on. Jumping to a conclusion based on minimal evidence is **overgeneralization.**

Red Herring Argument

Any time you think "That's beside the point" or "That's irrelevant," you're probably hearing a **red herring** argument. In this fallacy, the speaker dodges the real argument and intentionally digresses and introduces an unrelated side issue in an attempt to divert attention. The term derives from the days of fox hunting when a dead fish was dragged across the trail of a fox to set the dogs off in a different direction.[23]

False Analogy

A **false analogy** occurs when the two things compared are not similar enough to warrant the comparison. Particularly common are inappropriate World War II analogies such as Hitler, the Gestapo, Himmler, genocide, and Nazis.[24] For example, the Internet has more than 200 hits for the analogy "animal Auschwitz," which compares the treatment of animals to the treatment of Jews, gays, and other groups during the Nazi era. Arguably, the treatment of animals is sometimes terrible, but it is different in degree and kind from what happened in Nazi Germany.

False Dichotomy

The **false dichotomy** fallacy states the issue as an either-or choice, overlooking other reasonable possibilities. So you might hear "Either graduate from college, or work in a

overgeneralization a fallacy of induction; generalizing too broadly, given the evidence

red herring introducing a side issue with the intent of drawing attention from the real issue

false analogy comparing two things too dissimilar to warrant the conclusion drawn

false dichotomy an either-or fallacy that ignores other reasonable options

low-paying job" or "Either you are for us, or you are against us." Such false dichotomies overlook the range of possibilities between the two extremes.

In summary, arguments are fallacious when they fail to provide evidence or present faulty evidence for the claim. Fallacies also attack the messenger instead of countering the message. Fallacies of analogy, causation, and induction are common. Learning to recognize irrelevant digressions and false choices will help you think more critically about the arguments you make and those you hear every day.

Student Learning: Book Website
This Stop and Check activity can also be found on the book's website, where it's located under "Chapter Resources."

Teaching Tip
Sophia On-Line Philosophy Courses has a page on Pathos, which includes a list of emotions that persuasion can appeal to and a link to texts of three famous speeches that use an appeal to pathos. See http://www.molloy.edu/academic/philosophy/sophia/aristotle/rhetoric/rhetoric2a_nts.htm. See also "Emotions in Rhetoric," http://www.molloy.edu/academic/philosophy/sophia/aristotle/rhetoric/emotions_ex2.htm. All URLs mentioned in the text are available as live, regularly maintained links on the book's website, located in the "Chapter Resources" list under "Web Links."

 STOP AND CHECK

IDENTIFYING FALLACIES

Working alone or with a group of classmates, copy the list of common fallacies presented on pages 340–342, and come up with an example of each. Use material from television shows or movies, personal experiences, letters to the editor, talk show callers, and the like. Share your examples with other class members.

If you need additional information, go to http://commfaculty.fullerton.edu/rgass/fallacy31.htm, a site sponsored by Dr. Robert Gass, University of California, Fullerton. He provides definitions and humorous examples of these and other common fallacies as well as an assignment and links to other sites that explain fallacious reasoning.

Include Pathos or Emotional Proofs

Contrast the following situations:

▶ You're listening to a speaker who has all her facts and figures straight, and she provides evidence that passes all the tests: Her examples are representative, her statistics come from reputable sources, and she cites knowledgeable experts. However, you still feel that there's no good reason for you to act. In other words, you're unmotivated—you are neither interested nor concerned.

▶ You're listening to a second speaker who similarly provides excellent evidence and sound reasoning. However, she links her topic to your core beliefs, values, personal goals, and emotions. You find yourself caring about her subject and wanting to believe and act as she proposes.

The second speaker realizes what good speakers have always known: **Motivation** is an internal, individualistic, or subjective factor that results when listeners understand how topics affect their lives in a personal way. That is, we look for emotional and psychological reasons to support our decisions. And in the end, our subjective reasons may be as influential as our logical ones. This demonstrates the power of emotions, which Aristotle called **pathos,** in reasoning.

Although you often respond subconsciously to emotional appeals, responses can be conscious, and your thoughts may run something like this:

motivation internal, individualized factor that results when we understand how topics affect our lives in a personal way

pathos appeals or reasons directed toward audience emotions

"She's right, that's *exactly how it feels* to go to bed hungry; we shouldn't let that happen!"

"Writing my resume carefully *will help me* get a better job."

"I have to protest over *such a fundamental issue* as freedom of speech."

"I've experienced *frustration* just like that! I can relate!"

Pathos relies on appeals to emotions and to needs.

Appeals to Positive Emotions

According to Aristotle, **emotions** are all the feelings that change people in ways that affect their judgment. Psychologists say we "approach" pleasurable emotions such as love, peace, pride, approval, hope, generosity, courage, and loyalty. We also feel good about our core beliefs and values, such as freedom and individualism. By appealing to positive feelings and values, you can often motivate your listeners to accept and act on your claims.

Narratives and examples are good ways to highlight emotions. In this speech excerpt, Marieta talks about international adoption. She was originally from the Philippines, but was adopted into an American home when she was a teenager.[25]

> You might be thinking that adopting an international child is a lot of work. Well, it is, but I believe it is worth it. My parents say that bringing me into their family is one of the most gratifying things they have ever done. And their generosity has obviously benefited me. If it were not for my parents, I would not be able to continue my college education. I wouldn't have any parents or sisters to call my own. As far as I know, I would probably still be in an orphanage because I wouldn't have a place to go.

Her personal story emphasizes generosity and hope as well as the underlying values of self-sacrifice for the good of others, education, family, and belonging. It provides a powerful argument for international adoption.

Appeals to Negative Emotions

Negative emotions are unpleasant, so we try to avoid feelings such as guilt, shame, hatred, fear, insecurity, anger, and anxiety. Appeals to negative emotions can be forceful, with sometimes disastrous results. Consider how effectively hate groups appeal to their audiences' weaknesses, rages, fears, and insecurities.

However, negative emotions are often useful. Fear, anger, and guilt, for instance, can motivate us to avoid real dangers—a fact that the campaign against drunk driving uses effectively. Think of a story you've heard or a television ad you've seen that shows adorable children killed by drivers who "just this once" drove while intoxicated. Don't they make you want to help solve the problem?

One way to arouse listener emotion is to use analogies. In this case, Mike Suzuki evokes anger in his speech against the use of Native American symbols as sports mascots.[26] He wanted fellow students (at a Catholic university that was undergoing a mascot change) to identify with the Native American perspective, so he employed the following analogy:

> Opponents feel that non-Indian people do not have the right to use sacred Indian symbols. Phil St. John, a Sioux Indian and founder of the Concerned American Indian Parents group, said the behaviors of Indian mascots at sporting events were comparable to a Native American tearing apart a rosary in front of a Catholic church. Can you imagine someone dressing up as the Pope and swinging a cross wildly in the air at one of our football games? This is how some Native Americans feel when their sacred symbols are used in sports.

As you might imagine, you can easily overdo negative appeals. For instance, excessive appeals to guilt or fear may turn off an audience. One audience member responded to a famous environmentalist activist's speech in this way:[27]

> [Her] presentation is meant to instill unease. In my case, she is succeeding, though not in the way she intends. She is making me worry . . . for the fate of this movement on which so much depends. As much as I want to endorse what I hear, [her] effort to shock and shame just isn't taking. . . . I find myself going numb.

He advises environmentalist speakers to evaluate the psychological impact of their appeals to fear and guilt and to present instead a "politics of vision" that connects environmental

emotions feelings that change people and affect their judgment; we tend to seek positive emotions and avoid negative ones

goals to positive emotions—to what is "generous, joyous, freely given, and noble" in people.

Appealing to Needs

One of the most widely cited systems of classifying needs follows the work of Abraham Maslow,[28] who ranked them into five levels, each building on the others. Everyone must satisfy basic physical needs for water, air, food, and shelter. After these needs are met, we need security and a feeling of safety, then love and belonging, followed by esteem, and topped off by self-actualization or the need to reach our potential. Here is a list of each level and some ways to address the needs of each one:

- *Basic needs:* Link your topic to your listeners' basic survival needs.
- *Security and safety:* Explain how to gain peace of mind, job security, safety, and comfort, better health, physical safety, and so on.
- *Love and belonging:* Show how your topic helps your listeners be better friends, creates a stronger community, or builds ties between people.
- *Esteem:* Demonstrate that you respect your listeners, and mention their accomplishments when appropriate. Find ways to make them feel competent to carry out your proposals. Let them know that their ideas, opinions, and concerns are significant.
- *Self-actualization:* Challenge your listeners to look beyond themselves and reach out to others. Encourage them to dream big dreams and accomplish unique things. The Army slogan "Be all that you can be" is an example of an appeal to self-actualization.

Marieta's speech on international adoption touched on many needs. Her adoptive parents provided a secure home where her physical needs were met. Being adopted gave her a sense of love, belonging, and esteem. In addition, she esteemed her parents for their generosity and kindness. And they reached outside themselves and did something significant for another human.

(To learn more about Maslow's hierarchy, do an Internet search for the exact term *Abraham Maslow*. Look for additional levels that other scholars have added to his hierarchy.)

Understanding Complex Motivations

As you can see, using pathos is complex, because needs, wants, emotions, and values overlap. As you create emotional appeals, keep in mind four important factors that result in motivational variation from individual to individual.[29]

1. *Sometimes you must choose between two desirable goals or feelings,* such as job security or the ability to reach your potential. In contrast, you may have to choose between two undesirable things, or "the lesser of two evils."
2. *Motives vary according to our circumstances.* Someone who's just ended a significant relationship may worry more about belonging and self-esteem than someone in a long-term relationship. What motivates you is different from what motivates your parents, and your parents, in turn, respond to different appeals than do your grandparents.
3. *Our responses often come out of mixed motives.* The alumna who donates out of loyalty to her school may also like the pride she feels when a building is named in her honor. An angry protest marcher may be acting out of underlying anxiety, fear, or frustration.
4. *Motivations are often group centered.* What we want for ourselves, we want for others, including our family, friends, members of our clubs, religious groups, schools, towns, states, society, and world. Consequently, a speech about child abuse in other countries can motivate listeners who want security for themselves and their own families, as well as for strangers.

Testing Emotional Appeals

Emotions, although essential, are not always trustworthy, so it is appropriate to examine them to see if they make sense. For example, if you use fear to motivate your audience, ask yourself if the fear is justified, or if you're making your listeners unduly fearful. Are you creating or playing on irrational fears? Excessive use of emotional appeals can cloud logical reasoning.

As a listener, ask questions such as these: "Why am I feeling guilty?" "Is my guilt reasonable?" "Is this speaker trying to manipulate me through my feelings?" "Although he is causing me to feel angry, is anger my primary emotion? Can it be that my underlying emotion is fear? Does this challenge to my cherished beliefs create anxiety that I am masking with anger?"[30]

Further, make sure emotion is used ethically. Generally, it is unethical to use emotional appeals in an attempt to bypass logical reasoning. For example, an appeal to national pride may create an argument for going to war in a way that clouds a more rational argument against military involvement. A speaker may use fear to motivate listeners to act for his own profit rather than for their own good.

Examine this ad. What rational appeals are here? What emotional appeals? Are the appeals balanced? Why or why not?

Develop *Ethos* or Speaker Credibility

A third type of **proof,** or reason to believe, comes from your personal qualities, as Chapter 5 points out. In fact, Aristotle[31] believed that your character—a proof he called *ethos*—is the most effective means of persuasion you possess. Here is his explanation of speaker credibility:

> Persuasion is achieved by the speaker's personal character [*ethos*] when the speech is so spoken as to make us think him [or her] credible. We believe good [people] more fully and more readily than others: this is true generally whatever the question is, and absolutely true where exact certainty is impossible and opinions are divided.

This means that people will place their confidence in you if they see you as personally believable, trustworthy, and of good character. Their inner dialogue or reasoning might look something like this:

> She really knows what she's talking about—she's obviously done her homework! And she seems to have good intentions towards me; I trust her. So, I believe her when she says that . . .

proof a reason to believe

ethos personal credibility or character traits that make a speaker believable and worthy of the audience's confidence

Teaching Tip
Ethos is a perception that listeners have of a speaker. Because it is a perception, it can be shaped by the speaker. Remind students of ways that a speaker can shape a positive impression, such as personal appearance, confidence, eye contact, gestures, and avoidance of vocalized pauses. Sophia On-Line Philosophy Courses has a page on Ethos that lists dimensions of a speaker's character that affect credibility. See http://www.molloy .edu/academic/philosophy/ sophia/aristotle/rhetoric/ rhetoric2b_nts.htm. All URLs mentioned in the text are available as live, regularly maintained links on the book's website, located in the "Chapter Resources" list under "Web Links."

In contrast, audiences frequently use the speakers' *ethos* as a reason not to believe their claims. The reasoning may run something like this:

> He has no clue as to what he is talking about. I feel he isn't being entirely up front.

> He seems so arrogant, like he really doesn't care about us. He just wants us to sign up for his pet project. I don't trust him. Therefore, I don't really trust his information about . . .

We evaluate speakers in four areas: good sense, good character, goodwill, and dynamism. You can increase your ethos by demonstrating these characteristics.

Demonstrating Good Sense

Good sense is a cluster of characteristics, made up of several components.

- *Intelligence:* Show that you have a broad understanding of your subject, complete with up-to-date information. Discuss related historical developments, and link your topic to contemporary national and international issues. Then, listeners will recognize that you're not bluffing your way through your speech.
- *Sound reasoning:* Support your claims with trustworthy evidence and logical connections between ideas. Avoid fallacies and unwarranted or excessive appeals to emotions.
- *Composure:* Demonstrate composure by maintaining your poise in a stressful situation. For example, if you become agitated, your audience may wonder why you can't control yourself. On the other hand, if you remain composed and controlled, they'll perceive you more favorably. However, note the differences in cultural expectations about composure described in the Diversity in Practice feature.

DIVERSITY IN PRACTICE
COMPOSURE IN OTHER CULTURES

CONCEPTS OF *ETHOS* depend on the cultural context. Credible speakers in the African American tradition tend to be forceful and emotional rather than calm and composed.[32] Good speakers are genuinely intense in their expression, and sometimes their emotions threaten to override the order and procedure common in the Euro-American style of public speaking. For this reason, listeners brought up in the Euro-American culture may consider them loud.

Similarly, Janice Walker Anderson[33] found that Arabs traditionally expected effective speakers to show their emotion and to heighten the audience's emotions through the rhythm and sounds of words. Overstating a case indicates the speaker's sincerity, not distortion; in contrast, a soft tone indicates the speaker is weak or dishonest.

Exhibiting Good Character

Vir bonum; dicendi peritus. Character counts. Your listeners will believe you more readily if they trust you, so demonstrate honesty, integrity, and trustworthiness by documenting your sources and giving facts that square with what they know to be true. Choose topics that matter to you, and stick by your convictions, even when they are unpopular. Politicians get into trouble when they appear to be poll driven and pander to different audiences, waffling from position to position according to what's popular instead of holding to their core beliefs.

Expressing Goodwill

Your listeners want to know you have them in mind, that you understand "their language." Kenneth Burke,[34] one of the 20th century's most respected rhetoricians, stressed the importance of "identification." According to Burke, a variety of "divisions" separate us, but **identification,** sometimes called **co-orientation,** can bring people with diverse beliefs and behaviors together.

But how do you identify with your audience? One way is to find areas of **common ground**—to emphasize similarities between you and your audience members. When you share beliefs, values, attitudes, and behaviors, it's easy to find areas of commonality to draw on. However, diversity issues make identification more challenging. When listeners are very diverse, search for commonalities and build on them. For instance, every audience shares with you the needs for safety and self-esteem. Watch the video of Barbara Bush's commencement address on the book's website, and notice how she emphasizes shared values with her audience.

Here, Susan Au Allen,[35] president of the U.S. Pan Asian American Chamber of Commerce, emphasizes common ground with her largely African American audience.

> So I salute you, a cherished ally. . . . We are Japanese, Filipinos, Chinese, Asian Indians, Koreans, Vietnamese, Laos, Thais, Cambodians, Hmongs, Pakistanis, and Indonesians. Each has a distinct beautiful ethnic cultural heritage, but our goals are the same as yours. We want to remove racial barriers, we want equal opportunity for our members, and we want to create greater horizons for those who follow.

Although you typically rely on commonalities, in some cases your differences will make you more credible, depending on the topic. For example, Gary suffered a stroke when he was seventeen years old; consequently, when he spoke about strokes and stroke victims, his words were much more persuasive because of his disability. Ariko spoke credibly about Japanese writing because she came from Japan.

Showing Dynamism

Dynamism, or forcefulness, is a fourth trait that influences credibility. (See Chapter 14.) It is linked to traits of extroversion, energy, and enthusiasm. This doesn't mean that you are not credible if you are introverted; however, your visible enjoyment of your topic, your enthusiasm, and your liveliness contribute to your ethos. Think of it this way: Aren't you more likely to believe someone who states ideas forcefully rather than apologetically?

In conclusion, other cultures may not name these proofs in Aristotle's terminology, but that does not mean they don't have them in some form. Across the globe, speakers address their listeners' rationality and their emotional responses, and they follow cultural ideas about what makes a speaker trustworthy.

© AP / Wide World Photos

Condoleezza Rice has credibility that is a combination of her experiences as provost of Stanford University, her doctorate in economics, and her positions as National Security Advisor (the first woman in that post) and as U.S. Secretary of State.

identification or co-orientation concerns shared among speakers and listeners that help overcome divisions and bring diverse people together

common ground specific areas or concerns that both speaker and audience consider important

STOP AND CHECK

EVALUATING ETHOS

Log on to www.americanrhetoric.com and read or listen to two of the top 100 speeches. Identify some ways the speaker demonstrates good sense, good character, goodwill, and dynamism.

Incorporate Principles and Forms of Invitational Rhetoric

In many cases, marshaling your best arguments will not resolve disagreements, especially on divisive issues like euthanasia and abortion. When others disagree heartily with your viewpoints, you may find it more satisfying to practice **invitational rhetoric,** a form of "sense making" identified by Sonia Foss and Cindy Griffin.[36] Rather than focus on winning an argument, invite your audiences into your world, to understand it as you do, and then invite them to present their own perspectives. Change may or may not result, but mutual understanding can be enhanced. Foss and Griffin identify three principles and two forms associated with invitational rhetoric.

Combining Three Principles

It is typical to think of traditional argument as verbal dueling with a winner and a loser; in contrast, invitational rhetoric focuses on mutual understanding and mutual influence based on the principles of equality, individual value, and self-determination. It's one way to develop a dialogical spirit as described in Chapter 3.

1. *Equality:* Rather than imposing your "superior" views on others, you see your listeners as equals. You don't select strategies to overcome their resistance; however, you do identify possible barriers to understanding and try to minimize or neutralize them. In short, you are open to one another's viewpoints.

    For example, say it's an election year. Your classroom contains active supporters of three presidential candidates. You all have formulated good reasons for your choices. As an invitational rhetor, you share the path you've traveled in making your decision, and you invite your classmates to share theirs.

2. *Nonhierarchical value of all:* By approaching your audience as equals, you respectfully look for the value in their conclusions as well as your own. You don't attempt to demean their position and point out their deficiencies, and you try to maintain a positive relationship with those who differ from you.

    Back to the election. By not considering yourself intellectually or morally superior by virtue of your viewpoint, you can respectfully recognize the value of your classmates' conclusions, because you work hard to see the point of their reasoning. There's no yelling, no put-downs, no character assassination of the various candidates.

3. *Self-determination:* Invitational rhetoric may or may not result in change. If your listeners change their opinions or their behaviors, it won't be because you shamed or scared them into accepting your views. And you may modify your own positions by considering their insights. In some instances, you and your listeners may agree to disagree while remaining mutually respectful.

    You and your classmates eventually split your votes, but regardless of who's elected, you have insights into the reasoning involved in each position, and you have learned more about working effectively in the political climate that will follow the election.

Including Two Forms

How does invitational rhetoric look in action? This alternative way of approaching issues typically takes two forms: offering perspectives and creating conditions that result in an atmosphere of respect and equality.

1. *Offering perspectives:* You explain what you currently understand or know, and you show a willingness to yield, examine, or revise your conclusions if someone offers a more satisfying perspective. When confronted with hostile or very divergent

viewpoints, **re-sourcement** is one way to respond creatively by framing the issue in a different way.

If this sounds complicated, read Gail Grobey's speech at the end of Chapter 15. In her narrative, Gail offers her perspective on not spanking children (to listeners who believed in spanking), and she reframes her daughter's discovery of a prescription pill. She calls it an *act of heroism* (saving the dog from danger) rather than buying into the *ownership frame* her daughter presents (it's mine, and you can't take it away).

2. *Creating conditions:* You can create conditions in which your audiences feel safe, valued, and free to offer their own perspectives in two ways. First, use **absolute listening,** or listening without interrupting or inserting yourself into the talk; this allows others to discover their own perspectives. Hear people out without criticism or counterarguments. Second, use **reversibility of perspectives.** While others are sharing their ideas, try to think from their perspectives instead of only your own. The Native American saying "Don't judge people until you've walked a mile in their moccasins" demonstrates perspective taking.

Invitational rhetoric, a form of reasoning often associated with women, is a model of cooperative, dialogical communication in which you and your audiences generate ideas. Because it is rooted in affirmation and respect, it's arguably an ethical way of coming to conclusions. Further, because you're not intent on controlling the ideas of others, you can disagree without figuratively going to war.

Summary

You draw upon a variety of reasoning strategies found in the canon of invention as you make simple daily decisions or argue about complex national policy questions. Although it is often impossible to prove a claim beyond any doubt, you have several resources when using reasoning to support your ideas.

Toulmin's linear model of reasoning shows that claims of fact, definition or classification, value, and policy are based on various kinds of evidence, with a connecting link or warrant and backing that justifies them. Listeners weigh the evidence, data, or grounds to see if it is sufficient and trustworthy enough to lead to the conclusion. To avoid overstating your claim, it is important to limit its scope by using qualifiers. Further, your arguments may be more persuasive if you rebut or counter the possible objections your listeners may have.

Aristotle presented three kinds of proofs thousands of years ago. The first, logos, or rational proof, comes from your words. Analogy, both figurative and literal, is reasoning by comparison. Inductive reasoning draws generalizations or conclusions from a number of examples. Then, deductively, generalizations are applied to particular cases. Finally, causal reasoning links things that exist in time in such a way that the second results from the first. All these methods require the application of specific tests; otherwise, they can lead to fallacious or faulty conclusions.

Pathos, or emotional proofs, involves appeals to your listeners' positive and negative emotions as well as their needs. The chapter presented five basic needs: survival, security, belonging and love, esteem, and self-actualization. Emotions combine to form motivations that are both complex and mixed.

The third proof, ethos, comes from personal credibility. To be believable, you should have good character, good sense, goodwill, and dynamism, but ideas about credibility vary across cultures.

Finally, an alternative way to make sense of complex issues is to practice invitational rhetoric based on equality, individual value, and self-determination rather than on control. You offer your perspectives and create conditions in which others are free to offer theirs. Absolute listening and reversibility of perspectives let you hear and learn from the viewpoints of others. Change may or may not result.

Student Learning: Workbook
To review this chapter, students can complete "Before You Take the Exam" in Chapter 18 of the *Student Workbook.*

re-sourcement creatively framing a divisive issue or viewpoint in a different way that may be less threatening

absolute listening listening without interrupting or inserting oneself into the talk

reversibility of perspectives an attempt to think from the other's perspective as well as one's own

STUDY AND REVIEW

The premium website for *Public Speaking* offers a broad range of resources that will help you better understand the material in this chapter, complete assignments, and succeed on tests. The website features

▶ Speech videos with critical viewing questions, various types of outlines, transcripts, and note cards

▶ Interactive practice activities, self quizzes, and a sample final exam

For more information about this text's electronic learning resources, consult your **Guide to Online Resources for Public Speaking** or visit http://communication.wadsworth.com/jaffe5.

KEY TERMS

The terms below are defined in the margins throughout this chapter. The book website also provides interactive flashcards and crossword puzzles to help you learn these terms and the concepts they represent.

Student Learning: Book Website
Under "Chapter Resources," students will find several tools for reviewing the information in this chapter, including a "Tutorial Quiz." You can also have them email you the results of this quiz as a participation or extra-credit activity.

argument 332
evidence, data, or grounds 333
assertions 334
warrant 334
backing 334
qualifiers 334
rebuttal 334
logos 335
analogy 335
reasoning by metaphor 335
parallel case or literal analogy 336
inductive reasoning 337
deductive reasoning 337
enthymeme 338
causal reasoning 339
fallacy 340
unsupported assertion 340
ad populum 340

ad hominem 340
post hoc 340
overgeneralization 341
red herring 341
false analogy 341
false dichotomy 341
motivation 342
pathos 342
emotions 343
proof 345
ethos 345
identification or co-orientation 347
common ground 347
invitational rhetoric 348
re-sourcement 349
absolute listening 349
reversibility of perspectives 349

APPLICATION AND CRITICAL THINKING EXERCISES

The exercises below are among the practice activities on the book website.

Instructor's Resource Manual
The *Instructor's Resource Manual* provides suggestions on how to use these critical thinking exercises.

1. Watch a movie or television show about a trial, and see if you can diagram the argument or case against the suspect using Toulmin's model. Who is arrested? For what (the claim)? On what evidence (the data or grounds)? What's the warrant (the link: causal reasoning, inductive reasoning, deductive reasoning, parallel case reasoning, testimony by a credible source, emotional arguments)? Is there backing for the warrant? Is the claim or charge limited or qualified? How? What are the rebuttal arguments (the defense)?

2. Find a letter to the editor in your local newspaper about a controversial topic. Identify the types of reasoning the author uses, and then evaluate his or her arguments. Do they pass the tests for reasoning given in the text? Assess the overall effectiveness of the argument.

3. Find a letter to the editor (refer to YanHong Krompacky's letter in Chapter 14) or an ad from a current magazine. How does it appeal to emotions (both positive and negative)? To needs?

4. Read the speech at the end of this chapter. Stop and answer the questions posed throughout.

5. With a small group of classmates, make a list of possible speech topics that relate to each of the levels of need in Maslow's hierarchy.

6. Watch a movie like *Twelve Angry Men,* or watch a clip of a movie speech found on **www.americanrhetoric.com**. Focus on the persuasiveness of the arguments stemming from logical and emotional appeals and from the credibility of the speaker(s).

7. Visit **www.ncpa.org/** and link to Debate Central or Both Sides. There you'll find a number of policy issues with links to further information on each topic. Using the Toulmin model as your framework, work with a partner to create a complete argument on a specific topic. Then refute the argument of another set of partners in a classroom discussion.

8. Stephen Toulmin is a major figure in argumentation. Do an Internet search for the exact term *Stephen Toulmin*. Find out more about this important thinker whose work is studied by beginning speakers across the nation and the globe. Be prepared to contribute to a class discussion about his ideas.

SPEECH VIDEO

Log on to the book website to watch and critique persuasive speeches such as Gail Grobey's "Spanking," Brittany Farrer's "Limiting Alcohol Ads," and Paul Southwick's "Embryo Adoption."

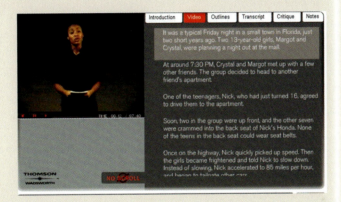

Student Speech with Questions

This speech contains both sound and faulty reasoning. To guide your analysis, stop throughout your reading and answer the questions inserted between points in the text.

THE BENEFITS OF HUNTING
Anonymous

Animals, I'm sure, have a place in everyone's heart. No one would like to see animals live pitiful lives and die by the hundreds from overpopulation and starvation. Well, this has happened before, and it could very well happen again if hunting is once again abolished by people who are uneducated about its true benefits.

If the welfare of animals means anything to you, it is essential that you listen closely to the biological facts that support hunting as being beneficial to wildlife, for in order to conserve wildlife, we must preserve hunting.

In the next few minutes, I will tell you about the damages resulting when people's right to hunt in certain areas is taken away. I will inform you of the uneducated ideas of animal activists and, finally, explain the differences between hunters and poachers.

a. *What do you think about the use of the phrases "I'm sure," "everyone," and "no one"? What effect does the use of the term "uneducated" have?*

b. *What claim is the speaker making?*

So many people are unaware of the damage that occurs to wildlife when hunting is taken away from a particular area. The best example of this happened in the state of Massachusetts. There, an animal rights group rallied and petitioned against deer hunting. Their efforts led to the banning of hunting in Massachusetts. During the period in which deer hunting was allowed, the deer population was around 100,000. Within the first year after the law was enacted, the population soared to 150,000.

Sounds good? Well, it wasn't! The overabundance of deer created a famine. Deer began to eat forest trees, gardens, and roots. They ate down to the foliage, leaving the plants unable to grow back the next year. Three years after the law went into effect the deer population went from 150,000 to only 9,000. It took the state ten years to return the deer population to normal. Eventually, the hunting ban was reversed, and the deer population has remained at its carrying capacity. I think it is hunting that plays a major role in keeping species from overpopulation.

c. What kind of reasoning is the speaker using? Does it pass the tests? Do you think her conclusion is obvious? Why or why not?

d. She says in her introduction that she will present biological facts about hunting. Does she do so to your satisfaction?

People often argue that animals were fine before man invented guns. However, before the white men came over here with guns, there weren't sprawling cities like Los Angeles and Portland to take up most of the animals' habitat. In those days, there was far more land for the animals to live on. Today, modernization has pushed the animals into a smaller wildlife area, leaving them less food and less room for breeding. Therefore, it is easier for the animals to overpopulate. Hunting has played a major role in keeping the animal population at a normal number. If hunting is taken away, the animals are sure to overpopulate.

It has been proven that humankind, even in its earliest form, has always hunted animals. Here in North America, before white people and guns came over, Indians hunted animals on a consistent basis. They killed hundreds of buffalo by herding them over cliffs every year. They caught school after school of salmon that migrated up the rivers. These hunts have always played a major role in population management, whether or not you choose to label it as a law of nature.

e. What argument does the speaker attempt to rebut? Does she do so to your satisfaction?

However, people argue that Indians needed to hunt animals to live, whereas today's North Americans don't need to kill animals to survive. So what if we can survive on fruit and vegetables? Humans are born omnivorous, meaning it is natural for us to eat both meat and plants. What is inhumane about eating an animal for food? Weren't we designed to do so?

f. Here is the second argument she attempts to counter or rebut. How well does she succeed? Explain your answer.

People also argue that the laws of nature will take care of animals. Hunting has always been a major part of the laws of nature. Without mountain lions to kill rabbits, the rabbit population would be a long-gone species because of overpopulation. Humans as well as mountain lions are animals. Our predation is as important to other animals, such as deer, as the mountain lion's predation is to rabbits.

g. What is the third argument the speaker attempts to refute? What kind of reasoning does she use?

h. Which of the three arguments do you think she did the best job of refuting? Which argument did she refute the least adequately?

Animal activists harass hunters all the time. These people have false perceptions of what hunting really is, and who hunters really are. At a rally against deer hunting, a woman speaker argued, "Hunters are barbarians who are in it for the kill. Hunters would use machine guns if they could. Plus, the deer are so cute." I think that argument is pathetic and holds absolutely no validity.

Another instance of hunter harassment occurred at Yellowstone National Park. An animal activist was not satisfied with only verbal harassment, so he struck the hunter on the head twice. Are animal activists really the peaceful and humane people they claim to be? And they still believe that hunters are bloodthirsty, crazy, and inhumane!

i. Do these two examples pass the tests for their use? Are they typical? How does the speaker generalize from them? How might she make her point instead?

Many of these misperceptions about hunters come from the association of hunters with poachers. Hunters are not poachers! Poachers are people who kill animals when they want, regardless of laws and regulations that were set to protect the animals. These are the kind of people who hunt elephants for their ivory tusks or kill crocodiles for their skins. Poachers kill deer in areas that are off-limits, during off-limit hunting seasons. These people are criminals who are extremely harmful to wildlife. Hunters would turn in a poacher in an instant if they caught one. Poachers give hunting a bad image in the eyes of the public. It's too bad that the animal activists don't go after the poachers who are extremely harmful to animals, and stop pointing a finger at hunters who follow the laws and regulations.

j. Why does the speaker contrast hunters to poachers? In what ways, if any, is this an effective argument?

If hunting is banned, just imagine a drive through the mountains on a road covered with emaciated skeletons of cadaverous deer who died of starvation. No longer can you take a picture of Bambi, your favorite deer that you saw every year at Yellowstone National Park. For Bambi and his family were overpopulated, and they slowly wilted away until their final day. Too bad there weren't a few healthy bucks taken by hunting that year to keep Bambi and family at a cozy carrying capacity where there was plenty of delicious food for all of them.

k. Here, the speaker uses a great deal of pathos. Identify emotional language and images. Is this effective? Why or why not?

The argument that animal activists use against hunting is fabricated mainly from emotions.

If they are personally against killing an animal, I can respect that. But they have no place trying to ban hunting. It is proven by biological facts that hunting is necessary for wildlife management. It provides millions of dollars that fund the construction of programs that help wildlife. It keeps species from overpopulating and starving to death. In order for wildlife to flourish at an optimum population number, hunting must continue to be a major part of wildlife management.

l. What does she put in her summary that does not appear anywhere else in her speech? If she had included it in the body of her speech and provided some evidence for that point, would her speech be stronger?

Questions

Now answer the following questions about the speech as a whole:

1. Overall, how would you grade the reasoning in this speech? Defend your grade.
2. How would you assess this speaker's credibility? How knowledgeable does she seem to be, and why? Does she show good sense throughout? Where (if at all) does she demonstrate goodwill toward listeners? Is there any way to assess her good character? Where (if at all) does she identify with her listeners?
3. How might you respond if you were an animal activist in her audience?
4. Where did you feel you would like to see sources cited?

A

SPEAKING IN SMALL GROUPS

THROUGHOUT THE WORLD, the ability to work well in small groups is essential in the classroom, as well in businesses and other organizations that regularly accomplish their tasks through cooperative work teams and groups. In fact, in a recent survey conducted by Pennsylvania State University, 71.4 percent of corporate executives polled listed the ability to work in teams as a desirable quality in recent graduates.[1]

Working in task-oriented teams often produces excellent results, but it can be frustrating, especially for those participants who are unaware of the dynamics inherent in group work. This appendix first presents some advantages and disadvantages of group work. Next, it gives specific tips for working in two types of groups: investigative groups and problem-solving groups. A description of formats commonly used in public presentations of group findings concludes this appendix.

Advantages and Disadvantages of Group Work

You've probably heard the saying "Two heads are better than one." In fact, some people who work on difficult problems believe "the more heads the better." However, if you're trying to accomplish a task with a group plagued by scheduling conflicts, dominating members, or nonparticipants, you may be tempted to work alone. Truth be told, the many advantages of group work must be balanced against the disadvantages.

Advantages of Group Work

Working in groups and teams has several advantages:[2]

▶ *Groups have access to more information and knowledge than do individuals working alone.* It's only reasonable to think that more people equals more experiences and more combined knowledge. For example, someone may have expertise in one area but lack it in another. She needs other group members to balance her out. Together, they can pool their resources and generate more information than they could produce individually.

▶ *The various viewpoints that participants bring to the group can help more creative ideas emerge.* By combining personalities and thinking and learning styles, the group as a whole can respond more creatively to an issue than if the solution relies on the ideas of only one person. Diversity within a well-functioning group also increases the members' understandings of various cultural perspectives that bear upon the issue.

▶ *Group work provides a deeper level of involvement and learning.* When all participants do research, discuss their findings, and listen to the information discovered by their teammates, the group can do three to four times as much research in approximately the same time as a single person working alone. Discussions also let group members ask and answer questions that clarify confusing ideas and sharpen critical thinking skills. Consequently, many people learn better in small groups.

▶ *Many people enjoy working in small groups.* People can be more motivated and have more positive attitudes when they don't deal with a subject or problem alone. Social interactions with others can make teamwork satisfying; not only do group members learn about an issue, they also learn about one another.

▶ *Working in small groups results in the co-creation of meaning.* Because of the nature of information sharing and decision making, small groups are inherently dialogical. Ideally, all members participate in discussing, refining, and evaluating ideas and solutions.

Appendix-at-a-Glance
This appendix is a concise discussion of speaking in group situations. First, it lists advantages and disadvantages of using a group to accomplish a task and looks at gender differences in group interactions. Then it describes the steps of investigative groups and problem-solving groups. It concludes with formats commonly used for public presentations.

Classroom Discussion / Activity
To help students apply the topic to their lives, ask them to offer examples of small groups in which they have participated.

Disadvantages of Group Work

Despite its advantages, group work has some disadvantages that you should anticipate.

- *Working in groups takes more time.* Scheduling meetings and working around the schedules of other busy people takes time which often frustrates task-oriented group members.
- *Some members of the group do more work than others.* Some group members may do less work than they would if they were responsible for the entire project. This results in tension within the group, and often the hard workers resent the slackers.
- *Some members of the group may monopolize the discussion and impose their ideas on others.* Dominators can take over a group if the members aren't careful. One reason is linked to personality: Some people are very extroverted and expressive. Another is linked to gender: Women often defer to men in mixed groups.[3]
- *There is a tendency toward groupthink.*[4] Groupthink happens when members try to avoid conflict by subtly pressuring themselves and one another to conform to a decision (which may be irrational and unwise). On a national and international level, American military officers in World War II failed to see the signs point toward a Japanese attack on Pearl Harbor, and the results were disastrous; in recent years, several world leaders convinced themselves and one another that Saddam Hussein had weapons of mass destruction in Iraq which required a war to eradicate them. As we now know, no weapons were found. Most decisions your group makes won't have such widespread implications, but you should strive to ensure that you aren't making a bad decision out of politeness or unwillingness to challenge the group's decision.

In summary, although group work offers many advantages, it also has disadvantages. Groups cannot avoid the time factor, but they can make attempts to use their available time together wisely. However, most disadvantages can be minimized if group members are accountable to one another, if all members have a chance to voice their opinion, and if they avoid agreement simply for the sake of peace.

DIVERSITY IN PRACTICE

MALE AND FEMALE TENDENCIES IN GROUP INTERACTIONS

IN HER BOOK *You Just Don't Understand: Women and Men in Conversation,* Deborah Tannen[5] identifies several differences in the conversational styles associated with males and females. John Cowan[6] traces these differences to boys' and girls' playground experiences, which he suggests are "at least a light-year apart." Remember, however, that male- and female-associated characteristics are tendencies, not absolutes, and men and women, especially college students, are probably more alike than different.[7] Nevertheless, Tannen's conclusions are widely discussed, and tendencies like the following have implications for communication in small group contexts.

- Men tend to engage in *Report Talk,* which is informative speaking that relies more on facts, figures, and definitions and less on personalized information. In contrast, women tend to engage in *Rapport Talk* that stresses relationships and personalizes information with examples and stories.
- Men's tendency is to pursue interactional goals aimed at gaining power, status, and respect— whether or not they offend others. Women, in contrast, tend to help others and build relationships between people. They are less concerned about winning an argument.

(continued)

- Men tend to speak in a *dominant way,* meaning that they interrupt and display their knowledge and expertise. They also control the topic and set the agenda. On the other hand, women express more agreement, making connections and smoothing relationships. Cowan[8] says that men offer "assertion followed by counterassertion," and women offer "inquiry followed by counterinquiry." Although women suggest more topics than men, men choose which topic to discuss.
- Men explain more than women, and their explanations are lengthy. Women can and do explain, but they have fewer opportunities to do so in mixed gender groups.
- Men speak more. Conversational time is one-sided in their favor. Women listen more and speak less in mixed gender groups.

To learn more about Professor Tannen's work, visit her Web page at www.george town.edu/faculty/tannend/ or search the Internet for *Deborah Tannen.* You'll find interviews, excerpts from her books, and other interesting information about gender differences that affect men's and women's talk in small groups.

**Student Learning:
Book Website**
All URLs mentioned in the text are available as live, regularly maintained links on the book's website, located in the "Chapter Resources" list under "Web Links."

Investigative Teams

Educators commonly ask students to team up to study a subject and present their findings to the entire class. For example, one study[9] concluded that biology students learn to do "science thinking" in small groups and that their classroom presentations hone the organizational and speaking skills they will use throughout their careers as scientists.

Investigative reporters (students and professionals alike) also team up to probe complex social issues. Because a seven- to ten-minute report (described in Chapter 16) can only overview a controversy, many instructors have students work in teams to study a significant issue in greater depth. Group members then present their findings in a more extended period of time. In addition, reporters for a news magazine such as *U.S. News & World Report* commonly work together on a major feature. One or two write the actual story, but the names of additional contributors are listed at the end of the article. Sidebars and smaller, supplementary stories, each written by a different member of the investigative team, surround the featured story.

The advantages of teamwork converge in investigative teams. Obviously, a team can cover a national issue in a national magazine much more thoroughly than a single reporter can. Similarly, students typically learn more and become more involved in a subject when they investigate it with others. The group shares the research burden, which allows a particular student to focus mainly on one area. Not only do team members learn more, others in the class benefit from the variety of perspectives they hear and the indepth coverage they get when the group shares its findings publicly.

To research and report a topic effectively, the team should have several meetings that progress from an initial get-acquainted session through the research stage to the final presentation.

First Meeting: Getting Acquainted

In your initial meeting, get to know one another and find out each person's interest, knowledge, and expertise regarding your topic. (This is a good time to exchange phone numbers or email addresses.) Leadership can develop informally, or you can designate someone to guide the meeting and keep people on task. An important role is *gatekeeper,* the person who makes sure that quiet people participate and that no one dominates the discussion. Another important role is *recorder,* the member who takes notes (minutes) on what transpires during the meeting.

During this meeting, divide your subject into subtopics, and have each member select specific aspects to research in depth. For instance, you might include a definition, the history, numbers and types of people affected, regions or areas affected, proposed solutions, or arguments for and against each solution.

For the group to be successful, it must hold members accountable. Consequently, before you adjourn, have group members identify a specific subtopic and specify the methods (such as interviews or library research) they plan to use to investigate it. Then set a date, place, and time (beginning and ending times) for the next meeting.

Additional Meetings: Discussing the Subject

Begin each new meeting by approving the minutes of the previous meeting. Organize your group's work by writing out an explicit *agenda*, an ordered list of the items you'll discuss. Proceed by holding team members accountable for summarizing their work and answering questions the others ask. After everyone has contributed, discuss the following: What questions do we still have as a group? Are there gaps in our research? If so, where? What patterns or recurring themes are we finding? Are we beginning to detect a way to organize our final presentation?

Continue to use the gatekeeper and recorder roles. In every meeting, focus on your final goal—to present your material publicly. To achieve this objective, cooperate on organizing ideas and outlining materials into a coherent form. Review organizational patterns (Chapter 9), and think of creative ways to introduce and conclude your presentation (Chapter 10). Identify possible visual aids (assigning a person to create each one), and put someone in charge of requesting the equipment you will need for your presentation.

Before the group separates, have all participants state specifically what they will do before the next meeting to forward the group's goals. Always conclude by setting a date, place, and time for your next meeting.

Final Meeting: Polishing the Presentation

In previous meetings you researched various aspects of a complex topic. You also used skills from the canon of arrangement or organization to shape your final product. Now, meet a final time to finalize all the details. Give each group member a written outline or record of what you've done. Rehearse the final presentation so that everyone knows her or his role, and iron out any glitches that arise. Check that visuals are made and equipment is ordered, and then congratulate one another on a job well done.

Problem-Solving Teams

Teaching Tip
For additional information on group decision making, consult the "decision making" page from Psychology Hyper Text at http://sun.science.wayne.edu/~wpoff/cor/grp/decmake.html.

What is a problem? Professor Jack Henson[10] defines "problem" as *the difference between what is* (the present condition) and *what should be* (the goal). In other words, a problem is the gap between what we have and what we want. We work with others to solve campus, local, national, and global problems. Campus, or local, issues include such things as military recruitment on campus, challenges to free speech, parking problems, and alcohol abuse. National and international issues such as environmental protection, global trade imbalances, elder abuse, and safe water gain our attention. When problems arise, we often form discussion groups, task forces, and committees in which we typically use a problem-solving method described a hundred years ago by the educator John Dewey and modified several times since.

The analytical, linear process presented here of appraising problems and generating solutions is typical of Euro-American culture, and similar methods are used globally. For example, the Africa Region's Knowledge and Learning Center reported that women's groups in Senegal also use a five-step process to solve community problems.[11] In many contexts, a structured, rather than a random, approach results in more effective group work. However, don't think of this process as strictly linear, proceeding only in one direction from point to point; your group may circle back to previous steps, and you may revise as you go along. What follows is a modification of John Dewey's original five steps.

Step One: Define the Problem

It's important at the outset to state the problem clearly. If you fail to do this, your work will be more difficult later, because it is hard to find a solution for something that is vague. Some problems are simple to define: "Whom shall we recommend to be hired as the new basketball coach?" is an obvious problem to solve after a controversial coach resigns. However, for most problems, you should narrow the topic and follow these three general suggestions:

▶ State the issue as a policy question, using the word *should*. For example, "Which athlete should we honor as outstanding gymnast?" "What should we do to enhance nighttime safety in the parking lots?"
▶ Leave the question broad enough to allow for a variety of answers; that is, use an open rather than a closed question. The yes or no closed question "Should the student council repair acts of vandalism in the student union building?" is less effective for group discussion than the open question "How should the student council ensure that campus buildings remain free from vandalism?"
▶ State the question as objectively as possible, avoiding emotionally charged language. "How can we get rid of this unfair grading system?" is less effective than "What changes, if any, should be made in the current methods of assigning grades?"

Step Two: Analyze the Problem

After you know the problem, begin collecting pertinent information using the guidelines described in Chapters 7 and 8. Look for the facts—including causes and effects—values, and policies that relate to your topic. Divide the relevant issues among group members and have them consult a variety of sources for information. Asking questions such as these will be helpful:

▶ What are the factual issues involved? What's the history of the problem?
▶ What causes the problem? Which are primary causes? What secondary factors contribute to it?
▶ What effects result from the problem?
▶ What values apply? Are ethical issues involved? In what respects?
▶ Are any relevant policies involved? Any historical precedents?

After completing these two steps, you're ready as a group to explore possible solutions.

Step Three: Set Criteria for Deciding on a Solution

Because solutions must be realistic in terms of time, money, and ease of enactment, set up standards for determining an acceptable solution before you even begin to suggest possible solutions. As part of your consideration, ask yourselves two vital questions:[12] (1) What must we do? That is, what is *required?* (2) What do we want to do? In other words, what is *desired?* For example, we must solve the problem with less than $10,000; we want to solve it with less than $5,000. We must have the policy in effect by the beginning of the next school year; we want to have it implemented by the end of the spring term. When you work within budget and time constraints, you'll automatically rule out some solutions as too costly or too time consuming.

Step Four: List Possible Solutions

During this period, your group should generate as many ideas as possible. Because you're seeking possibilities, don't worry if all these suggestions aren't practical. Withhold judgment until later. One common way to generate ideas is to *brainstorm*, in which group members offer a number of ideas for consideration. Consider using a mind map as described in Chapters 6 and 7 to record these ideas.

Here are some tips for a successful brainstorming session:

◗ Have a recorder write down all the suggestions, using a whiteboard, overhead transparency, or flip chart.
◗ Record all the ideas without evaluating them.
◗ Make sure each person in the group has an opportunity to contribute at least once.
◗ Piggyback off one another's ideas—that is, encourage group members to use one proposal as a jumping-off point for another.

After a successful brainstorming session in which everyone generates ideas, begin to evaluate each idea against the criteria you decided upon earlier. Often your brainstorming session will lead you to rethink your criteria. So don't hesitate to go back and make necessary revisions.

Step Five: Select the Best Solution

Now that your group has a good idea of the problem, has set criteria for a solution, and has generated a number of ideas, it's time to select the best solution. Begin to evaluate the suggested solutions against the criteria you set. You'll easily eliminate some ideas because they're too expensive, too time consuming, or don't fit your criteria for other obvious reasons. After you have pared down your options, analyze and weigh the merits of those that remain to find the one that members of your group can agree on.

Presenting Your Group's Findings

Whether your group investigated a topic or solved a problem, decide how you will report on your findings, both in writing and orally. First, summarize your work. Then present the information you've discovered or the solution you've chosen, justifying your choice. For problem-solving groups, provide information on why you predict the solution will work, why it will be cost effective, and why it will be easy to implement. Then present your findings to the audience who will most likely be involved in its implementation. In general, there are three basic ways to present your conclusions.

A Final Report

In this format, one member speaks for the entire group. A group giving an investigative report on a topic such as increasing nighttime safety in campus parking lots all gather data and work together to write up their findings, but only one member of the group actually speaks publicly.

The team members designate a presenter to define the problem for their audience and briefly explain relevant background information. Then the presenter summarizes the decision-making process, identifies the criteria decided on for the solution, describes alternative solutions that were considered, and explains and justifies the group's final choice.

To illustrate, let's look at ways a new nighttime parking policy might be announced. To communicate with the college leadership as well as the public, the task committee writes a final report that details the procedures used and gives the underlying rationale for the policy. The committee chairperson then presents these to the board of trustees and to the student council for approval. A press release generated from the final report goes to newspapers in the area. Television stations pick up the story and send reporters to interview the committee spokesperson to gain additional information about the new policy.

A Panel Discussion

In this format, all group members sit on a panel and discuss the issue in dialogical interactions. A leader or moderator asks a series of questions, and members take turns providing insights, with everyone contributing from his or her store of information and opinions. Afterward, the moderator may open the discussion to the audience and encourage listeners to talk with panelists during a question-and-answer period. In this way, the group and the audience cooperate in co-creating meaning.

Each member of a group that studied ways to improve nighttime safety in campus parking lots, does research on the topic. They all search for facts, find examples of what other schools have done, get quotations from experts and laypeople, interview or survey college students, professors, and teaching assistants, and discuss among themselves their personal opinions. In a group planning meeting, they share their findings and identify a series of questions to discuss; then on the day of their presentation, each member contributes to each question during their group's allotted half hour. Afterward, they invite audience questions.

The entire problem-solving group might appear in a "town hall" session on campus. There, in a free-flowing manner, each committee participant discusses the recommended safety policy and the process the group went through to reach it; the committee chair acts as emcee. After the proposal is presented, audience members can ask questions regarding implementation, cost, consequences, and so on.

A Symposium

In this format, each member of the group selects one aspect of the problem and prepares and delivers a speech about it. After the speakers have all finished, the moderator usually opens up the floor for a question-and-answer period.

If a group investigating the topic of nighttime safety in campus parking lots chooses a symposium format, they subdivide the topic, and assign each person one part. The first speaker leads off by describing the problem; the second overviews possible solutions. The third explains the chosen solution, and the fourth relates a case study of a college that implemented a similar policy. The final speaker provides a summary. After they finish, a moderator asks for audience questions.

To inform parents of a new nighttime safety policy on campus, the committee could present a symposium during Parents' Weekend. Interested family members then come to hear the task group members discuss their recommendations. One discusses the history of the problem. The next describes the campus-wide discussions that took place over a two-year period. A third details the specifics of the new policy, and the final speaker tells why the committee believes this solution is workable. Parents can then ask questions.

B

SPEAKING ON SPECIAL OCCASIONS

SPECIAL OCCASION SPEECHES are common at celebrations, solemn occasions, and occasions that reaffirm group values. Their purpose is to commemorate. They also have an *integrative function* that helps connect people to one another and to their shared goals.[1] Special occasion speeches reinforce and maintain the common belief-attitude-value cluster that influences the group's behaviors.

This appendix provides guidelines for speeches of introduction, farewell, announcement, award presentation and acceptance, nomination, commemoration or goodwill, and eulogy. The Diversity in Practice feature describes some aspects of organizational culture that affect your speech.

Introductions

When people first meet, they ask questions such as "Who is this person?" "What do we have in common?" "What background experiences bring her here?" Introductions are short speeches that provide people with the information they need to interact effectively. You may introduce a classmate, a newcomer to your workplace, or a speaker at a special event. Regardless of the type, keep your introduction brief. Chapter 2 provided guidelines for introducing a classmate. Here are some tips for introducing an unfamiliar person to your school or work environment:

▶ Provide the newcomer's name and job title.
▶ Give a few relevant details about the person's educational and occupational background as well as personal characteristics.
▶ Close by welcoming the newcomer to the group.

Here is a sample introduction of a new housemother to a fraternity. Notice that it briefly presents her qualifications and provides the fraternity brothers, to whom she's a stranger, with information about her background and some of her interests, which will help them relate to her.

> Today, we welcome our new housemother, Linda Butler-Jones. Linda joins us from another Sigma Phi Epsilon house in the great state of Texas. She graduated from the University of Florida, where she majored in psychology (which, when you think of it, is a good major for a housemom).
>
> Linda spent twenty years as a high school counselor, but after her children left for college, she went back to campus herself—this time as a fraternity housemother where she put her managerial and hostessing skills to good use. As you know, we rely on housemothers to plan our meals, etiquette classes, and social events. From what I've been told, the Sigma Phi Epsilon men in her former house were the best fed on campus, they were always exceptionally polite, and their social events were legendary—for all the good reasons.
>
> Now, after thirteen years in Texas, she's ready to move to the Pacific Northwest. And we are delighted to welcome her, knowing that her skills will help us fulfill our fraternity's motto of "Building Balanced Leaders for the World's Communities."
>
> Linda, we're glad you're here. We know you will be a great addition to our house.

To introduce a guest speaker, include some information about the occasion that precipitated the invitation as well as about the actual speaker. Here are some elements to include in such speeches:

- Greetings and/or a welcome to the group
- A statement about the occasion
- Announcement of the speaker's name and topic
- A brief account of the speaker's background, education, training, achievements, personality, or any other salient information that relates to the topic or the audience.

Afterward, be prepared to make a few remarks that provide closure. Briefly thank the speaker, and make a simple, short remark relating to the central idea of the speech.

You can watch and evaluate a sample introduction by Nathan Willingham of Missouri State University on the book's website.

Farewells

Saying good-bye is never easy, because departures cause disruptions that affect those left behind to a greater or lesser degree. This is true whether or not the person was well liked. For example, consider the emotions that arise when a popular professor leaves for a position in another university, a beloved rabbi retires, an unpopular manager is fired, or the seniors on the football team graduate. Because all these departures signal changes in an organization's social patterns, farewell speeches function to ease the inevitable changes that face both the departing individual and the group.

Individuals who leave bid the group or organization farewell, and a group member says good-bye on behalf of those who remain. Both speakers should express emotions—

especially appreciation, sadness, affection, and hope for the future. Balance the sadness inherent in the occasion by speaking about happy times; recounting humorous stories is one way to do this.

When you say farewell because you are leaving, include some or all of these elements:

▶ Remind group members of what they've meant to you personally.
▶ List some lessons you learned from being with them.
▶ Tell humorous stories that you'll carry with you as happy memories.
▶ Express both your sadness at leaving and your hopes for the future.
▶ Invite people to write or visit you in your new location.

When you bid farewell to someone who is departing, you speak not only for yourself but also for the group. Remember these elements in your speech:

▶ Recognize the person's accomplishments in the group.
▶ Recognize positive personal characteristics that you will remember.
▶ Use humorous anecdotes.
▶ Express your personal sadness and the group's sense of loss.
▶ Wish the person well in his or her new location.
▶ When appropriate, present a gift as a remembrance.

Announcements

Announcements keep individuals and groups knowledgeable about the goings-on of organizations and groups by providing facts about upcoming events or developments of interest. In clubs and organizations, businesses and faculty meetings, announcements are an agenda staple because they answer the questions "What's happening?" or "What's new?" Essential to these short speeches are details regarding who, where, when, and how much it costs, as the following outline of essential points shows:

▶ First, draw your listeners' attention to the event.
▶ Provide such details as who, what, when, and where the event takes place.
▶ Give both the costs and the benefits of attending.
▶ End with a brief summary of important information.

Here's a sample announcement:

Have fun and do good at the same time by attending the third annual Oregon Food Bank Benefit which will be held Tuesday, August 2, from 5:30–9:00 p.m. at McMenamins Grand Lodge in Forest Grove. Listen to the Big Band sounds of Swing DC and meet some representatives of the Oregon Food Bank, who will be there to take donations of cash or canned goods. The restaurant will donate half of all food and beverage receipts to the food bank. Children are welcome.

So help stop hunger in Oregon a week from Tuesday, from 5:30–9:00 p.m. in Forest Grove. For directions to the lodge, call 992-9533, or download a map from www.mapquest.com.

Classroom Discussion/ Activity
Have students select an announcement from the school's website (usually under "News" or "Press Releases") or the campus paper and turn it into an announcement speech that they present to the class.

Award Presentations

Award rituals express the common values of a group; we recognize meritorious work or character traits that embody our ideals. It's common to present recipients with a permanent memento of some sort. When you present an award, emphasize the group's shared beliefs, values, and commitments. In general, award presentations include these elements:

▶ Name the award and describe its significance. What personal traits or accomplishments does it honor? In whose name is it being presented? Why is it given? How often is it awarded? How are the recipients selected?
▶ Summarize the selection criteria and reasons the recipient is receiving the award.
▶ Relate the appropriateness of the award to the traits of the recipient.
▶ Express good wishes to the recipient.

Note, however, that some cultural groups rarely single out one individual to praise over others. (New Zealanders, for instance, have the saying "The tall poppy gets mown down.") Consequently, members of these groups may feel uncomfortable when their personal characteristics are publicly acknowledged. If this is the case, honor the entire group rather than a single individual.

Acceptance Speeches

Accept an award with a brief speech in which you express gratitude to those who selected you, thank other people who helped you become eligible for such an honor, and reinforce the cultural values that the award demonstrates, as these guidelines and sample acceptance speech show:

▶ Thank those who honored you.
▶ Acknowledge others who helped you.
▶ Personalize what it means to you.
▶ Express appreciation for the honor.

> Thank you, Professor Geffner, for those kind words, and thank you, committee, for selecting me as the Outstanding Speech and Hearing Student this year. As you know, many other students are deserving of honor for their scholarship and their service to the clients in our speech clinic, and I know that each one deserves recognition.
>
> Of course, no student can accomplish anything were it not for the support of a dedicated faculty—and the faculty here at St. John's University is outstanding. I have been impressed not only with their wisdom and skills, but also with the personal interest they all take in the life of each student who majors in speech pathology and audiology. Thanks also to my parents, who supported me both financially and emotionally through these past four years. I appreciate you all.
>
> Next year I will attend graduate school at Northwestern University. I'm sure that when I'm homesick for New York I will remember this honor and be inspired by your confidence in me.
>
> Thank you once again.

Nominations

Nominations are short persuasive speeches that do two things: (1) introduce your candidate to the group, and (2) present brief arguments explaining why she or he should be elected. Be sure to include the following elements:

▶ Name the office, and tell its importance to the organization as a whole.
▶ List the reasons the candidate is right for the office.

Two persuasive organizational patterns discussed in Chapter 17 are especially effective: (1) a direct method or statement of reasons pattern and (2) a criteria satisfaction pattern. When he nominated John Roberts as a new Supreme Court justice, President Bush set the following criteria:[5]

> And so a nominee to that court must be a person of superb credentials and the highest integrity, a person who will faithfully apply the Constitution and keep our founding promise of equal justice under law.

He then explained why his nominee met the criteria:

> John Roberts currently serves on one of the most influential courts in the nation, the United States Court of Appeals for the District of Columbia Circuit. Before he was a respected judge, he was known as one of the most distinguished and talented attorneys in America. John Roberts has devoted his entire professional life to the cause of justice and is widely admired for his intellect, his sound judgment and personal decency. . . . He's a man of extraordinary accomplishment and ability. He has a good heart. He has the qualities Americans expect in a judge: experience, wisdom, fairness, and civility. He has profound respect for the rule of law and for the liberties guaranteed to every citizen. He will strictly apply the Constitution in laws, not legislate from the bench. He is also a man of character who loves his country and his family. I'm pleased that his wife, Jane, and his two beautiful children, Jack and Josie, could be with us tonight. . . .

Commemorative Speeches

Commemorative speeches emphasize the audience's ideals, history, and memories. Although their basic purpose is to inspire and to reinforce beliefs and values, these speeches are often entertaining as well. Frequently, speakers representing an organization give special occasion talks; in fact, a single large corporation may annually provide speakers for more than 1,000 events. These representatives hope to create or increase goodwill toward their organization. Goodwill speeches are common at breakfast, luncheon, and dinner meetings, as well as at conventions and commencement ceremonies.

Although each speech is different, the following characteristics are typical:

▶ *Build the speech around a theme.* Find out in advance if one has already been selected for the occasion; if so, prepare your remarks around it. If not, select your own inspiring theme. Amari Howard built her classroom speech around the theme "no day but today," words from a song from the Broadway musical "Rent." You can watch and evaluate Amari Howard's speech on the book's website. Farah Walters,[6] President and Chief Executive Officer, University Hospitals of Cleveland, explains her theme in this excerpt from a keynote address she gave before an organization called WomenSpace.

> Before preparing these remarks, I asked the leadership of WomenSpace if there was anything special that I should address. I was told that there might be some interest in learning a little more about who I am and how I got to be the head of one of America's largest academic medical centers; and I was asked if I would give my assessment of where women are today in the professional world, and where I think women will be in the years ahead. I will touch upon those topics, but in a particular context.
> And that context is in the title of my talk—"In Celebration of Options."

▶ *Inspire listeners.* Inspiration is often linked to positive emotions and values such as hope, courage, respect, perseverance, and generosity. See how many positive emotions and values you can identify in this excerpt from Barbara Bush's[7] commencement address at Wellesley College:

Instructor's Resource Manual
Part I contains guidelines and an evaluation form for a tribute speech assignment.

Wellesley, you see, is not just a place, but an idea, an experiment in excellence in which diversity is not just tolerated, but is embraced. . . . Diversity, like anything worth having, requires effort. Effort to learn about and respect difference, to be compassionate with one another, to cherish our own identity, and to accept unconditionally the same in others. You should all be very proud that this is the Wellesley spirit.

You can watch and evaluate Barbara Bush's speech on the book's website. You'll also find its transcript on the website and in Appendix C.

▶ *Pay special attention to language.* To make your speech both inspiring and memorable, choose vivid, moving, and interesting words and phrases. Describe scenes in detail so that your hearers can form images in their minds; select words that are rich in connotative meanings. This excerpt from President Kennedy's[8] inaugural address shows the power of inspiring language.

And so, my fellow Americans; ask not what your country can do for you—ask what you can do for your country.

My fellow citizens of the world; ask not what America will do for you, but what together we can do for the freedom of man.

Finally, whether you are citizens of America or citizens of the world, ask of us here the same high standards of strength and sacrifice which we ask of you. With a good conscience our only sure reward, with history the final judge of our deeds, let us go forth to lead the land we love, asking His blessing and His help, but knowing that here on earth God's work must truly be our own.

You can watch John F. Kennedy's speech online at www.americanrhetoric.com. You'll also find the speech's transcript in Appendix C.

▶ *When appropriate, use humor.* For certain events, such as after-dinner speeches whose major purpose is to entertain, humor is almost essential. This example comes from the opening of Nora Ephron's[9] commencement address at Wellesley.

. . . [D]ear class of 1996, I am so proud of you. Thank you for asking me to speak to you today. I had a wonderful time trying to imagine who had been ahead of me on the list and had said no; I was positive you'd have to have gone to Martha Stewart first. And I meant to call her to see what she would have said, but I forgot. She would probably be up here telling you how to turn your lovely black robes into tents. I will try to be at least as helpful, if not quite as specific as that.

▶ *Be relatively brief.* These speaking occasions are generally not times to develop an extensive policy speech or to provide detailed information. Rather, they are times to state major themes that reinforce important values.

For further examples, go to http://dir.yahoo.com/Education/Graduation/Speeches/ and read or watch commencement addresses from a variety of speakers.

Eulogies

Eulogies are perhaps the most difficult speeches to give, because you probably knew the subject quite well. Don't worry about summarizing the person's entire life; instead, highlight things that celebrate the person's personality, and focus on sharing your feelings and your experiences to comfort other mourners. For example, here are some lines from Jonah Goldberg's eulogy for his father:[10]

. . . I think it would be a mistake to think my dad's wisdom and his humor were different facets of his personality. For him, "humor" and "wisdom" were different words for the same thing. After all, a sense of humor is merely the ability to see connections between things we haven't noticed before (while laughter is what we do when we realize that those connections should have been obvious all along.) Is wisdom really such a different thing?

Maybe it is, but it never really seemed to be in my dad.

Call it wisdom or humor, my dad saw the world through different lenses. . . . what was obvious for my dad was often insightful, profound, or hilarious to the rest of us. And, conversely, what was obvious to most people could be a complete mystery to him. To call my dad "handy" or overly burdened with street smarts would be a stretch.

Here are some guidelines:

▸ If you're the only person giving a eulogy, consult family members and friends for insights and anecdotes that capture essential personal characteristics. This also gives you an opportunity to find out if there is information the family prefers you *not* mention.

▸ Draw from your memories, and share appropriate feelings and experiences.

▸ Keep in mind your goal, which is to appropriately celebrate the deceased person's life by focusing on positive, memorable characteristics.

▸ Humor, used sensitively, can be appropriate and comforting.

▸ Consider using the wave pattern and organize your eulogy around a repeated theme like "Chet was creative . . ." or "John was a devoted friend . . ." or "Molly had enough energy for three people. . . ."

▸ Often, lines from poetry or the deceased's favorite lyrics work well.

▸ Don't worry about delivery. If you break down or otherwise show your emotions, your audience will be sympathetic. If you think losing control will be a problem, write out and read your eulogy, or speak with the person officiating beforehand and ask him or her to take over if you simply cannot continue. (For an example of an emotional eulogy, read Cher's speech at the memorial service for Sonny Bono, her former husband. It's available at www.americanrhetoric.com.)

▸ Keep it short. Unless you're told otherwise, limit your remarks to five to ten minutes.

In summary, special occasion speeches function to integrate the members of the group with one another and with the community in which they exist. You'll hear these talks in a variety of organizations—from clubs and volunteer associations to business, educational, and religious institutions. You may have numerous opportunities to introduce newcomers, present awards, give announcements, and make other short speeches on special occasions.

As noted throughout these appendixes, video of several special occasion speeches is available on or through the book's website: Nathan Willingham's introduction of actor John Goodman, Barbara Bush's commencement address at Wellesley College, a link to John F. Kennedy's inaugural speech, and others, such as Amari Howard's inspirational speech and Keisha Walkes' toast of Barbara Jordan.

Teaching Tip
For additional examples of eulogies (from Winston Churchill's eulogy of Franklin Roosevelt to Ronald Reagan's eulogy for the space shuttle Challenger crew), see Famous Eulogies at the Public Speaking Tips website: http://www.speaking-tips .com/Eulogies/. All URLs mentioned in the text are available as live, regularly maintained links on the book's website, located in the "Chapter Resources" list under "Web Links."

C

SAMPLE SPEECHES
Student Speeches

Overdose

Important event speech; Self-introduction (Chapter 2); speech topic from one's life experiences (Chapter 6)

Angela Bolin
Angela's assignment was to base her speech on an important event in her life. You can watch a video of Angela delivering her speech on the book's website.

Introduction

I. I should not be standing in front of you today.
II. Each of you has been ill at some time in your life.
III. My story is about a simple childhood illness, a mistake in a pharmacy, and a long, precarious hospital stay that influenced my decision to become a physician.

Body

I. My story begins with a simple sore throat when I was eight years old.
   A. My family physician prescribed an antibiotic.
   B. The pharmacy instead gave me Calan, an adult heart medication.
      1. SafeMedication.com says Calan relaxes the blood vessels so the heart doesn't have to pump as hard.
      2. In a few days I had consumed three times the adult dosage.
II. My parents rushed me to Cox North Hospital, where physicians began emptying my stomach before rushing me to Cox South Hospital.
   A. I spent five days in the intensive care unit.
   B. I then spent two days in a private room.
III. Pediahealth online pharmacy says no study has been done on the effect of Calan on children under 18.
   A. I interviewed my mother about the anticipated complications of Calan; she said they include heart, liver, and kidney failure.
      1. Overdose side effects listed on the HealthSquare website include congestive heart failure, slow heartbeat, heart attack, fluid retention, headache, low blood pressure, nausea, rash, shortness of breath, and upper respiratory infection, among other things.
      2. My mother said my heart alarm often went off because my heartbeat went below 40 beats per minute.
   B. My physicians did not expect me to live and told my parents not to get their hopes up.
IV. My parents turned to prayer.
   A. They alerted 500 students during a chapel service at Central Bible College.
      1. By the end of the day, these students had called their church prayer chains.
      2. Literally millions prayed for the little girl in Springfield.
   B. I believe these prayers pulled me through, and my doctors are still baffled at my recovery.

V. After this experience I want to heal others.
   A. I am a pre-med sophomore, planning to enter medical school in the fall of 2008.
   B. I plan to specialize in reconstructive plastic surgery.

Conclusion

I. If not for my illness, a pharmacy error, an overdose, and a hospital recovery, I would not be on my way to becoming a physician.
II. My ultimate goal is to save lives, just as my life was saved.

Dolphin Communication
Outline for an informative speech on a topic related to animals (Chapters 6 and 16)

Tanya Moser

Tanya's assignment was to prepare and deliver an informative speech with visual aids. Here is her content outline. Some sources are comparatively old, but the research has been going on for decades. Do you think older sources are still valid for this topic?

General Purpose: To inform

Specific Purpose: To inform my audience about research findings that show that dolphins engage in intelligent communication

Thesis Statement: Dolphins are intelligent animals that communicate with other dolphins and with human researchers.

Introduction

I. "Hoop Right Frisbee In": a dolphin trained to communicate with humans would know exactly what this meant.
II. The language barrier prevents us from communicating with animals, but dolphin studies show that we are not the only intelligent animals, and it is possible to communicate with some animals.
III. After I read an article for a writing class, I found several additional articles and books related to dolphin communication.
IV. I will explain the concept of dolphin intelligence, dolphin-to-dolphin communication, and dolphin communication with humans.

Body

I. Dolphins are intelligent and may be the animal closest to humans in this area.
   A. Dolphins have the highest brain-to-body size ratio of any nonhuman animal, which may mean they can process complex information (Forcier-Beringer, 1986).
   B. But intelligence is not entirely based on brain size.
      1. It is also related to how information is processed and used.
         a. Quickness and efficiency are important.
         b. So is flexibility, the ability to adapt to moment-by-moment happenings.
      2. Dolphins have both quickness and flexibility.
   C. Dolphins can mimic some human sounds.
      1. This indicates an ability to remember sounds.
      2. It also suggests the ability to communicate in an artificial language.
II. Dolphins communicate among themselves.
   A. Dolphins communicate through a system of whistles, clicks, rattles, moans, and squeaks (Dolphin Research Center, 2005).

1. Clicking sounds, used for navigation in deep waters, may convey messages.
   a. Pulsed squeaks can indicate distress.
   b. Buzzing clicks may indicate aggression.
2. The *New York Times* (2000) reports that dolphins exchange more than 1,700 whistles.
3. One hypothesis is that dolphins identify themselves through signature whistles (Hampton, 2003).
   a. Each one uses a distinctive whistle to identify itself to other dolphins.
   b. Mothers and calves find each other, even in groups of other whistling dolphins (Dolphin Research Center, 2005).
4. An article titled "Those Dolphins Aren't Just Whistling in the Dark" suggests they may pass down legends or stories (Sayigh & Payck, 1986).
   a. This seems a little far-fetched.
   b. However, animals seem to understand things in their own way.

III. Through training, captive dolphins have learned to associate sounds with objects and actions.
   A. In a study at the Dolphin Keyboard Communication Project at Disney's EPCOT Center in Florida, researchers used an underwater keyboard.

[Display transparency showing the nine-key keyboard.]

   1. Symbols on each of nine keys represented a specific object.
      a. The symbol was not a picture of the object.
      b. The keys could be moved so that dolphins could not memorize the location.

[Display second transparency, showing keys in a different position.]

   2. When dolphins pressed a key, a distinctive whistle was sounded, and they received the object associated with the key's symbol.
      a. They soon learned to associate symbol with object.
      b. Dolphins would give the "ball" whistle before pressing the key.
      c. With two items at once, such as a ring and a ball, they would make both whistles as they played with the objects.
   3. They remembered these sounds on a long-term basis.
      a. Researchers separated them from the keyboard for two years.
      b. When they saw it again, they happily began to whistle the various sounds.
   B. Dolphins could understand "sentences" that combined objects or actions they learned to associate with whistles.
   1. Two- to five-word sentences consisted of an indirect object, a direct object, and a connecting term.
      a. "HOOP RIGHT FRISBEE IN" meant, "Put the frisbee in the hoop on the right."
      b. Word order mattered (Dolphin Institute, 2002).
   2. Dolphins could understand a variety of word combinations.
      a. One instructor said "WATER TOSS," thinking this was nonsense.
      b. The dolphin quickly moved to the hose on the tank's railing and glided through it, sending out a spray of water.

Conclusion

I. In conclusion, we are not the only intelligent creatures on earth.
II. Dolphins are intelligent animals that communicate with one another and with humans through an invented "language" of whistles and clicks.
III. The next time you hear somebody talking to her dog as if it were a person, just think that she may know something about communicating with animals that dolphin studies hint at.

References

Curtis, P. (1987, January/February). Contact with dolphins. *Sea Frontiers*, 84–92.

Dolphin Institute. (2002). *Understanding language.* Retrieved November 7, 2005, from www.dolphin-institute.org/our_research/dolphin_research/understandinglanguage.htm

Dolphin Research Center. (2005). *Dolphin communication.* Retrieved October 31, 2005, from www.dolphins.org/Learn/COMMUN.pdf

Dolphin whistles offer signs of language ability. (2000, September 5). *The New York Times.* Retrieved October 30, 2005, from InfoTrac College Edition.

Evans, P. G. H. (1987). *The natural history of whales and dolphins.* New York: Oxford.

Forcier-Beringer, A. C. (1986, March/April). Talking with dolphins. *Sea Frontiers*, 84–92.

Sayigh, L. S., & Pyack, P. L. (1989, Spring). Those dolphins aren't just whistling in the dark. *Oceanus*, 80–83.

Self-Injury
Informative speech with several types of evidence (Chapters 8 and 16)

Caroline Valmont

Caroline's assignment was to research, outline, and deliver an informative speech, using several types of evidence and considering her audience. You can watch her deliver this speech on the book's website.

Specific Purpose: To inform my audience about people who intentionally injure themselves

Central Idea: Self-injury has several causes and effects, but there is help for those who seek it.

Introduction

I. Have you ever been so frustrated you wanted to pound something? [Hit the table.]
II. Many of us have inflicted pain on ourselves at least once in our lives, but probably not so seriously that it could be defined as self-mutilation.
III. When I heard about self-mutilation, I found it hard to understand why people would injure themselves, so I began to do research on the topic.
IV. Self-injury has several causes and effects, but there is help for those who want it.
V. Today, I will explain who self-mutilates, why they do so, the effects of self-injury, and the institutions and procedures used to deal with the problem.

Body

I. The television documentary "Can You See My Pain" (Hawley, 2000) defines self-mutilation in the following way.
  A. Self mutilation is the intentional harming of one's body; it entails cutting, scratching, abrading, or burning the skin, injecting or inserting foreign objects in the body, or ingesting toxins or alien substances.
  B. Self-mutilation is not suicide; individuals who hurt themselves only want to relieve some sort of inner pain; however, it may result in suicide.
II. Typically, self-injury begins in adolescence, although some injurers start in childhood and others wait until adulthood (Hawley, 2000).
  A. The stereotypical self-mutilator is a female Caucasian teen, from a middle-class dysfunctional home, doing poorly at school.
    1. For example, Brianna began cutting herself at age 14; now 17, her arms reveal many scars that mark out three years of emotional pain (Eller, 2004).
    2. Women are victims of society that pressures them to look, act, and dress in certain ways.
    3. Both male and female individuals in institutions such as prisons and juvenile detention centers have high incidences of self-injury.

4. Self injurers tend to have low self-esteem, feelings of inadequacy, or some psychological disorder.

5. Many come from a background that was sexually, emotionally, or physically abusive.

B. However, a May 2005 *Time* magazine article says this demographic is changing; some estimate up to 30% of self-injurers are male.

1. More now come from stable, two-parent homes, with no evidence of abuse.

2. Cutting is becoming more publicized due to confessions from celebrities like Angelina Jolie and Fiona Apple.

III. Now that we know who self-mutilates, we can ask why they do it.

A. Caroline Kettlewell, researching her book *Skin Game,* was fascinated to learn the connection between self-injury and a feeling of guilt in extreme cases.

1. From the time he was 13, a 30-year-old man had pressed and hit his eyeballs with his hand (Wetzler, 1980).

a. This began after he saw his mother naked and felt guilty.

b. It left him 60 percent blind, with a detached retina and cataracts.

2. Another 39-year-old man amputated his penis after a homosexual encounter.

3. Brooke started etching words she couldn't say to others on her stomach, which she called her "billboard" (Eller, 2004).

B. A May 2005 *Time* magazine article reports that self-mutilators cut either to feel more or to feel less.

1. People who are depressed, anxious, or have borderline personality disorder say they cut to kick-start feelings when they feel numb.

2. In contrast, other self-mutilators say their inner turmoil becomes so great that cutting themselves provides relief and calms them down.

3. For example, after Marissa's father left, she substituted cutting for her feelings, which she suppressed so as not to be a burden on her family (Eller, 2004).

Transition: Now that we have looked at what self-mutilation is, who does it, and why, let's see what can be done about it.

I. There are hotlines, hospitals, books, and rehabilitation centers for people who self-injure.

II. Organizations such as SAFE (Self-Abuse Finally Ends) Alternatives are structured inpatient programs that deal with all degrees of self-injurers.

A. Successful treatment involves a variety of methods.

1. Treating one disorder at a time is not as effective, because that allows another problem to dominate.

2. SAFE Alternatives does cognitive/behavioral work with patients' thoughts and actions.

3. SAFE Alternatives also emphasize interpersonal relationships and the use of words to solve the problems that lead to cutting.

B. Some therapists have their clients substitute harmful behaviors with a lesser degree of "infliction" for more harmful behaviors.

1. Examples include crushing ice in their hands or snapping a rubber band on their wrists.

2. These procedures may be frowned upon, but at least they don't leave scars.

Conclusion

I. Today we have looked at the problem of self-injury done by people who search for relief from traumatic experiences or stresses.

II. The solutions take time, but if you encounter a self-mutilator or if you are tempted to self-injure, there are places to get help.

III.   Your skin is something you should appreciate and respect.

IV.   As Caroline Kettlewell says in *Skin Game*, "Skin has a good memory. Skin is like the ground we walk everyday; you can read a whole history in it if you know how to look."

References

Eller, T. S. (2004, Winter). The razor's edge. *Christian Parenting Today*. Retrieved October 30, 2005, from InfoTrac College Edition.

Kettlewell, C. (2000). *Skin game*. New York: St Martin's Griffin.

Kluger, J. (2005, May 16). The cruelest cut: Often it's the ones teens inflict on themselves. *Time, 165*(20), 48.

Littig, E. & Thomas, D. (Producers). (2000). *Can you see my pain?* [Motion picture]. (Available from Northeastern Wisconsin In-School Telecommunications, 2420 Nicolet Drive, IS 1040, Green Bay, WI 54311)

Wetzler, J. M. (1980). *Description of guilt, delusional thinking, and sexual experience in a group of self-mutilators.* Seattle: University of Washington.

El Equipo Perfecto (The Perfect Team)

Narrative speech delivered in Spanish and interpreted into English (Chapters 13 and 15)

Uriel Plascencia; interpreter, Kelly Bilinski

Uriel's first language is Spanish, so he prepared a narrative speech in Spanish; before the speech, he worked with a fellow student, going over his speech with her. On the day he spoke, she translated his words as he paused between ideas. One key to speaking through an interpreter is to look directly at the audience at all times and to speak at your natural rate. As soon as the interpreter finishes one phrase, go directly into the next. Uriel might use longer phrases in some places and shorter phrases in others, depending on his point. To see an interpreted speech, watch the video of Uriel and Kelly delivering this speech on the book's website.

Cuando estaba en mi último año de Preparatoria, yo tuve buenos amigos. Nuestra amistad era muy fuerte que estábamos juntos mucho tiempo. (When I was a senior in high school, I had some very good friends. Our friendship was so strong that we spent a lot of time together.) *Nosotros éramos como un equipo en todos los aspectos porque estábamos en las mismas clases, hacíamos juntos nuestra tarea, practicábamos deportes y platicábamos mucho. Nosotros nunca tuvimos problemas serios.* (We were like a team in all aspects because we spent time in classes doing our homework, playing sports, and talking. We never seemed to have any serious problems.)

En el principio del segundo semestre, se abrió un campeonato de vóleibol. (In the beginning of the second semester, there were openings for intramural volleyball.) *Yo no pensaba estar en estos juegos porque yo estaba muy ocupado con mis estudios.* (I didn't think about being in those games because I was very busy with my studies.) *Dos de mis amigos hicieron un equipo y me invitaron a formar parte del equipo, yo acepté estar en el equipo.* (Two of my friends made a team and they invited me to be a part of the team; I decided to play with them.) *Ellos me dijeron la hora y el día de nuestros partidos.* (They told me the time and the days that we were supposed to play.) *Un día, ellos me llamaron por teléfono para saber si yo iba a venir al partido y yo les dije que sí.* (One day, they called me to find out if I was coming to the game, and I said yes.)

Antes del partido, ellos me dijeron que yo iba a jugar el segundo juego. (Before the game, they told me that I was going to play the second set.) *Cuando ellos terminaron de jugar el primer juego, yo fui a la cancha para hacer cambios y ellos no quisieron cambiarme.* (When they finished playing the first set, I came to the court to switch players, and they didn't want to switch the team.) *Ellos no quisieron que yo jugara con ellos.* (They didn't want me to play with them.) *Yo me sentí un poco mal y traté de entenderlos porque nosotros teníamos planes para el futuro.* (I felt a little bad, and I tried to understand because we had plans for the future.) *Ellos ganaron el juego y nos fuimos juntos de ahí. Ellos no se disculparon y no me dijeron nada acerca de esto.* (They won the game and we left from there together. They didn't apologize or even talk to me about it.)

Ellos me volvieron a llamar por teléfono para saber si yo iba a venir a los juegos finales y yo dije que sí. Yo fui muy emocionado a los juegos finales porque yo quería que fueramos los campeones. (They called me again to find out if I was coming to the finals and I said yes again. I came to the game very excited because I wanted to win the finals.) *Antes del juego, ellos me dijeron qua yo iba a jugar el segundo juego. Ellos me volvieron hacer la misma cosa que última vez.* (Before the game, they told me that I was going to play the second set. They made me the same promise as the last time.) *Yo fui a la cancha para hacer cambios y ellos no quisieron cambiarme.* (I came to the court to switch with another player, but then they didn't want to switch.) *Ellos me rechazaron enfrente de muchas personas porque había mucha gente durante los juegos finales.* (They rejected me in front of many people because there were a lot of people during the finals.) *Ellos insinuaron que no me necesitaban.* (They meant they didn't need me.) *Yo estaba muy decepcionado y me sentí muy estúpido enfrente de ellos. Yo me fui de la cancha y no pude entender por qué ellos me hicieron esto.* (I was very disappointed and I felt so stupid in front of them. I left the court, and I couldn't understand why they made this promise to me.) *Nosotros no habíamos tenido problemas y no supe cuál era el problema.* (We hadn't had any problems, and I didn't know what was wrong.) *Yo me esperé para ver si ellos ganaban* (I waited there to see if they would win) *pero no ganaron y me fui inmediatamente de ahí.* (but they didn't, and I left immediately.)

Yo estaba pensando todo el día acerca de cuál fue el problema porque yo pensaba que nuestra amistad era más fuerte que un estúpido juego. (I thought the whole day about what was wrong, because I believed our friendship was stronger than a stupid game.) *Ellos no podían decir que yo era un mal jugador porque yo era mejor que ellos.* (They couldn't say that I was a bad player, because I was actually a better player.) *Yo me sentí muy triste porque ellos no me habían hecho algo como esto antes.* (I felt very bad because they had made a promise like this before.) *Yo traté de entender la situación pero no pude.* (I was trying to understand the situation but I couldn't.)

Al siguiente día, (The next day,) *uno de mis amigos me estaba buscando para disculparse. El sabía lo que hizo y trató de explicarme y disculparse.* (one of these friends was looking for me to apologize. He knew what he had done and he tried to explain to me and apologize.) *Yo lo perdoné.* (I forgave him.) *Cuando me amigo trató de disculparse, yo no lo estaba escuchando. Yo estaba escuchando mi corazón y a Dios.* (When my friend was trying to apologize, I didn't listen to him. I was listening to my heart and God.) *Yo aprendí de Dios a perdonar y esta es la razón por que yo lo perdoné.* (I learned from God to forgive, and this is the reason why I forgave him.) *Nosotros somos amigos otra vez.* (We are friends again.) *El aprendió una lección y estoy seguro que él no lo volverá a hacer a nadie.* (He learned a lesson, and I am sure that he won't do this again to anybody.)

How to Write and Pronounce the Vietnamese Alphabet
Demonstration speech (Chapter 16) with a visual aid (Chapter 12)

NamKy Nguyen
NamKy's assignment was to give a short how-to or demonstration speech. He uses a document camera to display the letters as he writes them. A video of NamKy performing his speech is on the book's website.

General Purpose: To demonstrate

Specific Purpose: To show my audience how to write and pronounce the Vietnamese alphabet

Central Idea: Vietnamese is easy to write but hard to speak.

Introduction

I. *Xin chào các bạn!* Don't worry, I'm fine; I just spoke a bit of Vietnamese.
II. We live near Portland, which has many Vietnamese residents; Seattle has even more, and there are 80 million Vietnamese speakers in Vietnam.
III. Is Vietnamese like Chinese? Korean? No, it uses a modified Latin alphabet.
IV. I have had 16 years of writing, reading, talking, studying, and dating in Vietnamese, so I think I can consider myself as an expert here, no doubt.
V. In this speech, I'll illustrate the Vietnamese alphabet, pronounce the letters, and teach you some Vietnamese words.

Body

I. First, I will write and pronounce the 29 letters of the Vietnamese alphabet.
   A. [Pronounce each letter] a ă â b c d đ e ê g h i k l m n o ô ơ σ p q r s t u u' v x y
   B. Vietnamese is a tonal language; there are six different tones that change meanings.
     1. The six tones are level [ma], rising [má], falling [mà], dipping-rising [mă], rising-glottalized [mã], and low glottalized [mạ].
     2. For example, a level tone on *ma* means "ghost," a rising tone [má] means "mom."
     3. The tone changes the meaning; it can be the opposite.
II. Some common Vietnamese words are *Xin chao* [greeting—polite, respectful] and *Cam on* [thank you].

Conclusion

I. Today, I have showed you how to write and pronounce Vietnamese, and I taught you a couple of words.
II. The alphabet wasn't so hard, was it?
III. Have a great time when you meet a Vietnamese person and *Xin chao.*

A Toast to Barbara Jordan

Special occasion speech that emphasizes a value (Chapter 17 and Appendix B)

Keisha Walkes

This was a showcase speech given at Missouri State University. Keisha's tribute is a good example of a speech that aims "to commemorate." You can watch a video of Keisha delivering her speech on the book's website.

General Purpose: To commemorate

Specific Purpose: To pay tribute to the politician, educator, and leader, the late Barbara Jordan

Thesis Statement: Barbara Jordan had a tremendous impact on the views and beliefs of America and on the governance of the United States.

I. President Bush, members of Congress, distinguished guests, ladies and gentlemen: it is my pleasure to welcome you to the first Woman of the Century Awards Gala.
   A. We gather to chat, mingle, exchange pleasantries, and pay tribute to an extraordinary woman who has played many roles in her lifetime.
   B. She has been a politician, educator, inspirational speaker, and leader, whom Senator Barbara Boxer calls a pioneer and riveting orator.
   C. I think of her as the First Lady because of the many firsts she has pioneered.

Transition: Let's get to know something about our honoree.

I. Our awardee was born February 21, 1936, in Houston, Texas; as the daughter of a Baptist minister, she was practically raised in church.

II. She graduated magna cum laude from Texas Southern University in 1956.
   A. She received her law degree from Boston University.
   B. She has honorary doctorate degrees from 25 colleges and universities.
III. She has many firsts.
   A. She was part of the first debate team from a Black university to compete in the annual forensics tournament at Baylor College.
   B. She was the first Black elected to the Texas Senate.
   C. She was the first Black woman governor in U.S. history (she served for one day).

Transition: Let's now look at why she is our Woman of the Century.
   I. A Woman of the Century should be authentic as a leader.
      A. Jordan struggled to break the color barrier.
      B. She refused to accept her position as a "woman," and she spoke up.
II. A Woman of the Century should have integrity and moral resolve.
      A. Jordan spoke out for upholding the Constitution.
      B. She spoke out against discrimination due to color, gender, or class.
      C. Her powerful words as a member of the Judiciary Committee during Watergate made a difference in history.
III. A Woman of the Century should have initiative.
      A. Jordan emphasized Constitutional rights.
      B. She realized the importance of education about values.
      C. Her words reached many ears and showed that everyone could make a difference.

Transition: Now, the moment we've all been waiting for. [Propose toast]
   I. You yourself have agreed that a leader must have courage, must stand up for what he or she believes, and must be able to motivate.
   II. Thus, you have chosen this woman as a leader.
   III. Ladies and gentlemen, I therefore ask you to join me and raise your glasses in tribute to your leader, your Woman of the Century, the late Barbara Jordan.

Overconsumption of Sugar

This persuasive speech illustrates information in Chapters 17 and 18.

Hans Erian

Hans gave this persuasive speech in competitive speech tournaments as a representative of Chabot Community College. He won a silver medal at a national tournament for community college competitors. On the book's website, you can watch a video of this speech, given during the final round of the tournament,

General Purpose: To persuade

Specific Purpose: To persuade my audience that overconsumption of sugar is contributing to obesity and related diseases, but something can be done about it

Central Idea: Too much sugar can lead to obesity and Type II diabetes, but national awareness, plus personal commitment to good health, can help.

Introduction

   I. Fifteen-year-old Arnold Scott weighed three hundred pounds; he developed symptoms that led to a diagnosis of Type II diabetes.
      A. Type II diabetes, usually associated with adults, is increasing among children and leaving them vulnerable to blindness, heart and kidney disease, and stroke at ages as young as thirty (*Newsday*).
      B. Dr. Barbara Lindner of the National Institute of Diabetes, Digestive Diseases, and Kidney Diseases linked the rise in diabetes to a rise in obesity, and obesity is on the rise because of sugar.

1. The *Nationwide News* of August 21, 2001, reported that, of the ten most-bought foods bought at the supermarket, most are sugar-filled junk foods.
2. A Georgetown University study showed that 25 percent of adult calories come from sugar; for kids, it's closer to 50 percent.

II. The average person in this room consumes about 125 to 150 pounds of sugar per year.
   A. *Consumer Reports on Health* of August 2001 says that increases in blood sugar levels lead to increases in disease and death.
   B. Americans are consuming too much unhealthy sugar without realizing it.

III. Today we will explore two major causes of sugar overconsumption, then we'll examine negative effects, and finally we'll look at ways to nationally and personally deal with the problem.

Body

I. The two main reasons for increased consumption of sugar are ignorance and increased consumption of soda pop.
   A. The FDA and the sugar association have been fighting a linguistic tug-of-war since about 1970 over the definition of sugar.
      1. Fructose is the good sugar, the kind found naturally in fruit.
      2. Bad sugar, the kind in most foods, comes under names like sucrose, dextrose, and high fructose corn syrup, which may be confusing because of the word "fructose" in it.
      3. Common items in local stores can lead to confusion.
         a. Here's a cranberry-tangerine juice drink that we'd expect to be healthy, but the second ingredient is high fructose corn syrup.
         b. Wheaties include whole wheat, sugar—and also corn sugar and brown sugar, other bad sugars; can this be the breakfast of champions?
   B. The second reason is the increased consumption of soda.
      1. Coca Cola contains sucrose and has about ten teaspoons of sugar per pint.
      2. The consumption of soda increased by 43 percent to eighty-five gallons per year since 1987; that's 555 cans annually for every American (*San Jose Mercury News*).

Transition: Now that we've seen the increased use of sugar because of ignorance and soda pop, we will see the negative effects this is having on our health.

II. This amount of sugar is having a negative impact on our health.
   A. There is convincing new evidence between weight gain in children and the consumption of soda pop (*New York Times*).
      1. Obesity is directly linked to soda pop consumption, regardless of the amount of food you eat or lack of exercise.
      2. Perhaps this is because the body has trouble adapting to intense concentrations of sugar taken in liquid form.
   B. Obesity is linked to many diseases, including high blood pressure, high cholesterol, and heart disease, as well as cancer and diabetes.
      1. Obesity is now considered the number two killer in the United States because it causes cancer and other problems.
         a. Obese people are 70 percent more likely to get pancreatic cancer, which has a 95 percent mortality rate (*New York Times*).
         b. The U.S. Department of Health links it to post-menopausal breast cancer and colon cancer.
      2. Obesity is linked to diabetes.
         a. Since 1991, adult obesity has increased by 60 percent, and the percentage of overweight kids has doubled (*Hartford Courant*).

      b. Children and adolescents are developing Type II diabetes, a disease associated with people over forty-five years of age.

      c. Dr. Gerald Bernstein predicts that, if left unchecked, there will be five hundred million diabetics worldwide in twenty-five years, leading to a tidal wave of suffering and an avalanche of health care bills.

Transition: Now that we see that Americans are consuming too much sugar and it's destroying our health, we need to decrease our sugar intake.

III. We can do something on a national and a personal level.

  A. On a national level, we need to increase our awareness and decrease soda pop consumption.

    1. Kelly Brownwell, director of Yale University's Eating and Weight Disorders, recommends regulation of ads aimed at children to provide equal time for nutritional and pro-exercise messages.

    2. She also suggests changing the price of foods to make healthier foods less expensive than sugar-laden ones.

    3. Schools could disable the school vending machines during class time, strip them of sweets, or put a new tax on them, which may discourage students from buying sweets (*New York Times*).

    4. We might also impose a tax on soft drinks in general.

Transition: These are just a few ways to provide incentives for people to get healthy and eat less sugar.

  B. We would like to have someone else help us get healthy, but what is really needed is a personal commitment to health.

    1. Start off slow and follow Dr. Robert Owen's advice; he wrote *Optimum Wellness,* and he suggests you have dessert a few times a week or a can of pop a couple of times a week.

    2. In fact, the World Health Organization suggested that up to 10 percent of calories can come from sugar, but try to stick to healthy sugars.

    3. In addition, be a label reader.

Conclusion

I. Now that we have looked at the misconceptions regarding sugar and what they lead to, you can decrease your sugar intake.

II. This will prevent more people from ending up like Arnold Scott, who must take insulin injections just to stay alive.

No Day But Today

Amari's commemorative speech emphasizes an important cultural idea (Appendix B)

Amari Howard

Amari was assigned to create a speech that was based on an important quotation, poem, or lyric. She used song lyrics from the Broadway musical "Rent" as her theme. You can watch a video of Amari delivering this speech on the book website.

You are a 20-something New York artist struggling to make ends meet. You're freezing, hungry, and depressed because no one is buying your work; to top it all off, you have AIDS. However, you find a way to persevere through another day. This is the premise of the lives of the characters in Jonathan Larson's controversial musical "Rent."

    I was mystified by this play when I went to see it last December. The lyric "no day but today" embodies the play's message and has had a tremendous effect on my life.

Let's begin with background information about the play and its author. "Rent" is based on the life of struggling Bohemian artists in downtown New York City. According to sitefor-rent.com, its writer, Jonathan Larson, actually lived this type of life and wanted to document it and show that there could be optimism in a life of drug addiction, homelessness, and AIDS.

The song "Life Support" is a wonderful example of Larson's hope. It ends with the thought-provoking lyric, "no day but today."

Unfortunately, Larson died suddenly while the play was still in its final dress rehearsal, so he never got to see his dream come to fruition. The play, however, went on to be one of the most successful plays of all time. It won many awards, including a Pulitzer Prize.

Now that you know a bit about the play, let's talk about how and why it personally affected me.

Although I am not struggling to make it as I live the Bohemian life in New York, I have gone through something in my life that required a positive outlook. Even before watching the play, I applied the "no day but today" philosophy to my life.

My mother and best friend died when I was 14. Our last conversation had been a heated argument. I will never stop regretting that we didn't part on better terms. Since then, I have made extreme changes in my life to prevent such a situation from happening again. I try not to go to sleep while angry with someone for fear that I might not have a chance later to rectify the situation. Not a day goes by that I don't say "I love you" to the most important people in my life. I started living live every day as if it is my last; therefore, I live as if there is no day but today.

Harriet Martineau said, "You better live your best and act your best and think your best today, for today is a short preparation for tomorrow and all the other tomorrows that follow." This quote embodies Jonathan Larson's vision of the motivation that comes from knowing that we should strive to fully utilize every day. This philosophy of how to live has truly affected how I choose to live.

You do not have to be freezing, hungry, or depressed to persevere; you just have to realize that there is no day but today.

Professional Speeches

Tolerance, Love, and Cooperation: When I Think of Ramadan

Goodwill speech that emphasizes dialogue and illustrates the wave pattern (Chapters 3, 9, and Appendix B)

Fahri Karakas[1]
Fahri Karakas is on the Faculty of Management at McGill University in Montreal, Canada. This is the first main point in Karakas's speech, given at the Interfaith Dinner of Dialogue Foundation in Montreal, December 2004. It is a good illustration of the wave pattern.

. . . It is a great pleasure to share this celebration and dinner with you. We are hundreds of people here from various races, different religions, and diverse backgrounds. All of us united, committed, excited, and together under one roof. This is a vivid portrait of the cosmopolitan and multicultural Canadian society. A model of richness as a result of diversity. A living model of democracy and peaceful coexistence. I want to convey my sincere congratulations and thanks to Dialogue Foundation of Montreal for preparing this special occasion for us. I am especially impressed with our friends' sincerity, kindness, generosity, openness, and eagerness to learn. They have been very effective in educating me and others about international religious topics, as well as in promoting an open interfaith dialogue in Montreal.

In the first part, as a practicing Muslim, I would like to share with you a few words on my personal reflections on the month of Ramadan, Ramadan practices, and fasting experiences. Ramadan is commonly called the "Lord of Eleven Months." It is a very special month for Muslims filled with lots of blessings, happiness, love, and sharing.

Personally, I always remember missing Ramadan throughout the year. Ramadan is accepted as our lovely, kind, valued guest. Ramadan is welcomed with great joy, excitement, tranquility, and peace. When I think of Ramadan; I remember all values, people, times, and contexts— all very valuable to me.

When I think of Ramadan, I remember Turkey— my beloved country— the home bed (cradle) of 27 different civilizations. When I think of Ramadan, I remember Istanbul— the city I am in love with, with all its grandeur and mystery.

When I think of Ramadan, I remember special *iftar* (dinner) tents built on every corner in Istanbul— throughout the streets of Uskudar, Sultanahmet, and Eyup. *Iftar* tents are ready, welcoming you everywhere with great warmth. All people eat there as a family, as brothers and sisters, without any borders. Regardless of your status, wealth, race, and religion. All people experiencing perfect equality and sincerity. You are busy? In traffic? Could not reach home? Not have enough money? You just break your fast or have your dinner in the streets.

When I think of Ramadan, I remember my dear mother (and there are many of our friends who feel the same way I think)—my dear mother who cooked a lot of meals, so delicious Turkish cuisine, *tarhana* soups, *boreks,* and *kebaps,* for me. When I think of Ramadan, I remember being awakened by my father in the middle of the night at 4 am for *sahur* (midnight supper). I remember having, sharing our meal as well as our compassion and love together, in an original context in the middle of the night.

When I think of Ramadan, I remember fasting. And I remember— during the day of fasting— especially just before fast breaking, feeling so elevated, so purified, so excited, so awkward, so happy, like a baby. It is a peak experience. When I think of Ramadan, I remember my prayers. I remember being close to God. I remember the love of God— and being loved by God. "Yes, oh my God, you exist and you are the only one. I am your servant, you are my Lord. I am your lover, you are my beloved one. I am zero, you are the infinity. I am a droplet, you are the ocean."

When I think of Ramadan, I remember and reflect on:

- Self-discipline and spiritual strength,
- Compassion and helping poor people,
- Hunger and poverty around the world,
- The value of peace, dialogue and tolerance in all spheres of life,
- The value of treating people equally without bias,
- Brotherhood, sincerity, friendship, love and sharing,
- Self-sacrifice, devotion and idealism,
- Being a piece of soil for roses to flourish,
- Praying for the well being of humanity,
- The value of enabling others to live well instead of living well,
- The value of a noble way of living, serving both your country and humanity at large.

When I think of Ramadan; I remember the way of Sufism and the paths of Anatolian dervishes and Sufis: Ghazzalis, the Rabbanis, Yunus Emres, Bediuzzamans, and Rumis, who were all travelers on the road of spiritual happiness based on love, compassion, and dialogue. . . .

Inaugural

Commemorative speech notable for its effective use of language (Chapter 13, Appendix B)

John F. Kennedy[2]

President Kennedy's 1960 Inaugural speech, composed with the aid of speechwriter Ted Sorensen, is number two on www.americanrhetoric.com's list of 100 best speeches (behind Martin Luther King's "I Have a Dream" speech). It has become the standard to which other presidents aspire. You can watch it online at www.americanrhetoric.com.

Vice President Johnson, Mr. Speaker, Mr. Chief Justice, President Eisenhower, Vice President Nixon, President Truman, Reverend Clergy, fellow citizens:

We observe today not a victory of party, but a celebration of freedom— symbolizing an end, as well as a beginning— signifying renewal, as well as change. For I have sworn before you and Almighty God the same solemn oath our forebears prescribed nearly a century and three-quarters ago.

The world is very different now. For man holds in his mortal hands the power to abolish all forms of human poverty and all forms of human life. And yet the same revolutionary beliefs for which our forebears fought are still at issue around the globe— the belief that the rights of man come not from the generosity of the state, but from the hand of God.

We dare not forget today that we are the heirs of that first revolution. Let the word go forth from this time and place, to friend and foe alike, that the torch has been passed to a new generation of Americans— born in this century, tempered by war, disciplined by a hard and bitter peace, proud of our ancient heritage, and unwilling to witness or permit the slow undoing of those human rights to which this nation has always been committed, and to which we are committed today at home and around the world.

Let every nation know, whether it wishes us well or ill, that we shall pay any price, bear any burden, meet any hardship, support any friend, oppose any foe, to assure the survival and the success of liberty.

This much we pledge— and more.

To those old allies whose cultural and spiritual origins we share, we pledge the loyalty of faithful friends. United there is little we cannot do in a host of cooperative ventures. Divided there is little we can do— for we dare not meet a powerful challenge at odds and split asunder.

To those new states whom we welcome to the ranks of the free, we pledge our word that one form of colonial control shall not have passed away merely to be replaced by a far more iron tyranny. We shall not always expect to find them supporting our view. But we shall always hope to find them strongly supporting their own freedom— and to remember that, in the past, those who foolishly sought power by riding the back of the tiger ended up inside.

To those people in the huts and villages of half the globe struggling to break the bonds of mass misery, we pledge our best efforts to help them help themselves, for whatever period is required— not because the Communists may be doing it, not because we seek their votes, but because it is right. If a free society cannot help the many who are poor, it cannot save the few who are rich.

To our sister republics south of our border, we offer a special pledge: to convert our good words into good deeds, in a new alliance for progress, to assist free men and free governments in casting off the chains of poverty. But this peaceful revolution of hope cannot become the prey of hostile powers. Let all our neighbors know that we shall join with them to oppose aggression or subversion anywhere in the Americas. And let every other power know that this hemisphere intends to remain the master of its own house.

To that world assembly of sovereign states, the United Nations, our last best hope in an age where the instruments of war have far outpaced the instruments of peace, we renew our pledge of support— to prevent it from becoming merely a forum for invective, to strengthen its shield of the new and the weak, and to enlarge the area in which its writ may run.

Finally, to those nations who would make themselves our adversary, we offer not a pledge but a request: that both sides begin anew the quest for peace, before the dark powers of destruction unleashed by science engulf all humanity in planned or accidental self-destruction.

We dare not tempt them with weakness. For only when our arms are sufficient beyond doubt can we be certain beyond doubt that they will never be employed.

But neither can two great and powerful groups of nations take comfort from our present course— both sides overburdened by the cost of modern weapons, both rightly alarmed by the steady spread of the deadly atom, yet both racing to alter that uncertain balance of terror that stays the hand of mankind's final war.

So let us begin anew— remembering on both sides that civility is not a sign of weakness, and sincerity is always subject to proof. Let us never negotiate out of fear, but let us never fear to negotiate.

Let both sides explore what problems unite us instead of belaboring those problems which divide us.

Let both sides, for the first time, formulate serious and precise proposals for the inspection and control of arms, and bring the absolute power to destroy other nations under the absolute control of all nations.

Let both sides seek to invoke the wonders of science instead of its terrors. Together let us explore the stars, conquer the deserts, eradicate disease, tap the ocean depths, and encourage the arts and commerce.

Let both sides unite to heed, in all corners of the earth, the command of Isaiah— to "undo the heavy burdens, and [to] let the oppressed go free."

And, if a beachhead of cooperation may push back the jungle of suspicion, let both sides join in creating a new endeavor— not a new balance of power, but a new world of law— where the strong are just, and the weak secure, and the peace preserved.

All this will not be finished in the first one hundred days. Nor will it be finished in the first one thousand days; nor in the life of this Administration; nor even perhaps in our lifetime on this planet. But let us begin.

In your hands, my fellow citizens, more than mine, will rest the final success or failure of our course. Since this country was founded, each generation of Americans has been summoned to give testimony to its national loyalty. The graves of young Americans who answered the call to service surround the globe.

Now the trumpet summons us again— not as a call to bear arms, though arms we need— not as a call to battle, though embattled we are— but a call to bear the burden of a long twilight struggle, year in and year out, "rejoicing in hope; patient in tribulation," a struggle against the common enemies of man: tyranny, poverty, disease, and war itself.

Can we forge against these enemies a grand and global alliance, North and South, East and West, that can assure a more fruitful life for all mankind? Will you join in that historic effort?

In the long history of the world, only a few generations have been granted the role of defending freedom in its hour of maximum danger. I do not shrink from this responsibility— I welcome it. I do not believe that any of us would exchange places with any other people or any other generation. The energy, the faith, the devotion which we bring to this endeavor will light our country and all who serve it. And the glow from that fire can truly light the world.

And so, my fellow Americans, ask not what your country can do for you; ask what you can do for your country.

My fellow citizens of the world, ask not what America will do for you, but what together we can do for the freedom of man.

Finally, whether you are citizens of America or citizens of the world, ask of us here the same high standards of strength and sacrifice which we ask of you. With a good conscience our only sure reward, with history the final judge of our deeds, let us go forth to lead the land we love, asking His blessing and His help, but knowing that here on earth God's work must truly be our own.

An Indian's View of Indian Affairs
Example of narrative reasoning (Chapter 15)

Chief Joseph[3]

Chief Joseph of the Nez Percé *Indian tribe told this story on January 14, 1879, before a large gathering of Cabinet officers, congressional representatives, diplomats, and other officials. His speech shows that Congress has good reasons to act in behalf of his people.*

My name is *In-mut-too-yah-lat-lat* (Thunder Traveling Over the Mountains). I am chief of the *Wal-lam-wat-kin* band of *Chute-pa-lu,* or *Nez Percés* (nose-pierced Indians). I was born in eastern Oregon, thirty-eight winters ago. My father was chief before me. When a young man, he was called Joseph by Mr. Spaulding, a missionary. He died a few years ago. There was no stain on his hands of the blood of a white man. He left a good name on the earth. He advised me well for my people.

Our fathers gave us many laws, which they had learned from their fathers. These laws were good. They told us to treat all men as they treated us; that we should never be the first to break a bargain; that it was a disgrace to tell a lie; that we should speak only the truth; that it was a shame for one man to take from another his wife, or his property without paying for it. We were taught to believe that the Great Spirit sees and hears everything, and that he never forgets; that hereafter he will give every man a spirit-home according to his deserts: if he has been a bad man, he will have a bad home. This I believe, and all my people believe the same.

We did not know there were other people besides the Indian until about one hundred winters ago, when some men with white faces came to our country. They brought many things with them to trade for furs and skins. They brought tobacco, which was new to us. They brought guns with flint stones on them, which frightened our women and children. Our people could not talk with these white-faced men, but they used signs which all people understand. These men were Frenchmen, and they called our people *Nez Percés* because they wore rings in their noses for ornaments. Although very few of our people wear them now, we are still called by the same name. These French trappers said a great many things to our fathers, which have been planted in our hearts. Some were good for us, but some were bad. Our people were divided in opinion about these men. Some thought they taught more bad than good. An Indian respects a brave man, but he despises a coward. He loves a straight tongue, but he hates a forked tongue. The French trappers told us some truths and some lies.

The first white men of your people who came to our country were named Lewis and Clarke. They also brought many things that our people had never seen. They talked straight, and our people gave them a great feast, as a proof that their hearts were friendly. These men were very kind. They made presents to our chiefs and our people made presents to them. We had a great many horses, of which we gave them what they needed, and they gave us guns and tobacco in return. All the *Nez Percés* made friends with Lewis and Clarke, and agreed to let them pass through their country, and never to make war on white men. This promise the *Nez Percés* have never broken. No white man can accuse them of bad faith, and speak with a straight tongue. It has always been the pride of the *Nez Percés* that they were the friends of the white men. When my father was a young man there came to our country a white man (Rev. Mr. Spaulding) who talked the spirit law. He won the affections of our people because he spoke good things to them. At first, he did not say anything about white men wanting to settle on our lands. Nothing was said about that until about twenty winters ago, when a number of white people came into our country and built houses and made farms. At first our people made no complaint. They thought there was room enough for all to live in peace, and they were learning many things from the white men that seemed to be good. But we soon found that the white men were growing rich very fast, and were greedy to possess everything the Indian had. My father was the first to see through the schemes of the white men, and he warned his tribe to careful about trading with them. He had suspicion of men who seemed so anxious to make money. I was a boy then, but I remember well my father's caution. He had sharper eyes than the rest of our people.

Next there came a white officer (Governor Stevens), who invited all the *Nez Percés* to a treaty council. After the council was opened he made known his heart. He said there were a great many white people in the country, and many more would come; that he wanted the land marked out so that the Indians and white men could be separated. If they were to live in peace it was necessary, he said, that the Indians should have a country set apart for them, and in that country they must stay. My father, who represented his band, refused to have anything to do with the council, because he wished to be a free man. He claimed that no man owned any part of the earth, and a man could not sell what he did not own.

Mr. Spaulding took hold of my father's arm and said, Come and sign the treaty. My father pushed him away, and said: Why do you ask me to sign away my country? It is your business to talk about spirit matters, and not to talk to us about parting with our land. Governor Stevens urged my father to sign his treaty, but he refused. I will not sign your paper, he said; you go where you please, so do I; you are not a child, I am no child; I can think for myself. No man can think for me. I have no other home than this. I will not give it up to any man. My people would have no home. Take away your paper. I will not touch it with my hand.

My father left the council. Some of the chiefs of the other bands of the *Nez Percés* signed the treaty, and then Governor Stevens gave them presents of blankets. My father cautioned his people to take no presents, for after a while, he said, they will claim that you have accepted pay for your country. Since that time four bands of the *Nez Percés* have received annuities from the United States. My father was invited to many councils, and they tried hard to make him sign the treaty, but he was firm as the rock, and would not sign away his home. His refusal caused a difference among the *Nez Percés*. . . .

Chief Joseph continues the speech, detailing years of treaty negotiations between the Nez Percé and the whites. His conclusion recognizes that the inevitable has happened; his people are powerless against the white settlers. But his final plea is for equal justice under law for the Indian as well as for whites.

Mrs. Bush's Remarks at Wellesley College Commencement

Commencement address to a hostile audience (Chapters 17, 18, and Appendix B)

Barbara Bush[4]
You can watch a video of this speech on the book's website.

Administrators invited former First Lady Barbara Bush to speak at Wellesley College's commencement exercises, although students in the class wanted the novelist Alice Walker to speak. Facing a hostile audience, Mrs. Bush used humor to present her "goodwill" special occasion speech on Friday, June 1, 1990. After she thanked the president, recognized the platform party, the graduates, and the parents, she said:

More than ten years ago when I was invited here to talk about our experiences in the People's Republic of China, I was struck by both the natural beauty of your campus . . . and the spirit of this place.

Wellesley, you see, is not just a place . . . but an idea . . . an experiment in excellence in which diversity is not just tolerated but is embraced.

The essence of this spirit was captured in a moving speech about tolerance given last year by the student body president of one of your sister colleges. She related the story by Robert Fulghum about a young pastor who, finding himself in charge of some very energetic children, hits upon a game called "Giants, Wizards, and Dwarfs." "You have to decide now," the pastor instructed the children, "which you are . . . a giant, a wizard, or a dwarf." At that, a small girl, tugging at his pant leg asked, "But where do the mermaids stand?" The pastor told her there are *no* mermaids, and she says, "Oh, yes there are." She said, "I am a mermaid." Now this little girl knew what she was, and she was not about to give up on either her identity or the game. She intended to take her place wherever mermaids fit into the scheme of things. Where do mermaids stand? . . . *All* those who are different, those who do not fit the boxes and pigeonholes. "Answer that question," wrote Fulghum, "and you can build a school, a nation, or a whole world." As that very wise young woman said . . . "Diversity . . . like anything worth having . . . requires *effort*." Effort to learn about and respect difference, to be compassionate with one another, to cherish our own identity . . . and to accept unconditionally the same in others.

You should all be very proud that this is the Wellesley spirit. Now I know your first choice today was Alice Walker, known for *The Color Purple*. And guess how I know?

Instead you got me— known for— the color of my hair! Alice Walker's book has a special resonance here. At Wellesley, each class is known by a special color . . . for four years the Class of '90 has worn the color purple. Today you met on Severance Green to say goodbye to all of that . . . to begin a new and very personal journey . . . to search for your own true colors.

In the world that awaits you beyond the shores of Lake Waban, no one can say what your true colors will be. But this I do know: You have a first-class education from a first-class school. And so you need not, probably cannot, live a "paint-by-numbers" life. Decisions are not irrevocable. Choices do come back. As you set off from Wellesley, I hope that many of you will consider making three very special choices.

The first is to believe in something larger than yourself. . . . To get involved in some of the big ideas of your time. I chose literacy because I honestly believe that if more people could read, write, and comprehend, we would be that much closer to solving so many of the problems plaguing our society.

Early on I made another choice, which I hope you will make as well. Whether you are talking about education, career, or service, you are talking about life . . . and life must have joy. It's supposed to be fun!

One of the reasons I made the most important decision of my life . . . to marry George Bush . . . is because he made me laugh. It's true, sometimes we've laughed through our tears . . . but that shared laughter has been one of our strongest bonds. Find the joy in life, because as Ferris Bueller said on his day off . . . "Life moves pretty fast. Ya don't stop and look around once in a while, ya gonna miss it." I won't tell George that you applauded Ferris more than you applauded him!

The third choice that must not be missed is to cherish your human connections; your relationships with friends and family. For several years, you've had impressed upon you the importance to your career of dedication and hard work. This is true, but as important as your obligations as a doctor, lawyer, or business leader will be, you are a human being first and those human connections— with spouses, with children, with friends— are the most important investments you will ever make.

At the end of your life you will never regret not having passed one more test, winning one more verdict, or not closing one more deal. You will regret time not spent with a husband, a child, a friend, or a parent.

We are in a transitional period right now . . . fascinating and exhilarating times . . . learning to adjust to the changes and the choices we . . . men and women . . . are facing.

As an example, I remember what a friend said, on hearing her husband complain to his buddies that he had to babysit. Quickly setting him straight . . . my friend told her husband that when it's your own kids . . . it's not called babysitting!

Maybe we should adjust faster, maybe slower, but whatever the era . . . whatever the times, one thing will never change. Fathers and mothers, if you have children . . . they must come first. You must read to your children, you must hug your children, you must love your children. Your success as a family . . . our success as a society . . . depends *not* on what happens at the White House but on what happens inside your house.

For over fifty years, it was said that the winner of Wellesley's annual hoop race would be the first to get married. Now they say the winner will be the first to become a C.E.O. Both of those stereotypes show too little tolerance for those who want to know where the mermaids stand. So I want to offer you today a new legend: The winner of the hoop race will be the first to realize her dream . . . not society's dream . . . her own personal dream.

Who knows? Somewhere out in this audience may even be someone who will follow in my footsteps and preside over the White House as the president's spouse. I wish him well.

The controversy ends here. But our conversation is only beginning. And a worthwhile conversation it has been. So as you leave Wellesley today, take with you deep thanks for the courtesy and the honor you have shared with Mrs. Gorbachev and me. Thank you. God bless you. And may your future be worthy of your dreams.

REFERENCES

CHAPTER 1

1. Jensen, K. K. & Harris, V. (1999). The public speaking portfolio. *Communication Education, 48,* 211–227.

2. Veciana-Suarez, A. (2005, March 15). Speaker helps women find a balance. *The Miami Herald,* Retrieved February 2, 2005, from InfoTrac College Edition.

3. Richmond, V. P. & McCroskey, J. C. (1995). *Communication: Apprehension, avoidance, and effectiveness* (4th ed.). Scottsdale, AZ: Gorsuch Scarisbrick.

4. Dwyer, K. K. (1998). Communication apprehension and learning style preference: Correlation and implications for teaching. *Communication Education 47,* 137–150.

5. Beatty, M., McCroskey, J. C. & Heisel, A. D. (1998). Communication apprehension as temperamental expression: A communibiological paradigm. *Communication Monographs, 65,* 197–219.

6. Sawyer, C. R., & Behnke, R. R. (2002). Behavioral inhibition and the communication of public speaking state anxiety. *Western Journal of Communication, 66,* 412–423.

7. Roper Starch. (1999). How Americans communicate. Poll commissioned by the National Communication Association. Retrieved February 15, 2005, from www .natcom.org/research/Poll/how_americans_communicate.htm#not%20cheap.

8. Morreale, S., Spitzberg, B. H. & Barge, K. (2001). *Human communication: Motivation, knowledge, and skills.* Belmont, CA: Wadsworth.

9. MacIntyre, P. J., & MacDonald, J. R. (1998). Public speaking anxiety: Perceived competence and audience congeniality. *Communication Education, 47,* 359–365.

10. Peterson, M. S. (1997). Personnel interviewers' perceptions of the importance and adequacy of applicant's communication skills. *Communication Education, 46,* 287–291.

11. Reed, V. A. & Jernstedt, G. C. (2004). A tool for the assessment of communication skills. *Academic Exchange Quarterly, 8,* 106–111. Retrieved February 12, 2005, from InfoTrac College Edition.

12. Waugh, T. (2004, June). The tide is turning. Are you ready? *The Practical Accountant, 37,* 16–17. Retrieved February 12, 2005, from InfoTrac College Edition.

13. See the definition of "dialogist publicity" in K. Wahl-Jorgensen (2001). Letters to the editor as a forum for public deliberation: Modes of publicity and democratic debate. *Critical Studies in Media Communication, 18,* 303–320.

14. Veciana-Suarez, Speaker helps.

15. Allen, M., Berkowitz, S., Hunt, S., & Louden, A. (1999). A meta-analysis of the impact of forensics and communication education on critical thinking. *Communication Education, 48,* 18–30.

16. Call to Serve. (n.d.) Red white & blue jobs: Making a difference with your liberal arts degree (p. 1). Partnership for Public Service Booklet.

17. Gray, G. W. (1946). The precepts of Kagmenmi [sic] and Ptah-hotep. *Quarterly Journal of Speech, 31,* 446–454.

18. Smith, D. (1996, February). Discussion leader: Globalization of the general education curriculum. George Fox University, Newberg, OR.

19. Galvin, K. M., & Cooper, P. J. (2000). Perceptual filters: Culture, family, and gender. In K. M. Galvin & P. J. Cooper (Eds.). *Making connections: Readings in relational communication* (2nd ed., p. 32–33). Los Angeles: Roxbury.

20. Hart, R. P., & Burks, D. O. (1972). Rhetorical sensitivity and social interaction. *Speech Monographs, 39,* 90.

21. Pearce, W. B. (1989). *Communication and the human condition.* Carbondale: Southern Illinois University Press.

22. Wallace, K. K. (1955). An ethical basis of communication. *The Speech Teacher, 4,* 1–9.

23. Ong, W. J. (1982). *Orality and literacy: The technologizing of the word.* New York: Methuen.

24. Weider, D. L. & Pratt, S. (1990). On being a recognizable Indian. In D. Carbaugh (Ed.), *Intercultural communication and intercultural contacts* (pp. 45–64). Hillsdale, NJ: Lawrence Erlbaum.

25. Marsella, A. J. (1993). Counseling and psychotherapy with Japanese Americans: Cross-cultural considerations. *American Journal of Orthopsychiatry, 63,* 200–208.

26. Messenger, J. (1960). Anang proverb riddles. *Journal of American Folklore, 73,* 235.

27. Pennebaker, J. W., Rime, B., & Blankenship, V. E. (1996). Stereotypes of emotional expressiveness of northerners and southerners: A cross-cultural test of Montesquieu's Hypothesis. *Journal of Personality and Social Psychology, 70,* 372–380. See also E. M. Kao, D. K. Nagita, & C. Peterson. (1997. Explanatory style, family expressiveness, and self-esteem among Asian American and Euro-American college students. *Journal of Social Psychology, 137,* 435–444.

28. DePaulo, B. M., Blank, A. L., Swain, G. W. & Hairfield, J. G. (1992). Expressiveness and expressive control. *Personality and Social Psychology Bulletin, 18,* 276–285.

29. Kochman, T. (1990). Cultural pluralism: Black and white styles. In Carbaugh, *Intercultural communication,* 219–224.

30. Weider & Pratt, Recognizable Indian.

31. Jenefsky, C. (1996). Public speaking as empowerment at Visionary University. *Communication Education, 45,* 343–355. See also M. A. Jaasma. (1997, summer). Classroom apprehension: Does being male or female make a difference? *Communication Reports, 10,* 218–228.

32. Stewart, E. C. & Bennett, M. J. (1991). *American cultural patterns: A cross-cultural perspective* (rev. ed.). Yarmouth, ME: Intercultural Press.

33. Kochman, Cultural pluralism; Sullivan, P. A. (1993) Signification and African-American rhetoric: A case study of Jesse Jackson's "Common Ground and Common Sense" speech. *Communication Quarterly, 41,* 1–14; See also A. Wierzbicka. (1991). *Cross-cultural pragmatics: The semantics of human interaction.* Berlin: Mouton de Gruyter.

34. Becker, C. B. (1991). Reasons for the lack of argumentation and debate in the Far East. In L. A. Samovar & R. E. Porter (Eds.), *Intercultural communication: A reader* (6th ed., pp. 234–243). Belmont, CA: Wadsworth.

35. Ugwu-Oju, D. (1993, November 14). Pursuit of happiness. *New York Times Magazine.*

36. Pearce, *Communication.*

37. Arnett, R. C., & Arneson, P. (1999). *Dialogic civility in a cynical age: Community, hope, and interpersonal relationships.* Albany, NY: SUNY Press.

38. Schwandt, B. & Soraya, S. (1992, August 13–15). Ethnography of communication and *"Sprechwissenschaft"*—merging of concepts. Paper presented at the Ethnography of Communication Conference, Portland, OR.

39. Bavelas, J. B., Hutchinson, S., Kenwood, C. & Matheson, D. H. (1997). Using face-to-face dialogue as a standard for other communication systems. *Canadian Journal of Communications, 22,* 14 pp. [online.] Retrieved March 3, 2005, from http://info .wlu.ca/~wwwpress/jrls/cjc/BackIssues/ 22.1/bavel.html.

40. Bahktin is quoted in Wierzbicka, *Cross-cultural pragmatics,* 149.

41. Quoted (p. 352) in McGuire, M., & Slembek, E. (1987). An emerging critical rhetoric: Hellmut Geissner's Sprechwissenschaft. *Quarterly Journal of Speech, 73,* 349–400.

42. The transactional model appears in almost every communication text.

CHAPTER 2

1. Robinson, T. E. (1997). Communication apprehension and the basic public speaking course: A national survey of in-class treatment techniques. *Communication Education, 46,* 188–197.

2. Behnke, R. R. & Sawyer, C. R. (1999). Milestones of anticipatory public speaking anxiety. *Communication Education, 48,* 165–172.

3. Bippus, A. M. & Daly, J. A. (1999). What do people think causes stage fright? Naïve attributions about the reasons for public speaking anxiety. *Communication Education, 48,* 63–72.

4. Cicero, M. T. (1981). *Ad herennium: De ratione dicendi. (Rhetorica ad herennium).* (H. Kaplan, Trans.) The Loeb Classical Library. Cambridge, MA: Harvard University Press.

5. Staley, C. C. & Staley, R. S. (2000). Communicating in organizations. In Galvin & Cooper, *Making connections*, 287–294.

6. Quintilian. (1920–1922). *The instituto oratoria of Quintilian* (4 vols. H. E. Butler, trans.) The Loeb Classical Library. Cambridge, MA: Harvard University Press.

7. Style. (2005). *Compact Oxford English Dictionary*. Accessed January 26, 2005, from www.askoxford.com/concise_oed/style?view=uk.

8. Sawyer, C. R. and Behnke, R. R. (1999). State anxiety patterns for public speaking anxiety and the behavior inhibition system. *Communication Reports*, *12*, 33–41.

9. Behnke, R. R & Sawyer, C. R. (2001). Patterns of psychological state anxiety as a function of anxiety sensitivity. *Communication Quarterly*, *49*, 84–95.

10. Ibid. See also M. J. Young, R. R. Behnke, & Y. M. Mann. (2004). Anxiety patterns in employment interviews. *Communication Reports*, *17*, 49–57.

11. Howell. W. (1990). Coping with internal-monologue. In J. Stewart (Ed.) *Bridges not walls: A book about interpersonal communication* (5th ed, pp. 128–138). New York: McGraw Hill.

12. Bippus & Daly, Stage fright; See also MacIntyre & MacDonald, Public speaking anxiety.

13. Robinson, Communication apprehension.

14. Ayres and Hopf have been studying visualization for many years. See Ayres, J. & Hopf, T. S., (1989). Visualization: Is it more than extra-attention? *Communication Education*, *38*, 1–5.; Ayres, J. Hopf T., & Ayres, D. M. (1994). An examination of whether imaging ability enhances the effectiveness of an intervention designed to reduce speech anxiety. *Communication Education*, *43*, 256.

15. Ayres, J., Hopf, T., & Edwards, P. A. (1999). Vividness and control: Factors in the effectiveness of performance visualization? *Communication Education*, *48*, 287–293.

16. MacIntyre & MacDonald, Public speaking anxiety.

17. Finn, A. N., Sawyer, C. R. & Behnke, R. R. (2003). Audience-perceived anxiety patterns of public speakers. *Communication Quarterly*, *51*, 470–482.

CHAPTER 3

1. Plumb. P. (2002, Feb. 25). Seminar: Make disagreements more manageable. *Nation's Cities Weekly*, *25*, 7–8. Retrieved March 13, 2005, from InfoTrac College Edition.

2. Jensen, J. V. (1997). *Ethical issues in the communication process*. Mahwah, NJ: Lawrence Erlbaum.

3. Ibid.

4. Pearce, *Communication*.

5. Reported in C. Watters. (2003, May 20). Speaker disrupts Rockford College graduation. *Rockford Register* Star [online]. Retrieved May 21, 2003, from www.rrstar.com.

6. Dutton, B. (2001, December 20). Editorial one-sided [Letter to the editor]. *San Francisco Chronicle*, A22.

7. Porter, R. E. & Samovar, L. A. (1994). An introduction to intercultural communication. In Samovar & Porter, *Intercultural communication*, 4–25.

8. Berger, P. (1969). *A rumor of angels: Modern society and the rediscovery of the supernatural*. Garden City, NY: Doubleday.

9. Tannen, D. (1998). *The argument culture: Moving from debate to dialogue*. New York: Random House.

10. Berger, *Rumor*.

11. Gates, H. L. (1992). *Loose cannons: Notes on the culture wars*. New York: Oxford University Press.

12. Pearce, *Communication*. See also D. S. Grimes & O. C. Richard. (2003). Could communication form impact organizations; experience with diversity? *The Journal of Business Communication*, *40*, 7–28. Retrieved March 15, from InfoTrac College Edition.

13. Pearce, W. B. & Pearce, K. A. (2000). Combining passions and abilities: Toward dialogic virtuosity. *Southern Communication Journal*, *65*, 161–175.

14. Jensen, *Ethical issues*.

15. Yankelovich, D. (1999). *The magic of dialogue: Transforming conflict into cooperation*. New York: Simon & Schuster.

16. Pearce & Pearce, Combining passions.

17. Foss, S. & Griffin, C. (1995). Beyond persuasion: A proposal for an invitational rhetoric. *Communication Monographs*, *62*, 2–18.

18. Etzioni, A. (1996*). The new golden rule: Community and morality in a democratic society*. New York: Basic Books. (pp. 104–106).

19. Annan, K. (2001, February 5). Idea of "dialogue among civilizations" rooted in fundamental UN values, says Secretary-General in Seaton Hall address [Press release and text of address] [online]. Seaton Hall University, School of Diplomacy and International Relations, South Orange, NJ. Retrieved May 3, 2003, from www.un.org/Dialogue/pr/sgsm7705.htm.

20. Yankelovich, *Magic of dialogue*.

21. Mallory, B. L. & Thomas, N. L. (2003, Sept-Oct). When the medium is the message: Promoting ethical action through democratic dialogue. *Change*, *3*, *5*, 10–18. Retrieved February 12, 2005, from InfoTrac College Edition.

22. President Clinton is quoted on the organization's home page at www.seedsofpeace.org.

23. Seeds of Peace. About us. Accessed February 5, 2005. www.seedsofpeace.org/site/PageServer?pagename=aboutus.

24. Shalhoub-Kevorkian, N. (2001, March). Using the dialogue tent to break mental chains: Listening and being heard. Social Service Review, 75, p. 135. Retrieved April 27, 2005, from InfoTrac College Edition.

25. Tannen, *Argument culture*, 289.

26. Quoted in Bartanen, M. & Frank, D. (1999). Reclaiming a heritage: A proposal for rhetorically grounded academic debate. *Parliamentary Debate: The Journal of the National Parliamentary Debate Association*, *6*, 31–54.

27. Barrett, H. (1991). *Rhetoric and civility: Human development, narcissism, and the good audience*. Albany, NY: SUNY Press.

28. Jensen, *Ethical issues*.

29. Hexham, I. (1999). Academic plagiarism defined. University of Calgary Department of Religious Studies. Retrieved February 8, 2005, from www.ucalgary.ca/~hexham/study/plag.html.

30. Avoiding plagiarism. (Last updated 2001, October 25). UCDavis Student Judiciary Affairs. Retrieved February 9, 2005, from http://sja.ucdavis.edu/avoid.htm#guidelines.

31. Statistics. (2005). Retrieved February 8, 2005, from www.plagiarism.org/plagiarism_stats.html.

32. Many Internet sites explain plagiarism. In addition to Purdue's Online Writing Lab, see J. R. Edlund. (2001, October 25, last updated).What is "plagiarism" and why do people do it? University Writing Center. California State University, Los Angeles.[online].

33. Purdue Online Writing Lab. (2004). Avoiding plagiarism. Retrieved December 10, 2005, from http://owl.english.purdue.edu/handouts/research/r_plagiar.html.

34. Mason, W. (2005, May). *Make* it newish: E. E. Cummings, plagiarism, and the perils of originality. (E.E. Cummings: A biography) (Book Review). *Harper's Magazine*, *310*, 92–102. Retrieved December 10, 2005, from InfoTrac College Edition.

35. Kennedy, R. S. (1980). *Dreams in the mirror: A biography of E. E. Cummings*. Quoted in ibid.

36. Sawyer-Laucanno, C. (2004). E.E. Cummings, a biography. Quoted in US latest, MIT scholar.

37. Purdue Online Writing Lab.

38. Avoiding Plagiarism. (2001). UCDavis.

39. Southwick, P. (2004). Embryo adoption. In Jaffe. C. I. *Public speaking: Concepts and skills for a diverse society* (4th ed., pp. 389–391). Belmont, CA: Wadsworth.

40. Valentine, J. (2004). The *dun dun* drum. Student speech included in Appendix C.

41. Frist, B. (2004, August 31). Full text of the remarks of Senate Majority Leader Bill Frist. *The New York Times*. [online] Retrieved September 1, 2004, from .nytimes.com/2004/08/31/politics/campaign/01TEXT-FRIST>html.

42. This box draws from N. Carbone. (2001, December 3). Thinking and talking about plagiarism. Bedford St. Martins Technotes. Retrieved February 5, 2005, from http://bedfordstmartins.com/technotes/techtiparchive/ttip102401.htm.

43. Hunter, J. (1997). Confessions of an academic honesty woman. Grinnell College Writing Lab. [Online.] Accessed February 11, 2005. www.grinnell.edu/academic/writinglab/forum/con_hj.pdf.

44. Blakeslee, S. (1992, March). Faulty math heightens fears of breast cancer. *New York Times*, Sec. 4, pp. 1, 2.

45. Gardner, A. (2005, February 1). Women missing out on heart disease diagnoses and treatments. TheBakersfieldChannel.com. [Online.] Retrieved February 9, 2005,

from http://kero-tvhealth.ip2m.com/index.cfm?pt=itemDetail&Item_ID=116331&site_cat_id=7.

CHAPTER 4

1. Harris, D. (2001, September 3). Listen up!: Most of Mike Lazarus's service advisers are women. *Automotive News*, 75(5946), 2. Retrieved April 5, 2005, from InfoTrac College Edition.

2. The 25% efficiency percentage is widely quoted. See Roach, C. A. & Wyatt, N. J. (1995). Listening and the rhetorical process. In Stewart, *Bridges*, 171–176.

3. Maes, J. D., Weldy, T. B. & Icenogle, M. L. (1997, January). A managerial perspective: Oral communication competency is more important for business students in the workplace. *Journal of Business Communication*, 34, 6–14. Retrieved May 28, 2003, from InfoTrac College Edition.

4. Salopek, J. J. (1999). Is anyone listening? *Training and Development*, 53, 9, 58–60. Retrieved February 23, 2005, from Info-Trac College Edition.

5. Burley-Allen, M. (2001). Listen up: Listening is a learned skill and supervisors need it to improve their employee relationships. *HR Magazine*. Retrieved February 20, 2005, from InfoTrac College Edition.

6. Bentley, S. (1998, February). Listening better: A guide to improving what may be the ultimate staff skill. *Nursing Homes*, 47, 2, 56–59. Retrieved March 1, 2005, from InfoTrac College Edition.

7. Harris, *Listen up!*

8. Lundsteen, S. W. (1993). Metacognitive listening. In A. D. Wolvin & C. G. Coakley (Eds.). *Perspectives on listening* (106–123). Norwood, NJ: Ablex.

9. Ibid.

10. Edwards, R. & McDonald, J. L. (1993). Schema theory and listening. In Wolvin & Coakley, *Perspectives*, 60–77.

11. Tannen, D. (1989). *Talking voices: Repetition, dialogue, and imagery in conversational discourse*. Cambridge: Cambridge University Press.

12. Sitkaram, K. S. & Cogdell, R. T. (1976). *Foundations of intercultural communication*. Columbus, OH: Charles E. Merrill.

13. Ibid.

14. Daniel, J. & Smitherman, G. (1990). How I got over: Communication dynamics in the black community. In Carbaugh, *Intercultural communication*. See also A. L. Smith (Molefi Asanti). (1970). Socio-historical perspectives of black oratory. *Quarterly Journal of Speech*, 61, 264–269.

15. Kiewitz, C., Weaver, J. B. III, Brosius, H-B., & Weimann, G. (1997). Cultural differences in listening style preferences: A comparison of young adults in Germany, Israel, and the United States. *International Journal of Public Opinion Research*, 9, 233–248. Retrieved May 29, 2003, from Info-Trac College Edition.

16. University of Minnesota, Duluth. (2002, February 20). Listening skills. Student handbook [online]. Retrieved May 30, 2003, from www.d.umn.edu/student/loon/acad/strat/ss_listening.html.

17. Lundsteen, Metacognitive listening.

18. Ridge, A. (1993). A perspective of listening skills. In Wolvin & Coakley, *Perspectives*, 1–14.

19. Hybels, S. & Weaver, R. I. (1992). *Communicating effectively*, 3rd ed. New York: McGraw Hill.

20. Goodman, G. & Esterly, G. (1990). Questions—the most popular piece of language. In Stewart, *Bridges*, 69–79.

21. Becker, C. B. (1991). Reasons for the lack of argumentation and debate in the Far East. In Samovar & Porter, *Intercultural communication*, 234–243; See also K. Sueda. (1995). Differences in the perception of face: Chinese *mien-tzu* and Japanese *mentsu*. *World Communication*, 24, 1, 23–31,

22. Anonymous reviewer. (2004).

CHAPTER 5

1. Luce, B. (2002). Top of their class [Online]. *Columns: The University of Washington Alumni Magazine*. Retrieved December 15, 2002, from www.washington.edu/alumni/columns/june02/ honors1.html.

2. Holzman, P. (1970). *The psychology of speakers and audiences*. Glenview, IL: Scott Foresman.

3. Cipolla, B. (2000). Gift of language, gift of suffering: Papal voice a powerful tool. Catholic News Service. Retrieved April 28, 2005, from www.catholicherald.com/cns/voice.htm.

4. Hollingsworth, H. L. (1935). *The psychology of audiences*. New York: American Book Company.

5. Collier, M. J. (1994). Cultural identity and intercultural communication. In Samovar & Porter, *Intercultural communication*, 36–45.

6. Rothenberg, P. S. (Ed.). (1998). *Race, class, and gender in the United States*. New York: St. Martin's Press.

7. Collier, Cultural identity; O'Neil, D. (1999, September 21). Ethnicity and race: An introduction to the nature of social group differentiation and inequality [Online]. Retrieved April 23, 2003, from www.daphne.palomar.edu/ethnicity/default.htm.

8. Jaffe, C. I. (1995). Chronemics: Communicating mainstream cycles to Russian Old Believer children. *World Communication*, 15, 1–20.

9. Student demographics. (2005, November 2). LaGuardia Community College. Retrieved December 10, 2005, from www.lagcc.cuny.edu/facts/facts03/PDFs _profile/Fa_2005.pdf.

10. O'Neil, Ethnicity and race.

11. Marmor, J. (1996, December). Blurring the lines. *Columns*, 16, 8, 22–27.

12. Clinton, W. J. (2000). State of the Union. Address delivered to a joint session of Congress, January 27. Retrieved June 13, 2005, from http://clinton4.nara.gov/WH/SOTU00/sotu-text.html.

13. Morton, L. P. (1998). Segmenting publics: An introduction [Column]. *Public Relations Quarterly*, 43, 13, 33–34. Retrieved April 15, 2003, from InfoTrac College Edition.

14. O'Donovan, C. (1997, December). The X styles. *Communication World*, 15, 1, 17–20. Retrieved April 15, 2003, from InfoTrac College Edition.

15. Halstead, T. (1999, August). A politics for generation X. *Atlantic Monthly*, 284, 2, 33ff. Retrieved August 29, 1999, from InfoTrac College Edition.

16. Prensky, M. (1998, October). Bankers trust: Training is all fun and games. *HR Focus*, 75, 10, 11. Retrieved August 30, 1999, from InfoTrac College Edition.

17. Vogel, M. (2001, February). The I-generation: How managers can integrate this new employee base's unique skills and work behavior into their organization. AgriMarketing. Retrieved April 6, 2005, from www.agrimarketing.com/show_story .php?id=10093.

18. Andersen, J. R., & Nussbaum, J. F. (1987). The public speaking course: A liberal arts perspective. *Communication Education*, 35, 174–182.

19. America 2000: A map of the mix. (2000, September 18). *Newsweek*, 136, 12, 48.

20. Rokeach, M. (1972). *Beliefs, attitudes, and values*. San Francisco: Jossey-Bass.

21. Jaffe, Chronemics.

22. Levine, R. (1997). *A geography of time*. New York: Basic Books.

23. Tracy, L. (2005, March 1). Taming hostile audiences. *Vital Speeches of the Day*, 71(10), 306–313.

24. McCroskey, J. C. (1993). *An introduction to rhetorical communication*.(6th ed.). Englewood Cliffs, NJ: Prentice-Hall.

25. Weider & Pratt, Recognizable Indian.

26. Miller, A. N. (2002). An exploration of Kenyan public speaking patterns with implications for the American introductory public speaking course. *Communication Education*, 51, 2, 168–182.

CHAPTER 6

1. Southwick, P. (2005, April 13). Personal interview. Newberg, Oregon.

2. Christensen, M. D. (1998, March). An idea is only the bait. *The Writer*, 111, 20–21.

3. Bitzer, L. F. (1999). The rhetorical situation. In J. L. Lucaites, C. M. Condit, & S. Caudill (Eds.), *Contemporary rhetorical theory: A reader* (pp. 217–225). New York: Guilford; see also Vatz, R. E. (1999). The myth of the rhetorical situation. In Lucaites, Condit, & Caudill, *Contemporary rhetorical theory*, 226–231.

4. McKeon, R. (1998). Creativity and the commonplace. In T. B. Ferrell (Ed.), *Landmark essays on contemporary rhetoric* (pp. 33–41). Mahwah, NJ: Hermagoras Press.

5. Murray, D. M. (1998, May). Write what you don't know. *The Writer*, 111, 7–9.

6. Christensen, Idea.

7. Carrell, L. J. (1997). Diversity in the communication curriculum: Impact on student empathy. *Communication Education*, 46, 234–244.

8. Scofield, S. (1999, August). An end to writer's block. *The Writer*, 111, 7–9.

9. Augustine. (1958). *On Christian doctrine*:

Book IV (D. W. Robertson Jr., Trans.). New York: Liberal Arts Press.

10. Campbell, G. (1963). *The philosophy of rhetoric* (L. Bitzer, Ed.). Carbondale: Southern Illinois University Press. (Original work published 1776)

11. Porrovecchio, M. (personal email, 2005, March 29) reminded me of the influence of Campbell's psychological theories on his rhetoric.

12. Monroe, A. H. (1962). *Principles and types of speech* (5th ed.). Chicago: Scott Foresman.

13. Gwynne, R. (2005, March 12 last updated). Topic organization. University of Tennessee Knoxville. Accessed March 12, 2005. http://web.utk.edu/~gwynne/topic_organization.html.

14. Anonymous reviewer. (2005). College of Marin.

15. Gwynne, Topic organization.

16. Engnell, R. (1999). What is a central idea? Class handout for Introduction to Communication, George Fox University, Newberg, OR.

17. Griffin, C. W. (1998). Improving students' writing strategies; knowing versus doing. *College Teaching, 46,* 48–52. Retrieved April 16, 2003, from InfoTrac College Edition.

CHAPTER 7

1. Lieggi, L. (1999, July 20). Personal interview. George Fox University, Newberg, OR.

2. Rodrigues, D., & Rodrigues, R. J. (2000). *The research paper and the World Wide Web* (2nd ed.). Upper Saddle River, NJ: Prentice-Hall.

3. Harnack, A., & Kleppinger, E. (1998). *Online!: A reference guide to using Internet sources, 1998 edition* [Online]. New York: St. Martin's Press. Retrieved November 8, 2002, from www.smpcollege.com/online-4styles^help.

4. Baker, S. (2005, February 17). Don't fear the blog and the fury. *Business Week Online.* Retrieved March 16, 2005, from InfoTrac College Edition.

5. Hacker, D. (1998). *A writer's reference* (4th ed.). New York: Bedford/St. Martin's.

6. Unless noted otherwise, the information in this section comes from Finding information on the Internet: A tutorial. (2004, August 18, last updated). UC Berkeley—Teaching Library Internet Workshops. Retrieved August 12, 2005, from www.lib.berkeley.edu/TeachingLib/Guides/Internet/FindInfo.html.

7. Sherman, C. (2004, February 18). Yahoo! Birth of a new machine. Search Engine Watch. Retrieved August 13, 2005, from http://searchenginewatch.com/searchday/article.php/3314171.

8. Sherman, C. & Price, P. (2001). About this site. The Invisible Web Directory. Retrieved August 13, 2005, from www.invisible-web.net/

9. Miller, Kenyan public speaking patterns, 174.

10. Internet Source Validation Project. (1999, July). [Online]. Retrieved February 7, 2002, from www.stemnet.nf.ca/~dfurey/validate/termsi.html.

11. Hawkes, L. (1999). *A guide to the World Wide Web.* Upper Saddle River, NJ: Prentice-Hall.

12. Yu, H. & Young, M. (2004). An impact of web search engines on subject searching in OPAC. *Information Technology and Libraries, 23,* 168–181. Retrieved March 16, 2005, from InfoTrac College Edition.

13. Abram, S. & Luther, J. (2004, May 1). Born with the chip: The next generation will profoundly impact both library service and the culture within the profession. *Library Journal, 129,* 34–38. Retrieved March 16, 2005, from InfoTrac College Edition.

14. Yu & Young, Web search engines.

15. Miller, Kenyan public speaking patterns.

16. Hawkes, *Guide.*

17. Wikipedia. (2005). Wikipedia Encyclopedia. Retrieved April 9, 2005, from http://en.wikipedia.org/wiki/Wikipedia.

18. Reuters. (2005, April 8). Yahoo backs Wikipedia. Retrieved April 9, 2005, from http://today.reuters.co.uk/news/newsArticle.aspx?type=internetNews&storyID=2005-04-08T013855Z_01_HOL805922_RTRIDST_0_OUKIN-TECH-YAHOO.XML.

19. Vara, V. (2005, March 28). From Wikipedia's creator, a new site for anyone, anything. *Wall Street Journal,* B1, B6.

20. Paragraph 107: Fair use. (2004, April 30). Copyright Law of the United States of America. Title 17. Circular 92. Chapter 1. Retrieved March 18, 2005, from www.copyright.gov/title17/92chap1.html.

CHAPTER 8

1. For information that supports environmentalists' claims, search InfoTrac College Edition for articles that detail the scientific conclusions.

2. InfoTrac College Edition has many articles about Lomborg. For example, see Cowley, J. (2003, June 30). The man who demanded a recount. (Dissent). *New Statesman (1996), 132(4644).* 28–30. Retrieved April 30, 2005; West, W. (2003, February 18). Eco-doomsayers exact revenge on Lomborg. *Insight on the News,* 19(5), 56–57. Retrieved April 30, 2005). Pope, C. & Lomborg, B. (2005, July-August). The state of nature. (Debate). Foreign Policy, 149, 66–74. (Retrieved August 10, 2005).

3. Karim, A. T. (2002, May 1). Terrorism: Addressing its root causes [Comments made in a question and answer forum] "Islam, 9/11, and U.S. National Security." American Council for Study of Islamic Societies, College of William and Mary, Washington, D.C., March 4, 2002. *Vital Speeches,* 68, 14, 25–29.

4. Read, R. (2005, Spring). Reporting from a "calamity that defies description." *Nieman Reports,* 53, 1, 73–76. Retrieved June 3, 2005, from InfoTrac College Edition.

5. 100 questions and answers about Arab Americans: A journalists' guide. (2001). *Detroit Free Press.* Jobs Page. Retrieved June 13, 2005, from www.freep.com/jobspage/arabs/index.htm. Unless noted otherwise, the information in this box comes from this source.

6. Census and religious information from: Arab American Demographics. (2005). Arab American Institute. Retrieved May 28, 2005, from www.aaiusa.org/demographics.htm.

7. MacIntyre, A. (1981). *After virtue: A study in moral reasoning* (2nd ed.). South Bend, IN: University of Notre Dame Press.

8. Miller, Kenyan public speaking patterns, 178.

9. Eller, T. S. (2004, Winter). The razor's edge. (CPT Special Report). *Christian Parenting Today,* 17, 2, 34–39. Retrieved June 3, 2005, from InfoTrac College Edition.

10. Springen, K. (2004, June 7). Drastically downsized. *Newsweek,* p. 78.

11. Schrof, J. M. & Schultz, S. (1999, June 21). Social anxiety. *U.S. News & World Report,* 126, 24, 53.

12. Wilson, P. (1983). *Second-hand knowledge: An inquiry into cognitive authority.* Westport, CT: Greenwood.

13. LaWare, M. R. (1998). Encountering visions of Aztlan: Arguments for ethnic pride, community activism and cultural revitalization in Chicano murals. *Argumentation and Advocacy,* 34, 140–153. Retrieved June 13, 2005, from InfoTrac College Edition.

14. Wilson, *Second-hand knowledge.*

15. Kluger, J. (2005, May 16). The cruelest cut: Often it's the one teens inflict on themselves. *Time,* 165, 20, 48.

16. Ibid.

17. Tembo, M. S. (1999, April). Your mother is still your mother. *World and I,* 14, 4. Retrieved May 24, 2005, from InfoTrac College Edition.

18. Walters, F. (1992, November 15). In celebration of options: Respect each other's differences. *Vital Speeches of the Day,* 265–269.

19. Pitney, J. J. (1995, November 13). The Tocqueville fraud. *The Weekly Standard,* 1, 44–45.

20. Riley, J. & Ratchford, J. (1998). Americans expected to enjoy 25.6 million hot dogs during baseball season. National Hot Dog and Sausage Council. Retrieved June 6, 2005, from www.hot-dog.org/pr/pr_opening2000.html.

21. Lewis, R. (2002, August 27) How to Become a Good Googler. The Early Show. Retrieved June 13, 2005, from www.cbsnews.com/stories/2002/08/26/earlyshow/contributors/reginalewis/main519808.shtml.

22. Matthews, T. J., Hamilton, M. S., & Hamilton, B. E. (2002, December 11). Mean age of mothers, 1970–2000. National Vital Statistics Reports, 51(1). Retrieved August 10, 2005, from www.cdc.gov/nchs/data/nvsr/nvsr51/nvsr51_01.pdf.

23. Powell, E. A. (2005, May 25). Study shows modest decline in college student credit card debt. *Statesman-Journal.* Salem, OR, B1.

24. GFK NOP. (2005, June 15). World culture score. Index examines global media habits . . . uncovers who's tuning in, logging on, and hitting the books. Retrieved August 10, 2005, from www.nopworld .com/news.asp?go=news_item&key=179.

25. Powell, Modest decline.

26. National Center for Victims of Crime. (2000). *Crime and victimization in America, statistical overview* [Online]. Retrieved November 13, 2000, from http://www .ncvc.org.

27. Khan, L. A. (2002, January 15). A century of great awakenings: "We have learned much about ourselves." *Vital Speeches of the Day, 68(7),* 222–225.

28. McLain, F. J. (2001, November 1). The music in your soul. A celebration of life. A speech delivered at fall convocation, Queens College, Charlotte, NC, September 18, 2001 *Vital Speeches of the Day, 68(2),* 59–61.

CHAPTER 9

1. Impact Publications. (2001). Secret #24: Organize ideas for easy understanding. Winning the Job: Your Career Resource Center. Retrieved June 1, 2005, www.winningthejob.com/page2.php3?ID=150& Item=2397.

2. Miller, G. A. (1956). The magical number seven, plus or minus two: Some limits on our capacity for processing information. *The Psychological Review, 63,* 81–97. [Reprinted online.] Retrieved April 29, 2005, from www.well.com/user/smalin/ miller.html.

3. Young People's Trust for the Environment. (2001). Fact sheet: What is a tsunami? Retrieved June 1, 2005, from www.yptenc.org.uk/docs/factsheets/ env_facts/tsunami.html.

4. Bloch, M. (1975). *Political language and oratory in traditional society.* London: Academic Press.

5. Miller, Kenyan public speaking patterns.

6. Jorgensen-Earp, C. (n.d.), "Making other arrangements": Alternative patterns of disposition [Unpublished course handout]. Lynchburg, VA: Lynchburg College.

7. Jorgensen-Earp, Other arrangements.

8. Zediker, K. (1993, February). Rediscovering the tradition: Women's history with a relational approach to the basic public speaking course. Panel presentation at the Western States Communication Association, Albuquerque, NM.

9. Truth, S. (1997). Ain't I a woman? Modern History Sourcebook. [online]. Retrieved June 1, 2005, from www.fordham.edu/ halsall/mod/sojtruth-woman.html. Original speech delivered 1851, Women's Convention, Akron, OH.

10. Karakas, F. (2005, April 1). Tolerance, love, and cooperation: When I think of Ramadan. *Vital Speeches of the Day, 71(12),* 373–377.

CHAPTER 10

1. Statham, S. (2001, July 1). Dead man watching. *Vital Speeches of the Day, 67(18),* 563.

2. Quintilian, *instituto oratoria,* Chapter 2.

3. Davidson, J. (2001, November 15). Relaxing at high speed: You must take time. *Vital Speeches of the Day, 68,* 87–91.

4. Wirth, D. (1999, October 29) *Arachnophobia: Overcoming your fear* [Student Speech]. Goshen, IN: Goshen College.

5. Martin, T. (2001, November 1). I am fearfully and wonderfully made: Living is an adventure. Address delivered at the Westover School, Middlebury, CT, October 11, 2001. *Vital Speeches of the Day, 68,* 61–63.

6. Tinkler, H. (2001, January 1). The heart of the matter. Speech delivered November 16, 2004. Texas A & M. *Vital Speeches, 71,* 170–175.

7. Abdoo, R. A. (2004, November 15). Lessons in doing the right thing. Speech delivered October 14, 2004. University of Dayton. *Vital Speeches of the Day, 71,* 78–85.

8. Braithwaite, C. A. (1997). *Sa'ah Naagháí Bak'eh Hòzhóón:* An ethnography of Navajo educational communication practices. *Communication Education, 46,* 219–233.

9. Echo in introductions and conclusions. (n.d.) Instructional web page [Online]. Retrieved December 15, 1999, from www .stlcc.cc.mo.us/fv/webcourses/eng020/ testlocation/mensepage/Echo.html.

CHAPTER 11

1. Preparing the delivery outline. (1999, December 14). Riverdale School Speech Class, Upper Grades [Online]. Retrieved January 12, 2001, from www.teleport.com/ ~beanman/english/delivout.html.

2. Jorgensen-Earp, Other arrangements.

3. Thinking and learning skills. (1999). SNOW. University of Toronto. [Online]. Retrieved December 24, 1999, from http://snow.utoronto.ca/learn2/introll .html.

4. Irvine, J. J., & York, D. E. (1995). *Learning styles and culturally diverse students: A literature review.* (ERIC Document Reproduction Service No. ED382 722 UDO3046). Retrieved November 19, 1999, from http://ericae.net/faqs.

5. Giller, E. (n.d., accessed 1999, December 28). Left brain/right brain religion [Online]. Retrieved December 28, 1999, from www.sabbath.com/ acfl.htm; see also Riding, R., & Cheema, I. (1991). Cognitive styles—an overview and integration. *Educational Psychology, 11,* 193–215.

CHAPTER 12

1. Anonymous reviewer. (1994).

2. Neil Wolkodoff is quoted in C. Deherrera. (2002, May). Enhance your career by becoming a speaker. *IDEA Health & Fitness Source, 20 5,* 23–27. Retrieved March 21, 2005, from InfoTrac College Edition.

3. Jeremiah 13.

4. Reynolds, S. (1996, December). Selling to another language. *Communication World, 14,* 11. Retrieved March 21, 2005, from InfoTrac College Edition.

5. Wall, T. (2004, October). PowerPoint pitfalls that can kill an audience's will to stay

awake. *Presentations, 18(10),* 46(1). Retrieved March 21, 2005, from InfoTrac College Edition.

6. Ibid.

7. Muhovic, E. (2000). Visual aids for presentations. [Online.] Center for Managerial Communications, Denver University. Retrieved October 19, 2002, from www.du .edu/emuhovic/visualpresentations.html.

8. Deherrera, Enhance your career.

9. Davidson, W., & Kline, S. (1999, March). Ace your presentations. *Journal of Accountancy, 187,* 61. Retrieved October 29, 2002, from InfoTrac College Edition.

10. Becker, R. A. & Keller- McNulty, S. (1996, May). Presentation myths. *The American Statistician, 50,* 112–116. Retrieved April 23, 2005, from InfoTrac College Edition.

11. Anonymous reviewer (1994).

12. Doumont, J-L. (2005, Feb.). The cognitive style of PowerPoint: Slides are not all evil. *Technical Communication, 52,1.* 64(7). Retrieved March 20, 2005, from InfoTrac College Edition.

13. Put more power in your next presentation: Use a document camera. (2005). Presenters online. Retrieved March 23, 2005, from www.presentersonline.com/ technical/tools/documentcamera.shtml.

14. See Presentation tips: "Document camera." (2004, February 18). University of Wisconsin–Madison. Retrieved March 20, 2005, from www2.fpm.wisc.edu/ support/PresentationTips.htm.

15. Anonymous reviewer. (1994).

16. Hernandez, T. (2004, Dec.). Digital whiteboards allow design teams to capture plan markups. *Building Design & Construction, 45,* p 19–21. Retrieved March 20, 2005, from InfoTrac College Edition.

17. Anonymous reviewer. (1994).

18. Radel, J. (1999, July). Effective presentations. The University of Kansas Medical Center on-line tutorial series [Online]. Retrieved March 20, 2005, from http:// KUMC.edu/SAH /OTEd/jradel/effective .html.

19. Zielinski, D. (2003, Sept.). Go! Part two: Planes, trains and presenting: Secrets and strategies of speakers on the go. *Presentations, 47(4),* 17–28. Retrieved March 20, 2005, from InfoTrac College Edition.

20. Five keys to effective handouts. (1997, October 13). *Buffalo Business First* [online]. Accessed March 22, 2005. http://buffalo .bizjournals.com/buffalo/stories/1997/ 10/13/smallb3.html.

21. Readability. (n.d.) Planning, design, and production [Online]. Retrieved January 3, 2000, from http://ibis.nott.ac.uk/ guidelines/ch2/chap2-G-4.html.

22. Jacobs, K. (2005). Which fonts look good in presentations? Retrieved March 24, 2005, from www.microsoft.com/en-us/ assistance/HA011243941033.aspx.

23. Ibid.

24. The facts about fonts. (2003, December). *PR Newswire.* Retrieved March 21, 2005, from InfoTrac College Edition.

25. Using color to your marketing advantage. (2005, March 21). Great FX Business

Cards Web site. Accessed March 21, 2005. http://www.greatfxbusinesscards.com/colorandemotions.htm.

26. Ibid.

27. Detz, J. (1998, April–May). Delivery plus content equals successful presentations. *Communication World, 15*(5), 34–36. Retrieved January 20, 2000, from InfoTrac College Edition.

28. Anonymous reviewer. (1994).

29. Ibid.

CHAPTER 13

1. Asen, R. (1999, Winter). Toward a normative conception of difference in public deliberation. *Argumentation and Advocacy, 35*(3), 115–116. Retrieved from InfoTrac College Edition.

2. Berstein, D. (2002, June 20). Putting in a good word. *Design Week, 17, 25,* 10–11. Retrieved March 8, 2005, from InfoTrac College Edition.

3. Ibid.

4. Gozzi, R. (1990). *New words and a changing American culture.* Columbia, SC: University of South Carolina Press.

5. Liberman, M. (2004, February 15). 46 Somali words for camel. Language Log. Retrieved June 7, 2005, from http://itre.cis.upenn.edu/~myl/languagelog/archives/000457.html.

6. Barfield, O. (1973). *Poetic diction: A study in meaning.* Middletown, CT: Wesleyan University Press, p. 23.

7. Dialects doing well. (1998). InSCIght on Apnet. Retrieved March 12, 2003, from www.apnet.com/inscight/02181009/graphb.htm.

8. Gozzi, New words.

9. Police officer. (2002). Merriam-Webster online. Retrieved June 7, 2005, from www.m-w.com/cgi-bin/dictionary; Principal. (2002). Merriam-Webster online. Retrieved June 7, 2005, from www.m-w.com/cgi-bin/dictionary.

10. Ibid.

11. Ray, J., & Badle, C. (1993, February 3). Hosts of "Queer Talk" speaking on a talk radio call-in show. WABC, New York.

12. Delwiche, A. (2002, September 29). Propaganda: Euphemisms. Propaganda Critic. Retrieved August 20, 2005, from www.propagandacritic.com/articles/ct.wg.euphemism.html.

13. Johannesen, *Ethics.*

14. Currey, J., & Mumford, K. (2002, September 18) Just talk: Guide to inclusive language. University of Tasmania. Retrieved December 20, 2002, from http://student.admin.utas.edu.au/services/just_talk/Disability/disability.htm.

15. Emory University Department of Religion (2001, December 6). Statement on inclusive language. Retrieved December 20, 2002, from www.emory.edu/COLLEGE/RELIGION/about/statement.html.

16. Seiter, J. S., Larsen, J., & Skinner, J. (1998). "Handicapped" or "handi-capable"? The effects of language about persons with disabilities on perceptions of source credibility and persuasiveness. *Communication Reports, 11*(1), 21–31.

17. Freimuth, V. S., & Jamieson, K. (1979). *Communicating with the elderly: Shattering stereotypes.* Urbana, IL: ERIC Clearinghouse on Reading and Communication Skills.

18. Winans, J. A. (1938). *Speechmaking.* New York: Appleton-Century.

19. Currey & Mumford, Just talk.

20. Zimmerman, T., & Goode, E. (1994, October 3). The mind of Aristide. *U.S. News & World Report,* p. 32.

21. Pettit, R. (1990). *Who/what would you want in your band? Or why did I spend 25 years playing drums?* [Student speech]. Oregon State University.

22. Lamm, R. D. (2005). How to make an environmentalist. *Vital Speeches of the Day,* pp. 304–306.

23. Carnahan, J. (1999, June 15). Born to make barrels: Women who put their stamp on history. Address given at the Trailblazer's Awards Ceremony, University of Missouri, St. Louis. *Vital Speeches of the Day, 65,* 529–531.

24. Underwood, A. (2004, April 5). Doughnuts in the dark. *Newsweek,* p. 51.

25. Peters, D. (2000, May). Sweet seduction. *Chatelaine, 73*(5), 53. Retrieved December 15, 2002, from InfoTrac College Edition.

26. Reagan, R. (1986, January 31). Memorial service for the crew of the space shuttle *Challenger.* Houston. Retrieved December 15, 2002, from www.eulogywriters.com/challenger.htm.

27. Archambault, D. (1992, May 1). Columbus plus 500 years: Whither the American Indian? *Vital Speeches of the Day, 58,* 491–493.

28. Seattle. (1971). The Indian's night promises to be dark. In W. C. Vanderwerth. (Ed.). *Indian oratory: Famous speeches by noted Indian chieftains* (pp. 118–122). Norman, OK: University of Oklahoma Press. (Original work published 1853)

29. Osborn, M. (1997). The play of metaphors. *Education, 118,* 1, 84–87. Retrieved December 14, from InfoTrac College Edition.

30. Seattle, Indian's night.

31. Osborn, M. (1967). Archetypal metaphor in rhetoric: The lightdark family. *Quarterly Journal of Speech, 53,* 115–126. See also Osborn, M. (1977). The evolution of the archetypal sea in rhetoric and poetic. *Quarterly Journal of Speech, 63,* 347–363.

32. Lustig, M. W., & Koester, J. (1993). *Intercultural competence: Interpersonal communication across cultures.* New York: HarperCollins; see also Simons, G. F., Vazquez, C., & Harris, P. R. (1993). *Transcultural leadership: Empowering the diverse workforce.* Houston: Gulf.

33. Thiederman, S. (1991a). *Bridging cultural barriers for corporate success: How to manage the multicultural workforce.* New York: Lexington; see also Thiederman, S. (1991b). *Profiting in America's multicultural market places: How to do business across cultural lines.* New York: Lexington.

34. King, M. L., Jr. (1963). I have a dream. American rhetoric [Online]. Retrieved December 10, 2005, from www.americanrhetoric.com/speeches/Ihaveadream.htm.

CHAPTER 14

1. Montalbo, T. (1980). Churchill: A study in oratory. Seven lessons in speechmaking from one of the greatest orators of all time. The Churchill Centre. Retrieved June 9, 2005, from www.winstonchurchill.org/i4apages/index.cfm?pageid+814.

2. Laureates. (2005). The Nobel Prize in Literature 1953. Nobelprize.org. Retrieved June 14, 2005, from http://nobelprize.org/literature/laureates/1953.

3. This information comes from Montalbo, Churchill.

4. Goffman, E. (1959). *The presentation of self in everyday life.* Garden City, NY: Doubleday Anchor.

5. Bippus & Daly, Stage fright.

6. Arthur, A. (1997, July). Keeping up public appearances: Master the fine art of public-speaking and give a great presentation every time. *Black Enterprise, 27,* 12, 54. Retrieved December 20, 2002, from InfoTrac College Edition.

7. Molloy, J. T. (1976). *Dress for success.* New York: Warner Books.

8. Ekman, P. & Friesen, W. V. (1969). The repertoire of nonverbal behavior: Categories, origins, usage, and coding. *Semiotica, I,* 49–98.

9. Richmond, V. P. & McCroskey, J. C. (2000). *Nonverbal behavior in interpersonal relations* (4th ed.). Scottsdale, AZ: Gorsuch Scarisbrick.

10. Montalbo, Churchill.

11. Richmond & McCroskey, *Nonverbal behavior.*

12. Aristotle, (1954, 1984). *The Rhetoric.* H. R. Roberts (trans.). New York: The Modern Library.

13. Burgoon, J. K., Buller, D. B., & Woodall, W. G. (1989). *Nonverbal communication: The unspoken dialogue.* New York: Harper & Row; see also Ray, G. B. (1986). Vocally cued personality prototypes: An implicit personality theory approach. *Communication Monographs, 53,* 266–276.

14. Ibid.

15. Davidson, W., & Kline, S. (1999, March). Ace your presentations. *Journal of Accountancy, 187*(3), 61. Retrieved January 7, 2003, from InfoTrac College Edition.

16. Hypes, M. G., Turner, E. T., Norris, C. M., & Wollferts, L. C. (1999, January). How to be a successful presenter. *Journal of Physical Education, Recreation & Dance, 70,* 1, 50–53.

17. Montalbo, Churchill.

18. Humphrey, J. (1998, May 15). Executive eloquence: A seven-fold path to inspirational leadership. *Vital Speeches, 64,* 15, 468–471.

19. Hart & Burks, Rhetorical sensitivity.

20. Branham, R. J., & Pearce, W. B. (1996). The conversational frame in public address. *Communication Quarterly, 44,* 4, 423–439.

21. Brookhiser, R. (1999, November 22). Weird Al: A troubled and alarming vice president. *National Review, 60, 22*, 32–34. See also Shipman, C. (2000, December/January). Searching for Al. *George Magazine, 102*, 9.

22. Hypes, Turner, Norris, & Wolfferts, Successful presenter.

23. Ross, R. S. (1989). *Speech communication: The speechmaking system* (8th ed.). Upper Saddle River, NJ: Prentice-Hall.

CHAPTER 15

1. Endicott, J. (2003). The art of storytelling in presentations. Retrieved June 15, 2005, from www.presentersuniversity.com/courses_delivery_storytelling.php.

2. Watson, B. (1997). The storyteller is the soybean . . . the audience is the sun. *Smithsonian, 27*, 12, 60–67.

3. Wicker, B. (1975). *The story-shaped world: Fiction and metaphysics, some variations on a theme.* South Bend, IN: University of Notre Dame Press.

4. Cortese, A. (1990). *Ethnic ethics: The restructuring of moral theory.* Albany, NY: SUNY Press.

5. Fisher, W. R. (1984). Narration as a human communication paradigm: The case of public moral argument. *Communication Monographs, 51*, 1–22; Fisher, W. R. (1984). The narrative paradigm: An elaboration. *Communication Monographs, 52*, 347–367.

6. Barthes is quoted in Polkinghorne, D. E. (1988). *Narrative knowing and the human sciences.* Albany, NY: SUNY Press, p. 14.

7. Neile, C. S. (2005). Can storytelling save the world. Florida Storytelling Association. Retrieved June 21, 2005, from www.flstory.org/can_storytelling_save.htm.

8. Vergnani, S. A. (2003, March 14). Healing through storytelling. Columbia News Service. Retrieved June 20, 2005, from www.jrn.columbia.edu/studentwork/cns/2003-03-14/16.asp.

9. Ibid.

10. Neile, C. S. (2005). International Storytelling Center internship. The Woodrow Wilson National Fellowship Foundation. Retrieved June 20, 2005, from www.woodrow.org/phd/Practicum/neile.html; Neile C. S. (2003). War and peace and story. *Words of Wing, 6.* [online]. Healing Story. Retrieved June 20, 2005, from www.healingstory.org/articles/healing-story-articles.html.

11. Cassady, M. (1994). *The art of storytelling: Creative ideas for preparation and performance.* Colorado Springs, CO: Meriweather, p. 12.

12. Anokye, A. D. (1994, Fall). Oral connections to literacy: The narrative. *Journal of Basic Writing, 13*, 46–60.

13. Coste, D. (1989). *Narrative as communication.* Minneapolis: University of Minnesota Press.

14. Spangler, D. & Thompson, W. I. (1992). *Reimagination of the world: A critique of the new age, science, and popular culture.* New York: Bear & Company.

15. Sternberg, R. (1998). *Love is a story: A new theory of relationships.* New York: Oxford University Press.

16. Endicott, Art of storytelling.

17. Simmons, A. (n.d.). Six stories you need to know how to tell. International Storytelling Center. Retrieved June 15, 2005, from www.storytellingcenter.com/resources/articles/simmons.htm.

18. Keeshig-Tobias, L. (1990, January 26). Stop stealing native stories. *Toronto Globe & Mail*, A7.

19. Ibid.

20. Aristotle, *Rhetoric.*

21. Baum, N. (2003). A land twice promised. Retrieved June 20, 2005, from www.noabaum.com/land.html.

22. Stone, G. (n. d.). Promotional letter. New York: God's Love, We Deliver.

23. Kirkwood, W. G. (1992). Narrative and the rhetoric of possibility. *Communication Monographs, 59*, 30–47.

24. Torrance, J. (1998). Jackie tales: The magic of creating stories and the art of telling them. New York: Avon Books.

25. Cassady, *Art of storytelling.*

26. Burke, K. (1983, August 12). Dramatism and logology. *The Times Literary Supplement*, (p. 859).

27. Tannen, *Talking voices.*

28. Gergen, K. J. (1998). Narrative, moral identity and historical consciousness: A social constructionist account. Available manuscript. Retrieved December 27, 2004, from www.swarthmore.edu/SocSci/kgergen1/web/page/phtml?id=manu3&st+manuscript.

29. McNally, J. R. (1969). Opening assignments: A symposium. *The Speech Teacher, 18*, 18–30.

30. Burke, Dramatism.

31. Fisher, Human communication.

32. Fisher, Narrative paradigm; Fisher, Human communication.

CHAPTER 16

1. Virkler, S. (2005, February 27). Wind farm manager will be dinner speaker. *Watertown (NY) Daily Times*, p. n/a. Retrieved March 25, 2005, from InfoTrac College Edition.

2. Torres, N. L. (2005, May). Shout it from the rooftops: Ensure maximum exposure for your new product or service by becoming a public speaker. *Entrepreneur, 33*, 5, 98–99. Retrieved June 28, 2005, from InfoTrac College Edition.

3. Elmer-Dewitt, P. (1993, April 12). Electronic superhighways. *Time*, 50–55.

4. Davidson, J. (2005, January 15). Bombarded on all sides: Handling everyday information. (Speech delivered September 29, 2004.) *Vital Speeches of the Day, 71*, 7, 212–217.

5. Fancher, M. R. (1993, August 8). Will journalists travel on the information highway? *Seattle Times*, p. A2.

6. General Assembly of the United Nations. (1948, December 10). Universal Declaration of Human Rights. Retrieved June 28, 2005, from www.un.org/Overview/rights.html.

7. Gluckman, R. (2004, October 18). Beyond the Net's reach: A German firm says it has connected North Korea to the Web, only Pyongyang won't throw the switch. *Newsweek*, 40.

8. Maxwell, L. & McCain, T. A. (1997, July). Gateway or gatekeeper: The implication of copyright and digitalization on education. *Communication Education, 46*, 141–157.

9. Edwards & McDonald, Schema theory.

10. Quotation retrieved June 27, 2005, from www.quotedb.com/quotes/1382.

11. Mills, D. W. (2002). Applying what we know: Student learning styles. Retrieved June 27, 2005, from www.csrnet.org/csrnet/articles/student-learning-styles.html.

12. Budiansky, S. (1999, July). The truth about dogs. *Atlantic Monthly, 284*, 1, 39–41, 44+.

13. Patterson, M. (n.d.). Demonstrative speech (how to). Brazosport College. Retrieved January 22, 2000, from www.brazosport.cc.tx.us/~comm/demon.html.

14. Flynn, K, R, (n.d.). Demonstration or "how to" speech topics. Copia-Lincoln Community College. Retrieved June 28, 2005, from www.colin.edu/flynn/Speech/Demo_Speech.htm.

15. Nguyen, N. (2005, March). *Ha Noi, Thanh pho yeu dau* (my beloved city). Speech presented to COMM 100 class. George Fox University, Newberg, OR.

16. Miller, Kenyan public speaking patterns.

17. Rowan, K. (1995). A new pedagogy for explanatory public speaking: Why arrangement should not substitute for invention. *Communication Education, 44*, 235–250.

18. von Till, B. (1998, November). Definition speech. San Jose State University. Poster session. National Communication Association meeting, New York City.

19. Boerger, M. A. & Henley, T. B. (1999). The use of analogy in giving instructions. *Psychological Record, 49*, 2, 193. Retrieved January 23, 2000, from InfoTrac College Edition.

20. Gardner, H. (1993). *Multiple intelligences: The theory in practice.* New York: Basic Books.

21. Horsfall, S. (2005, Spring) The music of sub-Saharan Africa. Sociology of Music class notes. Texas Wesleyan University. Retrieved June 27, 2005, from http://web.txwesleyan.edu/sociology/horsfall/AfricaMu.html.

22. Goodall, H. L. & Waaigen, C. L. (1986). *The persuasive presentation: A practical guide to professional communication in organizations.* New York: Harper & Row.

23. Rubin, D. L. (1993). Listenability = oral-based discourse + considerateness. In Wolvin & Coakley, *Perspectives*, 261–268.

24. Rowan, New pedagogy.

25. Rubin, Listenability.

26. Thompson, F. T. & Grandgenett, D. J. (1999). Helping disadvantaged learners build effective learning skills. *Education 120*, 1, 130–135.

CHAPTER 17

1. Aristotle, Rhetoric.

2. Rubin, Listenability.

3. Ota, A. K. (1993, July 11). Japan's ambassador to U.S. set welcome new tone. *Seattle Times*, p. A12.

4. Mullins, D. (1993). Guest lecture. St. John's University, Jamaica, NY.

5. Festinger, L. (1957). *A theory of cognitive dissonance*. New York: Row, Peterson.

6. "Attitude." (n.d.). Definition retrieved July 5, 2005, from www.cogsci.princeton.edu/cgi-bin/webwn2.1.

7. This theory, developed by Fishbein and Ajzen, is summarized in Trafimow, D. & Finlay, K. A. (2001). Evidence for improved sensitivity of within-participants analyses in test of the Theory of Reasoned Action. *The Social Science Journal*, 38, 4, 629–638. Retrieved June 29, 2005, from InfoTrac College Edition.

8. Poss, J. E. (2001, June.) Developing a new model for cross-cultural research: synthesizing the health beliefs model and the theory of reasoned action. *Advances in Nursing Science*, 23, 4, 1–16. Retrieved July 6, 2005, from InfoTrac College Edition.

9. Anonymous reviewer (1994).

10. Monroe, A. H. (1962). *Principles and types of speeches* (5th ed.). Chicago: Scott Foresman.

11. Hunt, C. (2002, February). Service and therapy dogs. [Online.] Retrieved July 6, 2005, from www.cofc.edu/~huntc/service.html.

CHAPTER 18

1. Quoted in Quindlen, A. (2005, May 30). Life of the closed mind. *Newsweek*, 145, 22, 82.

2. Stewart, R. A. & Roach, K. D. (1998). Argumentativeness and the Theory of Reasoned Action, *Communication Quarterly*, 46, 2, 177+. Retrieved June 29, 2005, from InfoTrac College Edition.

3. Anonymous reviewer (1994).

4. Aristotle. *Rhetoric*, ¶1356, 356, 20.

5. Quintilian, *instituto oratoria*.

6. Ibid., XII: I, 1.

7. Toulmin, S. (1958). *The uses of argument*. Cambridge, UK: Cambridge University Press; Toulmin, S., Rieke, R, & Janik, A. (1984). *An introduction to reasoning* (2nd ed.). New York: Macmillan.

8. Hilliard, A. (1986). Pedagogy in ancient Kemet. In M. Karenga & J. Carruthers (Eds.). *Kemet and the African world view* (p. 257). London: University of Sankore Press.

9. McClain, F. J. (2001, November 1). The music in your soul: A celebration of life. Address delivered at Queens College, Charlotte, NC, September 18, 2001. *Vital Speeches of the Day*, 68, 2, 59–61.

10. Voth, B. (1998). A case study in metaphor as argument: A longitudinal analysis of the wall separating church and state. *Argumentation and Advocacy*, 34, 3, 127–139. Retrieved March 20, 2002, from InfoTrac College Edition.

11. Jaffe, C. I. (1998, November). Metaphors about the classroom. A paper presented to the National Communication Association, New York City.

12. Wicker, *Story-shaped world*.

13. Aristotle (1984). *Poetics* (¶1459, 5). (I. Bywater, Trans.) New York: The Modern Library. (Original translation published 1954).

14. Hilliard, Pedagogy, 287.

15. Sullivan, Signification.

16. Morris, H. J. (2002, June 17). League of their own. *U.S. News & World Report*, 131, 21, 50–51.

17. Griffiths, M. (1988). Feminism, feelings, and philosophy. In M. Griffiths & M. Whitford (Eds.). *Feminist perspectives in philosophy* (pp. 131–151). Bloomington: Indiana University Press; Jaggar, A. (1989). Love and knowledge: Emotion in feminist epistemology. In A. Garry & M. Pearsall (Eds.). *Women, knowledge, and reality: Explorations in feminist philosophy* (pp. 129–155). London: Unwin; McMillan, 1982).

18. Jaggar, ibid.

19. Griffiths, Feminism.

20. Frank, D. A. (1997). Diversity in the public space: A response to Stepp. *Argumentation and Advocacy*, 33, 195–197.

21. Dunbar, K. (2000). Gender, science & cognition [Online]. Retrieved July 5, 2005, from www.psych.mcgill.ca/perpg/fac/dunbar/women.html.

22. Asen, Toward a normative conception.

23. Gass, R. (1999). Fallacy list: SpCom 335: Advanced argumentation [online]. California State University, Fullerton. Retrieved July 5, 2005, from http://commfaculty.fullerton.edu/rgass/fallacy31.htm.

24. Engnell, R. A. (2001). Toward an ethic of evocative language: Contemporary uses of Holocaust-related terminology. *Southern Communication Journal*, 66, 312–322.

25. Cribbins, M. (1990). International adoption. [Student speech.] Corvallis: Oregon State University.

26. Suzuki, M. (1992, April 3). Native American symbols in sports. [Student speech.] St. John's University. Jamaica, New York.

27. Roczak, T. (1992, June 9). Green guilt and ecological overload. *New York Times*, p. A23.

28. Maslow, A. H. (1987). *Motivation and personality* (3rd ed.). San Francisco: Harper & Row.

29. Griffiths, Feminism.

30. Anonymous reviewer. (1994).

31. Aristotle, *Rhetoric*.

32. Kochman, Cultural pluralism.

33. Anderson, J. W. (1991). A comparison of Arab and American conceptions of "effective persuasion." In L. A. Samovar & R. E. Porter (Eds.). *Intercultural communication: A reader* (5th ed., pp. 96–106). Belmont, CA: Wadsworth.

34. Burke, Dramatism.

35. Allen, S. A. (1993, February 15). To be successful you have to deal with reality: An opportunity for minority business. *Vital Speeches*, 59, 271–273.

36. Foss & Griffin, Beyond persuasion.

APPENDIX A

1. Galvin & Cooper, Perceptual filters.

2. Beebe, S. A., & Masterson, J. T. (1990). *Communicating in small groups: Principles and practices* (3rd ed.). New York: Harper Collins; Cooper, P. J. (1995). *Communication for the classroom teacher* (5th ed.). Scottsdale, AZ: Gorsuch Scarisbrick.

3. Tannen, D. (1990). *You just don't understand: Women and men in conversation*. New York: William Morris.

4. Janik, I. (1971, November). Groupthink. *Psychology Today*, 43–46.

5. Tannen, *Don't understand*.

6. Cowan, J. (2000). Lessons from the playground. In Galvin & Cooper, *Making connections*, 307.

7. Grob, L. M., Meyers, R. A., & Schuh, R. (1997). Powerful/powerless language use in group interactions: Sex differences or similarities? *Communication Quarterly*, 45(3), 282–303.

8. Cowan, Lessons, 307.

9. Eisen, A. (1998). Small group presentations in teaching "science thinking" and context in a large biology class. *Bioscience*, 48(1), 54–57.

10. Henson, J. (n.d.). Problem solving using group challenges. Retrieved February 1, 2000, from www.bvte.ecu.edu/ACBMEC/p1998/henson.htm.

11. Sengalese women remake their culture. (1998, December). *IK Notes World Bank, No. 3* [Online]. Retrieved February 1, 2002, from www.africapolicy.org.

12. Kepner, C. H., & Tregoe, B. B. (1965). *The rational manager: A systematic approach to problem solving and decision making*. New York: McGraw-Hill.

APPENDIX B

1. Goodall, H. L. & Phillips, G. M. (1984). Making it in any organization. Upper Saddle River, NJ: Prentice-Hall.

2. Pacanowsky, M. E. & O'Donnell-Trujillo, N. (1983). Organization communication as cultural performance. *Communication Monographs*, 50, 126–147.

3. Bormann, E. G. (1985). Symbolic convergence theory: A communication formulation. *Journal of Communication*, 35, 128–138.

4. Ouchi, W. B. (1998, Fall). The concept of organizational culture in a diverse society [Online]. SIETAR International. Retrieved February 12, 2000, from http://208.215.167.139/sij-98-12/keynote03.htm.

5. Bush, G. W. (2005, July 19). Court in transition: Bush's announcement on the Supreme Court. Retrieved July 20, 2005, from www.nytimes.com.

6. Walters, Celebration.

7. Bush, B. (1990). Choice and change. Address delivered at Wellesley College commencement. Wellesley, MA.

8. Kennedy, J. F. (1960). (1961, January 21). Inaugural Address. Washington, D.C.

Retrieved November 8, 2005, from www.jfklibrary.org/j012061.htm.

9. Ephron, Nora (1996). Remarks to Wellesley College Class of 1996. www.wellesley.edu/PublicAffairs/Commencement/1996/speechesnephron.html.

10. Goldberg, J. (2005, June 17). The hop bird: My dad, 1931–2005. *National Review Online*. www.nationalreview.com/goldberg/goldberg200506170746.asp.

APPENDIX C

1. Karakas, Tolerance, love, and cooperation.

2. Kennedy, Inaugural address.

3. Chief Joseph's speech was originally published in (1879, April). An Indian's view of Indian affairs. *North American Review, 128(269).* 412–33. Retrieved November 8, 2005, from www.washington.edu/uwired/outreach/cspn/sense/part1%20pages/texts/josephview.htm.

4. Bush, B. Choice and change.

CREDITS

This page constitutes an extension of the copyright page. We have made every effort to trace the ownership of all copyrighted material and to secure permission from copyright holders. In the event of any question arising as to the use of any material, we will be pleased to make the necessary corrections in future printings. Thanks are due to the following authors, publishers, and agents for permission to use the material indicated.

Text Credits

Chapter 1. 15: Reprinted with permission.

Chapter 2. 18, 31: Mona Bradsher

Chapter 3. 40: Endorsed by the National Communication Association, November 1999. Reprinted by permission of the National Communication Association. **49:** Edwin Feulner, "Lay Your Hammer Down: Defend Your Convictions," Vital Speeches of the Day, 70(19) (July 15, 2004): 595–598.

Chapter 5. 85: Reprinted with permission.

Chapter 6. 103: Reprinted with permission.

Chapter 7. 128: Quianna Clay

Chapter 8. 152: Chris Russie.

Chapter 9. 169: Maria DiMaggio

Chapter 11. 196: John Streicher

Chapter 12. 227: Reprinted with permission.

Chapter 13. 237: www.CartoonStock.com **251:** Reprinted by arrangement with the Estate of Martin Luther King, Jr., c/o Writer House as agent for the proprietor New York, NY. Copyright 1963 Dr. Martin Luther King, Jr., copyright renewed 1991 Coretta Scott King.

Chapter 14. 262: YanHong Krompacky

Chapter 15. 285: Gail Grobey

Chapter 16. 305: Joshua Valentine

Chapter 17. 326: Courtesy of Brittany Farrer.

Chapter 18. 351: Anonymous

Appendix: 369: Reprinted by permission of Tanya Moser. **371:** Used by permission of Caroline Valmont. **373:** Uriel Plascencia; interpreter, translator Kelly Bilinski **374, 375:** Reprinted by permission of Keisha Walkes. **376:** Hans Erian (H.E. was on a WW speech video tape; WW owns all.) **378:** Reprinted by permission of Amari Howard. **379:** Reprinted by permission of Angela M. Bolin. **379, 382:** An Indian's View of Indian Affairs (1879).From Indian oratory: Famous speeches by noted Indian chieftans, by W. C. Vanderwerth. Copyright © 1971 by the University of Oklahoma Press, p. 259–284.

Photo Credits

Chapter 1. 2: © Lorna Owens/President, Lorna Owens Inc. **8:** top, © AP/Wide World Photos **10:** bottom, © David Young-Wolff/PhotoEdit **15:** © Thomson Learning

Chapter 2. 19: © Thomson Learning **22:** center, © Thomson Learning **28:** © Mary Kate Denny/PhotoEdit

Chapter 3. 34: © Visser Robert/CORBIS SYGMA **36:** © AP/Wide World Photos **39:** bottom, Courtesy of Seads of Peace Organization, www.seedsofpeace.org **42:** © University of Maine at Fort Kent/Jennifer Durepo. **44:** © Yoruba drum with stick, n.d., Wood, String, and Hide. The Trout Gallery, Dickinson College, Carlisle, Pennsylvania

Chapter 4. 54: © Jack Jaffe **56:** top, © Jacques Chenet/Woodfin Camp & Associates **61:** © George Fox University/Photo by Molly Boyle Arianne Reagor **63:** right, © AP/Wide World Photos **63:** left, © Jason Reed/Reuters/CORBIS

Chapter 5. 70: © AP/Wide World Photos **72:** © Spencer Grant/PhotoEdit **80:** © Jack Jaffe **82:** © AP/Wide World Photos

Chapter 6. 90: © Jack Jaffe **93:** © Steven L Raymer/Getty Images **97:** © Digital Vision/Getty Images

Chapter 7. 109: © Indiana University School of Law Library, Bloomington **112:** © Getty Images **115:** left, Courtesy Raven Sky Sports, www.hanggliding.com **115:** right, Courtesy United States Hang Gliding Association, Inc., www.ushga.org. Photo courtesy Paul Voight. **118:** © Tom Stewart/CORBIS **122:** Courtesy Bob Drudge. Copyright © 2003 Refdesk.com, www.refdesk.com

Chapter 8. 134: right, © AFP/Getty Images **134:** left, © AP/Wide World Photos **136:** © Ed Kashi/CORBIS **139:** © Charles Gupton/CORBIS **142:** © Clella Jaffe **146:** Courtesy Deirdre Steinberg **149:** © George Tarbay, NIU Media Services.

Chapter 9. 159: © NOAA Tsunami Warning Sign **162:** © AP/Wide World Photos

Chapter 10. 177: © Josh Nauman **180:** © Kevin Winter/Getty Images **183:** © Bettmann/CORBIS

Chapter 11. 194: © Peter Chapman Photography **199:** © Peter Chapman Photography

Chapter 12. 211: © Thomson Learning **220:** © Jack Jaffe

Chapter 13. 232: © NASA Marshall Space Flight Center (NASA-MSFC) **233:** © Reuters/CORBIS **239:** © JoelSimonImages.com **242:** © James L Stanfield/Getty Images **246:** © Kyle Krause/Index Stock Imagery/PictureQuest **248:** Josh Nauman

Chapter 14. 256: © Hulton-Deutsch Collection/CORBIS **261:** bottom left, © Thomson Learning **261:** bottom right, © Thomson Learning **263:** bottom, © AP/Wide World Photos

Chapter 15. 272: Laura Simms **274:** © Franz Lanting/Minden Pictures **276:** © Kenji Kawano **279:** Illustration from *Curious George Learns the Alphabet* by H.A. Rey. Copyright © renewed 1991 by Margaret E. Rey. Copyright assigned to Houghton Mifflin Company in 1993. Reprinted with permission of Houghton Mifflin Company. All rights reserved.

Chapter 16. 288: © Glen Allison/Getty Images **295:** © Charles Marden Fitch/SuperStock **298:** top, © Sean Sprague/PANOS Pictures **300:** © Susan Van Etten/PhotoEdit **304:** © Hillary Legget Carter

Chapter 17. 310: © Mary Clay/Getty Images **316:** © Creasource/Series/PictureQuest **317:** © Thomson Learning **321:** © Paul Conklin/Photo Edit **326:** © Thomson Learning

Chapter 18. 333: © Scala/Art Resource, NY **341:** © CORBIS **345:** Courtesy of WeMedia **347:** © AP/Wide World Photos **351:** © Thomson Learning

Artists' Credits for Mural Art

Cover: "Culture of the Crossroads" Mural © 1998 by Precita Eyes Muralists. Directed by Susan Kelk Cervantes. (McDonald's Building, 24th Street at Mission, SF, CA)

INDEX